ISAIAH

THE OLD TESTAMENT LIBRARY

Editorial Advisory Board

Brevard S. Childs

ISAIAH

Westminster John Knox Press
LOUISVILLE • LONDON

Book design by Jennifer K. Cox

First edition
Published by Westminster John Knox Press
Louisville, Kentucky

This book is printed on acid-free paper that meets the American National Standards Institute Z39.48 standard. ⊗

PRINTED IN THE UNITED STATES OF AMERICA

04 05 06 07 08 09 — 10 9 8 7 6 5 4 3

Library of Congress Cataloging-in-Publication Data

Childs, Brevard S.
    Isaiah : a commentary / Brevard S. Childs. — 1st ed.
        p.   cm.
    Includes bibliographical references and index.
    ISBN 0-664-22143-2
    1. Bible. O.T. Isaiah—Commentaries.   I. Bible. O.T. Isaiah. English. 2000. II. Title
BS1515.3.C48 2000
224'.1077—dc21   00-028993

This commentary is dedicated to Christopher R. Seitz,
cherished friend, brilliant interpreter, defender of the faith.

CONTENTS

Preface   xi

Abbreviations   xiii

Bibliography   xix

1. Introduction to the Book of Isaiah   1
2. Introduction to Isaiah 1—39   7
3. Introduction to Isaiah 1—12   9
4. Isaiah 1:1   11
5. Isaiah 1:2–31   12
6. Isaiah 2:1–4:6   23
7. Isaiah 5:1–30   37
8. Isaiah 6:1–13   49
9. Isaiah 7:1–25   60
10. Isaiah 8:1–22   69
11. Isaiah 8:23–9:6(7)   77
12. Isaiah 9:7–10:4   81
13. Isaiah 10:5–34   87
14. Isaiah 11:1–16   97
15. Isaiah 12:1–6   107

16. Introduction to Isaiah 13—23   113
17. Isaiah 13:1–14:32   117
18. Isaiah 15:1–16:14   128
19. Isaiah 17:1–18:7   133
20. Isaiah 19:1–20:6   139
21. Isaiah 21:1–17   145

22. Isaiah 22:1–25   154

23. Isaiah 23:1–18   162

24. Introduction to Isaiah 24—27   **171**

25. Isaiah 24:1–25   175

26. Isaiah 25:1–12   181

27. Isaiah 26:1–21   186

28. Isaiah 27:1–13   192

29. Introduction to Isaiah 28—35   **199**

30. Isaiah 28:1–29   201

31. Isaiah 29:1–24   211

32. Isaiah 30:1–33   220

33. Isaiah 31:1–9   229

34. Isaiah 32:1–20   234

35. Isaiah 33:1–24   242

36. Isaiah 34:1–35:10   249

37. Introduction to Isaiah 36—39   **259**

38. Isaiah 36:1–37:38   267

39. Isaiah 38:1–22   278

40. Isaiah 39:1–8   285

41. Introduction to Isaiah 40—55   **289**

42. Isaiah 40:1–11   293

43. Isaiah 40:12–31   303

44. Isaiah 41:1–42:13   311

45. Isaiah 42:14–43:21   327

46. Isaiah 43:22–44:23   337

47. Isaiah 44:24–45:25   344

48. Isaiah 46:1–47:15   356

49. Isaiah 48:1–22   367

50. Isaiah 49:1–13   379

51. Isaiah 49:14–50:11   387

52. Isaiah 51:1–52:12   397

53. Isaiah 52:13–53:12   407

54. Isaiah 54:1–17 424

55. Isaiah 55:1–13 431

56. Introduction to Isaiah 56—66 **439**

57. Isaiah 56:1–8 451

58. Isaiah 56:9–57:13 459

59. Isaiah 57:14–21 467

60. Isaiah 58:1–14 473

61. Isaiah 59:1–21 481

62. Isaiah 60:1–22 491

63. Isaiah 61:1–11 500

64. Isaiah 62:1–12 508

65. Isaiah 63:1–6 514

66. Isaiah 63:7–64:11(12) 519

67. Isaiah 65:1–66:24 526

Index **549**

PREFACE

When I was preparing a study on the book of Exodus during the late 1960s and early 1970s, the reasons for writing a commentary were entirely obvious. There had been no technical commentary on the book in English for over fifty years. In Germany, largely from fortuitous circumstances, a similar lacuna existed. In addition, the new insights of critical research, especially in terms of form criticism, history of interpretation, and theology, had not been adequately applied to this book. However, during the last thirty years the academic situation has dramatically changed. There is a plethora of biblical commentaries, both on Old and New Testaments, written from every possible perspective and on every level of popular and technical interpretation. For many within the biblical field, the publication of yet another commentary seems about the last thing needed.

My reasons for attempting a commentary on the book of Isaiah arise from several concerns. First, in spite of the large number of commentaries (Isaiah is particularly well represented), tremendous confusion still reigns regarding virtually every serious problem of interpretation. Of course, I am aware that certain aspects of exegesis have been done in an impressive manner. In the light of the exhaustive philological, historical, and text-critical research done on Isaiah, say, by Wildberger, Elliger, Oswalt, and Barthélemy, there is little need to rehearse once again many of the same issues. In my judgment, what is needed is a fresh interpretive model that does not get lost in methodological debates, and that proves to be illuminating in rendering a rich and coherent interpretation of the text as sacred scripture of both church and synagogue. It is interesting to note that von Rad's Genesis commentary in its semipopular format provided more stimulus for the post–World War II generation than did the elaborate, three-volume commentary of Westermann. Clearly the decisive issue of interpretation does not turn on its scope or level of technicality.

Second, the book of Isaiah presents a special challenge because of its length, complexity, and enduring importance for both Jews and Christians. The usual pattern of immediately dividing the book into at least two or three parts has had a deleterious effect on the interpretation of the whole. Even though many voices have expressed a similar concern over the last two decades, there have been no successful attempts to overcome the problem on the commentary level. I am, of course, aware that there have been several recent efforts toward this end, but from my perspective, these commentaries have not met the need.

Third, after having recently completed a lengthy project on biblical theology (1992), I am fully cognizant that its effect has been minimal on the field of biblical exegesis. Usually books on biblical theology have been relegated to a special subdiscipline, and thought to relate only to larger hermeneutical and theological concerns without any close relation to exegesis. Those engaged in biblical theology are often dismissed as "theologians," and not biblical interpreters. For my part, I have always considered biblical theology to be only an ancillary discipline that better serves in equipping the exegete for the real task of interpreting the biblical text itself.

Ever since I first began to teach the book of Isaiah in 1954, I have tried to keep abreast of the changing approaches to the book, which have moved through numerous stages of literary-critical, form-critical, redactional, and rhetorical analysis. I have learned much from each, yet I am also conscious that an eclectic mixing of methods does not offer a real solution. I also resist the practice of some immediately to characterize my approach as "canonical," since the label has only engendered major confusion. Frequently, I have had genuine difficulty in even recognizing those features that have been assumed by reviewers to be constitutive of my approach. I hope that this commentary will be judged on its own merits apart from any prior concept of what a "canonical" reading ought to entail. In a brief introduction I shall attempt to set forth a few broad guidelines of my thinking, especially in regard to the leading role that modern redactional analysis has assumed in Old Testament interpretation.

I have learned much over the years from many different commentators. Yet I especially acknowledge the work of W. A. M. Beuken of Leuven, whose illuminating articles and magisterial four-volume commentary in Dutch on chapters 40—66 have opened the way to a new era in interpreting the book of Isaiah.

Finally, I am exceedingly grateful for the time and energy that have been granted to me to write this commentary. During the last decade I have been afflicted with serious health problems at three different intervals. I am thankful that on each occasion I received a reprieve to continue the work.

New Haven
September 2, 1998

ABBREVIATIONS

AASOR	Annual of the American Schools of Oriental Research
AB	Anchor Bible
ABD	*Anchor Bible Dictionary*
AJSL	*American Journal of Semitic Languages and Literatures*
AnBib	Analecta biblica
ANET	J. B. Pritchard, ed., *Ancient Near Eastern Texts,* 3d ed., Princeton, 1969.
AOAT	Alter Orient und Altes Testament
ASTI	*Annual of the Swedish Theological Institute in Jerusalem*
ATD	Das Alte Testament Deutsch
AUSS	*Andrews University Seminary Studies*
AV	Authorized Version
BA	*Biblical Archaeologist*
BASOR	*Bulletin of the American Schools of Oriental Research*
BAT	Botschaft des Alten Testament
BBB	Bonner biblische Beiträge
BC	Biblical Commentary, ed. C. F. Keil, F. Delitzsch
BDB	F. Brown, S. R. Driver, and C. A. Briggs, *Hebrew and English Lexicon of the Old Testament,* Oxford, 1906
BEATAJ	Beiträge zur Erforschung des Alten Testaments und des Antiken Judentums
BET	Beiträge zur Biblischen Exegese und Theologie
BETL	Bibliotheca ephemerdium theologicarum lovaniensium
BHK	R. Kittel, *Biblia hebraica,* 3d ed., Stuttgart, 1937
BHS	*Biblia hebraica stuttgartensia,* Stuttgart, 1977
Bib	*Biblica*
BJRL	*Bulletin of the John Rylands University Library,* Manchester
BK	Biblischer Kommentar
BN	*Biblische Notizen*
BOuT	De Boeken van het Oude Testament
BSt	Biblische Studien, Neukirchen-Vluyn
BT	*The Bible Translator*

BTB	*Biblical Theological Bulletin*
BTFT	*Bijdragen: Tijdschrift voor Filosofie en Theologie*
BWANT	Beiträge zur Wissenschaft vom Alten und Neuen Testament
BZ	*Biblische Zeitschrift*
BZAW	Beihefte zur *Zeitschrift für die alttestamentliche Wissenschaft*
CBQ	*Catholic Biblical Quarterly*
CBSC	Cambridge Bible for Schools and Colleges
ConBOT	Coniectanea biblica, Old Testament
CSS	Cursus Scripturae Sacrae
CTLAT	*Critique Textuelle de L'Ancien Testament,* II, D. Barthélemy
DSBOT	Daily Study Bible, Old Testament
Ebib	Etudes bibliques
EgTh	*Eglise et Théologie*
EHAT	Exegetisches Handbuch zum Alten Testament
ET	English translation
ETL	*Ephemerides theologicae lovanienses*
ETR	*Etudes théologiques et religieuses*
EvT	*Evangelische Theologie*
ExpB	Expositor's Bible
ExpT	*Expository Times*
FAT	Forschungen zur Altes Testament
FB	Forschung zur Bibel
FOTL	Forms of the Old Testament Literature
FRLANT	Forschungen zur Religion und Literatur des Alten und Neuen Testaments
Fs	*Festschrift*
GKC	Gesenius' Hebrew Grammar, ed. Ed. E. Kautzsch, tr. A. E. Cowley, 2d ed. Oxford, 1910
GA	*Gesammelte Aufsätze*
GS	*Gesammelte Schriften*
HALAT	W. Baumgartner, *Hebräisches und Aramaïsches Lexikon zum Alten Testament,* 3d ed.
HAT	Handbuch zum Alten Testament
HBC	*Harper's Bible Commentary*
HCOT	Historical Commentary on the Old Testament
HDR	Harvard Dissertations in Religion
Herm	Hermeneia
HKAT	Handkommentar zum Alten Testament
HS	Die Heilige Schrift des Alten Testaments, ed. Feldmann
HSAT	*Die Heilige Schrift des Alten Testaments,* ed. A. Bertholet, 2 vols., 4th ed., 1922–23
HSM	Harvard Semitic Monographs

HSS	Harvard Semitic Studies
HTR	*Harvard Theological Review*
HUCA	*Hebrew Union College Annual*
IB	*Interpreter's Bible*
ICC	International Critical Commentary
IEJ	*Israel Exploration Journal*
Int	*Interpretation*
IntBC	Interpretation Bible Commentary for Teaching and Preaching
IOS	*Israel Oriental Society*
JAOS	*Journal of the American Oriental Society*
JBL	*Journal of Biblical Literature*
JBTh	*Jahrbuch für Biblische Theologie*
JJS	*Journal of Jewish Studies*
JNES	*Journal of Near Eastern Studies*
JPOS	*Journal of Palestine Oriental Society*
JQR	*Jewish Quarterly Review*
JR	*Journal of Religion*
JSOT	*Journal for the Study of the Old Testament*
JSOTSup	Journal for the Study of the Old Testament Supplement Series
JSS	*Journal of Semitic Studies*
JTS	*Journal of Theological Studies*
KAT	Kommentar zum Alten Testament
KeH	Kurzgefasstes exegetisches Handbuch zum Alten Testament
KHC	Kurzer Hand-Commentar zum Alten Testament
KD	*Kerygma und Dogma*
LXX	Septuagint
MT	Masoretic Text
NAB	New American Bible
NCB	New Century Bible
NEB	New English Bible
NEchB	Neue Echter Bibel
NF	Neue Folge
NICOT	New International Commentary on the Old Testament
NIV	New International Version
NJPS	New Jewish Publication Society (=Tanakh)
NRSV	New Revised Standard Version
NTS	*New Testament Studies*
NTT	*Nederlands Theologisch Tijdschrift*
OBO	Orbis biblicus et orientalis
OTE	*Old Testament Essays*
OTL	Old Testament Library
OTS	Oudtestamentische Studiën

OTWSA	Ou-Testamentiese Werkgemeenskap in Suid-Afrika
PEQ	*Palestine Exploration Quarterly*
PJ	*Palästina-Jahrbuch*
POS	Pretoria Oriental Series
POTT	*Peoples of Old Testament Times,* ed. D. J. Wiseman, 1973
POuT	De Prediking van het Oude Testament
RB	*Revue biblique*
RevScRel	*Revue des sciences religieuses*
RGG	*Religion in Geschichte und Gegenwart*
RHR	Revue de l'histoire des religions
RQ	*Revue de Qumrân*
RSV	Revised Standard Version
SANT	Studien zum Alten und Neuen Testament
SBL	Society of Biblical Literature
SBLDS	Society of Biblical Literature Dissertation Series
SBLMS	Society of Biblical Literature Monograph Series
SBS	Stuttgarter Bibelstudien
SBT	Studies in Biblical Theology
SJLA	Studies in Judaism in Late Antiquity
SJOT	Scandinavian Journal of the Old Testament
SJT	*Scottish Journal of Theology*
SPB	Studia postbiblica
ST	*Studia theologica*
TDOT	*Theological Dictionary of the Old Testament,* ed. G. R. Botterweck, H. Ringgren (English translation of *TWAT*)
ThB	Theologische Bücherei
TheolEx	Theologische Existenz Heute
ThStK	*Theologische Studien und Kritiken*
TLZ	*Theologische Literaturzeitung*
TRE	*Theologische Realenzyklopädie*
TS	Theologische Studien
TTS	Trierer theologische Studien
TTZ	*Trierer theologische Zeitschrift*
TWAT	*Theologisches Wörterbuch zum Alten Testament,* ed. G. R. Botterweck, H. Ringgren
TWNT	*Theologisches Wörterbuch zum Neuen Testament,* ed. G. Kittel
TynBul	*Tyndale Bulletin*
TZ	*Theologische Zeitschrift*
UF	*Ugaritforschungen*
VF	*Verkündigung und Forschung*
VT	*Vetus Testamentum*

VTSup	Vetus Testamentum, Supplements
WBC	Word Biblical Commentary
WF	Wege der Forschung
WMANT	Wissenschaftliche Monographien zum Alten und Neuen Testament
WO	*Die Welt des Orients*
ZAW	*Zeitschrift für die alttestamentliche Wissenschaft*
ZBK	Zürcher Bibelkommentare
ZNW	*Zeitschrift für die neutestamentliche Wissenschaft*
ZTK	*Zeitschrift für Theologie und Kirche*

SELECT BIBLIOGRAPHY

Commentaries on Chapters 1—66

J. Calvin, 1551
C. Vitringa, 1724
E. F. K. Rosenmüller, 1792
W. Gesenius, 1821
F. Hitzig, 1833
J. A. Alexander, 1846–47
F. Delitzsch, [4] 1886, BC, 1890
Ibn Ezra (d. 1167), ET Friedländer, 1873
J. Knabenbauer, CSS, 1881
T. K. Cheyne, 1889
G. A. Smith, ExpB, 1888–90, [2] 1927
A. Dillmann, KeH, 1890, [6] 1898
J. Skinner, CBSC, 1896–98
K. Marti, KHC, 1900
B. Duhm, HKAT, 1892, [4] 1922
F. Feldmann, EHAT, 1925–26
D. Kimḥi (d. 1230), ET L. Finkelstein, 1926
W. Hertzberg, 1936
J. Fischer, HS, 1937–39
E. J. Kissane, 1941–43
G. Fohrer, ZBK, 1960–65
E. J. Young, NICOT, 1965–72
A. Schoors, BOuT 1972–73
J. F. A. Sawyer, DSBOT, 1984, 1986
J. W. D. Watts, WBC, 1985, 1987
J. N. Oswalt, NICOT, 1986, 1997
J. A. Motyer, 1993

Commentaries on Chapters 1—39

G. B. Gray, ICC (1—27), 1913
O. Procksch, KAT, 1930

V. Herntrich, ATD (1—12), 1950
R. B. Y. Scott, IB, 1956
W. Eichrodt, BAT, 1960, 1967
O. Kaiser, OTL (1—12), [2] 1983; (13—39), 1974
H. Wildberger, BK, 1972–82
R. E. Clements, NCB, 1980
G. T. Sheppard, HBC, 1988
C. Seitz, IntBC, 1993

Commentaries on Chapters 40—66

C. C. Torrey, 1922
K. Budde, HSAT, 1922
P. Volz, KAT, 1932
U. E. Simon (40—55), 1953
H. Frey, BAT (40—55), [4] 1954
J. Muilenburg, *IB,* 1956
C. R. North, 1964
G. Fohrer, ZBK, 1964
J. D. Smart, 1965
G. A. F. Knight, 1965
J. L. McKenzie, AB, 1968
C. Westermann, OTL, 1969
P.-E. Bonnard, Ebib, 1972
R. N. Whybray, NCB, 1975
K. Elliger, H.-J. Hermisson, BK, 1978
W. A. M. Beuken, POuT, 1979–89
E. Achtemeier (56—66), 1982
R. J. Clifford (40—55), 1984
R. Kilian, NEchB, 1986–94
W. Grimm, K. Dittert (40—55), 1990
P. D. Hanson, IntBC, 1996
J. L. Koole, HCOT, 1997

1. INTRODUCTION
TO THE BOOK OF ISAIAH

Selected Bibliography

P. Ackroyd, "Isaiah I–XII: Presentation of a Prophet," *Congress Volume Göttingen,* SVTSup 29, Leiden 1978, 16–48; reprinted in *Studies in the Religious Tradition of the Old Testament,* London 1987, 79–104; **H. Barth,** *Die Jesaja-Worte in der Josia Zeit,* WMANT 48, Neukirchen-Vluyn 1977; **J. Barton,** *Isaiah 1–39,* OT Guides, Sheffield 1995; **W. A. M. Beuken,** "Jesaja 33 als Spiegelbild im Jesajabuch." *ETL* 67, 1991, 5–35; **D. M. Carr,** "Reaching for Unity in Isaiah," *JSOT* 57, 1993, 61–80; **B. S. Childs,** *Introduction to the Old Testament as Scripture,* London and Philadelphia 1979, 311ff.; *Biblical Theology of the Old and New Testaments,* London and Minneapolis 1992; "Retrospective Reading of the Old Testament Prophets," *ZAW* 108, 1996, 362–77; **R. E. Clements,** *Isaiah and the Deliverance of Jerusalem,* JSOTSup 13, Sheffield 1980; "The Unity of the Book of Isaiah," *Int* 36, 1982, 117–29; **C. Hardmeier,** "Jesajaforschung im Umbruch," *VF* 31, 1986, 3–31; **D. R. Jones,** "The Tradition of the Oracles of Isaiah of Jerusalem," *ZAW* 76, 1955, 226–46; **L. J. Liebreich,** "The Compilation of the Book of Isaiah," *JQR* 46, 1955/6, 259–77; 47, 1956/7, 114–38; **R. Rendtorff,** "Zur Komposition des Buches Jesaja," *VT* 34, 1984, 295–320; **J. F. A. Sawyer,** *The Fifth Gospel: Isaiah in the History of Christianity,* Cambridge 1996; **C. R. Seitz,** "Isaiah 1–66: Making Sense of the Whole," *Reading and Preaching the Book of Isaiah,* ed. C. R. Seitz, Philadelphia 1988, 105–26; **G. T. Sheppard,** "The 'Scope' of Isaiah as a Book of Jewish and Christian Scriptures," *New Visions of Isaiah,* ed. R. F. Melugen et al., JSOTSup 214, Sheffield 1996, 257–81; **B. D. Sommer,** *A Prophet Reads Scripture,* Stanford 1998; **M. A. Sweeney,** *Isaiah 1–4 and the Post-Exilic Understanding of the Isaianic Tradition,* BZAW 171, Berlin 1988; Isaiah 1–39, FOTL 16, Grand Rapids 1996; **M. E. Tate,** "The Book of Isaiah in Recent Research," *Forming Prophetic Literature, Fs J. D. Watts,* ed. J. W. Watts et al., JSOTSup 235, Sheffield 1996, 22–56; **J. Vermeylen,** "L'unité du Livre d'Isaïe," *The Book of Isaiah,* ed. J. Vermeylen, Leuven 1989, 11–53; **H. Wildberger,** "Jesaja, das Buch, der Prophet und seine Botschaft," *Jesaja,* BK x/3, 1982, 1509–1713; **H. G. M. Williamson,** *The Book Called Isaiah: Deutero-Isaiah's Role in Composition and Redaction,* Oxford 1994.

The interpretation of the book of Isaiah has gone through many important changes during the last hundred years. Because this history has been reviewed often (cf. Childs, *Introduction to the Old Testament,* 311ff.; Tate, 22ff.; Sweeney, *Isaiah 1–39,* 31ff.), there is no need to repeat it in detail, but merely to draw a few main lines.

The initial literary critical commentary of B. Duhm brought to bear on the text a new level of penetrating literary analysis, and his division of the book into three major parts (chapter 1–39; chapter 40–55; chapter 56–66) has been a major influence on the study of the book ever since. The application of form criticism to Isaiah, represented by scholars such as Wildberger and Westermann, sought to show the effect on the composition of traditional oral patterns and to break out of an impasse that developed when too great an emphasis fell on distinguishing between "genuine" and "non-genuine" passages (e.g., Marti). However, the approach did little to halt the atomizing of the book and at times even exacerbated its fragmentation. Most recently, new methodological approaches such as redactional criticism have sought to trace larger horizontal layers of editorial shaping. These approaches have discerned forces of redactional activity that have sought to lend a measure of coherence and unity to the diverse parts of the book of Isaiah as a whole (Vermeylen, 11ff.).

Within the last three decades the most creative work of Isaiah has fallen largely into this last category of redactional criticism for four reasons. First, the issue of the structure of the book has occupied much attention. Within the English-speaking world, P. Ackroyd's illuminating essay (1978) coined the phrase "presentation of a prophet." Ackroyd's concern was to go beyond the familiar issues of authorship and historical setting and to raise the question of how the editor wished to render his material. He argued that it was not by harmonizing the great diversity, but by the recognition of the full impact of the prophet on the editor, even when using different forms of presentation. Duhm had assumed that each of his larger divisions had developed mostly independently of each other and that only at a very late date were they joined. Now the emphasis shifted, not only to the presentation in the individual sections (1—12; 13—23; 36—39), but to the linking of chapters 33—35 and to the function of the parts within the whole (cf. Seitz, Sweeney *Isaiah 1—39*). The effect has been to raise a host of new and fresh interpretive questions.

Second, the emphasis on structural and editorial shaping is an indication of a major paradigm shift that has occurred regarding the very nature of prophetic literature. The shift involves the recognition of the force of textualization of the oral tradition into a written corpus. Whereas the earlier form critics tended to see the creative periods lying within the oral stage, later critics have discovered a continuing process of reinterpreting the written text. Whether this reinterpretation is called "extension" (*Fortschreibung*) or "midrash" (Clements, *Isaiah and the Deliverance*), it assumes that a corpus of written texts was continually evolving in response to changing historical forces. The result is that interpreters have become reluctant to eliminate verses as meaningless glosses, but to reckon with the possibility of an intentional expansion on the part of an editor.

Third, there has arisen a new interest in the book of Isaiah as a whole, but in a form that differs markedly from the traditional view that defended unity in terms of single authorship. In a well-known article ("The Unity of the Book of Isaiah") R. Clements outlined his understanding of the unity of Isaiah in terms of a redactional process in which at least four distinct layers can be identified: an eighth-century (preexilic), a seventh-century ("Josianic"), an exilic, and a postexilic redaction. This shaping process was largely driven by Israel's changing historical fortunes. In addition, one of the startling new developments within the last three decades has been the attention paid to different redactional layers within Second Isaiah, a collection that previously had been largely regarded as of one piece. It is now widely held that the concluding chapters of the book (65 and 66) are closely related to the first chapter, and that a conscious intention can be discerned toward uniting the various parts into some form of coherent literature as a whole (Liebreich, Compilation 259ff.).

Fourth, another feature of importance within the rubric of redactional criticism has been the role assigned to retrospective reading of the prophet. Whereas it was once thought that First, Second, and Third Isaiah could each be assigned to different historical periods with some consistency, now it has emerged that the earlier material has often been reinterpreted by the later. A growing consensus now suggests that the heart of the entire redactional process lies with Second Isaiah, whose influence reshaped First Isaiah and largely determined the form of Third Isaiah (cf. Rendtorff, Williamson). According to some new hypotheses, Second Isaiah has been assigned the role of transforming the inchoate material of First Isaiah by means of a retrospective interpretation in order to reflect the disastrous experience of the destruction of Jerusalem in 587. Clearly such an approach raises a great number of new and difficult interpretive issues (Childs, "Retrospective Reading").

In the light of these newer exegetical challenges in the field of Isaianic studies, I think that it is in order to set forth my own approach in this commentary. Although I have learned much from the many modern studies of the book of Isaiah and identify myself in many respects with the newer methods, I still have enough serious reservations over the state of the field as to wish to move in a different direction from that represented by both the left and right. My concern is to develop my interpretation of the book in an exegetical form rather than as a theological or hermeneutical tractate.

First, I remain deeply concerned with the unity of the book, which I agree cannot be formulated in terms of single authorship. In this respect, I differ from the traditionally conservative approach represented by E. J. Young, Oswalt, and Motyer, among others, which, in my judgment, results in a literary and theological flattening of the richness of the prophetic witness. I plan to develop a commentary on the entire canonical scope of the sixty-six chapters that the received tradition designated as the prophecy of Isaiah. By the term *canon* I am not merely addressing its formal scope, but including the quality of the theological testimony identified with the prophet Isaiah. A major question of concern is to develop in what sense one can truly speak of the canonical corpus as the word of God to Isaiah. The complexity of the issue is especially clear when one considers that the historical eighth-century prophet does not appear in the book after chapter 39. With the majority of modern scholars, I strongly doubt that the problem can be resolved by portraying the eighth-century prophet as a clairvoyant of the future. A much more subtle and profound theological reflection is called upon to do justice both to the unity and diversity of the biblical corpus.

Second, I agree with the modern redactional stress on the multilayered quality of the biblical text. However, in my opinion, it is fully inadequate to find the unity of this book in a succession of redactional layers, each with its own agenda, which are never ultimately heard in concert as a whole. To end one's critical analysis by outlining a seventh-, sixth-, and fifth-century redactional succession, each with an absolute dating, fails to reckon with the book's canonical authority as a coherent witness in its final received form to the ways of God with Israel. Ultimately, the analysis of distinct layers and compositional growth must be used to enrich the book as a whole, rather than to fragment it into conflicting voices of individual editors, each with a private agenda. In the end, it is the canonical text that is authoritative, not the process, nor the self-understanding of the interpreter.

Third, one of the most important recent insights of interpretation has been the recognition of the role of intertextuality (cf. Beuken). The growth of the larger composition has often been shaped by the use of a conscious resonance with a previous core of oral or written texts. The great theological significance is that it reveals how the editors conceived of their task as forming a chorus of different voices and fresh interpretations, but all addressing in different ways, different issues, and different ages a part of the selfsame, truthful witness to God's salvific purpose for his people. The fact that one cannot always determine the direction in which the intertextual reapplication flows is a warning against assigning too much importance on the recovery of sequential trajectories as the key to meaning.

Fourth, I remain critical of those interpreters who attempt to force exegesis into narrowly defined structuralist categories, or who restrict its only legitimate role to synchronic analysis. The relation of the synchronic and diachronic dimensions is an extremely subtle one in the Bible and both aspects must be retained (cf. Childs, *Biblical Theology,* 98ff.; 211ff.). Basically, my resistance to much of postmodern literary analysis derives from theological reasons. Although I have learned much from modern literary techniques, I differ in my theological understanding of the nature and function of scripture. I regard the biblical text as a literary vehicle, but its meaning is not self-contained. Its function as scripture is to point to the substance (*res*) of its witness, to the content of its message, namely, to the ways of God in the world. For this reason I remain highly critical of many modern literary proposals, which are theologically inert at best, and avowedly agnostic at worst.

Finally, regarding the place of the New Testament in an Old Testament commentary on Isaiah, the primary task of the latter is to hear the Old Testament's own discrete voice and to honor its own theological integrity. Yet as a Christian interpreter, I confess with the church that the Old and New Testaments, in their distinct canonical forms, together form a theological whole. However, to deal adequately with the New Testament far exceeds the scope of an Old Testament commentary and the ability of this author. Nevertheless, I have offered a few probes of crucial texts that have played a prominent role within Christian tradition. I am fully aware that the full task remains still to be undertaken.

In recent years there have been a few attempts made to trace the role that the book of Isaiah has played in various periods in the history of the Christian church. Many of these volumes are useful and filled with learning (e.g., J. F. A. Sawyer). Yet I remain critical of approaches that, when tracing the appropriation of the book of Isaiah, assume that the major forces at work were largely cultural. Often the concentration falls on the misuse of biblical texts. What is missing is the ability to see the effect of the coercion of the text itself in faithfully shaping the life of the church—its doctrine, liturgy, and practice—in such a way as to leave a family resemblance of faith throughout the ages. In search of this goal, the voices of the great Christian interpreters—Chrysostom, Augustine, Thomas, Luther, Calvin—remain an enduring guide for truthfully hearing the evangelical witness of Isaiah in a manner seldom encountered since the Enlightenment.

2. INTRODUCTION
TO ISAIAH 1—39 (FIRST ISAIAH)

A special introduction to First Isaiah is hardly necessary. The major introductory problems are covered in the commentary. There is a brief review of the major exegetical problems before each of the major sections: 1—12; 13—23; 24—27; 28—35; 36—39. In addition, the function of the sections is often summarized in the concluding chapter.

Following Duhm's initial division of the book as a whole into three parts, it was often assumed in popularizations of the critical approach that the material of First Isaiah was to be dated preexilic in contrast to the exilic and postexilic dating of Second and Third Isaiah. Of course, this is a major misunderstanding of Duhm, who pointed out from the start that a large amount of late material was found within this first division. He reckoned with a lengthy process extending from an eighth-century core, centered in chapters 6—8, to a late Hellenistic collection in chapters 24—27.

Much energy in recent times has focused on establishing the manner in which the very divergent sections of First Isaiah were formed into its final form of the book. Duhm's view was that the collection of chapters 1—39, along with Second Isaiah (chapters 40—55), had largely developed independently of each other, and only at a very late date had been joined. At this point much criticism has set in, and a great variety of new proposals have been made, including several that envision a process of mutual influence exerted among the various sections during most of the process of growth. Some of this controversy will be reviewed when it directly impinges on the interpretation, especially regarding the functions of chapters 33, 34—35, and 36—39.

In general, I remain much less certain than many that the precise stages in the compositional history of the book of Isaiah can be recovered. Moreover, I would also question whether these decisions play the exegetical importance that have been assigned to them. I recognize that some structural divisions are clearly intentional and of much importance (e.g., chapters 12 and 39). However, I wonder whether others share a fortuitous element in their positioning, and it is a modern anachronism to require a clear and rational reason for every structural division.

Perhaps the one example of a major revision of Duhm's classic distinction between the three Isaiahs is the recent case made for seeing the structure of the book of Isaiah falling into two basic parts, namely, chapters 1—33 and 34—66, and in assigning chapters 32—33, 34—35, and 36—39 to transitional roles in linking the two major sections. Sweeney (*Isaiah 1—39,* 43ff.) has recently summarized the major argument for this new structural analysis. Some of his points are well taken and of interest. However, in the end, I would judge that Duhm's divisions are still to be preferred. In addition to Duhm's literary and historical reasons for accepting chapters 1—39 as a discrete section, my major reason is a theological one. The sharp break between the collection of oracles in which the person of the eighth-century prophet is foundational for the tradition ends in chapter 39. Beginning with chapter 40, the message of the book functions in a different fashion apart from any role for the historical figure of Isaiah. Rather, the authority of the prophet continues and encompasses the remaining chapters, but in a strikingly different manner. To shift the major division to chapter 34 blurs this crucial shaping of the Isaianic corpus, and therefore I feel the hypothesis is to be rejected (cf. the commentary on chapter 40).

3. INTRODUCTION TO ISAIAH 1—12

Selected Bibliography

H. Barth, *Die Jesaja-Worte in der Josiazeit: Israel und Assur als Thema einer produktiven Neuinterpretation der Jesajaüberlieferung,* WMANT 48, Neukirchen-Vluyn 1977; **K. Budde,** *Jesaja's Erleben. Eine gemeinverständliche Auslegung der Denkschrift des Propheten* (Kap. 6, 1–9, 6), Gotha 1928; **R. E. Clements,** "The Prophecies of Isaiah and the Fall of Jerusalem in 587 B.C.," *VT* 30, 1980, 421–36; **M. A. Sweeney,** *Isaiah 1—39,* FOTL 16, Grand Rapids 1996, 65ff; **H. G. M. Williamson,** *The Book Called Isaiah: Deutero-Isaiah's Role in Composition and Redaction,* Oxford 1994.

Certainly one of the most complex and controversial portions of the book of Isaiah is the initial collection of oracles in chapters 1—12. There is general agreement that chapter 1 constitutes an introduction of some sort, but the scope covered by the superscription remains in dispute. Again, a wide scholarly consensus recognizes a closure in chapter 12, which is sharply distinguished from the succeeding oracles. However, the remaining structural elements of the section all present difficult problems that need to be addressed in detail. For example, how is one to explain the stark contrast between oracles of judgment and those of salvation, which are often juxtaposed in a brittle fashion (e.g., 2:6)? How is one to understand the present position within the book of Isaiah's temple vision in chapter 6? Is the repetition of an apparent refrain in 5:24 (and again in 9:12ff.) an indication of a literary interpolation?

Very early in the critical study of these chapters an important hypothesis was developed under the rubric of Isaiah's *Denkschrift* (memoir). Accordingly, it was argued that the earliest core of the book was to be found in chapters 6—8 and was basically derived from the prophet's own historical experiences. More recently, this hypothesis has come under increasing attack and the issue calls for close reexamination.

In his commentary of 1892, Duhm had assigned a goodly number of passages within chapters 1—12 to a postexilic date (e.g., chapter 4). His analysis still retains support from many. During the last few decades critical attention has tended to focus on discerning a widespread redactional reinterpretation of the earliest core of First Isaiah by an exilic author akin to Second Isaiah. This issue has been greatly sharpened by the writings of both Clements and Williamson.

The very influential book of H. Barth in 1977 mounted a case for a major redaction of First Isaiah during the reign of King Josiah in the late seventh century expressing opposition to Assyrian aggression. He reckoned that it extended from chapter 2 to at least chapter 32. Many scholars continue to support Barth's reconstruction (e.g., Clements, Sweeney), but probably with less confidence than earlier. At least enough uncertainty exists to require a fresh appraisal.

Finally, the continuing debate over Isaiah's "messianic" message turns largely on the analysis of texts within this initial collection: chapters 7, 8, 9, and 11. Although it is unlikely that a consensus of opinion will soon emerge, the importance of the problem again requires careful study.

4. Isaiah 1:1

The vision of Isaiah the son of Amoz, which he saw concerning Judah and Jerusalem in the days of Uzziah, Jotham, Ahaz, and Hezekiah, kings of Judah.

Selected Bibliography

O. Loretz, *Der Prolog des Jesaja-Buches* (1, 1–2, 5), Altenberge 1984, 13–23; **M. A. Sweeney,** *Isaiah 1—4 and the Post-Exilic Understanding of the Isaianic Tradition,* BZAW 171, Berlin 1988; **G. M. Tucker,** "Prophetic Superscriptions and the Growth of a Canon," *Canon and Authority: Essays in Old Testament Religion and Theology,* ed. B. O. Long and G. W. Coats, Philadelphia 1977, 56–70.

The superscription of the book designates its prophetic author, the nature of his message as divine revelation, the addressee as Judah and Jerusalem, and the time frame of his preaching. The latter spans the period from King Uzziah (783–742; cf. 6:1) through the reign of King Hezekiah (715–687). The heading *ḥāzôn* ("vision") is used in a weak sense comparable to Obadiah 1 and Nahum 1:1.

The major controversial issue turns on the question of how much of the succeeding parts of the book are covered by this initial superscription, which is generally recognized as part of a late editorial shaping of this corpus of prophetic material. Since there are other superscriptions also ascribed to Isaiah in 2:1 and 13:1, some scholars have limited the range of material covered by the first heading either to chapter 1 or to chapters 1 — 12. The reasons for assuming that the initial superscription is intended to include the entire book of Isaiah will emerge more clearly in the succeeding commentary. Briefly stated, the decision turns on the evidence of a process of intentional redactional rendering of the whole of the Isaianic material into a unified corpus.

The scholarly discussion regarding the scope of the material covered by the superscription has been dominated by the concern to determine the original redactor's intent. Few modern commentators would question the importance of this question, although it often remains impossible to arrive at a conclusion of certainty.

However, there is another aspect of the problem relating to the function of the superscription. In the final literary form of the book of Isaiah, 1:1 now introduces the entire book. Even if there were fortuitous literary and historical factors involved, the present position of the superscription affords it an important hermeneutical function. The fact that the dating of Isaiah's preaching is concluded with the reign of Hezekiah has important implications for the interpretation of chapters 40—66. Regardless of the many signs of post-Isaianic dating, the superscription functions to define the historical setting of the prophecy of Isaiah to the preexilic period and thus shapes the understanding of the later parts of the book as well. The reader is not encouraged to extend the historical setting of Isaiah's ministry beyond the reign of King Hezekiah (who dies at the end of chapter 39), but is instructed to interpret the material within the historical framework established by the superscription. Thus, the basic hermeneutical issue is posed at the outset. The reader is pressed to reflect on the nature of this prophetic corpus. Is there another way of understanding the prophetic claim of Isaianic prophecy for this entire collection when the prophet himself does not ever appear after chapter 39? This issue will be pursued further throughout the commentary, but especially in chapter 40 and following.

5. Isaiah 1:2–31

1:2   Hear, O heavens, and listen, O earth
            for the LORD has spoken:
        "Children have I reared and brought up,
            but they have rebelled against me.
3   An ox knows its owner
            and an ass its master's stall.
        Israel does not know,
            my people does not understand."
4   Ah, sinful nation,
            people laden with iniquity,
        brood of evildoers,
            depraved children.
        They have abandoned the LORD,
            spurned the Holy One of Israel,
        turned their backs on him.
5   Why will you be beaten anymore,
            that you persist in rebellion?
        Every head is sick
            and every heart afflicted.
6   From head to foot
            no spot is sound—
        wounds and welts
            and festering sores,

not cleansed or bandaged
   or soothed with oil.
7   Your land is desolate,
   your cities scorched with fire.
Before your very eyes foreigners strip your land—
   a wasteland overthrown by foreigners.[a]
8   And the daughter of Zion is left
   like a booth in a vineyard,
like a hut in a cucumber field,
   like a city under siege.
9   Unless the LORD of hosts
   had left us some survivors,
we would be like Sodom,
   no better than Gomorrah.
10   Hear the word of the LORD,
   you rulers of Sodom.
Listen to the instruction of our God,
   you people of Gomorrah!
11   "What need have I of all your sacrifices?"
   says the LORD.
"I am fed up with burnt offerings of rams,
   and the fat of stuffed beasts.
I have no desire for the blood of bulls,
   of sheep and of male goats.
12   Whenever you come to enter my presence—
   who asked this of you,
this trampling of my courts?
13   Stop bringing empty gifts;
   the smell of sacrifice is abhorrent to me.
New moons and sabbaths,
   and the calling of assemblies—
I cannot endure iniquity and sacred assembly.
14   Your new moons and fixed seasons
   fill me with revulsion;
they have become a burden to me.
   I cannot endure them.
15   When you lift up your hands in prayer,
   I will hide my eyes from you.
Even though you offer countless prayers,
   I will not listen.
Your hands are stained with blood.
16   Wash yourselves clean,

        remove your evil deeds
      from out of my sight.
        Cease to do evil,
17   learn to do good.
        Seek justice,
      aid the oppressed,[b]
        support the rights of the orphans.
      Plead the widow's cause.
18   Come, let us debate our case together.
        Though your sins are crimson,
      they can become white as snow;
        though they are red as dyed wool,
      they can become like fleece.
19   If you are willing and obedient,
        you will eat the good things of the land.
20   But if you refuse and rebel,
        you will be eaten by the sword,
      for the LORD himself has spoken."
21   How she has become a harlot,
        the faithful city!
      She was once full of justice,
        where righteousness dwelt—
      but now murderers.
22   Your silver has turned to slag.
        Your wine is diluted with water.
23   Your rulers are rogues
        and cronies of thieves.
      They all love bribes
        and chase after gifts.
      They do not defend the cause of the orphan,
        and the widow's case never reaches them.
24   Therefore, this is the declaration
        of the Almighty, the LORD of hosts,
      the Mighty One of Israel:
        "Enough! I will vent my anger on my foes;
      I will wreak havoc on my enemies!
25   I will turn my hand against you,
        and smelt away your dross as with lye,
      and remove all your impurities.
26   I will again make your magistrates what they once were,
        and your counsellors like those of old.

> Afterward you will be called
> City of Righteousness, Faithful City."
27 Zion will be redeemed by justice,
>   her repentant ones with righteousness.
28 But rebels and sinners together will be destroyed,
>   and those who forsake the LORD will perish.
29 For one will be ashamed of the oaks
>   in which you have delighted,
>   and disgraced because of the gardens
>   that you have coveted.
30 You will be like an oak with fading leaves,
>   and like a garden without water.
31 The strong man[c] will become tinder,
>   and his work a spark,
>   and both of them will burn together
>   with none to quench.

a. Emendation yields "like the overthrown of Sodom" (cf. Williamson, *The Book Called Isaiah*, 245).

b. The meaning of the clause is uncertain. Some suggest the translation, "restrain the violent."

c. The Hebrew *ḥāsōn* is uncertain (NEB, "the strongest tree"; NJPS, "stored wealth").

Selected Bibliography

J. Becker, *Isaias—der Prophet und sein Buch,* SBS 30, Stuttgart 1968, 45ff.; **J. Begrich,** "Die priestliche Tora," *Werden und Wesen des Alten Testament,* ed. P. Volz et al., BZAW 77, Berlin 1936, 63–80; **E. Ben Zvi,** "Isaiah 1:4–9, Isaiah, and the Events of 701 B.C.E. in Judah," *JSOT* 5, 1991, 95–111; **H. J. Boecker,** *Redeformen des Rechtslebens im Alten Testament,* Neukirchen-Vluyn 1964, 68ff.; **K. Budde,** "Zu Jesaja 1—5," *ZAW* 49, 1931, 16–40, 182–211; 50, 1932, 38–72; **D. Carr,** "Reaching for Unity in Isaiah," *JSOT* 57, 1993, 61–80; **B. S. Childs,** "Retrospective Reading of the Old Testament Prophets," *ZAW* 108, 1996, 362–77; **M. Delcor,** "Les attaches littéraires, l'origine et la signification de l'expression biblique 'prendre à temoin le ciel et la terre,'" *VT,* 1966, 8–25; **G. Fohrer,** "Jesaja 1 als Zusammenfassung der Verkündigung Jesajas," *Studien zur alttestamentlichen Prophetie* (1946–65), BZAW 99, 1967, 148–66; **Y. Gitay,** "Reflections on the Study of Prophetic Discourse: The Question of Isaiah 1 2—20," *VT* 33, 1983, 207–21; **B. Gosse,** "Isaïe 1 dans la rédaction du livre d'Isaïe," *ZAW* 104, 1992, 52–66; **J. Jensen,** *The Use of Torah by Isaiah,* CBQMS 3, Washington 1973, 68–84; **D. R. Jones,** "Exposition of Isaiah 1," *SJT* 17, 1964, 463–77; 18, 1965, 457–71; 19, 1966, 319–27; 21, 1968, 320–27; **L. J. Liebreich,** "The Compilation of the Book of Isaiah," *JQR* 46, 1955/56, 259–77; 47, 1956/57, 114–38; **O. Loretz,** *Der Prolog des Jesaja-Buches (1:1–2, 5),* Altenberge 1984; **R. F. Melugin,** "Figurative Speech and the Reading of Isaiah 1 as Scripture," ed. R. F. Melugin, M. A. Sweeney, *New Version of Isaiah,* JSOTSup 214, Sheffield 1996, 282–305; **L. G. Rignell,** "Isaiah Chapter 1," *ST* 11, 1957, 140–58; **M. A. Sweeney,** *Isaiah 1—4 and the Post-Exilic Understanding of the Isaianic Tradition,* BZAW 171, 1988, 101–33; *Isaiah 1—39,* FOTL 16, Grand Rapids 1996, 73–87; **J. Vermeylen,** *Du Prophète Isaïe à L'Apocalyptique,* I, Paris 1977, 37–111; **H. G. M. Williamson,** "Relocating Isaiah 1:2–9," *Writing and Reading the Scroll of Isaiah,* ed. C. C.

Broyles, C. A. Evans, VTSup 70, 1, Leiden 1997, 263–77; **J. T. Willis,** "An Important Passage for Determining the Historical Setting of a Prophet Oracle—Isaiah 1:7–8," *ST* 39, 1985, 151–69.

1. Structure, Genre, Setting, and Function

The chapter is made up of a series of smaller units that differ in meter, form, and historical background. Usually they are so divided: vv. 2–3; 4–9; 10–17; 18–20, 21–26; (27–31). The units do not stand in a chronological sequence. The description of Zion's physical desolation (vv. 7–8) now precedes the portrayal of Israel's opulent but empty cultic exercises (vv. 10–17) from an earlier period. Often a catchword connection is evident (cf. vv. 9 and 10).

Form-critically, different genres are represented, such as accusation (vv. 2–3), invective (vv. 4–9), torah instruction (vv. 10–17), trial summons (vv. 18–20), dirge and promise (vv. 21–26). Much energy has recently been expended in refining the analysis of the form and function of these various genres (cf. Sweeney, *Isaiah 1—39*). There is some justification for this attention because the discrete units have left traces from their prehistory. However, the major point to be made is that these separate units have been given a new function within a literary context that is distinct from their original role. They now form an introduction to the book as a whole. The determination of its present function is exegetically far more important than recovering an earlier oral stage.

It is a fortunate characteristic of the recent interpretation of chapter 1 that the importance of determining the literary function of the passage within the larger corpus has been recognized and pursued with great energy. Fohrer's well-known essay ("Jesaja 1") pointed in a fresh direction when he suggested that chapter 1 was an intentional composition, joined by catchwords that serve as a compendium (*Zusammenfassung*) of the preaching of Isaiah. It functioned to present a sequence of the prophet's major themes of sin, judgment, and possible salvation. Other commentators then spoke of the chapter as a "general preface and guide" (Clements), or as an exhortation calling for repentance (Sweeney, *Isaiah 1—4*, 119–23). More recently, Carr ("Reaching for Unity") questions whether chapter 1 is simply a summary, since so many important themes are missing. He suggests that it serves as an invitation to read what then follows. Most recently, Williamson ("Relocating," 264ff.) argues that nearly all of the parts of the chapter derived from a prior written form of the words of Isaiah. Williamson then seeks to demonstrate the close connection between 1:2b–3 and 30:9, between 1:4 and 5:7ff., and between 1:5–9 and 30:15–17. The argument remains, of course, speculative, but helpful in showing the high level of continuity of chapter 1 with the preaching of Isaiah, even when redactionally shaped.

Finally, there is general agreement that vv. 27–31 present a different sort of problem. Fohrer reflected the older literary critical perspective when he regarded vv. 27–28 as a gloss and vv. 29–31 a fragment of some kind (cf. below for a different approach). Scholars continue to differ in dating the redaction of the chapters to the exilic or postexilic age.

Regarding the question of the original historical setting of the subunits, the majority opinion assigns the material largely to the eighth century. In spite of the majority position, vv. 7–9 are thought most likely to reflect the period following Sennacherib's invasion in 701. Obviously the reference to Israel's excessive cultic activity (vv. 10–17) stems from an era prior to the later disaster.

Although the direction of recent research on chapter 1 has been often very illuminating, in my opinion much of it has not been fully on target. It has missed the dominantly theocentric function of the chapter. The focus is not on Isaiah, who remains solely a vehicle; nor does it fall primarily on Israel. Rather, the introduction focuses immediately and throughout the chapter on God. It recounts his overwhelming anger toward Israel, offers examples of the nation's rebellious behavior, and then turns to God's effort to bring his people into obedience. The chapter concludes with the exercise of God's will both to punish and to restore Zion according to his own purpose. The dirge over the city is ended through an eschatological reversal that restores the faithful city. Zion's redemption is not just a "possibility" (Fohrer) that is realized only by repentance, but a transformation derived solely from God, into which salvation Israel is invited to enter through true repentance.

2. Exposition

[1:2–3] The divine accusation begins within the widest possible context of calling the heavens and the earth to bear witness to God's charge made against his people, rebellious children, who, in spite of the loving care of a father, are without sense. The idiom of appellation appears also in ancient Near Eastern texts, but in Isaiah 1 it functions largely rhetorically and should not be linked in a heavy-handed way to a theology of creation. The accusation is made, not in forensic terms as a breaking of God's law, but in a parabolic form of wisdom. Israel has less understanding of its Lord than even the most stupid of domesticated animals. Still, the two different idioms, law and wisdom, bear testimony to the same subject matter: Israel's total alienation from its God to whom it owes its life and well-being.

Recent commentators have tended to stress the element of biblical diversity, suggesting that the Isaianic imagery of "royal ideology" is independent of the language of the Mosaic covenant. Yet the issue is more complex than first meets the eye. The initial formulaic appellation to the heavens and earth to bear testimony to God's charge (v. 2) has its closest parallel in the first verse of the Song of Moses (Deut. 32:1–43), which has been profiled with a narrative framework interpreting the call to heaven and earth to witness against Israel (31:28). Already in Deut.

4:26 in direct speech God calls heaven and earth to testify against Israel, but in chapter 31 the theme of Israel's coming apostasy is expanded. The Song of Moses calls upon the heavens and earth to witness to God's faithfulness and Israel's corruption (v. 4b). In fact, many of the themes of Isaiah are sounded in similar vocabulary. Israel is a "perverse nation," "children without faithfulness" (v. 20), "with no understanding" (v. 28), "from the vine of Sodom and from the fields of Gomorrah" (v. 32). God will punish them "with a foolish nation," and "scatter them afar" (v. 26). Yet the one who "wounds also heals" (v. 39) "and will vindicate his people" (v. 36). Delitzsch writes perceptively that the present of Isaiah corresponds to the future of the Song of Moses (56).

The hermeneutical point to make is neither that Isaiah is directly citing from Deuteronomy 32, nor is the Deuteronomist dependent on the prophet. Rather, the relationship is of a different order from a simple literary or redactional linkage. The intertextuality has arisen because finally the collections of the law and the prophets have been united within the body of Israel's scriptures, and thus for later readers—both Jew and Christian—a strong resonance has been unleashed between the two even though there is no hard evidence that an original intertextual connection was intended. Thus, while it is exegetically correct to stress the diversity between the law and prophets at an earlier time, it is equally important to recognize the coercion of the united biblical text toward revealing the coherence of the selfsame subject matter.

[4–9] The form of the unit is that of an invective delivered by the prophet, but it has been linked by association of context ("people," "children") with the preceding. The prophet chastises the people for doing evil, abandoning Yahweh, and treating him with contempt. The term *sin* (*ḥaṭṭā'āh*) is not a deviation from some ideal norm, or simply missing the mark, as often suggested, but in the context is directly related to rebellion against God by Israel's action. This produces the condition of a people "laden with iniquity" (*'āwôn*). The holiness of God is thus repudiated by a people whose entire life now reflects the exact opposite character (cf. Ps. 78:40ff.).

Often in prophetic speech an invective ushers in a harsh word of divine threat (e.g., Amos 6:4ff.), but the verses that follow describe a judgment already fallen. The imagery is of a rebellious slave who has been repeatedly beaten by his master. He is covered with bleeding wounds, bruises, and stripes, which have all begun to fester and sicken the entire body with infection. As yet no remedy for healing has been administered. The pus has not been wiped clean, the wounds have not been bandaged, no soothing oil has been applied. Then the imagery shifts abruptly to the land that lies desolate, with cities gutted by fire and ravished by foreign invaders. Jerusalem alone, "daughter of Zion," remains utterly isolated and forlorn, like an abandoned child, isolated and useless. Often commentators draw attention to Sennacherib's proud boast of shutting up Hezekiah "like a bird in a cage" (*ANET*, 288).

Then again the prophetic message shifts and a brief glimmer of light enters into the grim picture when the prophet focuses once more on God. Zion would have been extinguished (a subjunctive mode is introduced) were it not for the plan of God. The prophet does not here develop an elaborate theology of the remnant, but only hints at a "few survivors" who have escaped the devastation. This remnant—the leftovers—prevents Zion from being utterly destroyed like Sodom and Gomorrah. However, to interpret this verse simply as a postexilic addition, ascribing to the survivors a hope for political restoration, badly misses the heart of the prophetic message. Rather, an alternative to Israel's desolation is given in the form of confession. The remnant are the preserved of God and with them Isaiah personally identifies: "Yahweh had left us some survivors." There is a new life from the old. Within chapter 1 this note is only briefly sounded, but the theme will be developed in great length in the succeeding chapters.

[10–17] This unit opens with a sharp polemic against Jerusalem's thriving cultic practice. It is linked with the preceding oracle by a catchword, "Sodom and Gomorrah," but the imagery has shifted its focus to become now a symbol for a sinful people, indeed the antithesis of the people of God. Both the leader and the people of Jerusalem are indicted in the attack.

Much scholarly debate has occurred in an effort to determine precisely whether the genre stems from priestly, prophetic, or wisdom circles. The argument has become quite sterile without much exegetical illumination. All three strains are involved in some fashion, but the search for sharp, form-critical distinctions is quite fruitless. Like other prophets before him (1 Samuel 15; Amos 5), Isaiah confronts a multitude of worshippers who crowd into the temple to fulfill their sacrificial obligations. He is fully knowledgeable concerning the various types of sacrifice (holocaust, cereal offerings, etc.) as well as the various appointed sacral feasts. However, he mixes them all together, riding roughshod over careful priestly protocol, in order to reject them all as an abomination before Yahweh, indeed before the very God whom they believed had called for these forms of worship.

Israel's offerings are deemed "empty," "abhorrent," and its sacred liturgy a "trampling" in God's courts. God's reaction is portrayed in graphic language. He is "fed up," weary and disgusted before this tedious ordeal, and is even filled with "revulsion" toward Israel's carefully orchestrated rituals. To suggest with Kaiser that this outburst is a contrived construct from the early postexilic period is unconvincing. The attack rings with the same authority as does that of Amos (chapter 5) or Jeremiah (chapter 7), and represents a powerful minority voice within Israel's religion without any clear parallels from ancient Near Eastern sources. The older hypothesis from the nineteenth century that the prophets were opposed to sacrifice in principle has been generally rejected as misconstrued. The prophetic attack is highly specific—it even includes prayer (v. 15)—and is directed to this moment of deep religious distortion within Jerusalem.

Similarly, the remedy to this intolerable situation is offered in highly concrete imperatives, and is not a general ethical program that can be fixed within historical parameters. Before the Holy One of Israel, Israel must wash itself— "Your hands are stained with blood"—and remove these evil deeds from God's sight. Violence and pious assembly (v. 13) are intolerable before divine purity. Then God's demands for a radical reversal are stated in blunt, straightforward language, the meaning of which Israel is assumed to know, since the commands are addressed to the will: "Cease to do evil, learn to do good."

Next, specific examples follow that are heaped up in quick succession: "Seek justice, aid the oppressed, support the rights of the orphans. Plead the widow's cause" (v. 17). This is the "word of Yahweh" (v. 10); it is also torah, not in the strict sense of Mosaic formulation, but as imperatives commensurate with everything that Israel had learned from its long historical experience with its God. These are not universal ethical teachings, but a highly existential application of the divine will that had long since been revealed to Israel, and now delivered with a fresh poignancy to a corrupt, complacent, and self-righteous population.

[18–20] The unit is clearly separated from what precedes and follows. The language is forensic: "let us test each other," "let us come to a legal understanding," "let us debate our case together." The divine offer is conciliatory, but not at this juncture forgiving (cf. Boecker for the structure of a trial). The two subsequent clauses in v. 18 are to be rendered as conditional rather than construed as interrogative or ironical statements, which are less suited to the juridical context. Even though Israel's sins are grievous—crimson red—they can still be rendered free of blemish and pure. There is yet a chance, but placed before Israel is a clear-cut decision, one determined not by intention, but action. If obedient to the way of life prescribed by God, Israel can enjoy the gifts of the land. But if the people remain rebellious, the alternative is destruction by the sword. The purpose of God for his people has always been for salvation. Israel's future is not determined by some blind force of fate, but stands before the consequences of its own decision.

[21–26] There is general agreement that vv. 21–26 comprise a unit. The form is initially that of a dirge (cf. Isa. 14:4ff.; Ezek. 28:12ff.) which functions as an invective, and which is followed by a threat to God's enemies, concluding with a promise to Zion. The faithful city and dwelling place of righteousness, Zion, is now characterized as a harlot. The imagery shifts to silver becoming slag, and wine adulterated with water. The city has lost its purity. Then in v. 23 the figures are dropped in place of a literal portrayal of Zion's sorry condition. Both ruler and people are corrupt, engaged in bribery and theft. No one defends the rights of the abused orphan and widow.

As a result, Yahweh, Lord of hosts and Mighty One of Israel—both ancient terms associated with war—arises in anger against his enemies. The language of judgment returns to the earlier figure of dross, which is now smelted with fire and heat. Thus Yahweh resolves to restore Zion to its earlier state as a right-eous city with just judges and counsellors as at the beginning. The emphasis of the promise falls fully on the sole and magisterial decree of God to execute his will for Zion. The focus is completely theocentric and emerges from the divine decision. It is not pictured as a combined effort, dependent on Israel's willing-ness to cooperate, but is a part of God's future, both as envisioned and executed. For the shape of the book of Isaiah as a whole, it is highly significant that this eschatological note of redemption forms an integral part of the introductory chapters to the Isaianic corpus and is hardly an afterthought dictated by wish-ful thinking of postexilic editors.

[27–28] One of the most difficult aspects of chapter 1 turns on the conclud-ing verses. Duhm set the critical stage with his sharp literary analysis. Accord-ingly, vv. 27–28 reveal by their uneven meter and different concept of Zion's state of slavery that the verses are an exilic or postexilic addition. Certainly his argument is well taken that vv. 21–26 form a well-structured unity which comes to an end with an *inclusio* in v. 26. Recent conservative attempts simply to blend vv. 27–28 in a harmonious continuity (Watts, Motyer) have not recog-nized the extent of the problem. Modern redactional critics have argued that the sharp division made between the righteous and the sinners is foreign to Isaiah's thought, but rather characteristic of postexilic Judaism (cf. Isa. 59:17ff.; 65:3, 17). Also, the tension between the authentic government of Zion and its pres-ent corrupt rulers is different from the polarity described above (Vermeylen, 105ff.). As a result, the verses are seen as a retrojection of postexilic conditions into the eighth-century preaching of Isaiah.

Moreover, if the historical context has been correctly reconstructed, the pas-sage assumes that Jerusalem has already suffered judgment. The addition reflects the continuing tensions within the devastated city, which has not yet returned to normalcy (cf. Clements, Sweeney, *Isaiah 1–39*). In my opinion, there are major problems with this interpretation, which shares a characteristic failing of the usual approach to the retrospective reading of the prophets (cf. Childs). These various redactional approaches assume that a correct meaning of a text is only obtained by a referential reading based on a reconstructed lit-erary or historical context. The effect is to disregard the present function of this multilayered text within its canonical context.

In contrast, I would argue that vv. 27–28 are a good example of textual exten-sion (*Fortschreibung*). From the experience of the exile, Israel discovered a dif-ferent dimension of vv. 21–26. It was not that the Isaianic text had to be adjusted to fit the social realities of a later time, but exactly the reverse. From the coercion of the biblical text Israel learned how correctly to understand the new postexilic situation. Desolate Israel clung firmly as never before to the promised salvation of Zion and the final destruction of God's enemies. The scribal editor confirmed the promise of Isaiah as true: Zion—as far as it was truly Zion—would surely be redeemed. Moreover, this promised salvation would stem solely from God's justice (*mišpāṭ*) and from his righteousness (*ṣedāqāh*), not from Israel's virtue. Rebels and sinners who forsook Yahweh would not partake of this salvation of Zion, but be destroyed. Thus, this textual extension confirmed Isaiah's promise as true, and by using the vocabulary of Israel's later (postexilic) experience defined more clearly the implicit Isaianic concept of Zion as a faith reality, distinct from merely a political entity, but still containing the wicked along with the faithful. Finally, it is a crucial hermeneutical observation to note that the textual extension retained the initial eschatological perspective of vv. 21–26 and did not render it into an inert historical artifact from Israel's past, which is a failing of most retrospective interpretations.

[29–31] There still remains the problem of interpreting the final verses of the chapter. Duhm's proposal has considerable support that these verses were a fragment from a larger Isaianic polemic against the practices of a fertility cult found especially in the Northern Kingdom (Isa. 2:6ff.; Hos. 4:11ff.). Israel will be ashamed before its sacred trees and gardens, which do not give life. Such cultic worshippers are compared to decaying vegetation that will soon be consumed. These verses have been joined to v. 28 as an illustration of the fate of rebels and sinners. However, the connection is quite brittle. The shift from the third person plural (they) to the second person (you) can be somewhat eased if the first verb is construed as an impersonal. Clearly the redactor used vv. 29ff. as an illustration of the punishment of the wicked, who are bracketed by the repetition of the same adverb, "together" (vv. 28, 31).

The history of this editorial process remains somewhat obscure. If one assumes that a redactor used a genuine, eighth-century Isaianic fragment in vv. 29–31 and joined it with vv. 27–28 as an illustration of the judgment of the wicked, several problems emerge. How is one to conceive of an editor joining an ancient preexilic fragment to a postexilic extension in vv. 27–28? Clements feels that it is more reasonable to assume that vv. 29–31 constitute an even later addition than the extension in vv. 27–28 and that this addition was a redactional creation, not an ancient Isaianic fragment. The major case against Clements's hypothesis turns on the larger redactional shaping of the entire Isaianic corpus. There is much evidence to suggest that chapters 65—66 were edited in such a way as to conform to the themes, even specific vocabulary, of chapter 1 to form a massive literary *inclusio* to the entire book of Isaiah. The portrayal of the wicked still in Zion after its redemption in chapters 65 and 66 is patterned after 1:28ff. The direction of the intertextuality seems in this case to be from chapter 1 to chapters 65—66, especially since the content of vv. 29ff. shows no signs of postexilic retrojection.

In sum, the best solution appears to be to assume that a postexilic editor shaped his textual extension in two very different ways. Verses 27–28 are a textual expansion used to interpret the relation of the righteous and the wicked within the redeemed community. Verses 29–31 constitute a genuinely Isaianic fragment that served the editor as a graphic illustration of the judgment announced to the wicked who do not share in Zion's future. One cannot, of course, rule out the possibility that a postexilic form of cultic apostasy played a role in the editorial choice of this Isaianic fragment to illustrate a similar pattern of continuing rebellion against Israel's true worship.

6. Isaiah 2:1–4:6

2:1   The word that Isaiah son of Amos saw concerning Judah and Jerusalem.

2   It will happen in the latter days
      that the mountain of the house of the LORD
   will be set over all other mountains,
      and will be lifted high above the hills;
   and all the nations will stream to it.

3   Many people will go and say:
      "Come, let us go up to the mountain of the LORD,
      to the house of the God of Jacob,
   that he may teach us his ways
      and that we may walk in his paths."
   For out of Zion will go forth the law,
      and the word of the LORD from Jerusalem.

4   Thus he shall judge among the nations,
      and arbitrate for the many peoples;
   and they will beat their swords into plowshares
      and their spears into pruning hooks.
   Nation will not lift sword against nation,
      nor ever again be trained for war.[a]

5   O, house of Jacob!
      Come, let us walk
      in the light of the LORD.

6   Surely you have rejected your people,
   the house of Jacob,
      for they are full of diviners[b] from the east
        and of soothsayers like the Philistines,
        and they strike bargains with foreigners.

7   Their land is full of silver and gold,
      and there is no end to their treasures;
   their land is full of horses,
      and there is no limit to their chariots.

8   Their land is full of idols;
          they bow down to the work of their hands,
          to what their own fingers have made.
9   So humankind is brought low
          and all people will be humbled—
          do not forgive them!
10   Go into the rocks,
          and hide in the ground
     before the terror of the LORD,
          and from the dreaded splendor of his majesty.
11   Haughty human looks will be brought low,
          and the pride of men humbled,
     and the LORD alone will be exalted
          in that day.
12   For the LORD of hosts has a day of waiting
          against all that is proud and mighty,
          against all that is high to bring it low,
13   against all the cedars of Lebanon,
          tall and lofty,
     and against all the oaks of Bashan;
14   against all the towering mountains
          and against the high hills;
15   against every lofty tower
          and every fortified wall;
16   against all the ships of Tarshish,
          and against every stately vessel.
17   Human arrogance will be brought low,
          and the pride of men humbled;
     and the Lord alone will be exalted
          in that day.
18   As for the idols, they will vanish completely.
19   And men will enter caves in the rocks
          and the holes in the ground
     before the terror of the LORD,
          and from the dreaded splendor of his majesty
          when he rises to terrify the earth.
20   On that day men will fling away
          to the rodents and bats
     their idols of silver and their idols of gold,
          which they made to worship,
21   to enter the caves of the rocks
          and the cleft of the cliffs

before the terror of the LORD,
>and from the dreaded splendor of his majesty,
when he rises to terrify the earth.
22 Oh, stop glorifying man,
>who has only a breath in his nostrils.
>What is he really worth?
3:1 For lo, the sovereign LORD of hosts
will remove from Jerusalem and Judah
>>prop and stay,
every prop of food
>and every prop of water,
2 soldier and warrior,
>judge and prophet,
>soothsayer and elder,
3 the captain of fifty and man of rank,
>counsellor, magician, and enchanter.
4 And I will make mere boys their princes,
>and babes will rule over them.
5 and the people will oppress one another,
>man against man, neighbor against neighbor,
the young will bully the old,
>and the riffraff the honorable.
6 If a man seizes his brother
>in the house of his father (saying),
"You have a cloak,
>you be our leader,
take charge of this heap of ruins,"
7 he will cry out on that day, saying,
>"I have no remedy;
>in my house there is neither bread nor cloak.
You will not make me leader of the people."
8 For Jerusalem has stumbled
>and Judah has fallen,
because they have spoken and acted against the LORD,
>defying his glorious presence.
9 Their partiality and judgment testify against them;
>like Sodom they proclaim their sins.
They do not hide them.
>Woe upon them!
>They have earned their own disaster.
10 Tell^c the righteous it will be well with them,
>for they will enjoy the fruit of their deeds.

11   Woe to the wicked! All will go badly for him,
          for what his hands have done
          will be done to him.
12   Youths oppress my people
          and women rule over them.
      O my people, your leaders mislead you
          and confuse the direction of your paths.
13   The LORD takes his place in court;
          he rises to judge peoples.
14   The LORD brings an indictment
          against the elders and princes of his people:
      "It is you who has ravished the vineyard,
          the plunder from the poor is in your house.
15   How dare you crush my people
          and grind the faces of the poor?"
      says the Lord GOD of hosts.
16   The LORD says:
      "Because the daughters of Zion are so vain
          and walk with their necks extended,
          flirting with their eyes,
          moving with mincing gait
          and jingling feet,
17   the LORD will make bald
          the scalps of the daughters of Zion,
          and the LORD will uncover their foreheads.[d]
18   In that day the LORD will strip away the finery[e] of the
      anklets, the headbands, and the crescents; 19 the pendants,
      the bracelets, and veils; 20 the headdresses, the armlets,
      the sashes, the perfume boxes, and the amulets; 21 the
      signet rings and nose rings; 22 the festive robes and the
      capes and cloaks, the purses; 23 the lace gowns and linen
      garments, the turbans and shawls.
24   So instead of perfume there will be a stench;
          and instead of a girdle, a rope;
          and instead of well-set hair, baldness;
          and instead of a rich robe, sackcloth;
          instead of beauty, branding.
25   Your men will fall by the sword,
          your warriors in battle.
26   And her gates will lament and mourn,
          ravished, she shall sit upon the ground.
4:1   In that day, seven women will seize one man, saying,

> "We will eat our own food and provide our own
> clothing, only let us be called by your name.
> Take away our disgrace!"

2   In that day the branch of the LORD
>   will be beautiful and glorious,
>   and the fruit of the land
>   will be the pride and glory of Israel's survivors.

3   and those who remain in Zion
>   and are left in Jerusalem,
>   everyone enrolled in the book of life,
>   they will be called holy.

4   When the LORD has washed away
>   the filth of the women of Zion,
>   and cleansed the bloodstains of Jerusalem from its midst
>   by a spirit of judgment and by a spirit of purging,

5   then the LORD will create over the whole shrine
>   and over her festive gathering
>   a cloud of smoke by day
>   and a bright flame of fire by night;
>   for over all the glory there will be a canopy.

6   And there will be a booth for a shade by day
>   from the heat of the sun,
>   and a refuge and hiding place
>   from storm and from rain.

a. A textual comparison of vv. 2–4 with Micah 4:1–4 lies outside the scope of this commentary.

b. An object such as "diviners" (*qôs^e mîm*) appears to have fallen out by haplography (cf. *BHS*).

c. The MT is often emended to read "blessed" (*'ašrê*).

d. Clearly a euphemism.

e. The identification of the jewelry is uncertain.

Selected Bibliography

P. R. Ackroyd, "A Note on Isaiah 2, 1," *ZAW* 75, 1963, 320–21; **J. G. Baldwin,** "*Ṣemaḥ* as a Technical Term in the Prophets," *VT* 14, 1964, 93–97; **J. Becker,** *Isaias—der Prophet und sein Buch,* SBS 30, 1968, 49–50; **J. Blenkinsopp,** "Fragments of Ancient Exegesis in an Isaian Poem (Jes 2, 6–22)," *ZAW* 93, 1981, 51–62; **G. I. Davies,** "The Destiny of the Nations in the Book of Isaiah," *The Book of Isaiah,* ed. J. Vermeylen, Leuven 1989, 93–94; **G. von Rad,** "The City on the Hill," *The Problem of the Hexateuch and Other Essays,* ET New York 1966, 232–42; **G. T. Sheppard,** "Isaiah 1–39," *Harper's Bible Commentary,* New York 1988, 562–63; "The 'Scope' of Isaiah as a Book of Jewish and Christian Scriptures," *New Visions of Isaiah,* ed. R. F. Melugin and M. A. Sweeney, JSOTSup 214, Sheffield 1996, 257–81; **M. A. Sweeney,** *Isaiah 1–4 and the Post-Exilic Understanding of the Isaianic Tradition,* BZAW 171, 1988, 134–84; *Isaiah 1–39,* FOTL 16, Grand Rapids 1996, 87–112; "The Book of Isaiah as Prophetic Torah,"

New Visions of Isaiah, op. cit., 50–67; **H. Wildberger,** "Die Völkerwallfahrt zum Zion, Jes II 1–5," *VT* 7, 1957, 62–81; **H. G. M. Williamson,** *The Book Called Isaiah,* Oxford 1994, 150–55.

The central portions of this unit consist of harsh judgment oracles, at first directed more generally against human pride and idolatry (2:6–22), but then focused on the encroaching anarchy (3:1–15) and the desolation of Jerusalem's wealthy women (3:18–4:1). These prophetic proclamations of judgment have been bracketed at the beginning and end with two oracles of eschatological redemption of Zion, now cleansed of all its sin and impurity (2:2–5; 4:2–6).

Exposition

[2:1] There has been much discussion of the dating and function of this second Isaianic superscription. Initially it appears strange that the prophet is again introduced after 1:1. Generally it is held that this superscription is a redactional heading to the collection found in chapters 2 — 12 (cf. 13:1) that was specifically addressed to Judah and Jerusalem. Various theories about its exact age and relation to vv. 2–5 or 6 ff. remain the subject of debate. Usually 2:1 is thought older than 1:1 in terms of the book's redactional history. Ackroyd has suggested that the superscription in 2:1 refers only to the unit following in vv. 2–4 and not to a collection of ensuing oracles. However, this would be odd since usually such headings introduce larger prophetic collections. The general consensus is that 2:1 marked the beginning of a collection at some stage in the book's redactional growth.

[2–5] An initial problem that is crucial for interpreting this passage is establishing a proper context. The issue first surfaced in the older debate over the authorship of the passage in Isaiah because of its close parallel to Micah 4:1–4. Evidence for the priority of either Isaiah or Micah is inconclusive. It is possible that the passage predated both prophets and was accommodated by each collection in a slightly different form. Although the redactional age of the composition remains contested, the material of the passage is clearly ancient, even with mythopoetic roots, which has been encompassed with old Hebrew pilgrimage traditions (cf. Wildberger). Initially scholars attempted to establish a context within the biography of Isaiah. Duhm, followed by Eichrodt, assumed that the passage must be the swan song of the aged prophet at the end of his career because it would not fit within his largely judgmental preaching. Others rejected entirely Isaianic authorship and assigned it to a postexilic author as "nongenuine."

More recently, a growing scholarly consensus has emerged that such a biographical approach offers a misleading avenue into the problem on context. The relation between literary composition and authorial intent requires a far more subtle handling. There is every indication that the passage has been shaped editorially to function specifically within the book of Isaiah. This insight evokes a very different set of questions from the traditional ones of authorship and dating. The oracle's position is surely redactional, but this observation in itself tells the interpreter very little about its canonical function.

The initial question of redactional critics turns on determining the editorial intention in placing 2:2–4 at this position in the book. The issue is tied to the dating of this redactional activity, and on this issue commentators disagree. Sweeney (*Isaiah 1–39*, 95–96) argues for a date in the Persian period later than Second Isaiah. Williamson insists on a date congruent with Second Isaiah, which is used to support his theory of Second Isaiah as the redactor of First Isaiah. These differences in dating at first seem to be of little importance. However, what is significant and related to the issue of dating is the intent that is projected to explain the redactional role of the oracle. Thus, Sweeney speaks of the great tension in chapters 2–4, and he sees the major purpose of a postexilic editor to lie in acknowledging that the "ideal Jerusalem" of 2:1–4 had not been realized by the restoration of the Second Temple. Because of this disillusionment, the earlier hope of salvation was projected into the future, sometime in the mid-fifth century. Clements also places the redactional shaping in the fifth century, but sees the major purpose to relate the earlier Isaianic threats to the disaster of 587. The effect of this retrojection was to remove the threats as having been already fulfilled and thus to provide in 2:1–4 and 4:2–6 a note of future optimism.

In my opinion, both of these etiological (*post factum*) interpretations politicize the biblical material and flatten its theological dimensions by explaining its meaning as a later historical rationalization. The hermeneutical task of exegesis is indeed to take seriously the complex, multilayered quality of this text. However, it must also pursue the text's theological movement as the prophetic message was shaped into authoritative scripture in order to unfold the purpose of God with his people, precisely at a juncture when God's time intersected violently with Israel's.

At the outset, the initial phrase "it shall happen in the latter days" (v. 2) establishes the text's context as eschatological. It speaks of God's time, different in kind from ordinary time, and it signals immediately that there is no simple linear continuity between Israel's historical existence and the entrance of God's kingdom. Rather, into the old breaks the radical new. To contrast God's time as "ideal" and Israel's as "actual" (Motyer) is completely inadequate theologically and confuses the major exegetical problem of chapters 2–12, which turns on the stark juxtaposition of passages of salvation with those of judgment. Contrast 2:1–4, 4:2–6, 9:1–6, 10:20–27, 11:1–16, and 12:1–6 with 2:6–22, 3:1–4:1, 5:1–7, 5:8–30, and 9:8ff. Although these texts often represent different redactional layers, their start juxtaposition within the final form of the text is to be resolved theologically, not redactionally.

Verse 2 picks up the theme of the faithful city introduced in 1:21ff. The application of the ancient, Canaanite mythopoetic imagery of Zion being transformed into the highest of all mountains reflects the theme of a new creation, but one that bears the marks of God's original intention of primordial harmony of the universe (Gen. 2:10ff.). Jerusalem as the seat of the house of God now exerts an overwhelming attraction for the nations, which stream to it. Their purpose is then stated in direct discourse: "Let us go up . . . to the house of the God of Jacob that he may teach us . . ." The nations come not to be proselytized into the Hebrew religion—the concept of human religion is foreign to the text—but to learn from God. The form of this instruction is torah and the word of the Lord, which issue from Jerusalem.

Recently G. T. Sheppard ("Isaiah 1—39") has argued quite correctly that closer attention should be paid to the precise meaning of *tôrāh* in Isaiah. As is widely recognized, the term covers a wide semantic range of meaning including teaching, instruction, and law. Within the book of Isaiah it has often been argued that the term denotes simply the teaching of the prophets and that it was considered to be completely independent of the law of Moses (e.g., 8:16; 30:9). However, Sheppard has pointed out that in 2:3 the same word has been expanded in terms of the larger revealed Torah that became associated with the law of Moses in the Pentateuch. In passages such as 2:3, 8:20, 24:5, and in chapters 40—66, the term has been broadened to include by assumption the revealed Mosaic legislation as the divinely given norm for Israel. Accordingly, this development thus provides the warrant for the traditional Jewish interpretation that the book of Isaiah serves as a commentary on the Mosaic Torah.

Although I feel the force of Sheppard's canonical argument, it does not appear to be fully convincing. Indeed there is a broadening of the term evoked in part by the larger context of an expanding collection of sacred scripture. Yet I would argue that the semantic extension is not simply in terms of prophetic Torah being identified with the Mosaic. Rather, the subject matter of the prophetic message as divine truth continues to exercise a coercion on Israel such that the Mosaic Torah itself increasingly received its full meaning from the divine reality witnessed to by the prophets. On the one hand, the substance (*res*) of the prophetic polemic served to check all legalistic moves inherent in law (1 Sam. 15:22ff.). On the other hand, the unswerving appeal to the Mosaic Torah by the prophets (Jer. 7:1ff.; Mal. 4:4) blocked all attempts to mitigate the full force of the divine will that was given a concrete form at Sinai. In a word, both law and prophetic proclamation were expanded in terms of a deepening grasp of God's reality, but neither was subordinated in principle to the other. Of course, it was this understanding of the nature of Hebrew scripture that drove the apostle Paul to identify the divine truth of the entire Old Testament with the one reality made known through God in Jesus Christ (Rom. 10:1ff.).

In v. 4 God's role is described as adjudicating justly among the nations. His reign is universal in scope, and the "many peoples" portrayed as now living in peace and harmony are those who have gone to the mountain of the Lord to walk in his ways. The description of eschatological rule is not part of a human social program; indeed, the demonic threat of a return to war remains still virulent (Joel 4:9ff. = ET 3:9ff.). Rather, "the holy city, New Jerusalem descends out of heaven from God as a bride adorned for her husband" (Rev. 21:2).

The final exhortation of v. 5 is addressed to the house of Jacob and points both forward and backward. Israel stands poised either on the side of the nations who are seeking "the house of the God of Jacob" (v. 3), or on the side of the rejected disobedient people, "the house of Jacob" of v. 6. The prophet Isaiah identifies himself with his people in urging them, "let us walk in the light of the LORD," and thus truly be the house of Jacob. This ending, which differs from its parallel in Micah 4, offers a good illustration of how the author (editor) sought to address his hearers existentially in accord with the larger literary context of his message (cf. Williamson, 153).

[2:6–22] Textual and structural problems greatly encumber the interpretation of this passage. For some commentators, a deeply rooted distortion of the prophet's original message has been attributed to its process of transmission. Ever since Duhm's initial analysis in 1892, which he continued to polish in the subsequent editions of his commentary, a great variety of textual and structural reconstructions have been attempted. The warrant for such probes derives from what appears to be fragments of refrains. The clause "humankind is brought low and all people will be humbled" occurs with slight variations in 2:9, 11, 17 and in 5:15. Moreover, the sequence: "Yahweh alone will be exalted in that day," appears in a refrain-like repetition in vv. 11 and 17. Finally, there are clusters of lead words, such as the initial play on the word "full," followed by a polemic against everything "proud and mighty" (vv. 12–14), and ending with a focus on the destruction of idols (vv. 18, 20) and the "terror of Yahweh" (vv. 19, 21). Earlier commentators (e.g., Procksch) tried to reconstruct two originally independent oracles. More recently, attention has focused on patterns of redactional growth (Clements), but both approaches remain largely unilluminating.

It would be unwise to deny a complex transmission process at work. I do not dismiss the suggestion that verses such as 2:18–19 might possibly reflect the effect of the disaster of 587, but whether such a resonance derives from a redactional layer is impossible to prove. Above all, I question in this case whether a reconstruction of an original prophetic oracle is either possible or fruitful. The real issue rather turns on how this difficult, but far from incoherent, text now functions in its present form. Unfortunately, not much help has emerged from recent synchronic analyses (Watts, Motyer), which have often imposed modern literary categories to achieve a unified reading. One gains the impression of an interpreter forcing Shakespeare's rules for composing a sonnet upon the wild and unruly poetry of Walt Whitman. Finally, some commentators have despaired of finding any unified meaning and have characterized the chapter as a heap of unrelated fragments.

What we have in this passage is a devastating series of judgment pronouncements that describe the life and behavior of rejected Israel, moving rapidly from accusation to accusation. The land is full of soothsayers and "quack" prophets; it is saturated with the corrosive influence of foreigners, especially with the production of idols. Jerusalem seeks its security in armaments of horses and chariots, priding itself on its wealth. The prophet thus focuses his scathing attack on the people's pride and haughtiness. His speech erupts in a diatribe against all the symbols of human power and confidence. It extends to their strong walls of defense, ships, beautiful crafts, and even includes the mighty cedars of Lebanon and high mountains in which Israel glorified. It is, however, characteristic of Isaiah's God-saturated stance that his attack extends far beyond Jerusalem and Judah to be directed against all of humanity in general. A similar contrast between God and human beings, between spirit and flesh, continues to resonate throughout his entire career (cf. 31:3).

The vehement prophetic denunciation of Israel's manner of life does not arise from a conservative intolerance of foreign influences, but rather stems from a consistently awesome vision of God as creator. From a radically theocentric stance the prophet lays claim for Yahweh's complete sovereignty over his creation: "Yahweh alone will be exalted." The coming judgment is described as the entrance of God's day of reckoning. In this passage there is not yet mention of a foreign enemy, but the judgment is unleashed solely from God. He rises to terrify the earth (vv. 10, 19, 21). The manifestation of his glory as judgment is the reverse side of the revelation of his salvation (cf. chapter 6). The effect is that as the dimensions of God's time are portrayed, Israel and humanity in general are rendered smaller and smaller. "Humankind is brought low," its pride humbled and haughtiness shamed, and all its vaunted works rendered worthless. The result is utter terror, fleeing into caverns, sharing the filthy holes of bats and moles in the dirt, unable to endure the glory and splendor of God.

It becomes clear that the sharp literary discontinuity between vv. 2–5 and vv. 6ff. reflects more than a simple compositional problem, but touches on the basic hermeneutical discontinuity between *Heil* and *Unheil* (salvation and doom) in the book of Isaiah (cf. Herntrich). A radical discontinuity derives from the tension rather than from the subject matter itself. Reflection on the literary intertextuality of the chapter highlights the thematic discontinuity of two opposing visions of reality. In vv. 2ff. the one mountain containing the house of Yahweh is exalted as the highest elevation of all, whereas in vv. 12ff. the high mountain, lofty hills, and proud towers are symbols of human arrogance much like the Tower of Babel. In the first unit, the nations flow to the mount to learn of God; in the second, the land is filled with foreigners, traders, and soothsayers. In the first, the nations come to walk in God's paths; in the second, they worship their own inventions. In the one, the nations reject the weapons of violence; in the other, there is no limit to their horses and chariots. Finally, in the one, peace and harmony of God's reign issue; in the other, there is terror, fear, and humiliation. Naturally, it is difficult to determine how much of this effect is the result of conscious redactional intent and how much derives from the intertextual resonance generated by the larger canonical context. However, the very nature of scripture as a genre greatly relativizes the importance of making this distinction, which remains a central concern only to historical critics.

The present unit of 2:6–22, in spite of the unresolved problems of its literary composition, produces the effect of a tremendous orchestration of sounds. The drum beat of "full of . . . full of . . . full of . . ." is broken by an alternate cadence of "low, humble, hide." Then again the notes shift to profile the "proud, high, and lofty," which are then shattered in a crescendo of crashing sounds as God rises to terrify the earth, and the Lord alone is glorified in that day. A major criticism of all the various literary reconstructions is that, in the end, the readings are pale and insipid in contrast to the rough, awesome terror produced by the received text. This effect is only enhanced by the imperative interpolations: "do not forgive them" (v. 9); "go into the rocks" (v. 10), "stop glorifying man, who has only a breath in his nostrils" (v. 22). With this utterly theocentric focus, the reader finds the central pulse beat of Isaianic theology, and is led on inexorably to seek its source in the chapters that lie ahead.

[3:1–12] Although there is a larger thematic unity that loosely connects 3:1–4:1 — namely, the disastrous effects of the growing anarchy of Jerusalem — it does help exegetically toward sharpening the textual focus to treat each of the smaller units as an initially discrete entity.

The judgment oracle is directed specifically against Jerusalem and Judah, only the sequence is inverted from the two previous superscriptions. The semantic effect is inconsequential. Yahweh himself is stripping away the ruling classes of Jerusalem's society — the military, the judicial, the religious. These are the offices that give civil community stability and direction. In v. 1, reference to "every prop of food and every prop of water" appears to be a type of commentary on the phrase "prop and stay," which alters the original sense and could possibly reflect the later experience of the siege of the city in 587 (cf. 2 Kings 25:3). However, the observation remains uncertain since the connection of anarchy and famine are closely related (v. 7). The coming anarchy follows when irresponsible leaders take control. They are described as children and untrained. The result is that both justice and common civility become casualties. The irony of the situation is highlighted by describing the possession of a cloak as sufficient evidence of distinction to warrant a leadership role. The effect of their rule increases in society. Verse 9 speaks of the twisting of justice and of flagrant sin like that of Sodom, which they no longer are concerned to conceal. In vv. 10–11 there is an aside, first addressed to the righteous, then to the wicked. These verses could well be secondary in order to heighten the contrast within the suffering population, since v. 12 joins with the theme of v. 9. The passage closes with an elegy on the people.

The prophet again identifies with his people in their plight and heaps the blame on their leaders who have wrought this confusion and disorder.

[13–15] These verses reflect a different literary form from the preceding unity. The setting is forensic and Yahweh is pictured as a judge taking his seat in court to execute a judgment. Yet the thematic continuity between the units is close and the unit serves to intensify the attack on the leaders. From the mouth of God in direct discourse, the major blame for Jerusalem's condition is laid at the door of the elders and princes. Specific accusations in the style of prophetic invectives are hurled. The ruling classes are exploiting the poor and grinding them into the ground. The polemic shares much in common with Amos (e.g., 2:7) and Micah (e.g., 2:1ff.) and has a decidedly eighth-century flavor. The imagery of Zion as the vineyard is used, which resonates backward to 1:8 and forward to 5:1ff. God then identifies with his abused people in a heated confrontation (v. 15). The concluding formula, "says Yahweh, God of hosts," only adds to the solemn authority of the divine sentence.

[3:16–4:1] The passage is clearly set apart from the preceding unity by means of an introductory formula. Yet the formula is conventional and does not really match the prophetic oracle, which addresses Yahweh in the third person. The form used is that of an invective, which grounds the divine threat (v. 16) and follows with specific accusations. The women of Jerusalem are singled out to illustrate the indulgent, arrogant, and silly behavior of the wealthy, who will shortly suffer humiliation and shame. All the horrors of war—rape, disease, and famine—will replace the luxurious life of opulence and self-indulgence. Verses 18–23 appear to be a later prose expansion of the invective, which carefully catalogs in the greatest detail all the offending items from the female wardrobe and interrupts the cadence of the original oracle.

The verses that follow (3:25–4:1) are quite different in literary form from the preceding verses, but they were clearly understood as standing in closest continuity with the threat against the women of Jerusalem. Zion, the city, is portrayed as a woman who is about to suffer in war the death of her husband and the shame of widowhood. The concluding verse that portrays seven women pursuing one man in search of a husband returns to the earlier theme of social anarchy, when all the normal conventions have been disregarded and desperation reigns before the encroaching reality of shame and reproach.

[2–6] The passage again marks a sharp shift in content from the oracles of chapters 2—3. After Yahweh had executed his judgment and cleansed Jerusalem from its moral filth, a remnant that has survived will be deemed holy. Then God will again make the land glorious and Zion will become a city of sacred assemblies. Yahweh will manifest himself as at the exodus to protect his city and people.

The initial debate on this passage revolved around the questions of dating and unity. Duhm judged the style to be a clumsy, overladen form of very late prose. A few older commentators tried to salvage a preexilic nucleus, but shortly a wide consensus confirmed the passage as postexilic. The "ideology" of the unit was correlated with themes from late prophetic and priestly literature. The ritualistic and ethical concerns were thought to resemble Ezekiel, Third Isaiah, and Zechariah more than the prophet Isaiah (cf. G. B. Gray). Clements tried to extend this direction of interpretation further by assigning a motivation to the redactor. Accordingly, these verses were introduced by a late redactor to show that the threat to Jerusalem had passed.

Some of these critical observations may well be right. The style of the passage appears expansive and there are striking parallels with late biblical literature. Yet I would argue that the interpretation of these factors has been badly misconstrued, largely because of the assumption that a reconstructed historical context provides the only access to the passage's meaning. Clements's analysis not only historicizes the passage, but then alters the text's eschatological orientation into an etiological commentary on the past. Wildberger's form-critical focus results in a severe fragmentation of the passage without any substantive coherence.

The chief exegetical issue at stake again turns on the question of context. Crucial to correct interpretation is the recognition of the element of intertextuality. The passage has chosen words and themes from Israel's tradition that provide a resonance for the informed reader. In addition, the chapter is set within the specific literary setting of the book of Isaiah and contrasts the cleansed, redeemed, and purified community with the haughty, corrupt, and anarchic people of chapters 2 and 3. Finally, the passage reflects a holistic reading of Israel's entire prophetic corpus that combines a wide range of prophetic and priestly promises into one single story. In a word, one sees in chapter 4 every evidence of an interpretation that has been responsive to the coercion of the entire biblical text and is not just an expression of a given political or social ideology.

"In that day the branch of the LORD will be beautiful and glorious, and the fruit of the land will be the pride and glory of Israel's survivors." The phrase "in that day" is the third close reference to the formula (cf. 3:18; 4:1). The two prior usages serve largely to continue the future orientation of the judgment oracle. The dominant eschatological emphasis of 2:1–4 and 2:6ff. reverberates strongly in 4:2. Not just ordinary time is being extended, but God's time of eschatological judgment and salvation, which comprises one single reality without a fixed temporal sequence.

More difficult to determine is the meaning of the phrase "branch of Yahweh," which stands in parallel to "fruit of the land." The traditional Christian interpretation has followed the Targum in interpreting the phrase messianically. The warrant for this interpretation is in the clear messianic reference to the *ṣemaḥ* ("branch") in Jer. 23:5, 33:18, and Zech. 3:8, 6:12 (cf. Ps. 132:17). However, modern critics have been quick to point out the exegetical problems involved in this rendering. First, in the above "messianic" passages the "branch" is related to a scion of David, and not to Yahweh as in 4:2. Second, if the Messiah is the branch, who is the paralleled "fruit of the land"? As a consequence, the great majority of scholars (also Delitzsch) interpret the verse to mean that Yahweh promises a renewed fertility to the land, which will spring forth in the new period of Zion's redemption.

Once again, the interpretation depends on the question of proper context. From a strictly philological perspective, the literal rendering of the passage as a promise of renewed fertility and beauty to the land is not wrong. Yet the exalted style of the entire passage warns against a too flat and prosaic interpretation. At the very least, the promise of a beautiful and glorious increase of vegetation is playing on the eschatological theme of a return of paradise. Vineyards will be planted and their fruit eaten (Isa. 65:23). Zion will rejoice from the sheer abundance of food and drink (66:11). The wilderness will become a fruitful field (32:16). Zion will become a crown of beauty (62:3), and those eating of its fullness will praise Yahweh (62:9; cf. Hos. 14:5ff.; Amos 9:13ff.; Isa. 30:23).

In the same manner, once the term "branch" had become a technical term for the Messiah in later prophetic literature, it is difficult to imagine this earlier, nontechnical usage not accumulating a richer connotation than perhaps originally intended. Particularly does this move seem likely when one recalls that the passage has been linked intertextually with its larger Isaianic context. Had not Isa. 11:1 spoken of a "shoot" (*nēṣer*) from the stump of Jesse, which initiated the prophetic theme of the return of paradisal peace and harmony (vv. 6–9; cf. 65:21ff.)? Moreover, the use of the verb "create" (*bārā'*) raises the level of the imagery to that of a new divine creation, which starts over, as it were, after the cleansing of Jerusalem. In sum, in the present literary context within the book of Isaiah, the terms resonate with messianic reference both in terms of the messianic bringer of salvation (the "branch") and the return of paradise ("the fruit of the land"). Indeed, the very expansive, overlaid style of the unit is a further sign that this passage has acquired multilayered connotations when construed in the light of the larger corpus of scripture.

The same "surplus of meaning" can be discerned in the rest of this passage. Chapter 1 had spoken of God's purifying of the faithless city filled with blood by fire and heat (v. 15) in order to restore faithful Zion (vv. 24ff.). The prophet Isaiah himself, who confessed, "I am a man of unclean lips, and I live among a people of unclean lips," (6:5) was purified with a burning coal. Now "in that day" the purified site of the whole of Mount Zion will be covered along with her assemblies (4:5). The language is of the worshipping community called to a festival (cf. Ex. 12:16; Lev. 23:7–8), the celebration of which serves as a remembrance of Israel's deliverance throughout every generation.

The presence of the Lord is again manifested to Zion as to the wilderness generation by the accompanying cloud by day and flaming fire by night. The stress falls on the leading and protection of God in his glory, a continuing protection and shelter from danger. The sign of God's gracious presence is no longer confined to the Holy of Holies with its access only to the high priest, but the entire mountain is overshadowed as a sacred sanctuary. The postexilic note of peace and safety (Zech. 8:12; 14:11) is especially strong, as is the emphasis on the rising glory of God (Isa. 40:5; 60:2).

However, the most complete resonance of this eschatological theme encompassing the entire book of Isaiah is found in Rev. 21:22–27. The presence of God now replaces the temple and provides the light rather than the sun and moon (Isa. 60:19–20). By its light the nations walk (2:24) and bring into the city their wealth (60:11). The city gates are open continually (60:11). Only the pure enter its walk, those written in the book of life (4:3). Finally, Revelation 21 speaks of "the glory of God as its light and its lamp is the Lamb." Is this a reference to that "branch" in whose days Israel will dwell securely (Jer. 23:5–6)?

7. Isaiah 5:1–30

5:1   I will sing for my beloved
        a song about my friend concerning his vineyard.
    My loved one had a vineyard
        on a fertile hillside.

2   He broke up the soil, and cleared it of stones,
        and planted it with choice vines.
    He built a watchtower in it
        and even hewed out a winepress.
    Then he hoped it would yield good grapes;
        instead it yielded bitter grapes.

3   Now then, you dwellers in Jerusalem
        and men of Judah,
        you be the judge
    between me and my vineyard.

4   What more could have been done for my vineyard
        that I have not done for it?
    Why, when I hoped for good grapes,
        did it yield bitter grapes?

5   Now I will tell you
        what I am going to do to my vineyard.
    I will take away its hedge
        that it may be destroyed.
    I will break down its wall
        that it may be trampled.

6   And I will make it a desolation;
         it shall neither be pruned nor hoed,
     but thorns and thistles will grow.
         Then I will command the clouds
         not to rain on it.
7   For the vineyard of the LORD of hosts
         is the house of Israel,
     and the men of Judah
         are his pleasant plantings.
     He looked for justice,
         and behold, injustice,
         for righteousness, but behold cries of distress.
8   Woe to you who add house to house
         and join field to field,
     until no space is left
         and you alone inhabit the land.
9   In my hearing (swore) the LORD of hosts:
         "Surely great houses will become desolate,
     fine large houses without occupants.
10   For ten acres of vineyard
         will yield just one *bath,*
     and a field sown with a *homer* of seed
         will yield a mere *ephah.*"
11   Woe to those who rise early in the morning
         to run after their drinks,
     who stay up late at night,
         until they are inflamed by wine!
12   They have lyre and lute,
         timbrel, flute, and wine at their feasts,
     but they do not give a thought
         to the deeds of the LORD,
     and take no notice
         of the work of his hands.
13   Therefore my people will go into exile
         for lack of knowledge;
     their men[a] of rank will die of hunger
         and their masses will be parched with thirst.
14   Therefore Sheol has increased its appetite
         and opened its mouth, its limitless jaws,
     and down go the nobility and common people
         with her brawlers and revelers.

15 So humankind is brought low and men are humbled,
    and the eyes of the arrogant are depressed.
16 But the LORD of hosts is exalted in justice,
    and the Holy God proves himself holy in righteousness.
17 Then lambs will graze as in their meadows,
    and strangers[b] will feed among the ruins of the rich.
18 Woe to those who haul sin[c] with cords of deceit,
    who drag iniquity with wagon tackle,
19 who say: "Let (God) hurry,
    let him get on with his work
that we may see it.
    Let the plan of the Holy One of Israel
    be quickly fulfilled if we are to
    pay any attention!"
20 Woe to those who call evil good
    and good evil,
who present darkness as light
    and light as darkness,
who make bitter sweet and sweet bitter!
21 Woe to those who are wise in their own eyes,
    and clever in their own sight!
22 Woe to those who are champions at
    drinking wine,
and heroes in mixing drinks,
23 who acquit the guilty for a bribe,
    and deprive the innocent of his right!
24 Therefore, as straw is consumed by a tongue of fire
    and dry grass shrivels in the flame,
so their roots will rot
    and their blossom blow away like dust;
for they have rejected the law of the LORD of hosts,
    and despised the word of the Holy One of Israel.
25 Therefore the anger of the LORD burns
    against his people,
and he stretched out his hand
    against them and smote them,
so that the mountains shook;
    and their corpses were like refuse
    in the streets.
For all this his anger is not turned away,
    and his hand is stretched out still.

26   He will raise a signal to a nation far off,
        and he will whistle for those
        at the ends of the earth.
        See, they come with lightning speed!
27   Not one of them grows tired or stumbles,
        not one sleeps or dozes,
        not a belt comes loose at the waist,
        not a sandal thong breaks.
28   Their arrows are sharpened,
        and all their bows are drawn;
        their horses' hoofs are like flint,
        their chariot wheels like the whirlwind.
29   Their roaring is like a lion's;
        they roar like young lions,
        they growl and seize their prey,
        they carry it off and none can rescue.
30   And in that day they will roar over it
        like the roaring of the sea.
        And if one looks at the land,
        behold, darkness and distress,
        and the light is darkened by its clouds.

   a. The MT reads literally "men of hunger." It is often repointed as a verbal form of
mût, mētê, meaning "dying."
   b. Some emend the MT "strangers" to "sheep/goats."
   c. The imagery of v. 18 is unusual. NEB prefers to read with emendations: "who drag
wickedness like a tethered sheep and sin like a heifer on a rope."

Selected Bibliography

B. W. Anderson, "'God with Us'—In Judgment and in Mercy: The Editorial Structure of Isaiah 5—
10(11)," *Canon, Theology and Old Testament Interpretation, Fs B. S. Childs,* Philadelphia 1988, 230–45;
H. Barth, *Die Jesaja-Worte in der Josiazeit,* WMANT 48, 1977, 109–17; **J. Barthel,** *Prophetenwort und
Geschichte. Die Jesajaüberlieferung in Jes 6—8 und 28—31,* FAT 19, Tübingen 1997; **U. Becker,**
Jesaja—von der Botschaft zum Buch, FRLANT 178, Göttingen 1997; **E. Blum,** "Jesajas prophetisches
Testament. Beobachtungen zu Jes 1—11," *ZAW* 108, 1996, 547–65; 109, 1997, 12–29; **W. P. Brown,**
"The So-called Refrain in Isaiah 5:25–30 and 9:7–10:4," *CBQ* 52, 1990, 432–43; **K. Budde,** *Jesaja's
Erleben. Eine gemeinverständliche Auslegung der Denkschrift der Propheten (Kap 6, 1–9, 6),* Gotha
1928; **B. S. Childs,** *Biblical Theology of the Old and New Testaments,* London and Minneapolis 1992,
337–47; **J. A. Emerton,** "The Translation of Isaiah 5, 1," *The Scripture and the Scrolls, Fs A. S. Van der
Woude,* VTSup 49, 1992, 18–30; **C. Hardmeier,** "Verkündigung und Schrift bei Jesaja," *Theologie und
Glaube* 73, 1983, 119–34; **S. A. Irvine,** "The Isaianic Denkschrift: Reconsidering an Old Hypothesis,"
ZAW 104, 1992, 216–31; **H. Junker,** "Die literarische Art von Is. 5 1–7," *Bib* 40, 1959, 259–66; **T.
Lescow,** "Jesajas Denkschrift aus der Zeit des syrisch-ephraimitischen Krieges," *ZAW* 85, 1973, 315–31;
C. E. L'Heureux, "The Redactional History of Isaiah 5.1–10.4," *In the Shelter of Elyon, Fs G. W.*

Ahlström, ed. W. B. Barrick, J. R. Spencer, JSOTSup 31, Sheffield 1984, 99–119; **H. P. Müller,** "Glauben und Bleiben: Zur Denkschrift Jesajas Kapitel VI 1–VIII 18," *Studies on Prophecy,* VTSup 26, Leiden 1974, 25–55; **D. L. Petersen, K. H. Richards,** "Isaiah 5:1–7," *Interpreting Hebrew Poetry,* Minneapolis 1992, 81–88; **H. Graf Reventlow,** "Das Ende der sog. 'Denkschrift Jesajas,'" *BN* 38/39, 1987, 62–67; **W. Schottroff,** "Das Weinberglied Jesajas (Jes 5, 1–7): Ein Beitrag zur Geschichte der Parabel," *ZAW* 82, 1970, 68–91; **G. T. Sheppard,** "The Anti-Assyrian Redaction and the Canonical Context of Isaiah 1– 39," *JBL* 104, 1985, 193–216; **O. H. Steck,** "Bemerkungen zu Jesaja 6," *BZ* NF 16, 1972, 188–206, *Wahrnehmungen Gottes im Alten Testament,* ThB 70, Munich 1982, 149–70; **J. Werlitz,** *Studien zur literarkritischen Method,* BZAW 204, 1992; **W. Werner,** "Vom Prophetenwort zur Prophetentheologie: Ein redaktionskritischer Versuch zu Jes 6, 1–8, 18," *BZ* 29, 1985, 1–30; **G. R. Williams,** "Frustrated Expectations in Isaiah V 1–7: A Literary Interpretation," *VT* 35, 1985, 459–65; **J. T. Willis,** "The Genre of Isaiah 5:1–7," *JBL* 96, 1977, 337–62; **G. A. Yee,** "The Form Critical Study of Isaiah 5:1–7 as a Song and as a Juridical Parable," *CBQ* 43, 1981, 30–40.

1. Structure, Genre, and Function

There is wide agreement that vv. 1–7 comprise a unit with a clear introduction separating the verses from chapter 4, and with an obvious ending in v. 7. Much debate, however, turns on determining the exact genre of the song (cf. below).

At the outset, a major problem of the chapter turns on the relation of the song to the succeeding verses. A new and clearly defined form-critical series of woe oracles (invectives) extends from vv. 8–23, each beginning with *hôy*. These six woe oracles are of differing lengths, followed by two apparently judgment oracles in vv. 24–25. These verses in turn lead to a concluding oracle announcing the coming of a "nation far off" to execute God's judgment. In addition, there are numerous signs that the text of this series of oracles has suffered both expansions and contractions. Some commentators also argue for a dislocation in the sequences (e.g., Wildberger). The clearest examples of expansion lie in vv. 13 and 14, both beginning with a "therefore," and in vv. 15–16, which have a parallel from chapter 2. The exegetical decision of some of the older commentators to recover an original series through emendation and translocation has usually been judged unfruitful and too conjectural. The collecting and shaping process did not always preserve the oral pattern in which the prophetic invective was closely followed by a divine threat. Anderson has pointed out the rhetorical use of consecutive "therefores" and sought to demonstrate its literary effectiveness (Anderson, 234–35).

Even more perplexing is v. 25, which ends with an apparent refrain: "For all this his anger is not turned away, and his hand is stretched out still," a phrase recurring in a sequence found in 9:7ff. (ET 9:8ff.). Duhm, followed by many, thought that the beginning of the oracle had suffered a major loss since v. 25 does not attach smoothly to v. 24. The observation of the refrain in the verse provided the first evidence on which the famous *Denkschrift* (memoir) hypothesis has been built. Because this theory has been rehearsed many times, a review can be brief. Nevertheless, it has greatly affected how one interprets chapters 5 — 10.

2. The *Denkschrift* Hypothesis

Although elements of the theory go back to critical analyses of the mid-nineteenth century, the classic formulation derives from the studies of K. Budde. As originally formulated by him, 6:1–9:6 constituted a discrete collection of Isaianic oracles authored by the prophet himself that had been accidentally inserted into another early collection of oracles. The evidence for this theory rested on several observations:

a. A series of oracles directed against the Northern Kingdom can be clearly delineated by the presence of a common refrain occurring in 9:11, 16, 20; and 10:4: "for all this his anger is not turned away . . ." In addition, the refrain appears in 5:25, the effect of which is that the collection of visions comprising 6:1–9:6 has been bracketed by two parts of a single oracle.

b. A series of woe oracles against Judah begins in 5:8 and continues in vv. 11, 18, 20, 21, 22. Then following the series of refrains in chapter 9, there occurs another woe oracle in 10:4 that again serves to bracket the verses 6:1–9:6 as a discrete entity.

c. In addition to these formal literary arguments of a so-called "double *inclusio*," additional arguments from content were brought forth. First, chapter 6 was judged to be an autobiographical narrative of the prophet's initial call expressing his earliest prophetic experience. Because in most other instances the prophetic call occurs at the beginning of a book (e.g., Jeremiah, Ezekiel), it was argued that Isaiah's call in chapter 6 originally stood at the beginning of an early collection and was only later relegated to its present position as the book continued to develop. Second, the historical setting for the composition of a so-called *Denkschrift* (memoir) is given in 8:16ff., in which the prophet drew up a testimony of his message after it had been rejected, and committed it to his disciplines for posterity (cf. the parallel in 31:8ff.)

As a result of these arguments, the *Denkschrift* hypothesis has received wide acceptance and has greatly influenced the interpretation of chapters 5 — 10(11). Since the initial formulation of Budde and others, there have been two major refinements of the theory. First, it has been increasingly argued that the *Denkschrift* has undergone considerable expansion. Accordingly, most critical scholars conclude the memoirs at 8:18, and regard 8:19–9:6 as containing several later expansions. Other additions are also seen in 6:12–13, 7:15, and 7:18–25. Second, with the rise of redaction criticism the dislocations effective in the *Denkschrift* are not seen as accidental, but as part of intentional historical strategy. Probably the most persuasive arguments have been those of H. Barth and O. H. Steck. Because a major issue turns on the relation of chapter 6 to chapters 7—8, we shall return to this debate in the commentary on chapter 6. (For the most recent appraisal of the hypothesis, cf. Barthel, 37–48).

Although for years I accepted the *Denkschrift* hypothesis as persuasive, the theory has, in my opinion, become increasingly untenable for a variety of reasons. It is interesting to note that several other scholars have also begun to express their serious reservations (Reventlow, Irvine).

First, when the hypothesis was first proposed, it rested on the older literary-critical assumptions of accidental interpolation. The theory seemed to resolve tensions in the text that had occurred from several unintentional dislocations. The goal of critical exegesis was then to relate the reconstructed text directly to its true historical referent. Thus, each of the two series of woe oracles and refrains was separated and restored to its allegedly original literary sequence within a historical setting. In particular, the "call" narrative was removed from its present position in chapter 6 and placed at the beginning of the book as more historically accurate (Procksch, Eichrodt). The obvious weakness in this older literary-critical approach was in failing adequately to deal with the present literary form of the text as a literary composition with its own integrity, which may well have intended something of semantic significance in positioning Isaiah's experience at chapter 6 rather than chapter 1.

Second, the exegetical move of redactional criticism seemed to correct this hermeneutical flaw when it sought to discover an editorial intentionality for the form and function of these chapters. However, in practice an unresolvable tension has emerged, particularly in the work of Barth and Clements: to establish both a meaningful reading of the present form of the text within its literary context and at the time to use the dislocations from the *Denkschrift* hypothesis to trace the stages of a history of redactional reinterpretation.

Barth (114), for example, infers that the reason for the shift of 5:25 from the end of the sequence of refrains in chapter 9 to its present position turned on the need for a bridge to 5:26–29 in introducing the Assyrians before the "call." However, the emergence of the threat from the Assyrians before chapter 6 can be far more easily explained historically (cf. 2 Kings 15:19ff.) without this elaborate *Denkschrift* hypothesis of a retrojection from the late seventh century back to the eighth. Similarly, the so-called refrain in 5:25b (a single occurrence in chapter 5 hardly makes it a refrain!) follows in unbroken continuity with v. 25a and does not require the conjectures of Duhm and Clements that several cola before v. 25a have been lost. Or again, to suggest that the introduction of a woe oracle in 10:1ff. serves to extend to Judah the divine judgment once directed against the Northern Kingdom by means of a refrain, is obvious from the present form of the text without a complex dislocation theory.

Crucial to the redactional method is the hermeneutical assumption that the biblical text is only correctly interpreted when texts are calibrated according to a reconstructed editorial process. Thus, the true significance of the dislocation of the refrain in 5:25 is that the Josianic redaction of the late seventh century first introduced into the Isaianic corpus as an ideological construct the theme of the Assyrian threat before Isaiah's "call" in chapter 6. This theme had played no role in the earlier Isaianic core traditions. Moreover, because eschatological themes are consistently assigned to a subsequent postexilic redaction, 5:30 is relegated to a period after 587 according to this assumed redactional trajectory. As a result, the thematic movement within the present form of the book of Isaiah, which involves the prophet's interpretation of the "plan of Yahweh" for Israel and the nations, has been replaced by a critically reconstructed redactional scheme that runs roughshod over the canonical shape of the biblical text itself.

Third, there is one final use of the *Denkschrift* hypothesis, which generally falls under the rubric of rhetorical criticism. A brilliant example is found in B. W. Anderson's essay on chapters 6—10. Anderson seeks to explore literary techniques that he finds at work in the construction of the text. His observations regarding the rhetorical effect of the juxtaposition of two "therefore" oracles (5:13–14, 24–25) are quite illuminating. However, my major criticism of his approach is that his attention to rhetorical features tends to separate formal stylistic features from theological substance and can distract from the text's theological intentionality (its *skopus*) by focusing on largely peripheral, formal elements. Anderson is aware of the problem, but in an attempt to avoid this trap he has fallen back on unconvincing sociological theories of prophetic countercultural attacks on the "establishment," which are then anachronistically imposed on the text, according to leads offered by W. Brueggemann (cf. Anderson, note 20).

In sum, the *Denkschrift* hypothesis remains a significant attempt to explain some of the genuine tensions in the Isaianic corpus, but particularly in its redactional-critical appropriation suffers from such heavy theoretical ballast as to obscure rather than illuminate the biblical text. The effect of the hypothesis is even more egregious in its interpretation of chapters 6 and 7, which will be treated in the next section of the commentary.

3. Exposition

[5:1–7] There has been much discussion concerning the exact genre of this song. The problem lies in understanding the relation between the predominately wisdom components of a parable and the prophetic features of a judgment oracle. The very recognition of a unique mixture of literary traditions should guard against an unfruitful search for a formally consistent pattern with one genre. Attention to both form and function is crucial.

At the outset, the song is not a love song, as often rendered (e.g., RSV), but a song of a beloved one concerning his vineyard that is sung by another. Because the imagery is flexible and indeterminate, there is a danger of the reader losing the main drift of the unity. Is the reference to a vineyard intended to be understood literally or metaphorically or both? The initial appeal to a lover (*dôdî*) has led some to interpret the vineyard as a metaphor of love, like that found in the Song of Songs. But this line of interpretation is a distraction that is never developed within the text itself. Again, the role of the friend has been thought by some commentators (e.g., Junker) to reflect the convention of the "friend of the bride," as in later rabbinic tradition. However, this feature again, even if present, remains undeveloped and lies below the surface of the text. At most these elements of indeterminacy, which are constitutive of a wisdom saying, function to puzzle the audience, which expects one thing but then receives quite another, as the mood of entertainment and curiosity is quickly dispelled by the prophet.

Verses 1–2 outline briefly the content of the song, which turns out to be a complaint. The owner of the vineyard carefully planted a vineyard in the best soil. He used the choicest vines, prepared the ground, built a watchtower to guard it, and hewed out a vine vat to receive the expected juice. Greatly to his disappointment, the vineyard produced only bitter tasting grapes, unusable for wine. At this point the audience could still hear the song metaphorically as a veiled accusation of a marriage gone awry.

In v. 3 there is an unexpected shift of speakers. The owner of the vineyard now speaks in the first person. Moreover, the tone of the *māšāl* ("parable") calling to reflection is altered. Rather, the owner now seeks a judgment between himself and his vineyard. As an accusation he demands to know what more he could have done. The audience is now involved in making a decision. The owner thus forces them out of their neutral stance as they unknowingly pass judgment on themselves.

As in v. 3, the adverb of v. 5, "now," once again signals a shift. Before a response can be evoked the owner offers his own decisions in the form of a harsh judgment oracle: "I will tell you what I am going to do . . . . I will take away its hedge . . . . I will break down its wall that it may be trampled." The final threat of the judgment, "I will command the clouds not to rain on it," clearly reveals the true identity of the speaker.

The concluding verse then removes any possible doubt about the meaning of the song. The Lord of hosts is the owner; Israel and Judah are his vineyard. God looked for *mišpāṭ* ("justice"), behold *miśpāḥ* ("bloodshed"); for *ṣᵉdāqāh* ("righteousness"), behold, iniquity *ṣᵉʿāqāh* ("iniquity").

Part of the task of exegesis of the Old Testament within its larger canonical context is to be aware of the reverberations of a given passage within scripture. The echo of chapter 5 picks up where the "old song" had ended. God lays continual claim on the ownership of the vineyard, which the leaders have devoured (3:14). The theme of a "new song" of the vineyard is first sounded in chapter 27. The coming eschatological day of salvation will evoke a new litany of praise. God announces his intent as its keeper continually to maintain it night and day against all enemies. This theme is continued in 42:10, but it then enters into Israel's liturgy to become a persistent note of expectation and hope (Pss. 96:1; 98:1; 144:9; 149:1).

In the New Testament, Isaiah 5 is explicitly picked up in Jesus' parable of the vineyard and the wicked tenants (Matt. 21:33–46). Again a man plants a vineyard, sets a hedge about it, digs a pit, and erects a tower. However, then the focus of the parable diverges sharply from that of Isaiah 5 and directs its attention to the wicked tenants of the vineyard who refuse to give the owner his fruit. Finally, they lay claim for themselves on the vineyard by killing the son.

For the interpreter who takes seriously the witnesses of both testaments, the exegetical task requires theological reflection of the relation of the two. More is required than simply describing a history of interpretation, or of analyzing features of literary continuity. Rather, the task lies in relating the theological substance of both. The juridical parable of Isaiah 5 has a theological significance far beyond the sharp existential formulation of the prophet. The issue turns on Israel's special election. When the song is read in the light of the whole Old Testament corpus, it reverberates with the entire Mosaic witness to Israel as God's special possession (Ex. 19:3ff.; Deut. 7:6ff., etc.). Likewise, in Jesus' parable the point again turns on God's claim to receive fruits of righteousness from the people, which then evoked such a violent rejection from the tenants that they murder the son (Matt. 21:43). John 15:1–11 further develops a christological interpretation of the vineyard when he probes the source of Israel's true fruit. It lies in complete dependence of the branches on the vine. God, the Father, is thus glorified by the righteous fruit that the followers of Jesus Christ produce.

In reflecting on the theological resonance created by the imagery of the vineyard, what is particularly significant is the recognition that, undergirding the wide variety in the application of the metaphor, one dominant witness encompasses the whole: "Behold, I make all things new. . . . [T]hese words are trustworthy and true" (Rev. 21:5).

[8–30] The unit consists of six woe oracles, a classic form of prophetic speech in which the prophet attacks a particular evil practice, often using the continuous action of the Hebrew participle. Often the so-called invective form is followed by a divine threat of judgment, such as in the oath formula of v. 9 or in v. 13. At times, however, in the collecting and shaping of the oral tradition, a series of invectives are aligned without succeeding threats.

These oracles of chapter 5 are usually assigned to the early period of Isaiah's preaching, but they were not delivered at one historical moment, as becomes evident from the very different settings that are reflected. There is, for example, considerable overlap in content between vv. 11 and 12. Some commentators (e.g., Wildberger) have suggested a different sequence for the oracles, which may be more logical but not necessarily more original. It does appear that the woe series contains expansions. Verse 14 does not attach easily with v. 13, although the syntactical problem of referent is not insurmountable, as sometimes claimed. Verses 15–16 appear to be a secondary addition with close parallels in chapter 2. Yet the effect is to produce an intertextual resonance with v. 7 ("justice and righteousness") and thus to join the elements of the chapter closer together.

The first woe oracle (vv. 8ff.) is directed against the abuse of power by the wealthy who exploit the poor by driving them off their land. From the chilling story of Naboth's vineyard (1 Kings 21) one learns how deep was the tradition of the land as a sacred inheritance. Because the rich of Judah act as if they now own the land for their pleasure—"It is you who has ravished the vineyard" (3:14)—God now threatens to destroy it literally, both houses and crops.

The second oracle (vv. 11ff.) is directed against the self-indulgence of a wealthy class whose members waste their time in carousing and frivolity and have no regard for God's activity in the world, not perceiving his work as creator. This lack of knowledge, which introduced the book in v. 13 (cf. Hos. 4:1), has been greatly expanded, first in v. 3 by the threat of exile and dying of hunger and thirst, and second in v. 14 against the wealthy of Jerusalem, who are portrayed as sliding down into Sheol. Verses 15–16 pick up a refrain from 2:9 to strike again the note that God alone will be exalted and the proud brought low. The God of righteousness looked for justice, but found only iniquity within his vineyard, thus the fury with which his anger burns. Verse 17 concludes the original woe oracle with the theme of the strangers feeding among the ruins, which resonates with 1:7. The reading of the LXX—kids grazing among the rubble—is also a familiar image in Isaiah (e.g., 7:25).

Verses 18–19 attack those who are so heavy with sins that they drag their guilt and iniquity with ropes after them. They are the cynical crowd that mocks the preaching of Isaiah that God has a plan for Israel. They have no awe, but dare God "to do his thing." Whatever God does is judged by them to be irrelevant in their world.

Verse 20 attacks those who "call evil good and good evil." In the nineteenth century this oracle was interpreted in a highly philosophical manner as an attempt to relativize Israel's morality by blurring the ethical distinctions between good and evil. However, such a perspective is highly anachronistic and alien to Old Testament thought. Consequently, Wildberger finds it impossible to provide this accusation with a concrete setting unless the verse is coupled with vv. 23–24 and interpreted in terms of judicial abuse. Yet there is another interpretive option. Israel's wisdom literature affords a far closer analogy for the background of the prophetic accusation that does not entail a recording of the oracle. Proverbs speaks of the deceitful man as one who twists his speech

(17:30), who utters empty words without substance (26:24ff.; 28:24). Such evil dissemblance has severed all connections between words and reality. Yet evil is not good; darkness is not light. Woe to such pretense, which seeks to confuse truth and falsehood, integrity (*tōm*) with emptiness (*šāw'*).

Verse 21 continues a similar theme of the shrewd and wise in the ways of the world who think that they can order their own affairs through cleverness. Finally, v. 22 returns to the earlier theme of v. 11 and is directed against the excessive drinking of the rulers who ruthlessly twist the law to deprive the powerless of all legal protection. The issue is not one of general "civil rights," but the divine order of justice that God established for his chosen people. The parallel with Amos's similar accusations in 2:6ff. is striking. There Amos appears knowledgeable about the legal prescriptions from the ancient covenant code (Ex. 22:25). A judgment oracle follows in v. 24, with the coming destruction described with the metaphors of burning grass, of rotting roots, and of parched buds disintegrating like dust. Verse 24b, which again grounds the judgment in the rejection of "the law of Yahweh" and the "word of the Holy One of Israel," has often been removed as a Deuteronomic addition (cf. Amos 2:4). Yet the effect of the verse, regardless of its exact dating, is to provide a summary of the prophet's accusation that encompasses all the woes of chapter 5 in terms of rejecting the law and despising God. The verse also establishes through word play on "mountain" a contrast between wicked Jerusalem and true Zion (cf. 2:3).

As discussed earlier, the inclusion of v. 25 in this position has played a major role in the *Denkschrift* hypothesis. The verse is thought to be a fragment from a series of oracles in chapter 9 that all end in a refrain. Nevertheless, in spite of the recognition that the text of Isaiah has undergone a lengthy compositional development, the function of the "refrain" in v. 25—better described as intertextual resonance—differs markedly from its use in 9:7ff. In chapter 9 a historical review of God's punitive action in the past against the Northern Kingdom, which did not result in Israel's repentance, is offered. As a result, "for all this his anger is not turned away and his hand is stretched out still." Such use of a refrain following a historical review has its closest parallel in Amos 4:6ff.

In contrast, Isaiah 5 does not present a historical review, but rather a series of accusations of continuing abuses of Judah against God and his people that function as prophetic invectives calling forth judgment. These threatening oracles follow in vv. 24 and 25. Yet the anger of God, which has already resulted in punishment—v. 17 even speaks of exile—is not enough. The abuses in the vineyard still continue and thus God's anger continues to intensify. Even though he "smote them . . . and their corpses were like refuse," this judgment is still insufficient: "His anger is not turned away and his hand is stretched out still." The indictment in v. 25b is integrally related to the anger of v. 25a and is not a clumsy editorial interpolation. The judgment, which is predicted as still to come, is then described in vv. 26–30. God signals for a "nation far off," and the enemy descends. His appearance is pictured in mythopoetic imagery. A superhuman hoard of robotlike raiders descends on Jerusalem, much akin to Jeremiah's "enemy from the north" (Jer. 4:13ff.), who bring terrifying destruction. Their identity remains hidden and at this point they are not yet identified with the Assyrians. Then in v. 30 the subject and object of the growl continue from vv. 26–29. However, by means of the familiar eschatological formula "in that day," the judgment is extended into a cosmological dimension as primordial chaos returns.

To conclude: It is highly important that the chapter be read as a whole, and that vv. 1–7 and 8–30 be interpreted together. The major argument for this decision lies in the larger structure of the book and the decisive role assigned to chapter 5. The previous section (2:1–4:6) had shaped the earlier preaching of Isaiah in such a way as to emphasize the radically different visions of Zion. On the one hand, a vision of the righteous rule of God is presented in two oracles at the beginning and end of the larger section. On the other hand, between these brackets there emerges a sinful, proud, and chaotic society in active revolt against God's rule. In chapter 5 a new stage in God's dealing with Jerusalem is initiated by the "song of the vineyard." Because Zion has become hopelessly corrupt, God will render it a total waste. The following woe oracles in chapter 5 then catalogue in detail the grounds for the verdict and culminate in the coming of a final eschatological judgment, ushered in by a terrifying enemy. In chapter 6 the divine decision to destroy Israel is revealed to Isaiah in a heavenly vision and grounded in the holiness of God. Isaiah is commissioned to be a guarantee of destruction. The hardening process is then described in chapter 7 and 8 along with the emergence of a faithful remnant.

The point bears repeating that a major objection to the *Denkschrift* hypothesis is that it substitutes a different theological trajectory for these chapters and thus runs in the face of the canonical intent. It reorders the literary sequence according to a critically reconstructed redactional scheme that reflects a heavy ideological bias regarding the nature of biblical prophecy.

8. Isaiah 6:1–13

6:1   In the year that King Uzziah died, I saw the Lord seated upon a throne, high and exalted, and the skirts of his robe filled the temple. 2 About him were attendant seraphim. Each of them had six wings. With two he covered his face, with two he covered his feet, and with two he flew. 3 They were calling ceaselessly to one another:
"Holy, holy, holy is the LORD of hosts;
the whole earth is full of his glory."

4   And the threshold shook to its foundation at the sound of their cries,
     and the house was filled with smoke. 5 Then I cried:
          "Woe is me; I am lost!ᵃ
          For I am a man of unclean lips,
          and I live among a people of unclean lips.
          Yet my own eyes have beheld
               the King, the LORD of hosts."
6   Then one of the seraphim flew to me carrying a glowing coal that he
     had taken from the altar with a pair of tongs. 7 He touched it to my
     lips and declared:
          "Now that this has touched your lips,
          your guilt is removed
          and your sin is purged away."
8   Then I heard the voice of the Lord saying, "Whom shall I send and
     who will go for us?" And I said, "Here am I; send me." 9 Then he
     said, "Go, and say to this people: 'Keep hearing, but do not
     understand; keep seeing, but do not perceive.'
10   Dull this people's mind,
          stop their ears,
          and seal their eyes,
     lest they see with their eyes,
          and hear with their ears,
     and understand with their hearts,
          and turn and be healed."
11   Then I said, "How long, O Lord?" And he replied:
     "Until cities lie waste without inhabitants
     and houses without people,
          and the land is utterly desolate,
12   and the LORD removes the population far away,
          and the deserted sites are many
          in the midst of the land.
13   Though a tenth remains there,
          it will again be laid waste,
     like a terebinth or an oak,
          whose stump is left over even when felled.ᵇ
     Holy seed is its stump."ᶜ

     a. The frequent translation of *nidmêtî* as "silent" is far too weak for this verb.
     b. The Hebrew text of v. 13 is extremely difficult and has evoked countless attempts
at emendation. Cf. the reviews by Emerton and Barthélemy (*CTLAT*, 41–44). The most
widely proposed emendations (cf. *BHS*) are to read *'ăšērāh* ("Asherah") for *'ăšer*
(which), *bāmāh* (high place) for *bām* (in them), and to interpret *maṣṣebet* as "sacred

pole" rather than "stump." The textual debate greatly intensified with the discovery of the Qumran text 1QIs^a (cf. the exposition below).

c. The final colon is missing in the LXX.

Selected Bibliography

J. Barthel, *Prophetenwort und Geschichte. Die Jesajaüberlieferung in Jes 6—8 und 28—31,* FAT 19, Tübingen 1997, 37–117; **C. Brekelmans,** "Deuteronomistic Influence in Isaiah 1—12," in *The Book of Isaiah,* ed. J. Vermeylen, Leuven 1989, 167–76; **B. S. Childs,** "Retrospective Reading of the Old Testament Prophets," *ZAW* 108, 1996, 362–77; **J. A. Emerton,** "The Translation and Interpretation of Isaiah VI.13," *Interpreting the Hebrew Bible: Essays in Honor of E. I. J. Rosenthal,* ed. J. A. Emerton, S. C. Reif, Cambridge 1982, 85–118; **C. A. Evans,** *To See and Not Perceive: Isaiah 6:9–10 in Early Jewish and Christian Interpretation,* JSOTSup 64, 1989; **J. Gnilka,** *Die Verstocking Israels. Isaias 6,9–10 in der Theologie der Synoptiker,* SANT 3, Munich 1961; **N. Habel,** "The Form and Significance of the Call Narrative," *ZAW* 77, 1965, 297–323; **C. Hardmeier,** "Jesajas Verkündigungsabsicht und Verstockungsauftrag in Jes 6," *Die Botschaft und die Boten, Fs H. W. Wolff,* ed. J. Jeremias, L. Perlitt, Neukirchen-Vluyn 1981, 235–51; **F. Hartenstein,** *Die Unzugänglichkeit Gottes im Heiligtum: Jesaja 6 und der Wohnort JHWHs in der Jerusalemer Kulttradition,* WMANT 75, Neukirchen-Vluyn 1997; **R. Kilian,** "Der Verstockungsauftrag Jesajas," *Bausteine biblischer Theologie, Fs G. J. Botterweck,* ed. J. J. Fabry, BBB 50, Cologne 1977, 209–200; **R. Knierim,** "The Vocation of Isaiah," *VT* 18, 1968, 47–68; **T. Lescow,** "Jesajas Denkschrift aus der Zeit der Syrischephratischen Krieges," *ZAW* 85, 1973, 315–31; **L. J. Liebreich,** "The Position of Chapter Six in the Book of Isaiah," *HUCA* 25, 1954, 37–40; **J. L. McLaughlin,** "Their Hearts Were Hardened: The Use of Isa 6,9–10 in the Book of Isaiah," *Bib* 75, 1994, 1–25; **K. Nielsen,** "Is 6:1–8—8:18 as Dramatic Writing," *ST* 40, 1986, 1–16; **R. Rendtorff,** "Jesaja 6 in Rahmen der Komposition des Jesajabuchs," ed. J. Vermeylen, *The Book of Isaiah,* Leuven 1989, 73–82; **J. M. Schmidt,** "Gedanken zum Verstockungsauftrag Jesajas (Is. VI)," *VT* 21, 1971, 68–90; **O. H. Steck,** "Bemerkungen zu Jesaja 6," *BZ* 16, 1972, 188–206; **D. C. Steinmetz,** "John Calvin on Isaiah 6: A Problem in the History of Exegesis," *Int* 36, 1982, 156–70; **W. Werner,** "Vom Prophetenwort zur Prophetentheologie. Ein redaktionskritischer Versuch zu Jes 6, 1–8, 18," *BZ* 29, 1985, 1–30; **H. G. M. Williamson,** *The Book Called Isaiah,* Oxford 1994, 30–56; **W. Zimmerli,** *The Book of Ezekiel,* I, ET Hermeneia, Philadelphia 1979, 97–100.

The procedure in this section will be initially to sketch some of the major critical problems of the chapter that directly affect the interpretation, and to offer some preliminary suggestions on the proper direction to move toward resolution. Moreover, I plan to develop in detail an approach through an exposition of the passage in order to ground the position in exegesis. In a final summary an attempt will be made to draw together the implications for the interpretation of the larger unit.

1. The Critical Debate

a. The Literary Context. The initial problem is to interpret the significance of the present position of Isaiah's vision of God in chapter 6. Traditionally, it was thought that the order of chapters 1—5 proceeded largely according to a chronological sequence. Calvin took his lead from the superscription in seeing Isaiah active during the reign of King Uzziah and in holding these early oracles to be contained in chapters 2—5. Then only at the end of Uzziah's life did the prophet receive a second and more profound call.

However, with the rise of the *Denkschrift* hypothesis the major reason for the present position of Isaiah's "call" derived from the effect of the chapter's lengthy compositional history. Originally the call stood at the beginning of a small collection of oracles related to the Syro-Ephraimite war; however, with the expansion of the corpus this initial experience was relegated to chapter 6. On the basis of this critical assumption it was a common practice of commentators to restore the call to the beginning of the book (Procksch, Eichrodt). The shift to redactional criticism resulted in an attempt to supply intentional editorial reasons for its present place in the book. These have been previously discussed in the framing of the *Denkschrift* hypothesis in chapter 5 (cf. above). The redactional approach denies any chronological sequence in chapters 2—5, and, according to Barth and Clements, sees these chapters as reflecting later editorial layers from either the late seventh century or the post-587 period.

b. The Form-Critical Debate. One of the more important debates regarding the interpretation of chapter 6 is form-critical in nature. The issue turns about determining the genre of chapter 6. The background for the recent discussion derived from an influential analysis of Zimmerli in his Ezekiel commentary (1:97–100) in which he distinguished two forms of Old Testament call narratives. One is found in Exodus 3 (Moses), Judges 6 (Gideon), and Jeremiah 1 (Jeremiah). The recipient is initially reluctant to the divine call, offering reasons for refusal, but his reluctance is overcome, usually with the aid of a sign, and he is finally commissioned as a prophetic messenger. The other form has its primary textual example in 1 Kings 22 (Micaiah ben Imlah) and is set in the context of the divine council in which God deliberates with his court. The messenger, overhearing the conversation, volunteers, and is commissioned for a special task.

The argument in respect to chapter 6 turns on the question whether the divine encounter of Isaiah established an inaugural call. By "call" is meant an inaugural experience with God that resulted in his becoming a prophet. An important group of scholars has defended the view that chapter 6 conforms to the second rather than the first narrative pattern, and thus they reject the use of the term *call* for Isaiah. Wildberger sought to show that the vocabulary of sending was not present in the classic call narrative, but was constitutive of the commissioning pattern. However, the strongest argument for the commissioning form turned on the analysis of Knierim and Steck that chapter 6 was integrally bound to the Syro-Ephraimite war in chapters 7 and 8, and had been joined by the redactor of the *Denkschrift* in order to illustrate the effect of the hardening in the rejection of Isaiah's message by Ahaz and the people. A few modern scholars (e.g., Clements) share Steck's position, but also continue to refer back to chapter 6 as a call.

The issue at stake is more complex than usually considered. Indeed the parallels to the commissioning of Micaiah in 1 Kings 22 are striking. Yet there are many unique features in chapter 6 that diverge greatly from the commissioning pattern. In 1 Kings 22 there is no attention paid to the messenger apart from his role as executor of the commission. However, in chapter 6 a lengthy description, crucial to the entire chapter, is given before the commissioning scene. When Isaiah beholds God, he confesses in complete awe his own sin and guilt, and only after he has been cleansed is the commission delivered to him. In a word, Isaiah's role is, in some important sense, paradigmatic. His experience of "death and rebirth" is constitutive of his role in this chapter. In 8:18 Isaiah himself is named a "sign and portent" along with his "children." In this sense, there are features of a call and not just a commissioning parallel to Micaiah. As a consequence, the currently formulated polarity between call and commission does not address adequately the theological dimension of the text and needs to be approached from a different theological perspective.

c. Etiology and Retrospective Readings. The interpretation of chapter 6 has been greatly influenced by various theories of retrospective readings that claim to have discovered the key to the chapter's real function. Initially the warrant for this approach focused on the hardening motif of vv. 9–10: "Dull this people's mind, stop their ears, and seal their eyes." Already in the nineteenth century, commentators (G. A. Smith, later Gray) argued that no prophet could have begun his ministry with such a discouraged attitude. A psychological explanation suggested that later in life, when the prophet reviewed his own failure, he saw at work the hand of God and retrojected onto chapter 6 his inability to elicit a positive response as if it were a divinely ordered purpose. Although this classic psychological interpretation is no longer in vogue, its effect is still very much present in a slightly different garb. Herntrich and Wildberger still focus on the prophet's self-evaluation when they assign a major function of the narrative to be a legitimizing of Isaiah's role as prophet. However, this alleged concern also seems largely irrelevant to the text.

Much more prevalent than the psychological approach is a great variety of retrospective interpretations arising from redactional criticism. Steck, Barth, and Clements, among others, understand the core of chapter 6 to be a retrospective reading of the Syro-Ephraimite debacle, which perspective was read back onto chapter 6 as the chapters making up the *Denkschrift* were joined. Subsequently vv. 11–13 were added, which provided an even later retrojection. Clements draws important chronological inferences from the redactional shape, and feels that the present relationship between chapter 6 and 7–8 rules out the possibility of any Isaianic oracles from the reigns of Uzziah or Jotham preceding the confrontation with Ahaz. Even more radical implications are drawn by Kaiser and Werner, who seriously doubt that chapter 6 reflects the experience of the eighth-century prophet, but believe the narrative is a theological construct from the exilic or postexilic period under the influence of the Deuteronomistic school. By means of a complex redactional process the editors sought to encourage Judah toward faith in God after the disaster of 587. In a word, the historical conditions of postexilic Israel are retrojected back into the eighth century for allegedly ideological reasons.

Lest this criticism of these various modern theories of retrospective readings be misconstrued as being completely negative, let me quickly add that there are indeed genuine, retrospective components reflected in chapter 6, the recognition of which does not destroy the theological integrity of the chapter (Childs, and the careful theological formulation of Barthel, 461 ff.). The hermeneutical issue turns on how the process of retrojection is understood. It is certainly possible that the effect of the destruction of Jerusalem in 587 set up a resonance retrospectively within chapter 6. The radical formulation of the judgment of hardening—"houses without people . . . the land utterly desolate" (v. 11)— could well have been shaped in part by the events of 587, which were understood as the final outcome of Israel's hardening. Similarly, the rebirth of life from the stump (v. 13) resonates with the hope of the new and thus adumbrates chapters 40ff. (cf. Rendtorff, 73ff.). In sum, the elements of intertextual linking of the parts of scripture do not arise simply as literary constructs of self-serving editors, but from a profound wrestling with the coercion of the biblical text, continually instructing a community of faith in the meaning of its historical experiences, both past and future.

2. Exposition

The exegesis that now follows envisions as one of its major concerns to address the issues raised by the various modern readings of chapter 6, and it will try to distinguish between theologically legitimate and nonlegitimate uses of critical categories within the book of Isaiah.

[6:1–3] The vision of Isaiah is set chronologically in the year of King Uzziah's death. Because of several historical uncertainties, including his co-regency, there remains disagreement over fixing an absolute date. Those scholars following Albright's higher chronology generally assign his death to 742. Others, following the sequence preferred by Jepsen and Hanhart, prefer the year 736. However, as suggested by the unusual form of its introduction, there is reason to assume that more is intended than offering a conventional dating. Isaiah's vision is specifically anchored in Israel's history—it functions much like the inclusion of Pontius Pilate in the Apostles' Creed—but thereby a major turning point in God's dealings with Israel is being marked. From a strictly historical perspective the death of Uzziah certainly designates the end of an age of stability and the beginning of the Assyrian threat. But for the writers of the book of Isaiah, of much more significance is the nature of this turning point in God's history with his people. Chapter 6 is, above all, about a wholly different dimension of history: God's time as it enters into Israel's life according to a divine purpose. Chapters 2—4 had highlighted two different understandings of the administration of the world—the one controlled by human activity, the other according to God's rule. Chapter 6 now offers a massive, new theological grounding for this sharp polarity.

Isaiah "saw the Lord." The description of what then follows shows clearly the use of a special biblical idiom. What Isaiah saw was the "glory" (*kābôd*) of God, that is, his outer manifestation. The picture is dynamic and in motion. Very shortly just the tip of his robe envelops the entire temple. The author is not merely speaking metaphorically in consciously figurative language, but in a highly concrete fashion he reacts in an effort to render the reality whom he encountered. The imagery is initially that of the Jerusalem temple—doorposts, smoke, altar—but these are shortly transformed into a heavenly scene. God is revealed as king on a throne, dressed in a robe, with his attendants, the seraphim. Only in this passage do such seraphim appear. Using ancient Near Eastern parallels, scholars have found some apparent antecedents, especially from Egypt, of ferocious, serpent-like guardians of the sacred precincts. However, the parallels do not aid greatly in the interpretation of chapter 6 and provide, at best, some distant background. Here they are described in their function of serving God with covered face as they offer a continuous litany of worship.

It is the content of their hymn that is important: "Holy, holy, holy, is the Lord of hosts; the whole earth is full of his glory." His glory is his disclosed holiness; his holiness is his inner glory (Oetinger, Bengel). Holiness in the Old Testament is not an ethical quality, but the essence of God's nature as separate and utterly removed from the profane. Holiness, the "glory of his majesty," strikes terror in the unholy and proud (Isa. 2:19), but to his attendants awe and reverence. The seraphim call to one another in a continuous antiphony: "the whole earth is full of his glory." The seraphim offer worship and praise. Even at that moment, in the year of Uzziah's death, God rules and has always ruled. The whole world reflects his glory, even though sinful Israel and proud Assyria only recognize their own agendas. The prophet, living at the time of Uzziah's death and actively worshipping in the Jerusalem temple, is suddenly ushered into God's presence and given to experience a wholly different dimension of reality.

[4–12] "The house was filled with smoke." Was it that the temple's incense and burnt offerings took on a new heavenly appearance? The effect was only to add to Isaiah's terror. "Woe is me; I am lost!" He is awestruck, not because he is only a mortal before the infinite, but because he is a sinful human being, sharing the impurity of an entire nation. In the presence of the Holy One of Israel, he perceives his true state. The explicit juxtaposition of the prophet's own sinfulness with that of his people indicates that the focus was not just on the individual; rather, Isaiah shares the selfsame sickness as all of his people, both lost and corrupt.

Then one of the seraphim flies to him with a burning coal taken from the altar. The imagery of the temple continues, but the earthly temple has now been absorbed by the heavenly. He touches his lips, which is the vehicle of the word. His guilt is removed, his sin forgiven. No response from Isaiah is given. Indeed the focus throughout is not on the spiritual experience of the prophet or on what this ecstatic event meant to him. To focus on such individual, personal evaluations completely misses the point of the narrative. Isaiah has no time to revel in his private emotions. He is not concerned with reimagining God! Rather, only when his sin, seen in all its massive and objective reality, is removed can Isaiah hear the voice of God: "Whom shall I send and who will go for us?"

The imagery surrounding the commissioning is that of a divine court. God is consulting his entourage. The parallels with 1 Kings 22 are striking. The issue is one of sending a messenger on a special assignment. Whether this commissioning involves an inaugural call for the prophet is largely tangential to the concerns of the chapter. Isaiah's history with God, here being portrayed, is indeed important, even crucial, but how it fits into the prophet's biography is irrelevant.

Rather, the entire focus now falls on the content of the commission. Say to that people: "Keep hearing, but do not understand. Keep seeing, but do not perceive." Beyond this, the specific role of the deliverer of the message is spelled out. He is to dull their minds, stop their ears, and plaster over their eyes, unless by seeing, hearing, and comprehending, they might actually repent and be saved. The prophet is to be the executor of death, the guarantor of complete hardening. His very proclamation is to ensure that Israel will not turn and repent.

Needless to say, the subject of divine hardening is one of the most difficult topics in the Bible. It appears to run in the face of God's very nature. Does not the God of Israel will only good for his people? Was not the purpose of divine election to bestow life, not death? These theological issues are not easily resolved, but the search for resolution is certainly to be sought in exploring the biblical context.

a. The mystery of divine hardening cannot be explained by shifting the initiative to Israel, as if hardening were only an idiom describing how Israel hardened its own heart by disobedience. It is constitutive of biblical hardening that the initiative is placed securely with God in the mystery of his inscrutable will. Of course, it is equally clear that Israel's sinfulness formed the grounds for the judgment. The philosophical objection to a logical inconsistence that has been continually raised since the Enlightenment plays no role whatever in the Old Testament. The hard juxtaposition of divine initiative and Israel's guilt remains unmoved.

b. The commissioning of Isaiah is directed to "that people," namely, to sinful Israel. It occurred in a specific, concrete moment within the nation's history. The divine decree is not a universal judgment from which broader, theological implications respecting the world in general can be drawn, but is directed to Israel in all its particularity, to the Jews, to the people of God. Israel's *Heilgeschichte* has become Israel's *Unheilgeschichte*. The divine intent of election has been turned into a choosing for destruction (Amos 3:2).

c. The commission marks a turning point (*Wende*) in God's history with Israel. Isaiah learns that the divine sentence has already been decreed. Chapter 5 marks the transition. The vineyard will be destroyed. The hand of God is still stretched out in anger; the enemy has been summoned. Chapter 6 is integrally connected to this turning point and announces the same divine decision, only from a different vantage point. Chapter 5 had grounded Israel's destruction in its total disregard for God's justice and righteousness by those who despised the Holy One of Israel (v. 24). Chapter 6 brings the role of the prophet into play. To him has been revealed the true glory of the Holy One of Israel. Isaiah has experienced the eternally present rule of God in all its awesome and terrifying majesty. He has also experienced his own "death and rebirth" through an act of divine purification and forgiveness in order to perform Israel's destruction. His commission is not one of strategy of how he is to preach, but concerns the effect of his proclamation. The divine word of which he is the bearer will only result in rejection; Israel has been divinely hardened lest it were to seek to repent. Clearly to bring in a psychological or redactional theory of a retrospective coloring attributed to a failed ministry or to the subsequent political debacle is both to misconstrue the entire chapter as well as to destroy its theological import.

To this dreadful commission Isaiah does finally respond. He replies in the plaintive language of the Psalter: "How long, O Lord?" (v. 11). Surely there must be a limit to this divine judgment. The belief in divine mercy undergirds the entire Psalter. Then God replies to the prophet's intercession: "Until cities lie waste without inhabitants . . . and the land is utterly desolate." There is no merciful limit. The punishment is not pedagogical, but final. Israel's *Heilsgeschichte* has been concluded. The end has come (Amos 8:2).

[13] The concluding verse is made exceedingly difficult to interpret because of textual problems. The text from Qumran (1QIs^a) has evoked a variety of new proposals, such as that of the NEB: "like an oak or a terebinth, a sacred pole thrown out from its place in a hill-shrine," but the imagery so reconstructed is

unilluminating and unlikely. The MT, although difficult, remains still the most plausible: "It will again be laid waste, like a terebinth or an oak, whose stump is left over even when felled." The sentence remains still of unrelenting judgment. The old tree has been cut down and burned even as a stump.

Nevertheless, there is a different note struck in the final half line: "Holy seed is its stump." Because this colon is missing from the LXX, many commentators have eliminated the verse as a late postexilic gloss without value. However, the Greek text, especially of the book of Isaiah, cannot wield this kind of textual authority. A more convincing argument for its dating has been recently mounted by Williamson. He has noted that the expression "holy seed" occurs elsewhere in the Old Testament only in Ezra 9:2, where it is part of a complex process. Its usage there reflects a sophisticated exegetical technique for combining diverse Pentateuchal texts that had developed by the fifth century. Williamson concludes that v. 13 offers an analogy that must be seen as an editorial addition from this same postexilic period. My only disagreement with Williamson's formulation lies in his concluding sentence: "It must, therefore, be discounted from the remainder of our analysis" (35).

Actually what one finds in this concluding colon is an excellent example of a textual extension or *Fortschreibung*. This verse is not merely an "optimistic" gloss stemming from an editor's wishful thinking and thus to be eliminated to recover the *ipsissima verba* of Isaiah. Rather, it is a response to the coercion of the prophetic text on late scribal transmitters of the tradition. The addition is not an attempt to soften the message of destruction, but rather to pursue and to interpret the full dimensions of the biblical text. Indeed, Isaiah does not speak here of a remnant or of a pious group who escaped judgment. All of Israel must perish: "houses without people." The radical quality of this imagery resonates with the intensity of 587. There is no continuity from the old to the new. Yet Isaiah has himself emerged from his "death" and shortly names his son "a-remnant-will-return" (7:3). Thus the mystery of the remnant continues, and these ancient readers saw in the stump that remained standing when felled (cf. 11:1) the hope of the new. The force of the entire narrative of chapter 6, particularly in the larger context of chapters 1 — 12, strove for an exposition of the meaning of v. 13. The tree had been felled, but its stump still stands and in the stump is the holy seed waiting to sprout in God's time.

To summarize, chapter 6 plays a crucial role in the interpretation of chapters 1 — 12 because it points both backward and forward. It joins with chapter 5 in marking a decisive turning point in the divine plan for Israel. Chapter 5 had announced the destruction of the vineyard and the coming eschatological judgment summoned from afar by God. Chapter 6 then grounds the divine decree in the eternal rule of God who reveals his will as holiness. In the light of his revelation God commissions his prophet to execute his sentence of hardening. However, the prophet is not just an impersonal vehicle, but one who identifies with his people and whose cleansing by fire and whose restoration makes him the paradigm of the new arising from the old. The holy seed is its stump. Chapter 6 also points forward to chapters 7—9. Ahaz personifies the response of hardness to the promise of God offered to faith. At the same time, and interwoven with this unbelief, there appears a testimony to the emergence of a faithful remnant, which springs from the ashes of Israel's destruction, a new creation of God and his Messiah.

Redaction critics have correctly sensed in their analysis of these chapters an element of retrojection, but, in my opinion, they have misunderstood its significance. What is here present is not a tendentious reading back of a subsequent political agenda, but is part of a process of canonical shaping that stems from a holistic reading of the larger prophetic corpus. The witness to God continues to grow in richness and understanding. This true subject matter is then often extended to earlier portions of Isaiah without attention to the age of its discovery, but rather only to the truth of its witness when measured according to its theological substance. Thus the portrayal of God's rule in 2:1–4 and again in 4:2–6 resonates with elements of Isaiah's vision of chapter 6 and is grounded in the reality of God's eschatological rule, revealed to the prophet in chapter 6. Likewise, 2:6ff. also reverberates with the imagery of God's glory, but here revealed in terror (2:21). The point to emphasize is that canonical shaping develops from a holistic wrestling with the subject matter of the biblical text, and as comprehension grows through encounter with the living God it begins to infuse the entire book with a truthful witness to the one story of God's salvific purpose with Israel.

It is quite impossible to conclude an exposition of Isaiah 6 without some brief attention to the reverberations from the Old Testament text within the New Testament. First, for any careful reader of the New Testament it is fully evident that the Isaianic passages of Israel's hardening play a major role in interpreting the ministry of Jesus Christ, within both the Gospels and the letters of Paul. Fortunately, these texts have been studied in depth by Gnilka, among others. Again, the major point to make is that the appeal to the theme of hardening (Matt. 13:14ff.; John 12:40) as an interpretation of the negative reception of Jesus' teaching is not to be understood as a redactional coloring to explain a failed ministry. Rather, the response to Christ's preaching is seen as an integral part of the selfsame struggle of God with Israel already witnessed to in the entire Old Testament. The rejection and crucifixion of Jesus was the ultimate climax to a history that extended throughout Israel's history (Acts 7). Indeed, the mystery of Israel remains the death of the old and rebirth of the new. Paul picks up this same note in testifying that God—in spite of it all—has not rejected his people (Rom. 11:1ff.). In the course of his argument, he cites from Isa. 29:10 as a warrant for Israel's hardening (Rom. 11:8).

Second, the explicit reference in John 12 to Isaiah 6 calls for serious reflection. After citing the hardening verses, the evangelist proceeds: "Isaiah said this because he saw his glory and spoke of him" (v. 41). What could this possibly mean?

Traditional Christian exegesis has tended to interpret John's saying in a rather flat
and narrow fashion as if the New Testament were supplying the real object of the
prophetic vision—Jesus Christ—unfortunately missed by the Old Testament.
Long ago Calvin objected to this narrow interpretation that limited the vision to
the person of Jesus. Rather, he argued that in Isaiah 6 the prophet speaks of God,
the Lord, in an absolute manner. Yet Calvin is quick to add that God never revealed
himself to the Old Testament patriarchs apart from his eternal Word, the only
begotten Son. Calvin wisely resists Christian interpreters trying to prove from the
song of the seraphim that there were three persons in one essence in the Godhead.
He prefers using stronger evidence to support the doctrine of the Trinity. Yet at the
same time he confesses that it is indeed the triune God who is being worshipped
in the Old Testament. His strongest evidence does not derive from isolated proof
texts, but rather from a holistic reading of the entire canon of ancient Israel.

9. Isaiah 7:1–25

7:1 When Ahaz son of Jotham son of Uzziah was king of Judah, Rezin,
king of Syria, and Pekah son of Remaliah, king of Israel, marched on
Jerusalem, they were unable to prevail against it. 2 When the house
of David was told that Syria had allied itself with Ephraim, their hearts
and the hearts of their people trembled as the trees of the forest shake
before a wind. 3 But the LORD said to Isaiah, "Go out to meet Ahaz,
you and Shearjashub your son, at the end of the conduit of the upper
pool by the road to the Fuller's Field, 4 and say to him, 'Be firm and
keep calm, do not fear, and do not lose heart on account of these two
smoldering stubs of firebrands, at the fierce anger of Rezin and Syria
and the son of Remaliah. 5 Because Syria with Ephraim and the son
of Remaliah have plotted against you, saying, 6 "We will go up
against Judah and invade and conquer it, and we will set up the son of
Tabeel as king." 7 Therefore, the Lord GOD has said:
      "'It will not succeed,
      it will not happen,
8   for the chief city of Syria is Damascus,
          and the chief of Damascus is Rezin.
      (Within sixty-five years Ephraim will cease to be a nation)
9   and the chief city of Ephraim is Samaria,
          and the chief of Samaria is the son of Remaliah.
      If you do not stand firm in your faith,
          you will not stand at all.'"
10   The LORD spoke further to Ahaz: 11 "Ask a sign from the LORD your
God, from lowest Sheol[a] or from highest heaven." 12 But Ahaz said,

"I will not ask, and I will not test the LORD." 13 Then he retorted: "Listen, house of David! Is it not enough to try the patience of men? Will you also try the patience of my God? 14 therefore the Lord himself will give you a sign: a maiden is with child and she will bear a son, and will call his name Immanuel. 15 By the time he learns to reject the bad and choose the good, he will be eating curds and honey. 16 For before the child knows to reject the bad and choose the good, desolation will come upon the land of the two kings before whom you now cower. 17 The LORD will cause to come upon you and your people and your ancestral house such days as have not been seen since Ephraim broke away from Judah—the king of Assyria." 18 In that day, the LORD will whistle for the flies from the distant streams of Egypt and for bees from the land of Assyria. 19 They will all come and settle in the steep ravines and in the crevices of the rocks, and on all the thornbushes, and on the water holes. 20 In that day, the Lord will use a razor hired from beyond the Euphrates—the king of Assyria—to shave your head and the hair of your legs, and remove your beard as well. 21 In that day, a man will save alive a young cow and two sheep; 22 and there shall be such an abundance of milk, he will eat curds and honey. 23 In that day, every place where there used to be a thousand vines with a thousand pieces of silver will be turned over to thorns and briars. 24 One will go there only to hunt with bow and arrows, for thorns and briars will cover the whole land. 25 As for the hills that once were cultivated by the hoe, you will no longer go up there for fear of the briars and thorns; they will become places where cattle are turned loose and where sheep run.

a. There is a dual exegetical tradition regarding the interpretation of *š^e'ālāh*. It can be read as an imperative of *s'l* ("ask"). This is the interpretation generally followed in Jewish exegesis. It can also be read as a variant pointing of the noun *Sheol*. This latter option is generally preferred. Cf. Barthélemy (*CTLAT*, 46f.) for the textual history of the problem.

Selected Bibliography

R. Bartelmus, "Jes 7, 1–17 und das Stilprinzip des Kontrastes. Syntaktisch-stilistische und traditions-geschichtliche Anmerkungen zur Immanuel-Perikope," *ZAW* 96, 1984, 50–66; **J. Barthel,** *Propheten-wort und Geschichte. Die Jesajaüberlieferung in Jes 6–8 und 28–31,* FAT 19, Tübingen 1997, 118–83; **J. Becker,** *Isaias—der Prophet und sein Buch,* SBS 30, 1968, 56ff.; **M. Buber,** "The Theopolitical Hour," *The Prophetic Faith,* ET New York 1949, 126–54; **R. E. Clements,** "The Immanuel Prophecy of Isa. 7:10–17 and Its Messianic Interpretation," *Die Hebräische Bibel und ihre zweifache Nachgeschichte. Fs R. Rendtorff,* ed. E. Blum et al., Neukirchen-Vluyn 1990, 225–40; **C. Dohmen,** "Verstockungsvollzug und prophetische Legitimation. Literarkritische Beobachtungen zu Jes 7, 1–17." *BN* 31, 1986, 37–56; "Das Immanuelzeichen. Ein jesajanisches Drohwort und seine inneralttestamentliche Rezeption," *Bib* 68, 1987, 305–29; **G. Fohrer,** "Zu Jesaja 7, 14 im Zusammenhang von Jesaja 7, 10–22," *ZAW* 68, 1956,

54–56; **H. Gese,** "Natus ex virgine," *Probleme biblischer Theologie. Fs G. von Rad,* ed. H. W. Wolff, Munich 1971, 73–89; **E. Hammershaimb,** "The Immanuel Sign," *ST* 3, 1949, 124–42; **P. Höffken,** "Grundfragen von Jesaja 7, 1–17 im Spiegel neuerer Literatur," *BZ* NF 33, 1989, 25–42; **C. A. Keller,** *Das Wort Oth als "Offenbarungszeichen Gottes,"* Basel 1946; **R. Kilian,** *Die Verheissung Immanuels Jes 7, 14,* SBS 35, Stuttgart 1968; **M. Rehm,** *Der königliche Messias im Licht der Immanuel Weissagungen des Buches Jesaja,* Kevelaer 1968; **M. Rössel,** "Die Jungfrauengeburt des endzeitlichen Immanel. Jesaja 7 in der Übersetzung der Septuaginta," *JBTh* 6, Neukirchen-Vluyn 1991, 135–51; **D. Schibler,** "Messianism and Messianic Prophecy in Isaiah 1 – 12 and 28 – 33," *The Lord's Anointed: Interpretation of Old Testament Messianic Texts,* ed. P. E. Satterthwaite et al., Grand Rapids 1995, 87–104; **J. J. Stamm,** "Die Immanuel-Weissagung und die Eschatologie des Jessaja," *TZ* 16, 1960, 439–55; **O. H. Steck,** "Rettung und Verstockung. Exegetische Bemerkungen zu Jesaja 7, 3 – 9," *Wahrnehmungen Gottes im Alten Testament,* ThB 70, Munich 1982, 171–86; "Beiträge zum Verständnis von Jesaja 7, 10–14 und 8, 4," ibid., 187–203; **M. A. Sweeney,** *Isaiah 1 – 39,* FOTL 16, Grand Rapids 1996, 143–64; **W. Vischer,** *Die Immanuel-Botschaft im Rahmen des königlichen Zionfestes,* Zollikon-Zürich 1955; **P. D. Wegner,** *An Examination of Kingship and Messianic Expectation in Isaiah 1 – 35,* Lewistown 1992; **J. Werlitz,** *Studien zur literarkritischen Method. Gericht und Heil in Jesaja 7, 1–17 und 29, 1–8,* BZAW 204, Berlin 1992; **H. W. Wolff,** *Frieden ohne Ende. Jesaja 7, 1–17 und 9, 1–6 ausgelegt,* BSt 35, Neukirchen-Vluyn 1962.

1. The Function of Chapter 7 in the Context of Chapters 1 – 12

We have previously argued that chapter 6, first of all, points backward to chapter 5, and from a different perspective, both literarily and traditio-historically, confirms the message of Israel's destruction. The vineyard must be destroyed. However, chapter 6 bears terrifying testimony that this destruction derives already from a divine decision made in the heavenly council: these people are to be hardened so that they are unable to repent.

However, chapter 6 also points forward, and chapter 7 offers the first illustration of the hardening process at work in King Ahaz's rejection of the challenge of faith. In my judgment, the critical hypothesis of a *Denkschrift* (memoir) as offering a key to the redactional growth of these next chapters has greatly confused the interpretive issue. The third person form of chapter 7 strongly resists its being encapsulated within a larger autobiographical unit along with chapters 6 and 8. Chapter 7 does indeed continue the theme of hardening, but it also introduces other major themes that have been lost in the usual retrospective reading of these chapters. Above all, chapter 7 introduces the messianic hope associated with Immanuel and begins to develop the theme of the remnant, which had only been adumbrated in the earlier chapters (1:9; 4:1ff.; 6:13). In addition, these themes of chapter 7 are further expanded in an integral way in 8:1–9:7(6). They continue through chapters 10 and 11 and reach a crescendo in chapter 12, thus concluding the first major division of the book of Isaiah.

2. Structure

The chapter divides into three easily distinguishable units: 1–2; 3–17; 18–25. The last section comprises four independent eschatological sayings, each introduced by the formula "in that day," which appear further to interpret the prophetic oracle of vv. 10–17. More controversial is whether there is a temporal break after v. 9, or whether the same historical setting is assumed. The decision is not of major significance because, even though different notes are struck, the verses belong closely together in content. I prefer taking vv. 3–17 together as a single unit since the offering of a sign in v. 10 grows out of the exchange in vv. 3–9.

3. Internal Coherence

No one who has worked closely with this passage will underestimate the extreme difficulty of this chapter. The problems arise in part because of the long and controversial history of interpretation, and in part because of the significance of the chapter for the New Testament's christological formulation. However, an equally important reason turns on the multiple problems of understanding the internal coherence of the chapter in its present form.

There is a wide recognition that chapter 7 is a multilayered text that shows signs of growth and expansion. The crucial hermeneutical question turns on how one understands the depth dimension of this text in relation to it as a literary whole. How does a reconstructed diachronic level relate synchronically to the text's final form? The signs of editorial expansion that will have to be tested in detail in the exegesis appear at first in the larger historical setting provided by v. 1, which has been appropriated from 2 Kings 16:5. There is a further expansion in v. 8b that functions much like a parenthesis within the poetic oracle of vv. 7–9. Then again, elements of secondary textual expansion are thought to appear in vv. 15, 16b, and in the two references to the king of Assyria (vv. 17 and 20). Finally, there are signs of a secondary, literary relationship between vv. 15 and 22 involving the theme of "curds and honey," which will be further explored in the exposition below.

In my approach, the goal of interpretation is toward an understanding of the full richness of the various voices in this passage, but always in relation to the text's final form. In other words, the aim is not to try to reconstruct an allegedly original oracle of the prophet that can then be distinguished from later accretions within the final form that are judged to impair the text's logical coherence. Rather, my concern is to analyze how the coercion of the text from the hearing of the earliest levels of tradition evoked further interpretive activity from its editorial tradents who sought to register the continual effect of the whole on each single text.

4. Exposition

[7:1–2] Verse 1 has a close parallel in 2 Kings 16:5. Older commentators such as Delitzsch thought that the editor of the book of Kings had borrowed from Isaiah. However, a large modern consensus believes that the appropriation took place in the reverse direction. The verse serves to establish a larger historical context for the ensuing confrontation, even though the concluding clause, "they were unable to prevail against it," anticipates an outcome later than that reflected in vv. 3–17. Verse 2 prepares the reader for the encounter between Israel and Ahaz, and for the prophet's initial advice.

[3–9] Isaiah is commanded to meet King Ahaz on the highway to the Fuller's Field. It has often been argued that this is a later redactional feature which serves at the outset to contrast Ahaz with Hezekiah (36:2). However, it is much more likely that the historical setting was a genuine feature of the encounter, as was also the explicit presence of Isaiah's son, Shearjashub. The king was personally inspecting the city's highly vulnerable water supply in his deeply agitated state over the impending attack on Jerusalem. Isaiah seeks to calm the young king using the conventional formula of assurance, "do not fear." To this he adds his confident assertion that Ahaz has no reason to fear his two enemies, whose fury has already been exhausted. What remains is merely smoldering firebrands.

The logic of the succeeding sentence has called forth considerable discussion. The two coalition powers have devised an evil plan to conquer Jerusalem and to replace the legitimate Davidic king with their own puppet, Tabeel ("good for nothing"). To this threat the word of the Lord announces, "It will not succeed, it will not happen" (v. 7). Traditionally, vv. 8ff. have been taken as providing the grounds for this assurance. More recently, some scholars have suggested instead that these verses are to be taken as subjective clauses, namely, "it shall not stand . . . that the head of Syria will be Damascus and the head of Damascus Rezin . . . ." (cf. Kaiser). Although this rendering is syntactically possible, it is unlikely from its larger context. The best indication of the prophet's point is found in 31:3: "the Egyptians are mere human, not God." The plan of Judah's enemies will not prevail because "the chief city of Syria is Damascus. . . .[A]nd the chief city of Ephraim is Samaria." Occasionally it has been argued that the prophetic oracle is elliptical and it assumes as its "punch line" the ending, "but Judah's head is Jerusalem, and Jerusalem's head is Yahweh"; however, this addition appears unnecessary.

The climax of the oracle comes as a direct challenge to Ahaz for a response in faith to the promise of divine support: If you do not believe, you will not be sustained. The two verbs play on two different forms of the same Hebrew root 'mn ("prove faithful," "believe"). Ahaz is challenged to ground his action upon God's promise to support him before his enemies. Undergirding the promise lies the divine covenant made with the house of David (2 Sam. 7:12ff.), which had been directly threatened by the coalition (cf. v. 13). In a word, unless Judah, the people of God, understands itself as a theological reality—a creation of God and not merely a political entity—the state will have no future existence. King

Ahaz as the tradent of the Davidic promise is called upon to respond for himself and for his people to the reality of God's faithfulness.

Finally, there is wide agreement that the poetic oracle (vv. 7–9) has incurred a prose expansion in v. 8b which specifies that within sixty-five years Ephraim will be utterly destroyed. The present context provides no indication of the historical reference to this prediction or of its specific function within the oracle. The most frequent hypothesis conjectures that in roughly the years 670/69 the Assyrian kings, Esarhaddon and Ashurbanipal, had deported large number of Ephraimites, thus conclusively bringing to an end the existence of the Northern Kingdom. This scribal addition confirmed *post factum* the prophetic word of judgment spoken by Isaiah (cf. 2 Chron. 20:20ff. for a later reverberation of Isa. 7:9).

[10–17] One would expect the subject of this oracle to be Isaiah, especially from the larger context (cf. vv. 11 and 13), but the reference directly to Yahweh as the subject functions to emphasize the divine authority of the offer that follows. It is not merely a suggestion from the prophet, but an invitation from God himself to request a sign. Moreover, there are no restrictions placed on the scope of the sign, which can embrace the totality of the created world from Sheol up to the heavens. But Ahaz refuses to accept the offer and defends his refusal with his fear of putting God to the test. Taken by itself, his response seems to have the trappings of true piety before such an awesome decision. However, this possible interpretation is immediately excluded by the prophet's vehement response, which brands it as wearisome hypocrisy arising out of sheer unbelief (cf. 2 Kings 16:1–4). Recent attempts to interpret Ahaz's unbelief as a "communication breakdown" (Bartelmus) is hopelessly anachronistic and theologically inert.

Unfortunately, almost every word of the sign given in vv. 14ff. is controversial. At the outset, much turns on the understanding of the term "sign" (*'ôt*). Within the prophetic corpus, as distinct from the Priestly source of the Pentateuch (e.g., Gen. 9:12), a sign is a special event, either ordinary or miraculous, that serves as a pledge by which to confirm the prophetic word. The sign precedes in time the impending threat or promise, and prefigures the fulfillment by the affinity in content between the sign and its execution. In 1 Sam. 10:1ff. Samuel promises Saul that he will reign as prince to save his people from their enemies. The sign of confirmation is that he will be met on that very day by three different groups of persons, each bringing him good news. The occurrences climax with the coming upon him of the spirit of God. Conversely, in 1 Sam. 2:34 a threat is pronounced against the whole house of Eli, predicting its doom. The sign of the threat is that Eli's two sons will die on the same day as a pledge confirming the future destruction. With the possible exception of Ex. 3:12, the sign and the fulfillment do not coalesce (cf. Childs, *Exodus*, OTL, 56–60).

[14b] "A maiden (*'almāh*) is with child and she will bear a son, and will call his name Immanuel." This birth announcement formula is conventional, occur-

ring also in Gen. 16:11; Judg. 13:3, and in a Ugaritic text ("Nikkal," line 7). The participial form of the verbs receives its temporal reference from the larger context, and is best rendered with an epic present tense. The subject of the verb of naming is clearly a third person feminine form referring to the mother (*GKC* 74g, but cf. Gen. 16:11).

The term *'almāh* ("maiden") has in the past evoked much controversy, initially because of its translation in Greek by the LXX as *parthénos* ("virgin"), and its subsequent role in Matt. 1:23. The noun is derived, not from the root "to be concealed" as suggested already by Jerome, but from a homonym, meaning "to be full of vigor," "to have reached the age of puberty." Thus the noun refers to a female sexually ripe for marriage. The emphasis does not fall on virginity as such and, in this respect, differs from the Hebrew *bᵉtûlāh*. However, apart from the controversial reference in Prov. 30:19, the women in all the other references to an *'almāh* do actually appear to be virgins (e.g., Gen. 24:43; Ex. 2:8; Ps. 68:26). It is very unlikely that a married woman would still be referred to as an *'almāh*. In sum, the English translation of the Hebrew by the AV as "virgin" is misleading in too narrowly focusing on virginity rather than on sexual maturity. Conversely, the preferred modern translation of "young woman" (NRSV) is too broad a rendering since it wrongly includes young wives.

An additional uncertainty arises because the term *'almāh* occurs with the definite article. Syntactically this opens up a variety of possible options. It can denote a specific maiden either present or known from tradition. Or again, it can refer generically to a class of individuals, or even to an infinite number of maidens. The interpretation can only be determined from the larger context. In my judgment, the collective interpretation of the term as defended by Duhm and Kaiser undermines the function of the sign as described above and is to be rejected.

The mother gives the child the name Immanuel, God-with-us. The name does not occur elsewhere in the Old Testament, but the close parallels from the Psalter (46:8, 12) make clear that it is an expression of trust in the presence of God integral to Israel's piety. The attempt to locate the formula within a specific "holy war" context or within a liturgical festival remains highly speculative and is not exegetically helpful. One of the most significant features of this verse is the mysterious, even vague and indeterminate, tone that pervades the entire passage. The reader is simply not given information regarding the identity of the maiden, or how precisely the sign functions in relation to the giving of the name Immanuel. It is, therefore, idle to speculate on these matters; rather, the reader can determine if there are other avenues of understanding opened up by the larger context. Specifically, what is the significance of learning how the sign of Immanuel was interpreted from within the subsequent tradition in chapter 8 (cf. below)?

[15–25] I shall postpone detailed discussion of v. 15 for the moment and turn first to the larger problems of interpreting this section. The position has been argued often (e.g., Fohrer) that the sign is a pledge only of judgment, which secondarily has been construed with elements of promise to soften the announced destruction. The following reasons have been offered in support of this interpretation:

   a. The initial sign of the promise was rejected and replaced by a judgment oracle signalled by the adverb *lākēn* ("therefore").
   b. The final section of v. 16, "before [whose kings] you now cower" cannot originally be a modifier of the noun *hā'ᵃdāmāh* ("cultivated soil"), which is not a political designation. The clause was later added to turn judgment into promise.
   c. Verses 16 and 17 are connected asyndetically and lack an adversive *waw,* which v. 17 would require if a contrast in content were intended.
   d. The closest parallel to the sign in chapter 7 is found in 8:1–4, which has the clear structure of a straightforward judgment oracle.

In response, it must be conceded that initially there is considerable force to these arguments. The text of 7:14ff. is clearly multilayered in quality and does show signs of reworking from subsequent reflection. Yet to each of the arguments mounted one can also show grammatical, syntactical, and form-critical exceptions to these reconstructed oracular patterns. For example, there are instances which show that the semantic range of the noun *'ᵃdāmāh* ("soil") can be extended virtually to parallel *'ereṣ* ("country, land, territory"; cf. BDB 5). Again, there are examples in which the adverb *lākēn* does introduce oracles of promise (Isa. 28:16). Finally, the relative clause in v. 16b, often considered to be secondary, is syntactically fully in order.

However, an even more compelling reason for rejecting a reconstruction of the oracle that eliminates all features of promise lies in analyzing the manner in which this oracle was heard by its editors. In a word, if the true exegetical task does not lie in eliminating certain voices of the final form of the Hebrew text as nongenuine accretions, but rather in seeking to understand the effect of the text's own concern on the subsequent editorial shaping, then a very different set of questions and answers emerges.

The giving of the sign to Ahaz (vv. 10–17) is a continuation of the previous challenge for faithfulness to the promise of God given to the house of David in vv. 3–9. Ahaz's refusal to trust shattered the solidarity between the house of David and the people of God (v. 17). A wedge had now been driven within Israel that resulted in a tension both between the disobedient, empirical ruling Davidian and the true messianic representative of the throne of David (9:6[7]), as well as between faithless Israel destined for destruction and the faithful remnant who were signs of the new people of God (8:18).

It is this larger literary and theological context that accounts for the complex shaping of vv. 10–17. The sign of Immanuel, in striking contrast from the simply constructed sign oracle in 8:1–4, now has a double edge. For those of unbelief—Ahaz and his people—the sign is one of destruction (v. 17), but for those of belief, the sign of Immanuel is a pledge of God's continuing presence in salvation (v. 16).

Some of the complexity of the final form of the passage lies in the exegetical activity of those editorial tradents of the Isaianic tradition who struggled in response to the coercion of the text for further understanding of Gods's purpose with Israel. There are two main places in which this subsequent reflection can most clearly be discerned:

a. One textual expansion seeks to clarify the role of the sign of Immanuel. Verse 15, "By the time he learns to reject the bad and choose the good," interrupts the expected connection of v. 14 with the purpose clause of v. 16a, and duplicates the temporal marker of v. 16: "before the child knows to reject the bad and choose the good." The intention behind the expansion is clear. The sign of Immanuel ("God-with-us") must serve, not just as a pledge of judgment (v. 17), but also as a promise of the future, the sign of which the name anticipates by its content. It has long been recognized that the image of "curds and honey" has a dual meaning. It can be a symbol of desolation, when no food is left in a devastated arable land except the wild produce of the wilderness. However, it can also be a symbol of abundance, such as a land "flowing with curds and honey."

In the four concluding eschatological oracles (7:18–19, 20, 21–22, 23–24), devastation is spelled out in different imagery with the dominant theme being the return of briars and thorns in the place of pasture. In v. 21 the devastation is such that a man struggles for a subsistence level of life with a young cow and two sheep. Yet right at this point, the meaning of the imagery shifts. These few pitiful animals produce such an abundance of milk that all those survivors who are left now feast on curds and honey. The ancient sign of blessing, "a land flowing with milk and honey" (Josh. 5:6), returns for the remnant of the land.

The meaning is the same in v. 15. The sign of Immanuel is also the pledge of blessing. Within the same short period of time the blessings anticipated in the name will be visible for the faithful who believe in the messianic rule of God. The language of curds and honey testifies to the selfsame new eschatological reality as that of the great joy of the harvest in 9:3(2), or of the earth "full of the knowledge of the LORD as water covers the sea" (11:9).

b. The mysterious name of Immanuel in 7:14 receives clarification in two passages in chapter 8 that belong roughly to the same period of the Syro-Ephraimite crisis (cf. below). The judgment announced by Isaiah will come and cover the whole land, but the remnant has hope because the land belongs to Immanuel (8:8). Again in 8:9ff., in spite of the evil plans of distant nations their counsel will not prevail because God has so willed it through Immanuel (v. 10). In sum, Immanuel is no longer the unborn child of 7:14, but the owner of Israel's land and the source of the divine force that brings the plans of conspiring nations to naught (Ps. 2:1ff.). Notwithstanding the extraordinary mystery and indeterminacy surrounding the giving of the sign of Immanuel, there are many clear indications that it was understood messianically by the tradents of the Isaianic tradition, and shaped in such a way both to clarify and expand the messianic hope for every successive generation of the people of God.

10. Isaiah 8:1–22

1 Then the LORD said to me, "Take a large tablet and write on it in common script[a] 'For Maher-shalal-hash-baz.'" 2 And I got reliable witnesses, Uriah the priest and Zechariah the son of Jeberechiah, to attest for me. 3 Then I approached the prophetess, and she conceived and bore a son. Then the LORD said to me, "Call him Maher-shalal-hash-baz, 4 for before the boy learns to say 'my father' and 'my mother' the wealth of Damascus and the spoils of Samaria will be carried off to the king of Assyria."

5 The LORD again spoke to me: 6 "Because this people has rejected the gently flowing waters of Shiloah and melts in fear[b] over Rezin and the son of Remaliah, 7 therefore the Lord is bringing up against him the mighty floodwaters of the Euphrates — the king of Assyria with all his pomp. It will rise over all its channels, overflow all its banks, 8 and sweep through Judah like a flash flood reaching up to the neck, and its overflowing streams will spread across the entire breadth of your land, O Immanuel."

9   Band together,[c] O nations, and be broken;
        listen to this, all you distant lands.
    Arm yourselves, you will be dismayed;
        arm yourselves, you will be dismayed.
10 Hatch a plot, it will come to nothing.
        Plan a strategy, it will not succeed,
        because God is with us (Immanuel)!

11 The LORD spoke to me with his strong hand upon me, warning me not to follow in the way of this people, saying: 12 "Do not call conspiracy all that this people calls conspiracy, and do not fear what they fear, nor be in dread. 13 None but the LORD of hosts will you regard as holy.[d] Give reverence to him alone and hold him alone in awe. 14 He will be a sanctuary but also a stone of stumbling and a rock of offense to the two houses of Israel, a trap and snare to those living in Jerusalem. 15 And many will trip over these and fall and be injured, they will be snared and caught." 16 Bind up the testimony, seal the teachings among my disciples. 17 And I will wait for the LORD, who is hiding his face from the house of Jacob, and I will hope in him. 18 See, I and the children whom the LORD has given me are signs and portents in Israel from the LORD of hosts, who dwells on Mount Zion. 19 And when

they say to you, "Inquire of ghosts and familiar spirits who chirp and
mutter; should not a people inquire of its gods,[e] of the dead on behalf
of the living?" **20** To the law and to the testimony! Surely for one who
speaks thus, there will be no dawn. **21** They will roam the land,
distressed and hungry, and when they are famished, they will become
enraged and, looking upward, will curse their king and their God. **22**
They will look toward the earth, and see only distress and darkness and
terrifying gloom, and they will be thrust into utter darkness.

a. The expression *bᵉḥeret ᵉnôš* has an uncertain meaning, and is rendered in a variety of different ways: "with an ordinary pen"; "in a common writing."

b. The MT reads "the delight of Rezin." Various attempts have been made to retain
this text. NJPS transfers the phrase to v. 4. Sweeney ("On *ûm ᵉśôś* in Isaiah 8.6," 42ff.)
interprets it like an adjective describing the waters of Shiloah, but then eliminates v. 6b
as a gloss. Others interpret Israel, not Judah, as the subject and so explain the rejoicing.
Probably the decision to emend the text by replacing the *śîn* with a *sāmek* ("melt in
fear") best retains the coherence of the passage as a whole.

c. The verb *rō'û* is often emended with the LXX to read "know," or derived from different Hebrew roots such as *r"* or *rw'*. The MT is still to be preferred.

d. The MT "regard as holy" (*taqdîšû*) should not be emended to "regard as conspirator" (*taqšîrû*), so Duhm and Kaiser.

e. *Elohim* refers not to God, but deities, the "shades of the dead."

Selected Bibliography

P. Ackroyd, "Isaiah 1—12: Presentation of a Prophet." *Studies in the Religious Tradition of the Old Testament,* London 1987, 98–99; **K. Budde,** "Zu Jesaja 8, vers 9 und 10," *JBL* 49, 1930, 423–28; **R. P. Carroll,** "Translation and Attribution in Isaiah 8.19 f.," *BT* 31, 1980, 126–34; **C. A. Evans,** "An Interpretation
of Isa 8,11–15 Unemended," *ZAW* 97, 1985, 112–13; **K. Fullerton,** "The Interpretation of Isaiah 8 5–10,"
JBL 43, 1924, 253–89; **A. Jeppesen,** "Call and Frustration: A New Understanding of Isaiah viii 21–22,"
VT 32, 1982, 145–57; **C. A. Keller,** *Das Wort Oth,* Basel 1946; **H. Klein,** "Freude an Rezin," *VT* 30, 1980,
229–34; **A. Laato,** *Who Is Immanuel? The Rise and the Foundering of Isaiah's Messianic Expectations,*
Åbo 1988, 163–73; **N. Lohfink,** "Isaias 8, 12–14," *BZ* 7, 1963, 98–104; **G. Rignell,** "Das Orakel 'Maher-
salal Has-bas': Jesaja 8," *ST* 10, 1956, 40–52; **M. Saebø,** "Zur Traditionsgeschichte von Jesaja 8, 9–10,"
ZAW 76, 1964, 132–44; **O. H. Steck,** "Beiträge zum Verständnis von Jesaja 7, 10–17 und 8, 1–4," *TZ* 29,
1973, 161–78; **M. A. Sweeney,** "On *ûm ᵉśôś* in Isaiah 8.6," *Among the Prophets: Language, Image and
Structure in the Prophetic Writings,* ed. D. J. A. Clines et al., JSOTSup 144, Sheffield 1993, 42–54; *Isaiah
1—39,* FOTL 16, Grand Rapids 1996, 165–188; **C. F. Whitley,** "The Language and Exegesis of Isaiah 8,
16–23," *ZAW* 90, 1978, 28–42.

1. Structure, Form, and Historical Setting

Traditionally, chapter 8 has been divided into six units: vv. 1–4; 5–8; 9–10;
11–15; 16–18; 19–21. However, in spite of the signs of different literary forms,
the six units are generally thought to form a larger redactional whole. There is

an initial coherence of setting in that the units appear to relate to the aftermath of the confrontation of king and prophet in the crises evoked by the Syro-Ephraimite war.

Recently Sweeney (*Isaiah 1–39*) has argued for a different structural division. Verses 1–15 are attached to chapter 7 whereas vv. 16ff. are joined to the following oracle, 8:16–9:6. In my judgment this structural analysis does not commend itself for several reasons. The dominant literary feature of chapter 8 is the autobiographical style. Three times it is said, "Yahweh spoke to me" (vv. 1, 5, 11). Although this feature is often regarded as a major reason for postulating a *Denkschrift,* the sharp contrast of this style in chapter 8 with chapter 7 only increases one's doubts about the theory. The autobiographical style extends through vv. 16–18 and brings to a conclusion a movement begun in v. 1. By separating off vv. 16ff., one breaks the continuity of the narrative and also fails to reckon with the new beginning in chapter 9. Although it is possible to distinguish features of traditional oral patterns of speech in chapter 8 — Sweeney speaks of report, disputation, instruction — these form-critical categories are not much aid in understanding the narrative context. The focus of the chapter differs markedly from chapter 7 and is hardly just another duplicating sign sequence.

2. Exposition

[8:1–4] The historical setting of the passage falls in the period of the Syro-Ephraimite war. Attempts to be more precise do not seem particularly helpful toward rendering an interpretation. The unit consists of a sign oracle and is divided into two parts, vv. 1–2 and 3–4, which are joined by a repetition of the name Maher-shalal-hash-baz. The major exegetical problem lies in determining how the two parts relate. The close parallels to 7:14ff. are immediately apparent. Both contain sign oracles associated with the conceiving and naming of a child. The period of the physical development of the child serves as a temporal marker to set limits for the coming judgment from Assyria.

At first sight 8:1–4 seems quite straightforward in comparison with the series of mysterious and concealed references of chapter 7. Nevertheless, the problem of determining the coherence between the two parts of the passage has proven perplexing. Commentators generally seek to bring the passage's structure into conformity with chapter 7, either by construing the verb in v. 3 as a pluperfect, ("I had gone to"; Duhm, Kissane), or by rearranging the sequence of the verses (Gray). Neither solution is satisfactory. Sweeney seeks a redactional solution by making chapter 7 dependent on chapter 8, which is unconvincing and does not address the issue at stake in the structure of the passage.

The direction toward a more satisfactory solution was first pointed out by Keller. He observed two distinct usages of the sign oracles by the prophet. The first has been previously described in the analysis of chapter 7. The sign, which always preceded a prophecy of judgment or salvation, served as a pledge conforming its fulfillment and adumbrating its content. In contrast, the second usage of the sign was a form of symbolic action in which an event or a riddle was enacted. Its revelatory meaning only emerged when it was joined to a divine word of interpretation. For example, in chapter 20 Isaiah is commanded to walk naked and barefooted. Only after three years does the divine word explain the action: "Just as my servant Isaiah has walked stripped and barefoot . . . , so will the king of Assyria lead away stripped and barefoot the Egyptian captives" (vv. 3–4). In 8:1 Isaiah is instructed to write in a legible script a strange inscription on a large, publicly visible tablet: *mahēr-šālāl-ḥāš-baz* ("swift to come is the spoil, speedy is the prey"). He then secures two well-known, reliable citizens, Uriah and Zechariah, in order to establish through public witness the time of the writing of the inscription, whose meaning was incomprehensible to all.

Only after this action does Isaiah approach his wife to father a child. Then God instructs the prophet to name the child according to the mysterious inscription. The baby thus becomes a prophetic sign of imminent judgment. Before the child knows how to cry "Papa" or "Mama," the king of Assyria will destroy the two coalition powers of Damascus and Samaria. The two parts of the passage are thus united within the one prophetic sign of the child who incarnates the coming judgment.

The difficult question to resolve is the function of the sign as symbolic action in vv. 1–2. Wildberger argues that establishing the time of the inscription as being before the destruction of Damascus and Samaria functioned to demonstrate that those in Jerusalem still had the freedom to decide in faith, even though Isaiah held out little hope of a new orientation in the politics of Jerusalem. This interpretation appears too influenced by the sequence of chapter 7. Rather, chapter 8 established by the symbolic inscription and by its impartial witnesses that the decision of judgment had already been made in the heavenly council, and that Jerusalem's decision (v. 6) was only a confirmation of the divine hardening, first announced to the prophet in chapter 6. The judgment had fallen even though the mysterious inscription was incomprehensible to its readers until the naming of the child. The autobiographical style of the passage further links it to the hardening commission of chapter 6, but without the need of an elaborate *Denkschrift* hypothesis.

[5–8] Initially, there are some difficult textual problems to resolve in v. 6, especially where the MT reads "the delights of Rezin." There are a number of ways to retain the MT (cf. above), but each time at a high cost. The suggestion that Judah's holding "with delight to Rezin" refers to a dissident faction within Jerusalem that supports the attacking coalition partners lacks support from the rest of Isaiah and is a solution of despair. In my judgment, the suggested emendation in my translation best retains the coherence of the oracle.

The unit continues the autobiographical form and appears to be a threat (*Drohrede*). Yet the word is recorded as a word of Yahweh spoken to the prophet and serves to tie together vv. 1, 5, and 11 as the direct will of God to the prophet. It also serves to dispel the thought that salvation would naturally accrue to Judah with the destruction of the two coalition powers. Rather, because "this people" refuses the "waters of Shiloah," judgment follows Judah in devastating swiftness.

The narrative setting of the oracle reflects a time later than 7:10ff. when Isaiah challenged Ahaz to respond in faith to God's promise to the house of David. In chapter 8 the decision of unbelief has already been made. Isaiah uses the image of the "waters of Shiloah" to draw his analogy. A meager supply of water for Jerusalem arose from the spring at Gehon located on the west side of the Kidron valley and flowed by canals to pools at the lower east side of the city. The prophet uses the figure of this trickle of water to depict the seeming weakness of the divine promise in contrast with the awesome strength of Assyria, whose aid Ahaz had sought. But for the prophet, Assyria is just a tool of God's power (10:5), and because of Judah's despising the divine aid in favor of Assyria's, God turns the aid into terrifying judgment. Yahweh is bringing up the mighty waters of the Euphrates, not for salvation as assumed by Ahaz, but to sweep away Judah. They will overflow their banks, fill all its channels (wings) and reach to the very neck of the inhabitants of the land.

However, right at this critical juncture there is an editorial addition: "its overflowing streams will spread across the entire breadth of your land, O Immanuel" (v. 8b). Commentators differ on how to deal with the appeal to Immanuel. Often it has been removed as a pious gloss, or rendered as a sentence and joined with v. 9 (NJPS), or understood as a redactor's reinterpretation of 7:14. But these interpretations do not touch the heart of the issue. First of all, the addition of the name Immanuel to a prophetic threat is striking evidence that the transmitters of the tradition of chapter 7 have continued to reflect on the theological significance of the mysterious child of the promise. The reference in 8:8 also shows that Immanuel has remained not just a sign name, but now receives a definite profile and is addressed as the Lord of the land of Judah. Finally, the double-edged feature of the original promise of chapter 7 has continued. Immanuel partakes of the judgment enveloping the people and land of Judah, but the divine judgment executed by the Assyrians has its limits explicitly because of the reality of "God-with-us."

[9–10] This oracle has a very different literary form from the preceding oracles and addresses a different audience: "Band together, O nations, . . . listen to this, all you distant lands." The oracle has the form of a prophetic proclamation of defeat for the enemies, and its content runs parallel to 14:24ff. Various attempts have been made to reconstruct an exact traditio-historical setting (Saebø), and indeed the conventional language indicates that the idiom used has a prehistory. However, this oracle is hardly a fragment of a free-floating tradition summoning to holy war, nor does it stem from an alleged doctrine of Jerusalem's inviolability.

Rather, the oracle has been shaped to fit within its present literary context. It provides another side of the ongoing editorial reflection on the role of Immanuel in this present crisis. It is directed against all the nations, peoples from "far countries," who plan Israel's destruction. The theme of evil intrigue against God's anointed is certainly traditional (cf. Psalm 2), but its function here has received a concrete historical reference. The plans of Assyria, archrepresentative of Israel's enemies, will be thwarted. They will not stand, again because of Immanuel. Once more the profile of Immanuel has grown. God's people are offered a pledge of salvation, not from a theory of Jerusalem's inviolability, but because of God's manifested presence even in the midst of judgment. To suggest that such a hope is derived from an optimistic political climate generated by King Josiah's reign in the late seventh century is seriously to misunderstand the nature of biblical eschatology, which has neither a political nor psychological origin.

[11–15] The autobiographical style of vv.1 and 5 continues with an even heightened intensity: "when the LORD took me by the hand." The major point of the warning (*Mahnrede*) is clearly stated at the outset: "not to follow in the way of this people." There follows a specific instance of such unsuitable behavior that is addressed both to the prophet and to his followers: "Do not call conspiracy all that this people calls conspiracy, and do not fear what they fear" (v. 12).

In recent years there has been considerable discussion of the exact context for understanding the term "conspiracy." Lexicographically the nominal and verbal forms of the root *qšr* refer to treason, sedition, and internal political intrigue. External political activity against the state by another power is not included. Particularly in the period of the Syro-Ephraimite crisis, there is an explicit reference in 2 Kings 15:25 to Pekah's conspiracy to usurp the reigning king of Samaria (cf. also 2 Kings 17:4); however, the intrigue of the coalition against Ahaz cannot be termed a conspiracy. Traditional interpretation took its lead from the experience of the prophets Amos (7:10) and Jeremiah (32:1ff.), who were accused of treason because they prophesied defeat of the nation as a judgment of God. In contrast, more recently the case has been argued that there was an anti-Assyrian party within Jerusalem that opposed Ahaz's refusal to align himself with the coalition. As a consequence, this group was conspiring against him.

In my opinion, much of this debate has served as an unfortunate distraction from the main subject matter of the oracle. The divine warning does not turn on one form of political intrigue, which is never specified in the text itself. Rather, the warning is directed against all and everything that is surmised to be treason by the city's populace. As a result of such rumors the city is filled with great fear and foreboding of impending violence.

In contrast, the prophet is called upon to direct his attention to the real source of power and dread: "None but the LORD of hosts will you regard as holy." He is the one to fear; he is the object of terror. In a word, the true issue at stake is again between two visions of reality. Does the future lie in the throes of power politics and clever human machinations, which evoke fear and uncertainty? Or does the future lie with God, the Holy One of Israel, who is the real power to be reckoned with?

The majority of critical commentators, following Duhm, have felt that the contrast between fear of conspiracy (v. 12) and regard for God's holiness lacks coherence. By means of a conjectural emendation of v. 13 (cf. *BHS*) the sentence is rendered: "Yahweh of hosts, him you shall regard as a conspirator." In my opinion, there are several reasons why this emendation is not justified and the MT should be maintained (cf. Lohfink, 98ff.):

1. There is no textual support from variant textual traditions.
2. The reference to Yahweh as conspirator is a modern anachronistic concept that has no warrant from the Hebrew Bible itself. God is never viewed as a conspirator, even when his ways are mysterious.
3. The contrast between the false fear of conspiracy and the true fear of God is consistent with Isaiah's larger message. God's holiness is what evokes true terror (2:10, 14; 6:5–6).

The oracle concludes with the familiar double-edged form of prophetic proclamation. To the people Yahweh is a sanctuary, an idiom parallel in Ezek. 11:16. Conversely, God has become to both houses of Israel "a trap and snare" on which they will stumble and be broken.

[16–18] There has been general recognition that this unit brings to an end the prophet's confrontational proclamations arising from the Syro-Ephraimite crisis (7:1ff.). Isaiah appears to have withdrawn from the public debate in the face of the flat rejection of his message. He only surfaces again after Ahaz's death when a new phase of his activity begins during the reign of Hezekiah. Yet a number of difficult exegetical questions are at stake in the interpretation of this passage. What is the genre of the oracle? How directly is the message related to 8:1–15? How is one to understand the reference to "disciples" (*limmûdîm*) in v. 16?

First, the genre is neither a prophetic prayer to God nor a form of prophetic instruction. Rather, it is a type of "confession" with loose parallels to Jeremiah (20:11), Second Isaiah (50:7ff.), and the Psalter (27:1, 56:9[10]). Second, although some have recently argued (e.g., Clements) that vv. 16–18 are directly related only to 8:1–4, and that the material in vv. 5–15 is subsequent interpretive expansion, this view does not do justice to the movement of the chapter as a whole. Verses 16–18 do not speak of a written testimony as in 8:1, but the concerns of the passage are far broader and reflect the confrontation of chapter

7 as well. Finally, although the term *disciple* does not refer to a closely defined prophetic school as some have suggested, still it does suggest the presence of followers who have received the truth of his preaching and to whom Isaiah entrusts his teachings for preservation until a later time.

Because of the rejection of his message by Ahaz, whom the prophet has urged to respond in faith in the divine promises to David, Isaiah withdraws from a public role. However, he does not retreat in despair or self-introspection. Rather, he continues to hope in God with full confidence and chooses to wait until God no longer "hides his face" from Israel in anger. Moreover, Isaiah has been given signs of the promise of a new age. The function of the sign has already been discussed in chapters 7 and 8 as a foretaste of judgment for faithless Israel and as a pledge of promise to the faithful remnant. Each of the previous signs carried a double-edged message: Shearjashub, Immanuel, Maher-shalal-hash-baz. Moreover, Isaiah also included himself along with the "children" whom God had given to be "signs and portents" from the Lord who rules in Zion (8:18). He also personifies in his death from sin (6:7) the birth of a new people under God's rule. The sign is both a pledge of the future (chapter 7, but also a symbol that points to a concealed and mysterious reality (8:1ff.).

Finally, in this confession of Isaiah one can also discern the beginnings of a sense of "canon consciousness." By this is meant the prophetic witness that was not received when first proclaimed has been collected and preserved in faith for another generation. These collected testimonies retain their truth and authority in spite of the passing of time and continue to serve as God's word for a future age. Originally, Isaiah may have simply hoped for a better time in the future, but when this oracle was placed within the context of his larger literary corpus, there emerges with great force a relentless openness to the future, which has been propelled forward by an eschatological vision of the whole creation within the one divine purpose for Israel.

[19–23] This disputation oracle that concludes the chapter is extremely difficult to interpret, in part because of textual and philological problems, and, in part because of the lack of a clear literary and historical context.

Although there appears to be a new literary unit beginning in v. 19 that deals with a different subject matter, the repetition in v. 20 of the same terminology of "teaching and testimony" from v. 16—now in reverse order—points to a strong element of continuity and textual extension. Apparently some group in Jerusalem offered an alternative avenue to divine knowledge from that of the prophet. Why not inquire of ghosts and spirits from the realm of the dead? The Hebrew *'ôb* refers to familiar spirits from the world of necromancy that are conjured up through magical rites. Throughout its whole history following the settlement in the land, Israel fought a running battle against the inroads of such forms of superstition that were categorically prohibited by the Hebrew faith (Lev. 19:31; 20:6, 27; 1 Sam. 28:7, Isa. 19:3).

At a time of deep anxiety, the attraction of the forbidden spirits arose in direct challenge to the prophet's message. Isaiah's earlier appeal to the testimonies and teachings (v. 16) now receives a fresh application in response to a new fear. Whether this disputation stems from Isaiah's contemporaries or from a later literary actualization of the prophet's testimony by his disciples cannot be easily determined. There is no convincing evidence to suggest that the prominence given to the teachings (*tôrāh*) in v. 20 reflects a specific legal content rather than a general usage of the term, and therefore refers to the written corpus of postexilic Judaism. Rather, what is fully clear is that Isaiah's appeal to the teaching and testimony again returns to the only authoritative avenue by which to discern the divine will.

There then follows an intense polemic against the defenders of this form of magic. For those who hold to such a belief there will be only darkness without a dawn. These consequences are graphically spelled out. When pressed and hungry from the devastation of the land, they will grow outraged and curse their king and God. When they look skyward as they roam the land in despair, they will experience only darkness. Once again the theme of hardening, first sounded in chapter 6, returns. The judgment of God has not resulted in repentance, but only in the heightening of evil.

11. Isaiah 8:23–9:6(7)

8:23 Yet there will be no more gloom for those who were in distress. At first he brought into contempt the land of Zebulun and the land of Naphtali, but later he made glorious the way of the sea, the land beyond the Jordan, Galilee of the nations.[a]

9:1(2) The people walking in darkness
     have seen a great light;
on those living in the land of darkness
     a light has dawned.
2(3)   You have enlarged the nation
     and increased its joy.[b]
They rejoice before you
     as with joy at the harvest,
     as people exult when dividing the spoil.
3(4)   For the yoke that burdens them,
     the bar across their shoulders,

the rod of their oppressor,
you have shattered as on the day of Midian.
4(5) For every warrior's boot issued in battle,
and every garment rolled in blood,
will be burned as fuel for the fire.
5(6) For a child has been born for us,
a son has been given to us,
and the government will be on his shoulders,
and his name will be called:
"Wonderful Counselor,ᶜ Mighty God,
Everlasting Father, Prince of Peace."
6(7) Great shall the dominion be,
and boundless the peace,
upon the throne of David, and over his kingdom
to establish it, and to uphold it
with justice and righteousness
from that time on and forever.
The zeal of the LORD of hosts will accomplish this.

a. The text of 8:23 is extremely difficult and highly controversial (cf. the exposition below). The most thorough review in recent times is offered by J. A. Emerton. He succeeds in pointing out the full range of textual problems, but whether his own solutions can be sustained still remains debatable.

b. The MT reads "not have you increased." Either one can read the Qere *lô* ("to it") rather than the Kethib *lō'* ("not"), or emend by joining the two words to form *haggîlāh* ("joy") (*BHS*).

c. In spite of Delitzsch's defense of separating "wonder" and "counsellor," the MT accentuation supports the two into one name. However, Delitzsch is fully correct in rejecting the naming of the child as periphrastic designations of God (cf. NJPS). Cf. J. D. W. Watts's note on the variation among the versions (1:131).

Selected Bibliography

A. Alt, "Jesaja 8, 23–9, 6. Befreiungsnacht und Krönungstag," *Kleine Schriften zur Geschichte des Volkes Israel,* II, Munich 1953, 206–25; **H. Barth,** *Die Jesaja-Worte in der Josiazeit,* Neukirchen-Vluyn 1977, 141–77; **R. A. Carlson,** "The Anti-Assyrian Character of the Oracle in Is. ix 1–6," *VT* 24, 1974, 130–35; **J. A. Emerton,** "Some Linguistic and Historical Problems in Isaiah VIII.23," *JSS* 14, 1969, 151–75; **J. H. Hayes and S. A. Irvine,** *Isaiah, the Eighth-Century prophet: His Times and His Preaching,* Nashville 1987, 169–84; **J. Høgenhaven,** "On the Structure and Meaning of Isaiah VIII 23B," *VT* 37, 1987, 218–21; **G. von Rad,** "The Royal Ritual in Judah," *The Problem of the Hexateuch and Other Essays,* Edinburgh and New York 1966, 222–31; **M. A. Sweeney,** "A Philological and Form-Critical Re-evaluation of Isaiah 8:16–9:6," HAR 14, 1994, 215–31; *Isaiah 1–39,* FOTL 16, Grand Rapids 1996, 175–88; **J. Vollmer,** "Zur Sprache von Jesaja 9, 1–6," *ZAW* 80, 1968, 343–50; **P. Wegner,** "A Re-examination of Isaiah ix 1–6," *VT* 42, 1992, 103–12; **H. Wildberger,** "Die Thronnamen des Messias, Jes. 9, 5b," *TZ* 16, 1960, 314–32; **H. W. Wolff,** *Frieden ohne Ende, Jesaja 7, 1–17 und 9, 1–6 ausgelegt,* BSt 35, 1962, 53–90;

A. S. van der Wunde, "Jesaja 8, 19–23a als literarische Einheit," *Studies in the Book of Isaiah, Fs W. A. M. Beuken,* ed. J. van Ruiten and M. Vervenne, Leuven 1997, 129–36; **W. Zimmerli,** "Vier oder fünf Thronnamen des messianischen Herschers in Jes IX 5b.6," *VT* 22, 1972, 249–52.

Exposition

The extreme difficulty of interpreting this oracle is initially revealed by the continuing debate over determining the end of the former unit and the beginning of the next. In the MT 8:23 is understood as a continuation of the preceding oracle and is separated from the new oracle in 9:1–6. However, in the LXX, in a severely corrupted text, a major portion of v. 23 is thought to introduce the oracle in 9:1–6.

In 1950, the famous essay of A. Alt picked up on the Greek and Latin traditions, and it appeared for a time that he had conclusively tipped the balance in their favor. Alt thought that he could reconstruct a poetic strophe from 8:23aß–b, which formed the beginning of the royal enthronement oracle of 9:1ff., and which he assigned to the period immediately following the military incursions of Tiglath-pileser III in the years 734–32. More recently, Alt's literary reconstruction of 8:23 has been seriously called into question as far too speculative. Nevertheless, a majority of scholars still hold to seeing the second part of v. 23 as a prose introduction, probably shaped by an editor, which served as a bridge from the description of desolation and darkness to that of light and salvation.

The philological problems of v. 23 remain highly contested and the sharply divergent translations reflect this debate (cf. NJPS, NEB, NIV). First, because of a tension between the feminine form of the noun (*'ēt*, "time"), and its masculine adjectives ("former," "latter"), an alternative suggestion has been to translate the phrase as referring to earlier and later kings (NJPS), but this translation has not resulted in a coherent reading on which scholars can agree. Second, the geographical references do seem most likely a reference to the Hebrew equivalent of the three Assyrian provinces set up by Tiglath-pileser after the destruction of the Northern Kingdom, as Alt suggested. Thus the evidence for a historical setting in the period after 732 does seem to have been largely sustained. The Assyrian conquest forms the background of desolation and gloom against which the ensuing prophetic note of light and hope is sounded. Certainly Alt has shifted the consensus away from the postexilic dating of the oracle widely accepted in the nineteenth century and still defended by Kaiser and Kilian.

The oracle is structured to build up a high level of suspense by first announcing the dramatic shift from darkness to light for the people suffering oppression. Then the reasons for the change are outlined in three clauses (vv. 3, 4, 5), each introduced by *kî* ("because," "for"): the yoke of slavery has been broken, the weapons of battle removed, and a miraculous child has been born to rule. The burning issue of the identity of the child is closely tied exegetically to the genre of 9:1–6. On this question, scholars continue to differ widely.

Alt argued that the form and style revealed an authentic Isaianic succession oracle for the crowning of Hezekiah as king. (Some have preferred identifying the king with Josiah or even Ahaz.) The language of the accession oracle was deemed conventional and common to the royal enthronement tradition of the ancient Near East. Accordingly, the reference was not to a literal birth of a king but was the hyperbolic idiom of royal accession. The royal titles assigned to the child in 9:5(6) do indeed have strong parallels to the Egyptian coronation liturgy and refer to the qualities desired of a new monarch.

Yet at this juncture it is crucial to distinguish between the conventional language of the oracle and its biblical function within the book of Isaiah. To suggest that this oracle is simply hyperbolic, oriental language used to celebrate the accession of a new Israelite king is to historicize the biblical text and to overlook its role within the larger literary context. It is thus crucial that the interpretation not focus simply on the preliterary form of the text. To interpret this text as a historical vestige, moored in misguided hopes from Israel's past, is to misunderstand the canonical forces at work in shaping the prophetic tradition into a corpus of scripture directed to Israel's subsequent generations of faith. The oracle may well reflect the conventional language of its milieu, but far more significant for determining its meaning is to recognize the predominantly eschatological movement of the oracle.

In my opinion, it is a major misunderstanding of this passage to politicize its message and derive the oracle from an enthusiasm over the accession of one of Judah's kings. Sweeney's proposal (*Isaiah 1—39*, 18–19) that the Assyrian intervention against Pekah and Rezin was interpreted as Yahweh's purpose for Judah to reassert Davidic control over Northern Israel suffers from a similar historicizing assumption. Even to suggest that the climax of the oracle in v.6 supports such an alleged plan involves a massive demythologizing of its eschatological language.

The two verbs in 8:23aß are best rendered as contrasts in time: "first he brought into contempt" (*hēqal*) and later "he made glorious" (*hikbîd*; cf. Jer. 30:19). The perfect tenses remain difficult, but more than a chronological sequence is being depicted. Rather, two qualities of time, judgmental and redemptive, are being contrasted, which continue a major theme from chapter 7 onward. Sweeney (*Isaiah 1—39*, 186) speaks of "two contrasting positions," one that relies on the spirits of the dead, the other on Yahweh. The problem of the discrepancy of gender between noun and adjective in 8:23a is not without parallel in Hebrew. Verse 23 serves as a type of superscription to the oracle that follows, and anticipates both the humiliation and exaltation of the land by the use of the perfect form of the verbs.

Earlier we described the movement from the promise of Immanuel in 7:14 to a clearly messianic interpretation of his role in 8:8, 11. Now the son is described as coming in the period of Israel's deepest humiliation: "The people walking in darkness have seen a great light." The royal titles of kingship are conferred upon him: "Wonderful Counsellor, Mighty God, Everlasting Father, Prince of Peace." Each name brings out some extraordinary quality for the divinely selected ruler: a counsellor of unique wisdom and abundant power, endowed with enduring life, and the bringer of eternal peace. The description of his reign makes it absolutely clear that his role is messianic. There is no end to his rule upon the throne of David, and he will reign with justice and righteousness forever. Moreover, it is the ardor of the Lord of hosts who will bring this eschatological purpose to fulfillment. The language is not just of a wishful thinking for a better time, but the confession of Israel's belief in a divine ruler who will replace once and for all the unfaithful reign of kings like Ahaz.

To summarize: There is a narrative movement from 7:1–9:6 that portrays the rejection of the promise of God by the house of David and the resulting destruction of the people of God as divine hardening takes effect. Conversely, there emerges the hope of a faithful remnant, adumbrated by Isaiah's own experience of death and rebirth in chapter 6, and foreshadowed by the sign of Immanuel. This unfolding presentation of the entrance of God's rule in the midst of terrifying disasters culminates the history of the Syro-Ephraimite crisis with the messianic promise of chapter 9 and anticipates its ultimate expansion in chapter 11.

12. Isaiah 9:7(8)–10:4

9:7(8) The Lord has sent a word against Jacob,
    and it will fall on Israel,
8(9) and all the people will experience it—
    Ephraim and the inhabitants of Samaria—
    who say in pride and arrogance of heart:
9(10) "Bricks have fallen, but we will rebuild
    with dressed stones.
    Sycamores have been out down, but we will substitute
    cedars instead!"
10(11) So the LORD let the enemies of Rezin[a] triumph against
    them and stirred up their foes,
11(12) Aramaeans from the east and Philistines from the west,
    who devoured Israel with greedy mouths.
    For all this his anger has not turned back,
    and his arm is still stretched out.
12(13) But the people did not return to him who struck them, nor
    sought the LORD of hosts.
13(14) So on one day the LORD cut off from Israel head and tail,
    palm branch and reed.

14(15) The elders and the honored men are the head;[b]
　　　 the prophets, teachers of lies, are the tail.
15(16) For those who lead this people mislead them,
　　　 and those who are led have been confused.
16(17) Therefore the Lord will show no mercy to their young men,
　　　　 nor show compassion to their orphans and widows,
　　 for all are ungodly and wicked,
　　　 and every mouth pours out profanity.
　　 For all this his anger has not turned back,
　　　 and his arm is still stretched out.
17(18) For wickedness burns like a fire,
　　　 it consumes briars and thorns,
　　 it sets aflame the underbrush of the forest
　　　 so that it billows upward in a column of smoke.
18(19) By the fury of the LORD of hosts
　　　 the land has been scorched.
　　 Then the people became like devouring fire;
　　　 no one spares his brother.
19(20) On the right they snatch, but remain hungry;
　　　 on the left they devour, but are not satisfied.
　　 Each feeds on his own children's flesh.[c]
20(21) Manasseh devours Ephraim and Ephraim Manasseh,
　　　 and both of them against Judah.
　　 For all this his anger has not turned back,
　　　 and his arm is still stretched out.
10:1 Woe to those who execute evil writs
　　　 and issue oppressive decrees,
2   to deprive the poor of their rights
　　　 and rob the needy of my people of justice,
　　 making widows their prey, the fatherless their booty.
3   What will you do on the day of punishment,
　　　 when disaster comes from afar?
　　 To whom will you flee for help?
　　　 To whom will you leave your riches?
4   Nothing will remain but to cringe among the captives
　　　 or fall among the slain.
　　 For all this his anger has not turned back,
　　　 and his arm is still stretched out.

---

a. The MT reads "the enemies of Rezin." Often the name Rezin is deleted (*BHS*) and "enemies" is emended to "princes" (*śārê*).

b. Verse 14 is thought by some to be a later scribal gloss, but the cola are retained by a majority.

c. The MT reads "arm" and is often emended to "neighbor" (*rēʻô*) or to "seed" (*zeraʻ*).

Selected Bibliography

W. P. Brown, "The So-called Refrain in Isaiah 5:25–30 and 9:7–10:4," *CBQ* 52, 1990, 432–43; **J. L. Crenshaw,** "A Liturgy of Wasted Opportunity (Am. 4:6–12; Isa. 9:7–10:4; 5:25–29)," *Semitics* 1, 1970, 27–37; **H. Donner,** *Israel unter den Völkern,* VTSup 11, 1964, 64–75; **J. H. Hayes and S. A. Irvine,** *Isaiah the Eighth-century Prophet,* Nashville 1987, 184–94; **C. E. L'Heureux,** "The Redactional History of Isaiah 5:1–10:4," *In the Shelter of Elyon, Fs G. W. Ahlström,* ed. W. B. Barrick, J. R. Spencer, Sheffield 1984, 99–119; **M. A. Sweeney,** *Isaiah 1–39,* FOTL 16, Grand Rapids 1996, 188–96.

The passage consists of a prophetic proclamation of a divine judgment leveled against Israel that describes Ephraim's past calamities as unsuccessful in effecting its repentance. As a result, a refrain announcing God's continuing anger toward his people resounds through the entire oracle, extending to an indictment against Judah, which shares both in the selfsame wickedness and in the impending judgment.

1. Critical Exegetical Problems

A variety of problems face the interpreter of this passage. Who is the addressee of the oracles, the Northern Kingdom or Judah? What is the genre of the oracle? Are the verbs to be construed in a past or future tense, that is, as a historical retrospection of Israel's previous history, or as a prophetic oracle foretelling future judgment? In spite of a growing consensus in recent years that the passage reflects a historical perspective on the past and was directed originally to the Northern Kingdom alone, these issues are far from settled and call for a fresh analysis.

The structure of the unit is also contested and the decision made greatly affects the interpretation. According to the widely accepted *Denkschrift* hypothesis (cf. commentary on chapter 5), the original ending of the oracle of 9:7ff. is to be found in 5:25–30, and 10:1–4 should be joined with the other woe oracles of 5:8–24 (cf. Clements's reconstructed order of the units: 10:1–4a; 5:8–24; 9:8–21; 5:25–30). Because I do not agree that this hypothesis is convincing, a different interpretation will be suggested that seeks to do justice to its present structure.

Finally, in spite of the serious inadequacies of the *Denkschrift* hypothesis, there are clear signs of intentional editorial shaping that influence the manner by which the passage is construed. First, the placing of 9:7–10:4 directly after 9:1–6 would point to a larger function of this section within the book as a whole that is consistent with the pattern in chapters 2–12 of sharply juxtaposing oracles of salvation with those of doom. Second, the refrain found in 9:11, 16, 20, and 10:4 appears consciously to extend the divine judgment from Ephraim to Judah as well. Third, the problem of rendering the tenses of the oracle (cf. the succinct review by G. B. Gray, *Isaiah*, 181–82) points very likely to a text that has been reworked for a new function within a larger literary context. Fourth, the rather vague and confusing references to historical events, which have evoked endless interpretations of the intended referent, seem to suggest that they now function only as illustrations of something else of primary importance uniting the oracles.

2. Analyzing the Editorial Shaping

In my judgment, it is impossible to reconstruct the exact historical process of the redaction of this section. At best one can discern in the present form of the text indications of editorial shaping toward a theological rendering of the passage. The appeal to signs of the text's growth seems to me more convincing than, say, Delitzsch's attempt at a coherent reading through recourse to a theory of an "ideal" referent. The effort at probing into the text's depth dimension is justified insofar as it serves to illuminate the final form of the canonical text, rather than substituting a reordering of it in order to recover an original authorial intent within a reconstructed context.

The oral tradition lying behind the genre of 9:7ff. is akin to that of Amos 4:6ff., which recounts by means of repeated refrains God's attempt to bring Israel to its senses through a series of natural calamities, but to no avail. Yet the initial introduction, "The Lord has sent a word against Jacob" (v. 7), indicates at the outset that the passage has a different function. The historical calamities that occurred do not serve to bring Israel to repentance. Rather, the divine decision of hardening has already been made, and God's continuing anger against Israel is only confirmed by the arrogant response to the destruction of cities in v. 9. The fact that the disasters depicted in 9:7–22 are rendered by past tenses (perfects and imperfect consecutives) and by future tenses (imperfects and perfect consecutives) without any clear, larger syntactical pattern can best be explained by the function of the chapter. Its role is to trace the historical effects of the divine word, unleashed against Israel, extending from the past to the present and into the future. Yahweh's hand is still stretched out in anger. Although it is possible that this mixture of tenses appeared at its earliest literary stages, it seems more likely that the dominant force of the passage's portrayal of eschatological judgment increasingly tipped the balance of the verbs from the past toward the future.

This conclusion also seems supported by the redactional ordering of the final woe oracle (10:1–4) to function as the conclusion of the passage by the use of the same refrain (v. 4). It is, of course, obvious that the form of the woe oracle is different from the preceding units of 9:7–22. The invective, with its preponderance of participles, focuses on the present and the continuing habits of injustice that are now practiced by those who have become the actual addressees of the entire oracle. The function of the oracle as a whole thus extends the focus of God's history-creating judgment from the Northern Kingdom to Judah as the recipient of the selfsame anger. The only difference is that Ephraim's punishment appears already to have occurred historically, whereas Judah has not as yet experienced the final stage of its destruction. Theologically speaking, the temporal sequence of the judgment is immaterial—to this extent Delitzsch's "ideal" referent has a certain warrant—since both political entities share the same effect of God's anger and, in striking contrast to the portrayal of the promised messianic rule of God (9:1–6), represent the powers of sin, oppression, and darkness, who continue to oppose the will of God in arrogance and pride.

3. Exposition

The structure of the section is marked by the repeated use of the refrain: "For all this his anger has not turned back and his arm is still stretched out" (9:7–11; 12–16; 17–21; 10:1–4).

In v. 7 the LXX's translation of the word sent by God against Jacob as "plague" is textually a secondary repointing of the MT, but this reading does correctly catch the sense of a history of death that is being described. A divine word of judgment has been hurled at Israel that all the people will come to experience. The first strophe sets the tone of the whole. Destruction has started and cities have fallen, but Ephraim and the residents of Samaria have learned nothing from these first signs of impending doom. Rather, they respond in pride and arrogance. The destroyed buildings will be replaced by even more costly substitutes: dressed stones for bricks, cedars for common sycamore wood.

As a consequence, God will increase the pressure (v. 10[11]). He will raise the "enemies of Rezin" against them and stir up their enemies, the Aramaeans to the east and the Philistines to the west. The phrase "enemies of Rezin" has long presented difficulties to the interpreter. The "enemies of Rezin" would appear to be a circumlocution for Assyria, who was Rezin's archenemy. Rezin had taken the initiative in forming a coalition in order to oppose the inroads from the expanding Assyrians under Tiglath-pileser III. For most commentators, therefore, it seems more logical to see the reference to Israel's enemies in v. 10 as referring to Syria and Philistia in v. 11. As a result, the text of v. 10 is often emended (cf. textual notes). Yet it is also possible to interpret v. 10 as two loosely connected threats: Yahweh let the Assyrians triumph over Israel, and he also raised up his old enemies on both sides of her borders, the Syrians on the east and the Philistines on the right, in order to devour Israel.

The uncertainty in handling this minor text-critical problem touches on a more important problem regarding the passage as a whole. How are the historical references contained in the historical review to be understood? Older scholars, such as Delitzsch, commenced the review in the ninth century under Jehu. Others, such as Procksch, started in the period before the Syro-Ephraimite war, and sought to trace a historical trajectory from the offering of tribute to the Assyrians by Menahem, to the murder of Pekahiah, and to the outbreak of the Syro-Ephraimite war. Still others began with an alleged earthquake during the reign of Uzziah and ended the historical review with civil strife before the outbreak of the war (cf. Hayes and Irwine, 184ff.). Most recently, Sweeney (192ff.) argues that the historical events are arranged in reverse order, starting with the most recent events and extending backward to a period prior to the Assyrian invasion.

The inability to determine with any degree of certainty which historical events are being used raises the question whether these historical references serve another function within the oracle from that of establishing an exact historical sequence. The events referred to appear to be more topically ordered and illustrate a quality of chaos and confession, which Israel's political machinations have engendered. The word of divine judgment begins with destruction from without when old and new enemies are allowed to triumph over God's people.

Then in vv. 12ff. an inner disorder erupts, much like that portrayed earlier in 3:1ff. Because Israel did not retain its faith in Yahweh, Yahweh cut off its leadership from top to bottom, and allowed the disastrous effects of unscrupulous and self-serving rulers to wreck havoc on the community. As a result, the whole populace is characterized as godless and foolish as God withdraws his compassion even from the orphans and widows, and the whole nation plunges into sheer folly and deception.

The final descent into a moral and political abyss is pursued in the third invective (vv. 18ff.). Now wickedness is portrayed with the imagery of a brush-fire out of control, with huge billows of thick smoke rising from a scorched earth. The graphic figures evoke a memory of the burning villages of civil war, but also of the fiery wrath of God in response to the apostasy of his people. The calamities of the past have only intensified the hatred. Civil war has broken out among the tribes and each side turns to its neighbors in uncontrollable ferocity. They devour each other, but their mounting cruelty finds no limit, and only accelerates in its momentum. It is Manasseh against Ephraim, Ephraim against Manasseh, and both against Judah. The reference to Judah in v. 20 forms a literary bridge to the final invective in chapter 10.

Now the focus of the divine anger falls fully on the present and future (10:1–4). An invective, much like the form of 5:8ff., is directed against those in Judah, who have learned nothing from Ephraim's folly but rather use their special position to pervert justice. Most likely, the reference to those who "execute evil writs and issue oppressive decrees" is not to new laws that have been enacted. Rather, the accusation is directed against the judges and petty officials of the state who abuse the poor in the application of the law. Through directives and decrees, red tape and delay, they rob the widows and orphans of their rights, and through trickery render the judicial system into a heartless exercise for defrauding the vulnerable. For such a people there is no future. The tragic irony of their situation is summed up in three plaintive questions: What will you do? Where will you flee? To whom will you leave your riches? Then the prophetic answer is provided: Nothing remains but to crouch on the ground among the refugees awaiting certain death. Even then God's anger has not abated, but his hand is still extended in wrath against them.

This terrifying oracle of judgment, which will shortly expand to encompass the destruction also of mighty Assyria, has been placed in between the glorious visions of the righteous, messianic reign of God in 9:1–6 and 11:1–9. In these passages of hope the prophet begins with the promise of coming salvation to a people living in deep darkness of religious uncertainty and political violence (8:19ff.). He paints a picture of the coming of Israel's long-expected redeemer, whom God will establish on the throne of David to reign in righteousness from that time forth.

However, there is another side to this picture, and it is this contrast to the rule of God to which the prophet continually returns as an integral component of the promise. There is another reality in the world of human affairs that opposes the rule of God at every turn and lays claim in arrogance and pride to its own power and ambition. One cannot talk prophetically about the reality of the reign of God without addressing the present world of tyranny, evil, and violence, both within and without the people of God. The two visions of reality belong integrally together because there can be no new eschatological entrance of divine salvation unless there is also an eschatological exercise of divine judgment that destroys the power of evil as a demonstration of the righteous reign of God. This constant theme of the two opposing forces recurs throughout the entire book of Isaiah, whether in the juxtaposition of the faithful and unfaithful city (1:24ff.; 26:1ff.), or in Yahweh's disputation with the idols (41:21ff.), or God's battle with Edom (63:1ff.), until it climaxes in the final victory of the new heavens and earth (65:17ff.).

13. Isaiah 10:5–34

10:5 Woe, Assyria, the rod of my anger,
          the staff—it is in their hands[a]—of my anger.
6 Against a godless nation I send him,
          and against the people of my wrath I charge him,
    to take its spoil and to seize its booty,
          and to trample them down like the mud of the streets.
7 But this is not what he intends,
          this is not what he has in mind.

Rather, it is in his heart to destroy,
  and so cut off not a few nations.
8   for he says: "Are not my commanders all kings?
9   Was Calno any different from Carchemish?
      Or Hamath from Arpad,
      or Samaria from Damascus?
10 As my hand seized the kingdoms of the idols,
      kingdoms whose images excelled those of Jerusalem and
      Samaria—
11 shall I not deal with Jerusalem and her images
      as I dealt with Samaria and her idols?"
12 But when the Lord has finished all his work on Mount Zion and
    Jerusalem, he[b] will punish the arrogant boasting of the king of
    Assyria and his haughty pride.
13 For he says:
    "By my own might I have accomplished it,
      and through the capacity of my own wisdom;
    I have taken away the boundaries of peoples,
      and plundered their treasures.
      Like a mighty one I subdued the inhabitants.
14 My hand has seized the wealth of people like a nest;
      as one gathers abandoned eggs,
    so I gathered all the earth,
      and there was none that flapped a wing,
      or opened his mouth to peep."
15 Does an ax boast over him who hews it,
      or a saw magnify itself against him who wields it?
    As though a rod would wield him who lifts it,
      or as if a staff should lift that which is animate!
16 Therefore the LORD of hosts will send
      a wasting away of its fatness,
    and within his body a fever will burn
      like fire.
17 Then the light of Israel will become a fire
      and his Holy One a flame,
    and in one day it will burn up and consume
      his thorns and briars.
18 The glory of his forest and meadows will be destroyed,
      both body and soul,
      as when a sick man wastes away.
19 What is left over of the trees of the forest will be so
      little that even a child can count them.

20   On that day, the remnant of Israel and the survivors of the house of
      Jacob will lean no more upon him that smote them, but they will lean
      upon the LORD, the Holy One of Israel, in security. 21 A remnant will
      return to the mighty God. 22 Although your people Israel will be as
      the sands of the sea, only a remnant of them will return. Destruction is
      decreed, overflowing with retribution. 23 For the Lord, the LORD of
      hosts, is carrying out a complete destruction, as decreed, upon all the
      land. 24 Therefore, thus says the Lord, the LORD of hosts: "O my
      people, who dwell in Zion, do not fear the Assyrians when they strike
      you with the rod and raise the staff against you as the Egyptians did.
      25 For very shortly my wrath will come to an end, and my anger will
      be directed to their destruction." 26 Then the LORD of hosts will
      brandish his whip over them as when he struck Midian at the rock of
      Oreb, and he will raise his staff over the waters as he did in Egypt. 27
      On that day, its burden will depart from your shoulder and its yoke
      from your neck.

28   He has gone up from Samaria,ᶜ
          and come to Aiath;
      he has passed through Migron,
          at Michmash he deposited his baggage.
29   He has crossed over the pass,
          at Geba he camped for the night;
      Ramah trembles,
          Gibeah of Saul has fled.
30   Cry aloud, Bath-gallim;
          Listen, Laishah!
      Answer her, O Anathoth!
31   Madmenah has fled,
          the inhabitants of Gebim have sought safety.
32   This same day at Nob
          he will halt and shake his fist
      at the mount of the daughterᵈ of Zion
          the hill of Jerusalem.
33   Lo, the Lord, the LORD of hosts,
          will lop off the branches with terrifying power.
      The tall trees will be felled
          and the lofty ones cut down.
34   He will cut down the forest growth with an ax,
          and Lebanon with its majesty will fall.

a. Verse 5b remains difficult. The MT appears to separate the two parts of the construct. As a result, the phrase "in their hands" is often dropped (RSV) or emended. To

construe the *mēm* as an enclitic results in an odd sense: "hand of my wrath," which stands in tension with 5a.

b. The MT reads a first person pronoun instead of a third.

c. The sense of the MT is very strained: "the yoke will be destroyed because of fatness." The proposed emendation is a conjecture (cf. *BHS*).

d. Read with the Qere and many versions *bat* ("daughter").

Selected Bibliography

W. F. Albright, "The Assyrian March on Jerusalem, Isa. X, 28–32," AASOR 4, 1924, 134–40; **H. Barth,** *Die Jesaja-Worte in der Josiazeit,* WMANT 48, Neukirchen-Vluyn 1977, 21–58; **J. Becker,** *Isaias — der Prophet und sein Buch,* SBS 30, 1968, 60–61; **B. S. Childs,** *Isaiah and the Assyrian Crisis,* SBT II, London 1967, 39–44, 61–63; **D. L. Christensen,** "The March of Conquest in Isaiah X 27c–34," *VT* 26, 1976, 385–99; **G. Dalman,** "Palästinische Wege und die Bedrohung Jerusalems nach Jesaja 10," *PJ* 12, 1916, 37–57; **H. Donner,** *Israel unter den Völkern,* VTSup II, Leiden 1964, 30–38, 142–45; **K. Fullerton,** "The Problem of Isaiah, Chapter 10," *AJSL* 34, 1917–18, 170–84; **S. Mittmann,** "'Wehe! Assur, Stab meines Zorn' (Jes 10.5–9.13aß–15)," *Prophet und Prophetenbuch, Fs O Kaiser,* ed. V. Fritz et al., Berlin 1989, 111–33; **M. A. Sweeney,** "Sargon's Threat against Jerusalem in Isaiah 10.27–32," *Bib* 75, 1994, 457–70; *Isaiah 1–39,* FOTL 16, Grand Rapids 1996, 196–211.

1. Literary Context

As we have previously seen, the messianic promises of Isaiah that emerged during the Syro-Ephraimite crisis proceed along a trajectory from chapter 7 to chapters 9:1ff., culminating in chapter 11. The initial problem is to determine the interpretive function of separating chapters 9 and 11 by two lengthy composite oracles: 9:7–10:4 and 10:5–24. In regard to the first unit, we have already suggested that it reflects the same familiar Isaianic dialectic that always matches the promise of eschatological salvation with the present reality of Israel's persistent disobedience. Israel's failure to learn from past warnings results in the outstretched arm of divine judgment. The new reality of a community of faith in Israel does not emerge except from the ashes of destruction, and then as a sheer gift of divine mercy.

The second unit, 10:5–34, develops in a far more explicit sense the relation of the promised salvation to the nations, especially to Assyria, who personified the power of military power. Earlier the prophet had introduced the role of the "nation far off" (5:26) whom God summoned for his instrument of terrifying judgment. Now the full theological significance of this relationship to the purpose of God in establishing his rule over Zion within a messianic kingdom is explained.

2. Structure and Redactional Shaping

The passage can be divided into three larger units: vv. 5–19; 20–27a; 27b–34. Each of these units shows signs of being an editorial composition that was formed from smaller sections. The crucial exegetical task turns on how this editorial process is to be understood. At times one can determine with some degree of certainty the direction of the redactional reworking, which is usually in the form of interpretive expansion. At other times such knowledge is hardly available by which to establish the earlier and later levels of the text. Moreover, the growth of a passage through the influence of intertextuality (a force deriving from the effect of a holistic reading of the entire corpus) cannot easily be placed in a historical sequence. At best, a theoretical reconstructing of the shaping of a passage serves to aid in understanding the present form of the text according to all its contours, and to sensitize the eye of the reader to its thick texture. In sum, the exegetical goal lies in interpreting the shaped text, and not to fragment its structure diachronically in order to recover some larger entity lying beneath the surface. Clearly the methodological approach being offered stands in opposition to much of current redactional criticism, whether according to a conservative (Clements, Williamson) or radical model (Kaiser, Vermeylen).

3. Exposition

[**10:5–19**] At the outset, these verses present several difficult form-critical and redactional problems. The form of the oracle appears initially to be that of an invective (woe oracle), but the present shape of the text diverges strikingly from the classic lines of the woe oracle. Clearly the major shaping force was that of the peculiar content of the prophetic oracle, which altered the traditional oral form from the start. The role of Assyria is both positive and negative. Assyria is the executor of God's judgment against Israel, a note already sounded in chapter 5. One observes immediately the intertextual reference in v. 6: "to take its spoil and to seize its booty," which continues to interpret the original riddle of the child's name, Maher-shalal-hash-baz (8:3). However, the main function of the oracle is to describe the subsequent judgment of God on a nation whose actions exceed its divine role as an appointed instrument of divine punishment.

The prophet characterizes Assyria's own intentions of worldwide conquest by putting into his mouth words typical of all the boastful inscriptions of the famous Assyrian monarchs. Because of the specific mention of different historical conquests, commentators have seized on this material in an effort to date the prophetic oracle. Moreover, there is a general agreement regarding the dating of the conquered cities mentioned. Calno in northern Syria fell to Tiglath-pileser III in 738. Carchemish, a Hittite city, was conquered by Sargon II in 717 and Hamath in 720. Arpad was destroyed apparently twice, in 738 and in 720. Yet these dates tell us little about the date of composition of the original oracle, but at most establish a *terminus a quo* that favors a late period in Isaiah's ministry. The prophet's use of specific events is largely illustrative of Assyria's boastful claim to invincible power.

Of more exegetical importance is the observation that an oracle, which from a literary perspective appears to have once been a single speech in vv. 8–9 and 13–14, has now been divided into two separate speeches, each with its own introduction (vv. 8, 13). Verse 12 is a prose sentence that spells out the temporal sequence of God's plan with Assyria and also provides the warrant for his destruction from his haughty pride. In addition, vv. 10–11 show signs of some inner friction, both in style and content, and introduce the subject of idols into the speech. Several critical approaches have been used in an attempt to deal with the tension (Duhm, Fullerton, Eichrodt), but they share in common a concern to rid the text of anything deemed to be a later accretion.

A more fruitful exegetical approach would be to seek to determine both the cause and effect of these interpretive expansions. For example, what intention lies behind the division of the Assyrian speech into two distinct sections? The two parts now seem to make different points. Verses 8–11 serve to document the intent of the Assyrian monarch announced by the divine oracle in v. 7. His plan is to expand his world power without limits. Has he not already demonstrated his might against the idols of the nations, including those of Samaria and Jerusalem? Their idols are powerless before him. It has long been noticed that this Isaianic oracle has been influential in shaping the arrogant speech of the Rabshakeh (36:18ff.), whose recital of Assyrian conquests covers similar ground. However, a reverse direction of influence is also possible. The reference in vv. 10–11 to the impotence of the nation's idols, whose reputation even exceeded those of Samaria and Jerusalem, picks up the completely pagan perspective of the Rabshakeh. Moreover, the intent of Assyria is not only directly opposed to Yahweh's plan, which sets a sharp limit to Assyria's aggression, but vv. 10–11 now develop in addition the theme of the blasphemy of the one true God who is slandered by his being included with the impotent pagan gods.

The new prose introduction in v. 12 serves several interpretive moves. First, it places the role of Assyria as a tool of divine punishment within a clearly defined temporal pattern. This shift in Isaiah's description of the role of Assyria does not derive from a change in the prophet's own attitude (*contra* Procksch), but was a part of Yahweh's plan for Assyria from the beginning (14:24–27). Second, the line of Assyria's expansion is now drawn before Jerusalem. There is a limit to Yahweh's punitive work on Mount Zion and Jerusalem. The effect of this temporal periodization of v. 12 is that the "godless nation" of v. 6 now refers to the fate of Samaria. Verse 12 thus reflects a holistic reading of the deliverance of Jerusalem in chapters 36–37, which the Isaianic editor has used to sharpen the profile of God's purpose with Assyria.

The second part of the speech (vv. 13–14) focuses on the conflict no longer just between diverse plans, but between two opposing claims of divine sovereignty. The king of Assyria is boastful and arrogant of this great power. He views the world and its inhabitants solely as objects, passive and helpless, to be plundered at will. The climax of the divine response to this blasphemy comes in the calm words of the wise sage (v. 15) reminiscent of the sovereign detachment of chapter 18. Does a lifeless tool claim control over the person who wields it? With one word the foolishness of the boastful tirade against the true ruler of the universe is rendered absurd.

However, the present oracle does not end with a rhetorical question. A connection with a concluding judgment oracle (vv. 16–19) is made explicit by an introductory adverb, "therefore." Two very different metaphors are used to spell out the judgment that Yahweh now "sends" against Assyria who had been his erstwhile vehicle in the destruction of others. The one is of lingering sickness that slowly decimates its soldiers; the other is of a wildfire sweeping through a forest. For commentators to suggest that the two metaphors are hopelessly incompatible is to misunderstand a characteristic feature of Isaianic poetry, which continually creates a startling effect by a stark mixing of metaphors. The passage does appear to have reworked a variety of themes found elsewhere in the Isaianic corpus, especially from 17:4ff. and 19:14, but the effect on the whole is hardly a "muddle," as Gray suggested.

To summarize the interpretation of vv. 5–19: In the earliest level of the text the prophet addresses the role of Assyria as God's instrument within the one divine plan. The boastful Assyrian king is only a tool and has no power of his own. The subsequent reworking of this passage within its larger canonical context used themes from the later description of Assyria's defeat in chapters 36–37 in order to bring greater depth and sharpness to the Isaianic oracle. God's plan was to destroy godless Samaria and also to extend his work on Mount Zion, but limits were clearly established. Assyria, the blasphemer and symbol of human arrogance, would be cut down. However, to what extent Jerusalem would be spared in God's "work" on Mount Zion will be addressed in the subsequent verses.

[**20–27a**] The two prose passages that now follow (vv. 20–23; 24–27) are presented as an eschatological vision of the future. They both address the issue of the destiny of the remnant, but in distinct ways that relate to different aspects of the problem. The larger questions at stake concern the fate of the faithful remnant in the period of the continuing divine anger against Israel (9:7ff.), and the role of Assyria as an instrument of judgment (10:5ff.). It has long been observed that the style of these passages varies greatly from the usual poetic form of the Isaianic oracles. Consequently, historical critics have universally designated them as "nongenuine" and assigned them to a date later than the eighth century, either to a postexilic editor or to the Josianic redaction of the seventh century. However, as I shall argue, excessive attention to dating an oracle can often lead to obscuring a passage's actual function within a larger composition.

The distinctive feature of these two passages lies in the widespread usage of texts from the earlier Isaianic corpus. Because these passages appear to be offering actual interpretations of written texts and not just appealing to oral tradition, they have been frequently designated as "midrashic." From a strictly formal perspective there is some justification for the term, but, because this designation is prone to serious misunderstanding, it must be employed with great caution. Because of an erroneous grasp of the original function of midrash within classic Jewish exegesis, the term implies to most modern interpreters a fanciful, largely arbitrary, usage of biblical texts resting on superficial wordplays, which lack the theological depth of the original biblical authors (e.g., Duhm, Gray). However, if correctly understood, recognition of a particular biblical phenomenon, especially within the prophetic literature, is of great importance (cf. Childs, "Retrospective Reading of the Old Testament Prophets," 364 ff.). What is reflected in these passages is a serious wrestling with the substance of the Isaianic tradition, already in a largely written form, in an effort to interpret the content of the prophetic word in a changing context. The point is not that editors simply adjusted the tradition to meet new historical realities, but rather that the coercion of the authoritative biblical text itself pressed the believing community to explore the fuller meaning of the prophetic witness as an ongoing extension of divine revelation that guided its faith and practice.

For this reason, a basic hermeneutical error lies in assuming that by establishing the date of an oracle's composition one is able also to determine a text's true referent, which is then thought to reveal the redactor's own ideology expressed in the new interpretation. On this assumption great attention is paid to assigning these oracles to a seventh-century, "Josianic reduction" (Barth, Clements) or to a later postexilic editor (Duhm, Kaiser). Although accurate historical dating can at times be of exegetical significance, the crucial interpretive task lies in determining the narrative function to which such texts have been assigned, rather than in supplying a reconstructed setting apart from its present literary (canonical) context.

[20–23] These verses offer a profound struggle with the theology of the remnant by means of an interpretation of other parts of the Isaianic corpus. The passage is introduced as an eschatological vision that is linked by a catchword with v. 19, but which addresses the larger question raised by the prophet's message in 9:7ff. and 10:5ff. What is the future of the faithful remnant in the light of the continuing anger of God toward Israel and Assyria's role in the divine punishment? The remnant of Israel is not just what is left over (v. 19), but the people of God defined by its faith. In contrast to those of 9:13 who "did not turn to them who smote them," the remnant are those who confess the "Holy One of Israel" and have not despised his word (5:24). Yet the remnant of Israel is also characterized as the "survivors of Jacob" who are not exempt from the destruction of Israel, but share fully in the nation's judgment.

Nevertheless, the promise of Isaiah regarding the future of a faithful remnant is reiterated by God's instruction in 7:3 for Isaiah to take with him Shear-jashub ("a remnant will return"). The name of Isaiah's son carries a dual sense.

It is both a sign of judgment "only a remnant will return" and also a concrete pledge of a promise ("surely there will be a [faithful] remnant"). Moreover, this remnant will return to the prophesied messianic ruler of 9:5. Chapter 9 had spoken of the coming judgment and also of the coming eschatological reversal, but without a specific reference to the remnant. In vv. 20ff. its role is defined, but now an important corrective to a patriarchal promise is appended. Genesis 22:17 and 32:13 had promised that "the people of Israel will be as the sand of the sea" (cf. Hos. 2:1), but the promise is now restricted by a divine judgment: "Only a remnant of them will return" (v. 22). The reason is then given by a reference to Isa. 28:22: "I have heard a decree of destruction from Yahweh, God of hosts against the whole land." Destruction is decreed; God will make a full end (v. 23) when "the Holy God proves himself holy in righteousness" (5:16). Zion will indeed be redeemed by justice, that is, those in her who repent (1:27). The remnant will experience all the terrors of judgment, but the promise of new life through the destruction is affirmed. In sum, Israel receives an extension of divine revelation from the study of its scripture and a confirmation of its future as testified to by the prophet Isaiah.

[24–27a] The subject matter of the true people of God continues, and the second oracle is joined explicitly with a connective adverb, "therefore." However, the subject is approached from another direction and a different set of questions is being addressed. The second passage functions as a word of comfort by offering a conscious actualization of the promises of 9:1–6. The Lord of hosts speaks directly to the hard-pressed remnant of Jerusalem: "O my people, who dwell in Zion, do not fear the Assyrians when they strike you with the rod" (v. 24). The initial reference turns repeatedly to the rod of the oppressor (9:3), to the staff of God's fury (10:5), which was outstretched in anger against Israel (9:12ff; 10:4). But if the remnant is also to partake of this judgment, where then is the promise of survival? In response, the remnant is comforted (30:19ff.). There is a limit to the judgment (10:12). God's anger will come to an end, and it will now be directed toward destroying the destroyer (13:17; 14:24). God will wield his rod against them as he once smote Midian (9:3) and the Egyptians at the sea (11:15–16). In that day the yoke and the burden will be removed (v. 27), as promised in 9:3.

Duhm once argued that because of the late dating of many of the passages referred to in 10:20ff., the reference to Assyria could not be to Assyria of the eighth century, but must function here metaphorically as a cipher for the Syrian threat of the second century. With good reason few commentators have followed Duhm's hypothesis, since the only evidence derives from Duhm's initial assumption of a late Hellenistic dating. More recently, the historical referent has been ascribed to a Josianic redactor of the seventh century who was encouraged by Assyria's weakened position to hope for an imminent political change. Yet this seemingly more conservative alternative is hermeneutically of one piece with Duhm's. Both theories of reconstructed referents run roughshod over the narrative referent in chapter 10, which is clearly eighth-century Assyria. Nevertheless, Duhm is partially correct in at least recognizing the eschatological context of 10:20–27, which by its future orientation allows the promise of salvation for the remnant to serve as a word of comfort for every successive generation of the faithful, even when the threat of eighth-century Assyria has long passed.

[27b–34] This passage presents a series of difficult issues that are exacerbated by an initial textual problem in v. 27 (cf. textual notes). In the text's Masoretic form the introduction to the oracle has either been lost or garbled. In addition to the lack of a clear introduction, there is the sudden shift of literary style and the uncertainty as to the exact extent of the oracle. A few commentators (incorrectly in my opinion) have even argued that vv. 33–34 belong to the following oracle (Becker, 61; Barth, 64ff.).

The context of the oracle has to be inferred from the passage as a whole since no explicit setting is offered. What is clear, however, is the description of an army approaching Jerusalem, descending from the north with sudden and terrifying swiftness. The initial problem that has evoked decades of scholarly controversy turns on determining the historical background of the portrayal of the enemy's approach. The concrete features of the attacking army along with the great detail in picturing the geographical route of the march should caution the interpreter from immediately postulating a mythical construct of apocalyptic imagination.

Most commentators assume that the description reflects an actual historical invasion of Jerusalem, the knowledge of which is used by the prophet (or redactor) to fashion his message of an impending attack. The perplexing problem is that the route, which can be accurately reconstructed, is not the normal and readily accessible route southward from Bethel to Jerusalem that follows the watershed of the Ephraimite mountains. Rather, the route transverses the most rugged terrain possible, including the crossing of the *wadi es̩-s̩uwēnit,* which separates Michmash from Geba. A number of different historical invasions have been suggested as providing the geographical setting, such as the Assyrian invasion by Sennacherib in 701, Sargon's campaign against the Philistines in 712–11, or the attack by the Syro-Ephraimite coalition in 735. However, none provides a completely convincing model that matches the odd route depicted by the prophet (cf. Donner; Sweeney, "Sargon's Threat against Jerusalem").

In my opinion, this historical debate is of limited value in interpreting the passage. It aids to the extent in which the deviant path of attack described increases the effect of an unstoppable, invincible, and utterly terrifying enemy. Yet it is fully clear that the passage in its present form is a prophetic oracle, not a historical report. It is very possible that the geographical details derive from a memory of a past event, but recovering this particular invasion, even if possible, leaves the interpreter still a great distance from the meaning of the text.

The exegetical task remains crucial to determining how the prophet construed his material and to what end.

The enemy has taken on an eerie image, always addressed in the singular. The portrait of this colossus moving swiftly and with consummate ease over every possible barrier, and then emerging on the very outskirts of the city to shake its fist at Mount Zion, borders on the mythological. Of course, this portrayal should come as no surprise because already in 5:26 a terrifying, superhuman enemy was described who was about to execute cosmic judgment. Clearly prophetic imagination is at work in creating a highly existential atmosphere for the terrified inhabitants of Jerusalem, who are urged to flee before the attack on "this very day."

Then at the very last moment, in God's own time, the Lord of hosts will lop off the branches and fell the proud trees with an ax (cf. 10:15), and all the arrogant boasting of Assyria will be silenced. These verses thus climax the chapter by pulling together the great variety of images in a grand crescendo, leaving no doubt but that the righteous rule of God will indeed establish divine sovereignty over all human pretenses of world power. With this climax the way is now prepared for a full description of the victorious messianic reign that follows in chapter 11.

14. Isaiah 11:1–16

11:1   Then a shoot will come up from the stump of Jesse,
       and a branch will sprout from its roots.
2   The spirit of the LORD will rest on him:
       a spirit of wisdom and insight,
       a spirit of counsel and might,
       a spirit of knowledge and of the fear of the LORD.
3   He will delight[a] in the fear of the LORD.
    He will not judge by what he sees,
       nor decide by what he hears.
4   But he will judge the needy with righteousness,
       and decide for the meek of the earth with equity.
    He will strike the land[b] with the rod of his mouth,
       and slay the wicked with the breath of his lips.
5   Righteousness will be the girdle of his loins,
       and faithfulness the girdle of his waist.
6   The wolf will dwell with the lamb,
       and the leopard will lie down with the kid;
    the calf, the lion, and the fatling together,[c]
       and a little child will lead them.

7   The cow and the bear will graze,
          their young will lie down together;
          and the lion will eat straw like the ox.
8   A baby will play over a viper's hole,
          and an infant will put his hand into an adder's den.
9   They will neither harm nor destroy
          on all my holy mountain,
     for the earth will be full of the knowledge of the LORD
          as water covers the sea.
10   In that day, the root of Jesse will stand as a
     signal to the peoples. The nations will rally to him,
     and his resting place will be glorious.
11   In that day the Lord will reach out his hand a second
     time to recover the remnant that is left of his people
     from Assyria, from Egypt, from Pathros, from Ethiopia,
     from Elam, from Shinar, from Hamath, and from the
     coastlands of the sea.
12   He will raise a signal to the nations,
          and will assemble the exiles of Israel,
     and gather the dispersed of Judah
          from the four corners of the earth.
13   Then Ephraim's envy will vanish
          and Judah's harassment will end;
     Ephraim will not envy Judah,
          and Judah will not harass Ephraim.
14   They will swoop down on the slopes of Philistia
          to the west,
          and together plunder the peoples of the earth.
     Edom and Moab will be subject to them,
          and the Ammonites will obey them.
15   And the LORD will dry up^d the tongue
          of the Egyptian sea.
     He will raise his hand over the River
          with a scorching wind,
     and he will break it into seven streams
          so that it can be crossed dry-shod.
16   There will be a highway from Assyria
          for the remnant of his people left,
     as there was for Israel
          when they came up out of Egypt.

a. The exact meaning of the Hebrew is unclear (cf. exposition below).

b. The MT reads "land" (*'ereṣ*). An emendation often suggested for parallelism is to read *'ārîṣ* ("violent").

c. In place of "fatling together," a suggested emendation reads "they feed" (*yimrᵉ'û*).

d. The verb used by the MT, *ḥrm*, means literally "to put to the ban." A suggested emendation is to read *ḥrb* ("dry up").

Selected Bibliography

G. Barrois, "Critical Exegesis and Traditional Hermeneutics: A Methodological Inquiry on the Basis of the Book of Isaiah," *St. Vladimir's Theological Quarterly* 16, 1972, 107–27; **H. Barth,** *Die Jesaja-Worte in der Josiazeit,* WMANT 48, Neukirchen-Vluyn, 1977, 58–76; **J. Becker,** *Isaias — der Prophet und sein Buch,* SBS 30, 1968, 61–62; **G. I. Davies,** "The Destiny of the Nations in the Book of Isaiah," *The Book of Isaiah,* ed. J. Vermeylen, Leuven 1989, 97–98; **H. Gressmann,** *Der Messias,* FRLANT 26, Göttingen 1929, 246ff.; **H. Gross,** *Die Idee des ewigen und allgemeinen Weltfriedens im Alten Orient und im Alten Testament,* TTS 7, Trier 1967; **H.-J. Hermisson,** "Zukunftserwartung und Gegenwartskritik in der Verkündigung Jesajas," *EvT* 33, 1973, 54–77; **M. Rehm,** *Der königliche Messias im Lichte der Immanuel-Weissagungen des Buches Jesaja,* Kevelaer 1968, 185–234; **J. T. A. G. M. van Ruiten,** "The Intertextual Relationship between Isaiah 65.25 and Isaiah 11.6–9," *The Scriptures and the Scrolls, Fs A. S. van der Woude,* ed. F. García Martínez, et al., VTSup 49, 1992, 31–42; **J. Vermeylen,** *Du Prophète Isaïe à L'Apocalyptique,* I, Paris 1977, 269–80; **G. Widengren,** "Yahweh's Gathering of the Dispersed," *In the Shelter of Elyon: Essays on Ancient Palestinian Life and Literature in Honor of G. W. Ahlström,* ed. W. B. Barrick and J. R. Spencer, Sheffield 1984, 227–45; **H. G. M. Williamson,** *The Book Called Isaiah,* Oxford 1994, 125–132; **E. Zenger,** "Die Verheissung Jesaja 11, 1–10: universal oder partikular?" *Studies in the Book of Isaiah, Fs W. A. M. Beuken,* ed. J. van Ruiten et al., Leuven 1997, 137–47.

The chapter is divided into two main units, vv. 1–9 and 11–16, with v. 10 forming a connecting bridge between the oracles. In addition, there is a question regarding the integral unit of vv. 1–5 and 6–9.

1. Structure, Context, and Dating 11:1–9

In terms of form-critical analysis the unit is usually classified as an announcement of a royal savior, but this formal observation provides limited exegetical help. The oracle has not been seriously shaped by oral conventions, but rather by literary, innertextual forces, and is largely unique in its overall structure. The crucial interpretive issue turns on establishing a context. A historically referential reading is usually assumed to hold the key, and the many proposals run the gamut of options.

a. Duhm, somewhat surprisingly, defended the Isaianic origin, but then, appealing to a psychological explanation of its "idealistic" features, described the oracle as stemming from the prophet's old age. Others who also defend an Isaianic authorship interpret the oracle in a nonmessianic manner, attributing the language to a hyperbolic, royal court style (Scott).

b. The most frequent critical interpretation (e.g., Clements) assigns the whole to a postexilic age and assumes that the reference to the "stump of Jesse" refers to the destruction of the Davidic monarchy in 587.
c. More recent redactional studies (e.g., Becker, Barth) have tended to separate vv. 1–5 from 6–9, and assign only the latter section to a postexilic redactional layer, which was secondarily dependent on such late passages as Isa. 65:25 and Hab. 2:14.

It is obvious that many difficult hermeneutical issues are involved in establishing a context. How is one to evaluate exegetically the role of literary seams? How is the appropriate referent to be determined? How is one to interpret the important element of authorial and editorial intentionality, especially in relation to literary intertextuality?

The first issue to address relates to the unity of vv. 1–9. From a tradiohistorical analysis (in spite of Gressmann) it is difficult to make a convincing case that the two themes of a coming messianic ruler and the return to paradise have been linked in oral tradition. References to an eschatological covenant with the animals (cf. Hos. 2:18[20]) have no royal messianic component. Likewise, Scandinavian research in the history of religions (Bentzen, Widengren) that seeks to join king and tree of life within one mythological ideology is highly speculative and unconvincing in relation to Hebrew tradition.

Nevertheless, there is a conceptual unity to be found in vv. 1–9 within the present literary context of the book. The theme of a description in the original divine intent of creation appears in chapter 1 as a recurring leitmotif. The themes of the restoration of Zion (1:26), the eschatological assembly of the nations of the world at the sacred mountain (2:1–4), and the establishment of a righteous rule by a future messianic ruler (9:1ff.) are reiterated by means of intertextual references throughout 11:1–9 (cf. below). In sum, from the perspective of the present literary unity, both in terms of position and function within the larger book, vv. 1–9 must be treated as an integral unit.

The issue of dating the passage is also related to important hermeneutical questions. Although it is possible that the cutting off of the line of Jesse to a stump may refer to the destruction of the house of David in 587, it is not a self-evident conclusion to draw from the verbal sense of the text. The initial problem turns on the assumption that a historically referential reading is always called for in order to establish a proper context. Yet in terms of vv. 1–6 such a move first historicizes the text and then seeks to recover its meaning from the reconstructed postexilic setting. However, the movement of the text within the larger context of the preceding chapters proceeds on a different plane. It describes an accelerating dissolution of the house of David that is portrayed primarily in theological terms (1:9; 1:22ff.; 2:6ff.; 5:1–4). Various historical events are then used as illustrations of Israel's decay, but the history being described is, above all, focused on the alienation of the Davidic dynasty and the people of Israel from the rule of God over his creation.

The point to emphasize is that in chapters 1 — 11 the role of historical events greatly varies. In chapter 7 the historical context of the Syro-Ephraimite war of 734 is absolutely crucial for its interpretation, and the historical details have been assigned a centrality by the biblical text itself. Again, in chapter 9 the initial background for the messianic light that suddenly breaks forth (v. 1) appears to be the Assyrian conquest of Galilee, but even here very shortly the messianic promise far transcends the initial eighth-century setting. When one comes to chapter 11, the emphasis of v. 1 falls on the new life sprouting from the mutilated house of David, but an exact chronological setting is not given. Rather, the stress lies on the rebirth, which does not emerge from the proud Davidic dynasty but from the ancient, uncorrupted stem of Jesse. For commentators in this case to focus on reconstructing a historical context to provide the key for understanding runs the danger of so concentrating on a level behind the text as to miss the text's own theological witness. In sum, the importance of precisely dating 11:1–9 needs to be greatly relativized within the exegetical task.

The problem of understanding the redactional shaping of vv. 6–9 also involves similar hermeneutical issues. It has recently been argued by redactional critics that two late postexilic passages, Isa. 65:25 and Hab. 2:14, have been added to an earlier Isaianic core in 11:1–5 to expand the vision of the coming new *eschaton* by retrojecting themes from the postexilic period back into the proclamation of Isaiah (Barth, 60–62; Vermeylen, 275–76). Those defending this retrojection argue with considerable cogency that the transformation of nature into paradisiacal harmony is a characteristic of the postexilic age. Although a somewhat similar motif of the harmony of nature appears already in Sumerian literature (Enki and Ninḥursag), it is also true that this theme is rare in preexilic Hebrew literature (e.g., Hosea 2).

The discussion of the direction of intertextual dependency has recently been subjected to a penetrating analysis by van Ruiten (31ff.). Although the case for a redactional retrojection of 65:25 to chapter 11 has not been completely ruled out, van Ruiten has mounted a persuasive argument based on the specific details of the intertextual shaping of 65:25, which strongly supports the traditional view of the adopting by chapter 65 of the earlier text of chapter 11. Chapter 65 reflects many signs of a holistic reading of chapter 11.

Still, the problem of the function of 11:6–9 is not resolved by simply determining the direction of the intertextual influence. The use of literary intertextuality is far more subtle than usually assumed by redactional critics. It is one thing to determine the direction of influence that often remains a difficult task. It is another to understand its interpretive significance. But even if it were possible, the determination of the original direction of influence does not exhaust the function of the intertextual reference within a literary composition. In a word, within the book of Isaiah as a whole the direction of continuing influence of 11:1–9 is forward-moving to 65:25. The original direction, even if it were originally retrospective (in this case highly unlikely) has been reversed according to its present canonical function. Accordingly, chapter 65 serves as an echo of 11:9.

The hermeneutical justification for this claim lies in the role of intertextuality within the Old Testament. It serves as a response by its readers (editors) to the force of the text when it seeks critically to enrich earlier parts of the corpus from later texts as a means of clarifying and deepening a grasp of the substance to which scripture as a whole points. This concern is for the truth of the witness, which is measured by its faithfulness to its theological context rather than by modern criteria of testing the accuracy of a biblical text according to the original sequence of historical events. Above all, this interpretive process of reflection, constitutive of canonical formation, arises from the struggle with the coercion of the text itself and is not simply a vehicle for expressing a private agenda or of self-serving ideologies.

2. Exposition

Chapter 11 has been editorially positioned to form the culmination of a theological direction that commenced at chapter 6, moved through the promise of a coming messianic ruler in chapter 7, and emerged in chapter 9 with the portrayal of a righteous messianic king upon the throne of David. Chapter 11 offers both a correction and an exposition of the messianic reign. Lest one suppose an unbroken continuity between the house of David and the coming king—the encounter with Ahaz in chapter 7 had destroyed this possibility—chapter 11 begins with the end of the old. The Davidic dynasty had been cut off to only a stump. Not only did God fell the mighty power of arrogant Assyria (10:33ff.), but also the proud and corrupt house of David.

[1] From the old stump there comes forth a shoot of new life. The naming of Jesse signals a sure continuity with Israel's past, but serves as a reminder of David's humble beginnings and of a promise grounded in divine election rather than on human pride and royal pretension (2 Samuel 7). The metaphor of the stump also picks up textually the holy seed in the stump of 6:13. In the mystery of God's purpose after the hardening, after the destruction of the land, and after the unbelief of Ahaz, true Israel still has a future because of Immanuel. In sum, it is a striking characteristic of chapter 11 that all the various themes sounded in the previous chapter are pulled together to provide, as it were, a holistic reading of the entire Isaianic message.

[2] The following verse proceeds to describe the charismata suitable to the Messiah's high office. He is endowed by the spirit of God to be the bearer of "the whole fullness of divine powers" (Delitzsch). The gifts are set forth in three couplets: wisdom and insight, counsel and might, knowledge and fear of the Lord. The spirit is the source of all new life, and a contrast is immediately struck with old Israel who did not understand (1:3), and who heard but did not comprehend, who saw but did not perceive (6:9).

Wisdom (*hokmāh*) is the gift of practical ability and skill that derives from discernment. Thus Solomon, as a type of the wise king (1 Kings 3:9), is given wisdom in order to govern rightly, distinguishing good and evil. Counsel is the capacity needed for sagacious diplomacy among peoples, and is joined with the required power needed to achieve a goal. In contrast to Assyria's ruthless exercise of brute force, this counsel controls its use for establishing order and the welfare of those governed. Finally, the coming ruler is equipped with the spirit of knowledge and the fear of Yahweh. The knowledge of God (*da'at*) is the essence of the right relationship of a creature to its creator (Hos. 2:22[20]; 4:1). It is based on love and devotion that is able to recognize the works of God in the world, constant with his own glory and the welfare of humanity. The fear of the Lord expresses both the beginning and end of life, and issues in reverence and worship. It is a response corresponding to the holiness of God, epitomized in the heavenly liturgy of 6:3: "Holy, holy, holy . . . the whole earth is full of his glory."

[3a] The exact sense of v. 3 is not fully clear in the Hebrew. Often the verse is removed as a textual dittography (*BHS,* Wildberger). However, depending on how one translates the initial verb, the colon can be understood as a summarizing response to the prior attributes in v. 2: "his delight shall be in the fear of the LORD" (RSV), or as a transitional clause pointing ahead to the effects of his divine endowments: "He shall sense the truth by his reverence for the Lord" (NJPS).

[3b–5] These verses then portray the nature of the coming ruler's reign according to the will of God, which has been assured by his spirit-filled endowments. The dominant emphasis falls on the righteousness (*ṣedeq*) and equity toward the weak and vulnerable of the world. In this sense, vv. 1–9 continue a major theme introduced in 9:6ff. Again one hears the implied contrast with Israel's unrighteous behavior that resulted in oppression of the poor and senseless acts of violence (3:5, 14). For the prophet Isaiah, the coming of the messianic age is not construed as one of heavenly sweetness and light. Rather, the attributes of counsel and might in governing are exercised in forcefully constraining the wicked and adroitly discerning both the good and the evil of human society (v. 3b).

[6–9] The effect of the righteous rule of the Messiah is depicted in terms of an age of universal peace that embraces both the human and animal world. Often the imagery is described as a return to paradise (Herntrich), and such a concept of the return to the beginning in an eternal cycle is reflected in Virgil's

IV *Eclogue*. Although there are occasional hints in the primordial history of Genesis that the alienation from God also produced enmity between man and beast (3:15; 9:2ff.), this concept was never fully developed and only infrequently shimmers behind the text. Rather, the portrayal of universal peace in this chapter is set within an eschatological context (Hos. 2:20[18]) and is an expansion of the picture of the future harmony among the peoples who flow to the holy mountain (Isa. 11:9). The prophetic picture is not a return to an ideal past, but the restoration of creation by a new act of God through the vehicle of a righteous ruler. The description in vv. 6–9 is a massive extension of the promise in chapter 9 that focuses on the eschatological deliverance of God's people.

In chapter 11 the vision of the future is greatly expanded to include not only the nations but creation itself, in which the entire world, not only the righteous king and his people, is filled with the knowledge of Yahweh (v. 9). As has already been mentioned, the passage shares intertextuality with two other prophetic passages, Isa. 65:25 and Hab. 2:15. It is possible that the Isaianic oracle of chapter 11 has been redactionally enriched by bringing into this earlier passage elements from the most fully developed description of the new heavens and earth (65:17ff.). The effect is to interpret the promise of the prophet Isaiah with new clarity and profundity by an explicit appeal to a new creation. What Isaiah envisioned was not a return to a mythical age of primordial innocence, but the sovereign execution of a new act of creation in which the righteous will of God is embraced and the whole earth now reflects a reverent devotion "as water covers the sea."

[11–16] Because v. 10 performs a particular editorial function it will be treated following the discussion of vv. 11–16. There is general agreement that the oracle forms a unity, except for some secondary expansion in v. 11. The oracle is an eschatological promise introduced with the familiar formula "in that day" concerning the restoration of the remnant. Different aspects of Israel's redemption are then described. Preeminent is the return of the remnant who have been scattered to the ends of the earth. Cush (or Ethiopia) lies to the furthest south. Elam lies on the far east. Shinar (or Babylon) and Hamath refer to middle Syria, and the islands correspond to the Phoenician coastal area. Verse 12 speaks of a signal being raised for the nations when God assembles the banished of Israel from the four corners of the world. Verses 13–14 describe the new harmony between Ephraim and Judah, and together they conquer their old enemies, Philistia, Edom, Moab, and Ammon. Indeed, even Egypt and Assyria are smitten when the Lord prepares a highway from Assyria for the escape of the remnant, like at the first exodus, a theme developed in 35:8, 40:3ff., and 62:10.

There is virtual unanimity among critical scholars that the entire oracle is late exilic or postexilic. The reasons for this dating are the familiar ones: the historical setting of a worldwide diaspora, the strong dependency on Deutero-

Isaiah and other late texts (Obad. 19–21; Micah 7:7–20; and Zech. 10:3–12), and the hope for a reconciliation between the Northern and Southern King-doms. As a consequence of this dating, a few radical commentators see the ora-cle as a fully independent composition reflecting the concerns of a still later postexilic Jewish community and having no integral connection whatever with the messianism of 11:1–9 (e.g., Kilian, 91).

In addition, the oracle receives a very negative assessment from even gener-ally conservative commentators such as Herntrich and Eichrodt. They see in the passage an outpouring of late Jewish nationalism and a vicious attack on the nations that is far removed in tone from the message of Isaiah. Herntrich goes to great lengths to illustrate the need for Christians to develop a "canon within the canon" in order to deal with such an alleged misconstrual of the prophetic preach-ing of universal peace. While this issue presents a difficult problem that cannot be easily dismissed, it fails at the crucial juncture to address the editorial restraints that play such a large role in the phenomenon of canonical shaping (cf. below).

[10] The familiar formula "in that day" sets v. 10 apart from vv. 1–9. It is then followed by a repetition of the same formula to begin a new oracle in v. 11. The critical question concerns the relation of this verse to what precedes and follows. It has long been thought that the verse serves as a kind of com-mentary, but in recent years its function has been increasingly formulated in redactional terminology, which is to say, it is seen as part of an editorial process of shaping. Verse 10 appears to have conscious links with both the preceding and following oracles. It picks up the phrase "stump of Jesse" from v. 1 and combines it with the noun "signal" from v. 11. The crucial exegetical issue lies in determining the intention and effect of this redactional move.

Occasionally a commentator suggests that v. 10 represents a clumsy attempt to harmonize two conflicting oracles, but usually its role is taken more seri-ously. Eichrodt and Wildberger argue that v. 10 functions to extend the role of the Messiah in vv. 1–9 also to include the nations. The difference between a shoot "from the stump of Jesse, and a branch [that] will sprout from its roots" (v. 1) and "the root of Jesse" (v. 10) is deemed insignificant. At most the change shows a certain carelessness and that the terminology had developed to become a technical term for the Messiah. The branch has grown into a tall tree to serve as a worldwide signal. Further, it is argued by some that v. 10 functions to rein-terpret 2:1–4 in order to introduce a new messianic component to the assembly of the nations. Although this interpretation offers a serious option, in the end it cannot be sustained. Especially damaging to this interpretation is that it does not affect the reading of vv. 11–16, which are considered to be a nonmessianic vision of the remnant without connection to the earlier oracle.

Rather, it seems far more likely to take the change in the formula "root of Jesse" as a significant indication of its reinterpretation. The root of Jesse, which owes its life to the new life from the shoot, now represents the remnant of Israel, the new messianic society, which participates in the new age of salvation and peace. The important role of the faithful remnant that has continually occupied Isaiah in his proclamation is missing in vv. 1–9, but is now addressed editorially by means of intertextual interpretation. By picking up key words from vv. 1 and 12, v. 10 joins the two oracles together in a larger unit. The two oracles are thus construed mutually to interpret each other.

The initial effect, when read together intertextually, is that both the Messiah and his community are now integrally joined in 2:1–4 with the nations flowing to Zion. Isaiah 11:9 had joined the transformation of the holy mountain with the new messianic age. Verse 10 now introduces the remnant, the stump of Jesse, as a signal that the nations seek. The final clause, "his resting place will be glorious," further resonates with the description in 4:2–6 of the glorious abode of the survivors of Israel as the holy site of Mount Zion.

The second effect is that vv. 11–16 are now understood in closest conjunction with vv. 1–9 as a description of the restoration of the remnant as the messianic society, the root of Jesse. Indeed, if vv. 11–16 are read in isolation, there are notes struck that sound harsh and nationalistic (e.g., v. 14). But if the redactional intention of v. 10 is taken seriously, these verses are to be understood as part of the righteous rule of the new messianic society (11:4ff.). This "canonical" interpretation does not deny that some tension remains between the two oracles, but the direction of the redactor's interpretation seems quite clear.

There is one final aspect of significance in the redactional shaping of chapter 11. There is an apparent redactional force at work in construing the Isaianic corpus holistically, which would bring together into a larger unity the diverse themes of the reign of God, the coming of a promised messianic rule, and the emergence of a faithful remnant. It is often argued, however, that the eschatology of the book of Isaiah is highly diverse and inconsistent. Isaiah 2:1–4 speaks of a transformed Jerusalem without a Messiah or remnant, 4:2–4 of a purified Zion apart from a Messiah, 11:1–9 of a messianic age, but 11:11–16 of a restoration apart from a messianic vision. Usually this tension is resolved by establishing a historical development and assigning the various components to discrete redactional layers.

However, by careful attention to the function assigned to intertextuality through its lengthy editorial process, one can discern a very strong force emerging that sought to unify the prophetic proclamations into a coherent composition. Quite clearly, different literary restraints were at work in this canonical process from those operative in the modern world. Certainly no heavy-handed systematization of the prophetic oracles was attempted, but guidelines were carefully established that signalled points of resonance within the whole. Lying at the heart of this process was the theological assumption that this written literature was divinely inspired and authoritative for faith and practice. The biblical text was thus understood as a living vehicle inviting study and interpretation as the continuing revelation of God to the life and welfare of his people.

15. Isaiah 12:1–6

12:1   You will say in that day:
"I give thanks to you, O LORD;
    although you were angry with me,
your anger has turned away,
    and you have comforted me.

2   Surely God is my salvation;
    I will trust and not be afraid.
The LORD Yah[a] is my strength and song,
    and he has been my salvation.

3   With joy you will draw water
    from the wells of salvation,

4   and you will say in that day:
"Praise the LORD, call upon his name;
    make his deeds known among the nations;
    declare that his name is exalted.

5   Sing to the LORD, for he has done
    glorious things.
Let this be known in all the world."

6   Sing aloud and shout for joy.
    you inhabitants of Zion,
    for great in your midst
    is the Holy One of Israel.

a. Cf. Ex. 15:2 for the use of "Yah."

Selected Bibliography

W. A. M. Beuken, "Servant and Herald of Good Tidings: Isaiah 61 as an Interpretation of Isaiah 40–55," *The Book of Isaiah,* ed. J. Vermeylen, Leuven 1989, 414; **F. Crüsemann,** *Studien zur Formgeschichte vom Hymnus und Danklied,* WMANT 32, Neukirchen-Vluyn 1969, 227–28; **S. E. Loewenstamm,** "The Lord Is My Strength and My Glory," *VT* 19, 1969, 464–70; **J. Vermeylen,** *Du Prophète Isaïe à L'apocalyptique,* I, Paris 1977, 280–82; **H. G. M. Williamson,** *The Book Called Isaiah: Deutero-Isaiah's Role in Composition and Redaction,* Oxford 1994, 118–25; "Synchronic and Diachronic in Isaian Perspectives," *Synchronic or Diachronic? A Debate in Old Testament Exegesis,* ed. J. C. de Moor, *OTS* 34, Leiden 1955, 211–26.

Chapter 12 serves to bring to a conclusion the first section of the written corpus of Isaianic oracles by sounding the voice of faithful Israel in the idiom of the Psalter as an eschatological hymn of praise. The chapter offers a response to the great deeds of God's salvation to his people in Zion that were recorded in the previous eleven chapters.

1. Form, Structure, and Setting

The unit is divided into two parts, each with an introduction—"You will say in that day" (vv. 1 and 4)—which is then followed by a confession of praise in the style of direct discourse (vv. 1b–2; 4b–5). Verses 3 and 6 bracket the second confession and offer further theological grounding for the call of praise by the community of faith. Beuken (414) has suggested that the person addressed according to the editing of chapter 12 may be the prophet Isaiah himself, rather than the community. He finds a warrant in the singular address. This is an interesting suggestion, but it does not seem to be illuminating in the context of the chapter as a whole.

In contrast to the various oracular forms in the preceding chapters, chapter 12 is dominated by the psalmic language of Israel's liturgy. Usually the form is thought to reflect most closely the individual psalm of thanksgiving (e.g., Psalm 30; cf. the *Hodayoth* of Qumran). Nevertheless, the careful form-critical analysis of Crüsemann (227–28) has pointed out the sharp divergences from the conventional pattern of the thanksgiving psalm, especially in the verbal forms. It seems clear that the traditional conventions of the Psalter have been reused to shape an eschatological psalm of thanksgiving into a new vehicle for the prophetic proclamation of the book. In addition, there is another characteristic feature of the unit that is crucial in evaluating its role within the book. The passage is a veritable catena of citations and allusions from other sections of Isaiah, from Exodus, and the Psalter. For example, v. 1=Isa. 5:25; v. 2a=Ex. 15:2b; v. 2b=Ex. 15:2a; v.3=Isa. 35:10, 55:1; Ps. 105:41, 43; v. 4=Ps. 105:1, 148:13; v.5=Ex. 15:1, 21. This use of scripture naturally has wide implications for determining the nature of the redactional shaping of the passage as a whole.

Recently, Williamson (118ff.) has mounted a strong case for seeing Second Isaiah as the actual editor of portions of First Isaiah, including in particular chapter 12. He focuses on the well-known observations that demonstrate the marked affinities of the chapter in language, style, and content with Second Isaiah. I do not have any serious problems with his detailed philological and literary arguments. My difference is rather a hermeneutical one, which emerges when one inquires how this information is then used exegetically in his interpretation of chapter 12.

His identifying the redactor with Second Isaiah appears to provide for him a way of establishing a historical context for chapter 12. Since much is considered known about Second Isaiah, his identification as editor unlocks a wide interpretive framework that includes historical, literary, religious, and even pyschological insights into his ideology by which to interpret First Isaiah. Yet to adopt this approach opens up all the old pitfalls involved in the dependency on authorial intent, now broadened to include redactional as well. Once again, exegesis is directly built on the fragile and subjective foundation of literary and historical reconstructions.

Williamson concludes his discussion by stating that "the chapter functions just like the eschatological hymns of praise in 40—55" (123). This conclusion rests largely on the assumption of editorial identity and misses the unique literary and theological role of chapter 12. In the exegesis that follows, I shall try to discern the effect of the shaping of the final form of the biblical text in an effort to determine its function as a holistic witness within the larger canonical corpus.

2. Exposition

The redactional history of this passage is closely tied to the theological function of the chapter within its larger literary context. The chapter forms a conclusion to chapters 1—11 and brings to an end the first section within the book of Isaiah. It is not directly related redactionally to what follows in the oracles to the nations in chapters 13ff. (*contra* Vermeylen), but rather offers a holistic reading of the Isaianic message from the prior chapters.

The major point to make is that chapter 12 presents the voice of the faithful remnant of Israel responding to the great deeds of God, both in judgment and redemption, which had occupied the prophets throughout the former chapters. Up to now there had been the promise of a new community of faith that would emerge from the ashes of Israel's destruction, but the actual voice of the remnant had not been heard. The presentation of this voice of praise serves to confirm that the new society of faith was not merely a future promise, but was a present reality, made concrete first in the son Shearjashub (7:3), but above all in the sign of Immanuel (7:14). This community of faith confirms in liturgical praise its experience of God, and the choice of the idiom of the Psalter bears testimony to the liturgical actuality of the worship.

The hymn of thanksgiving begins by picking up the major theme of the preceding chapter: "I give thanks . . . although you were angry with me." Behind this confession resonates the continual refrain of the prophetic judgment: "Surely you have rejected your people" (2:6); "For all this his anger has not turned back and his arm is still stretched out" (9:11); "Destruction is decreed" (10:22). However, along with this acknowledgment of the divine punishment there sounds the word of forgiveness: "your anger has turned away, and you have comforted me" (12:1). Then there follows the remnant's response.

Had not God spoken, "do not fear the Assyrians when they strike you" (10:25)? From the experience of faith Israel answers: "God is my salvation. . . . I will trust and not be afraid" (12:2). The theme of salvation is repeated three times, not just as a promise extended, but a reality experienced: "God is my salvation" (v. 2). It is this experience of the redeeming mercy that evokes joy as an inexhaustible source of life-giving water. Moreover, as with the rest of the Psalter, the experience of salvation calls forth a witness to the rest of the world that bears testimony to the wonders of God's mighty works.

Of great significance is that in v. 2 Israel's hymn of praise is made through an appropriation of the "song of the sea" sung by Moses and his people following their deliverance from the Egyptians (Ex. 15:1ff.), and later used liturgically in Israel's continuing worship (Ps. 118:14). Thus an analogy is established between redeemed Israel after the deliverance from Egypt and the present remnant, who in their experience of faith already stand on a safe shore a second time after having been rescued from enemies and exile. Here the theme sounded most strongly is that of 11:11ff., the restoration of the remnant by the sheer might of its God.

The function of the language of the Psalter is to stress the actual response in worship by a present community of faith. Yet this is only one side of the response. The song of thanksgiving has been rendered into an eschatological hymn of praise: "You will say in that day . . ." (vv. 1 and 4). The salvation that the faithful community has experienced is only a foretaste of the coming deliverance of Israel. In the response of faith the reality of the divine presence, "God with us" (Immanuel), has been experienced, pointing to the full eschatological consummation of the kingdom of God. Israel can shout in joy because the Holy One of Israel, who has always reigned over his creation (6:3), even now shows himself mighty in the midst of his people (v. 6). The eschatological tensions of the chapter testify that the remnant already shares in that for which it waits in expectation. It was not a large step when the Christian church began to understand in a sacramental sense the tension between "already but not yet" as revealed in the Eucharist: "As often as you eat this bread and drink the cup, you proclaim the Lord's death until he comes" (1 Cor. 11:26).

To conclude, chapter 12 once again illustrates the unique role that intertextuality plays in the shaping of Israel's scriptures. Redaction critics have long pointed out that the style of citing from a catena of written texts, many of which are quite late, point to a postexilic editorial dating of the chapter. Yet as has been previously argued, the danger of misconstruing the exegetical significance of these correct literary observations is acute. Thus, it is seriously misleading to suggest that the text should now be interpreted within the new critically reconstructed exilic or postexilic setting in order to replace the fictive Isaianic context of the chapter with a historical ideology of some Jewish group of the Persian-Hellenistic period. Rather, the true exegetical context has been established by its literary function within the book.

The biblical editors felt free to portray the theological reality of the confessing remnant, which emerged in response to Isaiah's prophetic proclamation, in the language both of Israel's past—the deliverance from Egypt (Exodus 15)—and also of the future—the divine word of comfort (Isa. 40:1). Because the editors assumed the unity of the one selfsame divine reality at work throughout the history of salvation, the temporal significance of the age of the original oracles used in the portrayal is largely relativized and only serves to enrich and fill out with fresh colors the reality to which the biblical text now bears its eloquent testimony. For this reason, chapter 12 not only summarizes chapters 1—11, but also points forward in anticipation of the consolation of Second Isaiah (11:2=40:1).

16. INTRODUCTION TO ISAIAH 13—23

Selected Bibliography

P. A. H. de Boer, "An Inquiry into the Meaning of the Term *mś*," *OTS* 5, 1948, 197–214; **D. L. Christensen,** *Transformation of the War Oracle in Old Testament Prophecy,* HDR 3, Missoula 1975; **G. I. Davies,** "The Destiny of the Nations in the Book of Isaiah," *The Book of Isaiah,* ed. J. Vermeylen, Leuven 1989, 93–120; **H. Donner,** *Israel unter de Völkern,* VTSup 11, Leiden 1964; **M. Drechsler,** *Der Prophet Jesaja* II/I, Stuttgart 1849, 1–16; **S. Erlandsson,** *The Burden of Babylon,* ConBOT 4, Lund 1970; **H. S. Gehman,** "The 'Burden' of the Prophets," *JQR* 31, 1940–41, 107–21; **J. B. Geyer,** "Mythology and Culture in the Oracles against the Nations," *VT* 36, 1986, 129–45; **H. L. Ginsberg,** "Reflexes of Sargon in Isaiah after 715 B.C.E." *JAOS* 88, 1968, 47–53; **G. R. Hamborg,** "Reasons for Judgment in the Oracles against the Nations of the Prophet Isaiah," *VT* 31, 1981, 145–59; **J. H. Hayes,** "The Usage of Oracles against Foreign Nations in Ancient Israel," *JBL* 87, 1968, 81–92; **J. H. Hayes and S. A. Irvine,** *Isaiah: His Times and His Preaching,* Nashville 1987, 220ff.; **A. K. Jenkins,** "The Development of the Isaiah Tradition in Isaiah 13—23," *The Book of Isaiah,* ed. J. Vermeylen, Leuven 1989, 237–51; **L. J. Liebreich,** "The Compilation of the Book of Isaiah," *JQR* 46, 1955/56, 259–77; 47, 1956/57, 114–38; **D. L. Petersen,** "The Oracles against the Nations: A Form-Critical Analysis," *SBL 1975 Seminar Papers,* ed. G. McRae, Missoula 1975, 1, 39–61; **C. R. Seitz,** *Isaiah 1—39,* IntBC Louisville 1993, 115–71; **M. A. Sweeney,** *Isaiah 1—39,* FOTL 16, Grand Rapids 1996, 212–17; **H. G. M. Williamson,** *The Book Called Isaiah,* Oxford 1994, 156–83.

1. Structure and Genre

Initially the structure of the corpus appears quite clear, with nine superscriptions, each introducing a subunit of the oracles concerning the nations by means of the formula *maśśā'* ("oracle concerning"): 13:1; 15:1; 17:1; 19:1; 21:1; 21:11; 21:13; 22:1; 23:1. The new section, beginning with chapter 13, is set off from the preceding chapters. In addition, the corpus 13—23 is also carefully distinguished from the succeeding collection of chapters 24—27, although the close relation between the two sections will be discussed subsequently.

There has been a lengthy but still inconclusive debate over the exact sense of the term *maśśā'* (cf. Gehman, Scott, Erlandsson). Some have sought to connect it with the noun *burden,* and thus have designated its use within a superscription as a special type of judgment oracle. Others, citing Zechariah (9:1, 12:1), have argued for its being a neutral term for a pronouncement. Sweeney (222), following Weis, argues that the *maśśā'* pronouncement shares no overarching single genre. It is to be distinguished from a conventional oracle of judgment. Clearly the nations are not the direct addressees, but the oracle has another function which includes Israel. From one perspective, it is possible to see a distant relationship to the genre of the war oracle (Christensen), but this development, even if true, lies in the distant past and adds little to the interpretation of Isaiah. In its present literary setting, the oracles are directed primarily to Israel and designed to explain events in the world of affairs as an act of Yahweh. Thus, as has been frequently pointed out, these oracles are concerning the nations and not necessarily against them. This new theological function now overrides whatever antecedents may once have been at work. There seems to be no clear chronological order, but rather largely a thematic one.

Beside the clearly structural *maśśā'* form, there are a variety of other oracles within the corpus that stand outside the larger framework. Isaiah 14:24–27 is a summary-appraisal form concerning the fulfillment of Isaiah's word against Assyria. Isaiah 14:28–32 has its own superscription, which dates the oracle concerning Philistia in the year of King Ahaz's death (cf. also 17:12–14; 18;1–7; 20:1–6; 22:1–14; 22:15–25). On the basis of these divergent forms, some have sought to reconstruct a diachronic trajectory. However, regardless of whether one assigns the extraneous material to the early levels of growth, or whether one argues for a reversed move beginning with the *maśśā'* structure, the present form of the corpus has subordinated the extraneous material to the dominant perspective of the *maśśā'* pronouncement.

2. Setting, Redaction, and Function

The problem of determining the historical and literary setting of chapters 13—23 has evoked a lengthy debate. At the outset, it is evident that the concern with the nations is not confined only to these chapters. There are, of course, larger structural parallels in the prophetic books, such as Jeremiah 46—51, Ezekiel 25—32, and smaller scattered prophecies of a similar genre such as Amos 1:3–2:16 and Zeph. 2:4–15. Even more immediately relevant are the literary connections with Isaiah 11 and 12, which provide a transition to chapters 13—23 and which list Assyria, Egypt, Ethiopia, Philistia, Edom, Moab, and Ammon. There are also linguistic and thematic connections between chapters 13—23 and chapters 1—12. Especially the motif of the outstretched hand over the nations in 14:25 is thought to be allied to the refrain in chapters 5, 9, and 10.

A crucial problem of great significance in establishing a historical setting turns on understanding the relationship of Babylon to Assyria in chapter 13. With the rise of the historical-critical analysis of the book of Isaiah, particularly in the period following Duhm, it was assumed that the threat to Babylon by the Medes in chapter 13 would identify the period as the Neo-Babylonian kingdom of the sixth century, which was brought to an end by the Medes and Persians in

539. The terminus for dating chapter 13 was therefore set in the late exilic or early postexilic period. The presence of Assyrian oracles was derived from earlier fragments, some even attributed to the eighth-century prophet, which had been reinterpreted for later use within chapters 13—23. Especially chapter 14 was thought to have an original Assyrian context.

In 1970 Erlandsson's volume, *The Burden of Babylon,* offered a very learned attack on this critical hypothesis. He argued that the historical setting of chapters 13—23 was not that of the Neo-Babylonian era, but rather of the Assyrian period culminating with the attack on Jerusalem in 701. The description of Babylon in chapter 13 was of the kingdom of Merodach-baladan. In 705, with the death of Sargon, Babylon sought to throw off the Assyrian yoke, but in 702 Sennacherib successfully attacked and destroyed Merodach-baladan's city of Babylon. Again in 694 he fought and defeated the Babylonians, and in 689 Sennacherib finally brought Babylonian power to an end.

There are several strengths to Erlandsson's hypothesis:

a. It is able to explain the violent destruction of the city depicted in Isaiah 13, which did not even occur in 539.
b. It also addresses the issue of why Assyrian oracles appear in chapters 13 and 14 by offering a unified historical setting.

Nevertheless, there remain major problems with this reconstruction:

a. There is the serious historical problem that prior to the defeat of the Assyrian hegemony at the end of the seventh century the Medes were in alliance with the Babylonians against Assyria and were not enemies of Babylon.
b. Even more important, the description of Babylon in chapter 13 as the epitome of evil and world power is far more suitable to the age of Nebuchadnezzar than of Merodach-baladan. The entire role of the hated oppressor in chapters 13—23 is far from the Babylon depicted by Erlandsson at the end of the eighth and beginning of the seventh centuries.

For these reasons the majority of modern scholars reject Erlandsson's hypothesis which, however, continues to be defended by conservative interpreters such as Hayes and Irvine, and Oswalt.

Of course, once one has decided on a sixth-century setting for the major shaping of the corpus, then a host of difficult problems still remain that call for resolution. Particularly the hermeneutical problems at issue have been handled with great boldness and insight by C. Seitz (115–71). For example, how is one to understand the leap from the eighth to the sixth century? For what purpose was this collection of oracles so shaped within the book of Isaiah?

In the earlier literary-critical period, scholars tended to speak of "genuine" and "nongenuine" passages, which resulted in their fragmenting the corpus into a largely arbitrary collection of independent pieces. The great advantage of the recent redactional analysis is that an attempt is made to recover an editorial intention that shaped the corpus into a unified whole. From the perspective of the events of 587, of the exile, and of the rise of the Medes and Persians, the significance of Israel's history in reference to the world powers of Assyria and Babylon was interpreted retrospectively as consisting of the one theological purpose of God with his people.

The debate over the exact age of the redactional shaping of chapters 13—23 continues, and a case has been often mounted that the editorial perspective reflects much theological compatibility with that of Second Isaiah. The fall of Babylon is imminent and the coming of the Medes is seen as a fulfillment of Isaiah's prophecy (41:25). The influence of a theology akin to Second Isaiah is especially visible in the editorial links provided by 14:1–3, 22 in joining chapters 13 and 14.

Of greatest importance is that the shaping of chapters 13—23 anticipates the theology of Second Isaiah in envisioning a typological relation between the Assyrian and Babylonian oppressions. The issue is thus indirectly addressed that, in spite of the fulfillment of God's promise of destroying Assyria in Israel's land (14:24–27; chapters 36—37), Israel still faces a final humiliation before its final victory over Babylon. Particularly in chapter 14 one can see how the defeats of Assyria and Babylon were linked as an illustration of the coming victory of God's righteous rule.

The theology of chapters 13—23 is not just directed against the nations of the world. Rather, it has been long observed that there is also a positive theme, and a future is envisioned in terms of the encompassing of the nations within the sovereignty of God. Above all, this corpus as a whole functions as a witness to the ultimate victory of the rule of God. The theme of the day of the Lord picks up an eschatological hope of First Isaiah, which is then projected into a universalized form in the chapters that follow (24—27).

17. Isaiah 13:1–14:32

13:1 An oracle concerning Babylon that Isaiah son of Amoz saw.

2 Raise a banner on a bare hill,
  cry aloud to them.
 Wave a hand for them to enter
  the gates of the nobles.

3 I have summoned my purified ones,
  have commanded my mighty ones,
  to execute my anger,
  those who rejoice in my majesty.

4 Listen, a tumult on the mountains,
  like that[a] of a great multitude.
 Listen, an uproar of kingdoms,
  of nations assembling.
 The LORD of hosts is mustering
  an army for war.

5 They come from a distant land,
  from the end of the heavens—
 the LORD and the weapons of his wrath—
  to destroy the whole earth.

6 Wail, for the day of the LORD is near;
  it will come like destruction from the Almighty.

7 Then all hands will grow limp,
  and every man's heart will melt.

8 They will be overwhelmed with terror,
  pain and agony will seize them;
  they will writhe like a woman in labor.
 They will gaze in terror at each other,
  their faces flushed in fear.

9 Look, the day of the LORD is coming,
  cruel, with fury and anger,
 to make the earth a waste,
  and to destroy the sinners within it.

10 The stars and their constellations

will not give off their light.
The sun will be dark at its rising,
    and the moon will not reflect its light.

11   I will punish the world for its evil,
    and the wicked for their sins.
I will end the arrogance of the proud
    and humble the haughtiness of tyrants.

12   I will make people scarcer than fine gold
    and more rare than the gold of Ophir.

13   Therefore I will make the heavens tremble;
    and the earth will shake from its place
at the anger of the LORD of hosts,
    in the day of his burning wrath.

14   Like hunted gazelles,
    like sheep with none to gather them,
each will return to his own people,
    everyone will flee to his native land.

15   Whoever is found will be thrust through,
    and whoever is caught will fall by the sword.

16   Their infants will be dashed to pieces
    before their eyes;
their houses will be looted
    and their wives raped.

17   Behold, I will stir up the Medes against them,
    who do not value silver
    or have any delight in gold.

18   Their bows will shatter the young;
    they will show no mercy to infants,
    nor will they spare the children.

19   And Babylon, the glory of kingdoms,
    the proud splendors of the Chaldeans,
will be overthrown by God
    like Sodom and Gomorrah.

20   It will never be inhabited
    or dwelt in from generation to generation.
No Arab will pitch his tent there,
    no shepherd will pasture there.

21   But desert creatures will lie down there,
    and its houses will be full of owls.
There ostriches[b] will dwell
    and wild goats will dance.

22   Hyenas will howl in its towers

and jackals in the luxurious palaces.
Its time is close at hand,
    and its days will not be prolonged.

14:1 But the L ORD will have compassion on Jacob and will again choose Israel, and will settle them in their own land. Strangers will join them and attach themselves to the house of Jacob. 2 And the peoples will take them and bring them to their homeland; and the house of Israel will possess them as male and female slaves. They will take captive their captors and rule their oppressors. 3 On the day the L ORD has given you rest from your pain and sorrow and from hard service, 4 you will take up this taunt against the king of Babylon:

How the oppressor has met his end
    and the fury[c] ceased!

5 The L ORD has broken the rod of the wicked,
        the rod of the tyrant

6 that struck peoples in rage
        with relentless blows,
        crushing nations in anger
        and persecuting them endlessly.

7 The whole world is at rest and peace.
        It breaks out in singing.

8 Even pines and cedars of Lebanon
        rejoice at your fate saying,
    "Now that you have been laid low,
        No one comes up to cut us down."

9 Sheol below is stirred up
        to greet you at your coming;
    it rouses the shades to meet you,
        all who have been rulers on earth;
    it made all the kings of the nation
        rise from their thrones.

10 All of them will speak and say to you:
    "So you have become as weak as we,
        you have become like us!

11 Your pomp is brought down to Sheol,
        the sound of your lutes.
    Maggots are the bed under you
        and worms your blanket."

12 "How you are fallen from heaven,
        O Day Star,[d] son of Dawn!
    How you are cut down to the ground,
        you who laid low the nations!

13   You said in your heart,
          'I will ascend to heaven,
      above the stars of God.
          I will set my throne on high;
      I will sit in the mount of assembly
          in the far north;
14   I will ascend—ascend above the cloud banks.
          I make myself like the Most High!'
15   Instead, you are brought down to Sheol,
          to the bottom of the Pit.
16   Those who see you stare at you,
          they look closely at you:
      'Is this the man who made the earth tremble,
          and shook kingdoms,
17   who turned the world into a desert
          and overthrew its cities,
      who did not let his prisoners go home?'
18   All the kings of nations lie in state,
          each in his own tomb.
19   But you are cast out of your tomb
          like putrefied carrion.
      You are covered with the slain,
          those pierced by the sword,
      who sink to the stones of the Pit
          like a trampled corpse.
20   You will not join them in burial,
          because you have destroyed your land
          and killed your people.
      Let the offspring of the wicked
          never be mentioned again.
21   Prepare a slaughtering place for his sons
          because of the sins of their fathers,
      lest they rise and possess the earth
          and fill the face of the world with cities."
22   "I will rise up against them," says the LORD of hosts, "and will wipe
      out from Babylon her reputation and remnant, her offspring and
      descendants," says the LORD. 23 "I will make it a place for owls, a
      swampland, and I will sweep her with a broom of destruction," says
      the LORD of hosts.
24   The LORD of hosts has sworn, saying:
      "As I have planned, so will it be,
          and as I have purposed, so it will happen,

25 　　that I will break Assyria in my land
　　　　　　and will crush him on my mountains.
　　　　Then his yoke will be taken from them
　　　　　　and his burden will drop from their shoulders."
26 　　This is the plan prepared for the whole earth.
　　　　　　This is the hand that is stretched out against the nations.
27 　　For the LORD of hosts has formed a plan,
　　　　　　and who can frustrate it?
　　　　And his hand is stretched out;
　　　　　　who can turn it back?
28 　　In the year that King Ahaz died this oracle came
　　　　　　from God:
29 　　"Do not rejoice, all you of Philistia,
　　　　　　that the rod that struck you is broken,
　　　　for from the root of a snake will spring up a viper,
　　　　　　and its fruit is a flying serpent.
30 　　The firstborn of the poor will pasture,[e]
　　　　　　and the needy will lie down safely.
　　　　But I will kill your root with famine;
　　　　　　it will slay what is left of you.
31 　　Wail, O gate; cry out, O city;
　　　　　　quake, all Philistia.
　　　　For smoke comes out of the north,
　　　　　　and there is no straggler in its ranks."
32 　　What will he answer the envoys of that nation?
　　　　"The LORD has established Zion,
　　　　　　and in it, the wretched of his people find refuge."

　　　a. The Hebrew *dᵉmût* is difficult to render as an adjective, but the suggested emendation to *hᵃmôt* ("roaring") is unnecessary.

　　　b. The identification of the birds and animals is uncertain.

　　　c. The meaning of the Hebrew *madhēbāh* is unknown. Usually the word is emended to *marhēbāh* ("fury") (cf. LXX, 1QIsᵃ).

　　　d. *hēlēl* ("morning star"), often pointed *hēlāl* (*BHS*), is rendered "Lucifer" by the Vulgate.

　　　e. Verses 30a and 32b are often shifted to a position after v. 31.

Selected Bibliography

R. Bach, *Die Aufforderungen zur Flucht und zum Kampf im alttestamentlichen Prophetenspruch,* WMANT 9, Neukirchen-Vluyn 1962; **H. Barth,** *Die Jesaja-Worte in der Josiazeit,* WMANT 48, Neukirchen-Vluyn 1977, 103ff., 119ff.; **J. Begrich,** "Jesaja 14, 28–32," *GSAT,* ThB 21, Munich 1964, 121–31; **E. Bosshard-Nepustil,** *Rezeptionen von Jesaia 1–39 im Zwölfprophetenbuch,* OBO 154,

Freiburg, Göttingen 1997, 67–92; **H. Bost,** "Le chant sur la chute d'un tyran en Ésaïe 14," *ETR* 59, 1984, 3–15; **B. S. Childs,** *Myth and Reality in the Old Testament,* SBT I, 27, London 1960, 69–72; *Isaiah and the Assyrian Crisis,* SBT II, 3, London 1967, 128–36; **R. E. Clements,** "The Prophecies of Isaiah and the Fall of Jerusalem in 587 B.C.," *VT* 30, 1980, 421–36; "Isaiah 14, 22–27: A Central Passage Reconsidered," *The Book of Isaiah,* ed. J. Vermeylen, BETL 81, Leuven 1989, 253–62; **S. Erlandsson,** *The Burden of Babylon,* ConBOT 4, Lund 1970, 67–69; **K. Fullerton,** "Isaiah 14:28–32," *AJSL* 42, 1925–26, 86–109; **H. S. Gehman,** "The 'Burden' of the Prophets," *JQR* 31, 1940–41, 107–21; **B. Gosse,** *Isaïe 13, 1–14, 23,* OBO 78, Freiburg 1988; **M. Greenberg,** "Pharaoh in the Netherworld (32:17–22)," *Ezekiel 21–37,* AB, New York 1997, 659–70; **P. Grelot,** "Isaïe XIV 12–15 et son arrière-plan mythologique," *RHR* 149, 1956, 18–48; **H. Jahnow,** *Das hebräische Leichenlied im Rahmen der Völkerdichtung,* BZAW 36, Giessen 1923, 239–53; **O. Loretz,** "Der kanaanäisch-biblische Mythos vom Sturz des Sahar-Sohnes Helel," *UF* 8, 1976, 133–35; **J. W. McKay,** "Helel and the Dawn-Godess: A Re-examination of the Myth in Isaiah XIV 21–15," *VT* 20, 1970, 451–64; **M. A. Sweeney,** *Isaiah 1–39,* FOTL 16, Grand Rapids, 1996, 218–39; **G. A. Yee,** "The Anatomy of Biblical Parody: The Dirge Form in 2 Samuel 1 and Isaiah 14," *CBQ* 50, 1988, 565–86; **B. M. Zapff,** *Schriftgelehrte Prophetie—Jes 13 und die Komposition des Jesajabuches,* FB 74, Würzburg 1995.

1. Structure, Genre, and Redactional Layering

Generally this section is thought to be composed of two larger units, 13:2–22 and 14:4b–21. These have been linked together editorially by an initial superscription (13:1), and two redactional units, 14:1–4a and 22–23. Chapter 14 concludes with two separate oracles, vv. 24–27 and vv. 28–32. In 1980 Clements proposed seeing a number of subdivisions within chapter 13 often designated as fragments (*Isaiah,* 132). These smaller divisions were regarded as of particular significance because he saw in them a historical progression extending from the late eighth century revolts against Assyria led by Merodach-baladan (vv. 2–3), to an eschatological reinterpretation of events beyond 587 in the imagery of the day of Yahweh (vv. 9–16). He assigned the final oracle (vv. 17–22) to the period just preceding the capture of Babylon by the Medes and Persians in 539. In my opinion, the new editorial function of vv. 2–22 is so strong in shaping the unity of the larger section as to relegate these reconstructed subdivisions to the text's background.

A very different approach to the structure of chapters 13 and 14 has been very recently developed by Bosshard-Nepustil. On the basis of a complex redactional analysis he distinguishes three different layers within the text: a *Grundschrift* in 13:2–8, 14–16, followed by two additional levels of expansion in vv. 1, 9–13, and 17–22. He attempts next to trace the growth of a literary context, which was shaped by intertextual resonances with Isa. 10:27b–34 and Jeremiah 4—6. This analysis leads him to seek to recover a matching level of literary redaction in Isa. 21:1–10 and 22:1–14. Since the exegetical assumptions in Bosshard-Nepustil's work are so very different from those employed in this commentary, it is probably wise to leave a detailed assessment to the next generation of scholars (but cf. my commentary below on chapters 21 and 22).

The more critical issue is associated with an interpretation of chapter 13 by Clements and Seitz. It turns on whether or not one understands the "purified ones" of v. 3, whom God calls to execute his eschatological judgment, to be the Babylonians. According to this interpretation, an analogy is established here with 10:5ff. when God used the Assyrians as his agent of destruction before then destroying the very ones who had first served as his means of judgment. Accordingly, only in v. 17 does the reversal set in when the Medes are called upon to destroy Babylon.

Although this is a serious interpretive option, it is not in the end to be preferred. Rather, the more likely interpretation is the traditional one, which sees Babylon as the object of God's judgment rather than the means throughout the entire chapter. The reasons are as follows:

    a. The style used in the chapter is not one of chronological sequence, but rather a veiled, eschatological army is portrayed ushering in the day of Yahweh, which engulfs the entire world. Then v. 17 with its introductory particle, "behold" (*hinnēh*), pulls back the veil to reveal the solution to the mystery: It is the Medes executing the judgment on Babylon who constitute God's phantom army.

    b. The symbolism attached to Babylon is that of the sixth-century Neo-Babylonian empire, not the struggling forces of Merodach-baladan. The analogy with Assyria as "the rod of his anger" breaks down, since vv. 3–16 depict the final denouement of history and the defeat of cosmic evil.

The second major oracle of the section, 14:4b–21, is clearly a taunt song delivered against the king of Babylon. A rather convincing case can be made that this taunt song was originally directed against a hated Assyrian king. Sargon II is usually identified as the original referent since apparently his body was abandoned after he was killed in battle (cf. 14:19–20). In its present form the song is explicitly directed to the king of Babylon, and the transitional function of 14:1–2 shows that both 13:2–12 and 14:3–23 are presupposed. The theology expressed in 14:1–2—the election of Israel, the return to the land, the reversal of the role of the oppressor—are all elements that are similar to those of Second Isaiah. The effect of this editorial activity is to reveal clearly that the entire unit, 13:1–14:23, has been shaped in the exilic period, reflecting both the destruction of Jerusalem in 587 and also the expectation of deliverance from the Persians in the imminent future. This wide redactional consensus has been clearly described recently by Sweeney (212ff.). However, his assumption that the punishment of the nations is always portrayed as an act of Yahweh for some particular political purpose appears to me to unnecessarily historicize the material in too heavy-handed a manner. Although it may be useful at times for

Sweeney to distinguish carefully between a possible seventh-century, sixth-century, and fifth-century edition of these chapters, one is disappointed that this redactional scheme, dependent upon diachronic reconstruction, remains operative right to the end of his exegesis, and thus is never overcome by a theological construal of the final effect of the canonical process.

The redactional significance of 14:24–27 has long been evident, and has been developed even further in recent years (cf. Barth, Clements). Regardless of whether one is fully convinced that the passage once marked the conclusion of the so-called seventh-century Josianic redaction beginning in chapter 5, the intertextual relation to the refrain of the "outstretched hand" in chapters 5, 9, and 10 is clear. Thus the passage serves redactionally to unite the destruction of Assyria with its latter counterpart Babylon, and to join in the one plan of God the destruction of the arrogant oppressor from both the eighth and sixth centuries. It also joins well with the final oracle in 14:28ff., which warns Philistia in the year of King Ahaz's death that another military colossus will shortly arise from the north (v. 31).

2. Exposition

[13:1] The superscription in v. 1 marks the first of the nine *maśśā'* oracles in this corpus. However, it is different from the rest in its attribution to Isaiah, the son of Amoz. Thus it presents a clear parallel to 2:1 and initiates a well-defined corpus. As we shall see, there are other structural parallels between chapters 2— 12 and 13—23 that indicate larger redactional strategies (cf. below).

[2–5] The unit begins with a summons to battle: the raising of a banner, the cry to assemble, the waving of the hand, and the gesture to proceed. The army called by God is to enter as conquerors into the city of the princes. Yahweh summons his "purified ones," those rightly prepared for battle, to execute his wrath. The time is of excitement and tremendous action, but also mysterious. Those executing the divine judgment and those receiving it are undefined as yet. Nor is it wise immediately to supply a historical referent, lest the literary tension of the pronouncement be too quickly resolved. Yet there is a perceptive resonance in v. 3 with the summoning of mighty men to execute the divine anger (cf. 10:5).

The assembling and the goal of this phantom army is pursued with a host of new metaphors. The roar of multitudes mustering for war is deafening as God's army collects from the extremities of the heavens. The eerie description again is a reminder of the terrifying army of 5:26ff. that descends from the ends of the earth, roaring like a lion, and bringing cosmological darkness. However, the explicit goal of this apocalyptic army is made clear for the first time—to destroy the entire world.

[6–16] In this context of eschatological judgment, it is fully appropriate that the prophet describes its effects in the idiom of the "day of the LORD." Scholars have long sought to trace a trajectory in the growth of this concept, such as tying it to an original holy war tradition (cf. M. Saebø, *TWAT* III, 566ff.). However, the lack of hard evidence and the huge gaps between its occurrences obscure any certainty regarding its development. When it first appears in the eighth century (Amos 5:18–20), it is already well developed as a hope for Israel's favorable welfare. Amos, of course, destroys the people's false aspiration by construing the coming of the day of Yahweh as unmitigated judgment. When it occurs in Joel 1 and Zephaniah 1, its coming appears to arise from within a specific historical context. Then immediately a misfortune is turned into a divine judgment that continues to accelerate into a worldwide cosmological event: "a day of ruin and destruction, darkness and gloom" when "all the earth shall be consumed, indeed in a full end" (Zeph. 1:16ff.). A similar movement occurs in Isa. 2:6ff. with the terror of God obliterating all human pride and God alone being exalted in his day.

The author of chapter 13 exploits with apocalyptic intensity the terrifying effect on the earth's inhabitants of the cosmological disorder of darkness at noon and the shaking of the earth's foundation. There is no hope for escape from the sheer horror of the slaughter. The final description (vv. 14–16) leaves the arena of the heavenly judgment and returns to the description—all too well known in the ancient Near East—of the cruel massacre of a helpless people by an invading army: infants dashed on rocks, wives ravished, and houses looted. The way is thus prepared for the final section, which names the human agent of this divine judgment.

[17–22] The reference in v. 17 to the Medes as the executor of God's vengeance on the Babylonians immediately establishes a historical setting in the late sixth century. However, it is also significant that the coming of the Medes is portrayed as a still future event, and is not to be interpreted as a late postexilic retrojection of the events of 539 when Babylon actually fell. The nature of the prophetic oracle is misunderstood if it is simply rendered as a historical event describing the end of one political era and the beginning of another. Rather, the prophet speaks of God's time, which is close at hand, and of a divine purpose in history that receives its true significance as a demonstration of God's sovereignty over the nations. The claims of Babylon—its splendor, glory, and pride—are exposed as false. In full confidence, long before its demise is revealed for all to see, the prophet pronounces the imminent end of the oppressor.

[14:1–4a] It has long been observed that the function of these verses is to join two passages into a unified whole, each of which reflects a discrete literary history. While 13:2–22 speaks of Babylon's coming destruction in eschatological terms, 14:4ff. takes up an ancient taunt song to celebrate the fall of its arrogant ruler. Verses 1–4a make clear the implications of this divine action for Israel. God will again have compassion on Jacob and Israel and again elect (*bḥr*) his people. They will return to their own land, be joined by aliens, and their captors will now serve them.

Both the language used and the concepts developed are closely akin to those of chapters 40—55, which is further evidence against the position of those who defend a late eighth-century context for these chapters (Erlandsson, Oswalt, Hayes and Irvine). The editorial effect of this unity is to anticipate the full significance for Israel of God's sovereignty over the nations, which will receive its extended development in chapters 40—55. Thus chapters 13—23 are primarily a witness to God's rule, whereas chapters 40—55 focus on Israel's rebirth as the effect of this sovereignty. Yet the two themes are closely intertwined as the editor makes abundantly clear.

[4b–23] Ever since the classic form-critical analysis of H. Jahnow in 1926 (*Das hebräische Leichenlied*), there has been a wide consensus that the passage is a taunt song (*Spottlied*) directed against a mighty king (cf. Jahnow's metrical reconstruction of the poem, 240ff.). Moreover, the mocking is shaped into a parody of a conventional funeral dirge, such as one finds in David's lament over the death of Saul and Jonathan (2 Sam. 1:17ff.). Yet in the place of deep grief and profound sorrow over the death of a hero, Isaiah 14 reverberates with scorn and immense relief over the passing of a tyrant.

Verses 4b explodes with the sense of astonishment, followed by satisfaction that the fury of the oppressor has ceased. God has broken the rod of the wicked ruler who had ruled through fear and violence. Now the whole world can rest in quiet. Shortly the sense of freedom breaks into an emotion of sheer joy. The cedars of Lebanon—often the object of Assyrian plunder—are portrayed as sharing in the rejoicing. Then in the mythopoetic language of the underworld, the "shades" (*rᵉpā'îm*; *TWAT* 7, 625ff.) rise to greet in mockery the mighty kings who have become as weak as themselves. The contrast is between their former pomp and the horrible revulsion of lying on a bed covered with crawling worms and maggots.

The imagery shifts to the ancient mythology of the Day Star (*hēlēl*), who falls from the heights of the heavens to the earth. Long before the opening up of the ancient Near East in the nineteenth century, scholars had drawn parallels with Greek mythology related to Venus. Subsequently, other scholars appealed to the Babylonian-Assyrian myth of Ishtar's descent to the underworld (*ANET*, 106ff.). However, with the discovery of the Ugaritic texts, the evidence mounted for seeing a far closer parallel with Canaanite mythology. The name of the highest God was *'ēl 'elyôn,* and the seat of the deity was mount Zaphon. The most plausible reconstruction is of Helel's challenge to the power of Elyon who, when thwarted, was thrown down to Sheol. The myth depicts a cosmic battle between Helel and Elyon in the brilliant rise of the morning star in the heavens and its sudden dimming before the strengthening rays of the sun.

The biblical taunt gloats over the demise of the detested tyrant who made the earth tremble, overthrew cities, and refused to release his prisoners. Now he receives no honorable burial, but like a loathsome corpse is abandoned and desecrated. The final verse in the dirge reverts to outright cursing. May his descendants be obliterated and may his royal sons be slaughtered to end his evil line once and for all! Verses 22 and 23 conclude with a divine judgment oracle in the first person. The extent of the judgment is extended beyond that of its king, and is directed against the hated city that will be utterly eradicated along with its posterity.

In the scholarly debate much energy has been expended in seeking to determine exactly the original historical referent of the taunt song. The traditional view, still defended by Hayes and Irvine (*Isaiah,* 226ff.), identifies the king with Tiglath-pileser III, who indeed assumed the Babylonian throne after its conquest in 729. However, most scholars argue that the reference to the king of Babylon is a sixth-century redactional reinterpretation. Originally it had been directed against an earlier and much hated Assyrian king. Various Assyrian kings have been nominated, but the most widely accepted proposal is Sargon II, especially because his death appears more closely to parallel that of the taunt (vv. 19–21).

From an exegetical perspective, the hermeneutical significance of the reapplication of the taunt serves several functions in the chapter. First, from the literary side the taunt against the arrogant pagan king prepares the way for the two concluding oracles, vv. 24–27 and 28–31. The one confirms God's plan to destroy Assyria, the other warns the Philistines not to rejoice prematurely over Assyria's demise because already a new enemy has arisen. Second, from a theological perspective the intertwining of Assyria and Babylon editorially highlights that within the divine purpose both foreign powers are joined and represent within the stages of human history the selfsame reality of arrogance, which God's kingship is in the process of destroying and will in the end fully succeed as victorious.

[24–27] The majority of earlier critical commentators has thought that this oracle was misplaced and should be joined to the invective in 10:5–15 (cf. Procksch). More recently, critics have assigned the passage to an anti-Assyrian layer that was then attributed to a "Josianic" redaction of the seventh century (Barth, Clements). This theory is not to be dismissed out-of-hand but, at best, is a reconstruction lying deep in the background of the editorially shaped text. The crucial exegetical task turns on assessing the present literary and theological function of the present text in chapter 14.

The passage, which has a very strong resonance with Isaiah 10, has been shaped in the form of a "summary-appraisal" (cf. Childs, *Isaiah and the Assyrian Crisis,* 128ff.). It serves to summarize and to confirm Yahweh's decision to destroy Assyria. The plan of God that the prophet announced in chapter 10 is being fulfilled: "his hand is stretched out." The passage further establishes the typological link between Assyria and Babylon. Just as God's plan against Assyria has unfolded and Assyria has been destroyed, so also the promise to include equally arrogant Babylon is part of the selfsame promise.

[28–32] The oracle begins with a superscription setting it in the year that King Ahaz died. A variety of critical problems has arisen from this heading.

Kaiser (*Isaiah 13—39*, 49ff.), following earlier critical leads, dismisses the setting as secondary and unhistorical, but the effect of this decision is to open the way to free speculation when projecting other settings (e.g., a late Hellenistic age). A more serious problem with the superscription is that the exact year of Ahaz's death is contested. The school of Albright opts for the year 715, that of Begrich for 725. In spite of this element of historical uncertainty, it does seem clear that the Philistines are being warned not to take comfort in the apparent death of an Assyrian oppressor since his successor will be even worse. Of course, it would be possible to fit the warning to a variety of different historical scenarios in the late eighth century, depending on whether one chooses Tiglath-pileser III's death in 727 or Sargon II's in 705. In both cases the real concern of the prophet's warning comes in v. 32. To those messengers from Philistia who plot intrigue against Assyria during a period of royal transition, the prophet counsels neutrality with such an alliance. He bases his opposition here not on shrewd calculation, but on Israel's faith in God's promise to Zion. Here alone is true refuge and safety found.

The sharp tension that we noted in chapters 13 and 14 continues in this final oracle. Clearly 14:28–32 arose in an Assyrian historical context. A direct reference to Babylon is fully missing. Yet the redactional shaping of the chapter as a whole functions to provide the needed literary momentum for continuing the analogy between Assyria and Babylon. The message is the same "canonically," whether proclaimed in the eighth or sixth centuries. God's sovereignty extends over all the nations, and he provides salvation for the pious of his people through his enduring promise to Zion.

18. Isaiah 15:1–16:14

15:1 An oracle concerning Moab.
    Ar in Moab is laid waste,
        destroyed in a night!
    Kir in Moab is laid waste,
        destroyed in a night!
2   Dibon went up to its temple,[a]
        to its high places to weep;
        Moab wails, Nebo and Medeba.
    Every head is bald,
        every head is shorn.
3   In its streets they are covered with sackcloth;
        on the roofs, in its squares,
        they all howl, streaming with tears.

4   Heshbon and Elealeh cry out,
         their voice is heard as far as Jahaz.
     Therefore the armed men[b] of Moab shout,
         and their heads grow weak.
5   My heart cries out over Moab;
         her fugitives flee down to Zoar,
         to Eglath Shelishiyah.
     For they go up the ascent of Luhith weeping;
         on the road to Horonaim
         they mourn their destruction.
6   The waters of Nimrim are a desolation;
         the grass is dried up, the green has gone,
         vegetation has vanished.
7   So their wealth and supplies
         they carry over the wadi of Willows.
8   The cry has encircled the whole of Moab;
         their wailing reaches as far as Eglaim,
         even to Beer Elim their wailing!
9   The waters of Dimon[c] are full of blood,
         but I will bring even more on Dimon—
     a lion for the fugitives of Moab
         and for the remnant in the land.
16:1 Send a lamb to the ruler of the land[d]
     from Sela, by way of the desert,
         to the mount of the Daughter of Zion.
2   Like fluttering birds
         pushed from the nest
     are the daughters of Moab
         at the fords of the Arnon.
3   "Give us counsel,
         make a decision.
     Make your shade like night
         at high noon.
     Hide the fugitives;
         do not betray the refugees.
4   Let Moab's outcasts remain with you;
         be a shelter for them
         against the aggressor."
     For the oppression has ceased
         and the destruction ended;
         violence has vanished from the land.

5   And a throne will be established in mercy,
        and one will sit upon it in faithfulness,
                from the tent of David,
                a judge who seeks justice
                and is zealous for righteousness.
6   We have heard of the pride of Moab,
                how proud he was,
        his arrogance, pride, and conceit—
                but this boasts are empty!
7   Therefore let Moab wail,
                let everyone wail for Moab.
        Mourn and grieve
                for the raisin cakes of Kir Hareseth.
8   The fields of Heshbon wither,
                and the vines of Sibmah;
        the lords of the nations
                have trampled down its branches
        that once reached Jazer
                and spread toward the desert.
        Their shoots spread out
                and reached to the sea.
9   Therefore I weep with the weeping of Jazer
                and for the vine of Sibmah.
        O, Heshbon and Elealeh,
                I drench you with tears
        because the shouts have ended
                over your ripened fruit and your harvest.
10   Rejoicing and gladness are gone
                from the orchards.
        In the vineyards no songs are heard;
        no one treads out wine in the presses,
                for I have caused the shouting to cease.
11   My heart moans like a harp for Moab,
                my inward parts for Kir Hareseth.
12   When Moab appears at the high place,
                he will become weary;
        when he comes to pray at his sanctuary,
                it will be to no avail.
13   This is the word that the LORD has already spoken in the past. 14 But
        now the LORD says, "Within three years, as a servant under contract
        would count them, the glory of Moab will be despised, in spite of its
        huge population, and those left will be few and weak."

a. Many emend the MT's reading of *bayyit* ("house") to *bat* ("daughter").

b. The MT's reading *ḥᵃluṣê* ("armed men") is often emended to *ḥalṣê* (*"loins"*) to provide better parallelism.

c. The LXX and 1QIsᵃ read "Dibon."

d. The genitive is ambiguous and can be read as subjective or objective.

Selected Bibliography

J. R. Bartlett, "The Moabites and Edomites," *POTT,* ed. D. J. Wiseman, London 1973, 229–58; **D. L. Petersen,** "The Oracles against the Nations: A Form-Critical Analysis," *SBL 1975 Seminar Papers,* ed. G. McRae, Missoula 1975, I, 50ff.; **E. Power,** "The Prophecy of Isaias against Moab," *Bib* 13, 1932, 435–51; **W. Rudolph,** "Jesaja XV—XVI," in *Hebrew and Semitic Studies, Presented to G. R. Driver,* ed. D. Winton Thomas, W. D. McHardy, Oxford 1963, 130–43; **Thomas G. Smothers,** "Isaiah 15—16," *Forming Prophetic Literature, Fs J. D. W. Watts,* ed. J. W. Watts, P. R. House, JSOTSup 235, Sheffield 1996, 70–84; **M. A. Sweeney,** *Isaiah 1—39,* FOTL 16, Grand Rapids 1996, 240–52; **A. H. Van Zyl,** *The Moabites,* PDS 3, Leiden 1960.

Exposition

The oracle concerning Moab is introduced with a superscription that serves to incorporate it within the larger *maśśā'* framework of chapters 13—23. It also concerns the nations. The literary structure of the oracle is far from clear, and this uncertainty also creates difficulty in achieving a coherent interpretation. In general, there is agreement that the passage can be divided into three units in addition to a conclusion: 15:1–9 is a lament occasioned by an attack on Moab; 16:1–5 offers a prophetic proposal to Moab to seek refuge in Judah; 16:6–11 continues a further lament in the light of Moab's pride; 16:12–13 concludes with two subsequent interpretations respecting Moab's future.

Great difficulty emerges in trying to follow the logic of the movement within the passage. The genre of chapter 15 and 16:8ff. is that of the lament, and has only subsequently been rendered editorially into prophetic pronouncement (*maśśā'*). The lament in chapter 15 appears to be that of the prophet's because of the use of a first person pronoun (v. 5), and it expresses a genuine sorrow over Moab's devastation. The real difficulty lies in the transition in 16:1–5. The unit appears to be a proposal by the prophet to the emissaries of Moab on how to secure protection for the refugees from Judah. Verse 1 suggests that a suitable gift be sent to Judah to the ruler of the land (the imperative verbal form should be retained) that would accompany those making the request for sanctuary. The role of v. 2 in this context is not fully clear and has often been attached to v. 9. However, if the voice in v. 1 is the prophet's, it can be understood as a further recognition of Moab's extreme plight. The actual request for sanctuary comes in vv. 3–4a: "be a shelter for them against the aggressor."

How is one then to understand what follows in vv. 4b–5? The RSV includes these verses as a continuation of the same speech begun in v. 1 to be made by the emissaries of Moab seeking refuge. The NRSV reveals a different interpretation by ending the first speech with v. 4a and assigning vv. 4b–5 to another voice. The decision is affected by how one construes the content of vv. 4b–5. Those commentators who understand it as an appeal to Israel's messianic hope regard it as impossible in the mouth of Moab's emissaries. Others understand it as an assumed condition that sanctuary in Judah implies also political submission to the authority of Judah. A messianic interpretation does not seem to fit coherently in this context, and is removed by some as being an incoherent, late expansion. With the NRSV, I choose to assign vv. 4b–5 to the voice of the prophet and in continuation of his initial advice in v. 1 rather than seeing it as an explicit messianic allusion.

Isaiah 16:6–11 appears to be a response to the plea for sanctuary in Judah. The connection, however, with vv. 1–5 is not very smooth, but little is gained by joining vv. 6ff. directly to chapter 15 and assigning vv. 1–5 to a later secondary expansion. The response in vv. 6ff. is a rejection of Moab's regret. The grounds given for Judah's refusal is Moab's "arrogance, pride, and insolence." As a result, the lament of Moab will continue into the future. The first person voice of the prophet returns in vv.9ff.: "My heart mourns like a harp for Moab" (v. 11). Verse 12 summarizes the nation's plight, focusing on the futility of its pagan gods to deliver.

Probably the concluding verses succeed in bringing the oracle into the larger structure of the *maśśā'* collection of chapters 13—23. A reinterpretation is offered in v. 31 that designates the preceding material as a "word that the LORD has already spoken in the past." This former word is given explicitly a new function in the present ("now"). Within three years the threat against Moab will be fulfilled and Moab's glory will be reduced to a pitiful remnant. The effect is that the previous laments over a military invasion are interpreted as a divine judgment against the nation, and her distress will continue into the future. In the present context of the chapter, especially following the warnings to the Philistines, the prophetic word functions to alert Moab that an even greater oppressor, namely the Babylonians, lies in the future as God's new agent of judgment.

Much of the difficulty of understanding this passage lies in the inability to establish its original historical setting. Because of the enormous geographical specificity some commentators assign the passage to the seventh-century period of Josiah's reforms, when the king sought to restore the traditional claims of the old Davidic empire. This passage would then provide prophetic legitimation to Judah's political ambitions. In my opinion, this theory is not to be ruled out of court, but it remains highly speculative. To what extent it aids in interpreting the present function of the text within the corpus of chapters 13—23 can be debated. It does help in establishing a larger pattern in which the roles of Assyria and Babylon are linked as part of a single divine purpose in revealing God's continuing sovereignty over the nations.

19. Isaiah 17:1–18:7

17:1 A pronouncement concerning Damascus.
  Behold, Damascus will cease to be a city;
    it will become a heap of ruins.
2 The cities of Aroer[a] will be forsaken;
    they will be a place for flocks;
    they will lie down undisturbed.
3 The fortress will disappear from Ephraim,
    and sovereignty from Damascus.
  The remnant of Aram will be like
    the glory of the Israelite, says the LORD of hosts.
4 In that day the glory of Jacob will dwindle,
    and the fatness of his flesh will waste away.
5 It will be as a reaper harvests standing grain,
    and gathers the ears by the armful,
    or gleans in the Valley of Rephaim.
6 Only gleanings will be left in it,
    as when one beats an olive tree:
  two or three berries at the very top,
    four or five on its fruitful boughs,
      declares the LORD, God of Israel.
7 In that day, men will turn to their Maker, and their eyes will look to the Holy One of Israel. 8 They will not turn to altars that their own hands made, and they will not regard sacred posts and incense stands that they themselves fabricated.
9 In that day their fortress cities will be like the deserted sites that the Amorites and the Hivites[b] abandoned because of the Israelites, and there will be desolation.
10 Truly you have forgotten the God of your salvation,
    and have not remembered the Rock of your refuge.
  Therefore, though you set out attractive plants
    and plant strange slips,
11 though you make them sprout on the day
    you plant them,
  and on the morning of planting them
    you force them to blossom;

yet the harvest will disappear
    in the day of sickness and great pain.

12   Ah, the roar of many peoples
    that roar like the roaring sea.
The raging of nations that rage
    like the rage of mighty waters.

13   Though the nations roar like surging waters,
    when he rebukes them, they will flee away,
driven like chaff before the wind on the hill,
    and like tumbleweed before a gale.

14   At sunset, sudden terror!
    By morning, it is gone.
This is the portion of those who loot us,
    the lot of those who plunder us.

18:1   Ah, land of whirring wings
    beyond the rivers of Ethiopia,

2   which sends envoys by sea
    in papyrus boats over the waters.
Go swift messengers,
    to a nation tall and smooth-skinned,
to a people feared near and far,
    to a nation of strange speech[c] and oppression,
    whose land is divided by rivers.

3   All you inhabitants of the world
    who live in the earth,
when a banner is raised on the mountains, look!
    When a trumpet sounds, listen!

4   For this is what the LORD said to me:
"I will remain quiet and observe
    from my dwelling place,
like dazzling heat in sunshine,
    like a cloud of mist in the heat of harvest.

5   For before the harvest, when the bud is fully developed
    and the blossom becomes ripened grape,
he will cut off the shoots with
    pruning hooks,
and will lop off the spreading branches.

6   They will all be left to the mountain vultures
    and to the beasts of the earth;
the birds will feed on them all summer,
    and the wild animals all winter.

7   At that time gifts will be brought to
        the LORD of hosts
     from a people tall and smooth-skinned,
        from a people feared near and far,
     a nation of strange speech and oppressive,
        whose land is divided by rivers,
     to the place of the name of the LORD of hosts—
     Mount Zion.

    a. The LXX reads "forever"; cf. *BHS* for the suggested emendation.
    b. The translation follows the LXX. The MT reads "the Horesh and the Amir."
    c. The MT is unclear. Usually it is connected to 28:10 as a form of gibberish.

Selected Bibliography

B. S. Childs, *Isaiah and the Assyrian Crisis*, SBT II/3, London 1967, 50–53; M. Delcor, "Le problème des jardins d'Adonis dans Isaïe 17, 9–11 à la lumière de la civilisation Syro-Phénicienne," *Syria* 55, 1978, 371–94; **H. Donner,** *Israel unter den Völkern*, VTSup 11, Leiden 1964, 38–42; **B. Gosse,** "Isaïe 17, 12–14 dans la rédaction du livre d'Isaïe," *BN* 58, 1991, 20–23; **M. Sweeney,** *Isaiah 1–39*, FOTL 16, Grand Rapids 1996, 252–62; **G. Wanke,** *Die Zionstheologie der Korachiten*, BZAW 97, Berlin 1966, 113–17.

1. Form, Function, and Setting

Chapter 17 has caused great problems in the past and has often been dismissed as largely enigmatic. Even when claiming a "kerygmatic unity" in vv. 1–11, Wildberger follows the older literary analysis in fragmenting the passage into a variety of smaller units, which, in addition, have also suffered incomprehensible glosses (v. 2). Kaiser proceeds in this same exegetical tradition in positing a series of largely independent oracles. Clements argues for a complex redactional growth, assigning vv. 12–14 to a Josianic redaction, vv. 7–8 to postexilic additions, and v. 9 to a subsequent etiological commentary. Generally, but not always, it is assumed that the original oracle of vv. 1–6 is of Isaianic origin. However, the present editorial shaping is thought to derive from a much later period and its final redactional function has not become very clear.

Major credit goes to M. A. Sweeney (252ff.) for finally making sense of chapter 17 along with chapter 18. His initial contribution was in demonstrating that the overarching structure of the unit extends from 17:1 to 18:7, a position intuited by J. A. Alexander (*Commentary on Isaiah,* 2:331) but without adequate evidence. Sweeney mounts three arguments in determining the scope:

    a. The *maśśā'* superscription of 17:1 extends to 19:1, and is missing
       in chapter 18.

b. The two chapters are closely joined thematically by a common agricultural imagery (17:4–6, 10–11; 18:3–6).

c. The *maśśā'* form typically includes reference to Yahweh's action in human affairs, which is provided by chapter 18.

Although there is generally agreement that the setting of 17:1–6 reflects the period of the Syro-Ephraimite war (732), it is also clear that the material in both chapters has been editorially shaped into its present form. Verses 7–8 offer an eschatological word of hope in the language most often associated with Second Isaiah, and the verses are set in contrast to vv. 9–11, which depict Israel's idolatry. The parallels to 1:28ff. would seem to place the passage most likely also in a preexilic setting akin to vv. 1–6.

The form, function, and setting of vv. 12–14 remain all highly contested. Scholars are divided in either assigning the unit to an early, inherited Zion tradition used by the prophet, or relating it directly to Sennacherib's invasion of 701, or attributing it to a subsequent retrojection from either the seventh or fifth centuries. The mythopoetic language of the victory over the sea has long been recognized, but this observation does not in itself determine the age or function of the present oracle. Sweeney has made a good case that the passage is hardly an independent fragment, but has been redactionally shaped to its present literary context by means of a continuation of the agricultural imagery.

Chapter 18 is almost universally interpreted as an independent oracle of judgment directed against Ethiopia. Some disagreement continues over whether it refers to the earlier (713–711) or later period (705–701) of Hezekiah's political intrigue against the Assyrians. However, Sweeney's contribution lies in demonstrating that the oracle of chapter 18 is not an independent oracle directed against Ethiopia, but rather against Judah within the context of chapter 17. Its function has been shaped by the overarching *maśśā'* pronouncement (17:1) in which Yahweh's sovereignty is finally recognized by the nations (18:7).

2. Exposition

[17:1–3] The superscription (v. 1) offers a pronouncement concerning Damascus, which at first appears highly suitable for a section of oracles to the nations. Yet the focus on Damascus is somewhat contrived since it is almost immediately transcended in the units that follow in chapters 17 and 18.

The first three verses concern Damascus, but already the link with the Northern Kingdom is made in v. 3 with the inclusion of Ephraim. The oracle pronounces judgment above all on Damascus. The city will cease to be. The link with the Northern Kingdom assures that the historical reference is to the period of the Syro-Ephraimite war. The destruction of Damascus is pictured as having not yet occurred, but lying in the imminent future. Verse 2 mentions the cities of Aroer, which causes some difficulty in interpretation. There are several cities with this name in the Old Testament (Josh. 12:2; 13:9; 1 Sam. 30:28), but all seem far from Syria. Often the clever emendation of Lagarde has been accepted ("its cities are deserted forever"; cf. *BHS*), which does indeed make good sense. The final phrase in v. 3, "like the glory of the Israelite," serves not only further to tie the destruction of the coalition together—it is a futile glory—but also provides a literary transition to the succeeding judgment against Jacob.

[4–6] This oracle is given an eschatological setting ("in that day"), which confirms the prophetic imminence of the word. The formula has an integral function in the unit, and thus differs from its repetition in vv. 7 and 9, which serve as conventional links of literary expansions. The demise of the Northern Kingdom is portrayed in a series of images: the wasting of the flesh, the reaper of the harvest, and the gleanings of fruit trees. What is left will indeed be only a sparse remnant (*šeʾār*).

[7–8] These verses are often assigned to a later redaction because of their language and content, which reflect themes common to Second Isaiah (cf. 41:6–7; 43:3; 44:2; 51:13; 54:5). Yet these phrases are not confined only to Second Isaiah; many appear in First Isaiah as well (1:4; 2:6–22; etc.). However, the pattern of shifting without mediation from judgment to eschatological salvation is used so frequently as an editorial technique especially in First Isaiah that it tends to support a redactional shaping of the larger passage. Another sign of an editorial hand is the reference to humanity in general in v. 7 (*hāʾādām*), showing awe to its Maker, rather than its being an appeal to a faithful Jewish remnant. Thus, these verses fit well into a section concerned with the nations' recognition of Yahweh (18:3ff.).

[9] This verse appears to be a prose addition and is only connected thematically with vv. 10ff. Just as once the early inhabitants of the land—probably to be read with the LXX's "Amorites and Hivites"—abandoned their cities before the invading Israelites, so now the Northern Kingdom's cities will experience a similar fate.

[10–11] These verses continue the theme of Israel's loss of memory of what God has done for his people. The idiom is most common in Deuteronomy (6:12; 8:11), and is there joined with the metaphor of the rock, a term appearing frequently in the psalms in a variety of contexts to depict divine aid and comfort (18:47; 31:3; 89:27). The contrast to the unchanging strength and stability of the God of Israel is made with the ephemeral attraction of the dying and rising deities of the Adonis cult, which sprout with the spring rains, but perish in the heat of the summer.

[12–14] This oracle is not a classic woe oracle directed against the nations, but more an exclamation calling attention to a tumultuous invasion, much like a herald's cry. The imagery is ancient, with roots in the Canaanite mythopoetic language of the battle with Yam, the sea (cf. Pss. 46; 48; 76). Yet the chaos motif has been joined early with the *Völkerkampf* motif. Some recent commentators have objected vigorously to seeing its source as an ancient Zion tradition and would rather see it as arising from a later reflection on the event of 701. However, from the intensity of the imagery, which is strikingly different from Isaiah 36—37, it is more likely to be derived from ancient mythopoetic tradition than from a poetic adaption of a single historical event. The finality of the defeat of the nations is achieved by the use of a summary-appraisal form (v. 14b). The subject, identified as "us," reveals that the nations are not being addressed, but rather God's people to whom divine protection is guaranteed against all its enemies. Sweeney (260) has made a persuasive case that this oracle, whatever its origin, has been shaped to perform an integral function within the larger literary section.

[18:1–7] The oracle found in these verses is introduced without a superscription, but rather with an exclamation. The focus has shifted dramatically from Syria to the "land of whirring wings beyond the rivers of Ethiopia." In spite of some recent attempts to see in the imagery of whirring wings a reference to sailing ships (NEB), the traditional understanding as a reference to the abundance of insects still seems preferable. The historical setting appears to reflect the period of Hezekiah's attempt to enlist support from various smaller states in order to resist Assyrian aggression (31:1ff.). Usually v. 2 is understood as a description of the exchange of envoys between the two countries, Judah and Ethiopia. Ethiopia sends its emissaries by way of the Nile on boats of papyrus designed for these calm waters.

However, major difficulties arise when the sending of the "swift messengers" in v. 2 is seen as a continuation of a diplomatic mission from Ethiopia. First, the verb "go" (*lᵉkû*) does not carry the meaning of "return," which would be expected if the messengers were interpreted as Ethiopian envoys returning to a nation "tall and smooth-skinned" "whose land is divided by rivers." Second, why would the Ethiopian emissaries be sent to their own people? This apparent confusion has been resolved by Sweeney, who mounts a persuasive case for seeing the "swift messengers" (v. 2b) to be Judah's envoys. They are distinct from those sent by Ethiopia in v. 2a. This reading has the effect of altering the major force of the oracle, which is then not directed against Ethiopia.

Instead, the message in v. 3 to all the nations of the world is to observe when a signal is given. Then they will recognize Yahweh according to his action. Far above the fever of busy diplomatic intrigue, God views the world in calm rest from his heavenly dwelling before he acts. At the right time, just before the harvest, he will trim the shoots with pruning hooks and hack off the spreading branches. In the context of the chapter the imagery can only mean that of judgment against Judah, not Ethiopia. God will not support the planned rebellion, which will surely fail.

Verse 7 serves as a concluding statement that returns to the theme of Ethiopia's ambassadors and to a mighty and conquering nation. At that time, that is, after Yahweh has executed his judgment on Judah, Ethiopia will offer a tribute to Yahweh on Mount Zion. The gift represents an act of submission to the sovereignty of Yahweh as Lord to which the Ethiopians now bear witness as a result of Yahweh's intervention. Verse 7 is not a late scribal gloss, but integral to the editor's intention in shaping the entire passage as a testimony to God's future rule over the nations of the world.

20. Isaiah 19:1–20:6

19:1 A pronouncement concerning Egypt.
Look, the LORD rides on a swift cloud
　　and is coming to Egypt.
The idols of Egypt will tremble before him,
　　and the heart of the Egyptians will dissolve before him.
2 I will incite Egyptian against Egyptian,
　　brother will fight against brother,
neighbor against neighbor,
　　city against city, kingdom against kingdom.
3 The spirit of the Egyptians
　　within them will be drained,
　　and I will frustrate their plans.
So they will consult the idols and sorcerers,
　　the mediums and wizards.
4 And I will deliver the Egyptians
　　into the hand of a harsh master,
and a ruthless king will rule them,
　　says the Lord, the LORD of hosts.
5 The waters of the sea will dry up,
　　and the rivers will be parched and bare.
6 Its canals will turn foul,
　　and the streams of Egypt's Nile
　　　will diminish and become dry,
　　reeds and rushes will decay.
7 There will be bare places[a] by the river
　　on the banks of the Nile,
and everything sown along the river
　　will wither, blow away, and vanish.
8 Fishermen will mourn and wail;
　　all who cast lines into the Nile
and those who spread nets on the water
　　will lose their strength.
9 The flax workers will also be dismayed,
　　the combers[b] and weavers of white cloth.

10   Her weavers are crushed
        and all the wage earners sick at heart.
11   The officials of Zoan are complete fools;
        the wisest counsellors of Pharaoh
            give stupid advice.
      How can you say to Pharaoh,
        "I am a son of the sages,
        a disciple of ancient kings?"
12   Where then are your wise men?
      Let them tell you, and let them discover
        what the LORD of hosts has planned against Egypt.
13   The princes of Zoan have been fools,
        and the princes of Memphis deceived.
      The cornerstones of her tribes
        have led Egypt astray.
14   The LORD has poured into them
        a spirit of confusion;
      they make Egypt stagger in everything
            she attempts,
        as a drunkard staggering in his vomit.
15   There is nothing Egypt can do,
        either by head or tail,
        palm branch or reed.
16   In that day the Egyptians will be like women. They will tremble with
      fear before the hand that the LORD of hosts raises against them. 17 And
      the land of Judah will be the dread of the Egyptians. They will quake
      whenever Judah is mentioned because of what the LORD of hosts is
      planning against them.
18   In that day five cities in Egypt will speak the language of Canaan and
      swear allegiance to the LORD of hosts. One of them will be called
      "City of the Sun."c
19   In that day there will be an altar to the LORD inside the land of Egypt
      and a pillar to the LORD at its border. 20 They will serve as a sign and
      a witness to the LORD of hosts in the land of Egypt, so that when they
      cry out to the LORD against their oppressors, he will send them a savior
      and defender to deliver them. 21 For the LORD will make himself
      known to the Egyptians, and the Egyptians will acknowledge the LORD
      in that day. They will serve him with sacrifices and offerings; they will
      make vows to the LORD and fulfill them. 22 The LORD will first afflict
      Egypt and then heal them. They will turn to the LORD and he will
      respond to their prayer and heal them. 23 In that day there will be a
      highway from Egypt to Assyria. The Assyrians will go to Egypt and

the Egyptians to Assyria. The Egyptians and the Assyrians will worship together. 24 In that day Israel will be a third partner along with Egypt and Assyria, a blessing on the earth, 25 whom the LORD of hosts has blessed, saying, "Blessed be Egypt my people, and Assyria my handiwork, and Israel my inheritance."

20:1 In the year that the Tartan, sent by Sargon king of Assyria, came to Ashdod and attacked and captured it— 2 at that time the LORD spoke through Isaiah son of Amoz, saying "Go, and take off the sackcloth from your loins and the sandals from your feet." And he did so, going stripped and barefoot— 3 The Lord said, "Just as my servant Isaiah has walked stripped and barefoot for three years as a sign and portent against Egypt and Ethiopia, 4 so will the king of Assyria lead away stripped and barefoot the Egyptian captives and Ethiopian exiles, both young and old, with uncovered buttocks, to Egypt's shame. 5 Those who trusted in Ethiopia and boasted in Egypt will be dismayed and put to shame. 6 In that day the inhabitants of this coastland will say 'Look, this is what has happened to those on whom we relied, those to whom we fled for help and rescue from the king of Assyria! How then can we escape?'"

a. The meaning of *'ārôt* is unclear. Often it had been understood as "bare places" (BDB, 788, NRSV). Wildberger (*Jesaja*, 701) argues for a possible Egyptian loan word, meaning *die Binsen* = reeds.

b. Probably the *'athnāḥ* should be moved to the previous word (*BHS*). Some would also emend the verbal form to provide a smoother reading (*HALAT*, 1269).

c. The MT reads *heres* ("destruction"). Several Hebrew manuscripts, including 1QIsᵃ, read *ḥeres* ("sun"). This latter textual tradition is followed by the Targum and Vulgate. The reading above is therefore widely accepted as a reference to Heliopolis.

Selected Bibliography

L. Bonner, "Rethinking Isaiah 20," OTWSA 22–23, 1979–80, 32–52; **E. Bosshard-Nepustil,** *Rezeptionen von Jesaia 1–39 im Zwölfprophetenbuch,* OBO 154, Freiburg, Göttingen 1997, 35–36, 119–25; **T. K. Cheyne,** "The Nineteenth Chapter of Isaiah," ZAW 13, 1893, 125–28; **H. Donner,** *Israel unter den Völkern,* VTSup 11, Leiden 1964, 113–16; **S. Erlandsson,** *The Burden of Babylon,* ConBOT 4, Gleerup 1970, 80–81; **J. H. Hayes and S. A. Irvine,** *Isaiah, The Eighth-Century Prophet: His Times and His Preaching,* Nashville 1987, 257–71; **J. F. A. Sawyer,** "'Blessed Be My People Egypt' (Isaiah 19.25): The Context and Meaning of a Remarkable Passage," *A Word in Season, Fs W. McKane,* ed. J. D. Martin, P. R. Davies, JSOTSup 42, 1986, 57–71; **M. A. Sweeney,** *Isaiah 1–39,* FOTL 16, Grand Rapids 1996, 263–276.

1. Structure, Setting, and Function

Once again the recognition of the correct scope of the passage by Sweeney (263) on the basis of the pronouncement form (*maśśā'*) provides an important literary advance over prior analyses. It overrides the topical divisions according to content that join together chapters 18—20 because of a common Egyptian theme.

Chapter 19 is best divided into three units: vv. 1b–10; 11–15; and 16–25. Many of the earlier commentators sought to subdivide the initial verses into smaller oracles (vv. 1–4; 5–10), but the larger theophanic announcement renders this division unnecessary. Very diverse material of both judgment and blessing is contained in vv. 16–25, which is linked by the repetition five times of the formula "in that day."

The most crucial structural issue turns on one's evaluation of the role of 20:1–6. Until quite recently this prose chapter was separate from chapter 19 as an independent unit. Yet the case is very strong that the symbolic act of the prophet at the time of the siege of Ashdod is integrally related to the threatened conquest of Egypt by the Assyrians in chapter 19. Isaiah's symbolic act serves as a prophecy that anticipates Egypt's impending demise (cf. Sweeney, 264).

There is general agreement that the authorship of 19:1–15 is different from that of vv. 16–24, although there remains much controversy over the exact nature of these latter oracles. Usually these verses are ascribed to a postexilic period as a subsequent extension to the original prophecy of vv. 1–15, which foretells of political chaos. The parallel imagery of 11:11ff. points in this direction. Various attempts have been made to describe in more detail the setting of the original oracle. It is very difficult to be certain because internal strife was a recurring condition in Egyptian life during the entire latter part of the eighth century. The frequent appeal to a "universalism" in the religious outlook of 19:18ff. as a means of dating is extremely dubious, not only because of an assumed trajectory from an earlier to a later period, but also because the chapter's depiction of the relation of Israel to the nations is far removed from the modern concept of universalism. The oracles in 19:18ff. appear rather to be an intertextual extension of the prophecy of 2:2–4.

A variety of problems have surfaced in relation to the interpretation of 20:1–6 that are crucial for understanding the entire passage. The third person style of vv. 1–6 would indicate that the narrator does not derive from Isaiah, but offers an account concerning the prophet. Sweeney (272–73) offers several general arguments for assigning it to a seventh-century, Josianic redaction. Although this theory should not be too quickly dismissed, the evidence remains very fragile for his degree of certainty.

The central hermeneutical issue lies in the reuse of an original narrative regarding the defeat of Ashdod by the Assyrians under Sargon in 711. Isaiah's activity in chapter 20 of walking stripped and barefoot was originally offered as a sign-act related to the assault of the Philistine city by the Assyrian commander. However, a shift has occurred in 20:3, and now the act functions as a prophecy directed to the future defeat of Egypt in chapter 19, which was legitimated by the fulfillment of this earlier word against Philistia. However, there is a further adaptation of the oracle that has been pointed out by Seitz (144). A new linkage has affected the role of the Philistines, who are now spoken of as the inhabitants of the coastland. Because a similar terminology appears in Second Isaiah (41:5; 42:4) as the larger context of an eschatological hope in Yahweh's divine sovereignty over the nations, it is likely that there is an additional editorial broadening of the term and that the coming world judgment depicted in chapter 20 is shaped by the overarching themes of the *maśśā'* pronouncement of chapters 13—14.

Recently a very different redactional hypothesis respecting these chapters has been mounted by E. Bosshard-Nepustil (1997), who has pursued an approach first initiated by O. H. Steck. In my judgment, there are so many initial assumptions required to gain access to this approach as to make it unsuitable for further pursuit in this commentary. Undoubtedly, there are some astute exegetical observations made, but the complexity of his redactional hypothesis gives one considerable pause.

2. Exposition

[19:1–10] The unit is a theophanic announcement of the coming divine judgment against Egypt. The imagery of God's riding on a swift cloud is common in the Psalter (18:11; 104:3) and has ancient Near Eastern analogues. The judgment follows in a first person divine oracle with threats unfolding in a series of disasters. God stirs up civil wars and political unrest in Egypt, destroying the counsel of the idols and wizards and delivering the nation over to a harsh master. Although one can easily posit an Assyrian reference to the final threat, the text offers no further specificity. The reader will note the irony in the description of hard service (Ex. 1:14) with which the Egyptians had once afflicted the Israelite slaves.

Many of the older form critics (e.g., Wildberger) note that the first person oracle concludes with a closing formula in v. 4b. There is also a shift in the imagery in vv. 5–10, and the effect of the divine judgment on Israel's physical state is pursued. The Nile dries up, which destroys the life of the farmer, fisher, textile worker, and the poorest day laborer. Nevertheless, the oracle is best understood as part of the initial announcement and the latter verses simply spell out the consequences of the judgment.

[11–15] Both in form and content, a new unit begins in vv. 11–15 when a taunt is leveled against Pharaoh and his counsellors. In spite of the Egyptians' vaunted claims of being the source of true wisdom, the prophet ridicules their foolishness. Yahweh has rendered their knowledge helpless. They stagger like a drunken man, wallowing in their own filth, a description that reminds one of Isaiah's confrontation with the inebriated prophets and priests of 28:7ff. Egypt's wise men are confused because they do not understand the plan of God for Egypt.

[16–25] The concluding unit of the chapter consists of five prose oracles, apparently once independent, each linked with the formula "in that day." The first oracle (vv. 16–17) stands apart from the rest in its being still judgmental in nature, as if it served to summarize the preceding verses. The Egyptians will quake with fear before the land of Judah. They will be terrified because of Yahweh's purpose toward them.

However, the four succeeding oracles are different in nature and are largely positive in relating Egypt and Israel. Verse 18 projects a future in which five cities in Egypt will speak "the language of Canaan" and offer loyalty to Yahweh. The oracle appears to describe Jews living in Egypt who have attracted proselytes, which is implied in the terminology of "swearing allegiance." There has been great effort made in trying to provide a more precise historical context for this oracle. It has long since been pointed out that Jeremiah (44:1, 15) spoke of four places in Egypt to which Jews had fled in the sixth century. Later, the fifth-century letters from Elephantine revealed the extent of a Jewish presence there, particularly in the form of mercenaries and their families. One city is named in the MT, *'îr haheres* (v. 18), which means "city of destruction," but this sense is perplexing within the context of the larger oracle. However, a number of Hebrew manuscripts including 1QIsᵃ from Qumran reads *heres* ("sun"), a reading supported by the Targum and Vulgate. *Heliopolis* is the Greek for "City of the Sun," which carries the Egyptian name of On (Gen. 41:50; Ezek. 30:17). The theological point thus appears to be that even in the city of Re, the Egyptian sun god, the "language of Canaan" is spoken by those professing loyalty to the God of Israel.

Verses 19–22 continue the promise of the spread of the true worship of Yahweh in Egypt. In that day there will be an altar of Yahweh inside the land of Egypt and monuments on its borders. Clements (171) reads this statement as a *post factum* legitimation of a situation already existing at the time of the prophecy. From this perspective some have linked the word to the temple of Leontopolis reported in Josephus, which was established in the second century. Again there is evidence of a temple at Elephantine in the fifth century. Still, it is too hypothetical to insist on a specific etiological basis. The erecting of pillars as evidence of gratitude has parallels from the early patriarchal stories (Gen. 28:18) and should not be overinterpreted as providing evidence for religious conflict. What is remarkable is that now the God of Israel will respond to Egypt's cry of deliverance and will send a savior to rescue as he once had done for the oppressed Israelite slaves. They will also come to know Yahweh and respond with a suitable worship.

The language of the highway from Egypt to Assyria facilitating easy travel between the two countries is akin to the eschatological oracle of Isa. 11:16. However, there the focus is on the exiles of Israel repeating the exodus from the diaspora once experienced by their forebears when leaving Egypt. Here the highway serves to aid both the nations of Assyria and Egypt to worship together the God of Israel, which strikes a resonance with the promise of the nations'

assembly in 2:2–4. The unit closes with a remarkable extension of divine blessing on Egypt and Assyria, both of whom traditionally represented Israel's arch-
enemies and source of oppression.

[20:1–6] The account of the prophet's symbolic action is reported in a prose
style and is integrally connected with chapter 19. The central problem of the text
lies with the chronological sequence of vv. 1–3. Verse 1 reports the Assyrian
attack and capture of the Philistine city of Ashdod by Sargon in 711. Verse 2 links
the command to Isaiah to walk naked and barefooted with the same time as in v.
1. Finally, v. 3 interprets his symbolic act as a sign against Egypt and Ethiopia.

Several commentators have sought to straighten out the chronological
sequence by either removing v. 1 as secondary to the narrative (Wildberger,
749–50) or positing that the oracle once belonged to an earlier collection, which
would explain the disorder (Eichrodt, *Herr der Geschichte,* 77). Initially some
of the problem of coherence can be resolved if v. 2 is understood as an awkward parenthesis and the formula "at that time" is not unduly pressed. Obviously the broad meaning is that some time before the fall of Ashdod the prophet
received the command to perform a sign-act, which was then fulfilled with the
fall of Ashdod. Form-critics have correctly argued that the form of the sign-act
follows the classic pattern: command, execution, interpretation. Originally the
symbolic action was directed to the Philistines and warned Judah not to participate in political revolt against Assyria.

The element that causes the difficulty is that the oracle has been reinterpreted.
The sign-act is now used as a "sign and portent" against Egypt and Ethiopia.
Indeed, both the subsequent Assyrian kings, Esarhaddon and Ashurbanapal, did
attack and subdue parts of Egypt. However, the point of the reapplication of the
sign-act is not to be immediately historicized. Rather, it turns on the "inhabitants
of this coastland" confessing their helplessness in escaping the might of Assyria.
Some have interpreted the referent to be the Philistines, but this meaning is odd
since the Philistines had already learned of Egypt's impotence by 711. More
likely is the observation that the editor has once again broadened his scope to fit
this incident into the framework of his oracles concerning the nations (chapters
13—23; cf. Seitz, 144–45). "Inhabitants of this coastland" points to those distant
nations (41:5; 42:4) who are helpless before God's sovereignty, which executes
judgment on the world by means of the Assyrians and Babylonians.

21. Isaiah 21:1–17

21:1   A pronouncement concerning the Wilderness of the Sea.[a]
       Like whirlwinds from the Negeb,
            it comes from the desert,
            from a land of terror.

2   A harsh vision has been told to me:
         the plunder is plundering,
         the destroyer destroys.
     Go up, Elam! Advance, Media!
         I have put an end to all the striving[b] she caused.
3   Therefore my loins are seized with anguish.
     I am gripped with pain
         like a woman in labor.
     I am shattered by what I hear,
         I am bewildered by what I see.
4   My mind is confused,
         horror convulses me;
     the twilight I desired
         has turned into my violent shaking.
5   They set the tables,
         arranging the rugs,[c]
     they eat and drink.
     Get up, you officers!
         Grease the shields!
6   For thus the Lord said to me:
     "Go, post a watchman
         and let him report what he sees.
7   When he sees chariots,
         horsemen in pairs,
     Riders on donkeys,
         or riders on camels,
     let him be alert,
         fully alert."
8   Then the watchman[d] cried out:
     "Day by day I stand on my watch, O Lord,
         and every night remain at my post.
9   Look, riders come,
         horsemen in pairs!"
     Then he answered,
         "Fallen, fallen is Babylon,
     and all the images of her gods
         lie shattered on the ground!"
10   O my people, crushed on the
         threshing floor.[e]
     What I have heard from the
         LORD of hosts, the God of Israel,
         I announce to you.

11   A pronouncement concerning Dumah.
      One calls to me from Seir,
         "Watchman, what is left of the night?
         Watchman, what is left of the night?"
12   The watchman replies,
         "Morning will come, but also the night.
         If you will ask, then ask,
         but come back again."
13   A pronouncement concerning Arabia.
      In the thicket, in the scrub country,
         you will dwell.
      O caravans of Dedanites,
14   bring water for the thirsty.
      You inhabitants of Tema,
         bring food for the refugees.
15   For they have fled from the sword,
         before the whetted sword,
      from the bent bow,
         and from the heat of battle.
16   For thus said the Lord to me:
      'Within one year, fixed like a hired worker's contract, all the glory of
      Kedar will be ended.
17   and those left of the archers, the warriors of Kedar, will be few, for the
      LORD God of Israel has spoken."

a. There have been numerous emendations suggested by commentators, but the MT
is to be retained (cf. the exegesis).

b. The noun *'anḥātāh* ("sighing") fits with difficulty into the context. It has frequently
been emended (cf. *BHK*), or its normal semantic range extended.

c. The meaning of *ṣāpōh* remains conjectural (cf. *HALAT*[3], 978 for bibliography).

d. The MT *'aryēh* ("a lion") is almost universally emended to *hārō'eh* ("the seer")
and has the support of 1QIs[a]. NJPS retains the MT by supplying a comparative preposition, a solution first proposed by Ibn Ezra.

e. The MT reads "my threshed one, child of the threshing floor."

Selected Bibliography

R. Bach, *Die Aufforderungen zur Flucht und zum Kampf in alttestamentlichen Prophetenspruch*,
WMANT 9, Neukirchen-Vluyn 1962; **W. E. Barnes,** "A Fresh Interpretation of Isaiah xxi 1–10," *JTS* 1,
1900, 582–92; **E. Bosshard-Nepustil,** *Rezeptionen von Jesaia 1–39 im Zwölfprophetenbuch*, OBO 154,
Freiburg/Göttingen 1997, 23–42; **J. A. Brinkman,** "Elamite Military Aid to Merodach-baladan II," *JNES*
24, 1965, 161–66; **R. E. Clements,** "The Prophecies of Isaiah and the Fall of Jerusalem in 587 B.C.," *VT*
30, 1980, 421–36; **W. H. Cobb,** "Isaiah XXI 1–10 Reëxamined," *JBL* 17, 1898, 40–61; **P. Dhorme,** "Le

désert de la mer (Isaïe, XXI)," *RB* 31, 1922, 403–6; **S. Erlandsson,** *The Burden of Babylon,* ConBOT 4, Lund 1970, 81–95; **K. Galling,** "Jesaia 21 im Lichte der neuen Nabonidtexte," *Tradition und Situation, Fs A. Weiser,* ed. E. Würthwein and O. Kaiser, Göttingen 1963, 49–62; **J. B. Geyer,** "The Night of Dumah (Isaiah XXI 11–12)," *VT* 42, 1992, 317–39; **B. Gosse,** "Le 'moi' prophétique de l'oracle contre Babylone d'Isaïe XXI, 1–10," *RB* 93, 1986, 70–84; **J. H. Hayes and S. A. Irvine,** *Isaiah, Eighth-Century Prophet: His Times and His Preaching,* Nashville 1987, 271–76; **P. Lohmann,** "Das Wächterlied Jes 21, 11–12," *ZAW* 33, 1913, 20–29; **A. A. Macintosh,** *Isaiah XXI: A Palimpsest,* Cambridge 1980; **J. Vermeylen,** *Du Prophète Isaïe à l'Apocalyptique,* 1, Paris 1977, 326–32; **J. Zarins,** "Dumah," *ABD* 2, 239–40.

1. Structure and Genre

Chapter 21 contains three pronouncement (*maśśā'*) superscriptions (vv. 1, 11, 13). These three have been brought together to form a larger unit. The discrete superscriptions protect the integrity of the three pronouncements, yet the context and historical connection are such that the Dumah oracle (vv. 11–12) and the one concerning Arabia (vv. 13–17) could hardly have functioned apart from vv. 1–10. Commentators have long debated to what extent the enigmatic, veiled references in 21:1, 11 and 22:1 have exerted a cohesive force in the formation of the present composition.

The structure of vv. 1b–10 appears, in general, clear. Verses 1b–4 set forth a report of an attacking enemy, which is given to the prophet in the first person as a vision. It pictures the terrifying approach of an invader. The reader is not told who the enemy is, nor who is being attacked, only that Elam and Media are involved in some manner (v. 2). The prophet's reaction is then depicted in vv. 3–4 as one of great anguish and distress. The second part of the oracle (vv. 5–10) relates a divine command to post a watchman, and his report of the approach of riders is recounted. The climax of the oracle comes with the announcement of the fall of Babylon, which is confirmed with a direct word of the LORD to the prophet.

The structure of the Dumah oracle (vv. 11–12) extends the imagery of the watchman. It consists of a somewhat enigmatic question followed by the watchman's response. The final oracle of the chapter (vv. 13–17) consists of a request to offer aid to fugitives in the Arabian desert who have fled from battle. Then the prophet receives a first person oracle that within a year the glory of Kedar will be ended. The oracle is again confirmed as the direct word of the LORD.

2. The Historical Setting and Redactional Function of vv. 1–10

The most controversial problem in interpreting chapter 21 turns on establishing a historical context. Two alternative proposals dominate the debate.

The first option represents the classic modern historical critical hypothesis that assigns vv. 1–10 to the sixth century, around 540. It refers the attacking force to events associated with Cyrus and to the fall of the Neo-Babylonian empire. The commands in v. 2, directed to Elam and Media, are construed as part of the assault against the city of Babylon. This position has been defended by Procksch, Eichrodt, Clements, and Wildberger, among others. However, there are a number of troubling problems associated with this interpretation. From a literary perspective, it is odd that the prophetic reaction to the attack on Babylon is one of pain and anguish (vv. 3–4). Usually, the Judean response to Babylon's defeat is great relief and joy (14:12ff.; 47:1ff.; Jer. 50:8ff.). From a historical perspective, Elam no longer existed as a separate entity following its defeat by the Assyrians in 647/6, but it was absorbed into the Persian empire. What kind of role would it have played in 540?

The second option, initially defended in various forms by Cobb and Barnes a hundred years ago, and recently revived with fresh evidence by Erlandsson, Hayes and Irvine, and Sweeney, relates vv. 1–10 to the various Assyrian campaigns against the Babylonian chieftain, Merodach-baladan, in the late eighth century. Some of these scholars focus on Sargon II's conquest of Babylon in 710, others on Sennacherib's victory over Merodach-baladan in 700. Sweeney in *Isaiah 1—39* (282–83) offers a significant refinement by focusing on Sennacherib's campaigns against Babylon and the various Arab tribes in the northeastern desert west of Babylon in 691–89. Sweeney's interpretation serves to illuminate the last two oracles in the chapter as well. The major historical problem levelled against this second interpretive option is that Elam and Media were always considered enemies of Assyria, and it is difficult to reconcile their fighting against Babylon (cf. 22:6). Traditionally, this objection has been met by suggesting that scattered elements of these two tribes might have served as Assyrian mercenaries.

In addition to these two leading hypotheses, there has also emerged a third, initially represented by Kaiser and Kilian (cf. below). Accordingly, chapter 21 is a late apocalyptic passage and Babylon functions only as a cipher, thus as a literary construct lacking any specific historical reference. However, within the last decade this approach to the text as a literary construct has been extended and greatly radicalized. The new impulse arises from the school of O. H. Steck and has been developed in reference to chapters 21 and 22 by Bosshard-Nepustil.

At the outset, Bosshard-Nepustil accepts as evident that the present form of chapter 21 reflects the fall of Babylon in 539 and that earlier traditions from the eighth century, often deemed inaccessible, form a transparency for this sixth-century event. Yet the energy driving this approach has now moved in a different direction by attempting to reconstruct the development of its literary context (*Textbereich*) because a genuinely historical reference is no longer recoverable (33). It emerges as a construct formed by multiple literary layering. By means of a highly complex, often tortuous, literary analysis, two layers are reconstructed in vv. 1–10 on the basis of allegedly internal tensions. These layers are then coordinated with paralleled layers discovered in chapters 13 and

22. A commentary is not the place for a detailed criticism, but needless to say, I find the approach highly speculative and basically unilluminating (cf. Childs, "Retrospective Reading of the Old Testament Prophets").

In spite of the strengths of the two dominant historical theories, the problem has not been fully settled. Moreover, a variety of more recent literary and hermeneutical issues have been raised that further complicate the situation. For example, what has been the effect on the interpretation of chapter 21 of the later editorial *maśśā'* framework, and how does chapter 21 now function within the section of chapters 13—23? Or again, even if one assumes an eighth-century context, how have the later events, culminating in the destruction of 587, affected the redactional shaping and subsequent rendering of the chapter? Has an intertextual resonance with Habakkuk 1, Isaiah 47, and Jeremiah 50—51 influenced the interpretation of this text?

There have been two recent attempts to address these problems. In a very thorough monograph, A. A. Macintosh has argued that chapter 21 can best be described as a "palimpsest," that is, it reflects in its final form both an original eighth-century level and a subsequent sixth-century reinterpretation. Undoubtedly, Macintosh has opened up many fresh insights and has wrestled hard with the presence of these two layers. Nevertheless, in my opinion, there are serious problems involved with his imagery of a textual palimpsest. It is far too static a concept and does not deal with the entire problem of reader-response. That is to say, there is a dimension of ambivalence and fluidity within the present form of the text that allows it to be heard in different ways according to different resonances. Moreover, the multilayered quality of chapter 21 is not unique to this chapter alone, but is a characterization of the entire section of chapters 13—23.

The second major attempt at addressing the complex exegetical and hermeneutical problems of chapter 21 has been offered by C. Seitz (157ff.). Seitz argues that chapter 21 stands in a consciously dialectical relation with chapter 22. Both chapters share an element of mystery and both have been shaped to function within the larger *maśśā'* section of chapters 13—23 in order to defend God's sovereignty over the nations. The effect of this shaping has been to shift the emphasis away from specific historical circumstances to a new topical concern with the proper response to military assault and to the mixed message of partial defeat and victory (162). While I fully agree with much that Seitz describes as the topical effect of the final rendering of these two chapters, I would argue that one should not move too quickly away from the concrete historical references, even when, as he says, "strict chronological organization has taken a backseat to other concerns in the final presentation of chapters 21—22" (167).

My own exegetical attempt is addressed initially to the historical situation at the end of the eighth century. Assyria presses its attack on Judah's ally, Merodach-baladan. In a prophetic vision the prophet foresees Babylon's defeat, which evokes Judah's anguish. This earlier level within the present text has not been systematically replaced. There remains a crucial eighth-century witness, consonant with Isaiah's continual preaching, which warns of the futility of putting faith in human alliances, even with Merodach-baladan, Elam and Media.

However, the biblical text has not remained static, but has been subjected to a variety of new forces. The historical experiences of Judah, which extended from the end of the eighth century to the fall of Jerusalem in 587 and beyond, have left an impact on the way that earlier encounters with Assyria and Babylon were understood (cf. Cements). This new resonance is picked up in an intertextual relation with other prophetic passages such as Habakkuk 1, Isaiah 46—47, and Jeremiah 50. There are many other examples within the prophetic corpus of a new hearing of earlier words because of the later experiences of Israel with the nations (cf. especially Isaiah 1—12).

In addition, there is a literary reflection of Israel's ongoing experiences in the redactional ordering of the various prophetic oracles. The careful structuring of chapters 13—23 has arranged diverse texts within an overarching pattern concerning the nations. In many different ways earlier and later texts have been combined, and a theological testimony has been made that consciously relates the Assyrian and Babylonian histories with Israel's destiny.

Finally, a proper interpretation of these multilayered texts must take seriously into account the larger theological and hermeneutical issues at stake. Seitz correctly emphasizes that the genre of prophetic vision is not accidental for these chapters, but serves to bear witness to the unfolding of God's own historical purpose in judgment on the nations by means of a medium most suitable to the prophetic word: "the historical distance from the prophet Isaiah to the actual fall of Babylon is covered, without doing violence to the integrity of Isaiah's known historical location" (166). By focusing on the substance of the message, on its theological content, a given text can bear witness to the selfsame divine truth even when its composition extended over a lengthy sequence within human history. It is this living quality of the biblical text that is constitutive of its being designated as sacred scripture, that is, a continuing authoritative guide to the faithful regarding of the ways of God in the world.

3. Exposition

[21:1–10] The oracle is introduced by means of an enigmatic *maśśā'* superscription "concerning the Wilderness of the Sea" (*midbar-yām*). Countless emendations have been suggested that have been rehearsed too frequently to require repeating (cf. Macintosh, 4ff.; Barthélemy, *CTLAT* 152–53). The most persuasive suggestion has been recently refined by Sweeney (280–81), who picks up an earlier proposal that the territory ruled by Merodach-baladan is generally referred to in Akkadian as *mat tamti* ("land of the sea"). Sweeney then defends this identification against objections by showing that the noun *midbār* relates to a region's placement on the borders of a settled area, and refers either to desert or steppe. Consequently, *midbar-yām* is an appropriate Hebrew designation for the border areas ruled by Merodach-baladan.

[1b–2] The opening verses portray an approaching enemy in the language of a terrifying whirlwind suddenly sweeping in from the desert. It becomes clear that this is part of a harsh vision revealed to the prophet, which he relates in a first person oracle. No specific name of the invader is given; it is only described with a powerful sound of alliteration: a "plunderer plunders," a "destroyer destroys."

The commands that follow next provide at least some historical context: "Go up, Elam! Advance, Media!" The chief difficulty lies in determining the intention of the commands. Are these shouts of war urging on the Elamites and Medians to attack Babylon? This interpretation would provide a strong warrant for a sixth-century setting depicting the imminent collapse of the Neo-Babylonian empire led by Cyrus. Or are the commands rather "shouts of encouragement to Elamites and Medians defending against an attacker" (Sweeney, 281), which interpretation would rather support an eighth-century dating?

The interpretation of v. 2a is further affected by the ensuing difficulty in understanding v. 2b. The MT reads, "I have caused all her sighings to cease." Who is the speaker and to whom is the word addressed? Commentators have long been aware that major difficulties abound in reaching a decision. For those who think that Elam and Media are part of an anti-Assyrian force in support of Babylon, it makes little sense to speak of God's ending Babylon's sighing. Therefore, Macintosh emends the verb to serve as a command as in v. 2a: "Bring an end to all questions." The NEB renders it, "No time for weariness!" Others seek a broader construal of the noun to convey a meaning of despair: "I have put an end to all hope," that is, the resistance of Babylon against the Assyrians will fail. For those who see the setting as Cyrus's impending attack on Babylon, the verse presents no difficulty. It simply promises that the suffering caused by the Babylonians against Judah will cease.

[3–4] These verses depict the prophet's emotional reaction of deepest anguish upon receiving the harsh vision. This response offers the strongest warrant for defending an eighth-century setting. Babylon under Merodach-baladan is an ally and Judah's last hope against Assyria. Thus, to learn of Babylon's defeat is seen as a painful revelation. Wildberger (77–78), who consistently defends a sixth-century setting, is forced to fall back on a general psychological interpretation to explain the prophet's reaction to the vision of Babylon's defeat.

[5–10] The description in v. 5 of the total lack of preparation by the army and its officers for the coming assault continues to call forth a very mixed interpretation depending on the previously construed setting. For those working with an eighth-century setting, the description of smug complacency refers most likely to the ineffective resistance of the anti-Assyrian coalition. For those assuming a sixth-century setting, the description is of the prideful Babylonians, indeed, as depicted in Daniel 5, on the very night their city was captured by the Persians. In the light of these two conflicting interpretations, one sees the force of Seitz's attempt to overcome the impasse by shifting the semantic level (157ff.). He argues that this verse, along with its parallel in 22:1ff., simply serves to illustrate a pattern of inappropriate, complacent deportment, with the specific historical details falling into the background.

The concluding scene gives a divine command to post a watchman who is to observe and to warn. His report is then dramatically recounted. He sees riders approaching, coming in pairs, and the climactic announcement is delivered: "Fallen, fallen is Babylon." The addition of the smashing of her idols and of shattering them on the ground add to the note of her utter destruction (cf. 46:1ff.). The intensity of the tone announcing Babylon's fall far exceeds the defeat of Merodach-baladan, but resonates with the immensity of Babylon's final demise found in Isaiah 13—14 and Jer. 51:8. God has finally defeated the hated oppressor of Israel. In v. 10 the prophet addresses his own people, "crushed on the threshing floor," and confirms that what has happened carries the authority of God's direct word.

[11–17] Chapter 21 ends with two further, brief *maśśā'* oracles, vv. 11–12 and 13–17. Both the historical context and the similarity of content indicate that these oracles form an integral part with the preceding unit of vv. 1–10. It is doubtful that the final oracles ever functioned apart from their present literary connection.

The pronouncement concerning Dumah continues the theme of a watchman's vision. The noun *Dumah* designates a place name often identified as an oasis in the north central desert or Arabia (modern al-Jauf). The oracle fits well into the context of an invasion of the Assyrians by Sennacherib against the northern inhabitants of the Arabian desert. Almost immediately interpreters attached a symbolic meaning to the name, which can be rendered "silence" and conveys an atmosphere of mystery common to the chapter. The LXX connected Dumah directly with Edom reading *idumaea*.

Commentators have long struggled with the exact sense of the question and its answer. Macintosh is thorough in tracing the lengthy history of interpretation (45ff.). Some have interpreted its meaning to signal that morning will come, even though there will also be night; others that the day has indeed come and the period of night is over. A more likely interpretation sees the question inquiring as to how much longer Israel's oppression will last, that is, how much of the night is still left. The watchman assures the questioner that morning will surely come, but that night will also return. He does not know a timetable for the sequence. The question must be continually asked.

The oracle concerning Arabia contains two parts. The first, vv. 13b–15, requests that help be given to those refugees fleeing battle. The second part, vv. 16–17, concerns a prophetic word announcing the defeat of Kedar in the northern desert, which fulfills a judgment of Yahweh. The oracle appears to extend the defeat of Judah's allies by the Assyrians in subjugating the entire desert area and its nomads west of Babylon in 691–689. Like other nations with pretenses of glory and power, Kedar's wealth will also be removed—as God had vowed.

To summarize, chapter 21 raises the hermeneutical problem of interpreting the prophetic message to a new level of intensity. This exegesis has attempted to demonstrate that the chapter is a multilayered text and reflects a density of witnesses arising from Israel's history of experience with God. It appears that two major events, one in the eighth century and one in the sixth, are reflected, and that the one prophetic text served to disclose the divine will for his people in both. The later level of witness heard a fresh word in the earlier, specifically in terms of Judah's oppression under hated Babylon. However, the later level has not obliterated the first, but rather subtly shifted its focus to accommodate the intensity of Judah's subsequent experience of God's deliverance.

Macintosh has done well in trying to show how the text functioned in both the eighth and sixth centuries. However, the exegetical task is incomplete by his leaving the two reconstructed layers without connection. The final form has joined the two, indeed in a fashion quite unique within the corpus of chapters 13—23, and has assigned integrity to both. I would agree with Seitz that the combined text has altered the semantic level of the witnesses and has shaped the material into a dialectic between partial victory and partial defeat. The mystery of God's will remains that there is both morning and light, and that the length of darkness left for Israel remains unanswered.

The haunting question for Israel is left open, and the prophet continues to address his people as those crushed on the threshing floor (v. 10). The uniqueness of chapter 21 is not only in shifting the semantic level in the final form of the text, but in providing two different historical experiences that continue to supply content in their diversity to the dialectic relation between victory and defeat, both within the sovereign rule of God. The two levels within the text are not to be left in isolation, like a palimpsest, but as two poles of the dialectic forcing a reader's response to a pattern within the reign of God that continues to illuminate future events for God's faithful people who live in the age of light and of darkness.

22. Isaiah 22:1–25

22:1 A pronouncement concerning the Valley of Vision.
       What is the matter with you
             that all of you have gone up on the rooftops?
2   You boisterous, noisy city, exuberant town!
       Your slain have not been slain with the sword,
             nor your dead from battle.

3 All your rulers have taken to their heels,
       they have fled far away.
   All of those found[a] have been captured,
       seized without their bows.
4 Therefore I say, "Don't look at me,
       let me weep bitterly;
       do not try to comfort me
       over the ruin of the daughter of my people."
5 For the Lord GOD of hosts has a day
       of panic, trampling, and confusion
   in the valley of vision,
       raising a shout[b] and crying out to the mountains.
6 Elam bore the quiver
       with war chariots[c] and horsemen.
       Kir drew the shield from its cover.
7 Your choicest valleys were full of chariots,
       and horsemen took their stand at the gates.
8   Then he removed the covering of Judah.
   You looked in that day to the weapons
       in the Forest House,
9   and you saw the many breaches in the city of David.
   then you collected the waters of the lower pool,
10   and you listed the houses of Jerusalem
       and pulled down the houses to make the wall more defensible.[d]
11 You made a reservoir between the two walls
       for the water of the old pool,
   but you took no thought of him who planned it,
       and paid no attention to him who designed it long ago.
12 For the Lord GOD of hosts called on that day
       for weeping and mourning,
       for baldness and girding with sackcloth.
13 Instead, frivolity and fun,
       slaying cattle and slaughtering sheep,
       eating flesh and drinking wine.
   "Let us eat and drink for tomorrow we die!"
14 The LORD of hosts has revealed himself in my hearing.
   "Surely this will not be forgiven you until you die,"
       says the Lord GOD of hosts.
15 Thus says the Lord GOD of hosts, "Go say to this steward, to Shebna,
   who is over the household, 16 'What are you doing here and who gave
   you the right to cut out a grave for yourself, hewing your grave on the
   heights and carving a resting place in the rock? 17 Look, the LORD is

about to take hold of you and hurl you away, O you mighty man.ᵉ He
will surely twistᶠ you. 18 He will roll you up tightly like a ball and hurl
you into a far country. There you will die, and there will be your
splendid chariots, you disgrace to the house of your master. 19 For I
will remove you from your office and you will be ousted from your
position. 20 "'In that day I will summon my servant Eliakim, son of
Helkiah. 21 I will clothe him with your robe and fasten your sash on
him, and put your authority in his hand. He will be a father to the
inhabitants of Jerusalem and to the house of Judah. 22 I will place the
key of the house of David on his shoulder, and what he unlocks none
may shut, and what he locks none may open. 23 I will anchor him like
a peg into a secure place, and he will be a throne of honor for the house
of his father. 24 All the glory of his family will hang on him, the
offspring and the offshoot, all the small vessels, from bowls to jars.
25   In that day, says the LORD of hosts, the peg that was anchored in a
secure place will give way. It will be cut down and fall. And the
weight it supports will collapse, for the Lord has spoken.'"

a. On the basis of the LXX, the MT is often amended to "mighty one" (cf. *BHS*), but
the parallel in 13:15 tends to support the MT.

b. The MT *meqarqar qir* is a *hapax legomanon* and has traditionally been translated
"battering down walls." Recently, on the basis of Ugaritic and Arabic cognates, a verbal form has been conjectured, meaning "to shout or make a noise."

c. The MT *'ādām* ("man") is not to be emended to "Aram," as often suggested, but
serves to distinguish chariot from riders.

d. The verb *baṣṣēr* conveys the sense of making the defensive wall less accessible
by removing houses built at its base.

e. Often the MT *gāber* is repointed as *gibbôr* ("strong man"), but the meaning is similar. Others emend to *beged* ("garment").

f. The meaning of the Hebrew verb in this context is unclear. It occurs with an intran-
sitive sense of "wrap oneself" (1 Sam. 28:14). Others accept a meaning of "shake out"
(NEB).

Selected Bibliography

R. Amiran, "The Water Supply of Israelite Jerusalem," *Jerusalem Revealed: Archaeology of the Holy
City, 1968–1974,* ed. Y. Yadin, Jerusalem and New Haven, *IEJ* 1976, 75–78; **E. Bosshard-Nepustil,**
Rezeptionen von Jesaia 1–39 im Zwölf-prophetenbuch, OBO 154 Freiburg/Göttingen 1997, 42–92; **B.
S. Childs,** *Isaiah and the Assyrian Crisis,* SBT II/3, London 1967, 22–27; **R. E. Clements,** "The Prophe-
cies of Isaiah and the Fall of Jerusalem in 587 B.C.," *VT* 30, 1980, 421–36; **H. Donner,** *Israel unter den
Völkern,* VTSup 11, Leiden, 1964, 126–32; **J. A. Emerton,** "Notes on the Text and Translation of Isaiah
XXII 8–11 and LXV 5," *VT* 30, 1980, 437–51; **S. Erlandsson,** *The Burden of Babylon,* ConBOT 4, Lund

1970, 95–97; **J. H. Hayes and S. A. Irvine,** *Isaiah, The Eighth-Century Prophet: His Times and His Preaching,* Nashville 1987, 277–87; **R. Martin-Archard,** "L'oracle contre Shebnâ et le pouvoir des clefs. Es. 22, 15–25," *TZ* 4, 1968, 241–57; **T. N. D. Mettinger,** *Solomonic State Officials: A Study of the Civil Government Officials of the Israelite Monarchy,* ConBOT 5, Lund 1971, 70–110; **M. A. Sweeney,** *Isaiah 1–39,* FOTL 16, Grand Rapids, 1996, 288–302; **J. D. W. Watts,** "Excursus: Hezekiah's Pools and Waterworks," in *Isaiah 1–33,* Waco 1985, 282–86; **J. Willis,** "Historical Issues in Isaiah 22, 15–25," *Bib* 74, 1993, 60–70.

1. Structure, Setting, and Function

The passage is introduced with a *maśśā'* superscription that extends to 23:1. Initially the question is raised of why oracles concerning Jerusalem and its officials should be included within the larger section of chapters 13—23, which concerns the nations. The linkage of two very different sorts of oracles together under the same rubric, vv. 1–14 and 15–25, also poses the question of the editor's intention in so shaping his material. The answer to these questions will depend largely on how one proceeds in the critical analysis of the whole chapter.

Duhm's division of the first oracle into two sections, vv. 1–8a and 8b–14, continued to dominate the discussion for a half century. He interpreted vv. 2b–7 as referring to a future event that the prophet experienced in a sudden vision in reaction to the joyful celebration of the people to the city's perceived military deliverance. In contrast, vv. 8b–14 were interpreted as an announcement of punishment directed to Jerusalem because of its inappropriate behavior and lack of true faith in respect toward events that had already occurred. More recently, interpreters have virtually formed a consensus in maintaining that all the reflections of vv. 1–14 are of past events and that the issue turns on the strikingly different response to the deliverance of the city by people and prophet.

There is also wide agreement that the historical setting points to the period of Assyria's military aggression toward the close of the eighth century. A debate continues whether the event of the army's siege and withdrawal fits better with Sargon's campaign against the Philistines and other anti-Assyrian members of the coalition in 711 (Hayes and Irvine, Oswalt) or matches more closely with Sennacherib's siege of 701, depicted in 2 Kings 18:13ff. (Bright, Eichrodt, Clements). The latter option is generally preferred. It should, however, be noted that nowhere in chapter 22 is Assyria explicitly mentioned, and it can only be inferred from the larger context of chapters 13—23. The absence does caution against attempting to correlate the biblical text too closely with one putative historical event whose reconstruction provides the key to the interpretation. Although Assyria appears clearly to be the historical referent, it remains to be decided exegetically whether it functions in the background or foreground of the prophetic message.

In recent years the redactional analysis of the text has received great attention. There are many commentators who feel that the text of chapter 22 has remained entirely moored editorially to its original 701 setting (e.g., Eichrodt, Wildberger). Even Sweeney does not reckon with a subsequent redactional reinterpretation that would point the text literarily beyond its original eighth-century function. Likewise, Seitz argues that there is very little evidence of a substantial 587 redaction of chapter 22. However, to conclude *a priori* that there is a lack of later editorial shaping strikes one as a bit odd because of the pattern that has emerged in chapters 13—23 of a consistent attempt to link the Assyrian and Neo-Babylonian periods as parts of the one divine purpose of God respecting Israel and the nations.

For this reason alone, it is not unexpected that several modern scholars contend strongly for seeing a major Babylonian redactional layering (e.g., Clements, Kilian). Clements argues forcefully that the original prophecy of Isaiah is found in vv. 1–3 and 12–14, relating to the events of 701 when Hezekiah surrendered to Sennacherib (2 Kings 18:13–16). He then posits several post-587 additions, the first being an expansion in v. 4, the next in vv. 8b–11, and finally one in vv. 5–8a that filled out the description of God's judgment on Jerusalem by the Babylonians in 587. The major force for this etiological shaping stemmed from the tension between the conflicting fortunes of Jerusalem experienced in 701 and in 587. As a warrant for this redactional hypothesis, Clements points to v. 4: "the ruin of the daughter of my people," which, he argues, only occurred literally in 587. Again, the "battering down of walls" (v. 5; see textual notes) is alleged to fit the situation of 587 better than 701. Finally, the reference to soldiers from Elam and Kir is thought to corroborate a Babylonian setting. Of course, each of these points has been strongly contested by those defending an exclusively 701 setting (Hayes and Irvine). In my opinion, the etiological force exerted by the tension between 701 and 587, although present, does not play the major role claimed by Clements (cf. below).

Very recently, Bosshard-Nepustil has greatly radicalized this earlier critical position. Basically he argues that there is no direct correlation between the description in chapter 22 and any one historical event. Rather, an initial reference to events of 701 has been shaped to serve as a transparency to those of 587. In this, he would agree with Clements, even though his literary analysis differs.

According to Bosshard-Nepustil, the transition has been achieved by an expansion in v. 7 and by an intertextual reference to a variety of passages such as Isaiah 36—37 and Jeremiah 52 to form a literary context parallel to a reconstructed level in Isa. 21:1–10. The perspective that sought to portray an analogy between 701 and 587 was construed from an even later period just prior to the fall of Babylon in 539. Undoubtedly, there are here occasionally some interesting insights, but overall the approach is based on the assumption that there is no discernable connection between the Isaianic text and its putative historical referent. At best what emerges is a highly complex reconstruction of a literary construct. In my opinion, this approach results in a massive dehistoricizing of the text and very quickly runs into the sands of turgid obfuscation.

In contrast to these two approaches, I would argue that there is a third interpretive position that does more justice both to the initial historical reference in the text as well as to its editorial shaping. At the outset I would agree with the first position (e.g., Seitz) that there are no clear signs of a major editorial reinterpretation as suggested both by Clements and Bosshard-Nepustil. The alleged signs of tension in the present text between 701 and 587 are greatly exaggerated.

Nevertheless, I would argue that according to its present canonical role, the passage was heard by its editor, even in all its historical specificity, as also foreshadowing the event of 587. Not only does the superscription reveal a visionary dimension in the future, but the harsh indictment of Judah in v. 14 could only be understood as pointing to its fulfillment in 587. Regardless of whether or not an etiological element exerted a force in its compositional history, canonically speaking the text functions prophetically toward the future, not the past, as Calvin correctly discerned. In a word, it is not a subsequent redactional intrusion that results in "the two-layered nature of the text" (Oswalt) or its "transparency to 587" (Bosshard-Nepustil), but rather the narrative structure of a canonical corpus that comprises a holistic unified story of God's purpose in history for his chosen people. Recognition of the biblical text as scripture prepares the reader for the rich resonance that a holistic interpretation evokes, and functions without sacrificing the text's original historical mooring for a literary construct. Moreover, the inclusion of vv. 15–24 within the same pronouncement superscription would indicate that a relationship exists between the two parts and that a parallel was being drawn between the impending fall of unfaithful Jerusalem in v. 14 and the collapse of the house of David symbolized by Eliakim (v. 25).

The structure of vv. 1–14 is quite complex and its subdivisions reflect different emphases with a somewhat rough quality in the connections. Verses 5–8a portray a military attack on the city retrospectively as a manifestation of God's "day." Verses 8b–11 describe Judah's own attempt at defense unconcerned with any divine purpose. Verses 12–14 return to the theme of vv. 1–4, but conclude with a devastating indictment. The three subsections are linked by the catchword "day" (vv. 5, 8b, 12). Nevertheless, there is a sense of unity ultimately in the passage. Some of the difficulty derives from the perspective moving back and forth in time from present to past to future. Furthermore, the focus shifts from the prophet's reaction to the people's continued misplaced frivolity and to the finality of God's indictment.

Sweeney's (289ff.) attempt to bring greater form-critical precision to the subdivision has not always been successful, in my opinion. The formula "therefore I say" (cf. Ps. 30:7; 39:2; 40:8) shows that the oracle is already one step removed from being a real disputation. I also doubt whether vv. 5–14 can be accurately described with the category of "refutation." Finally, it can be questioned whether vv. 15–25 relate to vv. 1–14 by providing the grounds for the initial disputation. In sum, although the passage has a narrative coherence, the traditional form-critical patterns do not appear very helpful in its interpretation; similarly the appeal to literary layering has not been persuasive.

2. Exposition

[22:1a] The superscription "a *maśśā'* concerning the Valley of Vision" remains perplexing. From a formal perspective, it appears to be derived from v. 5 as a catchword, and thus reflects a certain parallel with 21:1. However, there is no geographic valley so named around Jerusalem, and whatever its original meaning in v. 5, it now appears to function symbolically in rendering events surrounding the attack on Jerusalem as a prophetic foreshadowing of the future.

[1b–4] The tone is that of a reproach, although the idiom is akin to a disputation. The city's inhabitants have assembled on the rooftops to observe the withdrawal of the besieging enemy. Although unnamed, the reference to the Assyrian invasion under Sennacherib in 701 provides the most likely historical setting. The prophet bitterly rejects their exaltation. Jerusalem has nothing to celebrate. Its inhabitants did not win a victory, but shamefully capitulated, fleeing in panic even before the battle. Often this description has been linked with the Assyrian report of the desertion of Hezekiah's mercenaries (*ANET,* 288). Verse 4 contrasts the people's exuberance with the prophet's despairing reaction to what he describes as "the ruin of the daughter of my people." To understand the idiom as depicting only physical destruction, and thus fulfilled only in 587, is being overly literalistic.

[5–8a] The tone abruptly shifts to describing retrospectively the attack of the enemy as the manifestation of a divine purpose. God's "day" was not the expected deliverance (Amos 5:18ff.), but a time of tumult, confusion, and battering down of walls. The description far exceeds the siege of Jerusalem but addresses the devastation wrought in the entire land, with Assyria overrunning all of Judah at will. The references to Elam and Kir have frequently been used as a warrant for establishing a historical setting in 587 (cf. Clements), since traditionally Elam was an enemy of Assyria and an ally of Babylon. Yet there are other interpretive options (e.g., Wildberger, 818–19), especially that of seeing Elamites serving as mercenaries in the Assyrian army. There is no evidence here to suggest a massive redactional overlay in this largely coherent passage. The passage ends in v. 8 with the ominous note that what has transpired stems from a divine decision to withdraw his protective covering from Judah. Even with its high degree of historical specificity from 701, the text begins to resonate the ultimate destruction of Judah, which is set in stark contrast to God's earlier promise of protection (37:33–35).

[8b–11] Again the tone abruptly shifts, this time to the desperate attempt of the inhabitants of Jerusalem to prepare a defense. The temporal sequence precedes the reported attack in vv. 5ff. Jerusalem looked to its weapons, to the repairing of the walls, and to ensuring its fragile water supply for the impending siege (cf. Amiran, Watts). The prose style of these verses contrasts both with what precedes and follows, and may reflect some subsequent expansion. However, the explicit contrast in v. 11 between Jerusalem's elaborate plans and those of God is essential in establishing the coherence of the whole.

[12–14] Verse 12 returns to the theme of vv. 1–4 and articulates precisely the main theme of the oracle. The miraculous deliverance by God of the city has been basically misunderstood by its superficial inhabitants. Instead of reacting in weeping and mourning, Jerusalem responded with a behavior that flagrantly manifested its continuing disregard for God's will for the nation. Judah had learned nothing from the Assyrian threat to its life from which God had delivered his people. The indictment is given in a solemn *Auditionsbericht* revealing God's terrifying decision in the ears of the prophet: "this will not be forgiven you until you die."

For readers of the whole canonical corpus of Isaiah, there can be little doubt that the threat anticipates the future destruction of the nation. It is this dimension of transparency that ultimately accounts for the inclusion of 22:1–14 within the oracles concerning the nations (chapters 13—23). In its unfaithful response to the deliverance of 701, Israel demonstrated that it was no different from its pagan neighbors in failing to reckon with the plan of Yahweh.

[15–25] The final oracle addresses a prophetic judgment against Shebna (vv. 15–19) and the subsequent installation of his replacement in Eliakim. Verse 25 then reports the ultimate demise even of Eliakim. The oracle is unique in the book of Isaiah in being directed specifically to an individual, and its meaning and function in chapter 22 are fraught with difficulty.

Shebna, who is described with the title of "steward" (*sōkēn*) and is "over the household," is attacked by the prophet in a bitter confrontation for having built himself a splendid, private tomb. The prophet announces the divine judgment against this act of arrogance in the most violent language possible. Shebna will have no need of such splendor because God will hurl him far from the land, where he will die in shame because of the abuse of his office. Commentators debate at length on the exact nature of the controversy. Some argue that the issue turns on a political difference between Isaiah and Shebna and that Shebna supported the anti-Assyrian alliance with Egypt in opposition to the prophet's advice. Others, such as Clements (190), propose an elaborate redactional history by which to tie in Josiah's attempt to increase the support for the house of David in the seventh century.

Although it is certainly possible that there was a political or sociological dimension to Shebna's demise and Eliakim's installation, the problem emerges that very little of this background has been supplied by the biblical text. It therefore seems idle to speculate when even the identity of the two individuals cannot be established with full certainty. It is true that 36:3 speaks of Eliakim's being "in charge of the palace," while Shebna is named only as "scribe," but even when one accepts the identity of the two figures as likely, it is still impossible to reconstruct a historical scenario from this sparse information.

The chief exegetical task turns on trying to discern the function to which the removal of Shebna and the installation of Eliakim have been assigned within the framework of the *maśśā'*. Shebna is condemned because of the abuse of his office that he exploited to his own personal glory. Such behavior was deemed by the prophet unacceptable within the household of God. Whether Shebna represented a political position opposed to Isaiah's or whether there was personal animosity between them are factors irrelevant to the witness of the text. Conversely, Eliakim is called God's "servant," and assigned all the trappings of the sacred office. To him is given the key of royal Davidic authority to provide a seat of honor to his ancestral house. Verse 24 continues the theme of the heavy responsibilities of his office. He will carry the entire weight of his father's house, both matters large and small. Often this portrayal has been interpreted in a negative sense, of nepotism from which his authority will collapse. However, the literary break first comes in v. 25 with a fresh introduction. God announces that in the future (the same catchword, "in that day," returns) the peg on which his sure authority rests will give way and fall. The reader is not given a reason, rather the verse appears to signal the end of the line of royal Davidic authority. To argue as some commentators (Sweeney) that the collapse described in v. 25 must actually refer to Shebna is quite out of the question from the context.

The inclusion by the editor of two very different sets of oracles, vv. 1–14 and 15–25, within the one *maśśā'* superscription raises the crucial issue of canonical intention. The most likely interpretation is that an analogy is being drawn between the public display of unbelief in vv. 1–14 and the private abuse of a divine calling in vv. 15–25. In both cases, a response to divine grace has been flaunted that calls forth the full intensity of God's judgment. Moreover, v. 14 had spoken of God's removal of his protection of Judah. Now v. 25 speaks of the collapse of the secure place of Davidic authority. The breaking of Eliakim's position appears to refer symbolically to the imminent end of the Davidic dynasty, which functions to extend the response in 701 as a transparency of the end of Judah's existence as a nation.

23. Isaiah 23:1–18

23:1   A pronouncement concerning Tyre.
         Wail, O ships of Tarshish,
             for Tyre is destroyed without house or harbor.[a]
         From the land of Cyprus
             word has reached them.
2   Be still, inhabitants of the coast,

and you merchants of Sidon;
your messengers[b] have crossed the sea.

3   Over many waters your revenue came,
from the grain of Shihor,
the harvest of the Nile.
You were the traders to the nations.

4   Be ashamed, O Sidon, for the sea has spoken,
the stronghold of the sea,[c] declares:
"I am as one who has never labored;
I have not given birth.
I have neither reared sons nor
brought up daughters."

5   When the word reaches Egypt,
they will be in anguish over the news from Tyre.

6   Cross over to Tarshish;
wail, you inhabitants of the coast.

7   Is this your city of celebration,
whose origin is from the ancient past,
whose feet have taken her to settle in distant lands?

8   Who has planned this against Tyre,
the giver of crowns,
whose merchants are princes,
whose traders were the honored of the earth?

9   The LORD of hosts has planned it,
to defile all glorious beauty,
to humble all the honored of the earth.

10   Till[d] your land like the Nile,
O daughter of Tarshish,
for there is no longer a harbor.[e]

11   He has stretched out his hand over the sea,
and made its kingdoms tremble.
The LORD has given an order concerning Canaan
to destroy her strongholds.

12   He said, "You shall not celebrate again,
O virgin daughter of Sidon, now crushed!
Arise, cross over to Cyprus—
even there you will not find rest."

13   Look at the land of the Chaldeans. (This is a people who no longer
exists, whom the Assyrians designated for wild animals.) They raised
up their siege towers, stripped their palaces, and turned it into a ruin.[f]

14   Wail, you ships of Tarshish,
your fortress is destroyed.

15   In that day Tyre will be forgotten for seventy years, like the span of one king's life. But at the end of seventy years, it will happen to Tyre as in the song of the prostitute:

16   "Take a harp, go about the town,
        long forgotten harlot.
     Play sweetly, sing many songs,
        that you may be remembered."

17   At the end of seventy years, the LORD will deal with Tyre, and she will return to her trade and prostitute herself with all the kingdoms on the face of the earth. 18 But her profits and earnings will be consecrated to the LORD. It will not be stored or hoarded. Rather, her profits will go to those who abide in the presence of the LORD for abundant food and fine clothing.

a. The NEB emends *mibbô'* to *mabo'* to specify an entry port.

b. The reading "messengers" is an emendation supported by 1QIs^a. The MT reads "those who go over the sea have filled you," which the NJPS renders as "you were filled with men who crossed the sea."

c. Some translators omit the phrase as a dittography.

d. The MT reads *'ibrî* ("overflow"). With the textual support of the LXX and 1QIs^a, the text has been emended to *'ibdû* ("work" or "till").

e. The MT reads *mēzaḥ* ("girdle" or "restraint"), which has been emended to *māḥōz* ("market, harbor").

f. For the difficulties of translation, consult the exposition below.

Selected Bibliography

T. K. Cheyne, *Introduction to the Book of Isaiah,* London 1895, 138–45; **S. Erlandsson,** *The Burden of Babylon,* ConBOT 4, Lund 1970, 97–102; **T. Fischer and U. Rüderswörden,** "Aufruf zur Volksklag in Kanaan (Jesaja 23)," *WO* 13, 1982, 36–49; **J. H. Hayes and S. A. Irvine,** *Isaiah, The Eighth-Century Prophet: His Times and His Preaching,* Nashville 1987, 287–93; **J. Lindblom,** "Der Ausspruch über Tyrus in Jes. 23," *ASTI* 4, 1965, 56–73; **W. Rudolph,** "Jesaja 23, 1–14," *Festschrift für Friedrich Baumgärtel,* ed. J. Hermann, Erlangen 1959, 166–74; **M. A. Sweeney,** *Isaiah 1–39,* FOTL 16, Grand Rapids 1996, 302–11; **G. E. Watson,** "Tribute to Tyre (Is. XXIII 7)," *VT* 26, 1976, 371–74; **C. F. Whitley,** "The Term Seventy Years Captivity," *VT* 4, 1954, 60–72; **H. W. Wolff,** "Der Aufruf zur Volksklage," *ZAW* 76, 1964, 48–56.

1. Structure, Genre, Setting, and Function

The pronouncement oracle (*maśśā'*) clearly divides into two main sections, vv. 1–14 and 15–18. The first oracle deals with the overthrow of Tyre, the second with its restoration. Traditionally, the first oracle has been further subdivided: vv. 1–5; 6–9; 10–14 (cf. Skinner, 185). There is a certain logic in this division because the oracle first addresses the homeward bound ships of Tyre that hear the dreadful news. Next, attention turns to the general inhabitants of the coastlands, urging them to flee and seek refuge elsewhere. Finally, the concluding verses focus on Yahweh's purpose to bring down the powerful.

Nevertheless, this division is not fully satisfactory. It separates vv. 8–9 from 11–12, both of which treat Yahweh's plan. Sweeney offers a different structural analysis that has many illuminating features. He proposes to see six commands (vv. 1b, 2–3, 4–5, 6–9, 10–13), each followed by a line providing the basis for the command. Yet the emphasis on command tends to overshadow the genre of the whole, which is a communal lament. Moreover, the term *command* can inadvertently flatten the considerable variety of functions continued in the different imperatives. There is also the structural issue that v. 13 (cf. below) as a prose sentence appears to interrupt the connection with v. 14. In the end, the subdivisions in vv. 1–14 are quite fluid and the recovery of a precise structure should probably not be pressed too hard. More important is the move from the lament to its theological interpretation within the plan of God.

The attempt of Duhm, Procksch, and others to distinguish sharply between an original oracle against Sidon and another against Tyre has not been helpful. Rather, the interaction between Sidon (vv. 2, 4, 12) and Tyre (vv. 5, 8) confirms that the larger area of Phoenicia is the concern of the oracle, and it is natural that the focus alternates between its two chief cities.

Verses 15–18 are set apart by the introductory formula "in that day." In contrast to the overthrow of Tyre, these verses speak of seventy years of abandonment before its future restoration. Using an old popular "harlot song" (v. 16), the city is pictured as again plying its trade, but this time in the service of Yahweh.

The genre of vv. 1–14 has traditionally also been a subject of debate. The issue turns on whether the oracle is a future-oriented prophetic threat, perhaps of Isaianic origin (Kissane, Rudolph), or a reflection of a past event. The majority view has favored the latter position, which has received further support from Wolff's more detailed analysis of the unit as a communal lament closely akin to Joel 1:5–14. Still, one can hardly deny that within the larger literary context of the book the oracle retains a strong future-oriented role as a prophetic word testifying to God's continuing purpose for the nations of the world.

At least since the time of Vitringa, much energy has been expended in trying to determine the historical period into which the destruction of Tyre in Isaiah 23 falls. Generally speaking, four different epochs have been defended as providing a correlation with the events depicted in the biblical text.

a. The attack upon Phoenicia by the Assyrians in 705–701 under Sennacherib has been defended by Rudolph and Erlandsson. This position usually involves a defense of Isaianic authorship.

b. Scholars such as Wildberger and Vermeylen continue to relate the event to an Assyrian attack, but prefer a date under Esarhaddon (681–669). Naturally, no claim to Isaianic authorship is made.

c. Others opt for the Persian period and connect the destruction to the capture of Sidon by Artaxerxes III (Ochus) in 343. This dating is defended by Duhm and Kaiser.
d. There are those who find the complete destruction of Tyre only realized by Alexander the Great in 332. Lindblom (69ff.) further develops his theory in support of this late Hellenistic dating by arguing that Assyria had become a symbolic name for the Seleucid kingdom.

In my opinion, much of this effort at establishing a historical setting to the biblical text by means of a direct correlation with historical events has been frustrated. The rhetorical nature of the prophetic oracle makes such direct correlation difficult at best. The function of the biblical text is seldom illuminated by a crude hermeneutic of such direct referentiality.

In addition, there is a further complication. Verse 13, which appears to offer the one key to a precise historical reference within chapter 23, is generally acknowledged to be extremely obscure, if not wholly unintelligible. Solutions offered for interpreting v. 13 fall into two different approaches.

The first tries to render the received MT as well as possible in spite of the need for some interpretive straining. Usually the text is translated: "Behold, the land of the Chaldeans; this people is no more; the Assyrians . . . have destroyed it" (so Skinner, Erlandsson, Sweeney). This historical reference to the late eighth century thus serves as a warning to Tyre. Then again, a very different rending apart from any explicit emendations is suggested by the RSV (cf. Cheyne, 140). It translates as follows: "Behold the land of the Chaldeans! This is the people; it was not Assyria. . . .They (the Babylonians) made her (Tyre) a ruin." According to this reading, v. 13 offers an interpretation, dating from the sixth century or later, that explicitly links the destruction of Tyre to the Babylonians rather than to the Assyrians. The major difficulty is that this translation runs roughshod over Hebrew grammar, besides ignoring the Masoretic accentuation (cf. below).

The second major approach to v. 13 is to resort to emendations. In the mid-nineteenth century Ewald sought to resolve the problem by emending "Chaldeans" to "Canaanites" (cited by Delitzsch, 411), whose land the Assyrians destroyed. However, surely the most brilliant emendations were proposed by Duhm in his 1892 commentary. He first emends "Chaldeans" to "Kittim," that is, the Phoenicians in the islands and coastlands of the Mediterranean, and then interprets Yahweh to be the subject of their judgment. The central portion of the verse he reads as an antiquarian gloss that attempts to locate the origins of Phoenicians: "This is a people designated to be seafarers." The solution is enticing because of its simplicity, but the cost of such a radical intrusion into the text is high. Subsequent commentators, such as Kaiser, have offered minor refinements to Duhm's solution.

My own solution (cf. below) is freely acknowledged to be tentative. It attempts to resist emendations of the MT as far as possible and rather argues that there are additional, cumulative reasons for taking seriously a Babylonian setting for vv. 1–14.

First, the MT tradition maintains unequivocally the reference to the Chaldeans, a term consistently associated with the Neo-Babylonian empire (cf. 13:19 in contrast to 39:1). Second, there is a persistent pattern in chapters 13—23 that addresses Yahweh's sovereignty over the nations in terms of both the Assyrians and the Babylonians (cf. chapters 13—14; 17—18; 19—20; 21; 22). The nature of their relationship is made in different ways, but frequently the events in the late eighth century associated with Assyria are rendered editorially in such a manner as to effect a transparency with the Babylonian era. The various exegetical attempts—largely by conservative commentators—to restrict the historical references solely to the Assyrian era have not been sustained (cf. above), but a Babylonian shaping is everywhere maintained within this larger section. Finally, in both Jeremiah and Ezekiel the destruction of Tyre has always been assigned to the work of the Babylonians (cf. Jer. 27:3; 47:4; Ezekiel 29—32). In sum, chapter 23 continues the notes sounded in chapter 13 that the eschatological denouement of history is linked to the demise of Babylon.

The setting of vv. 15–18 speaks of destroyed Tyre lying fallow for seventy years before her restoration. The reference may be to Jeremiah 25. Most likely, this appendix is of a later date than vv. 1–14, but whether it should be related *post factum* to the restoration of the city by Ptolemy II in 274, which is determined by a loose calculation from the city's fall to Alexander in 332, is far from clear.

Seitz (169) offers an interesting explanation for the final position of the oracle concerning Tyre as the conclusion of the section of chapters 13—23. Tyre was regarded as the nation without peer in respect to its glory and honor, yet its status did not escape the judgment of God. Accordingly, the prophetic section is bracketed by the greatest powers on land and on sea, to emphasize the supreme sovereignty of God's word over all the nations of the world.

2. Exposition

[**23:1–14**] The *maśśā'* concerning Tyre encompasses a communal lament in vv. 1–14 that is developed by means of a series of imperatives, directed to different recipients, in reaction to Tyre's demise: wail, be still, be ashamed, cross over, till. Usually the basis for the imperative follows immediately.

The first to hear of the disaster are the ships of Tarshish, who are now deprived of a home port. The mention of Tarshish, located on the southwestern coast of Spain, immediately calls to mind the extent of Phoenician trade. Then the news is heard by Tyre's ships from Cyprus, the last port of call before returning home. Next, the range of those affected is broadened further. The inhabitants of the Phoenician coast are called to respond in awesome silence before the dreadful report. The effect on Sidon is closely intertwined with that of Tyre and not carefully delineated. Its merchants also traversed the sea. They were the traders of the world and reaped their revenue from transporting the harvest of Egypt. Sidon is compared metaphorically to a barren woman who can never have children. Sidon, whose life was derived from the sea, is likened to one who will have no future progeny but has dried up. Even distant Egypt is in anguish over Tyre's fate, with whom its own livelihood is closely bound. The lament focuses on the contrast between a proud, ancient city whose merchants prowled the earth in honor and power, to its present status of dishonor and shame.

[8–12] The major theological theme of the chapter is sounded in v. 8. How did this all happen? The prophet answers in a confession, which builds in its momentum to a resounding climax. Yahweh, the Lord of hosts, has planned it. The theme of God's sovereign purpose in the history of the nations runs through the entire section, and is consonant with the message of Isaiah. The language of his supreme control is portrayed in a typical biblical idiom: "he has stretched out his hand over the sea" (Ex. 7:19; 8:6; Isa. 14:26), "[he has] made its kingdoms tremble" (Ezek. 31:16; 38:20), "he has given an order concerning Canaan to destroy her strong holds" (Ps. 89:41; Lam. 2:5).

Some commentators have speculated that v. 10 seems out of place and is unclear in its intent. According to the MT, the sense appears to be that with the destruction of Tyre there are no longer any restrictions. The term used is "girdle." However, if the text is emended, as many suggest, the appeal is that the traders should turn from their prior activity of trade to one of agriculture, and cultivate their soil like the Egyptians do theirs. It is not necessary to reorder the position of the verse since it now functions rhetorically to strengthen the expanding theme of Yahweh's new order. In v. 12 Yahweh speaks directly to the change that has transpired. The time for exultation by Sidon has passed; the era of rest and security is over. The oracle ends in v. 14 by returning to the initial theme of v. 1: "Wail, you ships of Tarshish, your fortress is destroyed."

[13] Finally, a word about v. 13, called a *crux interpretum*. The prose style of the verse, which interrupts the poetic structure of the unit, would indicate that the verse was not initially an integral part of the oracle. It serves as a subsequent interpretation, but one that must nevertheless be taken with equal seriousness.

The initial attraction to the RSV's translation, "Behold the land of the Chaldeans! This is the people; it was not Assyria," lies in its providing a clear interpretive option. Accordingly, a later editor—probably after the fall of Babylon in 539—sought to make clear to his readers that the destruction of Tyre, described in chapter 23, was not caused by the Assyrians but by the Babylonians. However, the crucial problem is that this English translation cannot be philologically justified.

In the first place, the Masoretic accentuation of a *zakēph* separates the verbal clause *lō'hāyāh* from the noun "Assyria," which serves as the subject of the following relative clause, and joins it with the preceding subject *zeh hā'ām*. Secondly, the verb *hāyāh* does not function syntactically in this context as a simple copulative, but denotes lack of existence. The nation has become as nothing. I have therefore translated the line: "Look at the land of the Chaldeans." The next two cola are then to be read as a parenthesis: "This is a people who no longer exists, whom the Assyrians designated for wild animals." Next, v. 13b continues with Chaldeans as the subject: "They raised up their siege towers . . . and turned it (Tyre) into a ruin."

The function of the verse within the context of vv. 1–14 is to draw an analogy between mighty Babylon and glorious Tyre, both of whom suffered destruction at the hands of Yahweh, Lord of hosts. The verse thus provides a late sixth-century actualization of the oracle against Tyre, which is consonant with the dominant editorial shape of chapters 13—23.

[15–18] The appendix to chapter 23 speaks of the restoration of Tyre after a period of seventy years. The editor makes use of a popular folk song depicting an aging harlot attempting to attract clients. Like the harlot, Tyre will again recover, but her revenue will now be dedicated to Yahweh. This concluding theme is found throughout the oracles concerning the nations, namely, that the nations in the future will bring tribute to Yahweh and be reconciled to the God of Israel (16:5; 18:7; 19:21).

24. INTRODUCTION TO
ISAIAH 24—27

Selected Bibliography

G. W. Anderson, "Isaiah xxiv—xxvi Reconsidered," *Congress Volume, Bonn 1962,* VTSup 9, Leiden 1962, 118–26; **R. J. Coggins,** "The Problem of Isaiah 24—27," *ExpT* 90, 1979, 328–33; **J. Day,** "A Case of Inner Scriptural Interpretation: The Dependence of Isaiah xxvi. 13–xxvii. 11 on Hosea xiii. 4–xiv. 10 (Eng. 9) and Its Relevance to Some Theories of the Redaction of the 'Isaiah Apocalypse,'" *JTS* 31, 1980, 309–19; **G. Fohrer,** "Der Aufbau der Apokalypse des Jesajabuches (Jesaja 24—27)," reprinted in *Studien zur Alttestamentlichen Prophetie (1949–1965),* BZAW 99, Berlin 1967, 170–81; **M.-L. Henry,** *Glaubenskrise und Glaubensbewährung in den Dichtungen der Jesajaapocalypse,* BWANT 86, Stuttgart 1967; **D. G. Johnson,** *From Chaos to Restoration: An Integrative Reading of Isaiah 24—27,* JSOTSup 61, Sheffield 1988; **J. Lindblom,** *Die Jesaja Apokalypse: Jes. 24—27,* Lund 1938; **P. Lohmann,** "Die selbständigen lyrischen Abschnitte in Jes 24—27," *AZW* 37, 1917–18, 1–58; **W. R. Millar,** *Isaiah 24—27 and the Origin of apocalyptic,* HSM 11, Missoula 1976; **B. Otzen,** "Traditions and Structures of Isaiah XXIV—XXVII," *VT* 24, 1974, 196–206; **O. Plöger,** *Theocracy and Eschatology,* Oxford 1968, 53–78; **H. Ringgren,** "Some Observations on Style and Structure in the Isaiah Apocalypse," *ASTI* 9, 1973, 105–15; **W. Rudolph,** *Jesaja 24–27,* BWANT 62, Stuttgart 1933; **R. Smend,** "Anmerkungen Zu Jes. 24—27," *ZAW* 4, 1884, 161–224; **M. A. Sweeney,** "New Gleanings from an Old Vineyard: Isaiah 27 Reconsidered," *Early Jewish and Christian Exegesis: Studies in Memory of William Hugh Brownlee,* ed. C. A. Evans and W. F. Stinespring, Atlanta 1987, 51–66; "Textual Citations in Isaiah 24—27: Toward an Understanding of the Redactional Function of Chapters 24—27 in the Book of Isaiah," *JBL* 107, 1988, 39–52; **J. Vermeylen,** *Du Prophéte Isaïe à l'Apocalyptique,* I, Paris 1977, 349–381.

Few sections within the book of Isaiah have called forth such a wide measure of scholarly disagreement on their analysis and interpretation as have these four chapters. The issues of contention cover a wide range of subjects.

First, the relation of these chapters to the rest of the book has long been debated without a clear resolution. Ever since Duhm's initial analysis, these chapters were considered largely *sui generis,* with little or no connection with the book as a whole. The exegetical effect was that commentators felt constrained to analyze these chapters independently of any close literary or historical connection derived from the larger prophetic book. One of the characteristics of recent scholarship has been to call into question this assumption of independence and to explore again some fresh proposals for the role of these chapters within the whole Isaianic corpus.

Second, the presence or lack of structural coherence has evoked many widely differing evaluations. Duhm's attempt to distinguish sharply between eschatological prophecy and liturgical songs has received considerable affirmation even when successive attempts were made to refine and modify his basic hypothesis (e.g., Procksch, Lindblom). Within more recent times, form-critical, redactional, and philological models have emerged, adding to the diversity (Vermeylen, I, 349ff.; Millar; Fohrer).

Third, the dating of these chapters has extended from the eighth to the second centuries. Because historical references are consistently vague and stylized, other techniques have been sought. Thus, using the metrical analysis of the Harvard school, Millar has sought to establish a probable historical setting. Plöger has tried to exploit new information concerning inner-Jewish sectarian conflicts from the Hellenistic period to recover some broad lines for a setting. Most often a thematic trajectory of apocalyptic motifs has been sketched into which chapters 24—27 have been set. Yet in spite of the energy expended no consensus has emerged.

Because this history of interpretation has been reviewed many times (cf. Kaiser, Millar, Johnson), it does not seem necessary to cover this same ground once again. Certainly this decision is not meant to imply that the past efforts are worthless. The careful text-critical work, say, of Rudolph, retains value, even when his more radical structural reordering of the text has not commended itself.

Two basic assumptions running throughout this scholarly history need again to be critically scrutinized. The first is that chapters 24—27 are without a real literary context and should be treated therefore in isolation from the whole. The second is the assumption that the biblical text can be matched directly to given historical events in order to bring the vague biblical references into sharper focus in a reconstructed context. In my judgment, both of these assumptions are deeply flawed and account, to a larger extent, for the continuing impasse.

Fortunately, new directions have been undertaken recently by Johnson, Seitz, and Sweeney. First, in differing ways a literary context has been sought for chapters 24—27 in relation to a larger canonical corpus. Seitz has attempted to discern the proper temporal perspective of each chapter within a larger prophetic narrative. Sweeney has been successful in discovering the significance in the widespread reuse of material in citations from earlier portions of the book.

Second, the search for a historical setting has tried to take seriously the eschatological nature of these texts. The texts are not timeless tractates, but present different aspects of a temporal sequence in which time is measured according to divine *kairoi*. The voice of faithful Israel is sounded in response from within specific moments of this history, whether as experiencing the full judgmental wrath on the world (chapter 25) or as rejoicing in the signs that deliverance is near (chapter 26).

Third, recent attempts, such as that of Seitz, have correctly assessed the theological substance of the prophetic witness of these texts, not as interesting religious concepts, but as divine admonition and encouragement to a community of faith living under great pressure and struggling to discern in its historical experiences the ways of God in human lives.

Moreover, it is not by chance that the section of chapters 24–27 follows chapters 13–23, concerning the nations. The previous section of prophecy had dealt with the purpose of God in exercising his sovereignty over the nations. This corpus had begun with the prophet's eschatological vision of the day of Yahweh (chapters 13–14), which was described as intersecting with the fall of Babylon and which epitomized the arrogance and pride of earthly powers. The ruler of Babylon who claimed to ascend to heaven was cut down (chapter 14). The biblical editor saw in Babylon's destruction the fulfillment also against mighty Assyria as part of the selfsame challenge to God's righteous rule. Then followed in great particularity God's exercise of his sovereignty over Moab, Damascus, Egypt, Philistia, and Tyre.

However, right at this juncture one sees the striking differences of chapters 24–27 both in form and content. Babylon is not mentioned even once. Rather, the eschatological focus of these chapters has raised their sights to the ultimate purpose of God in portraying the cosmological judgment of the world and its final glorious restoration. Moreover, the redemption of Israel is depicted as emerging from the ashes of the polluted and decaying world. Not just a remnant is redeemed, but the chapter recounts the salvation of all peoples who share in the celebration of God's new order when death is banished forever (25:8).

Much continuing debate has centered on the controversial issue of whether these chapters should be designated apocalyptic (Millar, 1ff.). A crucial component of the problem is involved in defining what one understands by the term and how one applies the concept to the interpretation. By characterizing this literature as apocalyptic, it is often then assumed that the classic apocalyptic book of Daniel provides a context akin to chapters 24–27. However, to read Isaiah through this lens runs immediately into difficulties. Indeed, Isaiah 24 does share an interest in the end time, but many of the features characteristic of full-blown apocalyptic are missing. Thus, the Isaianic writer does not leave the realm of history in portraying a coming new order. There is no concern with mysteries known only to the initiated or to hidden numbers pointing to heavenly secrets that call for a special interpreter. For these reasons many recent commentators have rejected the term *apocalyptic* as inappropriate for these chapters.

Nevertheless, there are some special features in chapters 24–27 that, if correctly interpreted, can rightly be designated as apocalyptic, in my opinion. The focus of these chapters is on the final, eschatological judgment by God of cosmic evil. These chapters look forward to the entrance of the kingdom of God (24:23), as do many of the other prophetic oracles; however, there is an extreme tension between the dying of the old age and the entry of the new that is not characteristic of the prophets (Hosea 14; Amos 9; Micah 4). Above all, the suffering community of Israel is instructed on life lived between the two ages. The perspective often fluctuates between participating in the suffering of the whole world (24:16b) and in entering into the celebration of the new in God's eschatological banquet (25:6).

A crucial problem in these chapters is the way the writers seek to retain historical specificity in a real world of oppressive rulers and proud cities, yet at the same time to view events as representative of a larger pattern within God's eschatological purpose. There is in these chapters a typological, even didactic, quality that sets them apart from chapters 13—23, and accounts for the frustration of commentators to pin down one series of empirical, historical events.

Finally, an important characteristic of chapters 24—27 is that the portrayal of God's final purpose is made by means of a reuse of the entire corpus of Isaianic material. Much credit goes to Sweeney ("New Gleanings" and "Textual Citations") for uncovering the larger interpretive significance of this practice. Often in the past, in failing to see the functions of the holistic reading of the Isaianic tradition by these chapters, especially of chapters 1–12 and 13–23, the larger literary coherence has been missed and the theological category of prophecy and fulfillment overlooked.

In sum, there are few sections within the book of Isaiah that illustrate more clearly the importance of interpreting the Old Testament scriptures as canon. To neglect such interpretation results in a failure to grasp how Israel's understanding of God grew and deepened as it continued to reflect on its sacred writings, provided a guide to later generations regarding the ways of God in the past, in the present, and finally into the future.

25. Isaiah 24:1–25

24:1   Behold, the LORD will empty out the earth
        and devastate it,
    and he will twist its surface
        and scatter its inhabitants.
2   There will be no difference
        for priest and for layman,
        for master and for servant,
        for mistress and for maid,
        for buyer and for seller,
        for borrower and for lender,
        for debtor and for creditor.
3   The earth will be completely laid waste
        and utterly spoiled,
        for the LORD has spoken this word.
4   The earth shrivels and withers,
        the world languishes and grows sick,
        the exalted[a] of the earth languish.
5   The earth has been polluted
        by its inhabitants;
    they have destroyed the laws,
        violated the statutes,
        broken the eternal covenant.
6   Therefore a curse consumes the earth,
        and its people must bear their guilt;
    therefore the inhabitants of the earth dwindle,
        and only a few are left.
7   The new wine fails, the vine withers,
        and all the merrymakers sigh.
8   The gaiety of the tambourines is silent,
        the noise of the revelers has stopped,
        the joyful harp is stilled.
9   No one drinks wine with singing;
        beer has turned sour to those drinking it.

10   The city of chaos lies desolate;
         every house is barred so no one can enter.
11   There is an outcry in the streets
         for lack of wine.
         The sun has set on all joy.
         All gladness is banished from the earth.
12   Devastation alone is left in the town,
         the gates are battered to ruins.
13   For thus it will be on the earth
         and among the nations,
      as when an olive tree is stripped,
         or when only gleanings from the vintage are left.
14   They raise their voices, shouting for joy;
         they proclaim the majesty of the LORD from the west.
15   Therefore glorify the LORD in the east;
         in the islands of the sea, the name of the LORD,
         the God of Israel.
16   From the ends of the earth
         we hear singing:
         "Glory to the Righteous One."
      But I said, "I waste away,[b] I waste away!
         Woe is me!
      The treacherous act treacherously,
         the treacherous deal very treacherously."
17   Terror, pit, and trap
         await you who dwell on earth!
18   Whoever flees at the sound of the terror
         will fall into the pit.
      Whoever climbs out of the pit
         will be caught in a trap.
      The windows of heaven are opened,
         the foundations of the earth tremble.
19   The earth will be broken up,
         the earth is split apart,
         the earth is violently tottering.
20   The earth staggers like a drunkard,
         it sways back and forth like a hut.
      Its sins weigh heavily on it,
         and it will collapse, and not rise again.
21   In that day, the LORD will punish
         the host of heaven in heaven,
         and the kings of the earth on earth.

22   They will be gathered in a dungeon,
         together as prisoners in a pit.
      They will be shut up in prison
         and after many days punished.
23   Then the moon will be confounded
         and the sun ashamed,
      for the LORD of hosts will reign
         on Mount Zion and in Jerusalem,
      and he will reveal his glory before his elders.

   a. With a slight repointing (cf. *BHS*) the RSV obtains more balanced imagery.
   b. This usage is unique to the Old Testament. It is often understood along with some versions as "my secret" (Kaiser). Others relate it to the *rzh* ("leanness"). From its context it appears to be an idiom paralleled to "Woe is me."

Selected Bibliography

D. G. Johnson, *From Chaos to Restoration,* JSOTSup 61, Sheffield 1988, 19–47; **O. Plöger,** *Theocracy and Eschatology,* ET Oxford 1968; **M. A. Sweeney,** "Textual Citations in Isaiah 24–27: Toward an Understanding of the Redactional Function of Chapters 24–27 in the Book of Isaiah," *JBL* 107, 1988, 39–52; **J. Vermeylen,** *Du Prophète Isaïe à l'Apocalyptique,* I, Paris 1977, 352–61; **P. Welten,** "Die Vernichtung des Todes und die Königsherrschaft Gottes: Eine traditionsgeschichtliche Studie zu Jes 25, 6–8; 24, 21–23; und Ex 24, 9–11," *TZ* 38, 1982, 129–46.

1. Structure, Form, and Genre

   The classic literary-critical analysis of chapter 24 generally divided the chapter into two major parts: vv. 1–13 and 14–23. However, the more significant move arose with the proposal to distinguish a history of textual growth proceeding through three or four redactional stages (cf. Wildberger, Vermeylen, Clements). Verses 1–6 and 14–20 are thought to form the basic stratum (*Grundschrift*) to which three further additions are detected (vv. 7–9, 10–12, 13). Duhm's initial distinction between eschatological oracles and later songs continues to play a role in the projection of different layers (vv. 21–23), although there is little consensus on when and how the expansions occurred.
   Within the last decade two impressive analyses defending the overall unity of the composition have been made by Seitz and Sweeney. In different ways, both seek to understand the complex movement of the chapter in relation to its larger literary coherence within the book of Isaiah, especially in its reinterpretation of prior prophetic traditions. Seitz's analysis gains its strength by tracing the imagery of the Noachic covenant and in developing its theological implications. Sweeney offers a detailed structural analysis, and joins the two main

parts within the traditional form-critical categories of prophetic announcement of judgment (vv. 3–13) and prophetic disputation (vv. 14–23).

In respect to its historical setting, Seitz sees a very close relationship between chapters 24—27 and 13—23. He is prepared to see chapters 24—27 as a culmination of the same Babylonian redaction, that is to say, an editorial intention expressing a common interest in Babylon as world judge. For Seitz, the author of chapters 24—27 stands at a historical moment when Babylon is at its greatest strength and as God's agent threatens to waste the earth (178). Sweeney also reckons with a sixth-century dating for the composition of the present form of the chapter, specifically about the time of the return of the exiles to Jerusalem in the early Persian period. He uses as evidence the universal outlook of these chapters, the affinites with Second-Isaiah, and the citation of prophetic passages outside of Isaiah, including Hosea, Jeremiah, Amos, and Micah. In sum, both Seitz and Sweeney reject the earlier attempts to characterize this chapter as apocalyptic literature that arose out of a setting akin to the book of Daniel. This position on dating the chapter continues to accrue wide support.

2. Exposition

[24:1–3] These verses introduce both the larger collection (chapters 24—27) as well as chapter 24 with a prophetic announcement of God's will to destroy the earth, twisting its shape and scattering its inhabitants. The punishment that follows will occur in total disregard for status, and the universal scope of those embraced in its judgment is emphasized by removing all distinctions between slave and master, buyer and seller, creditor and lender. In sum, it embraces all of the earth's inhabitants cutting across social, economic, and political standing. The utter finality of the divine decision is stressed by means of the formula: "the LORD has spoken this word."

However, the formula plays more than a conventional role and functions as a retrospective link with the chapters that have preceded. The parallels in language and content with chapter 13 spring immediately to view. Chapter 13 had spoken about "destroying the whole earth" (v. 5), "making the earth a waste" (v. 9), and "punishing the world for its evil" (v. 11). The intensity of the eschatological language is similar. In both chapters the judgment is all inclusive; in both it involves the earthly into the cosmological; in both it has resulted from a divine assault against the evil of the earth.

There is no indication that two different historical movements are being portrayed. Rather, one finds an all-encompassing apocalyptic consummation of human history announced. In typical biblical terminology the focus falls on the quality of a divine act of bringing the old age to an end. Yet there are differences in the accounts. Chapter 13 envisions the eschatological end of world history coinciding with the fall of Babylon, the archenemy. The "day of the LORD," in which finally the wrath of God is unleashed against all human arrogance, is identified with God's historical intervention against Babylon. It is a final consummation of a quality of judgment only foreshadowed in the overthrow of Sodom and Gomorrah (13:19).

[4–13] In chapter 24 the apocalyptic nature of the event is the same. Yet there is a characteristic difference in its depiction that continues to shape the entire chapter, indeed the entire collection of chapters 24—27. Verses 4–13 begin to expand the grounds for the divine decision by developing the theological grounds for the universal condemnation. The issue no longer turns on the specific sins of Babylon, but rather on a dimension of evil that causes both heaven and earth to grow sick. The earth has become polluted from the violation of God's laws and disregard of his statutes. Because of the mention of divine law, some commentators have proposed that the prophet is referring to the Mosaic covenant, yet this interpretation is very unlikely. The immediate reference to breaking the "everlasting covenant" offers a linguistic warrant for seeing rather a reference to the covenant with Noah (Gen. 9:16). In addition, the scope of the account is not limited to Israel, but includes the entire world. The curse lies upon the whole world, and its inhabitants suffer the guilt. Seitz has correctly seen that the imagery that extends throughout chapter 24 is most compatible with the Noachic traditions. "God saw that human wickedness was so great in the earth that every imagination was only evil continually" (Gen. 6:5). In Genesis, God wrought a new beginning in history; in Isaiah, he announced its end.

There is another feature of chapter 24 that confirms the paradigmatic quality of the apocalyptic portrayal. Verse 10 speaks of the "city of chaos." No further identification is offered, but the imagery of the city continues to function as a major feature of these chapters (24:10; 25:2; 26:5; 27:10). Only in 26:1 is it given a positive connotation as a "strong city," a bulwark of salvation. Various identifications of the city have been proposed, including Jerusalem, Babylon, and Samaria (cf. Sweeney, "Textual Citations," 43). Yet this historicizing move of interpreters seeks to provide a specificity that is precisely missing in the biblical text. In fact, it is the representative presentation of earthly human power, locked in deadly conflict against the entrance of God's righteous reign, that is constitutive of the function of these chapters.

There is another crucial factor to be observed when interpreting these verses. The parallels between chapters 17 and 24 of Isaiah have long been noticed, but much credit goes to Sweeney ("Textual Citations," 42ff.) for working out the implication of this reuse of earlier passages within chapters 24—27. Thus, 24:13 cites closely 17:6a: "as when an olive tree is stripped, or when only gleanings from the vintage are left." In chapter 17 the oracle condemns the Northern Kingdom for its role in the Syro-Ephraimite war. Yet as Sweeney notes, the imagery of judgment has been transferred from focusing exclusively on Israel to including all the nations. Yet, of equal importance, Sweeney observes that the reapplication of chapter 17 is not an arbitrary move, but is rather based on a holistic reading of all of chapter 17, indicating that Israel's punishment will be followed by judgment against the nations as well.

[14–16] The interpretation of vv. 14–16 has emerged as one of the most controversial in chapter 24. The introduction of the pronoun "they" has caused some commentators to argue that v. 13 actually begins this unit, thus providing an antecedent in the imagery of a remnant. However, this move is very unlikely and cannot be sustained either in form or content. The debate continues whether the pronoun refers to various unnamed peoples throughout the world (Sweeney, *Isaiah 1–39,* 328) or to a Jewish diaspora. Wildberger immediately historicizes the reference to the Jewish diaspora of the Persian period. Others opt for a later, Hellenistic one (cf. Johnson, 36ff. for a review of proposals). Frequently, a psychological ploy is offered (Plöger, 58), suggesting that the prophet is objecting to a superficial, premature joy on the part of Jews as a reaction to the nations' troubles.

In my judgment, these options fail to reckon adequately with the paradigmatic nature of the theological depiction of God's purpose with Israel and the nations. The idiom used in describing the rejoicing is such that the subject of the celebration can only be Israel. The singing for joy over the majesty of Yahweh and the giving of glory to the name of the God of Israel imitate the essentials of Israel's true voice of praise. The parallels with 12:3–6 and 42:10–12 clearly demonstrate that this is the proper idiom for the "new song" in responding to the entrance of God's promised new order. The issue at stake is certainly not its superficiality but its false timing. Chapter 24 describes the moment of apocalyptic judgment on the world within God's economy. The old age is coming to an end. Both the hosts of heaven and the king of the earth must be destroyed before the rule of God on Mount Zion can be inaugurated (v. 23).

This theological point is made abundantly clear in the reaction of the prophet in v. 16b (cf. 22:4). Israel has misread the signs of the times. The prophet is in anguish because the execution of the divine judgment on the entire world still lies ahead. Verse 16b establishes the grounds for the prophet's reaction with an allusion to 21:2: "a harsh vision . . . the plunder is plundering, the destroyer destroys." As in the case of Babylon in 21:2, v. 16 points to the time when the attackers will deal treacherously with the enemy. However, this event still lies ahead, and the fall of this apocalyptic enemy is made in universal terms.

[17–23] This interpretation appears to be confirmed by the succeeding verses. The oracle announcing the extent of the approaching judgment continues the litany of destruction started in vv. 1–3 with mounting intensity. Yet the assigning of vv. 14–16 to a redactional intrusion is to misunderstand the movement of the chapter as a literary whole, and thus to render a coherent unity into disconnected fragments.

The terror that is to fall encompasses all the inhabitants of the earth (v. 17). The motif of escaping one danger only to succumb to an even worse fate (v. 18) was already employed by Amos (5:18ff.), and it serves to emphasize the inevitability of the coming catastrophe. The parallels with 13:9ff. confirm further that a quality of apocalyptic final judgment is being presented that is not confined to one historical moment. The imagery of "the windows of heaven" being opened is akin closely to the flood (Gen. 7:11), but the darkening of the sun and moon (v. 23) within the context of a cosmic shaking is stock-in-trade for depicting the coming of Armageddon (Jer. 4:23; Ezek. 38:19ff.; Joel 4:15 [3:15]; Rev. 16:17ff.; 18:21ff.). The language of being brought down to a pit (v. 22) is reminiscent of the taunt against the mighty king of Babylon (14:15ff.).

The goal of God's judgment of the world is reached in v. 23: "The Lord of hosts will reign on Mount Zion and in Jerusalem, and he will reveal his glory before his elders." This climax also signals the beginning of God's new order and its effect on the faithful of the world, both among Israel and the nations (v. 6).

26. Isaiah 25:1–12

25:1   O LORD, you are my God.
      I will exalt you and praise your name,
          for you have done wonderful things,
          plans from of old, faithful and sure.
2   For you have turned a city into a heap,
          the fortified town into a ruin,
      the stronghold of foreigners into rubble.
          It will never be rebuilt.
3   Therefore a strong people will honor you,
          cities of ruthless nations will fear you.
4   You have been a refuge for the poor,
          a refuge for the needy in his distress,
      a shelter from the rainstorm,
          a shade from the sun's heat.
      For the blast of the ruthless is like
          a flood against a wall.[a]
5   Like the sun's heat in the desert,
          you subdue the roar of the foreigners.
      Like burning heat in the shade of a cloud,
          the song of the ruthless is vanquished.
6   On this mountain the LORD of hosts
          will prepare a rich feast for all peoples,
      a banquet of choice wines,

　　　　fat meat full of marrow,
　　　　and of rich wines well strained.

7　　And he will destroy on this mountain
　　　　the shroud that is draped
　　　　over the faces of the peoples,
　　　　the covering spread over all the nations.

8　　He will swallow up death forever.
　　　The Lord GOD will wipe away the tears
　　　　from all faces;
　　　he will end the reproach of his people
　　　　in all the earth,
　　　for it is the LORD who has spoken.

9　　It will be said on that day:
　　　　"This is truly our God.
　　　　We have waited for him
　　　　and he has delivered us.
　　　　This is the LORD on whom we have waited.
　　　　Let us rejoice and be glad in his salvation."

10　　The hand of the LORD will rest on this mountain.
　　　　Moab will be trampled upon in his place,
　　　　as straw is trampled in a manure pit.[b]

11　　He will spread out his hands in it,
　　　　as a swimmer stretches out his hands to swim.
　　　God will humble his pride
　　　　in spite of the skill[c] of his hands.

12　　the high walled fortifications he will bring down
　　　　and lay them low;
　　　he will level them to the ground, into the very dust.

　　a. The MT, translated by the RSV "a storm against a wall" (*qîr*), is pronounced by Wildberger to be "impossible." He emends with a majority (NJPS, NEB, etc.) to read *qôr* ("winter"). However, the MT, although unusual, is not impossible, and can be understood as a violent flood pounding a wall (cf. Delitzsch, Oswalt, and Barthélemy, *CTLAT*).

　　b. The Hebrew word is a *hapax legomenon*. NJPS interprets it as the proper name of a village near Jerusalem, Madmenah. The traditional rendering derives the noun from the root *dmn* ("to fertilize a field").

　　c. The meaning is unclear and perhaps related to "crafty" or "skilled."

Selected Bibliography

J. A. Emerton, "A Textual Problem in Isaiah 25, 2," *ZAW* 89, 1977, 64–73; **R. Martin-Achard,** "'Il engloutit la mort à jamais.' Remarques sur Esaïe 28, 8a," *Mélanges bibliques et orientaux en l'honneur*

de M. Mathias Delcor, ed. A. Caquot et al., Neukirchen-Vluyn 1985, 283–96; **P. Welton,** "Die Vernichtung des Todes und die Königsherrschaft Gottes; Eine traditionsgeschichtliche Studie zu Jes 25, 6–8; 24,
21–23; und Ex 24, 9–11," *TZ* 38, 1982, 129–46; **H. Wildberger,** "Das Freudenmahl auf dem Zion: Erwägungen Zu Jes. 25, 6–8," *TZ* 33, 1977, 373–83; **B. Wodecki,** "The Religious Universalism of the Pericope Is. 25:6–9," *Goldene Äpfel in silbernen Schalen,* ed. K.-D. Schunck and M. Augustin, BEATAJ 20,
Frankfurt 1992, 35–47.

1. Structure, Genre, and Function

The passage is usually divided into two parts, vv. 1–5 and 6–12, with several additional subdivisions suggested for the second unit (e.g., vv. 6–8; 9–10a;
10b–12). These later moves are not of great importance in themselves, and it is
generally acknowledged that the turn from the apocalyptic judgment in chapter 24 has occurred in chapter 25. At times it has been argued that 25:1–5 is an
interpolation that breaks the continuity with vv. 6ff., but this hypothesis is very
subjective, going back ultimately to Duhm's separation of apocalyptic
announcements and liturgical songs. The evidence for translating vv. 6–12 as
a prose unit (RSV) has not been widely accepted, and the NRSV correctly renders it as poetry.

Most commentators understand chapter 25 to be Israel's response to the
announced fall of the strong city. Some have stressed that a contrast has been
consciously made between an inappropriate response in 24:14ff. and a properly
faithful one in 25:1–5. The confession of a voice of praise is followed by the
announcement of a festival of joy celebrating the new order of God's rule. The
point is explicitly made that not only Israel but all peoples are included in the
feast. Yet, lest it be thought that a picture of universal salvation is being presented, vv. 10ff. end with the exclusion of Moab, whose pride keeps the nation
outside the community of faith.

In my opinion, the diverse literary forms have been carefully shaped into a
coherent composition that, following the lead of chapter 24, offers a paradigmatic presentation of Israel's proper response to the announcement of both catastrophic world judgment and God's ultimate plan for the redemption of Israel
and the nations. Moab functions within this composition, not as a misplaced literary fragment but as a representative symbol of ontological resistance to God's
purpose for his creation, and because of its continuing pride, Moab falls outside the arena of salvation.

2. Exposition

[25:1–5] The opening verses are classified form-critically as a psalm of
thanksgiving. The psalm is cast in the first person singular. It is generally
assumed that the singular voice is a representative of the larger worshipping
community. As evidence it has been pointed out that the individual song of

thanksgiving in Psalm 30 carries the superscription, "a song at the dedication of the temple," from which one can infer that the individual voice was a normal vehicle for corporate worship. Still, it is important to recognize how persistent, even dominant, the voice of the individual remained in Israel's worship. It would seem that for Israel the most elemental form of confession was the *credo:* "O Lord, you are my God" (v. 1). However, the ease with which the plural form is introduced (vv. 9; 26:1) confirms the easy continuity between the singular and plural.

The psalm shares the conventional components of Israel's worship of praise. God is exalted for his "wonderful things" (*pele'*), which are the great divine acts of salvation—sometimes "supernatural," sometimes not—revealing the hand of God at work on Israel's behalf. The psalmist is aware that the intervention of God is not accidental but follows a divine plan, thus demonstrating his faithfulness and constancy.

Although the form of the thanksgiving psalm is conventional in following an inherited pattern, there are several indications that it has been carefully shaped to serve in its present position within the corpus of chapters 24—27. The divine plan is specifically related to the destruction of the "fortified town," thus establishing a link with the previous chapter (24:10). Once again the city is unnamed and the representative role already established. Yet there is a deep resonance in the background to the fall of Babylon in the emphasis, "it will never be rebuilt" (13:20; 14:22). The joyful reaction of other peoples to the fall of the oppressor also functions as a reminder of 14:7: the whole world breaks into singing. It is also significant to note with Sweeney ("Textual Citations," 45–46) that vv. 4–5 appear to cite 4:5b–6, which had described the protective shelter from the heat of the day and from hail and rain. The author of chapter 25 makes use of these elements of hymnic thanksgiving in describing the overthrow of the fortified city. It is not fully clear whether only Zion is being protected because the poor and needy are not identified. The reference to "all peoples," who celebrate on the mountain in v. 6, might well suggest a more inclusive referent.

[6–8] These verses return to the theme sounded in 24:23. Following the destruction of the "city of chaos," which symbolizes the end of the old order of violence and pride, the Lord of hosts now reigns on Mount Zion, revealing his glorious presence. On this mountain, namely Jerusalem, Yahweh inaugurates a festival to celebrate his coronation. As in Deut. 14:26, a joyous festival demands the best of meat and drink. But most significant, it is explicitly stated that the new order of divine rule includes "all peoples." This emphasis is infrequent in chapters 24—27, but the theme grows in strength throughout both Second and Third Isaiah (56:6ff.; 60:1ff.; 66:18ff.).

The removal of the covering cast over all peoples (v. 7) has evoked some discussion. Some have suggested that it refers to spiritual blindness, but more fitting in the present context of a festival would be to see the veil of mourning replaced by a garment of celebration. Some commentators have argued that the description in v. 8 of the abolishing of death is out of place, since it exceeds the very earthbound description of a festival and projects the scene into an otherworldly hope of eternal life. Although it is true that such a "heavenly" description is unique in chapters 24—27, it is very difficult, if not impossible, to date with any accuracy the sudden entrance of a new theme. Moreover, when one considers that there is a representative, paradigmatic intention running through these chapters, such an ultimate formulation of the rule of God as without death and sorrow cannot be ruled out of court. Only in Isaiah's final chapters (65 and 66) is the theme of a new heaven and new earth fully developed (65:17ff.; 66:22–23), but the hope of a radical new world order apart from evil and sickness has been adumbrated throughout the entire Isaianic corpus. Although it is possible to see here a subsequent literary retrojection, the effect of this hypothesis, even if true, is not of crucial interpretive importance.

[9–12] The next verses set up a contrast between Israel's confession and Moab's exclusion. At first it might seem logical to interpret the prayer as one made by "all peoples" as in v. 6, but this reading is unlikely. Indeed, God includes the peoples in his invitation, but the voice that responds to God's salvation uses explicitly the idiom of faithful Israel. The formulation of obedient worship as "waiting for God" permeates the Psalter (25:3, 5, 21; 27:14; 37:34), but also is a major motif in all sections of Isaiah (8:17; 30:18; 33:2; 40:31; 49:23; 59:9; 60:9; 64:4). It denotes an attitude of eager expectancy of God's promised salvation. Particularly in the Psalter, part of the worshipper's intense sorrow lies in the perceived failure of its realization. The psalmist's faithfulness lies in hanging on patiently (37:7; 69:3). Similarly, in the book of Isaiah, faith involves waiting for the light when only darkness reigns because of God's hiding his face (8:17). The joy expressed in 25:9 is that the period of waiting is finally over as God's salvation is experienced. The divine blessing on those who have waited has been indeed realized.

For some commentators the announcement of Moab's continuing punishment is deemed highly inappropriate and attributed to a Jewish author's deep hatred of Moab (cf. Isaiah 16; Jeremiah 48; Zephaniah 2). That there was a long-standing animosity between Israel and Moab cannot be denied, but this observation does not sufficiently address the function of this passage in chapter 25. Rather, another paradigmatic move is being made, which culminates in the final verse of the book (66:24). The universal restoration of God's creation as portrayed by the prophet does not remove all tension between good and evil.

The mystery of God's salvation of the world is such that the possibility of rejecting God's invitation remains. In chapter 25 Moab is singled out, not for personal spite, but as the symbol of arrogance and pride that rejects the inclusion of all nations under the rule of Yahweh, Lord of hosts. Needless to say, this same *skandalon* is part of the offense of the gospel within the New Testament (Rev. 20:14; 21:27).

In sum, the modern ideology of religious universalism, characterized by unlimited inclusivity, is far removed from the biblical proclamation of God's salvation (cf. Seitz, 192).

27. Isaiah 26:1–21

26:1 In that day this song will be sung in the land of Judah:
        We have a strong city;
          he makes salvation its walls and ramparts.
2   Open the gates for the entry
          of the righteous nation that keeps the faith.
3   The calm mind you will keep in perfect peace
          because it trusts in you.
4   Trust in the LORD forever,
          for the LORD, the LORD, is
          an everlasting rock.
5   He humbles those who dwell on high;
          he will lay low the fortified city.
        He will lay it low to the ground,
          even leveling it into the dust.
6   Feet trample it,
          the feet of the poor,
          the steps of the lowly.
7   The way of the righteous is level,
          smooth[a] the path of righteousness
          which you lay.
8   Yes, in the paths of your judgments,
          O LORD, we wait for you.
        We long for your name
          by which you are called.[b]
9   My soul yearns for you in the night,
          even my spirit within me seeks you early.[c]
        For from your judgments upon the earth,
          the inhabitants of the world learn righteousness.
10   When shown favor,[d] the wicked does not learn
          righteousness.
        In an upright land, he acts perversely
          and does not see the majesty of the LORD.

11   O LORD, your hand is lifted up,
          but they do not see it.
      Let them see your zeal for your people
          and be ashamed.
      Let the fire for your enemies
          consume them.
12   O LORD, you will establish our well-being;
          all our works you have accomplished for us.
13   O LORD, our God, other lords beside you
          have ruled over us,
          but your name alone do we honor.
14   They are dead, they can never live;
          the shades will not arise.
      Therefore you punished them,
          and wiped out all memory of them.
15   But you have added to the nation, O LORD.
          You have added to the nation; you are honored.
          You have enlarged the borders of the land.
16   O LORD, in their distress they came to you.
          they poured out whispered prayers
          because your punishment fell on them.^e
17   As a woman with child about to give birth
          writhes and screams in her pangs,
          so we become because of you, O LORD.
18   We were with child, we writhed in pain,
          but we gave birth as if only to wind.
      We have brought no deliverance
          to the earth.
          The inhabitants of the world have not fallen.^f
19   But your dead will live;
          my dead bodies^g will rise again.
      Awake and rejoice, dwellers in the dust,
          for your dew is the dew of lights.
      You let it fall on the land of the shades.
20   Go, my people, enter your chambers,
          and shut your doors behind you.
      Hide yourself for a little while
          until his wrath passes.
21   See, the LORD is coming forth from his place
          to punish the people of the earth for their sins.
      The earth will disclose its bloodshed
          and will no longer conceal its slain.

a. The word *yāšār* is not to be construed as a vocative, "O straight one."

b. *zēker* here is not "memory," but the pronounced name.

c. *BHS* emends to "morning" to improve the parallelism.

d. The meaning is obscure. The use of this form as a conditional is highly unusual, but preferable to the various emendations suggested.

e. The second line is extremely difficult and without a clear solution. Cf. the lengthy discussion by Oswalt, I, 483–84, and Barthélemy, *CTLAT,* 183ff. Either one can extensively emend in several places, or attempt to interpret the MT as well as possible.

f. The literal meaning is "to fall," but some construe the verb metaphorically, "to be born."

g. The suffix is often emended to "their bodies" (*BHS*), but some see here an influence from Ps. 49:15.

Selected Bibliography

H. Birkeland, "The Beliefs in Resurrection of the Dead in the Old Testament," *VT* 3, 1950/51, 60–78; **J. Day,** "A Case of Inner Scriptural Interpretation," *JTS* 31, 1980, 309–19; **G. Fohrer,** "Das Geschick des Menschen nach dem Tode im Alten Testament," *KD* 12, 1968, 249–62; **D. M. Fouts,** "A Suggestion for Isaiah xxvi 16," *VT* 41, 1991, 472–75; **E. Haenchen,** "Auferstehung im Alten Testament," in *Die Bibel und Wir,* Tübingen 1968, 73–90; **D. G. Johnson,** *From Chaos to Restoration,* JSOTSup 61, Sheffield 1988, 67–84; **R. Martin-Achard,** *De la mort à la résurrection,* Neuchâtel 1956, 101–12; **H. D. Preuss,** "'Auferstehung' in Texten alttestamentlicher Apokalyptik (Jes. 26. 7–19, Dan. 12. 1–4)," *Linguistische Theologie* 3, 1972, 101–72; **J. F. A. Sawyer,** "Hebrew Words for the Resurrection of the Dead," *VT* 13, 1973, 218–34; **M. A. Sweeney,** *Isaiah 1—39,* FOTL 16, Grand Rapids 1996, 337–44.

1. Structure, Genre, and Function

Usually the unit is divided into two parts, vv. 1–6 and 7–21 (Wildberger, Kaiser, Clements), although different schemes of subdivision have also been suggested. In terms of genre, vv. 1–6 is classified as a psalm of trust or as a victory song, whereas the last section is analyzed as a communal complaint. Sweeney designates the entire chapter as a community complaint, while trying to recognize the great variety of form-critical components within his subdivisions.

The problem is that the crucial interpretive issues of the chapter are not greatly affected by these formal classifications. Seitz puts his finger on the central question at stake when he writes, "this question of proper temporal perspective is more pressing than the matter of diverse genre within the chapter" (193). Of course, this issue remains a basic concern for those who seek to defend a coherent movement in chapters 24—27 rather than seeing the chapter as an indiscriminate collage of apocalyptic utterances mixed with diverse songs and reflecting a wide expanse of historical periods. It strikes the reader as particularly perplexing that the preceding chapter speaks of the "fortified city" of

Israel's oppressor as having already been destroyed, of an eschatological feast in the presence of God for all peoples, and even of a vision of death being abolished in the new age of God's rule on the holy mountain.

Seitz tries to soften the stark contrast between these chapters by rightly pointing out that it is a characteristic feature of many psalms not to fix fully the temporal movement within God's economy. Thus the psalmist can praise God at one point for victory and then conclude that the final victory still lies in the future (Psalm 25). Or again, the psalmist typically fluctuates in his condition from calm confidence to compliance bordering on despair. While this observation is certainly true, a question remains about whether this insight is fully adequate for interpreting the apparent lack of coherence in these chapters.

Up to this point, I have argued the case for seeing chapters 24—27 as a paradigmatic presentation of life lived in the end time. The approach of these chapters certainly cannot be described correctly as a systematic abstraction of their material. The particularity of the presentation remains sharply contoured by means of the imagery of apocalyptic speech and the conventions of liturgical language. Yet there appears to be an intentional distance established from those specific historical events, which are rendered as illustrations of larger patterns. In a word, there is a distinct typological flavor given to the account. Babylon is never mentioned, but a "city of chaos" receives its just punishment. Judgment comes not from a specified enemy, but rather terror encompasses the world as God opens up "the windows of heaven." Jerusalem is not named the strong city where God inaugurates his salvation—what other city could possibly play this role?—but rather we hear only of a city waiting for the righteous to enter. Finally, salvation is not presented as an escape from earthly oppressors, but as a life with God apart from death and human decay.

The effect of this manner of literary composition is that its coherence does not lie in a linear temporal sequence in which the righteous are sharply removed from the wicked and the new age always succeeds the old. Rather, the chapter is organized in an aspectual, typologizing manner, and a different scenario is unfolded in each chapter even when similar conventions are used that often overlap in context. For example, there is much similarity in the genre and content of 25:1–6 and 26:1–6. Yet in chapter 25 the appropriate response to God's approaching judgment is followed by a portrayal of a "heavenly" festival. In contrast, in chapter 26 the faithful response in prayer to God's judgment of the lofty city (v. 5) is followed by a lengthy reflection of this same community of faith, but under oppression from the wrath of God, which is still felt (26:20).

In sum, chapter 26 offers a great variety of conventional forms, but in the end it results in a highly theological presentation directed to the faithful, who testify to the effect of God's victory, yet still experience the full weight of divine and human judgment. God's salvation has been truly experienced; his righteous rule is confessed. Yet ultimately salvation is depicted in terms that transcend any one experience. Chapter 25 speaks of a life removed from death, while chapter 26 of the promise of resurrection to life even after the suffering of death.

2. Exposition

[26:1–6] The opening verses share elements in the form of a song of victory and of trust. In many ways the unit continues the themes sounded in 25:1–5. It speaks of God as a strong bulwark, a refuge for the faithful, and it testifies to God's power to bring low human arrogance. Nevertheless, there are distinct features that begin to provide a distinct form and function.

The unit is portrayed as an eschatological song, much like 12:1ff., but sung in the land of Judah. A plural, first person voice sings praise to God, who has established a strong city of salvation as walls and bulwarks. It must, of course, be Jerusalem, but it remains unnamed. Its gates are opened to the righteous nation that keeps faith. By now describing the participants of God's salvation in terms of a righteous nation, one again hears a note that also serves to define those sharing a festive meal in God's presence. The net is extended wide enough for all the nations, and yet those characterized as God's people are always identified by a response of righteousness. Those invited into the city of salvation are further described. They are the recipients of "perfect peace"— God's *šalôm*—who are grounded in him through God's faithfulness in his calling forth human faith.

The indicative is then characteristically followed by an imperative in v. 4: "Trust in the LORD forever." He is an enduring support, an abiding source of unchanging stability on whom one can lean. Moreover, there is a warrant for this trust. God has already demonstrated his purpose in overcoming the ways of the wicked and in debasing the human pride of the lofty city. The poor and needy experience these moments of victory. By comparing 25:1–5 with 26:1–6 one senses the subtle shift of focus in the latter. The spiritual state of those within the gates of salvation has been depicted as peaceful and secure.

[7–21] This same theme of the path of the righteous is continued in the unit that follows: "The way of the righteous is level, . . . smooth the path of righteousness." However, the reader is unprepared for the description of this path that pursues the way of God's laws. The faithful community emerges as still waiting for its salvation. There is also the yearning for God's presence that pervades the entire Psalter. The grounds for this request is also shared by the psalmist that the inhabitants of the world learn of God's righteousness (96:10ff.; 119:46).

Then immediately a dissonant note is sounded. Even when God's favor is shown to the wicked, they do not understand its true source. Rather, they continue to deal dishonestly and do not see the majesty of God. The glorious world of God's rule described by the psalmist is not visible to all. His pain is directed to God: "your hand is lifted up, but they do not see it" (v. 11). Your works are clearly manifest, but the wicked do not recognize them. The conventional notes of the complaint are then sounded: "Let them see your zeal for your people. . . . Let the fire for your enemies consume them." The same pattern of life before the end is acknowledged to be still operative. The wicked are still at work. Israel is still oppressed by other lords. Yet the community of faith continues to confess its loyalty solely to Yahweh. It expresses its confidence that the wicked will not endure but, like the dead, mere shadows of existence, they will be cut off. Yet the righteous nation will live and increase in size in the land in order to reflect God's glory.

[16] Seitz (194) correctly recognizes that a real break occurs in v. 16. Although frequently in chapters 24—27 the prophetic vision described is the situation after the final eschatological day of judgment, Seitz argues that in 26:16–21 the status of the believer is viewed temporally before the day of wrath. I would argue that according to this typology, life for faithful Israel in the end time continues to share paradoxically most of the elements of the time prior to the end. That is to say, even when the faithful confess to have seen the hand of God at work on their behalf and the signs of the rule of God in righteousness have been manifested, the community is situated "between the times." The old is passing; the new has not yet come in its fullness.

In v. 16 the faithful community is described pouring out to God a whispered prayer in great anguish. It was because of what God had done that the expectancy was so high. The faithful "we" compares itself to a false pregnancy. In spite of the pangs and the excitement of a new birth, nothing but empty wind is brought forth (cf. Day, 311 and Hos. 13:13). Israel's deepest frustration arises because nothing seems to have been accomplished: "We have brought no deliverance to the earth. The inhabitants of the world have not fallen." All the divine promises of the new age and of Israel's transforming of the world have not been realized.

[19] What follows in v. 19 has been designated a *Heilsorakel,* the classic form of divine reassurance that salvation will come. It is the literary vehicle for much of Second Isaiah's proclamation of God's purpose for the redemption of Israel and the world (41:14ff.; 43:1ff.). Yet the promise of v. 19 transcends all the promises of Second Isaiah and has been composed specifically for the larger context of chapter 26. The hope for those living between the times is now projected beyond the grave to a resurrection of life, a final victory over death itself. Scholars have long debated whether the promise is only for the rebirth of the nation (cf. Ezek. 37:1ff.), or whether the hope includes the resurrection from the dead of the individual as well. This sharp distinction arose in the nineteenth century within the Old Testament guild when a certain trajectory of the history of Israel's religious concepts was widely accepted as valid. Many now agree

that this scholarly distinction is quite irrelevant for understanding the function of the promise within the context of chapter 26. The point being made is that the ultimate status of the believing community of Israel, which lives at an intersection of two dispensations within God's economy, is not determined by the rules of the old age. The sign of the new is not that pain and misery cease, but that the promised life in God's kingdom extends even beyond the grave. For the first time clearly in the Old Testament we hear of God's light penetrating into the land of the shades (*r*^e*pā'îm*) (cf. Psalm 139). It is not by chance that in both Judaism and Christianity the belief in God's ultimate victory has incorporated as a cornerstone of faith a confession in the resurrection of the dead, which sustains the faithful who await the consummation of the age.

[20–21] The final two verses of chapter 26 contain a prophetic word of encouragement directed to "my people." The imagery returns to that of the Noachic covenant. The command is given to "enter your chambers," to "shut your doors" behind you (Gen. 7:16) and to hide "for a little while," until the wrath has passed. Again the assurance is given that God is indeed coming to execute punishment for the world's iniquity with its dreadful consequences. When the early church responded to the promise of Jesus, "Surely I am coming soon," with the affirmation, "Amen, come quickly Lord Jesus" (Rev. 22:20), it was sharing the selfsame stance of the Old Testament saints by living expectantly between promise and fulfillment.

28. Isaiah 27:1–13

27:1   In that day the LORD will punish
      with his hard, great, and fierce sword,
    Leviathan, the twisting serpent;
      he will slay the dragon of the sea.
2   In that day,
    a delightful[a] vineyard, sing of it!
3   I, the LORD, watch over it;
      I water it constantly.
    I guard it day and night
      that no harm will come to it.
4   I have no anger.[b]
    Would that I had thorns and thistles!
      I would do battle[c] against them;
    I would set them all on fire.
5   Or let them lay hold of my protection;
      let them make peace with me;
      let them make peace with me.

6 In days to come[d] Jacob will take root.
　　Israel will blossom and put forth shoots,
　　and fill all the world with fruit.
7 Was he beaten as his beaters have been?
　　Was he slaughtered in the same degree
　　as his slaughterers?[e]
8 Measure by measure[f] you contended with them
　　in sending them away.
　　He removed them with his fierce blast
　　in the day of the east wind.
9 Therefore by this the guilt of Jacob
　　will be atoned for,
　　and this will be the full fruit of
　　the removal of his sin:
　　when he makes all the altar stones
　　like chalkstones crushed to pieces,
　　no Asherah or incense altars
　　will be left standing.
10 For the fortified city stands desolate,
　　a dwelling abandoned and forsaken,
　　like the wilderness.
　　There a calf grazes, there it lies down
　　and strips its branches.
11 When its twigs become dry, they are broken off;
　　women come and make fires of them.
　　For this is a people without understanding;
　　therefore their Maker has no compassion
　　on them,
　　and their Creator shows them no favor.
12 In that day the LORD will thresh out [the peoples] from the flowing
　streams of the Euphrates to the wadi of Egypt, and you will be gathered,
　one by one, O you Israelites. 13 And in that day, a great horn will be
　sounded, and those who were lost in the land of Assyria and those who
　were scattered in the land of Egypt will come and worship the LORD on
　the holy mountain in Jerusalem.

a. Some manuscripts read *ḥmr* ("wine") instead of *ḥmd* ("delight"). Cf. Barthélemy, *CTLAT,* 188–92, for the evidence.

b. The NEB emends the MT to read "wine."

c. Most commentators, including Delitzsch, connect the phrase with the succeeding verse against the Hebrew accentuation.

d. The Hebrew text has been slightly emended (cf. *BHS*).

e. The Hebrew of v. 7 is very clumsy, calling forth many suggested improvements through repointing.

f. The Hebrew word $b^e sa'ss^e ah$ is unknown. Traditionally in the versions (except the LXX) it is taken as a contraction of *bis'āh* $s^{e'} \bar{a}h$ ("measure by measure"). However, many prefer to reconstruct a verbal form (e.g., NJPS "to assail"). Others find an Arabic cognate, *sa' sa'* ("to drive on with cries").

Selected Bibliography

J. Day, *God's Conflict with the Dragon and the Sea,* Cambridge 1985; **C. H. Gordon,** "Leviathan: Symbol of Evil," *Biblical Motifs: Origins and Transformations,* ed. A. Altmann, Cambridge, Mass., 1966, 1–9; **H. W. M. van Grol,** "Isaiah 27, 10–11: God and His Own People," *Studies in the Book of Isaiah, Fs W. A. M. Beuken,* ed. J. van Ruiten and M. Vervenne, Leiden 1997, 195–209; **H. Gunkel,** *Schöpfung und Chaos,* Göttingen 2 1921; **E. Jacob,** "Du premier au deuxième chant de la vigne du prophète Esaïe: Réflexions sur Esaïe 27, 2–5," *Wort-Gebot-Glaube: Beiträge zur Theologie des Alten Testaments, Fs W. Eichrodt,* ed. H.-J. Stoebe et al., Zürich 1970, 325–30; **D. G. Johnson,** *From Chaos to Restoration,* JSOTSup 61, Sheffield 1988, 85–96; **O. Kaiser,** *Die mythische Bedeutung des Meeres in Ägypten, Ugarit, und Israel,* BZAW 78, Berlin 2 1962; **O. Plöger,** *Theocracy and Eschatology,* ET Oxford 1968, 71–75; **E. Robertson,** "Isa. xxvii 2–6," *ZAW* 47, 1929, 197–206; **M. A. Sweeney,** "New Gleanings from an Old Vineyard: Isaiah 27 Reconsidered," *Early Jewish and Christian Exegesis: Studies in Memory of William Hugh Brownlee,* ed. C. A. Evans, W. F. Stinespring, Atlanta 1987, 51–66; *Isaiah 1–39,* FOTL 16, Grand Rapids 1996, 344–58; **J. Vermeylen,** *Du Prophète Isaïe à l'Apocalyptique,* I, Paris, 1977, 377–78; **M. K. Wakeman,** *God's Battle with the Monster,* Leiden 1973.

1. Structure, Genre, and Function

There is general agreement that the chapter divides into the following units: vv. 1; 2–5(6); 7–11; 12–13. The heart of the chapter lies in the reinterpretation of Isaiah 5, the "song of the vineyard." Usually it is thought that v. 6 offers the prophet's interpretation of the divine speech. Among the moderns only Wildberger attempts (unsuccessfully) to link v. 6 to the unit that follows. Verse 1 is a separate oracle that is joined thematically with the rest of the chapter (cf. below). Verses 12–13 conclude both chapter 27 and the larger corpus, chapters 24—27, on a note of promise and restoration of the people of Israel on Mount Zion.

The most controversial segment of the chapter remains vv. 7–11. The interpretation of these verses is made even more difficult by the uncertainty of the Hebrew text. The translation of v. 8 is tentative at best, but other problems remain, such as the interchange between masculine and singular suffixes, which continue to evoke confusion. A major difficulty, greatly affecting the interpretation, lies in determining a historical setting. Often it has been argued that the passage reflects a Northern Kingdom tradition and has a compositional history distinct from the rest of the chapter. Vermeylen (I, 37–38) argues that the writer was using earlier material in order to relate the fate of the former Northern

Kingdom and its capital in Samaria with God's reconciliation of Judah. Following this line of thought, the fortified city in v. 10 is identified with Samaria and the reference to a people without understanding (v. 11) refers to its inhabitants. The passage would be used redactionally to reflect the ongoing Jewish-Samaritan conflict and interpret etiologically why their ancestors were rejected by God. This elaborate hypothesis is overly speculative and hardly fits into the larger context of chapter 27.

Although it is unwise to be dogmatic about the interpretation of these difficult verses, it would seem prudent to take one's lead from the passage as a whole. There seems to be a definite coherence in the passage if these verses can be understood as a positive message to Judah. Sweeney proposes seeing the oracle as addressing Israel's defeatist attitude by means of a disputational genre. Although one can quibble about whether the passage can be rightly pressed into this mold, v. 7 does raise a highly existential question in response to the reinterpretation of the allegory (vv. 1–6). Has God really been just in his judgments? What follows is a legitimation of God's punishment in removing Israel's guilt as measured by restraint. Jacob's future is then contrasted with the fortified city, the symbol of arrogant human power. Its inhabitants have no discernment. God will show them no compassion.

In this reading there is a coherent movement that ends on the eschatological note of the forgiveness of God and the assembling of the scattered diaspora of the world to the sacred mountain as promised by Isaiah (2:2ff).

The larger interpretive question remaining concerns the intention of the editors in the shaping of this chapter within the corpus. Up to now, I have sought to present the view that these chapters are consistently construed with a didactic, even typological goal, namely, to admonish and instruct a community of faith living in the end time. This is to say, the setting is placed at the juncture between two dispensations within the economy of God. The Jewish community has experienced the catastrophic judgment of Babylon, the symbol of arrogant human power, but also the first fruits of a new age of God's divine rule. However, in spite of the reality of the new, much of the old continues. Chapters 25 and 26 wrestle with the theological question of situating temporally the people of God both before and after the judgment of God. The community that rejoices in its salvation in 25:6 finds itself in chapter 26 still waiting for God's presence and yearning for light. The chapter thus seeks to address the faithful in this confusing context on how to live between the times. The corpus of chapters 24–27 does not use a simple, unilinear scheme or offer a one-dimensional temporal sequence. Rather, the issue is approached from different angles in an effort to do full justice to the reality of God's continuing presence as promised.

Within the structure of chapter 27 one can discern a coherent line of thought setting forth God's encouragement to his people.

a. Verse 1 uses the language of myth to announce that in God's time he will destroy the reality of evil in all its ontological dimensions. He will destroy not only historical forms of evil, but strike against its cosmic source once and for all.

b. Verses 2–6 return to the divine judgment respecting Israel as God's special possession, and confirm that the divine decision has been reversed. Israel is no longer under God's wrath, but rather God's total protection. The nation will thrive and its fruits fill the whole world.

c. Verses 7–11 address the issue of Israel's guilt in relation to those nations now under God's judgment. Israel has been rightly punished in just measure, but full atonement awaits its obedient response. In contrast, those who oppress Israel, symbolized in the fortified city, are now desolate. Their people still are without understanding in spite of having experienced the just wrath of God.

d. Verses 12–13 confirm that in God's time Israel will be gathered and those lost and scattered will return to worship Yahweh on the holy mount of Zion.

In sum, chapter 27 establishes a sequence within God's purpose. It serves to interpret the past judgment and the future promise in the light of God's announcement of his renewed pledge of commitment and assurance of victory. It thus situates Israel's life within the period of living with the promise of being God's special vineyard. Yet Israel's full purification from its past guilt awaits its producing fruits of righteousness according to the laws of God.

It is important to note that chapter 27 does not set up an *ordo salutis,* but it is typically apocalyptic in starting with the final judgment and covers only the interval between the final eschatological collision between the old and the new, between Israel's being already saved but not yet. This theological intention also accounts for the inability of the interpreter to find one specific historical setting, since the focus consistently falls on a typology of God's eternal purpose for his people that transcends one single historical moment in Israel's experience.

2. Exposition

[27:1] The chapter is introduced with the eschatological formula "in that day," which is then repeated in vv. 2, 12, and 13 in order to bind together the diverse units. Verse 1 is a discrete unit, both in form and content, and separated from what precedes and follows. Yet its mythological reference to the slaying of the dragon, Leviathan, has an important function in the oracle. Long before the discovery of the Ugaritic texts in northern Syria, the ancient myth of Tiamat (or Rahab), the sea monster, was known in the creation traditions of Israel.

In his famous book, *Schöpfung und Chaos* (1921), Gunkel had worked out the mythological relation between *Urzeit* and *Endzeit*.

With the discoveries of the Ugaritic texts the larger Canaanite roots of the ancient Near Eastern myth became far clearer. It recounted the battle of Baal, lord of the earth, to conquer the sea god, Yam, Lotan, and the seven-headed dragon (cf. Kaiser, 74ff.). Although the myth has been thoroughly demythologized within the Old Testament, it continued to function as mythopoetic imagery in Ps. 74:14; 104:7ff.; Isa. 51:9; and Job 40:25. However, as is evident from Isaiah 27, the imagery still carries a residual intensity and serves to address the basic ontological problem of primordial evil. The apocalyptic promise of the new age of divine rule is signalled by the slaying of the dragon (cf. Rev. 12:1ff.).

[2–6] The next compositional unit forms the heart of the chapter and consists of a reinterpretation of the song of the vineyard (5;1–7). The new song is recounted in the first person as a divine speech, but is then given an interpretation by the prophet in v. 6. The original song of chapter 5 can best be classified as a parable (*māšāl*), but in chapter 27 it has been rendered into an allegory. Each component is picked up and assigned a new meaning.

Accordingly, instead of the garden being left on its own, now Yahweh is its keeper. Instead of its dying from drought, now God himself waters it constantly. Instead of thorns and thistles being a sign of punishment and neglect, now they have become symbols of Israel's enemies against whom God fights. Instead of the garden being filled with cries of oppression and bloodshed, now it is the focus of God's peace. Instead of a verdict of final judgment, now God has no wrath left toward his people. Thus Jacob is not a wasteland, but a plant taking root with blossoms filling the whole world (cf. the parallel imagery in Ps.80:9; Hos. 10:1; and 14:4ff.).

[7–11] The break in the continuity of thought caused by vv. 7–11 is both sharp and unexpected. A serious question is raised that appears to question the equality of justice meted out to Israel in comparison with the nations: "Was [Israel] beaten as his beaters have been? Was he slaughtered in the same degree as his slaughterers?" Sweeney understands this rhetorical question as part of a disputation that challenges Israel's defeatist attitude (*Isaiah 1–39*, 349). I tend to feel that the function of the oracle is didactic from the start by forcing a negative response to the query. The prophet raises the issue of God's purpose in his past acts of judgment by evoking the reflection of his addressees. Wherein lay the difference between God's handling of his people and the nations?

[8] Unfortunately, the text of v. 8 remains highly obscure. Probably the decision by Barthélemy to retain the traditional interpretation "measure by measure" still remains the best choice and has the support of most of the ancient versions (cf. textual notes). The larger point made in v. 8 appears fairly clear. God did punish Israel, whether "with restraint" or "by assailing them" (NJPS),

and he removed them from the land. The punishment served to atone for the guilt of Jacob, but Israel's full cleansing would occur only when it responded by removing the remaining signs of pagan worship. In contrast, the punishment of the nations is completely lacking in a pedagogical intent.

[10–11] The verses that follow remain controversial and the interpretation greatly depends on the larger construal adopted. For some commentators the description of the deserted, fortified city in v. 10 is a reference to Jerusalem, and a parallel is drawn to 1:7–9. Others identify the city with the destruction of Samaria and tie the interpretation to the continuing struggle in the Persian and Hellenistic periods between rival Jewish parties. However, neither of these interpretations develop adequately the theme raised at the beginning of the oracle in v. 7.

Only when one interprets vv. 10–11 as a contrast to vv. 7–9 does the movement within the passage become coherent. The solitary city remains a quintessential symbol of earthly power and oppression. In contrast to the divine punishment of Israel in the past, which was measured, disciplinary, and directed toward Israel's ultimate redemption, those inhabitants of the destroyed city remain a people without discernment who will experience no favor from God. In sum, there is no general, universal salvation celebrated in the Old Testament, but the option of rejecting the kingship of God remains a terrifying and real possibility.

[12–13] The oracle concludes with the same eschatological formula, "in that day," which is used to introduce both verses. Much like the conclusion of chapter 11, the goal of God's purpose is formulated in the promised ingathering of Israel from its dispersion among the lands of its conquerors. Little significance can be attached to the lack of any mention of Babylon. Nor can the fact of a Jewish diaspora provide any real historical specificity. The hope of the final return to Zion of all Israel, one by one, remains the enduring goal of every Jew in every generation whose identity is still shaped by the promises of scripture.

29. INTRODUCTION
TO ISAIAH 28—35

Selected Bibliography

H. Barth, *Die Jesaja-Worte in der Josiazeit,* WMANT 48, Neukirchen-Vluyn 1977; **J. C. Exum,** "Isaiah 28—32: A Literary Approach," *SBL 1979 Seminar Papers,* II, Missoula 1979, 123–51; **C. R. Seitz,** "A King Will Reign in Righteousness: Isaiah 28—39," *Isaiah 1—39,* IntBC Louisville 1993, 203–8; **J. Vermeylen,** *Du Prophète Isaïe à l'Apocalyptique,* I, Paris 1977, 383–438; **H. G. M. Williamson,** *The Book Called Isaiah,* Oxford 1994, 184–239.

The section comprising chapters 28—35 is bracketed by clearly structured collections both in the preceding (chapters 24—27) and following (chapters 36—39) instances. The highly controversial question arises of how to assess the role of these intervening chapters. Scholarly opinion diverges greatly in the overall evaluation.

Fortunately, there are some initial elements of agreement on which to build further. It is commonly recognized that chapters 28—33 are characterized in a formal sense by a series of woe oracles (28:1; 29:1; 29:15; 30:1; 31:1; 33:1). One can infer from this feature that at an earlier stage within the compositional history there was probably a collection of these similarly structured oracles. It is also evident from the initial unit (28:1–4) that the oracles date from a period before the fall of the Northern Kingdom and extend to those events in the reign of Hezekiah that climaxed with Sennacherib's attack in 701. Traditional interpreters drew the implication that the "authentic" oracles of the eighth-century prophet thus comprised two main collections of oracles, the earlier in chapters 2—11 focusing on the Syro-Ephraimite war, the later in chapters 28—33 on events leading up to the Assyrian invasion of 701.

The modern interest in the redactional history of the formation of the book of Isaiah as a whole has resulted in a host of new questions being raised about the function of these chapters. Thus, Sweeney's analysis (*Isaiah 1—39,* 353ff.), building on the earlier analysis of H. Barth, seeks to sketch a history of the section's redactional growth that follows his familiar three-stage trajectory. He sees an eighth-century layer of genuine Isaianic oracles receiving a seventh-century Josianic redaction that served to highlight the emergence of a royal savior. The final shaping in a fifth-century edition largely affirmed the intention of the Josianic redaction. As I have indicated before, I find this method of simply juxtaposing three reconstructed layers from different ages inadequate as an interpretive solution because it does not address the effect of this shaping on the text as a whole. One is left only with fragments arranged in a historical sequence.

A very different solution has been developed recently by Williamson (184ff.), who has built upon some earlier reflections by Vermeylen. He suggests that the corpus of chapters 28—31, which lacks any superscription, was not intended to provide a new section but was a continuation of the oracles against the nations in chapters 13—23. The continuity between the chapters had been broken by the later interpolation of chapters 24—27. Whatever merit this hypothesis might have, it is built on a diachronic reconstruction that does not reckon with the present synchronic function of chapters 28—33. In the final form of the book it is difficult to regard the theory as illuminating, since in both its form and context chapters 28—33 certainly function in striking contrast to chapters 13—23.

Even greater controversy over these chapters turns on how one understands the role of chapters 32—35. These issues will be addressed below in the individual chapters. While I do not question the legitimacy of attempting to recover the history of the growth of the Isaianic corpus as a whole, much of the recent research remains futile, in my judgment, when it assigns the key to the interpretation to various theoretical reconstructions. The crucial exegetical question remains, regardless of how deeply one probes behind the present text, whether one can in the end discern any element of coherence in the rendering of the chapters in their final form.

From my perspective on chapters 28—32, I do not rule out the likelihood that unintentional, fortuitous factors to which the interpreter has no access may have contributed to the assembly and positioning of these chapters. In a word, I do not believe that every structural division stems from an editorial decision. Rather, I would argue that what one can determine is the manner in which these chapters, however originally collected, have been shaped into a larger didactic composition. These chapters at least now stand at some distance removed from an oral stage of the tradition. The large amount of wisdom material points to a lengthy reflective process in which the chapters were shaped toward a holistic reading of earlier Isaianic material. The canonical force of an accumulated corpus of authoritative tradition sought to show how the earlier prophecies were fulfilled in the events preceding Assyria's attack on Jerusalem. In the context of the narrative sequence of chapters 28—32, Isaianic oracles were reused to reinterpret the events of Hezekiah's reign. The influence of chapters 36—39 was then retrojected back to chapters 28—32. The editors of these chapters constantly employed techniques of intertextual referencing to offer a vision of a righteous ruler of chapter 32, set in contrast to the chaotic governance of chapter 3. I will also argue that chapters 34—35 further this holistic reading by setting up a resonance with major themes taken from both before and after these chapters.

30. Isaiah 28:1–29

28:1 Woe to the proud crown of the drunkards of Ephraim,
    and to the fading flowers of his glorious beauty,
  set on the head of a fertile valley
    of those overcome by wine.
2 See, the Lord has one at his bidding
    who is powerful and strong,
    like a hailstorm, a destructive tempest,
  like a storm of massive overflowing waters,
    he will hurl it forcefully to the ground.
3 That crown, the pride of Ephraim's drunkards,
    will be trampled underfoot.
4 And the fading flower of his glorious beauty,
    set on the head of the fertile valley,
  will be like an early fig before the summer harvest;
    whoever sees it devours it
    as soon as it is in his hand.
5 In that day the LORD of hosts will become
    a crown of glory,
    and a diadem of beauty for the remnant
    of his people,
6 and a spirit of justice to him who sits in
    judgment,
  and strength for those who turn back the battle
    at the gate.
7 But these also stagger from wine
    and reel from liquor.
  Priest and prophet stagger from liquor.
    They are confused from wine;
    they are dazed by strong drink.
  They are muddled in their visions;
    they stumble when rendering judgments.
8 For all the tables are covered with vomit,
    and there is not a space without filth.

9   "Who is he trying to teach?
          To whom is he explaining his message?
      To children weaned from their milk,
          those just taken from the breast?
10   That same senseless refrain,ᵃ over and over,
          now here, now there!"
11   Very well then, with foreign lips and alien tongue
          the Lord will speak to this people,
12   to whom he had said,
          "This is the resting place, let the weary rest;
      this is the place of repose."
          But they refused to listen.
13   So then the word of the LORD will be to them
          that same senseless refrain, over and over,
          now here, now there,
      so that they will go and fall backward
          and be broken, and snared, and captured.
14   Therefore hear the word of the LORD, you scoffers,
          who rule this people in Jerusalem.
15   Because you boast,
      "We have made a covenant with death,
          and concluded a pact with Sheol.
      When the overwhelming scourge sweeps by,
          it will not reach us;
      for we have made lies our refuge,
          and falsehood our shelter."
16   Therefore, thus says the Lord GOD,
      "Behold, I am laying in Zion a stone,
          a massive stone, a precious cornerstone of sure foundation,ᵇ
          the one who trusts shall not waver.
17   And I will make justice the measuring line
          and righteousness the plumb line.
      Hail will sweep away the refuge of lies,
          and the waters will overflow your shelter."
18   Then your covenant with death will be annulled,
          your pact with Sheol will not stand.
      When the overwhelming scourge sweeps by,
          you will be beaten down by it.
19   Every time it passes through
          it will catch you.
      It will pass through morning after morning,
          day and night,

and it will be sheer terror to understand
    the message.
20   The bed is too short for stretching out,
    and the blanket too narrow for wrapping up.
21   For the LORD will rise up as he did on
    Mount Perazim;
   he will rise up as in the Valley of Gibeon
    to do his work—strange is his work!
   And to perform his task—alien is his task!
22   Therefore do not scoff,
    lest your bonds be tightened;
   for I have heard a decree of destruction
    from the Lord GOD of hosts against the whole land.
23   Listen and hear my voice,
    pay attention and hear what I have to say.
24   When a farmer plows for planting,
    does he plow all the time?
   Does he keep on breaking up
    and harrowing the soil?
25   When he has leveled the surface,
    does he not sow caraway and
    scatter cummin?
   Does he not plant wheat in a row,
    barley in a strip,
    and spelt in a patch?
26   For God instructs him
    and teaches him the right way.
27   So too, caraway is not threshed with a sledge,
    nor is a cartwheel rolled over cummin,
   but caraway is beaten out with a stick,
    and cummin with a rod.
28   Grain must be ground for bread,
    so one does not keep threshing it.
   Even if he drives the wheels of his cart over it,
    his horses do not crush it.
29   All this is ordered by the LORD of hosts.
    His counsel is wonderful,
    his wisdom marvelous.

a. The Hebrew *ṣaw lāṣāw ṣaw lāṣāw* is thought to be either senseless gibberish or the sound of children reciting the alphabet.
   b. Cf. the exposition for a discussion of the architectural terminology.

Selected Bibliography

W. A. M. Beuken, "Isaiah 28: Is It Only Schismatics That Drink Heavily? Beyond the Synchronic versus Diachronic Controversy," *Synchronic or Diachronic?, OTS* 34, 1995, 15–38; **J. C. Exum,** "A Literary Approach to Isaiah 28," *SBL 1979 Seminar Papers,* 2, Missoula 1979, 123–51; **J. J. Jackson,** "Style in Isaiah 28 and a Drinking Bout of the Gods (RS 24.258)," *Rhetorical Criticism, Fs James Mulenburg,* ed. J. J. Jackson and M. Kessler, Pittsburgh 1974, 85–98; **L. Köhler,** "Zwei Fachwörter des Bausprache in Jesaja 28, 16," *TZ* 3, 1947, 390–93; **J. Lindblom,** "Der Eckstein in Jes. 28, 16," *Interpretationes ad Vetus Testamentum Pertinentes Sigmundo Mowinckel,* Oslo 1955, 123–32; **D. L. Petersen,** "Isaiah 28, a Redaction Critical Study," *SBL 1979 Seminar Papers,* 2, Missoula 1979, 101–22; **J. J. M. Roberts,** "Yahweh's Foundation in Zion (Isa. 28:16)," *JBL* 106, 1987, 27–45; **A. van Selms,** "Isaiah 28:9–13: An Attempt to Give a New Interpretation," *ZAW* 85, 1973, 332–39; **J. W. Whedbee,** *Isaiah and Wisdom,* Nashville 1971, 53–55.

1. Form and Function

The major exegetical task turns on determining the thematic coherence of this whole passage, which has been carefully crafted together into a unity. This task, however, is dependent on decisions regarding the history of composition that emerge from form-critical, redactional, and literary analysis. Four distinct units (vv. 1–6; 7–13; 14–22; and 23–29) have been linked together through a lengthy history of development. Crucial to this process has been the reuse of Isaianic material, largely from texts of an earlier corpus, to provide an important intertextual relationship.

A basic hermeneutical issue centers on how one evaluates the high level of symbolic language of the chapter. J. C. Exum (1979) offers an illuminating analysis of the interaction of metaphors and similes within the passage, but her study remains largely on the literary level. D. Petersen (1979) adds an important redactional analysis and attempts to trace the growth of the different strata with an eye on how the parts were secondarily rendered into a whole. He has made an important contribution in showing the extent to which earlier Isaianic texts have been taken up and reinterpreted within the new composition. However, in my judgment, more attention still needs to be paid to the theological forces exerted by a growing corpus of authoritative Isaianic material that increasingly shaped the presentation of the prophetic message into a canonical whole.

2. Exposition

[28:1–6] The unit opens with the conventional ejaculation of the woe oracle (*hôy*). The form is familiar from chapter 5 when a series of invectives was directed against the leaders of Judah. Although there is a formal parallel, there are important differences in usage. First, 28:1 serves to introduce a new collection of passages within the book following the oracles of the nations in chapters 13–23 (24–27). Isaiah 28:1, 29:1, 29:15, 30:1, 31:1, and 33:1 all begin with a woe marker. This fact would seem to confirm the hypothesis that the ejaculation stems from a conscious redactional strategy rather than its only being an original component of the oral tradition. Second, this initial passage is filled with allusive symbolic references, and as a closely honed literary composition is somewhat distant from the direct confrontational style of Amos or the earlier oracles of Isaiah.

The oracle begins with a denunciation of the proud crown of the drunkards of Ephraim. It comes as no surprise that drunkenness, especially among the rulers, is sharply criticized by the prophet (cf. 5:22). Rather, what is unexpected is a transition in the form of a double-entendre from the drunkards of Ephraim to the crown at the head of the rich valley, namely, the city of Samaria. The fading flowers in the garland of the drunkards is thus carried over as a suitable metaphor for the decadence of the capital. From the verses that then follow it is clear that the main thrust of the invective is directed against Samaria. The metaphorical shift from the drunkards to the senseless folly of the city functions well since both are represented as losing a once glorious beauty. The reference to Samaria as the head of Ephraim had already been given in 7:9, which foretold its inevitable destruction. Similarly, the imagery of the overflowing waters is closely related to the threat of 8:7 symbolizing Assyria. The veiled reference to the crown in v. 1 is then picked up and expanded in v. 3. Samaria with its fading glory at the head of the fertile valley in Galilee will be trodden underfoot and, in a shift of imagery, will be suddenly devoured like a tasty morsel.

Verses 5–6 introduce a new perspective to the passage. The familiar eschatological formula "in that day" establishes a different context from the previous judgment oracle directed to Samaria. At the same time, the continuity with vv. 1–4 is made certain by the explicit use in v. 5 of the crown imagery of vv. 1 and 3. In direct contrast to the "fading flower of its glorious beauty," now the picture is of the Lord of hosts becoming a "crown of glory, and a diadem of beauty" to the faithful remnant. Equally important, this eschatological promise to the people of God is further developed into a positive note by an intertextual reference to 4:2–4. Verse 5 repeats the "beauty" ($s^eb\hat{i}$) and "glory" of 4:2, which is promised to the remnant, namely, the "survivors of Israel" in 4:2. Moreover, only in 4:4 is there reference to the "spirit of justice" found in 28:6.

Usually within a redactional-critical analysis the interest in intertextual references falls on determining from such exegetical techniques and from literary seams the age of the editorial commentary. Verses 5–6 are thus judged to be extremely late additions because of dependency on equally late passages such as 4:2ff. Further evidence confirming this assessment is found in the intrusive nature of vv. 5–6, which appears to separate an original catchword connection between vv. 4 and 7. Although I do not deny that the attempt to track a temporal sequence within redactional layering can at times be exegetically significant,

in most cases the recovery of the history of a text's composition is less important exegetically than the effect of the shaping on the interpreted whole.

What then is the theological significance of the carefully structured oracle of
vv. 1–4 along with its eschatological reinterpretation in vv. 5–6? Recognition of
the redactional shaping of this first unit offers strong evidence for the concern
of the tradents of the Isaianic material that the prophetic voice in this new collection of oracles follows in close continuity with the Isaianic message that preceded. The oracle in vv. 1–4 serves to introduce a new corpus of oracles that are
largely set at a subsequent period in Judah's history after the Syro-Ephraimite
crisis and that led ultimately to the Assyrian attack on Jerusalem in 701. The initial oracle in chapter 28 begins with judgment on the Northern Kingdom and
summarizes the prophetic warning to the proud leaders of Ephraim before it
draws the analogy between Israel's destruction and Judah's. An essential note
in this new collection of oracles (chapters 28–32) focuses on the foolishness of
trusting in alliances with foreign nations when only in God's wisdom and purpose is there true salvation. Thus the warning of divine judgment now directed
to Judah and to Hezekiah is described most often in the wisdom terminology of
folly and stupidity, a theme already sounded in the book's prologue (1:2–3).

Equally important is the prophetic word of assurance that God has provided
a hopeful future for a faithful remnant also depicted in the language of wisdom.
It is therefore not by accident that the scribal editors portray this word of hope
with explicit references to other texts of promise from an earlier written collection (4:2–4). This intertextual reference thus prepares the way for the two
major themes of judgment and salvation of the remnant that resonate throughout chapter 28.

If one seeks to dissect these redactional references diachronically, assigning
some to earlier and others to later literary strata, the result is often to destroy
the holistic rendering that the final shaping seeks to impart. The hermeneutical
point to stress is that the redactional technique of literary intertextuality only
functions when the resonances are left unimpaired by linear diachronic
restraints, and when two different texts mutually interpret each other within a
canonical whole. Critical discovery of the seam in v. 5 sensitizes the reader to
the holistic intent of the editor. It does not serve as a warrant for reassigning the
unit to another level of interpretation governed by a reconstructed history of
composition.

[7–13] Verse 7 appears to be an editor's shaping of the succeeding independent oracle in order to link it consciously with the threat against the drunkards of Ephraim. The clear intention is to draw an analogy between the behavior
and ensuing fate of the Northern Kingdom and that of present Judah. What then
follows in the oracle seems to be a genuine confrontation between Isaiah and
drunken officials, prophets and priests, which erupts in a verbal exchange. It is
also quite clear that the report of the confrontation in vv. 7ff. indicates some lit-

erary distance from the actual historical encounter and does not reflect the direct immediacy of, say, Amos with Amaziah in Amos 7:10ff. One notices the third person pronouns in vv. 12–14 in contrast to the second person usage in Amos.

More recently, both Petersen and Exum have defended a reading of Yahweh as the intended subject of v. 9, but this suggested interpretation results in construing v. 9 as a rhetorical question by the prophet, which seems strained. The description of a drunken orgy in vv. 7–8 sets a highly realistic background for the abusive and incoherent retort of Isaiah's adversaries. "Who does he think we are to require his instruction? Are we merely children? All we ever hear from the prophet is the same tired old gibberish: *ṣaw laṣāw ṣaw lāṣāw!*" Much scholarly energy has been expended in an effort to explain the scene of debauchery. Was it a particular cultic festival, or a mantic technique carried to extremes? A resolution of this issue is of little consequence in understanding the scene's function within the present narrative. Within chapter 28 both groups of senseless inebriates—regardless of how they reached that condition—fail to discern in their stupidity the impending divine judgment sounded in the prophetic word. Similarly, not much is gained by supposing that the gibberish is derived from an imitation of children reciting the alphabet.

What is important in this gibberish used to mock the prophet is his ironical response. To a people who refused to hear the divine offer of salvation (v. 12; cf. 30:15), the word of God will be turned into gibberish for them, and from the lips of alien conquerors they will hear the same incomprehensible nonsense: *ṣaw lāṣāw ṣaw lāṣāw!* The editor of the oracle then concludes the unit by offering an intertextual commentary from 8:15: "they shall fall and be broken; they shall be snared and taken." The two passages are linked by a similar response of rejection of the prophetic message. In both instances the divine promise is turned into judgment from a fearful God whom they refuse to comprehend.

[14–22] This oracle is the most complex unit within the chapter. It consists of elements of a classic judgment oracle with a call to attention, the grounds for the verdict, and the ensuing execution of the sentence (vv. 14–15, 17b–19). To this is joined several additional verses of commentary (vv. 20–22). The most difficult form-critical task lies in assessing the oracle of promise found in vv. 16–17a. From the perspective of classic form-critical analysis there can be little doubt but that the oracle of promise reflects all the elements of a separate oracle originally distinct from the invective-threat, which brackets it on both sides. Nevertheless, it is equally clear that the larger editorial shaping of this chapter has combined these two oracles into an organic unity. As a result, the same dialectic between the judgment of the drunkards of Ephraim (vv. 1–4) and the promise of glory and beauty to the remnant (vv. 5–6) is continued and expanded in vv. 16–17a.

The oracle opens with a word of judgment directed again to the scoffers of Jerusalem, but now identified specifically with the leaders of the people. The grounding of the threat is made by the familiar technique of quoting from the accusers' own words, but here obviously their words have been rendered as a caricature of their proud self-confidence. It is possible that the "covenant with death" and "pact with Sheol" are caustic references to an alliance with Egypt and its chthonian gods, but the prophetic intent is clear apart from a reconstructed historical reference. The leaders' well-calculated plans for protection through clever machinations are the height of folly and will shortly be swept away in sheer terror.

However, embedded in the prophetic invective-threat is a promise, which is introduced as a direct speech of Yahweh (v. 16). Three smaller problems of interpretation have engaged scholars regarding this verse. The first turns on the text and grammar of the verb, the second on the exact meaning of the architectural imagery, and the third respecting the role of the appeal to faith. Of course, the resolution of the central problem regarding the meaning of the foundation stone in the context of the chapter is only affected in part by one's decision on these other issues.

The first problem turns on the form of the verb *yissad* ("to lay a foundation"). The MT points the verb as a piel perfect, preceded by a particle *hinnî*. This construction is grammatically possible, but extremely rare. It would be translated: "Behold, I am the one who laid a stone for a foundation." However, normally the *hinnēh* particle would call for a participle that is found in Qumran texts (1QIs^a=*mysd*; 1QIs^b=*ywsd*). Similarly, the Targum and various Greek translations support the participle. The participle form is to be preferred. Still an interesting question remains as to the relationship of v. 16 with 14:32, which offers the closest parallel to the MT pointing of v. 16.

The second problem involves the interpretation of several obscure architectural terms in the verse. There have been several philological attempts to understand *bōḥan* as an Egyptian loanword designating a particular hard stone (schist gneiss) used for statues and buildings. While such an interpretation is not impossible, it still remains conjectural. The most recent discussion by Roberts (29ff.) has made a stronger case for another Egyptian loanword meaning "fortress." He has offered support in the Qumran literature from several passages dependent on 28:16. The emphasis on the solidarity of the structure as a fortress fits very well with the rest of v. 16. One might have thought that the noun *bōḥan*, even if originally a Egyptian loanword, had been heard as a form of the Hebrew verb *bḥn* ("to test"), but this suggestion finds no support from the Greek or Latin versions. Of particular interest is the Targum's messianic interpretation, which lays its stress on the strength of the future king: "I am about to appoint in Zion a king, a strong king, powerful and terrible." Obviously other intertextual factors are involved in this rendering other than philology.

The third problem relates to the translation of the final colon. The verb *'mn* (hiphil) means to trust or to believe in what someone says (cf. 2 Chron. 20:20).

More controversial is the interpretation of the second verb, *yḥyš*, which is usually rendered "to be in haste." It is likely that this verb modifies the believer rather than the foundation with a meaning such as, "to be alarmed," "to depart in fear." The suggestion has been made that this final half-line would be viewed as an inscription written on the foundation stone itself according to a common ancient Near Eastern practice. While certainly possible, there is no strong internal evidence for this attempt at a further sharpening of the text. More significant are the intertextual references from 7:9 (cf. 8:11ff.), which offer a positive reformulation of an earlier oracle.

The difficult and larger question remains in understanding the theological significance of the stone that God is laying in Zion. The interpretive proposals are numerous and extend from a reference to the temple, to Zion, to the Davidic monarchy, to the remnant, or to faith itself (cf. Oswalt, *Book of Isaiah*, 1:518). Certainly it is inadequate to see in the promise a reference to the founding of the temple or to the securing of the Davidic dynasty. Rather, God is in the process of laying a new foundation stone that is unmovable before the overwhelming scourge of coming judgment. The stone is not faith itself, which remains the means offered for establishing oneself on the promised rock of salvation.

The key to the meaning of the verse lies in the larger context, not only of chapter 28, but of the book as a whole, which provides the content of the imagery. Isaiah 1:26 had first spoken of a restored city, a city of righteousness, and this note of justice and righteousness immediately follows in v. 17 as a continuing commentary on the building metaphors of v. 16. Chapters 7 and 8 had challenged King Ahaz to establish himself in faith on God's promise to the house of David that he had rejected. But a sign had been given to a remnant who believed and who clung to the promise in the midst of overflowing judgment (8:8, 10). The same theme of God's presence bringing both judgment for unbelief and salvation for faith is pictured again in 8:14–15 with God as a sanctuary and also a stone of offense on which many "will be snared and caught" (cf. 28:13).

As we have seen, this same dialectic has shaped vv. 1–4 and 5–6 in chapter 28. Moreover, the remnant in v. 5 has been linked with the pride and glory of the survivors in 4:2–4. The remnant in these chapters is not just a future promise, but a concrete reality that has already emerged as a new creation through faith during the period of Israel's judgment.

The effect of this intertextual interaction of passages is that the initially ambiguous foundation stone of 28:16 serves as a metaphor unifying central themes that have been nuanced in different ways throughout the book (cf. the discussion in chapter 11). The symbolism of the stone encompasses the reality of the new community, a faithful remnant, which is a foretaste of the coming righteous reign of God and which is ushered in by the promised messianic rule of Zion. Within this organic whole various aspects of the promise have been highlighted in a variety of ways in different texts. Isaiah 14:32 spoke of Zion as having been established in the past as a refuge for the remnant, whereas 28:16 envisions the establishment in Zion of a sure foundation, which extends into the future. At times the stone is a pledge of security for faith; at other times it is a rock of stumbling for unbelief (8:11ff.). Some texts of the corpus lay emphasis on the remnant as a creation of God, others on the remnant as a sign of the eschatological community. The error of earlier interpreters has been in trying to isolate only one feature from within this larger whole without adequate attention to the dynamic interplay of texts that together comprise the truth of the prophetic proclamation.

The oracle closes with several sentences of commentary that portray the inability of Judah to confront the full dimensions of the impending disaster. The bed is too short and the covering too scant to allow any comfort. Then the oracle returns to the earlier demonstrations of divine power when God had destroyed Israel's enemies on Mount Perazim and in the valley of Gibeon with hail and water. However, now God arises against his own people to execute his terrifying plan. Strange and alien is this plan, incomprehensible to a people who consider themselves wise. Therefore, do not scoff; the end has been decreed.

[23–29] The final oracle has long been recognized as a wisdom unit that strives to draw a sapiential lesson from the carefully ordered activities of a farmer, both in preparing the soil for planting and in reaping the benefits when the crop is ready for harvesting. There has been considerable debate on the exact nature of this wisdom genre. Should it be described as a parable (*māšhāl*), and does it arise from a disputational setting?

The oracle describes the succession of carefully executed activities by the farmer to prepare the ground for sowing his seed. The soil is ripped open by the plow. Then the large clods of soil are broken up and the surface leveled. The seed is placed in a carefully planned order with the wheat in rows in the middle, and the less valuable spelt assigned to the borders. This wisdom in agricultural skills is then attributed to God, who in Hebrew tradition is the source of all true knowledge. The implied lesson is that the striking changes in the way in which the soil is handled—ripped open, broken up, leveled—is not at all inconsistent, but belongs to a larger agricultural plan. Then a similar description of the variety of activities is portrayed as the farmer gathers in the harvest. Each crop calls for special handling. Dill is not threshed with a threshing sled, but beaten out with a stick. Similarly, one does not drive a cart over wheat intended for bread. Again the point is made that each crop calls for a different handling, but all according to a purpose. Verse 29 summarizes the lesson of the analogy. All this comes from Yahweh of hosts who is wise and deliberate.

An issue of critical debate is whether the prophet is here defending the coherence of his message against accusations from his opponents that he has altered his message. Some wish to relate his defense to an alleged shift in his political attitude toward the security of Jerusalem before Assyrian attack. However, this interpretation is influenced far too much by modern scholarly theories and does not arise from the text itself. Others see the prophet's defense of his message as a further extension of his earlier confrontation with the scoffers of vv. 7ff.

In my judgment, the analogy being drawn does not focus on the prophet and on the alleged inconsistencies of his preaching, but is thoroughly theocentric. The transition is made in v. 21: "the LORD will rise up . . . to do his work." Strange and alien is this work. Yet the final oracle makes clear that even as the farmer's activity seems strange and incoherent as he first tears open the ground before sowing his seed, so also Yahweh's apparently violent acts of judgment also follow a wise purpose. In his own time and according to his own counsel he will also bring forth suitable fruits from his creation (cf. 4:1). Because of this vision of the new eschatological reality lying behind all of the divine action, the editors of the book have continually projected this hope into every part of the book and allowed its different portrayals to resonate harmoniously in spite of the very great span of time that is reflected in the literary composition of the Isaianic corpus.

31. Isaiah 29:1–24

29:1   Woe, Ariel, Ariel,
      city where David camped.
  Add year to year;
      let your cycle of feasts continue.
2   And I will afflict Ariel,
      and there will be moaning and sighing,
      and she shall be to me like Ariel—a fiery altar.
3   And I will camp against you all around.
      I will encircle you with assault towers,
      and set up siege works against you.
4   Then from out of the ground you will speak
      from low in the dust your words will come.
  Your voice will sound from the ground like a ghost's.
      Out of the dust your voice will chirp.
5   Like fine dust will be the multitude of your enemies,[a]
      and like flying chaff the multitude of the ruthless.
  Then suddenly, in an instant,
6   you will be visited by the LORD of hosts
  with thunder and earthquake and great noise,
      with windstorm and tempest and the flames of fire.

7   Then the multitude of nations
         that fight against Ariel,
     all her attackers and the siege works against her,
         and those who afflict her,
     will be like a dream,
         a vision in the night.
8   It is like one who is hungry
         and dreams he is eating,
         but he awakens to find he is still hungry.
     Or when a thirsty man dreams he is drinking,
         but awakens faint and still parched.
     So will be all the multitudes of nations
         that fight against Mount Zion.
9   Act stupidly and be stupified!
         Act blindly and be blinded!
     Be drunk, but not from wine;
         stagger, but not from liquor.
10   For the LORD has spread over you
         a spirit of deep sleep,
     and has shut your eyes, the prophets,
         and covered your heads, and seers.
11   For all prophecy has become for you like the words of a sealed
     document. If it is given to one who can read and he is asked to read it,
     he will say, "I cannot because it is sealed." 12 And if the document is
     given to one who cannot read and he is asked to read it, he will say, "I
     cannot read."
13   And the Lord said:
     "Because these people come near to me
         with their mouth,
         and honor me only with their lips,
         but their hearts are far from me,
     and their worship of me has been
         rules of men learned by rote;
14   therefore I will again do marvelous things
         with this people,
         wonderful and marvelous;
     and the wisdom of its wise will vanish,
         the discernment of the discerning will be lost."
15   Woe to those who go to depths
         to hide their plans from the LORD,
         who do their work in dark places
         and say, "Who sees us, who will know?"
16   How perverse of you!

Should the potter be regarded as the clay?
should the thing made say of its maker,
"He did not make me,"
and that formed say of him who formed it,
"He does not understand anything."

17 Is it not in a little while,
Lebanon will be transformed into a fertile field,
and the fertile field seem like a forest?

18 In that day the deaf will hear
the words of a scroll,
and out of gloom and darkness,
the eyes of the blind will see.

19 Once more the humble will rejoice
in the LORD,
and the needy will exalt
in the Holy One of Israel.

20 For the ruthless will vanish,
and the scoffer disappear,
and those who wait for evil
will be cut down,

21 those who make a man out to be guilty with a word,
who lay a trap for the defender in court,
and with false testimony deprive
the innocent of justice.

22 Therefore, thus says the LORD who redeemed Abraham,
concerning the house of Jacob:[b]
"No more will Jacob be humiliated;
no longer will their faces grow pale.

23 For when he sees among them his children,
the work of my hands,
they will sanctify my name,
they will sanctify the Holy One of Jacob,
and stand in awe of the God of Israel.

24 And those who err in spirit will
come to understanding,
and those who murmur will accept instruction."

a. The MT reads "strangers."
b. Emendation reads "YHWH, God of the house of Jacob." (cf. *BHS*).

Selected Bibliography

B. A. Asen, "The Garlands of Ephraim: Isaiah 28, 1–6 and the *Marzēaḥ*," *JSOT* 71, 1996, 73–87;
W. A. M. Beuken, "Isa. 29, 15–24: Perversion Reverted," *The Scriptures and the Scrolls, Fs A. S. Van*

der Woude, ed. Garcia Martínez et al., *VTSup* 49, 1992, 43–64; **J. C. Exum,** "Of Broken Pots, Fluttering Birds and Visions in the Night: Extended Simile and Poetic Techniques in Isaiah," *CBQ* 43, 1981, 331–52; **S. Feigin,** "The Meaning of Ariel," *JBL* 39, 1920, 131–37; **L. Laberge,** "The Woe-Oracles of Isaiah 28 — 33," *EgTh* 13, 1982, 157–90; **M. Pope,** "A Divine Banquet at Ugarit," *The Use of the Old Testament in the New and Other Essays. Studies in Honor of W. F. Stinespring,* ed. J. N. Efrid, Durham 1972, 170–203; **M. A. Sweeney,** *Isaiah 1–39,* FOTL 16, Grand Rapids 1996, 373–86; **J. Werlitz,** *Studien zur literaturkritischen Methode. Gericht und Heil in Jesaja 7, 1–17 und 29, 1–8,* BZAW 204, Berlin 1992.

The oracle is made up of different individual units that have been editorially shaped to form a unified passage. The chapter continues the theme of chapter 28, namely, the strangeness of God's plan with Israel and the inability of a stupified and hardened people to comprehend it.

1. Structure and Movement

The passage divides into three larger units: vv. 1–8; 9–14; 15–24. Each unit shows signs of literary tension and editorial expansion, which will be analyzed in detail below. On the synchronic level there is a clear movement rendering the unit into a literarily coherent whole. Verses 1–8 depict the strangeness of God's work, which first lays siege to Jerusalem and humiliates its inhabitants with great distress. Suddenly without motivation there is a reversal and the divine judgment falls on the hordes who are attacking the city. Verses 9–12 pick up the theme of the blindness and stupor of the inhabitants who are unable to comprehend what is happening. Verses 15–24 return to the theme of the failure of the leaders of Judah to comprehend God's purpose as they engage in their own secretive plans for political survival. This portrayal of utter ignorance then forms the background for a radical transition in vv. 17ff. as God intervenes to transform both the darkness of the corrupted world and the folly of its inhabitants, the house of Jacob.

2. The Redactional Shaping of the Chapter

The narrative setting of the chapter seems quite clear. The theme of the inability of Judah to comprehend God's strange plan is continued from the previous chapter. Chapter 29 begins with God's initiating an attack on Jerusalem in order to cause Ariel great distress, but then suddenly shifting to the city's deliverance. This narrative setting presupposes Assyria's continuing threat against Judah and leads up to the failure of Sennacherib to conquer the city (chapters 36—37).

However, the real hermeneutical problem of the chapter first arises when the history of composition is broached. There are a variety of tensions in the text that are unexplained if the interpreter simply remains on the synchronic, literary level. First, there are striking duplications within the unit of vv. 1–8 that seem to go beyond merely a stylistic feature (cf. 4a // 4b; 7 // 8), but appear more like secondary reworking and expansion. Second, it is difficult to determine whether v. 5 is part of the description of the initial attack on the city or whether it belongs to the beginning of the divine deliverance. Third, what is the form and function of vv. 1–8? It is most infrequent in Isaiah for oracles of judgment and salvation to be organically joined on the earliest oral level. Fourth, the language and imagery of vv. 17ff. reflect elements most common in Second and Third Isaiah. Similarly, vv. 7–8 appear to share a *post factum* influence from the events of 701. Does this mean that behind the synchronic literary coherence of the chapter there is a complex, diachronic dimension that reflects a lengthy history of composition extending into the postexilic age that is radically at odds with the present literary narrative?

The usual way of resolving these problems is to revert to a redactional-critical hypothesis (cf. Vermeylen, Clements). Accordingly, vv. 1–4 represent the primary level of the text and originally functioned as a judgment oracle. Then at a subsequent date—whether in the seventh, sixth, or fifth century is debated—a redactor reinterpreted the original intent by transforming it into an oracle of promise. Next, at an even later postexilic period another redactor spelled out a description of the divine reversal in the apocalyptic language of Second and Third Isaiah (vv. 17ff.). These later expansions were retrojected back onto a core of Isaianic tradition to form a seemingly coherent literary narrative. However, it is generally assumed that the text's real meaning is only recovered by assigning each text to its properly reconstructed-redactional age (Vermeylen, 401ff.). As a result, the narrative framework of Isaiah's prophecy is generally interpreted as a late construct that reflects in its final form largely the ideology of the latest redactors (cf. Sweeney, 383f.).

In response I would argue for a very different understanding of the growth of the Isaianic corpus. The complexity of the problem of relating oracles of judgment and oracles of promise has already been seen in chapters 1 — 12. The two components of the prophet's message were simply juxtaposed, often within a brittle context without a smooth literary relationship (e.g., 2:1–5, 6ff.). Yet there is no compelling evidence to suggest that only the message of judgment was primary and that the element of promise was always secondary from a later redaction. Rather, in chapters 1 — 12 the form and function of the oracles in their traditionally oral state were a major force in determining the larger shape of the textualized, literary composition, which developed as the individual oracles were collected. At the same time there emerged clear components within the larger narrative framework of the prophet's proclamation, namely, God's plan for Israel's judgment, signs of a promised faithful remnant, and the ultimate destruction of Assyria. Moreover, these elements continued to be repeated and reinforced throughout chapters 1 — 12 within a constantly recurring pattern even when the relationship remained often fragmentary. Thus, God had decreed the destruction of sinful Israel by the hand of Assyria, yet in the midst of this judgment a remnant would emerge, who in turn would bear witness to the divine destruction of the destroyer, namely Assyria. Throughout chapters 1 – 12 this recurring pattern emerged on the primary level of the tradition and appeared in strikingly different ways within this collection (cf. the exegesis above of chapters 1, 6, 7, etc.).

There was another factor at work in the history of composition. As the oracles of Isaiah were collected, treasured, and shaped into a written literature, the developing corpus was constantly being enriched by continual expansion until it finally reached a stabilized form. Often these expansions and additional commentary emerged as a response to the coercion of earlier texts within the context of interpreting new communal experiences. In the introduction to the book of Isaiah in this commentary, this process of *Fortschreibung* (editorial expansion) was described. The editors who shaped the literary collection had little interest in preserving a historical record of the sequence of prophetic proclamations, but felt free to retroject later oracles into earlier passages in order to bring clarity and deeper understanding to the context of the original oracles. For example, the prophecy in chapters 2 – 3 of the judgment of God on proud Israel appears to have picked up vocabulary from the terrifying punishment inflicted on the nation by the exile. Conversely, the portrayal of exalted Jerusalem in 2:1–4 or the hope of the return of the diaspora (11:10ff.) uses the language of those who later experienced the fulfillment of earlier promises. The point to emphasize is that the prophetic oracles developed as they were used authoritatively by those who treasured them as scripture, and they continued to address the changing needs of each new generation as the vehicle of divine revelation. Because the major force in the history of growth was the continued impact on the Jewish community of the reality of God mediated through its authoritative writings, it is a fundamental misunderstanding to attribute the development within the prophetic corpus merely to extrabiblical sociological or historical influences.

In the light of this understanding of the redactional process, a different interpretation of the history of chapter 29 is now possible. Verses 1–8 have been shaped into a unified oracle illustrating the strangeness of the purpose of God, who both attacks and defends Jerusalem. The unit is not to be fragmented into a primary oracle of judgment and a secondary addition of salvation (*contra* Duhm, Clements, et al.). At the same time it is certainly also possible that some of the imagery of Assyria's defeat of 701 (37:29ff.) has *post factum* influenced the idiom of the enemies' frustration in vv. 7–8.

Then again, in understanding the shape of vv. 15–24, the same pattern of a reversal occurs from the blind ignorance of darkness (vv. 15–16) to that of praise and comprehension by those dwelling in the enlightened instruction of God (vv. 17ff.). The oracle (vv. 15–16) still retains the original shape of a wisdom disputational oracle. However, vv. 17–24 reflect a different compositional history. First, the language of reversal is couched in a terminology largely reminiscent of Second and Third Isaiah (cf. 32:15; 35:1ff.; 60:5; 66:14). Second, vv. 17–24 are carefully constructed in relation to chapters 28 and 29 in order to present the transformation as a direct reversal (note v. 18: "deaf will hear" // 28:12; 14:23; v. 20: "ruthless" // 28:20; v. 20: "scoffer" // 28:14, 22; v. 24: "err in spirit" // 28:7). In addition, there is a remarkable contrast made between the people who do not honor God (v. 13), on whom "a deep sleep" has fallen (v. 10), and the community of those who "stand in awe," who sanctify the name of God, and who come to true understanding (29:23–24). This form of textual interpretation would indicate that the editors have made use of exegetical techniques largely developed in the postexilic period in order to clarify and confirm the nature of the promise of renewal from the fuller experiences of a later generation.

The theological implication to be drawn from this analysis is that the proper role for the study of the diachronic dimension of the text lies not in fragment-ing or in replacing the synchronic level, but in using a recovery of a depth dimension for increasing an understanding of the theological substance that constitutes the biblical narrative itself. When an earlier generation used the term *kerygmatic,* it was expressing a similar concern.

3. Exposition

[29:1–8] The oracle opens with an editorial "woe" (*hôy*) as in 28:1, but the lit-erary form that follows does not reflect the classic prophetic conventions of invec-tive and threat. NEB renders it "alas." The oracle is addressed to Ariel, which is clearly identified in v. 8 as Mount Zion. This name presents an old crux and the author's intention in using it is not fully evident. The most frequent interpretation is that Ariel is the hearth of God, part of the altar for burnt offerings. The reference to David's encampment remains somewhat ambiguous. It could denote a hostile reference to David's initial siege of the old Canaanite city, or again be a reference to sacred Zion as David's city. Probably the former interpretation is to be pre-ferred. However, immediately Ariel is commended to continue and even to increase its cultic activity, an imperative that can only be meant ironically. Then without any accompanying invective God announces that he will now encamp against his holy city in order to distress it. A battery of assault weapons associated with the Assyrian army is then enumerated: encirclement, attack towers, and siege works. The effect is to crush the city. The outcome is grimly portrayed by means of literary repetition: dust, dirt, and the ghostly voice of a spirit barely audible. Most likely v. 5ab should be understood as part of Israel's distress.

Then a dramatic change in the city's fate is announced: "Then suddenly, in an instant . . ." There is an initial ambiguity in the term "visited," which could at first be construed as a continuation of the judgment. All the terms are usually associ-ated with destruction: thunder, earthquake, whirlwind, tempest, and devouring fire (cf. 30:30). However, v. 7 makes it clear that the divine violence is directed against the multitudes who are attacking Jerusalem. Moreover, the campaign is also associated with the theophany of Yahweh at Sinai, and is a powerful reminder of the nature of Israel's creative God, who is still at work. The emphasis on the destruction of the enemies does not fall on then describing Zion's salvation, but rather on the frustration of the attackers. Their efforts are like an unparalleled dream in the night without any reality, which vanishes into nothing at daybreak. The description resonates with the portrayal of Sennacherib's experience: "when the people arose the next morning—there were all the dead bodies." Then Sennacherib "broke camp and withdrew" (37:36–37).

The significance of the interpretation of 29:1–8 lies in the recognition that this oracle has been shaped as a continuation of the theme of the strangeness of God's purpose sounded in chapter 28. The seeming incomprehensibility of God's first attacking and then delivering Jerusalem does not derive from a tendentious redactional process that tries to replace a "pessimistic" message with an "optimistic" one. Rather, the complexity of the oracle derives from its basic theological content. God both kills and brings to life. The description of God's plan provides explanatory reasons; it is not dependent on Israel's response, but is derived solely from the mystery of God's hidden counsel.

[9–12] The short oracle that follows continues the theme of Israel's inability to comprehend. This theme has been sounded from the beginning of the book (1:2–3), but is now intensified by a return to the subject of Israel's hardening (6:9ff.). Israel is commanded to "act stupidly and be stupified," to "act blindly and be blinded." Then the reason is given for Israel's senseless behavior. God has drugged them with deep sleep and rendered them blind. Formulated in this astonishing paradox, the oracle sets forth the theological complexity of the prophetic understanding of hardening. The perverse and stupid behavior that has been initiated by Israel's rejection of God's will derives ultimately from a prior decision of divine judgment. Although it is possible that the identification of the prophets and seers in v. 10 is a subsequent editorial commentary that has interpreted the oracle specifically in reference to 28:7ff., these additions have nothing to do with an alleged allegorical interpretation by misguided redactors.

Verses 11–12 function as a further secondary prose commentary to vv. 9–10. The message of God to Israel has become a closed document that is either sealed or given to someone who cannot read. It is of interest to observe in this comment that divine revelation has now been carefully related to the vehicle of a written scroll. The effect of hardening is that Israel can no longer understand its scriptures. Certainly this development would indicate a later stage in the history of the text's growth.

[13–14] Verse 13 commences with a new introductory formula. Then in classic prophetic style it grounds the impending threat with an invective. The prophetic attack focuses on a form of false piety reminiscent of Hosea (7:14; 8:2; 10:1–2) and Micah (3:11; 6:6ff.). The worship of God has become perfunctory and superficial. Judah is only going through the motions devoid of any true devotion (cf. Isa. 58:2ff.), a routine of following religious customs, not in bringing sacrifices of praise. But once again, the threat takes a surprising turn as the theme of God's strange purpose returns. God responds to Israel's senseless behavior with a promise to do wonderful and marvelous things. Three times the root *pl'* is used, which is often translated "to perform a miracle." However, in the Old Testament a miracle is not some purely supernatural event, but rather something that evokes surprise and astonishment by which God is revealed as its source. Ordinarily the deliverance of Israel from Egypt is the primary illustration of God's working a "marvelous thing," (Micah 7:15). In v. 14 the "marvelous things" are not spelled out—for this the reader will have to wait—other than to indicate that God's wisdom will render utterly foolish the pretenses of those who claim to hear knowledge. Usually in the Old Testament this is a conjunction between human and divine wisdom. The former is the expression and vehicle of the latter. But in v. 14 a sharp contrast is being made, which subsequently serves as a warrant for a fuller exposition by the apostle Paul in 1 Cor. 1:18ff. of true wisdom from God and the pretenses of human pride.

[15–21] Traditionally, vv. 15–16 were considered an independent oracle akin to the two that precede it. However, more recently a more convincing case has been made (e.g., Sweeney) that vv. 15–16 are literarily linked with the verses that follow. Initially the repetition of the woe particle suggests the beginning of a new unit parallel to 29:1 and 30:1. Also the context is different from the previous oracle and reflects a prophetic polemic against leaders who are engaged in secret political maneuvering. The background appears to be similar to that of 30:1ff. and most likely relates historically to the period of Hezekiah's struggle for independence from Assyria after 715. Their stupidity lies in thinking that their plans were unnoticed by God. The prophet comments, "How perverse of you!" What utter foolishness to confuse the creator with his creation. The imagery of the ax trying to vaunt itself over its wielder occurred earlier in 10:15, and recurs also in Second Isaiah's caricature of idol worship in 44:9–10.

However, this common wisdom theme receives a different function in 29:15 and provides a background for a portrayal of God's new creation. Some modern commentators find the transition from an attack against political intrigue (vv. 15–16) to the transformation of nature (v. 17) to be incoherent (e.g., Eichrodt), but this assessment misses the genuine point of comparison. God, who is so misunderstood by those who struggle with their petty political machinations and discount the divine, is the one who will shortly demonstrate his true creative power to their detriment.

"Very shortly" (10:25) God, the creator, will transform the world of his creation, which the "ruthless," "the scoffer," and "those who wait for evil" have turned into gloom and darkness (29:20)—a reference surely to v. 15. In a portrayal that closely parallels 32:15ff., Lebanon will soon be changed into a fruitful field.

Then in contrast to the deafness and blindness of the old age, the deaf will hear and the blind see. The humble, who are oppressed by the ruthless, will experience joy in a recreated world of peace and justice (32:16ff.). Although the language of vv. 17–21 portraying the new age is that of chapters 35 and 40ff., the hope of a new age bringing light in place of darkness lies deeply embedded in the primary layer of Isaianic proclamation (9:1ff.; 14:24–27).

[22–24] The concluding verses are often thought to be an even later addition. The introduction in v. 22 does indeed set these verses apart from vv. 17–21. Part of the difficulty lies in the Hebrew text, which is often repointed to read "thus says Yahweh, the God of the house of Jacob." However, the real difficulty of this verse lies on a deeper level. It turns on the sudden reference to the redemption of Abraham, an idiom that appears nowhere else in the Hebrew Bible. Of course, one could argue that the expression should not be pressed too hard, but rather taken as a loose paraphrase of God's constant concern for Abraham throughout the patriarchal tradition.

Perhaps the key for discovering the intention of these verses lies in the repetition of the name of Jacob. Often the name Jacob is used simply in parallel with Israel (27:6) in order to denote the people of God, who are descended from the eponymic patriarch (Ps. 46:12). Yet there are other times in which the reference to the house of Jacob seems to be a conscious reference to all of Israel, both the Northern and Southern kingdoms (Isa. 2:3). It is significant to observe that the formula "the Holy One of Israel" occurs some twenty times in the book of Isaiah, but only in v. 23 is there a reference to "the Holy One of Jacob." The initial reference to "Abraham, concerning the house of Jacob" may therefore serve to emphasize the unity of one people of God, including Ephraim. If this were the case, vv. 22–24 have expanded the portrayal of the reversal of Israel's fortunes by consciously including reference to Jacob. One could also infer that the shaping of vv. 17–24 included a reversal of the oracle in 28:1ff. concerning the drunkards of Ephraim. They also will stand in awe of the God of Israel and come to an understanding of his wisdom (v. 24).

32. Isaiah 30:1–33

30:1   "Woe to the rebellious children," declares the LORD,
        "who make plans against my will,
    weaving alliances, but not of my spirit,
        thus heaping sin upon sin.
2   They go down to Egypt
        without consulting me,
    to seek refuge in Pharaoh's protection
        and shelter under Egypt's wing.

3 Therefore Pharaoh's protection will result in your shame;
   Egypt's shelter will bring disgrace.
4 Though his officials are in Zoan
   and his envoys reached as far as Hanes,
5 everyone will be humiliated
   by a people that cannot help them,
 that brings neither aid nor profit,
   but only shame and disgrace."
6 An oracle on the beasts of the Negeb:
 Through a land of hardship and anguish,
   of lionesses and roaring lions,
   of vipers and flying serpents,
 they carry their wealth on the backs of asses,
   their treasures on the humps of camels,
   to that people that cannot help them,
7 to Egypt whose help is completely worthless.
   Therefore I have called her,
   "Rahab who sits still."[a]
8 And now, go write it on a tablet for them;
   inscribe it in a record
 that for the days to come
   it may be a witness forever.
9 For they are a rebellious people,
   deceitful children,
 children who are unwilling to hear
   the instruction of the LORD;
10 who said to the seers, "Do not see,"
   and to the prophets, "Do not prophesy
   to us what is right.
 Tell us pleasant things, prophesy delusions.
11 Leave the way, turn aside from the path.
   We will hear no more
   about the Holy One of Israel."
12 Therefore, thus says the Holy One of Israel:
 "Because you have rejected this message
   and trust in oppression and deceit,
   depending on them,
13 therefore this sin will become for you
   like a crack and bulge in a high wall,
   whose collapse comes suddenly and swiftly.
14 It will shatter in pieces like pottery,
   which is smashed so violently

that no shard is left among its fragments
     for scooping coals from a hearth
     or dipping water out of a cistern."

15   For thus said the Lord GOD,
          the Holy One of Israel:
          "In repentance and rest is your salvation,
          in quietness and trust your strength,"
          but you refused.

16   You say, "No! We will speed on horses";
          therefore you will speed—in flight;
     and "you will ride on swift mounts";
          therefore swift will be your pursuers.

17   A thousand take flight before the threat of one,
          at the shout of five you will flee,
     until you are left
          like a flagstaff on a mountaintop,
     like a signal post on a hill.

18   Therefore the LORD waits to be gracious to you.
          Truly he rises to show you compassion,
          for the LORD is a God of justice
     Blessed are all those who wait for him.

19   O people of Zion, who dwell in Jerusalem, you will weep no more. He
     will be gracious to you at the sound of your cry; as soon as he hears, he
     will answer you. 20 Though the Lord gives you bread with sorrow and
     water with oppression, yet your Teacher will not hide himself any
     longer, but your own eyes will see your Teacher. 21 Your ears will hear
     a word behind you, saying, "This is the way, walk in it," whether you
     turn to the right or to the left. 22 Then you will treat as unclean your
     idols overlaid with silver and your images covered with gold. You will
     throw them away like a menstrual cloth, saying, "Out of my sight!"

23   He will send rain for the seed you sow in the ground, and the grain from
     the land will be rich and plentiful. In that day your cattle will graze in
     wide pastures. 24 The oxen and asses that work the soil will eat salted
     fodder that has been winnowed with pitchfork and shovel. 25 On
     every high mountain and lofty hill there will be streams running with
     water on a day of great slaughter, when towers fall. 26 The light of the
     moon will become like the light of the sun, and the light of the sun will
     be seven times brighter, like the light of seven days, when the LORD
     binds up the injuries of his people and heals the wounds he inflicted.

27   Behold, the name of the LORD comes from afar,
          with burning anger and thick clouds of smoke.[b]
     His lips are full of wrath
          and his tongue is like consuming fire.

28 His breath is like a raging torrent
      reaching up to the neck,
   to sift the nations with the sieve of destruction,
      and to place on the jaws of the peoples a bridle
   that leads them to ruin.
29 But for you there will be a song
      as on the night when a festival is celebrated.
   And there will be rejoicing
      as when people go up with flutes
   to the mountain of the LORD, to the Rock of Israel.
30 The LORD will cause his majestic voice
      to be heard,
   and will make his descending arm to be seen
   in furious anger and consuming flame,
      with cloudburst, rainstorm, and hail.
31 The voice of the LORD will shatter Assyria;
      with his rod he will strike.
32 And every stroke of the rod of punishment
      that the LORD lays upon them
   will be to the music of timbrels and lyres
      as he attacks them with blows of his arm.
33 Topheth has long been prepared;
      it has been made ready for the king.[c]
   Its fire pit is deep and wide,
      with fire and wood in abundance.
   The breath of the LORD, like a stream of burning sulfur,
      sets it ablaze.

a. Cf. below for the textual problem.
b. The Hebrew is unclear.
c. Emendation reads "Molech" (cf. Heider, 897).

Selected Bibliography

W. A. M. Beuken, "Isaiah 30: A Prophetic Oracle Transmitted in Two Successive Paradigms," *Writing and Reading the Scroll of Isaiah,* I, ed. C. C. Broyles and C. A. Evans, Leiden 1997, 369–97; **B. S. Childs,** *Isaiah and the Assyrian Crisis,* SBT, II/3, London 1967, 32–33, 35ff., 46ff.; **H. Donner,** *Israel unter den Völkern,* VTSup 11, 1964, 132ff., 155ff.; **K. Galling,** "Tafel, Buch und Blatt," *Near Eastern Studies in Honor of W. F. Albright,* Baltimore 1971, 207–33; **G. Heider,** "Molech," *ABD,* 4, 895–98; **R. F. Melugin,** "Isa. 30:15–17," *CBQ* 36, 1974, 303–4; **K.-D. Schunck,** "Jes. 30, 6–8 und die Deutung der Rahab im Alten Testament," *ZAW* 78, 1966, 48–56; **M. A. Sweeney,** *Isaiah 1–39,* FOTL 16, Grand Rapids, 1996, 386–401; **W. Werner,** *Eschatologische Texte in Jesaja 1–39. Messias, Heiliger Rest, Völker,* FB 46, Würzburg 1982, 97–103.

Against a rebellious people who seek protection through alliances with Egypt rather than through trust in the Holy One of Israel, the prophet is commended by God to write down his prophecy of destruction as a witness for future generations. Yet for those who wait for the promised salvation, God will come with burning fury against the nations and restore the afflicted of Zion.

1. Structure and Redactional Shaping

Many units of the chapter appear to have originated as independent oracles and follow the conventional forms of oral prophetic speech: vv. 1–5; 8–11; 12–14; 15–17. The invective-threat pattern dominates in these oracles. Nevertheless, in the present textual form of the chapter, the individual units have been reworked into the larger literary composition (cf. vv. 1–17) by means of various connecting devices. For example, vv. 1–5 are linked with vv. 6–7 by the repetition of the clause "people that cannot help them" (vv. 5 and 6). Again, v. 8 is joined in an immediate temporal sequence with what precedes. Further, v. 11 is linked to v. 12 with an adverb, "therefore," and also with a catchword in v. 12, "Holy One of Israel." The same messenger formula recurs in v. 15 as if further to expand on the accusation of despising the word by filling in with an example of blatant arrogance (v. 16). Finally, the linkage continues even in the later expansions as v. 18 is joined to v. 19 with a repetition of the verb "to be gracious."

The effect of this literary construction is to portray in a striking contrast the total destruction of those refusing God's protection and the faithful in Jerusalem who await the promise of deliverance. Verse 18 first sounds the note of redemption, which is then developed in an extravagant manner by a prose passage (vv. 19–26) in the apocalyptic idiom of the end time.

The oracle in vv. 27–29 offers a very different tradition of coming judgment with a terrifying picture of the fury of God reminiscent of the language of Molech. The same description of an overflowing flood reaching up to the neck was used earlier to depict Judah's punishment. In v. 28 the same judgment is now directed against the nations. This picture of judgment has then been expanded by the addition of an extended passage. Commentators are divided over whether these verses are to be rendered as prose or poetry. They depict a liturgical festival in praise of God's theophanic presence and a prophetic threat against his enemies (cf. Childs, 46ff.).

2. Exposition

[30:1–5] Verse 1 continues the series of woe oracles that began in chapter 28. The structure of the oracle follows generally the pattern of the invective-threat. The divine speech designates the addressee and often the grounds for the ensuing polemic. The historical context clearly reflects the period of political intrigue against the Assyrians in the reign of Hezekiah. Commentators differ over whether this attempt to forge an alliance with Egypt refers to the earlier revolt initiated by Ashdod (714–12) or to the events leading up to the invasion of Sennacherib in 701. The references to Zoan (Tanis) in the delta and to Hanes (Anusis) in Middle Egypt point to the period when the twenty-fifth Ethiopian dynasty controlled both Lower and Upper Egypt. Isaiah 18:1ff. spoke of a similar diplomatic exchange, although the date of the events of chapter 18 most likely preceded that of chapter 30. Isaiah contrasts Yahweh's plan with that of Judah's rulers, which he describes as "heaping sin upon sin." Some commentators explain the reference to sin as stemming from the role of foreign deities in the ritual sealing of treaties, but the reason is not made explicitly in the text. Judah's seeking security from Egypt rather than from Yahweh would be grounds enough for the prophet's harsh theological condemnation (cf. v. 12).

The same wisdom vocabulary of chapters 28—29 recurs in the prophet's description of the folly of a plan that is worthless and of no help. Such political maneuvering can only result in shame and disgrace. It is difficult not to see this condemnation of a faulty foreign policy as involving an implicit criticism of King Hezekiah even though his name is not explicitly mentioned. That Hezekiah is later portrayed as a model of a faithful king in contrast to Ahaz in chapters 36—39 does not in itself exclude an earlier condemnation. In addressing the oracle to "rebellious children," the theme of the book's prologue (1:2–3) is further continued as illustrating again the same pattern of Israel's rebellion against its only true Master.

[6–7] The oracle carries a superscription (*maśśā'*) reminiscent of those in chapters 13—23. Various attempts either to emend the MT text or to remove the connotation of a superscription (Wildberger) are not helpful. The exact prehistory of this unit is not fully clear, but on a redactional level the oracle has been carefully related to the preceding oracle by the repetition of the theme "a people that cannot help them" (vv. 5 and 6). The oracle even carries the flavor of a mild taunt. It describes a caravan laboriously traversing the wilderness, which is filled with dangers and terrors. Its beasts of burden—wordplay on the superscription—are heavily loaded with treasures intended to incur favor from the Egyptian court. Some commentators have tried to pinpoint the historical background by arguing that the reason for not using the easy coastal route south stems from its prior occupation by the Assyrians. This explanation is possible but speculative.

The point of the oracle is to reinforce the woe oracle of vv. 1–5. In spite of the great effort to acquire military assistance, Egypt is a useless ally. The sarcastic characterization of v. 7b has called forth much debate. The MT is awkward, but intelligible: "Are they Rahab?—sitting still!" The most frequently accepted emendation (*BHS*) suggests a repointing of the consonants to render,

"Rahab who sits still." In both readings the point is clear. Egypt is a monster incapable of doing anything, or to shift the metaphor, only a "paper tiger."

[8–11] The oracle that follows next assumes a narrative connection. The prophet is commanded to write down his message as a witness to later generations of the truth of his proclamation. The initial difficulty of interpretation turns on the unspecified antecedent of the suffix in v. 8. Does the "it" refer to a preceding object in vv. 6–7, or even to vv. 1–5? Or does it relate to what then follows in vv. 9ff.? The solution is further complicated by the two terms "tablet" (*lûªḥ*) and "record" (*sēper*). Are two actions of writing involved or only one? If the writing was to be on a tablet (cf. 8:1ff.), one would expect only a few words, such as "Rahab who sits still," but this solution does not fully match the intention of a written testimony that is to confirm an event occurring in the future.

First, only one act of writing is involved. The term *sēper* can also designate a tablet, that is, a single leaf (Ex. 17:14; Neh. 7:5). Second, the closest parallel to v. 8 is not found in 8:1, but rather in 8:16ff. In the light of the refusal of his message to Ahaz, the prophet counsels his disciples to collect his words for a later time when God is no longer hiding his face from Israel through their hardening. Likewise in chapter 30, the prophet is to register in writing his message as a witness to its truth for a later generation. The unexpected antecedent thus relates in a more general way to the following prophecies of impending judgment. The reference in vv. 9ff. to a people who cannot hear and yet demands "pleasant things" rather than the truth points to a subsequent time when the hardening has passed and Israel can again hear God's word, which is now despised (v. 12).

[12–17] It is difficult to determine the extent of each individual oracle, but this issue is of little importance in this chapter, which the editors have shaped into a larger unit by frequent repetition of the adverb "therefore" (vv. 12, 13, 18). Verse 12 begins with a messenger formula and links the response of the "Holy One of Israel" to his rejection in v. 11. Then the grounds for the judgment are again rehearsed (v. 12) that precede the prophecy of devastating judgment. The metaphors of a bulging wall and a shattered potter's vessel are especially effective in portraying irreversible destruction without hope of minor repairs. Verse 15 repeats again a message formula, reciting, as it were, the heart of Isaiah's message of trust in God through a quiet, unshakeable faith. Israel's response of unbelief is characterized by direct discourse and with a punishment to match each crime: "You say, 'No! We will speed on horses'; therefore you will speed—in flight." The language of humiliating defeat picks up the traditional language of holy war (Deut. 7:24; 11:25; Josh. 1:5, etc.) and then reverses it: A thousand of you will flee before one of your enemies. The result is that Judah is left "like a flagstaff on a mountaintop," a description that calls to mind Isaiah's prophecy in 1:8.

[18–26] Verse 18 begins again with the connective adverb "therefore," as if what follows is a logical consequence of what has preceded. But the connective is hardly logical nor expected. In vv. 15–17 a direct speech oracle by Yahweh climaxes in a harsh judgment. What follows then in v. 18 is a prophetic reassurance that God waits to be gracious and to show mercy, for he is a God of justice. A rather close parallel occurs in 1:27. Both these verses have in common God's promise of redemption to those who repent by turning to him, and both sound the note of God's justice. Moreover, it is significant that v. 18 appears to reflect the same level of redactional shaping as that of the preceding oracle (vv. 12–17). An indication of its role as a primary tradition lies in the subsequent exegetical expansion in vv. 19–26, which forms a catchword connection between v. 18 and v. 19 to develop the earlier theme into a baroque description of restoration. The implication is that the same tension between judgment and salvation that has repeatedly occurred in chapters 1 — 12 continues, along with its characteristic brittle linkage within the primary redactional layer.

The section that follows in vv. 19–26 reflects a different literary style. *BHK* judges it to be a prose addition; *BHS* seeks to render it as poetry. There are several close parallels within First Isaiah that are also generally attributed by commentators to a secondary redactional layering (10:20ff.; 25:6ff.; 32:15ff.). The sequence for describing the coming age of salvation follows the usual conventional pattern. God who has afflicted his people now turns from judgment to forgiveness. Blindness gives way to sight; hardening to obedience. Israel responds to the instruction of God by casting away its idols as unclean refuse (cf. Ex. 32:20). Finally, the restoration of the created order is portrayed as a return to fruitful crops and rich flocks of sheep and cattle. Even the light from the moon and sun is altered in the new future world as a sign commensurate with a people healed of its wounds. The only unfamiliar image is the reference to the "Teacher" in v. 20, which is quite rare. Yet within the literary context of chapters 28 — 30, with its strong wisdom stamp, the formulation should come as no great surprise. Isaiah 28:26 had spoken of the way of the farmer who is taught by God in wisdom. In contrast to the rebellious sons who would not hear the instruction (torah) of God (v. 9), those who dwell in Zion now are guided on their path by one who directs his obedient people with a gentle word (v. 21).

[27–33] This powerful oracle has long puzzled commentators with its unusual mixing of images. It opens with a description of God's coming from afar with burning anger and fury, a reminder of the great theophanic hymns of the Psalter (e.g., 18:8ff.). In Psalm 18 the mythopoetic description of God's riding the clouds and thundering from heaven is followed by his intervention to rescue a faithful soul who prays to God for deliverance. In contrast, in this final oracle of Isaiah 30 the theophanic vision is directed against the Assyrians, who will be consumed with burning fire on the burning place of God's sacred mountain. At the same time the destruction of the enemy evokes in Israel the joy of a festival.

The form-critical problem at stake is that elsewhere on the level of primary Isaianic tradition the literary forms of the threat and promise are not combined in this manner (cf. Childs, 47ff.). Moreover, rather than suggesting that the entire oracle is a postexilic construct, a more persuasive interpretation would be to recognize elements of ancient, theophanic tradition that depict Yahweh's coming in judgment of Assyria. At some later date—possibly postexilic—in response to the cumulative effect of God's promise as the ultimate goal of the divine plan for Israel, an explicit word of this promise was joined to the dominant note of threat against the nations. The result is that at this later stage of canonical shaping, the two elements of judgment and salvation in First Isaiah that most frequently were simply juxtaposed have been fused into an integral whole as part of the one divine purpose.

To summarize, a major concern of the interpretation of chapter 30 has been to do justice to the present form of the prophetic text while at the same time paying close attention to the signs of redactional growth within the text. How is it possible to render a unified interpretation of a redactored text without sacrificing its integrity by an appeal to countless redactional strata? Sweeney's learned monograph on First Isaiah serves as a convenient foil. Following his complex redactional analysis, he first offers a reading from a reconstructed eighth-century context, then one from the seventh century, and finally one reflecting late postexilic apocalyptic concerns. Such an approach seems to be basically unsatisfactory because it ends up fragmenting the canonical text equally as severely as did the nineteenth-century literary-critical approach of Duhm or Marti. It is also largely theologically inert.

Fortunately, there has recently emerged a major exception to the usual fragmentation of the chapter. W. A. M. Beuken has offered a brilliant new interpretation that has been able to recover the literary coherence of chapter 30 in a remarkably fresh fashion. Beuken seeks to demonstrate how the prophecy of Isaiah in vv. 1–17 has been actualized at a later date by expanding the original oracle by means of two different paradigms. In vv. 18–26 the imagery used is of a journey under God's leadership; in vv. 27–33 the imagery is of the theophany on the mountain of Yahweh. Of particular importance has been Beuken's success in recovering the broader context of the entire collection of chapters 28—33.

In my commentary, in contrast to those who would fragment the chapter, I have argued that the different layers of the present text are to be seen as reflecting the accumulated experience of a faithful community with God through the lenses provided by Israel's sacred scriptures. In the later levels of compositional growth the message of divine judgment and salvation are organically linked in a way that was at first, on the primary level of the tradition, unclear. However, increasingly the prophetic message gained in clarity as the anticipated eschatological salvation was painted with colors enriched by later apocalyptic imagery to form an organic whole. Hermeneutically speaking, it is crucial to understand how the major force in the shaping of the prophetic corpus derived from the experience by Israel of an ongoing encounter with God mediated through scripture rather than through the

direct influence of allegedly independent events of world affairs. It is precisely this
filtering process of scriptural reflection on the ways of God that gave a coherent
meaning to the changing life of Israel in the world of human affairs.

33. Isaiah 31:1–9

31:1   Woe to those who go down to Egypt for help,
      who rely on horses,
   and put their trust in the number of chariots,
      and in the great strength of their riders,
   but do not look to the Holy One of Israel,
      or seek help from the LORD.

2   Yet he too is wise and brings disaster.
      He does not take back his word,
   but will arise against the house of the wicked,
      and against the allies of those doing evil.

3   For the Egyptians are human, not God;
      their horses are flesh and not spirit.
   When the LORD stretches out his hand,
      he who helps will stumble,
   and he who is helped will fall,
      and both will perish together.

4   For thus the LORD said to me,
   as a lion—a great beast—growls over his prey,
      and, when the shepherds gather against him,
   is not frightened by their shouts
      nor daunted by their clamor,
   so the LORD will come down
      to do battle against[a] Mount Zion and its heights.

5   Like hovering birds, so the LORD of hosts
      will shield Jerusalem.
   He will protect and deliver it;
      he will spare and rescue it.

6   Return to him, O children of Israel, from whom you have so fully
revolted, 7 for in that day everyone will reject his idols of silver and
gold, which your sinful hands have made.

8   Then Assyria will fall by a sword, not made by man,
      and a sword, not of man, will devour him;
   and he will flee from the sword,
      and his young warriors will be put to forced labor.

9   His rock will dissolve in terror,

and his officers will panic at the sight of the banner,
declares the LORD, whose fire is in Zion,
whose furnace is in Jerusalem.

a. Cf. below concerning this translation.

Selected Bibliography

M. L. Barré, "Of Lions and Birds: A Note in Isaiah 31.4–5," *Among the Prophets: Language and Structure in the Prophetic Writings,* ed. P. R. Davies and D. J. A. Clines, JSOTSup 144, Sheffield 1993, 55–59; **H. Barth,** *Die Jesaja-Worte in der Josiazeit,* WMANT 48, Neukirchen-Vluyn 1977, 77–92; **B. S. Childs,** *Isaiah and the Assyrian Crisis,* SBT II/3, London 1967, 57–59; **G. Eidevall,** "Lions and Birds as Literature: Some Notes on Isaiah 31 and Hosea 11," JSOT 7, 1993, 78–87; **J. C. Exum,** "Of Broken Pots, Fluttering Birds and Visions in the Night: Extended Simile and Poetic Technique in Isaiah," *CBQ* 43, 1981, 336–38; **G. Sauer,** "Die Umkehrung in der Verkündigung Jesaja," *Wort-Gebot-Glaube, Fs W. Eichrodt,* ed. H.-J. Stoebe, Zürich 1970, 277–95; **M. A. Sweeney,** *Isaiah 1–39,* FOTL 16, Grand Rapids 1996, 401–8.

The oracle condemns those who, thinking themselves wise, seek protection from Egypt rather than from the Holy One of Israel. Yet God alone is God and qualitatively different from man. He is truly wise and will both judge the wicked with disaster and protect Jerusalem from the assaults of the Assyrians.

1. Form, Structure, and Redaction

The oracle once again begins with the conventional *hôy* of the woe oracle. Yet the form in chapter 31 is not simply a copy of prophetic oral speech, as often assumed by classic form-critics. Although certain formal characteristics continue, the oracle has been shaped by other substantive forces and the present literary composition reflects its own integrity. As has been previously observed in the section of chapters 28–32, the literary effect of a written composition is everywhere present. Eichrodt even speaks of an "indirect" quality to this oracle, which indicates that the present form of the text is a literary product and not just a collection of unmediated oral units.

One notices, for example, the strong wisdom element in v. 2, which is a feature uncharacteristic of the prophetic invective-threat. In v. 2 this component plays a central role in the present function of the oracle, and sets immediately a contrast between Yahweh's wisdom and the clever intrigues of those negotiating with Egypt. Then again, the theological reflection on the nature and power of God reveals that the form of the invective lies deep in the background, not in the foreground, of the text. Recently, Sweeney (402–3) has recognized these peculiar features in the oracle and has designated the structure of chapter 31 as a parenetic form, which was designed to persuade its audience in a particular course of action. However, the description of this unit as parenesis is not fully on target and should rather be restricted to vv. 6–7. Actually the element of persuasion is a minor one since for the writer the die has already been cast. In sum, the oracle outlines the wise response of God according to his sovereign plan (v. 2aß) to the continuing foolishness of human machinations. The future is firmly in the hand of God, who exercises his will in judgment and salvation.

The most difficult structural problem turns on the coherence of the chapter as a whole. It has usually been argued that vv. 1–3 are "authentic" to Isaiah and reflect a primary Isaianic tradition apart from some minor expansions. However, vv. 4–5 are thought to be hopelessly incoherent. Verse 4 speaks of a divine intent to destroy Zion, whereas v. 5 expresses just the opposite position in proclaiming Yahweh's protection. Clements's solution is typical of a modern redactional approach when he retains v. 4 as genuinely Isaianic, but assigns vv. 5 and 8–9 to a seventh-century Josianic redactor who retrojects the events of 701 onto this fragment of the original author. Verses 6–7 are then considered postexilic and represent two separate glosses. Fortunately, there has recently been a reaction to this rather extreme form of textual fragmentation (cf. Seitz).

I would argue that, although vv. 1–3 do reflect an independent oracle, it is closely joined to vv. 4–9. The initial oracle portrays the wise plan of God in response to Israel's failure to consult him who "does not take back his word" (v. 2). The stress is on God's wisdom, which embraces both the judgment and the salvation of his people. Recognition of the basic theocentric focus guards against setting these two elements in stark opposition and then feeling constrained to order them within a developmental redactional scheme. Verses 6–7 are indeed a prose interjection (cf. 2:5), which offer an existential appeal to Israel to turn from the path of sheer folly and to embrace the salvation extended to those who renounce idolatry.

2. Exposition

[31:1–3] The initial oracle continues the series of woes that is characteristic of the larger section of chapters 28 — 33. It parallels the language and content of 30:1–5. The historical setting falls in the same general period of 705–701 leading up to the invasion of Sennacherib. Some commentators argue that chapter 31 is slightly later than chapter 30, and may follow the disastrous defeat of the Egyptian army at Eltekeh, which dashed the last hopes of foreign aid. Certainly the mood is somber: "both will perish together" (v. 3).

For the prophet Isaiah the issue at stake in Jerusalem's search for pagan alliances is a theological one. Israel's leaders trust in chariots and horsemen and feel that events in the real world do not relate to religious faith. They do not look to the Holy One of Israel or inquire after his will. Yet Yahweh is truly wise and has the capacity to effect disaster. The controversy is over the wielding of power. Israel's leaders appear to agree with the nations that the only real force lies in military strength. Israel's leaders thus share a basically pagan perspective, which resonates with the speech of the Rabshakeh in chapters 36—37. Are not all the gods impotent?

Then the prophet strikes at the heart of this arrogance. The Egyptians, like the Assyrians, are only human; they are not God. Their horses are flesh and not spirit. The contrast does not rest on a dualistic distinction between the material and spiritual worlds, nor between a visible human and an invisible spiritual realm. Although Isaiah does follow a sapential convention in using the generic term for deity (*'ēl*) in contrast to humankind (*'ādām*), he fills this polarity with a biblical content. He is not talking about a class of gods, but only of Yahweh, God of Israel. The contrast is between the Creator and his creation. Yahweh is the source of the spirit, the dynamic divine power that gives life to his creation. All creation lies dead and inert until the life-giving breath of God infuses it with life (Gen. 2:7). God brings forth both good and evil. His word goes forth and accomplishes its end (Isa. 55:10–11). "He does not take back his word" (31:2). When he now arises in judgment, all who lay claim on his creative prerogative will be destroyed. Both the one seeking and the one giving it will perish (v. 3).

[4–9] The introductory formula of v. 4 no longer functions to present a private oracle of Yahweh (8:11), but within its new literary structure provides direct divine authority to the prophetic proclamation that follows. The theocentric focus of the oracle is crucial for its proper interpretation and serves as a corrective against the misplaced debate over whether the prophet returned to a theory of Zion's inviolability after an earlier period of announcing its utter destruction.

The chief exegetical problem turns on the relation of v. 4, which compares Yahweh to an attacking lion in a thoroughly hostile action, to v. 5, which appears to reverse Yahweh's relation to Jerusalem by means of a simile of hovering birds that shield against danger. The attempts of commentators to resolve this problem are numerous and fall into different categories:

  a. The traditional interpretation (AV, RSV, NEB) translates the verb *liṣbō' 'al* in a positive fashion, "to fight for," and sees the action of Yahweh in v. 4 to be a part of the same protective action as v. 5. The difficulty of this interpretation is that the Hebrew verb with its preposition is used consistently in a negative sense, "to fight against" (cf. Num. 31:7; Isa. 29:7; Zech. 14:12). Moreover, the image of the attacking lion seems out of place as a protective symbol, even if the stress falls on the lion's tenacity (cf. Hos. 5:14; Isa. 5:29; Nah. 2:12). Wildberger's attempt to separate the verb from its preposition in order to construe it in a positive sense cannot be sustained syntactially.
  b. Other commentators suggest either to delete portions of the text in order to remove the tension (Duhm, Scott), or claim that part of

vv. 4 and 5 have been lost (Eichrodt). Several propose that the sequence of the verses be reordered in order to eliminate the problem (Procksch). The great variety of these emendations only illustrates the high level of subjectivity involved.

c. Most recently a redactional solution has been confidently defended (Vermeylen, Barth, Clements). Accordingly, at a later date a redactor retrojected from the events of 701 the hope of a reversal of Jerusalem's fortunes, thus changing an original negative oracle (v. 4) into a positive one (v. 5). A most trenchant criticism of this two-stage scheme of redaction has been offered by Seitz (223), who argues that the categorizing for oracles as unequivocally negative or positive badly skews the prophet's intent and misses the genuine tension of his message.

As a consequence of this debate, I would offer a different exegesis from my earlier effort (*Isaiah and the Assyrian Crisis,* 57ff.), which isolated a form-critical analysis from its present literary structure seen as a whole. First of all, I would still insist that the translation of the verb in v. 4 demands a negative connotation, "to fight against" (cf. NJPS). However, the imagery of God's doing battle against Zion and the house of evildoers has already been a major theme in the preceding chapters. The oracle against Ariel in chapter 29 shared exactly the same pattern. Yahweh attacks Jerusalem, laying siege and humiliating the city before the sudden, unexplained reversal in 29:6. Similarly, 30:13 speaks about the ruthless shattering of the city because of its iniquity, but then concludes with the note in v. 18 of God's waiting to be gracious. Finally, 31:2 speaks of God's bringing disaster, not calling back his earlier words, and arising against the house of the wicked.

The key to the tension is first given in the parable (28:23ff.), which discloses the strangeness of God's purpose with Israel. This theme is then developed further in both chapters 29 and 30, and continued in chapter 31. The major point is that the Isaianic message does not consist of a tension between pessimistic and optimistic opinions of the prophet, or between competing redactional construals of earlier and later periods. Such a developmental trajectory renders an understanding of the true dimensions of the text virtually impossible. Rather, the issue is a complex theological one that emerged already in the prologue of the book (1:2–3). How is such a lack of understanding of God by Israel possible? Increasingly in the reflective style of the sage, chapters 28—33 focus on the folly of Israel in rejecting the merciful intervention of God, which can only result in utter destruction. Yet from the disclosure of God's revelation of his purpose in creation, there remains an unswerving hope of salvation that is fully incomprehensible to human sinfulness, blinded as it is in folly and arrogance. The prophet does not offer a systematic theological tractate, but a profound struggle with a continuing encounter with God that resonates through the entire corpus as a consistent witness. Israel's judgment and Israel's redemption cohere in God's purpose even when it often appears mysterious and incomprehensible to human logic.

The destruction and rebirth of Jerusalem is also closely joined to the divine verdict on Assyria that was God's chosen vehicle of judgment (chapter 10) but that also personified the arrogance of claiming sovereignty over the whole created world. In v. 8 Assyria's destruction is again announced, but the means of its destruction is made even clearer: "a sword, not of man, will devour him!" His stronghold and his powerful fighting force will be of no avail. Defeat comes from the Lord, whose coming in terrifying force had been announced in 30:27ff. Israel, not Assyria, has a Rock of protection (30:29), and Jerusalem becomes the furnace in which the refuse is burned.

[6–7] Finally, a word regarding vv. 6–7 is in order. There has been much recent discussion about whether Isaiah has a message of repentance (cf. Sauer). Usually when the word appears in Isaiah it is used to signal Israel's inability to repent. Nor is the theme frequently found in the prophet's preaching. The hardening of Israel has closed the door and only a restoration from the side of God renders a change possible. Nowhere in Isaiah's proclamation is this rebirth made contingent on Israel's decision to return (*contra* Fohrer).

Nevertheless, the appeal for repentance is not to be dismissed out of hand. Its note is sounded not only in 31:6–7, but elsewhere in key junctures within the book (e.g., 2:5). Its particular function is crucial for a proper understanding. Always after God's plan has been described and his will for Israel and the nations has been announced, then Israel is challenged to respond to the One who has embraced it. In v. 7 the inclusion of an eschatological context picks up the earlier note of Israel's utter despair (2:20), but now sees it as a promise of a time when all the false gods will indeed be despised when Israel emerges as a restored people.

34. Isaiah 32:1–20

32:1 When a king reigns in righteousness
    and princes govern with justice,
2 each will be like a hiding place from the wind,
    a shelter from rainstorms;
like streams of water in a desert,
    like the shade of a massive rock
in a parched land.
3 Then the eyes of those who see will not be closed,
    and the ears of those who hear will listen.

4   The mind of the reckless will have good judgment,
         and the tongue of the stammerers will speak readily
     and distinctly.
5   The fool will no more be called noble,
         nor the scoundrel said to be honorable.
6   For the fool speaks nonsense
         and his mind is busy with evil plots.
     He acts perversely
         and speaks falsely against the LORD,
     so that he leaves the hungry unsatisfied
         and withholds water from the thirsty.
7   The methods of the scoundrel are wicked.
         He devises evil schemes
     to destroy the poor with lies,
         even when the cause of the needy is just.
8   But he who is noble devises noble things,
         and by noble deeds he stands.
9   Rise up, you women who are at ease,
         and listen to my voice.
     You complacent daughters,
         hear what I have to say.
10   In little more than a year,
         you who feel confident will shudder,
     for the grape harvest will fail,
         and the fruit harvest will not come.
11   Tremble, you women who are at ease,
         shudder, you complacent women!
     Strip yourself naked,
         put sackcloth around your waists.
12   Beat your breasts
         for the pleasant fields,
         for the fruitful vines,
13   for the soil of my people,
         growing up in thorns and briars;
     yes, for all the joyous houses
         in the joyful city.
14   For the palace will be forsaken,
         the tumultuous city deserted.
     The citadel and the tower will become
         a wasteland forever,
     the delight of wild asses,
         a pasture for flocks;

15   until the spirit on high is poured out on us,
      and the wilderness is transformed into a fertile field,
      and the fertile field seems like a forest.

16   Then justice will dwell in the desert
      and righteousness will live in the fertile field.

17   For the effect of righteousness will be peace,
      and the result of righteousness,
      quietness and confidence forever.

18   Then my people will dwell in peaceful homes,
      in secure dwellings,
      in undisturbed places of rest.

19   And the forest will sink and vanish,
      and the city will be utterly laid low.[a]

20   Happy are you who sow beside every stream,
      and let your cattle and asses range free.

a. The meaning of the verse is very obscure. The NEB follows Driver's philological emendation: "it will be cool on the slopes" (cf. NIV: "though hail flattens the forest"). Perhaps more cautious is the above rendering, followed also by the RSV and NJPS. Cf. Barthélemy, *CTLAT,* for the full debate.

Selected Bibliography

H. Barth, *Die Jesaja-Worte in der Josiazeit,* WMANT 48, Neukirchen-Vluyn 1977, 211–15; **T. K. Cheyne,** *Introduction to the Book of Isaiah,* London 1895, 172–80; **H.-J. Hermisson,** "Zukunftserwartung und Gegenwartskritik in der Verkündigung Jesaja," *EvTh* 33, 1973, 54–77; **H. W. Hertzberg,** "Die Nachgeschichte alttestamentlichen Texte innerhalb des Alten Testaments," reprinted in *Beiträge zur Traditionsgeschichte und Theologie des Alten Testaments,* Göttingen 1962, 78–80; **J. J. M. Roberts,** "The Divine King and the Human Community in Isaiah's Vision of the Future," *The Quest for the Kingdom of God: Studies in Honor of George E. Mendenhall,* ed. H. B. Huffmon et al., Winona Lake 1983, 127–36; **B. Stade,** "Jes. 32, 33," *ZAW* 4, 1884, 256–71; **G. Stansell,** "Isaiah 32: Creative Redaction in the Isaian Traditions," *SBL Seminar Papers* 1983, 1–12.

The passage outlines the blessing of a government ruled in righteousness, which is contrasted with the anarchy of folly and ungodliness. The complacent women of Jerusalem are threatened into impending disaster until the Spirit of God transforms the desolate land into a quiet resting place for the faithful.

1. Structure, Context, and Editorial Shaping

There is general agreement that the passage divides into three sections: vv. 1–8; 9–14; 15–20. There are some additional problems regarding further subdivisions on which there is less consensus.

The problems of literary context, historical dating, and integrity of content remain highly controversial. One is struck by the very different kinds of material without any immediate sense of coherence between vv. 1–8 and 9–14 and between vv. 1–8 and 15–20. Many commentators argue that only the unit of vv. 9–14 has a concrete historical setting that could be assigned to the eighth-century prophet. Yet even this oracle, which contains mostly a threat against the complacent women of Jerusalem, has an obvious problem. In contrast, say, to 3:16ff., it seems to lack specificity. There are no grounds for reproof other than a general accusation of complacency. Nevertheless, a majority of commentators hold this oracle to be the core around which two later brackets have been added: vv. 1–8 and 15–20.

The major problem with vv. 1–8 turns on the issue of whether this is a messianic passage that announces the coming of a future royal ruler much like chapters 9 and 11. The style and content seem quite removed from these earlier eschatological passages. This unit is couched in wisdom language and seems to portray an ideal state of good government with a king and princes ruling with justice. Then the verses that follow in 4ff. closely follow the idiom of Proverbs in contrasting wise and foolish behavior. In addition, vv. 6–8 appear to be a subsequent scribal interpretation of the key words in v. 5, namely, "fool," "scoundrel," and "noble."

In recent times the most frequently defended interpretation of the chapter has been by means of a redactional process (Barth, Clements, Sweeney, Stansell). Accordingly, around the core tradition of vv. 9–14 has been added in vv. 1–5 a redactional layer from the seventh century—the so-called Josianic redaction—which focused its proclamation on the destruction of Assyria and the impending salvation of Israel. Some scholars hold that vv. 15–20 continued this same seventh-century redactional layer; however, others (e.g., Vermeylen, Stansell) would assign this last section to an even later postexilic addition, which sought to overcome the disappointment from the Josianic debacle by reformulating the promise in more eschatological imagery. In my opinion, these various redactional schemata are highly unsatisfactory. Not only are they very speculative in seeking to evoke from the text precise historical information by which to form a compositional trajectory, but the exegetical effort is to shatter the passage's literary integrity by claiming to reconstruct three distinct levels within a process. Is there another avenue for access into this difficult passage?

Initially, the lead is given by the position of chapter 32 in the larger context of the section, chapters 28—33. It has long been noticed that this section in general reflects a different style from chapters 1—12. Its oracles are at least one step removed from the oral stage of the tradition and seem reworked into a larger didactic composition by means of a substantial component of wisdom terminology. The common thread running through these chapters is the stupidity and foolishness of Israel in failing to comprehend the plan of God that entails the punishment of haughty Israel, then the destruction of Assyria, and finally the exaltation of restored Zion.

Chapters 32 and 33 form a particular climax to the previous chapters when they recapitulate the same elements of the divine plan before turning in a different direction in chapters 34—35, which furnish a bridge with Second Isaiah. Both chapters 32 and 33 follow in general the same larger pattern of recounting Israel's deep trouble, the threat of the enemy, and the vision of the coming salvation. However, the material making up the two chapters is different in terms of tradition-historical development and is only redactionally joined within the book's literary context. Chapter 32 is very strongly shaped by wisdom terminology, whereas chapter 33 is largely liturgical in nature. Chapter 33 appears to be influenced by chapter 32, especially in terms of the reference to the king and the peaceful habitation, which it picked up and further extended; however, chapter 32 seems independent of chapter 33.

There is one final feature in interpreting chapters 32 and 33 that has increasingly emerged as crucial for gaining access to these unusual forms. Both chapters, in somewhat different ways, share a common exegetical approach, namely, they attempt to offer a holistic reading of the prior Isaianic corpus, which is then adapted and creatively actualized in order to show how the earlier prophecies are about to be fulfilled in the events preceding the Assyrian attack on Jerusalem during the reign of Hezekiah. The precise exegetical technique used in chapter 33 will be described in the next chapter. Here attention will focus on chapter 32.

I argue in my exposition that the holistic reading of the Isaianic tradition is largely retrospective, but occasionally also points forward by the use of language and themes characteristic of chapters 40ff. At times chapter 32 employs virtual citations from earlier prophecy to make a fresh proclamation (e.g., 32:15 // 29:17). At other times, individual themes are picked up that resonate with previous motifs, such as the closing of the eyes and ears (32:3 // 29:9–10; 30:10; 6:9ff.). Then again, key words from a bundle of metaphors are reused, such as in the portrayal of the protection offered as a key in 32:2, which picks up the same words of "shelter," "shade," and "rainstorm" from 25:4. The term "joyful city" (v. 13) occurs only here and in a previous reference in 22:2, a reference that can hardly be accidental.

However, the boldest interpretation is to suggest that the juxtaposition of the theme of a righteous governance instead of a state of chaotic reign (vv. 1–8), followed by a threat to the complacent women of Jerusalem (vv. 9–14), derives from a holistic reading of chapter 3, in which similar themes are joined. The argument is cumulative in nature since the reuse of exact linguistic parallels is not present. Support will be sought from the scribal style and literary function of the material, which grows in clarity in the succeeding chapter.

The hermeneutical implication in this move is that the context for interpreting chapter 32 does not lie in a historical reconstruction or a redactional trajectory, but in its setting as a literary, indeed theological, construct that offers a fresh prophetic rendering of Isaianic tradition. In a word, the shaping of the text reflects the canonical force of an accumulated corpus of authoritative tradition that has been reused as a vehicle for an actualization of the selfsame divine purpose. It is, of course, possible to draw some historical conclusions regarding the dating of this final literary formation. The literary form of chapters 32–33 points to the end of the editorial growth of the book, but this information is of subordinate value in determining the meaning of the passage.

2. Exposition

[32:1–8] Commentators are divided on whether this passage announcing a king who will rule in righteousness should be considered messianic or nonmessianic. At first the debate was carried on in terms of its dating, whether the passage is genuinely Isaianic or later. Duhm led the way for its messianic interpretation by arguing that, like 9:1ff. and 11:1ff., chapter 32 could also be derived from the final period of Isaiah's ministry when in his old age. Very shortly, Isaianic authorship was largely denied by critical commentators, but the designation as messianic was continued, even though the passage was regarded as bland and individualistic (Wildberger). Most recently, Barth and Clements have argued for a seventh-century redaction in which traditional messianism was reformulated in terms of an idealization of King Josiah. Others choose to identify the royal figure with Hezekiah; however, it is a question whether anything is gained by historicizing the text in this way.

Another group of scholars has opted for a nonmessianic interpretation. The evidence for this interpretation turns largely on the strikingly different style in chapter 32 when compared with the announcement of a coming eschatological ruler such as in 9:1 and 11:1ff. Then again, the predominant wisdom language describes a situation rather than a historical event in which good government is restored. Nowhere else in the other messianic passages do the princes play a significant role along with the king.

In my opinion, both of these interpretations contain elements of truth, but neither has been able to bring forth a convincing portrait of the whole. The nonmessianic interpretation has rightly tried to assess the effect of the peculiar wisdom style, which lacks the eschatological intensity of the prophetic promises of chapters 9 and 11. The same features that were noticed in chapters 28–31 of an indirect relation to the level of oral tradition are further evidenced in chapter 32. The reflective, mediated style of the wisdom teacher is apparent, in which a didactic emphasis falls on the restoration of righteous governance. The portrait of the just rule by king and princes is couched in the same idiom as

God's righteous rule of 25:4: a hiding place, a covert from the storm, and a shade in a dry land.

In v. 3 a sign of a righteous society continues to be developed, which plays on the earlier theme of Israel's hardening (6:9; 29:18). No more will the eyes of those who see be closed, nor their ears stopped. Those once thoughtless and reckless will have sound judgment, and the speech of stammerers will be fluent (perhaps a reference to 28:7ff.). Verse 5 next contrasts the new condition of right governance with one in which the fool is called noble and the villain is deemed honorable. The three lead words in v. 5, "fool," "noble," and "scoundrel," are then further expanded in vv. 6–8. The exposition is carried out in the characteristic idiom of wisdom literature, with frequent parallels from the books of Proverbs and Ecclesiastes (e.g., Prov. 12:16; 26:4). The conclusion to be drawn is that vv. 1–8 have been influenced by a scribal school that has continued to shape the prophetic literature with the language of the wisdom tradition.

In addition, I would argue that there is another important influence at work on the editors of chapter 32 that is fully compatible with the redactional evidence from this section of the book. The editors have brought to bear earlier Isaianic material that is now rendered in a holistic fashion. The closest parallel to the description of a society opposed to this ideal form of right government is given most clearly in chapter 3. In contrast to the righteous rule of king and princes (*śārîm*), Isaiah pictured "boys" serving as princes, youths insulting elders, and villains debasing the noble (3:4–5). Leadership is foolishly offered to whoever still owns a coat. The result of such chaotic conditions in terms of social injustice (vv. 14ff.) is closely paralleled to the wicked abuse of the poor and the needy in 32:7.

[9–14] The coherence of the previous unit is suddenly broken off by the introduction of a different subject matter. The form of the new oracle is a threat against the complacent daughters of Jerusalem that is dominated by imperatives: hear, tremble, strip, gird, lament. Several things have puzzled commentators in this oracle. One misses signs of a concrete audience, which is very different from similar polemics directed earlier against the women of Israel in Amos 4:1ff. and Isa. 3:16ff. Moreover, the grounds for the harsh quality of the condemnation, usually given in a prophetic invective, are also missing. The only reproof is their complacency, and therefore scholars have searched in vain for evidence that would help to establish a historical context.

Again I would suggest that the editors of 32:9ff. have made use of a literary context found in chapter 3. Verse 12 had already introduced the role of women as an indication of the chaotic state in Jerusalem: "women rule over them." Could the literary context of chapter 3 within the corpus of Isaianic writings account for the transition in chapter 32 from vv. 1–8 to 9–14? This hypothesis might explain also the peculiar distance of the oracle from the usual patterns of oral speech. There are two other references in this unit that also show a scribal interest in using older material from the Isaianic corpus. First, vv. 12–13 speak of the "fruitful vines for the soil of my people, growing up in thorns and briars." The allusion appears to be to the song of the vineyard in 5:1–7 and is a holistic rendering of the passage rather than a midrashic one focusing on individual words. Second, the threat of coming destruction seems to pick up the tradition in chapter 22 of a "joyous city" (*qiryāh 'allīzāh*, v. 2 // 32:13), which will shortly be punished for its precipitous folly.

[15–20] The final section again offers another sharp reversal. In contrast to the threat of judgment in vv. 9–14, the message shifts dramatically to a new age of salvation and renewal. A redactional link joins the two units: "*until* the spirit on high is poured out on us." The striking factor is that this linkage is made in v. 15 by means of a virtual verbal citation from 29:17 that also introduces the radical shift from judgment to salvation: "(until) Lebanon will be transformed into a fertile field, and the fertile field seem like a forest."

There are several important implications to be drawn from this citation of 29:17. First, it makes clear that the transition is to the eschatological, messianic age. Whereas it was unclear in 32:1ff. whether the initial oracle was messianic or nonmessianic, the editorial shaping makes it now apparent that vv. 1–8 are to be understood messianically. Of course, this editorial rendering of the tradition does not in itself invalidate the observations of those defending a nonmessianic reading that the concern of the passage is for good government. For this reason both the messianic and nonmessianic interpretations have important support from different parts of the chapter. The interpretive impasse has arisen because of an initially false polarity between messianic and nonmessianic, which has informed the debate.

Verses 15ff. place the emphasis on the coming salvation initiated by an outpouring of the divine spirit. A new age results in which both the natural world and human society are transformed. The divine change is characterized by justice and equity, a term familiar throughout the book of Isaiah for the messianic age. Stress is laid particularly on the peace, security, and freedom of the new age (cf. 30:23ff.). The radical change in both nature and society is also a hallmark of Isaiah's vision of the new age of God's rule (2:1ff.).

However, it is equally important that this eschatological vision of the future be balanced by the notes sounded in 32:1ff. The prophetic message is not simply concerned with the miraculous intervention of God's kingdom. Israel's messianic king is not conceived of as a heavenly, eschatological redeemer who brings history to an end. Rather, he is one who rules and governs a nation "upon the throne of David, and over his kingdom . . . with justice and righteousness" (9:6[7]).

The value of good government and general human civility is a high concern of Isaiah's message. This is to say that the kingdom of God and the kingdoms of this world are not held apart in a radical sectarian polarity, but are seen together as two sides of one truth. In order properly to understand prophetic theology, it is crucial to see that the kingdom of God is indeed to transform the entire world and that sacred and secular society are held together in an integral unity. This prophetic witness remains an important check against an otherworldly apocalyptic move that would see no real bridge between the church and the world. Exactly at this point there is a serious theological disagreement between the theology of the Protestant Reformers and the heirs of Pietism.

35. Isaiah 33:1–24

33:1   Woe to you, O destroyer who has not been destroyed,
         you betrayer who has not been betrayed.
     When you have done your ravaging, you will be ravaged.
         When you have finished betraying, you will be betrayed.
2   O LORD, be gracious to us; we wait for you.
         Be our strength every morning,
         our salvation in time of trouble.
3   From the roaring sound peoples flee;
         when you rise up, nations scatter.
4   Spoil is gathered as locusts gather;
         like a swarm of locusts men leap on it.
5   The LORD is exalted, for he dwells on high.
         He will fill Zion with justice and righteousness.
6   He will be the stability for your times,
         the abundance of salvation, wisdom, and knowledge.
         Fear of the LORD is his treasure.
7   Look how brave men[a] cry in the streets,
         the envoys of peace weep bitterly.
8   The highways are deserted, no one travels.
         Treaties are broken, their witnesses are despised,
         no one is respected.
9   The land is parched and withered;
         Lebanon is disgraced and decayed.
     Sharon has become a desert,
         and Bashan and Carmel drop their leaves.
10   "Now I will arise," says the LORD,
         "Now I will lift myself up,
         now will I be exalted.
11   You conceive hay;
         you give birth to straw.
         Your breath is a fire that will consume you.

12 Peoples will be as if burned to lime,
        like thorns cut down that are set on fire."
13 You who are far away, hear what I have done.
        You who are near, acknowledge my power.
14 Sinners in Zion are afraid;
        trembling has seized the godless:
    "Who of us can dwell with the devouring fire?
        Who of us can dwell with everlasting burnings?"
15 The one who walks in righteousness
        speaks what is right,
        rejects profit from extortion,
        keeps his hand from receiving bribes,
        stops his ears from listening to violence,
        shuts his eyes against looking at evil—
16 such a one will dwell on the heights;
        his refuge will be fortresses of rocks,
        with food provided, and drink assured.
17 Your eyes will see a king in his beauty,
        and view a land that stretches in all directions.
18 Your thoughts will ponder the former terror:
        "Where is the counter of taxes?
        Where the weigher of tribute?
        Where is the one in charge of the towers?"[b]
19 You will no more see those arrogant people,
        the people of an incomprehensible speech,
        stammering in a language that cannot be understood.
20 Look upon Zion, the city of our appointed feasts.
        Your eyes will see Jerusalem,
    a peaceful habitation, an immovable tent,
        whose stakes will never be uprooted,
        nor any of its ropes broken.
21 For there the LORD in his majesty will be for us
        like a place of broad rivers and streams,
    where no warships can sail
        and no mighty vessels travel.
22 For the LORD is our judge,
        the LORD is our prince,
    the LORD is our king.
        He will deliver us.
23 His rigging[c] hangs loosely;
        it cannot hold the mast secure
        or keep the sails spread.

Then an abundance of spoil will be divided,
even the lame will carry off plunder.
24 And none there will say, "I am ill,"
and the sins of the inhabitants will be forgiven.

a. The text is difficult and highly contested. Some emend to read "men of Ariel."
Delitzsch, accepted by RSV, reads "warrior," citing 2 Sam. 23:20 and 1 Chron. 11:22.
Cf. Barthélemy, *CTLAT,* 231–32 for the complete debate.
b. The sense of the final colon is unclear: literally, "who counted the towers."
c. The meaning of the verse is obscure. The MT reads "your rigging." The translation of the last lines is also unclear and many possible emendations have been suggested.

Selected Bibliography

W. A. M. Beuken, "Jesaja 33 als Spiegeltext im Jesajabuch," *ETL* 67, 1991, 5–35; **T. K. Cheyne,** *Introduction to the Book of Isaiah,* London 1895, 162–72; **B. S. Childs,** *Isaiah and the Assyrian Crisis,* SBT II/3, London 1967, 112–17; **H. Gunkel,** "Jesaia 33, eine prophetische Liturgie," *ZAW* 42, 1924, 177–208; **J. H. Hayes and S. A. Irvine,** *Isaiah, The Eighth-Century Prophet: His Times and His Preaching,* Nashville 1987, 360–70; **S. Mowinckel,** *Psalmenstudien II,* Kristiana 1922, 235–38; **J. J. M. Roberts,** "Isaiah 33: An Isaianic Elaboration of the Zion Tradition," *The Word of the Lord Shall Go Forth. Fs D. N. Freedman,* ed. C. L. Meyers and M. O'Conner, Winona Lake 1983, 15–25; **M. A. Sweeney,** *Isaiah 1–39,* FOTL 16 6, Grand Rapids, 420–32; **J. Vermeylen,** *Du Prophète Isaïe à l'Apocalyptique,* I, Paris 1977, 429–38; **H. G. M. Williamson,** *The Book Called Isaiah,* Oxford 1994, 217–39.

The chapter, consisting of very different liturgical forms, has been shaped into a unified presentation of Isaiah's vision of the future after the threat from the great enemy has been overcome. God intervenes in majesty on Israel's behalf and promises to those who walk righteously a share in Zion's restored status as a place of divine presence and secure dwelling.

1. Structure, Context, and Editorial Shaping

The decisive modern essay on chapter 33 has been that of Gunkel in 1924, who built onto some initial insights of Mowinckel. Gunkel first reviewed the scholarly efforts of the late nineteenth century to interpret the lack of a rational order in which the mood shifted suddenly from complaint to joy, from the past tense to the future, and from third-person address to first. He felt that he could bring coherence by applying a form-critical method and thus recovering the text's original sociological setting. Indeed he was highly successful in demonstrating the presence of discrete literary genres (woe oracle, communal lament, theophanic oracle, entry liturgy, and prophetic promise). He then argued that these various genres functioned as a unified prophetic liturgy within the cultic life of the late Jewish community. The liturgy presupposed the destruction of

Jerusalem and awaited the restoration of Zion when oppressors would be destroyed, Jerusalem restored, and Zion reestablished under the kingship of Yahweh.

Gunkel's thesis has been widely accepted with minor modification for at least fifty years, but increasingly some new critical voices have been raised. First, there is really no hard evidence for a liturgy, and thus his theory remains at best a brilliant piece of speculation. Second, a very different picture of exilic and postexilic Judaism has emerged since Gunkel's era. The cultic theory of Mowinckel and Gunkel has greatly receded, and in its place an emphasis on scribal editorial activity has moved to the forefront, especially in the exilic and postexilic periods. Actualization of the past was not carved out primarily through cultic means, but above all through the reuse of the growing written corpus of authoritative scripture. As a result, many recent commentators have argued that Gunkel's genres constitute a level below the surface of the present written composition, and various attempts have been made to recover the redactional process involved in this development. The danger in this new model is that some interpreters have returned to a literary analysis akin to a pre-Gunkel period and have again atomized the text into numerous redactional layers.

I would argue that redactional critics have correctly seen that chapter 33 is not a cultic libretto, but that the conventional forms, once shaped by oral tradition, now are in the background of the present text. These forms have been editorially reshaped into a literary composition. However, the hermeneutical and exegetical problem lies in determining how this shaping has been carved out. Even more than in chapter 32, chapter 33 shows a high degree of intertextual reinterpretation. Chapter 33 reflects the common Isaianic pattern of Israel's desolation by enemies, of divine deliverance, and of the establishment of the rule of God, but it does so by reusing prior prophetic and psalmnic tradition, which it joins into a holistic interpretation with events taken from its continuing experience with God. In the context of the narrative sequence of chapters 28–32, earlier Isaianic oracles are reused to reinterpret the events leading up to the attack on Jerusalem during the reign of King Hezekiah. Although it has previously been pointed out that occasionally influences from chapters 36–39 have been retrojected back into chapters 28–32, by and large, the major textual influences came from chapters 1–12 and 13–27. The implications for dating the final literary composition will be dealt with below.

The position I have briefly outlined had been largely formulated when I first read the 1991 essay of W. A. M. Beuken of chapter 33. His brilliant article rivals in importance that of Gunkel. Beuken not only lays his major emphasis upon the intertextual reuse of written canonical tradition, but offers an intriguing hypothesis of chapter 33 as a "mirror text" (*Spiegeltext*). This is to say, there is a recognized literary genre that performs a unique function of highlighting a holistic dimension of a narrative through a subtle form of repetition and mirror imaging of an entire sequence of texts. The important implication of this hypothesis is that the context from which to interpret chapter 33 is no longer seen as a reconstructed cultic liturgy, nor as a redactional process involving distinct historical layers, but as a synchronic setting within the book of Isaiah. The less important issue of whether Beuken's theory of "mirror text" can be accepted in all its details can be delayed until the concluding summary of this chapter. Clearly this is a radically new model of interpretation for which one can only be grateful.

Very recently there has appeared another learned attempt, by Williamson, to interpret chapter 33 (221ff.). In his treatment he agrees in part with Beuken, but the focus of his research is very different. He goes to great lengths to date components of the oracle in his effort to support his larger redactional theory that Second Isaiah was the redactional editor of First Isaiah. He attempts to prove that chapter 33 served the editor as a transition to his own material of chapters 40 – 55. I do not doubt that Williamson has made some interesting observations, but his reading of the chapter is an oblique one, both to the concerns of this commentary and to chapter 33 as well, and this will not be pursued further.

2. Exposition

One of the major tasks of the exegesis will be to present evidence for asserting that the dominant function of the chapter is intertextual reinterpretation.

[**33:1**] Chapter 33 opens as a familiar woe oracle, but now addressed to an unnamed destroyer who will shortly be destroyed. The further stipulation that when he has ceased his destructive activity divine judgment will fall also on him calls to mind the clear reference to Assyria in 10:12 and 14:24ff. However, that Israel's enemy can at the same time be multidimensional arises from the observation of the occurrence of the same two doubly formed verbs *šdd* ("destroy") and *bgd* ("deal treacherously"), which has its verbal parallel in 21:2. Nowhere else in the Old Testament does this word pair occur. Further, Beuken argues that 33:1 is built on 21:2 both synchronically and diachronically. Since in chapter 21 the enemy is identified with the fall of Babylon (v. 9), a typological relation between Assyria and Babylon is here envisioned, which was apparent already in chapter 14 (cf. 24:16).

[**2**] The juxtaposition of the two Hebrew verbs in v. 2a also occurs in 30:18–19. An equally close parallel is found in 8:17, which reflects a similar confessional form. The confessional form again occurs in 25:1ff. and 12:1ff. In the latter passage the note of salvation (v. 2) resonates in 33:2. The motif of rescue coming in the morning hour is also a familiar hope of Israel (Ps. 46:6). Beuken correctly points out the theological significance of the voice of the faithful anticipating salvation in 12:1ff., which is now being confirmed in a thanksgiving song of 33:2.

[3] Following the plea for help in v. 2, there follows the description of God's theophanic entrance. The effect is paralleled to the flight and the roar of the nations in 17:12ff. and in the theophany of 30:27–28a.

[5–6] The theme of Yahweh's exalted position on high is familiar from 2:11, 17 and 12:4; however, the description in vv. 5b–6 is far closer than just a thematic parallel. The description of Yahweh's rule of righteousness and equity (cf. 1:27) in terms of "wisdom," "knowledge," and "fear of Yahweh" has a striking intertextual referent in 11:1–10.

[7–9] The initial phrase in v. 7 involves a very difficult text-critical problem (cf. textual notes), and thus it is unwise to overemphasize the issue of intertextuality. If one follows the frequent emendation and reads "people of Ariel," then the play on 29:1 is obvious. Beuken pursues an interesting approach in comparing the level of intertextual resonance if other textual options are accepted. His probe would favor a reference to Ariel in 33:7, but the results can hardly be conclusive and caution is called for in this case.

A more convincing intertextual parallel occurs between vv. 8b–9 and 24:3–7. The complaint over the chaotic conditions of the land is closely related to the apocalyptic description in 24:3–7 and shares a number of striking verbal parallels including "the land is parched and withered" (v. 9), and "treaties are broken" (v. 8). Interestingly, 35:2 portrays the transformation of nature in an eschatological reversal by picking up from 33:9 the reference to Lebanon, Sharon, and Carmel, a geographical parallel that only occurs in these two passages. Beuken includes in his list several alleged intertextual references to Second Isaiah, but none seem to be fully convincing, although a distant allusion is certainly possible.

[10–13] The reference in v. 10 to Yahweh's arising, lifting up, and being exalted has a thematic connection with 2:6–22, but there are no exact verbal parallels. The explicit emphasis in the verse to the advent "now" could perhaps be interpreted as a fulfillment of an earlier anticipation, but the evidence is inconclusive and should not be pressed.

[14–16] The form of these verses was long since identified by Gunkel as a "temple entry liturgy" such as is found in Psalms 15 and 24. Worshippers seeking entrance into the sacred temple area follow a convention of first requesting admission and being given the moral qualifications required for entry. The Isaianic text is apparently using this ancient liturgical form in a fresh metaphorical way to make the point that those who wish to share in the coming "peaceful habitation" of Zion must reflect a righteous way of life separated from violence and bloodshed that accords with the holiness of God's presence within the city.

[17–24] Much debate turns on the interpretation of the word "king" (v. 17) in the context of chapter 33. A large number of commentators insist that Yahweh is clearly meant and appeal for their strongest warrant to v. 22: "For the LORD is our judge, the LORD is our prince, the LORD is our king." Additional support for this interpretation is then adduced from a historical argument—

namely, that in the late postexilic period, hope in an earthly messianic king had failed and now resided solely in God's eschatological rule.

In my judgment, both arguments are not fully convincing. Rather, I would suggest that the reference to a king is an intertextual reference to 32:1. The appeal to his beauty is a conventional attribute of the reigning king according to ancient Near Eastern royal ideology (Psalms 45 and 72). The verses that then follow (vv. 17bff.) describe an earthly kingdom and continue to make use of the language of "peaceful habitation" found in 32:17ff. The righteous reign of God's anointed will not be encumbered by a search for military power ("the one in charge of the towers," v. 18), nor by a peace negotiated through treaties ("the weigher of tribute'). Nor will his rule be any longer threatened by an insolent people speaking a foreign tongue. Here the reference is to the Assyrians of 28:11, but may also have picked up additional coloring from the Rabshakeh's speech in chapter 36. Certainly his behavior was traditionally regarded as the epitome of insolence and arrogance (37:23ff.). However, to identify the king of v. 17 with Hezekiah is an unwarranted historization of the text.

The concern of the text is rather to offer a very different interpretive commentary on the coming events. Indeed, there will be the anticipated messianic king, but his function remains as always to serve as an earthly representative of Israel's true heavenly king. Jerusalem will be transformed because Yahweh will be "for us" in all his majesty. Most assuredly, Yahweh is Israel's judge, ruler, and above all, king. This reference has clearly in mind the prophet's vision of Yahweh's majestically reigning over his creation as king (6:1ff.). The attempt to separate along a redactional trajectory the hope of a messianic king from one solely restricted to God's reign fragments the theological unity of the biblical text, which is maintained in different and subtle ways throughout the entire book.

The concluding verses in the chapter are difficult to interpret both because of textual problems and because of the apparent lack of coherent context. These difficulties have called forth a variety of textual emendations and interpretations. Probably the emendation suggested by the NJPS is the least intrusive. It interprets the loose tackle of v. 23 as belonging to the enemy and understands the passage to mean that Jerusalem will be made inaccessible to its foes, as if surrounded by an impossible sea. The concluding theme of God's removing all illness through his forgiveness was adumbrated in 30:19ff., but only developed at great length in 65:17ff.

To summarize the chapter: The major credit for correctly interpreting chapter 33 goes to Beuken, who has convincingly demonstrated the crucial role that intertextuality has played in both summarizing and creatively reinterpreting the major themes of the prophetic message in a fresh manner. His appeal to a literary technique of "mirror image" has greatly sharpened the debate. However, I am hesitant fully to embrace the application of this alleged genre to chapter 33, lest it also introduce unnecessary and even misleading features into the exegesis. I am thinking especially of Beuken's discussion of the relation of narrative—a crucial component of the "mirror text" genre—and prophecy. Rather than attempting to interpret the ability of the prophetic text to absorb retrospective and prospective elements into his message as a special literary technique, I would prefer interpreting this phenomenon as theologically constitutive of Old Testament prophecy and thus also reflected in texts that are only peripherally related to the genre of a "mirror text" (cf. Childs, "Retrospective Reading of the Old Testament Prophets").

This hesitancy in no way detracts from the major contribution of Beuken in recovering a "canonical context" (according to my terminology) from which to offer a holistic reading of the chapter, rather than positing a reconstructed cultic or redactional setting. In this regard, I do not feel that Sweeney's generally positive evaluation of Beuken's essay has fully grasped the extent to which his own largely form-critical, historical, and redactional categories have been severely undermined by Beuken's approach to this chapter.

Although I think that the issue of the dating of chapter 33 has been greatly relativized in importance by the newer understanding of its literary context (this is not really grasped by Roberts), there are still some historical implications to be drawn from this highly developed exegetical technique. The evidence of this growth would establish the age of the shaping of the final form of chapter 33 most likely in the Persian or postexilic periods. The critical question of how the chapter functions in relation to chapters 1—32, 34—35, and 40ff. will be examined later in the commentary.

Equally important are the hermeneutical implications to be drawn from the manner by which chapter 33 was shaped. A very different model for interpreting the Old Testament prophetic books in general has begun to emerge. Crucial for the transmission process is the recognition that the prophetic voice has been extended to the next generation by means of its contextualized form within a written corpus of prophetic scripture. In chapter 33 the literary technique of intertextuality has reached a very developed stage with both a retrospective and prospective focus, that is, pointing backward and forward. Yet the transmission process, while greatly enriching the density of the original Isaianic proclamation from the wider perspective of the editors, has not shattered the narrative structure within which the material functions. The newly redactored literary form has retained the larger historical context of Isaiah's ministry leading up to the Assyrian attack on Jerusalem.

36. Isaiah 34:1–35:10

34:1 Draw near, O nations, and listen,
    pay attention, you peoples!
Let the earth and its inhabitants hear,
    the world and all that comes from it.

2   For the LORD is angry at all the nations,
        and furious at all their hosts.
    He has sentenced them, delivering them over to slaughter.

3   Their slain will be thrown out,
        and the stench of their corpses will rise.
    The mountains will be soaked with their blood.

4   All the hosts of heaven[a] will fade away,
        and the skies will be rolled up like a scroll.
    And all their host will fade away,
        like withered leaves on the vine,
    like shriveled fruit from the fig tree.

5   For my sword will be drunk[b] in the heavens.
        See, it descends for judgment upon Edom,
        upon the people I have doomed.

6   The sword of the LORD is saturated with blood;
        it is gorged with fat,
        with the blood of lambs and goats,
        fat from the kidneys of rams.
    For the LORD has a sacrifice in Bozrah,
        a great slaughter in Edom.

7   Wild oxen will fall with them,
        and young steers with mighty bulls.
    Their land will be soaked with blood,
        and their soil will be saturated with fat.

8   For the LORD has a day of vengeance,
        a year of retribution for Zion's cause.

9   Its streams will be turned to pitch,
        and its soil into brimstone.
    Its land will become burning pitch.

10   Night and day it will never be extinguished;
        its smoke will rise forever.
    From generation to generation it will lie desolate;
        no one will ever pass through it again.

11   But the owl[c] and buzzard will possess it,
        the hornbill and the raven will dwell in it.
    He will measure it with a line of chaos,
        and with weights of emptiness.

12   Its nobles[d]—there is no kingdom there to proclaim;
        all its princes will vanish.

13   Thorns will grow up in its palaces,
        nettles and briars in its fortresses.

It will be a haunt of jackals,
    a home for ostriches.
14   Devils will meet with hyenas,
        goat-demons will cry to each other.
    There also the night creatures will take repose
        and find a resting place.
15   There the arrow-snake[e] will nest and lay eggs.
        She will brood and hatch in its shade.
    There also the kites will be gathered,
        each with its mate.
16   Search and read from the scroll of the LORD.
        Not one of these is missing,
        none will be without a mate.
    For it is his mouth that has commanded,
        and his spirit has gathered them.
17   He has cast his lot for them;
        his hand has distributed it to them with the line.
    They will possess it forever,
        from generation to generation they will dwell in it.
35:1 The desert and the parched land will be glad.
        The wilderness will rejoice and blossom;
        like the crocus, 2 it will burst into bloom.
        It will also rejoice and shout.
    The glory of Lebanon will be given to it,
        the splendor of Carmel and Sharon.
    They will behold the glory of the LORD,
        the splendor of our God.
3   Strengthen the feeble hands,
        and steady the tottering knees.
4   Say to those who are fearful,
        be strong, fear not.
    Behold, your God!
        He will come with vengeance,
    with divine retribution;
        he will come and save you.
5   Then the eyes of the blind will be opened,
        and the ears of the deaf unstopped.
6   Then will the lame leap like a deer,
        and the tongue of the dumb shout for joy.
    Waters will gush in the wilderness,
        and streams in the desert.

7   The burning sand will become a pool,
    and the parched land springs of water.
    In the place of jackels, where they live,[f]
    grass will spring up with reeds and rushes.
8   A highway will be there
    that will be called the Holy Way.
    No one unclean will pass along it.[g]
    It will be for them who walk in the way,
    and the fools will not go on it.
9   No lion will be there,
    nor shall any ravenous beast come upon it.
    They will not be found there;
    only the redeemed will walk on it.
10   The ransomed of the LORD will return,
    and come to Zion with singing.
    Everlasting joy will crown their heads.
    Joy and gladness will overtake them,
    and sorrow and sighing will disappear.

a. *BHS* suggests emending to "hills" for the sake of parallelism.

b. Some read the verb *r'h* ("see") instead of *rwh*. A qal form is preferable to a piel.

c. The various birds and creatures are conjectural; cf. a Hebrew lexicon for the various proposals.

d. The position of "nobles," whether on the end of v. 11 or beginning of v. 12, remains debated.

e. The noun *qippôz* is a *hapax legomenon* with uncertain meaning. NEB translates "sand-partridge." Cf. Wildberger's continuing doubts for a resolution.

f. The meaning of the Hebrew is unclear.

g. The text seems to be in some disorder (cf. Barthélemy, *CTLAT*).

Selected Bibliography

J. R. Bartlett, "Edom and the Fall of Jerusalem 587 B.C.," *PEQ,* 114, 1982, 13–24; **W. A. M. Beuken,** "Isaiah 34: Lament in Isaianic Context," *OTE* 5, 1992, 78–102; **G. I. Davies,** "The Destiny of the Nations in the Book of Isaiah," *The Book of Isaiah,* ed. J. Vermeylen, Leuven 1989, 93–120; **B. Dicou,** "Literary Function and Literary History of Isaiah 34," *BN* 58, 1991, 30–45; *"Edom, Israel's Brother and Antagonist,"* JSOTSup 169, Sheffield 1994; **H. Donner,** "'Forscht in der Schrift Jahwes und lest.' Ein Beitrag zum Verständnis der israelitischen Prophetie," *ZTK* 87, 1990, 285–98; **K. Elliger,** *Deuterojesaja in seinem Verhältnis zu Tritojesaja,* BWANT 4/11, Stuttgart 1933; **B. Gosse,** "Isaïe 34–35. Le chatiment d'Edom et des nations, salut pour Sion," *ZAW* 102, 396–404; **V. Lauterjung,** "Zur Textgestalt von Jes. 34, 16," *ZAW* 91, 124–25; **C. R. Matthews,** *Defending Zion: Edom's Desolation and Jacob's Restoration (Isaiah 34–35) in Context,* BZAW 236, Berlin 1995; **J. Muilenburg,** "The Literary Character of Isaiah 34," *JBL* 59, 339–65; **M. Pope,** "Isaiah 34 in Relation to Isaiah 35, 40–66," *JBL* 71, 1952, 235–43; **R. B. Y. Scott,** "The Relation of Chapter 35 to Deutero-Isaiah," *AJSL* 52, 1935, 178–91; **O. H. Steck,** *Bereitete Heimkehr. Jesaja 35 als redaktionelle Brücke zwischen dem Ersten und dem Zweiten Jesaja,*

SBS 121, Stuttgart 1985; **M. A. Sweeney,** *Isaiah 1–39,* FOTL 16, Grand Rapids 1996, 434–54; **V. Tanghe,** "Der Schriftgelehrte in Jes 34, 16–17," *ETL* 67, 1991, 338–45; **C. C. Torrey,** *The Second Isaiah,* Edinburgh 1928; **J. Vermeylen,** *Du Prophète Isaïe á l'Apocalyptique,* 1, Paris 1977, 439–46; **H. G. M. Williamson,** *The Book Called Isaiah,* Oxford 1994, 213–20.

1. Structure and Editorial Shaping

Although critics in the nineteenth century (Duhm, Cheyne) argued for a late postexilic dating of chapters 34 and 35 and considered them to be an appendix to the collection of chapters 1 — 33, the modern critical debate regarding these chapters was launched in 1928 when Torrey proposed that they were written by Second Isaiah and were subsequently displaced by the insertion of chapters 36 — 39. Several well-known lexical studies (Scott, Pope) tended to support Second Isaiah's authorship.

A newer approach was ushered in with a shift away from questions of authorship to those of redactional intent. Elliger's careful study confirmed the relation of chapters 34 and 35 to both Second and Third Isaiah, but concluded that this redactional layer was not composed by either of the above Isaianic authors. Most recently there has been a veritable explosion of redactional studies (Vermeylen, Gosse, Beuken, Dicou, Sweeney) that has sought to investigate the editorial function of these chapters within the larger framework of the book of Isaiah as a whole. In distinction from the earlier lexical studies, there has been widespread agreement that the literary parallels adduced must be critically evaluated rather than being merely counted. For example, are the vocabulary affinities between chapters 34 and 40 — 66 to be given precedence over the large number of words in chapter 34 that are not found in chapters 40 — 66? Or again, what role does one assign to apparent similarities of syntax and style?

As a result, a much more complex and subtle picture of intertextual relationships has emerged. Chapter 34 is not so clearly connected to chapters 40 — 66 as is chapter 35; nevertheless, there are strong parallels to chapter 13 and especially to chapter 63. Beuken has made a strong case that chapter 34 reflects both retrospective and prospective connections including signs that the entire corpus of the Isaianic collection appears to have influenced its shaping. In contrast, chapter 35 relates only occasionally to chapter 34 (cf. 35:4b // 34:8; 35:7 // 34:13), but it largely shares a perspective directed toward the future, closely related to 40 — 55 and 56 — 66. Although chapters 34 and 35 appear once to have had independent compositional histories, they now function redactionally as a diptych to form an editorial bridge combining the first part of Isaiah with the second. The two major themes of the chapters, namely, the divine judgment of the nations and the return of the redeemed to Zion, point both backward to the earlier Isaianic prophecies as well as forward to the ensuing chapters.

2. Hermeneutical Problems at Stake in the Interpretation

At this juncture a major methodological problem arises. It is one that has frequently engaged this commentary and that is directed to commonly held assumptions of modern redactional criticism. Although I fully agree that the composition of the book of Isaiah developed over a lengthy period and that the narrative sequence of the book is not coterminous with its compositional history, it remains very doubtful that the meaning of the biblical text can be determined by direct recourse to a diachronic reconstruction of its redactional history.

The most ambitious form of redactional criticism of chapter 35 has been recently expounded by O. H. Steck, who has developed an elaborate hypothesis about the role of chapter 35 as a literary construct that was written as a bridge passage to join the two major parts of the book into a whole. It is very difficult to engage this highly learned redactional thesis in a brief fashion. The problem is that Steck's thesis regarding chapter 35 is a complete package resting on his larger redactional theories. If one does accept, for example, his understanding of the growth of First Isaiah and Second Isaiah as largely individual collections only later to be joined by chapter 35, his detailed arguments remain unconvincing. Similarly, when he envisions a horizontal redactional strand extending from chapter 35 back to 11:1–16; 27:12–13; and forward to 62:10–12, he makes redactional moves that for many remain far from persuasive. In sum, for the purpose of this commentary a debate over his oblique reading of the chapter does not seem useful. I have similar reservations with Sweeney's analysis (447ff.), which falls back into a form of historically referential rending, depending on alleged indices of fifth- and sixth-century events that, at the very most, lie deeply buried in the background of the present text.

Far more promising is the lead offered by Beuken (78ff.), who is concerned to show how chapters 34—35 have rendered a holistic reading of the book by an intertextual use of various parts of the book. Crucial to the debate is that one does not too quickly attempt to reconstruct historical trajectories within levels of intertextuality, since linkages are at times clear but at other times far less so.

The basic hermeneutical point to make is that the context from which a text is finally understood is not a reconstructed historical or redactional one, but is that of the written corpus of Isaianic scripture. To be sure, this corpus is far from monolithic and often a chorus of voices can be heard, but the exegetical task is to hear these voices of scripture in the configuration in which they have been canonically shaped. To the extent that a diachronic reconstruction of a text aids in interpreting the multilayered form of a witness, it can be useful, but diachronic reconstructions recovered from editorial seams do not hold the key to understanding the sense of the shaped text.

The discovery that even within so-called First Isaiah there are many late voices (exilic and postexilic), as is the case with both chapters 34 and 35, is an important confirmation that the canonical ordering of the book of Isaiah into a holistic witness stretched over many centuries. The authentic witness of the book of Isaiah has not been made in terms of a single authorial identity, but rather the living prophetic word extends deeply into the postexilic period. Isaiah 40:8 offers the best theological warrant for this position: "The grass withers, flowers fade, but the word of our God stands forever."

3. The Function of Chapters 34 and 35

I judge that a convincing case can be made that chapters 34 and 35 together form a bridge between chapters 1—33 and 40—66. Both chapters show a high level of intertextuality with other parts of the book, and together the two chapters function as two halves of one whole. Chapter 34 is linked largely with chapters 1—33, especially with chapters 13 and 24, and therefore is predominately retrospective in its editorial function. However, there is a major exception to this characterization, namely, its close tie to chapter 63. Moreover, the lack of a strong link with chapters 40—55 suggests that at some stage chapter 34 was independent of chapter 35. In contrast, chapter 35 has its closest ties with Second and Third Isaiah (chapters 40—55, 56—66). Although it does share with chapters such as Isaiah 12 the language of Second Isaiah, the predominant direction of its perspective is toward the future, not the past. The imagery of chapter 35 is dominated by the imagery of Second Isaiah (the glory of God, v. 2; the opening of the blind eyes, v. 5; the highway for the redeemed to pass, vv. 8ff.), and even a verbal citation of 51:11 occurs in v. 10.

The two chapters function together as diptych even though there is no explicit syntactical linkage made. The relation is that of a reverse correspondence and together they summarize the two major parts of the Isaianic corpus: God's power over the nations, and the exaltation of Zion for the salvation of Israel. The crucial decision to make regards the peculiar function of these chapters in their present position. Chapter 34 picks up from chapters 13—23 the call to the nations to bear witness to God's sovereign power and to his imminent cosmological retribution. The geographical sweep is far broader than in chapters 28—33. Already the rod of punishment has been transferred from Assyria to Babylon (13:15), and the proud boasting of Assyria before its destruction (chapters 36—37) is paralleled by the taunt against the king of Babylon (chapter 14).

In the light of this tendency to transcend the specific enemies of Israel's past into one of universal eschatological judgment, it comes initially as a surprise to find the ensuing verses of chapter 34 focused exclusively on the destruction of Edom, a nation not included in chapters 13—23. Yet clearly Edom functions within the chapter as the representative of the hostile enemy of Israel par excellence, the symbol of all that evokes the divine wrath. Its destruction is portrayed in the language of the overthrow of Sodom and Gomorrah in vv. 9–10. However, now the final judgment extends even beyond the destruction of Assyria (chapters 36ff.) and of Babylon (chapter 39) to foreshadow the ultimate purpose of God. In chapter 34 the judgment of Edom that precedes the redemption of Zion still lies in the future. Yet it is certain and can be confirmed from scripture itself (34:16). Moreover, chapter 34 also points referentially forward to chapter 63 in which the divine judgment of Edom has already occurred and now lies in the past.

The same typological tendency to transcend the specificity of earlier texts and to extend the prophecy in a more radically eschatological move can also be seen in chapter 35. The same imagery of Second Isaiah recurs—the eyes of the blind opened, the transformation of the wilderness, the highway for the returnees— yet the images have increasingly taken on a metaphorical tone. The highway is not just a means of improving the route home, but now is portrayed as a holy path reserved for the pure of heart.

This particular shaping of the two chapters also explains why chapters 34— 35 were placed before, and not after, chapters 36—39. The latter chapters were not just a historical appendix transferred from the book of Kings, but already have been shaped to anticipate the coming of the Babylonian exile following the period of Assyrian threat and pointing to the death and rebirth of the nations (cf. the exposition on chapters 36ff.). The form and function of chapters 34 and 35 in their present literary position within the book projects the divine plan beyond both these historical periods and focuses on the final eschatological exaltation of Zion and the entrance into the ultimate joy of the kingdom of God (v. 10).

4. Exposition

[**34: 1–17**] The nations are summoned to hear the indictment, to witness their destruction. The structure of what follows is determined by the particle *kî* ("for") in vv. 2, 5, 6–7, and 8, which sets forth the grounds for the execution of Yahweh's anger against Edom and demonstrates that the oracle against the nations (vv. 1–4) is integrally joined with Edom's destruction. The unit begins with the anger of Yahweh toward the nations, portrayed as an apocalyptic slaughter. It progresses from the description of God's cosmic sword, gorged with fat, and continues to the great sacrifice in blood-soaked Edom. The description culminates with the ultimate execution of Yahweh's day of vengeance. Edom is turned into the burning inferno of Sodom, a land of fire, brimstone, and eternally rising smoke. The repetition of the phrase "from generation to generation" in vv. 10 and 17 encapsulates the tone of finality. The imagery of limitless destruction is extended by means of piling up of figures of utter waste: none will pass through it, only unclean beasts inhabit this wilderness, the threat of chaos (*tōhû wābōhû*, Gen. 1:2) hangs over it, there is "no kingdom there."

The most extended symbol of desolation is that of the land being inhabited only by repulsive creatures: jackals and hyenas, the arrow-snake and kites gather. The closest parallel to these particular birds and beasts is found in 13:17ff., which describes the desolation wrought on Babylon by the Medes. Not only does the list overlap in large measure, but the same imagery of Sodom and Gomorrah, barren for all generations, recurs. The fact that the same imagery regarding Babylon is now extended to Edom is a further warrant for the representative role that Edom has assumed in God's final destruction of the enemy.

Much recent debate has been evoked regarding the interpretation of v. 16. The clause "Search and read from the scroll of Yahweh," is extremely perplexing. For one thing, it appears to interrupt the sequence of v. 15b, which joins to v. 16b. Again, it is argued that the imperative to seek and read reflects a much later scribal terminology unknown until the Hellenistic period. For such reasons, Wildberger and Beuken eliminate the words as a disturbing gloss. In my opinion, even though they might be a subsequent editorial expansion—the evidence is not decisive—the clause should not be eliminated as insignificant. Rather, it reflects an exegetical activity, perhaps expressed in the terminology of a later period, but one we have been observing with increasing frequency throughout the preceding chapters of Isaiah, which was designated as intertextuality. The point is that the reader is urged to find confirmation to the prophecy of Edom's destruction by looking elsewhere in scripture. The exact scope of the "scroll of Yahweh" is not stated in the text, and some (e.g., Calvin) have identified it with the Pentateuch. I am rather inclined to see it as a reference to the earlier prophecies of Isaiah, especially to chapter 13.

Other commentators (Procksch, Eichrodt) are disturbed that the appeal to confirm a prophetic judgment in v. 16 must refer to something more significant than the presence of unclean animals in the land of Edom. By transferring v. 17 to before v. 16, it is argued that the issue originally turned on a confirmation of the destruction of the land of Edom. However, I do not think that the suggested emendation is necessary, especially if one understands the intertextual function of the enumeration of the animals from chapter 13, which is used to signal a concrete fulfillment of the prophetic threat.

[35:1–10] Without the use of any specific syntactical markers to bind the two chapters together, chapter 35 immediately launches into an elaborate portrayal of the salvation of Israel. The imagery is not only closely related to that of chapters 40ff.—the desert blossoming, the joyful singing, the seeing of Yahweh's glory—but the vocabulary of v. 4 offers a parallel to 40:9–10: "Behold, your God! He will come."

The call to take courage (v. 3) before the imminent salvation is entirely famil-iar from Second Isaiah (cf. 43:1ff.), as is the opening of the eyes of the blind and the healing of the lame (vv. 5–6; cf. 40:5; 42:7). What is different in the shap-ing of the tradition of Second Isaiah in chapter 35 is that the imagery of the return to Zion has been extended far beyond the concrete historical situation depicted in chapters 40ff. To be sure, the strongest continuity with the return to Zion has been maintained when 34:10 cites 51:11. Nevertheless, there is a broader, metaphorical construal of the imagery. The highway is called "the Holy Way." Not all the refugees from Babylon are pictured returning on this highway, cer-tainly not the unclean and foolish. Rather, the use by chapter 34 of the imagery anticipates the refinements of the promise from the final chapters of the book in which God is pictured dwelling with only the one "who is repentant and hum-ble in spirit" (57:15ff.). Moreover, salvation is not merely deliverance from Babylonian captivity, but rather sharing in God's new creation (65:17ff.). Isaiah 35:10 picks up this same theme, "sorrow and sighing will disappear," which is finally elaborated in its fullest form in chapter 65.

37. INTRODUCTION TO
ISAIAH 36—39

Selected Bibliography

P. Ackroyd, "An Interpretation of the Babylonian Exile: A Study of II Kings 20 and Isaiah 38—39,"
SJT 27, 1974, 329–52; reprinted in *Studies in the Religious Tradition of the Old Testament,* London
1987, 152–71; "Isaiah 36—39: Structure and Function," *Von Kanaan bis Kerala. Fs J. P. M. van der
Ploeg,* ed. W. C. Delsman et al. AOAT 211, 1982, 3–21; reprinted in *Studies in the Religious Tradition,*
105–20; "The Biblical Interpretation of the Reigns of Ahaz and Hezekiah," *In the Shelter of Elyon, Fs
G. W. Ahlström,* ed. W. B. Barrick and J. R. Spencer, Sheffield, JSOTSup 31. 1984, 247–59; reprinted
in *Studies in the Religious Tradition,* 181–92; **M. L. Barré,** "Restoring the 'Lost' Prayer in the Psalm
of Hezekiah (Isaiah 38:16–17b)," *JBL* 114, 1995, 385–99; **C. T. Begg,** "2 Kings 20:12–19 as an Element of the Deuteronomistic History," *CBQ* 48, 1986, 27–38; **J. Begrich,** *Der Psalm des Hiskia,*
FRLANT 42, Göttingen 1926; **E. Ben Zvi,** "Who Wrote the Speech of Rabshakeh and When?" *JBL* 109,
1990, 79–90; **J. Bright,** "Excursus I. The Problem of Sennacherib's Campaigns in Palestine," *A History
of Israel,* 3d ed., 1981, 298–309; **J. A. Brinkman,** "Merodach-Baladan II," *Studies Presented to A. Leo
Oppenheim,* Chicago 1964, 6–53; **D. M. Carr,** "What Can We Say about the Tradition History of Isaiah?
A Response to Christopher Seitz's *Zion's Final Destiny*," *SBL 1992 Seminar Papers,* 583–97;
B. S. Childs, *Isaiah and the Assyrian Crisis,* SBT II/3, London 1967; "Psalm Titles and Midrashic Exegesis," *JSS* 16, 1971, 137–50; **R. E. Clements,** *Isaiah 1—39,* NCB, Grand Rapids and London 1980;
*Isaiah and the Deliverance of Jerusalem: A Study of the Interpretation of Prophecy in the Old Testa-
ment,* JSOTSup 13, Sheffield 1980; "The Prophecies of Isaiah and the Fall of Jerusalem in 587 B.C.," *VT*
30, 1980, 421–36; "The Isaiah Narrative of 2 Kings 20:12–19 and the Date of the Deuteronomic History," *Essays on the Bible and the Ancient World, Fs I. L. Seeligmann,* ed. A. Rofé and Y. Zakovitch,
Jerusalem 1983, 3:209–20; "The Prophecies of Isaiah to Hezekiah Concerning Sennacherib: 2 Kings
19:21 // Isaiah 37:22–35," *Prophetie und geschichtliche Wirklichkeit im Alten Israel, Fs S. Herrmann,*
ed. R. Luvak and S. Wagner, Stuttgart 1991, 65–78; "Isaiah 14, 22–27. A Central Passage Reconsidered," *The Book of Isaiah,* ed. J. Vermeylen, Leuven 1989, 253–62; "The Politics of Blasphemy," "*Wer
ist wie du, Herr, unter den Göttern?*" *Fs O. Kaiser,* ed. J. Kottsieper et al., Göttingen 1994, 231–46;
M. Cogan and H. Tadmor, *II Kings,* AB, New York 1988; **C. Cohen,** "Neo-Assyrian Elements in the
First Speech of the Biblical Rab-šaqê," *IOS* 9, 1979, 32–48; **P.E. Dion,** "Sennacherib's Expedition to
Palestine," *Église et Théologie* 26, 1989, 5–25; **H. Frei,** *The Eclipse of Biblical Narrative,* New Haven
1974; **F. J. Gonçalves,** *L'Expédition de Sennachérib en Palestine dans la littérature hébraïque anci-
enne,* Ebib ns 7, Paris 1986; **J. W. Groves,** *Actualization and Interpretation in the Old Testament,*
SBLDS 86, Atlanta 1987; **C. Hardmeier,** *Prophetie im Streit vor dem Untergang Judas,* BZAW 187,
Berlin 1990; **S. Horn,** "Did Sennacherib Campaign Once or Twice against Hezekiah?" *AUSS* 4, 1966,
1–28; **M. Hutter,** *Hiskija König von Juda,* Graz 1982; **C. Jeremias,** "Zu Jes. xxxviii 21f.," *VT* 21, 1971,
104–11; **O. Kaiser,** "Die Verkündigung des Propheten Jesaja im Jahre 701," *ZAW* 81, 1969, 304–15;
A. H. Konkel, "The Sources of the Story of Hezekiah in the Book of Isaiah," *VT* 43, 1993, 462–82;
A. Laato-Åbo, "Hezekiah and the Assyrian Crisis in 701 B.C.," *JSOT* 2, 1987, 49–68; **C. van Leeuwen,**
"Sanchérib devant Jérusalem," *OTS* 14, 1965, 245–72; **R. Liwak,** "Die Rettung Jerusalems im Jahr 701
v Chr.," *ZTK* 83, 1986, 137–66; **B. O. Long,** *2 Kings,* FOTL 10, Grand Rapids 1991; **A. R. Millard,**
"Sennacherib's Attack on Hezekiah," *TynBul* 36, 1985, 61–67; **N. Na'aman,** "Sennacherib's 'Letter to
God' on His Campaign to Judah," *BASOR* 214, 1974, 25–39; **H. S. Nyberg,** "Heskias Danklied Jes. 38,

9–20," *ASTI* 9, 1974, 85–97; **I. Provan,** *Hezekiah and the Book of Kings,* BZAW 172, Berlin 1988; **E. Ruprecht,** "Die ursprüngliche Komposition der Hiskia-Jesaja-Erzählungen und ihre Umstrukturierung durch den Verfasser des deuteronomistischen Geschichtswerkes," *ZTK* 87, 1990, 33–66; **C. R. Seitz,** *Zion's Final Destiny: The Development of the Book of Isaiah: A Reassessment of Isaiah 36–39,* Minneapolis 1991; "Account A and the Annals of Sennacherib: A Reassessment," *JSOT* 58, 1993, 47–57; **K. A. D. Smelik,** "Distortion of Old Testament Prophecy: The Purpose of Isaiah xxxvi and xxxvii," *OTS* 24, 1986, 70–93; **B. Stade,** "Miscellen, Ammerkungen zu 2 Kö, 15–21," *ZAW* 6, 1886, 156–92; **O.H. Steck,** *Bereitete Heimkehr. Jesaja 35 als redaktionelle Brücke zwischen dem Ersten und dem Zweiten Jesaja,* SBS 121, Stuttgart 1985; **M. A. Sweeney,** *Isaiah 1–39,* FOTL 16, Grand Rapids 1996; **J. Vermeylen,** "Hypothèsis sur l'origene d'Isaïe 36–39," *Studies in the Book of Isaiah, Fs W. A. M. Beuken,* ed. J. van Ruiten and M. Vervenne, Leuven 1997, 95–118; **H. G. M. Williamson,** *The Book Called Isaiah,* Oxford 1994; **W. Zimmerli,** "Jesaja und Heskia," *Studien zur alttestamentlichen Theologie und Prophetie,* GA II, Munich 1974, 88–103.

1. New Perspectives on Old Problems

Since my early monograph in 1967 (*Isaiah and the Assyrian Crisis*), there have been many changes in the interpretation of chapters 36—39. These have arisen from a development of new critical tools and from a new set of questions that have been put to the text.

First, Ackroyd broke fresh ground in the early 1970s by showing the role that chapters 36—39 played as a redactional bridge joining First and Second Isaiah. His insights were shortly taken up and expanded with new redactional analyses. Soon it became apparent that the growth of the entire book of Isaiah was equally involved.

Second, the interrelationship between the individual chapters emerged as much more complex than originally thought. The reigning assumption that the chapters were a simple appendix taken from Kings has been seriously challenged, and this debate has spurred a fresh examination of the discrete function of these chapters in the two collections (Isaiah and the Deuteronomistic History).

Third, in spite of the gains made in sorting out apparently different sources, traditions, and redactional layers, especially in chapters 36—37, new attention has now been directed to the need of a synchronic reading that would take seriously the literary shaping of the final form of the text. Indeed, the problem of how the diachronic and the synchronic dimensions of a text relate has become a major hermeneutical concern.

Ever since W. Gesenius's commentary (1821), a wide consensus has argued that the paralleled accounts of 2 Kings 18—20 and Isaiah 36—39 could best be explained by assigning priority to Kings, which was only secondarily taken over by Isaiah. The issue of the direction of influence appeared especially important because of the addition in 2 Kings 18:14–16, shortly designated the A account, which had a close parallel in the Assyrian annals of Sennacherib. The A account in Kings was thought to provide the basic historical perspective on the events of 701 from which the subsequent accounts could be measured.

This widely accepted position has been recently challenged by Smelik among others. He argues that the Isaiah account is primary and only secondarily adopted by the Deuteronomistic History of Kings. Clearly, if this interpretation could be successfully defended, a very different trajectory of these chapters would emerge. The A account of Kings would no longer be assured a central role, but another genre analysis would be possible (cf. Seitz, "Account A").

Smelik has mounted the following reasons for proposing the priority of Isaiah over Kings respecting the traditions of chapters 36—39:

a. This is the only place in Kings when a prophet, whose oracles have been recorded in one of the books of the Latter Prophets, appears in a narrative context. In contrast, the book of Isaiah contains other narratives in which Isaiah figures prominently.
b. The sequence in chapters 38—39 of Hezekiah's sickness and recovery, followed by the visit of Merodach-baladan, which is chronologically out of order, fits coherently with the larger structure of Isaiah in providing a bridge to chapters 40ff. However, the same cannot be said for the overall structure of Kings.
c. The story of the king's illness is better composed in Isaiah than in Kings and demonstrates the dependence of the latter account on the former.

In the scholarly debate that has followed this challenge, Smelik's thesis, followed in part by Seitz, has not, in my judgment, been sustained (cf. e.g., Gonçalves, Sweeney, Williamson). The compelling evidence that has been levelled against Smelik derives from several different perspectives:

a. The argument that the arrangement of chapters 36—39 can only be understood from the perspective of the book of Isaiah has been contested with the countercharge that it also fits within the larger pattern of the Deuteronomistic History. (Cf. the attack of Williamson [208] on Groves's formulation: "in 2 Kings 18—20 this climactic awareness of the exiles leads to—nothing.")
b. The date formulae in chapters 36—39 are at home in the Deuteronomistic corpus rather than in Isaiah. Many details of the chronology point to the priority of Kings, such as the fifteen-year extension of Hezekiah's life, which appears to be calculated from a knowledge of the years of his entire reign found only in 2 Kings 18:2.
c. The argument that 2 Kings 18:14–16 is a later interpolation has not been sustained by such detailed studies as Gonçalves, who found that vv. 14–16 are integrally connected with v. 13. The more likely hypothesis is that vv. 14–16 have been deliberately omitted by Isaiah.
d. The argument that the story of Hezekiah's sickness and recovery in Isaiah 38 has priority over its parallel in 2 Kings 20:1–18 because it is better composed has also not been confirmed (cf. the exposition below).

Nevertheless, the challenge evoked by this debate with Smelik and Seitz has offered a major contribution because it has successfully demonstrated the complexity of the problem, which had previously not been adequately recognized. Thus, in the present form of chapters 36—39 this collection does fit better with Isaiah than with Kings. It most certainly forms a bridge to Second Isaiah. However, what now seems evident is that from an original nucleus the tradition was shaped in different ways by the editors of both Kings and Isaiah. In the present parallel form one can see redactional elements from both of these tradents. The shaping process thus moved in both directions. The chronological formula "the fourteenth year of King Hezekiah" (2 Kings 18:13 // Isa. 36:1) is certainly consistent with the Kings tradition that has also entered into the shaping of chapter 38—namely, the fifteen-year extension of Hezekiah's life. While the arrangement of chapters 36—39 fits well in the redactional intention of Isaiah, it is not the case that it is totally incompatible with the editorial concerns of Kings but is connected with the Babylonian conquest in chapter 24 that fulfilled the prophetic word, and with the fate of Jehoiachin in chapter 25. In sum, the complexity of the redactional evidence has taken the edge off Smelik's most important argument in support of Isaiah's priority, but it has also forced a reexamination of the traditional critical assessment of these chapters that had underestimated the unique contribution of the Isaianic form of the witness.

The second major question of the new debate turns on the analysis of the compositional history of Isaiah 36—37 // 2 Kings 18—19. Ever since Stade and Duhm mounted arguments that chapters 36—37 consisted of two different accounts of the events of 701, several factors entered in a widely accepted source-critical analysis. It was generally assumed that account A (2 Kings 18:14–16), which did not appear in Isaiah but had a close parallel in the Assyrian annals, was the most accurate historical account of 701. Further, many argued that account A formed the basis in some fashion for the expansion of the stories that followed in both Kings and Isaiah. Smelik and Seitz have both challenged the use of the A account as foundational, and have sought to understand Isaiah's account independently of Kings. Once this move was made they denied that there was a real traditio-historical basis for dividing the subsequent B account (2 Kings 18:17ff. // Isa. 36:1ff.) into a B¹ and B² version.

Both of these issues are significant and have evoked much discussion within the last two decades. First, the critical consensus that has emerged does not support the attempt to discount the historical value of the A source, as if it were part of a later redactional issue within Kings. Rather, there is widespread agreement that it has been intentionally removed by the editor of the Isaiah recension because of a redactional intent in its portrayal of Hezekiah as a model king. Second, the argument has not received great support that the B account in Kings and in Isaiah is a unified account of one literary piece. The older source-critical analysis has largely been sustained insofar as it has pointed out the very diverse aspects of the story. Not only did there appear to be two distinct accounts, but there are very different emphases in B[1] and B[2] (cf. Childs, Gonçalves).

Yet once this has been said, the older source-critical approach has been modified and broadened. The problem of distinct voices is far from being fully settled, and both Smelik and Seitz have opened up a new vista of interpretation. They have rightly made a case that the presence of repetitions and literary conventions function well on the synchronic level without an appeal to sources. In my opinion, however, literary coherence on the synchronic level in itself cannot be used to refute in principle the presence of sources on the diachronic level. The balance of this evidence thus supports the presence of at least two voices, whether sources or redactional layers. Yet Smelik and Seitz have correctly observed that the older source analysis did not take seriously the synchonic dimension of the final form of the text. Thus, they shifted the hermeneutical focus to the effect of the unified text on the reader. How was the text construed once B[1] and B[2] were joined? This issue must certainly be addressed in more detail below.

In addition, there has been new attention paid to the relationship of the two layers, B[1] and B[2]. In my earlier work (*Isaiah and the Assyrian Crisis*), I defended the autonomy of both sources. In the light of Gonçalves research (373ff., 445ff.) it now seems more plausible to see a literary dependency of B[2] upon B[1]. The striking parallels in language seem to evidence that B[2] made use of B[1] not just in an oral state, but in some form of a written text for his expansion. I am thus prepared to speak of B[1] and B[2] as redactional layers rather than independent literary sources, but this distinction is not exegetically crucial as long as diachronic growth is recognized.

The exact age of the redactional layers remains hotly debated. Frequently it has been emphasized that the two anachronisms present in respect to Tirhakah and Sennacherib's death would seem to indicate that even B[1] lies at some temporal distance from the events of 701. In my earlier monograph I argued that B[1] reflects an earlier and later face. I still hold that the tensions within the text do not support the hypothesis of a free creation of one another, but that B[1] has continued to be reworked from a postexilic historical core by a subsequent Deuteronomistic layering. B[1] is still very much shaped by a historical coercion of the events, which cannot be simply replaced by the imaginative construal of an editor. In my judgment, B[2] is here quite different in style and content and, in spite of Williamson's argument (196–97) against seeing evidence of language akin to Second Isaiah, does reflect a later period of redaction.

Equally important has been the observation of a level of intertextuality that had not been adequately recognized before. It has long been seen that the Rabshakeh's claim of being sent by Yahweh is related in some fashion to Isaiah's preaching (chapter 10). Also the explicit reference to Hezekiah's removal of Yahweh's altars calls for an evaluation of the source of this information. In the exposition below, I shall defend the position that the speech of the Rabshakeh is not simply a free creation of the redactor and without any serious connection with the historical events of 701 (e.g., Hardmeier, 145ff.), but has an important element of historical verisimilitude.

This same issue leads to the ongoing debate regarding the historicity of these accounts. This issue revolves in part on the datings of the redactional levels of B^1 and B^2, which in turn is much influenced by the redactional role assigned to these chapters within the composition of the book as a whole (cf. below). I shall defend the case for a preexilic component in the B narrative, but largely for different reasons from those mounted by Seitz. In the older debate of the 1950s and 1960s, various estimates of the historical referentiality of the whole were closely related to one's initial literary theory. J. Bright (298ff.), following an interpretation defended by W. F. Albright among others, suggested that the A account of Hezekiah's capitulation (2 Kings 18:14–16), and the subsequent deliverance of Jerusalem, reflected two different historical campaigns. However, there is now a wide scholarly consensus that this reconstruction is highly unlikely and lacks any clear archaeological support for a second invasion in 688.

In contrast to Bright's hypothesis, the more widespread option of a critical reconstruction is the one defended most vigorously by Clements (*Isaiah and the Deliverance of Jerusalem*). Accordingly, the A account confirmed by the Assyrian annals describes the actual historical events of 701 that ended in Hezekiah's capitulation. The subsequent B account is a later midrashic expansion that turned defeat into victory. As I argued already in 1967 (*Isaiah and the Assyrian Crisis,* 14–15), I do not feel that this position is historically compelling, redactionally defensible, or theologically adequate (cf. also the criticisms of Wildberger and Gonçalves).

2. The Relationship among Chapters 36—39

Before turning to the central issue of the function of this corpus as a whole within the book of Isaiah, it is necessary to address briefly the relation of the individual parts. There is agreement that chapters 36 and 37 belonged originally closely together. The same cannot be said for chapters 38 and 39. Chapter 38 is only very loosely related to chapters 36 and 37 by means of a vague chronological formula, "in those days." Moreover, 38:6 // 2 Kings 20:6 imply that the deliverance of Jerusalem reported in chapters 36—37 still lay in the future. This would indicate some likely chronological dislocation within the larger narrative. The sickness theme is then picked up in chapter 39, but the linkage seems wooden. The function of chapter 38 is determined largely by its relation to the Kings parallel as well as the poetic expansion of the "writing of Hezekiah" (38:9–20), which is lacking in Kings.

It has long been noticed that in chapter 39, the visit of Merodach-baladan seems chronologically out of place. Merodach-baladan was the leader of the Babylonian opposition to the Assyrians in the late eighth century, but passed from historical sight after his defeat in 703. Ackroyd has made a strong case that the order of chapters 36—39 is a theological rather than chronological one, and the corpus has been shaped to form a literary bridge from the Assyrian period to the Babylonian in chapters 40ff. ("An Interpretation of the Babylonian Exile," *Studies*, 152ff.).

To summarize: Chapters 36—39 appear to have once had their own independent traditio-historical development. However, their shaping has been determined in the final editorial form by the role assigned to them within the book as a whole, namely, to serve as a bridge from the Assyrian to the Babylonian periods. This editorial role is widely accepted, but the dating for this redactional arrangement continues to be hotly debated.

3. The Forces Shaping Chapters 36—39

Several basic questions have emerged that have over the years dominated the debate over the role of chapters 36—39:

a. How is one to understand the traditions of the deliverance from Assyria (chapters 36—39) in relation to the preaching elsewhere in the eighth century of the prophet Isaiah, who seemed to foresee largely judgment? How is one to explain the shift in the proclamation of Isaiah from judgment to salvation as is dramatized in chapters 36—37?

b. How is one to explain the many signs in the prophetic text that the events of 701 were read in close contact with 587 (cf. Clements, "The Prophecies of Isaiah and the Fall of Jerusalem in 587 B.C.")? If the two events were linked in some fashion, how was the connection made and what was the direction of the influence—forward, backward, or both?

c. One major factor that has been repeatedly mentioned is the typological pattern established between Ahaz in 734 and Hezekiah in 701. One king is the model of unbelief and defeat, the other of faith and victory. If this relationship is one of antithesis, how can Hezekiah be a link with chapters 40—66 when 587 demonstrated a radically different outcome from 701? In other words, in what possible way could the example of 701 serve to illuminate 587?

d. Closely associated with this problem is the relation of chapters 36—39 to the formation of chapters 1—35 and 40—55. Is there not a better option than that of Duhm, who posited that the separate sections of the book developed independently of each other and that only very late, when First and Second Isaiah were fully formed, were chapters 36—39 introduced as a bridge? Many have recently sought to see the influence of Second Isaiah on the formation of

First Isaiah, whether as the actual redactor of First Isaiah
(Williamson) or as one of the many subsequent redactional layers
of the whole book (Steck).

The various hypotheses for resolving these complex issues are greatly
affected by one's overall concept of the true purpose of the entire book. Seitz
defines the view of a forward direction from First Isaiah to Second Isaiah, and
he envisions the concern for Zion's final destiny as explaining the massive
expansion of the corpus in Second and Third Isaiah proceeding from its relation to First Isaiah. Others use an etiological model and see the forces in shaping the book, including the introduction of chapters 36—39, to lie in a concern
for the restoration of the Davidic monarchy, or even in providing advice by way
of an analogy addressed to Zedekiah's political decisions (Hardmeier). Finally,
others like Sweeney are content simply to describe a trajectory of redactions
(seventh-century Josianic, sixth-century Babylonian, fifth-century Ezra-
Nehemiah), which in a loose sense run parallel with the Deuteronomistic and
post-Deuteronomistic editors, each with a discrete agenda.

I shall be making the case for the role of chapters 36—39 to link First and Second Isaiah, much like Ackroyd, but then pursuing the implications for the whole
of the book, including Third Isaiah. It is very possible that in an early form of
chapters 36—37 Hezekiah was indeed contrasted with Ahaz, which explains the
extremely favorable portrayal of Hezekiah in the B[2] layer, and the omission of
his capitulation in the A report. Yet by the time of the Chronicler, Hezekiah's role
has been subordinated, especially in the light of 587, and the Chronicler describes
the king as flawed (2 Chron. 32:25) in spite of his "acts of faithfulness."

Chapters 36—39 were construed after 587 both to confirm First Isaiah's
prophecy of breaking Assyria in the land (14:24ff.), but also to project God's
final purpose with Zion by fulfilling the word of Isaiah in chapters 40—66. The
redactional issue of determining exactly when chapters 36—39 entered with the
corpus and how much of First Isaiah had been already literally shaped is
hermeneutically not of primary importance for the task of interpretation. Its
major function within the book as a whole is to confirm the promise of First
Isaiah, yet to link chapters 1—35 with 40—55. The initial expansion of the Isaianic tradition in chapters 40—55 has related to the eschatological promises
contained in First Isaiah's message, but now formulated in terms of the old and
of the new. The function of chapters 36—39 was then shaped further in the
period of Third Isaiah by linking together chapters 1 and 65–66, and by projecting the future of Zion into an eschatological hope in which the deliverance
from Babylon (Second Isaiah) was now rendered as only an illustration within
God's total purpose for his people (Third Isaiah).

38. Isaiah 36:1–37:38

36:1^a In the fourteenth year of King Hezekiah, Sennacherib king of Assyria came up against all the fortified cities of Judah and took them. 2 And the king of Assyria sent the Rabshakeh from Lachish to King Hezekiah at Jerusalem with a large army. And he stood near the conduit of the upper pool, by the road to the Fuller's Field. 3 And there came out to him Eliakim, the son of Hilkiah, who was in charge of the palace, and Shebna the scribe, and Joah, the son of Asaph, the recorder.

4 The Rabshakeh said to them, "You tell Hezekiah: 'Thus says the great king, king of Assyria: On what do you rest this confidence of yours? 5 Do you suppose^b that mere words are strategy and power for war? On whom do you now rely that you have rebelled against me? 6 You are relying on Egypt, that broken reed of a staff, which will pierce the hand of anyone who leans on it. That's what Pharaoh king of Egypt is like to all who rely on him. 7 But if you then say to me, "We rely on the LORD our God," is he not the very one whose shrines and altars Hezekiah got rid of, telling Judah and Jerusalem, "You must worship before this altar?" 8 Come now, make a wager with my master, the king of Assyria. I will give you two thousand horses, if you can put riders on them. 9 How then can you repulse a single captain among the least of my master's servants, when you rely on Egypt for chariots and horsemen? 10 Moreover, have I come to attack and destroy this land without Yahweh's sanction? Yahweh himself told me: Go up against this land and destroy it.'"

11 Then Eliakim, Shebna, and Joah said to the Rabshakeh, "Please speak to your servants in Aramaic, for we understand it; do not speak to us in Judaean in the hearing of the people on the wall." 12 But the Rabshakeh replied, "Was it to your master and to you that my master sent me to speak these words? It was meant precisely for the men that are sitting on the wall, who are doomed with you to eat their own dung and drink their own urine."

13 Then the Rabshakeh stood and shouted out with a loud voice in Judaean: "Hear the words of the great king, the king of Assyria. 14 Thus says the

king: Do not let Hezekiah deceive you, for he cannot save you. 15 Do not let Hezekiah make you rely on Yahweh, saying: 'The LORD will surely save us; this city will not fall into the hand of the king of Assyria.'" 16 Do not listen to Hezekiah. This is what the king of Assyria says: Make your peace with me and come out to me. Then every one of you will eat from his own vine and fig tree and drink water from his own cistern, 17 until I come and take you away to a land like your own, a land of bread and wine, of grain fields and vineyards. 18 Do not let Hezekiah mislead you by saying, 'The LORD will save us.' Did any of the gods of the other nations ever save their land from the king of Assyria? 19 Where are the gods of Hamath and Arpad? Where are the gods of Sepharvaim? Have they delivered Samaria out of my hand? 20 Who of all the gods of these countries has been able to save his land from me? How then can Yahweh save Jerusalem from my hand?" 21 Then they were silent and did not answer him a word, for the king's command was not to answer him.

22 Then Eliakim son of Hilkiah, the overseer of the palace, Shebna the scribe, and Joah son of Asaph the recorder, went to Hezekiah with their clothes rent and reported to him what the Rabshakeh had said.

37:1 When King Hezekiah heard this, he rent his clothes and covered himself with sackcloth, and went into the house of the LORD. 2 He sent Eliakim, the overseer of the palace, Shebna the scribe, and the senior priests, clothed with sackcloth, to the prophet, Isaiah son of Amoz. 3 They said to him, "Thus says Hezekiah: This day is a day of distress, of rebuke, and of disgrace. Children have come to the birth, but there is no strength to deliver them. 4 Perhaps the LORD your God had heard the words of the Rabshakeh whom his master the king of Assyria has sent to mock the living God and that he will mete out judgment for the words the LORD your God has heard. Therefore pray for the remnant that still survives."

5 When the servants of King Hezekiah came to Isaiah, 6 Isaiah said to them, "Tell your master, 'This is what the LORD says: Do not be afraid of what you have heard, how the servants of the king of Assyria have blasphemed me. 7 Behold, I will put a spirit in him, so that he will hear a rumor and return to his own land; and I will make him fall by the sword in his own land.'"

8 The Rabshakeh returned and found the king of Assyria fighting against Libnah, for he had heard that the king had left Lachish. 9 Now the king heard concerning Tirhakah king of Ethiopia, "He has set out to fight against you." When he heard it,[c] he sent messengers to Hezekiah, saying, 10 "Tell this to King Hezekiah of Judah: Do not let your God on whom you rely deceive you by promising that

Jerusalem will not fall into the hand of the king of Assyria. 11 Surely you have heard what the kings of Assyria have done to all the countries, completely destroying them. And will you be delivered? 12 Did the gods of the nations that were destroyed by my forefathers deliver them—the gods of Gozen, Haran, Rezeph, and the people of Eden who were in Telassar? 13 Where is the king of Hamath, the king of Arpad, the king of the city of Sepharvaim, or of Hena or Ivvah?"

14 Hezekiah received the letter from the messengers and read it. Then he went up to the house of the LORD and spread it out before the LORD. 15 And Hezekiah prayed to the LORD: 16 "O LORD of hosts, God of Israel, enthroned between the cherubim, you alone are God over all the kingdoms of the earth. You have made heaven and earth. 17 Incline your ear, O LORD, and hear, open your eyes and see. Hear all the words that Sennacherib has sent to blaspheme the living God. 18 It is true, O LORD, the kings of Assyria have laid waste all the people and their lands. 19 They have thrown their gods in the fire and destroyed them because they are not gods, but only the work of human hands, wood and stone. 20 Now, O LORD our God, save us from his hand so that all kingdoms of the earth may know that you alone, O LORD, are God."

21 Then Isaiah son of Amoz sent a message to Hezekiah: "This is what the LORD, the God of Israel, says: Because you have prayed to me concerning Sennacherib king of Assyria, 22 this is the word that the LORD has spoken concerning him:

> The virgin daughter of Zion
>   despises and mocks you.
> The daughter of Jerusalem
>   wags her head behind you.

23 Whom have you blasphemed and slandered?
>   Against whom have you raised your voice
> and haughtily lifted your eyes?
>   Against the Holy One of Israel!

24 Through your messengers you have blasphemed the Lord,
>   and you have said,
>   'With my many chariots
> I have ascended the heights of the mountain,
>   to the very heights of Lebanon;
> I have cut down its tallest cedars,
>   the choicest of its pines.
> I have reached its highest peaks,
>   its densest forest.

25   I have dug wells
          and drunk the waters there.
      With the soles of my feet
          I have dried up all the streams of Egypt.'
26   Have you not heard?
          Long ago I ordained it.
      In days of old I planned it;
          now I have brought it to pass,
      that you should turn fortified cities
          into heaps of ruins.
27   Their people, deprived of strength,
          are dismayed and shamed.
      They are like plants of the field,
          like tender grass,
      like grass sprouting on the housetops,
          withered before it is grown.
28   But I know where you stay
          and your comings and goings,
          and how you have raged against me.
29   Because you have raged against me,
          and because your arrogance has reached my ears,
      I will place my hook in your nose
          and my bit in your mouth,
      and I will turn you back by the
          road on which you came.
30   "This will be the sign for you: This year you will eat what grows of
      itself, and in the second year what springs from that. But in the third
      year sow and reap, plant vineyards and eat their fruit. 31 And the
      surviving remnant of the house of Judah will take root below and
      produce fruit above. 32 For out of Jerusalem will come a remnant,
      and out of Mount Zion a band of survivors. The zeal of the LORD of
      hosts will accomplish this."
33   "Therefore, thus says the LORD concerning the king of Assyria:
      He will not enter this city
          or shoot an arrow here.
      He will not advance toward it with shields
          or throw up a siege ramp against it.
34   By the way that he came, he will return;
          he will not enter this city, says the LORD.
35   I will defend this city and save it,
          for my sake and for the sake of David my servant."
36   Then the angel of the LORD went forth and slew a hundred and eighty-

five thousand in the Assyrian camp. When the people arose the next morning, there were all the dead bodies. 37 Then Sennacherib king of Assyria broke camp and withdrew. He returned to Nineveh and dwelt there. 38 While he was worshipping in the temple of Nisroch his god, Adrammelech and Sharezer, his sons, struck him dead with the sword, and escaped to the land of Ararat, and Esarhaddon his son succeeded him as king.

a. The many variants in the MT between Isa. 36:1–39:8 and 2 Kings 18:13–20:19 are carefully analyzed by Wildberger, 3:1484–95 in a synoptic comparison. The purpose of this commentary is primarily to focus on the discrete shape of Isaiah's account.

b. Read with Qumran (*BHS*).

c. 2 Kings 19:9 has the variant *wayyāšob* ("he returned = again").

Exposition

"In the fourteenth year of King Hezekiah, Sennacherib king of Assyria came up against all the fortified cities of Judah and took them." The initial regnal summary stands isolated in Isaiah, but is a part of a chronological sequence in 2 Kings 18. The dating in the fourteenth year has continued to evoke difficulty. The problem lies in attempting to reconcile the attack by Sennacherib in 701 in 2 Kings 18:13 with the dating of Hezekiah's accession in 2 Kings 18:1. No consensus has emerged on a resolution.

A far more pressing problem arises when the Kings parallel with the introductory formula of Isaiah relating Sennacherib's attack is immediately followed by an account of Hezekiah's capitulation (the so-called A account, 18:14–16), which is missing in Isaiah. In recent years the point has been frequently emphasized (Smelik, Seitz) that it is a mistake methodologically to interject immediately the problem of the A account into the interpretation of Isaiah. The effect is to skew the exegesis in a historical direction without first giving attention to Isaiah's own rendering of the story. I think that this argument has much in its favor, and the problem of the capitulation of Hezekiah reported in Kings can be postponed until Isaiah's form of the text is closely examined. However, it is widely agreed that the lack of the A account in Isaiah is intentional, and not due to a fortuitous textual error.

In my earlier monograph of 1967 (*Isaiah and the Assyrian Crisis*), I followed the nineteenth-century leads of Stade and Duhm in distinguishing between two different sources in the B account that followed. The earlier source, designated B[1], was analyzed as extending from 2 Kings 18:17–19:9a, 36–37 // Isa. 36:1–37:9a. The later account, B[2], was identified as 2 Kings 19:9b–35 II Isa. 37:9b–36. There were some minor variations in the source analysis, especially regarding the seam between B^1 and B^2 (cf. Gonçalves, 373ff., 445ff.), but in general a common literary analysis was upheld. In my earlier analysis, I then attempted to examine carefully the differences between the two sources and I projected a diachronic development extending from B^1 to B^2. I argued that B^1 reflected both an earlier and a later face; the former a pre-exilic historical memory, the latter a Deuteronomistic influence. I assigned B^2 to a subsequent period, probably the postexilic age, with linguistic parallels to Second Isaiah, especially in 37:22ff.

While I think that this diachronic approach has retained some useful value, it does suffer from a major deficiency, which both Smelik and Seitz have emphasized. It does not adequately address the synchronic dimension of the combined text. This is a legitimate complaint, even if one now prefers to speak of redactional layering rather than literary sources. Nevertheless, I do not agree with Smelik's argument that because of the possibility of rendering the text as a coherent literary composition, the synchronic reading undercuts the case for seeing an earlier, diachronic diversity. Without adequate recognition of a history of development the danger can be acute of flattening the tensions and subtle nuances that are clearly present. Nor do I agree with several modern redactional critics who characterize chapters 37 — 38 as the "free composition" of editors, an imaginative construct without any recognizable relation to the events of 701 (*contra* Hardmeier). Similar difficulties attend the host of other etiological interpretations (e.g., Clements) that posit redactional construals which can be neither readily proven nor disproven.

[36:1–22] The first three verses introduce the report of the confrontation between the Rabshakeh and King Hezekiah before Jerusalem. It is significant that the scene is set at the conduit of the upper pool on the highway to the Fuller's Field (v. 2). This location could, of course, simply indicate that the meeting took place at that spot outside the city that controlled its crucial water supply (7:3ff.). However, in the recounting of the ensuing events there is a clearly antithetical typology developed between the response of Ahaz in 734 and Hezekiah in 701 to the threat of a hostile siege.

Chapters 36 and 37 are structured by a close repetition of a similar pattern:

1.	36:1–3	Report of an Assyrian invasion
	4–10	First threat of the Rabshakeh
	(11–12)	Interruption: speak in Aramaic
	13–20	Assyrian threat continued
	36:21–37:4	Hezekiah's response: call for prayer
	5–7	Isaiah's assurance and announcement of punishment
2.	37:8–9a	Report on Assyrian strategy
	9b–13	Second threat by Assyrian messengers
	14–20	Hezekiah's response: prayer

21–35		Isaiah's assurance
	21–29	Prophetic taunt
	30–32	Sign for remnant
	33–35	Promise to Zion
36–38		Fulfillment of judgment on Assyrians

The passage is characterized by continuous narrative that joins together a series of speeches. The Rabshakeh is first introduced as a messenger who delivers in the conventional formula the direct speech of the Assyrian king: "Thus says the great king, king of Assyria." However, the message that follows does not follow the traditional patterns of oral speech. Rather the speech oscillates between threats, taunts, arguments, and counterarguments. In my 1967 monograph (*Isaiah and the Assyrian Crisis*), I proposed seeing the speech as fitting the ancient Near Eastern pattern of diplomatic disputation (79–80). This form-critical category helps explain the shifting argument, the lack of logical consistency, and the exceedingly aggressive stance of the Rabshakeh in adapting his negotiating techniques to the opponent's actual or imagined weaknesses.

In the first speech, the Rabshakeh tries to show the hopelessness of resistance against Assyria. He points out the unreliable support of Egypt and mocks Judah's ability to mount a serious military force. Two arguments are especially startling. How can you rely on Yahweh when Hezekiah has offended him by removing his altars (v. 7)? And do you realize that Yahweh himself commanded the Assyrian king to destroy your land (v. 10)? Commentators have offered in general two main interpretations. The Rabshakeh seems to be intimately apprised of Judah's internal affairs, and he appears even to cite the prophet Isaiah's own words (10:5ff.). Smelik (78ff.) has developed the thesis that the writer has used a literary device in order shortly to demonstrate to the reader the falsehood of the Assyrian king by means of his obvious distortion of Old Testament prophecy. Long (214) characterizes these two Assyrian arguments as an irony directed to the Hebrew reader who understands the comedy of such a flagrant misunderstanding.

Although I do not doubt that there is acute literary imagination at work in the shaping of the narrative, there are features in the story that, in my judgment, reflect a genuine historical memory. Literary critics immediately respond that the realistic element to the story can just as easily be attributed to authorial imagination. Certainly this is true in modern literature, but the case is not as clear for biblical literature. This is to say that there are certain restraints on Israel's creative imagination. Narratives are shaped by traditional conventions and corporate memory, which is not typical for modern Western culture. Thus, it is frequent for a biblical writer to have Israel's enemies confess the power of Yahweh (Ex. 14:25), or conversely to poke fun at the impotence and the folly of idols (1 Kings 18:27; Isa. 44:9ff.). But it is rare for a Hebrew author to construe a pagan misunderstanding of Israel's God in an ironical fashion (cf. 1 Kings 20:23). I would therefore not rule out an element of genuine historical memory in this instance, particularly when the pagan misunderstanding of the Rabshakeh conforms to a genuinely ancient Near Eastern context of diplomatic disputation. The frequently used term "realistic narrative" (cf. H. Frei) does not adequately reflect the massive historical coercion exercised upon the biblical writers.

The narrative interruption described in vv. 11–13 certainly serves to increase the suspense of the encounter and to raise the stakes within the story. The sheer crudity of the Assyrian response reflects a pattern of intimidation with a credible historical warrant, and is a different level of realistic depiction from the conventional responses of both the pious king and resolute prophet (37:1–8). The point of this argument is not to mount a conservative apologetic that links the truth of a biblical narrative to a maximal claim for historicity. Rather, it is a protest against a recent tendency in biblical circles to attribute all skillful narrative to a redactor's free imagination apart from any mooring in the life of historic Israel. I would thus still defend the view that the so-called B¹ account (36:1–37:9a) reflects both an older and younger face. Accordingly, the reference to Hezekiah's removal of the altars strikes me as basically early, but it has now been construed as cultic centralization, which is a Josianic or Deuteronomistic component (2 Kings 23:4ff.).

The continuation of the Rabshakeh's harangue in vv. 13ff. following the interruption from the Jerusalem delegation now shifts the focus more directly toward isolating Hezekiah from his people. Thus the attack: "Do not let Hezekiah deceive you"; do not rely on him; do not be misled. The Rabshakeh's accusation focuses directly on Yahweh's impotence to deliver. He is just like all the other deities who have failed (v. 18b). But then a carrot is offered to soften the harsh threat: "Make peace and you can live in a land as rich as your own." Again words of deception! As Ackroyd long ago demonstrated (168), the Rabshakeh's language is in effect a parody on the divine promise to Israel of the land that God would give his people.

[37:1–9a] The response of the Judaean delegation and of King Hezekiah is of the deepest anguish, signalled by the rending of clothes and the tearing of sackcloth. The request for the prophet to intercede in prayer is hesitant, uncertain, and tentative. "Perhaps God will hear . . . ?" The theme of the Rabshakeh's mockery of Yahweh is sounded clearly for the first time, and will shortly be greatly expanded. Isaiah's response is a word of assurance. God has indeed heard the mockery. He promises not only that Sennacherib will be enticed to return to his own land, but that he will also be killed by the sword.

One of the consistently difficult problems arising from the dividing of the account into two sources, B¹ and B², has been in interpreting the so-called seam in 37:8–9. The problem has been complicated by a textual variant between 2 Kings 19:9b (yāšob = "return," "again") and Isa. 37:9b (yišma‘ = "hear"). The Kings reading seemed to support the joining of two sources, especially when rendered "again." Recently there have been several attempts to suggest a unified literary reading without an appeal to sources. Long (224) interprets vv. 8–9a to be "a typical framing repetition" by referring v. 9a syntactically to v. 8: "he [the king] had heard concerning Tirhakah . . . (v. 9b) and he [the Rabshakeh] went back." The suggestion is of interest and resolves the problem of having the rumor of Tirhakah the cause for again sending messengers to Hezekiah. However, this interpretation only really works with the Kings text.

For his part, Smelik interprets the threefold repetition of the verb "hear" as a stylistic device linking vv. 8–9 with v. 7 in a deliberately ambiguous attempt to suggest that Sennacherib would withdraw before Tirhakah. In my opinion, this highly sophisticated reading is not fully convincing. Still, both Long and Smelik do offer a reasonably coherent reading of vv. 8–9 within a putative unified narrative.

[9b–12] Whether one opts for an original or for a redactional unity in the story, the text's meaning is largely shaped by the parallel structure of the two threats. The second threat is delivered this time by a letter, which is a viable ancient Near Eastern vehicle. What is striking are both the continuities and discontinuities in the renewed form of intimidation. Instead of being warned against Hezekiah's deception, the full force of the attack falls now on Yahweh's deception: "Do not let your God deceive you with his empty promise of deliverance." The issue at stake now focuses on the one theological issue: the power of Assyria as the power of Yahweh. The mocking of the God of Israel is egregious blasphemy. The taunt again cites the same destroyed cities as earlier (2 Kings 18:34) and links Yahweh with all the other powerless deities.

[14–20] The response of Hezekiah also takes a greatly heightened form. Rather than first appealing to Isaiah for an intercessory prayer, the king prays directly and immediately to his God, stressing again the mockery of Yahweh by Sennacherib. Moreover, the prayer picks up conventional theological formulations that recall the aggressive monotheism of Second Isaiah. The gods that were burned by the kings of Assyria are all false deities. In contrast to the one living God they are no gods at all (40:9; 45:5, 14). Let Yahweh save Israel that all the kingdoms of the earth may learn "you alone, O LORD, are God." (v. 20)

[21–29] The reply of God to Hezekiah through the prophet then follows in a lengthy poetic oracle that is greatly expanded over that of the earlier account. God has indeed heard the mockery. Assyria's arrogance has come to his ears (vv. 23, 29). The king of Assyria is quoted in a style that accurately reflects the pompous, self-aggrandizement of countless victory steles: "With my many chariots I have ascended heights of the mountains. . . . I have cut down its tallest cedars. . . . I have dried up all the streams of Egypt (vv. 24–25). Now the issue is no longer one of military strength between armies or of clever diplomatic strategy, but is a theological one. Who actually controls the world? Sennacherib is not only a deceiver, but a blasphemer. Because he does not acknowledge Yahweh or his plans from of old, God will cut him down in his arrogance. He will turn him back on the way from which he came.

The age of this oracle has long been debated. Recently both Williamson (194ff.) and Seitz (*Zion's Final Destiny*, 116ff.) have contested the widely held consensus that the influence of Second Isaiah is present. For the actual interpretation of the passage this critical debate is not crucial, but it arises largely from concerns with larger redactional theories regarding the function of chapters 36—39. Regardless of its exact dating, the passage is a taunt song, filled with familiar themes from both First and Second Isaiah that speak of the blasphemy of God, of Yahweh as the Holy One of Israel, and of the fulfiling of the divine plan of old. It functions to climax a broad Isaianic witness to the nature of the God of Israel, which will shortly be confirmed in judgmental action (37:36–38).

[30–35] Next a sign is given to the surviving remnant of Judah. The theme evokes an intertextual resonance with Isaiah's son Shearjashub ("a remnant will return") in 7:3 and continues with the sign of Immanuel ("God-with-us"). Within three years vineyards will again be planted in Judah, and out of Jerusalem will go forth a band of survivors. Then an oracle of judgment is given that most probably once joined directly to v. 21, but now has been shaped by a new introductory messenger formula in v. 33. Assyria will not mount a siege, indeed not even shoot an arrow into the city. God will defend the city "for the sake of David." The divine promise to David, which was crucial to Isaiah's challenge to Ahaz for faith (7:6ff.), is again confirmed.

[36–38] Finally, the promised divine judgment against Assyria is fulfilled (cf. 14:24–25). "The angel of Yahweh went forth and slew a hundred and eighty-five thousand in the Assyrian camp." So Sennacherib departed for his home, and while worshipping his god Nisroch in Nineveh he was slain by his sons. Usually the date for this assassination is set at 681 B.C. when his son Esarhaddon assumed the throne, some twenty years after the attack on Jerusalem.

In conclusion, there is need for theological and hermeneutical reflection on the form and function of the entire account in chapters 36—37. Perhaps the best way to set up the hermeneutical issue is to contrast two opposite interpretations of the climactic destruction of the Assyrians in 37:36.

E. J. Young (*Isaiah*, 2:505) represents the traditional, conservative position. He writes: "The destruction of the Assyrian army is not to be accounted for on naturalistic terms but as the result of a supernatural, miraculous action of God performed through His angel. With one stroke or blow, as it were, the angel brought death into the camp. No mere natural phenomenon accomplished this, but only the sovereign power of the one true Lord, who controls heaven and earth."

In contrast, Clements represents a widely accepted liberal, critical approach, which describes the events as a "theological embellishment," "a piece of theological coloring," and an exaggeration far removed from the real world. The reader is instructed "in a world come of age" that "our knowledge of history . . . shows us unmistakably that angels do not come from heaven to slay the enemy" (*Isaiah and the Deliverance of Jerusalem*, 26).

I confess not to be satisfied with either of these two options, the supernatural-istic or the naturalistic. On the one hand, I would argue against the supernatural-istic because it fails to observe closely the literary form of the chapter, that is, the distinctive shaping and careful nuancing of the theological witness. Rather, it assumes that the author is writing in the genre of historical report and that the meaning of the angel's smiting of the Assyrian army is that of a historical force comparable to other natural catastrophes, of course, raised to the nth degree. Meaning is thus secured by correlating the biblical text with its historical refer-ent, supplied here by supernatural intervention. On the other hand, Clements's naturalistic position assumes that the sole forces shaping historical events are controlled inexorably by the natural laws of cause and effect. Thus, one can sim-ply deduce that any appeal to another force is a legendary elaboration, dictated by wishful thinking, mythical projection, or simplistic religious belief.

In contrast to both of these interpretive options, I would contend that Isaiah's prophecy in chapters 36—37 is a truthful witness to God's deliverance of Israel. The only interpretive question is to understand what is the content of this wit-ness and how it is achieved.

As I have attempted to show in my exegesis of chapters 36—37, the initial setting of the account is fully anchored in the real world of history. The world of the Rabshakeh is a historical personification of military strength, arrogance of power, and brutal intimidation as the chief goal. The Assyrian does not reckon with Yahweh or with any of the deities as a real force to oppose him. The history setting of chapter 36 is clear even if one provisionally omits the account in Kings of Hezekiah's capitulation to Sennacherib (A account), which in tone is simply more of the same. Most of chapter 36 relates the speech of the Rabshakeh with its threats, deception, and sheer arrogance. Hezekiah and his emissaries are portrayed in great fear, and almost persuaded by the "way of the world." However, Hezekiah still has a memory and a small window opened to God: "Perhaps God may have heard this challenge and will act." Of course, Isaiah the prophet is fully confident that God will intervene.

In the second account (37:8ff.), as we saw, the real confrontation is greatly sharpened. The issue is not between just two military powers, but their con-frontation is now posed completely as a theological contest. Sennacherib has mocked the living God. He discounts God's power completely and boasts of his own prowess. The entire biblical witness is now shaped to address this chal-lenge. But how does one describe a battle between heaven and earth, one that pits the power of the living God against human hubris?

The biblical writer uses another literary medium to describe the confronta-tion. God's action is portrayed apart from all natural causes, without reference to human agencies. There is no appeal to plague or storm. Rather, sheer evil is smashed by the direct hand of God in the conventional idiom of the *malak YHWH,* his divine personification. God himself thus slew the enemy, and when the army awoke, there were a hundred eighty-five thousand corpses around them. What is striking in this presentation is that there are no references to intermediary causes. To suggest that a plague was involved is to go beyond the text and misconstrue the witness. The biblical writer's point lies elsewhere and is formulated apart from any natural explanations. His is a confession: God indeed brought victory to his people, as he had promised.

The writer feels constrained to employ a particular style when he shapes this confessional history, a history that embraces both the world of God and that of humankind. However, once the confessional witness to God's faithfulness has been made, the writer returns to the world of human affairs. Sennacherib, king of Assyria, withdrew and returned to Nineveh, where secular historians also record that he was slain by his sons. Likewise, secular history—accounts quite apart from Israel's faith—confirms that Jerusalem was not sacked in 701. Yet how one evaluates this event depends on the reader's stance. It can be explained as a pious legend apart from empirical evidence, or one can identify with Israel's testimony in confessing that God did indeed save Jerusalem as he promised.

39. Isaiah 38:1–22

38:1 In those days Hezekiah became ill and was at the point of death. The prophet Isaiah son of Amoz came to him and said, "Thus says the LORD: Put your affairs in order, because you are going to die. You will not recover."

2 Thereupon Hezekiah turned his face to the wall and prayed to the LORD, **3** and said: "Please O LORD, remember how I walked before you faithfully and with complete devotion, and have done what is good in your eyes." And Hezekiah wept profusely. **4** Then the word of the LORD came to Isaiah. **5** "Go and tell Hezekiah, 'Thus says the LORD, the God of your father David: I have heard your prayer and seen your tears. I will add fifteen years to your life. **6** And I will deliver you and this city from the hand of the king of Assyria and defend this city. **7** And this is the sign to you from the LORD that the LORD will do the thing that he has promised. **8** I will make the shadow cast by the sun recede ten steps on the stairway of Ahaz.'" So the sunlight receded the ten steps it had descended.

9ᵃ A writingᵇ of Hezekiah king of Judah when he had been sick and had recovered:

10 I said:
I must depart in the prime of my life.
I have been consigned to the gates of Sheol
    for the rest of my years.

11 I said: I shall never see the LORD
    in the land of the living.
No longer will I look upon humans again
    among these inhabiting the world.[c]

12 Like a tent of shepherds
    my dwelling has been plucked up
    and taken from me.
Like a weaver I have rolled up my life.
    He has cut me off from the loom;
day and night you made an end of me.[d]

13   I bring forth sounds[e] until the morning,
but like a lion he has broken all my bones;
    day and night you made an end of me.

14 I chirped like a swift or crane,[f]
    I moaned like a dove.
My eyes grew weak as I looked to heaven.
    I am distressed; O Lord, be my support.

15 What can I say?
    He has spoken to me and then done it.
I will walk humbly[g] all my years
    because of the bitterness of my soul.

16 Lord, by such things[h] men live,
    and my spirit finds life in them too;
you have restored me to health
    and let me live.

17 Surely it was for my own good
    that I endured such suffering.
You saved my life from the pit of destruction.
    You have cast behind you all my sins.

18 For Sheol cannot praise you,
    nor can death extol you.
Those who go down to the pit
    cannot hope for your faithfulness.

19 The living, only the living, can give you praise,
    as I do this day;
    fathers tell their children of your faithfulness.

20 The LORD will save me,
    and we will sing with stringed instruments
    all the days of our lives in the LORD's house.

21 Then Isaiah said, "Let them take a cake of figs, and apply it to the boil
and he will recover." 22 Hezekiah asked, "What will be the sign that
I will go up to the house of the LORD?"

a. Isa. 38:9–20, the psalm of Hezekiah, exhibits an extremely difficult and controversial Hebrew text. The reader is referred to the following secondary sources: J. Begrich, *Der Psalm des Hiskia*, FRLANT, 42, Göttingen 1926; and D. Barthélemy, *CTLAT* 2:263–77.

b. Often emended to a psalm classification, *miktām* (e.g., Ps. 16:1).

c. The MT reads "cessation." One should probably read *ḥeled* ("world"), but cf. Barthélemy, *CTLAT*.

d. The meaning is uncertain (NJPS, "make whole").

e. The meaning is uncertain (cf. Barthélemy, *CTLAT*).

f. The exact species are uncertain (cf. Jer. 8:7).

g. There is much debate on the Hebrew root. This translation opts for *ddh* (cf. *HALAT*, 205).

h. The MT reads "on account of them they live."

Exposition

Much of the modern debate regarding the interpretation of chapter 38 has turned on the highly complex problem of relating it to its parallel in 2 Kings 20. There are two major variations within the two paralleled accounts. Isaiah's version is much shorter throughout than 2 Kings 20, but it adds the psalm of Hezekiah (vv. 9–20). There are also numerous minor differences (cf. below).

It has been generally assumed by historical-critical research that determining the diachronic relation between the two forms of the tradition is crucial for its correct interpretation. Moreover, it would be difficult to contest that the interpretation of each is affected by the decision regarding the direction in which the borrowing took place. Yet once the importance of this history of the growth of the text has been affirmed, the hermeneutical caveat must also be sounded that ultimately the integrity of each of these two witnesses according to their present form must be respected and vigorously pursued.

The problem of determining the priority between the versions of Kings and Isaiah is complicated by the different structures of the two. In the Kings account two different motifs are juxtaposed: the illness and recovery of Hezekiah (vv. 1–7) and the sign affirming the promise (vv. 8–11). Nevertheless, the inner coherence is unclear. Verse 7 ends the episode with the announcement that with the laying on of the cake of figs, Hezekiah recovered. (The LXX sought to harmonize v. 7 with v. 8 by reinterpreting the Hebrew preterite into a future tense: "that he may recover.") Then v. 8 has Hezekiah request a sign that he would be healed and go up to the temple on the third day, which should logically have preceded v. 7.

In contrast to Kings, Isaiah 38 has a unified sequence in vv. 1–8, with the requested sign preceding his healing. Yet, following the prayer of Hezekiah (vv. 9–20) two additional verses are added (vv. 21–22), which pick up the theme of the cake of figs and a request for a sign that he would go up to the temple.

Whereas earlier commentators have generally assumed the priority of the Kings account and regarded Isa. 38:21–22 as evidence of a late editorial harmonization, more recently Smelik (72), followed in part by Seitz (*Zion's Final Destiny,* 162ff.), has argued that Isaiah's version has the priority by virtue of its clear structure, and that Kings is a confused and secondary expansion. Whereas Smelik concedes to the majority opinion that v. 22 is a late scribal addition, Seitz has argued instead for the literary integrity of v. 22 within Isaiah's version of the story, and that Isaiah's two signs have been secondarily conflated into only one sign by Kings.

Without pursuing in detail the lengthy responses of Sweeney, Carr, Clements, and Willliamson, I think it fair to say that a broad consensus has emerged against Smelik in maintaining the priority of 2 Kings 20 over against Isaiah 38. Central to this assessment are the following points:

a. The rearrangement in Isaiah sought to smooth out the difficulty of 2 Kings 20:7 by removing it to the end of the chapter, which indicates that the text of Kings was earlier (cf. Cogan and Tadmor, 156–57).

b. Jeremias (104ff.) has shown that the subsequent removal of 2 Kings 20:7–8 to the end of the chapter by Isaiah's editor has garbled features of the original Kings account in Isa. 38:5–8, thus confirming the trajectory defended by Cogan and Tadmor.

c. The detailed text-critical analysis of Konkel (462ff.) supports the priority of Kings over Isaiah.

However, once the diachronic direction of the text's growth has been established, this decision does not rule out the legitimate concerns of both Smelik and Seitz that a synchronic reading of Isaiah in its present form determine its own unique function within the prophetic book as a whole. (Cf. B.O. Long's *2 Kings* for the most serious attempt at a synchronic reading of the Kings version.)

There has long been debate over the genre and setting of the story of Hezekiah's sickness and recovery. It has often been classified as a novella or legend, but these classifications help little. Occasionally attempts have been made to reconstruct an earlier version of the story in which a healing miracle was attributed to a prophet and later expanded to link the miraculous sign to the deliverance of Jerusalem (cf. Kaiser). This type of speculation appears to have won little support.

It has long been pointed out that the promise of deliverance to Hezekiah in v. 6 assumes that the divine rescue has not yet taken place. Jerusalem is still under siege as Hezekiah lies on a sick bed. The same theme of a future deliverance occurs also in 2 Kings 20:6. Regardless of an alleged original setting, the story in Isaiah 38 has been redactionally joined loosely to what preceded—"in those days"—and again to the emissary event in chapter 39. If the story is read on its synchronic level, perhaps Long's interpretation (*Kings,* 2:238) seems the most illuminating. He suggests overcoming the chronological tension by construing vv. 8–11 in 2 Kings 20 as an attempt to fill in a perceived gap in the earlier narrative in order to indicate that before his recovery Hezekiah had asked for a sign confirming his healing. This appears also to be the function of Isa. 38:22 according to the pluperfect translation of the NRSV.

The most significant redactional feature of the Isaianic version remains the positioning and shaping of the thanksgiving psalm in 38:10–19. Some have argued that the song was composed for its role in chapter 38; however, as it will be argued below, a more likely hypothesis is that an earlier form of the psalm has been intentionally adopted to give the sickness of Hezekiah a far larger typological significane.

[**38: 1–8, 21–22**] The story of the king's sickness is loosely connected by a temporal formula to the preceding narrative. Commentators push the connection beyond its narrative intent when they seek to establish an absolute dating calculating that his reign of twenty-nine years (2 Kings 18:2), when extended by fifteen years, would place his illness around 701. Not only is there controversy over the initial date of his reign (2 Kings 18:1), but the narrator in chapter 38 has avoided giving an exact chronology. However, what is clear is that in both the paralleled accounts of Kings and Isaiah (20:6 and 38:6) the deliverance of Jerusalem still lies in the future.

A crisis is evoked when Isaiah announced the king's imminent death. Hezekiah is deeply distraught, prays to God for recovery, and reminds God of his faithfulness in the past. Then the prophet receives a second word. God has heard Hezekiah's prayer and will add fifteen years to his life. He will deliver Hezekiah and Jerusalem out of the hands of the king of Assyria. The account of this scene is considerably longer in Kings than in Isaiah. In Kings, Isaiah has gone out of the "middle court" and is called back to deliver his message. Whether one can observe any specific editorial intent in the Isaianic abbreviation is unclear. The shorter Isaiah account does not really intensify the speed of the divine response, but only shortens the portrayal of the reversal of the divine will respecting Hezekiah. Even the omission by Isaiah of God's defense "for the sake of my servant David" appears insignificant and is already implied in Isa. 38:5.

The difference between the two accounts is much more pronounced and significant in what then follows. In 2 Kings 20:7 Isaiah brings a cake of figs, lays it on the infection, and Hezekiah recovers. Confusion then arises when a sign is given after the healing has occurred (vv. 8–9). However, the logical order of having the sign precede the healing occurs in the Isaiah account. In the extended Kings account, the king is given a choice of sign—here there is an intertextual resonance with Ahaz—whereas in the abbreviated Isaiah account no choice is given, but the shadow turns back in reversal of its normal order. Those interpretations that see in Isaiah's portrayal of the king a heightened idealization of the character of Hezekiah appear to me to be overly subtle.

The disturbing factor in the seemingly straightforward account of Isaiah over against Kings comes, however, at the conclusion of the psalm of Hezekiah in vv. 21–22. The complexity of the problem has been briefly discussed earlier. Two elements from 2 Kings 20 have been added as an appendix to Isaiah's account: the cure of the boil by a cake of figs and the sign of going up to the temple. In the light of the earlier discussion, especially with the conclusion from the textual and literary evidence that 2 Kings 20 has the priority over Isaiah's account, the various attempts to posit two originally distinct signs have been widely discounted. Quite correctly, most critical commentators speak of a dislocation caused by a later redactor's attempt to supplement Isaiah's shorter version from 2 Kings (cf. Delitzsch).

Yet it is still important to press on beyond the task of reconstructing the diachronic growth of the text and to address the synchronic effect of the present "dislocated text." One of the lasting contributions of Ackroyd's illuminating articles on these chapters was that he raised the issue of the effect of the reader on the present form of the text ("An Interpretation of the Babylonian Exile," *Studies,* 164). The RSV appears at first to take undue liberty with the Hebrew verb form when rendering the tense as a pluperfect ("Now Isaiah had said . . . "), but this translation is attempting to bring out the narrative effect of these verses on the reader of the whole passage. Long's interpretation of 2 Kings 20:8–11, which is also a passage without a smooth literary join, runs parallel to the function of 38:21–22: "Reading this epistle as filling a gap in the earlier narrative we may understand that before his recovery Hezekiah (had) asked for a sign to confirm that he would be healed by Yahweh" (*2 Kings,* 238). Such a reading is not to be dismissed as a conservative apologetic seeking a seamless reconstruction, but a modern literary approach to a difficult text that explores how its coherence would have been sought by later readers who are aware of a larger canonical corpus of paralleled texts.

[9–20] A final and crucial task toward understanding chapter 38 turns on the interpretation of the psalm of Hezekiah, which has been bracketed by the prose account of the sickness and recovery of the king (vv. 1–8; 21–22). There is no better passage by which to illustrate the new set of questions that modern interpreters have posed to the text.

In 1926 Joachim Begrich wrote a definitive study of the psalm of Hezekiah, which revealed both the great strengths and weaknesses of the form-critical approach of Gunkel. After a painstaking reconstruction of Hebrew text to its "original form," Begrich offers an analysis of the genre of the psalm, concluding that it is an individual song of thanksgiving which accords with the conventional form of the familiar examples of the Psalter (e.g., 18; 30; 32; 34; Jonah 2). The psalm begins with a description of the need, which evokes the cries of lament. In his suffering the psalmist flees to Yahweh, and a plea for God's attention is given. The psalmist then turns to confession, and he recounts the intervention of Yahweh and his deliverance. The high point of the psalm is reached when the psalmist concludes with the announcement of his thankoffering.

According to Begrich, the element of lament ends in v. 14, which looks to the past, but in v. 15 the moment of deliverance begins. The psalmist is no longer like those in Sheol who cannot praise God, but he renders his thanksgiving to God "this day" for his salvation. He participates with the worshipping congregation in praise to God.

Part of the difficulty of Begrich's analysis is that this interpretation is greatly shaped by his prior decision regarding the literary genre. Thus in the troublesome v. 15, Begrich emends the MT to read, "I will give thee thanks" 'ôdekkā), using as his warrant that his reading is essential to the form-critical pattern of the thanksgiving psalm. As a result, one leaves his analysis with the impression that the actual form of the psalm does not fit as neatly into his categories as he assumes. The element of lament seems far more pervasive and not all contained in a retrospective viewing. Still there is a wide agreement that the unit is largely a thanksgiving psalm with a very strong lament component.

Begrich then seeks to determine the setting of the psalm and decides that the psalm did not arise from the circle of Israel's temple singers, but had a private setting about which one can learn little. Begrich argues that the psalm originally had an independent life (its date is uncertain) and was only secondarily accommodated to the Hezekiah story. He finds no exegetical significance in the conventional superscription connecting the psalm to Hezekiah's illness (cf. Childs, "Psalm Titles," 137ff.). Then again, Begrich's discussion of the corporate reference ("we") remains trapped in the older form-critical debate between Balla and Smend (*Der Psalm,* 65). He insists in seeing only an individual referent and fails to recognize the shift of focus from the recovery of Hezekiah to that of the larger community of faith.

It is precisely at this juncture that modern scholarship has moved in a different direction from Begrich. Initially the credit goes to Ackroyd ("An Interpretation of the Babylonian Exile," *Studies,* 165ff.) for first pointing out the integral literary connection that the psalm now forms with the chapter as a whole, indeed with the larger Isaianic corpus. While most critical scholars would agree with Begrich that the psalm was not originally composed for its position in chapter 38, most would now concede that the psalm has been assigned a unique function with Isaiah. In a word, the reader perceives that a typological relationship has been set up between the sickness and recovery of Hezekiah and the judgment and restoration of the people of Israel. In this sense, there is a parallel movement made with chapter 39. The metaphors of being brought back from the pit and those used in Lamentations and Jeremiah for the experience of exile easily extend the initial focus on the king to a larger corporate entity of the nation. In this way the addition of the psalm of Hezekiah, which is missing in Kings, shapes the function of Isaiah 38 and serves along with chapter 39 to point to a longed for restoration beyond the nation's disaster.

40. Isaiah 39:1–8

39:1 At that time Merodach-baladan son of Baladan, king of Babylon, sent envoys[a] with a letter and a gift to Hezekiah, for he had heard that he had been sick and had recovered. 2 Hezekiah received the envoys gladly and showed them his treasure house—the silver, the gold, the spices, and the fragrant oils—and all his armory and everything that was found in his storehouses. There was nothing in his palace or in all his realm that Hezekiah did not show them. 3 Then the prophet Isaiah came to King Hezekiah, and said to him, "What did those men say to you? From where have they come to you?" Hezekiah said, "They have come to me from a far country, from Babylon." 4 He said, "What have they seen in your palace?" And Hezekiah replied, "They have seen everything there is in my palace. There is nothing in my storehouses that I did not show them."

5 Then Isaiah said to Hezekiah, "Hear the word of the LORD of hosts: 6 The time is coming when everything in your palace, which your fathers have stored up to this day, will be carried off to Babylon. Nothing will be left behind, says the LORD. 7 And some of your descendants, your own flesh and blood, born to you, will be taken away to serve as eunuchs in the palace of the king of Babylon." 8 Then Hezekiah said to Isaiah, "The word of the LORD that you have spoken is good." For he thought, "There will be peace and security during my lifetime."

a. The MT reads "letters" (cf. *BHS*).

Exposition

There have been attempts of late to establish the historical setting of chapter 39 by means of its reference to Merodach-baladan. His history is well documented (cf. Brinkman). Marduk-apla-iddini ruled Babylon during the years 722–710 and 704–703. Although some commentators have continued to defend the earlier period of his reign as the background for the sending of emissaries to Hezekiah about 711 (cf. Cogan and Tadmor), the great majority of scholars argue for the later period of 703. It is largely thought that the presence of emissaries matches more closely with the extent of Hezekiah's involvement in the 701 revolt. Accordingly, it is argued that the narrative order of Isaiah 36—39 is not chronological (cf. below).

The more difficult problem turns on the traditio-historical development of this text. Clements contends that chapter 39 is preexilic because of its focus on Jehoiachin and the Davidic dynasty rather than on the destruction of the temple in 587. However, the issue is complex because it involves the whole issue of the Deuteronomistic History as well. Recent redactional studies have emphasized the different editorial shaping of the material largely held in common. The different function of 2 Kings 20:12–19 // Isaiah 39 within the two corpora is significant. In 2 Kings the Deuteronomistic editor focuses on the prophecy/fulfillment motif (24:2ff.), the role of Jehoiachin (25:27ff.), and the possible restoration of a Davidic dynasty. In contrast, Isaiah never mentions Jehoiachin, but the major function of the chapter turns on establishing a bridge from the Babylon of Merodach-baladan to the Babylon of Nebuchadnezzar. It is difficult to imagine the shaping of Isaiah 39 apart from knowledge of 587.

It is very possible that the real historical reason for the visit of the emissaries of Merodach-baladan was to establish an alliance with Hezekiah in the years preceding the revolt against Assyria in 701; however, this putative historical motivation lies in the background of the text and has been subordinated to the narrative shaping of the visit to establish a literary link with chapters 40—55. Some have suggested that the primary function of chapter 39 was to establish a rationale for why Jerusalem was protected in 701 but not in 587, but this interpretation is largely motivated by a redactional theory that is not supported by the narrative of chapter 39 itself (cf. below).

The case has been made earlier that the individual chapters, 36—37, 38, and 39, have undergone a separate traditio-historical development. Nevertheless, these chapters have been finally linked together editorially in a clear fashion. The overarching effect of the unit for the reader is that chapters 36 and 37 are also brought within the orbit of chapters 38 and 39, and therefore the entire section functions as a literary bridge to chapters 40ff. The larger problem for the entire Isaianic corpus of why Jerusalem was saved in 701 but punished in 587 is not handled by chapters 36—39, but only addressed subsequently by both Second and Third Isaiah.

The sending of emissaries from Merodach-baladan to Jerusalem is loosely linked to the preceding events with the temporal formula "at that time." The link is made explicit with chapter 38 by means of the reference to Hezekiah's sickness and recovery. The emissaries arrive with letters and a present. It is difficult to imagine that the visit was simply a social call. Yet no deeper motivation proceeds from the perspective of Hezekiah, who welcomes them.

The naïveté depicted of Hezekiah appears, however, to be a literary device for the narrator, who uses the technique of Isaiah's questions to raise the significance of the visit to an importance far exceeding that of a courtesy call. No reader would imagine that the prophet was also so naïve as to be unaware of the nature of the visit. "What did those men say to you? From where have they come?" Ackroyd rightly emphasizes the full significance of Hezekiah's response: they came from "a far country, from Babylon," both of which sounded a resonance with earlier prophetic texts of threat and exile. Then the prophet asks, "What have they seen in your palace?" It is nowhere stated why Hezekiah had shown them his treasures. Second Chronicles 32:25 infers that his action stemmed from pride, but Isaiah 39 is silent on this point. Long argues that "a reader comes to understand that Hezekiah strikes a bargain with the Babylonians which God abhorred", but no clear inference from Isaiah's reaction can be drawn. Rather, the full weight of the narrative falls on their "seeing everything." The same theme is repeated: "There is nothing in my storehouses that I did not show them." Then the significance of the repetition becomes clear as the prophetic judgment is sounded in the same words: "Everything in your palace . . . will be carried off to Babylon. . . . Nothing will be left behind."

Various commentators have sought to explain why the punishment was so severe in light of the offense. Kaiser cites parallels to show that boasting of one's riches was conceived of as an arrogance that always evoked divine wrath. Others suggest that viewing another's property is tantamount to possessing it, and that it was so interpreted by the prophet.

For my part, I am unconvinced that these explanations help in understanding the judgment. The very fact that the narrator of the chapter is unwilling to proceed in these directions should check the need for supplying reason. The writer's emphasis rather falls on establishing a link from one event to another. The judgment that was shortly to occur was not by accident or even directly evoked by the king's misdeed, but unfolded according to a divine plan. This theme clearly emerges in the response of Hezekiah to the prophet. Ackroyd ("An Interpretation of the Babylonian Exile," *Studies,* 157ff.) has mounted a persuasive case against interpreting it as a smug response that the judgment will not personally affect him. Rather, it is an acceptance of the divine will in which Isaiah's form of the response (39:8) emphasizes the certainty of divine blessing at least in his lifetime.

To suggest that chapter 39 provides a link retrojected from the period after 587 is correct only to a point. However, its theological function is far deeper. It forms a connection with the message of the "new things" promised Israel by Second Isaiah, and his message of a divine purpose at work unfolds precisely in reference to the "old things" of First Isaiah. Exactly how God proposes to extend his blessings to a destroyed and exiled people calls for the entire message of Second Isaiah (chapters 40 — 55). Chapters 36 — 39 provide a final link to the next dispensation in the economy of God, but the exact content of the promise and its fulfillment will have to wait for the announcement of the good news of chapter 40 by the prophetic evangelist.

41. Introduction to Chapters 40—55 (Second Isaiah)

Selected Bibliography

J. **Becker,** *Isaias—der Prophet und sein Buch,* Stuttgart 1968; **J. Begrich,** *Studien zu Deuterojesaja* (1938), reprinted in ThB 20, Munich 1963; **W. A. M. Beuken,** *Jesaja,* II, POT, Nijkerk 1979, 1983; **B. S. Childs,** "Retrospective Reading of the Old Testament Prophets," *ZAW* 108, 1996, 362–77; **R. E. Clements,** "The Unity of the Book of Isaiah," *Int* 36, 1982, 117–29; "Beyond Tradition-History: Deutero-Isaianic Development of First Isaiah's Themes," *JSOT* 31, 1985, 95–113; **A. B. Davidson,** "The Book of Isaiah, chapters xl—lxvi," *The Expositor,* II/6, London 1883, 81–269; **S. R. Driver,** *An Introduction to the Literature of the Old Testament,* Edinburgh 8 1908, 230ff.; **B. Duhm,** *Das Buch Jesaja,* Göttingen 1892; **K. Elliger,** *Deuterojesaja in seinem Verhältnis zu Tritojesaja,* BWANT 63, Stuttgart 1933; **H.-J. Hermisson,** "Deuterojesaja-Probleme, Ein kritischer Literaturbericht," *VF* 31, 1986, 53–84; "Einheit und Komplexität Deuterojesajas. Probleme der Redaktionsgeschichte von Jes 40—55," *The Book of Isaiah,* ed. J. Vermeylen, BETL 81, 1989, 287–312; **R. F. Melugin,** *The Formation of Isaiah 40—55,* BZAW 141, Berlin 1976; **R. D. Merendino,** *Der Erste und der Letzte. Eine Untersuchung von Jes 40—48,* VTSup 31, Leiden 1981; **J. Muilenburg,** *Isaiah 40—66,* IB, 5, 1956, 381ff.; **H. D. Preuss,** *Deuterojesaja. Eine Einführung in seine Botschaft,* Neukirchen-Vluyn 1976; **R. Rendtorff,** "Zur Komposition des Buches Jesaja," *VT* 34, 1984, 295–320; **J. Skinner,** *Isaiah: Chapters XL—LXVI,* Cambridge 1906; **G. A. Smith,** "The Date of Isaiah 40—66," *The Book of Isaiah,* II, London, 1884, 1–26; **O. H. Steck,** *Gottesknecht und Zion. Gesammelte Aufsätze zu Deuterojesaja,* FAT 4, Tübingen 1992; **M. A. Sweeney,** *Isaiah 1—4 and the Post-Exilic Understanding of the Isaianic Tradition,* BZAW 171, Berlin 1988; **C. C. Torrey,** *The Second Isaiah,* Edinburgh 1928; **J. Vermeylen,** "L'Unité du livre," *The Book of Isaiah,* ed. J. Vermeylen, BETL 81, Leuven 1989, 11–53; C. Westermann, "Sprache und Struktur der Prophetie Deuterojesajas," *Forschung am Alten Testament,* ThB 24, Munich 1964, 92–170; **H. G. M. Williamson,** *The Book Called Isaiah,* Oxford 1994.

There is no more powerful example of the impact of the historical-critical method on the study of the Old Testament than the challenge to the traditionally held unity of the book of Isaiah. Since this history has been reviewed many times and is readily available in the standard handbook, the discussion can be brief.

The credit for successfully mounting a theory for dual authorship of the book of Isaiah is usually attributed to the work of J. C. Döderlein (1775) and J. G. Eichhorn (1778–83). Three major arguments emerged for assigning chapters 40—66 to a sixth-century author.

a. The historical setting of chapters 40ff. appears to reflect an exilic period after the fall of Jerusalem in 587 and the ensuing deportation of the Judaean captives.

  b. There are striking differences in language, style, and concepts
     between the first and second parts of the book, which can be most
     easily explained by positing two different authors.
  c. If chapters 40ff. were spoken by an eighth-century prophet to the
     needs of an exiled people some one hundred fifty years in the
     future, it would be a situation without parallel in the rest of the Old
     Testament.

However, the specific argument that seemed to carry the most weight, especially in the English-speaking world (cf. Davidson, 81ff.; Smith, 9; Skinner,
xixff.), turns on the logic of chapters 41—48. The coming of Cyrus is not presented as a future prediction, but rather as proof that the prediction of him has
been fulfilled. On the basis of his former prophecies concerning Cyrus, which
have been realized and can readily be confirmed by all, the prophet then makes
a future prediction in 44:24ff. and 45:1ff. The logic of the prophetic argument
demands that the audience of the prophet's words stands at a point in the sixth
century when the former prediction is viewed as part of history.

At the close of the nineteenth century, Driver still felt the need to mount an
extended case for the historical-critical position. However, by the beginning of
the twentieth century this position was increasingly taken for granted. Moreover, for better or for worse, the hermeneutical principle became axiomatic that
a biblical book could only be properly understood when interpreted in the light
of its original historical setting. Of course, since this setting was often far from
obvious, the critical axiom led to an increase in historical speculation in the
search for an exact historical referent. The same hermeneutic was employed by
conservative commentators when they speculated on alleged eighth-century
contexts for the corpus.

As is now well known, one of the major contributions of Duhm's commentary of 1892 was in distinguishing chapters 40—55 (Second Isaiah) from chapters 56—66 (Third Isaiah). One of the effects of this hypothesis was that—with
a few notable exceptions—the essential unity of Second Isaiah appeared to
receive even greater confirmation. With the rise of the form-critical method, the
analysis of Begrich in 1938 seemed also further to confirm the oral patterns of
prophetic speech still at work in the composition of this collection. If there were
criticisms, they came from those scholars who still preferred to extend the literary unity to the entire second part of the book (chapters 40—66), such as Torrey and Muilenburg.

Nevertheless, beginning roughly in the 1970s, important changes in the
approach to chapters 40—55 became increasingly evident:

First, attempts were made, initially by Westermann, followed by Melugin,
to overcome the inevitable fragmentation of Second Isaiah that stemmed from
form-critical analysis. Both of these scholars were able to demonstrate that the

traditional oral forms of the preexilic prophets had often been modified in the process of literary composition and that larger "kerygmatic" units had emerged. In sum, these scholars were successful in challenging the assumption that Second Isaiah had delivered his oracles orally much like Amos or First Isaiah. Rather, they posited actual literary compositions instead of collections of once discrete oracles.

Second, equally important were the new redactional-critical studies that not only challenged the assumption of an authorial unity to chapters 40—55, but projected different hypotheses regarding the compositional history of the corpus. Possibly the earliest concerted attempt at a fresh redactional analysis was that of Elliger in 1933, who sought to distinguish passages in chapters 40—55 that he attributed to Third Isaiah. During the hegemony of the form-critical approach in the immediate post–World War II period, Elliger's book lay somewhat dormant, but within the last decades, it has contributed to a veritable explosion of redactional studies of Second Isaiah. Particularly noteworthy are the efforts of Steck, Hermisson, Merendino, Clements, Rendtorff, Vermeylen, and Sweeney. In the English-speaking world the monograph of Williamson has stimulated interest with his hypothesis that Second Isaiah was the actual editor shaping literarily the traditions of First Isaiah into book form. Clearly the redactional approaches have varied considerably and no real consensus has yet emerged (cf. some of my reservations in "Retrospective Reading," 363ff.).

Third, another new direction in the study of Second Isaiah can be characterized by its emphasis on intertextual references within the Isaianic corpus as a key to its interpretations. Again there has been much diversity of approach under this rubric of "intertextual exegesis," but the most significant work has been provided by Beuken in his magisterial Dutch commentary on chapters 40—66.

There is one final aspect to the problem of Second Isaiah that can hardly be omitted because of its continual importance. Already in his commentary of 1892 Duhm had separated from the material of Second Isaiah a group of passages designated as "servant songs" (42:1–4; 49:1–6; 50:4–9; 52:13–53:12). Thus he laid the foundation for later redactional analysis that sought to interpret a portion of Second Isaiah independently of the corpus as a whole. Needless to say, the issue of the servant songs still remains a hotly debated problem without a wide consensus for its resolution.

In sum, the assumed authorial unity of chapters 40—55 that dominated the field for decades has been seriously eroded in the minds of many. Blocks of material such as the polemic against the making of idols (44:9ff.) and the Cyrus oracles (44:24; 45:1ff.) have been interpreted redactionally as belonging to once independent redactional layers, which at times are extended well beyond the scope of Second Isaiah. However, rather than continuing to sketch the broad lines of the present interpretive debates, the reader is urged to pursue the problems in more detail by means of the commentary that follows.

42. Isaiah 40:1–11

40:1 Comfort, comfort my people,
      says your God.
2 Speak tenderly to Jerusalem
      and declare to her
  that her term of service is over,
      that her iniquity has been pardoned,
  that she has received from the LORD's hand
      double for all her sins.
3 A voice cries:
  "In the wilderness prepare the way of the LORD,
      make level in the desert a highway for our God.
4 Let every valley be raised up,
      every mountain and hill made low.
  Let the uneven ground become smooth
      and the rugged places a plain.
5 And the glory of the LORD will be revealed,
      and all flesh as one will see it,
      for the mouth of the LORD has spoken."
6 A voice says, "Cry!"
  Another asks,[a] "What shall I cry?"
  All flesh is grass,
      and all its strength[b] like a wildflower.
7 The grass withers, flowers fade
      when the breath of the LORD blows on them.
      Surely the people are grass.
8 The grass withers, flowers fade,
      but the word of our God stands forever.
9 Get up to a high mountain,
      O Zion, herald of good tidings.[c]
  Lift up your voice with might,
      O evangelist Jerusalem
      Lift it up, do not fear.

Say to the cities of Judah
"Behold. your God."
10   See, the Lord GOD comes in power,
and his arm triumphs for him.
See, his reward is with him,
and his retribution before him.
11   Like a shepherd he will feed his flock,
gathering them in his arms;
he will carry them in his bosom,
gently leading those with young.

a. The translation is that of the MT. The LXX and 1QIsᵃ read "and I said" (*BHS*). Cf.
Petersen, 20.
b. The exact meaning in this context is contested (cf. Kuyper).
c. The syntax of *mᵉ baśśeret ṣiyyôn* is debated. The LXX, Targum, and Vulgate and
render it as an accusative object = "good tidings to Zion" (cf. 41:27; 52:7). Others take
it in apposition (cf. 41:14) = "herald of good tidings" (Delitzsch, Dillmann, Torrey).

Selected Bibliography

J. Begrich, *Studien zu Deuterojesaja,* ThB 20, Munich 1963; **F. M. Cross,** "The Council of Yahweh in
Second Isaiah," *JNES* 12, 1953, 274–77; **R. W. Fisher,** "The Herald of Good News in Second Isaiah,"
Rhetorical Criticism, Fs James Muilenburg, ed. J. J. Jackson and M. Kessler, Pittsburgh 1977, 117–32;
N. Habel, "The Form and Significance of the Call Narratives," *ZAW* 77, 1965, 297–323; **N. Kamano,**
"New Prophecy Is Not Actually New: Canonical Function of Isaiah 40:1–11 Reconsidered," *Yale Divin-
ity School Seminar Paper 1993* (unpublished); **L. Krinetski,** "Zur Stilistik von Jes 40, 1–8," *BZ* 16, 1972,
54–69; **L. J. Kuyper,** "The Meaning of *ḥsd,* Isa. xl6," *VT* 13, 1963, 489–92; **O. Loretz,** "Mesopotamis-
che und ugaritische-kanaanäische Elemente im Prolog des Buches Deuterojesaja (Jes 40, 1–11)," *Orien-
talia* 53, 1984, 284–96; **R. F. Melugin,** *The Formation of Isaiah 40–55,* BZAW 141, 1976, 82–86; **D.
L. Petersen,** *Late Israelite Prophecy,* Missoula 1977; **G. von Rad,** "*kiplayim* in Jes. 40, 2: Äquivalent?"
ZAW 79, 1967, 80–82; **C. R. Seitz,** "The Divine Council: Temporal Transition and New Prophecy in the
Book of Isaiah," *JBL* 109, 1990, 229–47; "How Is the Prophet Isaiah Present in the Latter Half of the
Book? The Logic of Chapters 40–66 within the Book of Isaiah," *JBL* 115, 1996, 219–40; **H. J. Stoebe,**
"Überlegungen zu Jes 40, 1–11," *TZ* 40, 1984, 104–13; **J. M. Vincent,** *Studien zur literarischen Eige-
nart und zur geistigen Heimat von Jesaja, Kap. 40–55,* Bern 1977, 197–251.

In the prologue of chapter 40 God announces his will for a new dispensation
toward Israel of forgiveness, peace, and restoration. His redemptive message is
then proclaimed from the heavenly council as a confirmation of the truth of his
word, and redeemed Jerusalem is called as a herald of the good tidings.

1. Structure and Context

The initial verses of the prologue, vv. 1–8, have often been divided into smaller
units, either according to a form-critical (Begrich) or rhetorical-critical analy-

sis (Muilenburg): vv. 1–2; 3–5; 6–8. However, from their style, content, and movement, vv. 1–8 clearly function as a unit within chapter 40. Somewhat more controversial is whether vv. 9–11 also constitute part of the prologue. I shall argue below that these verses do form part of the prologue, even serving as its climax. As is often the case in Second Isaiah, the creative force of the author in shaping the content of his prophetic proclamation allowed him to employ a traditional literary genre (a herald's cry) in a fresh fashion for his own kerygmatic goals.

The more difficult and truly the decisive exegetical question turns on establishing the context for the prologue's interpretation. One's decision fundamentally affects the understanding of both the passage and the whole of Second Isaiah. The problem, of course, emerges because of the lack of any superscription, which usually introduces a new prophetic collection. To suggest that it has been lost in transmission is a completely speculative thought and highly misleading. It is also clear from the attempts of the LXX and the Targum to supply an alleged addressee ("priests"; "prophets") that the problem was recognized.

One characteristic way of establishing a context, which increasingly emerged as the majority opinion once the authorship of chapter 40 was assigned to an anonymous prophet of the sixth century, was to see the prologue as a call narrative of a new prophet. However, apart from the difficulty of introducing a first person pronoun into v. 6 according to the LXX's reading, the unit lacks most of the elements of a traditional call and shares a host of anomalies, such as the unidentified voices of vv. 3 and 6.

A much more compelling reconstruction of a context was proposed by Cross in 1953. Cross argued that vv. 1–8 reflect a genre that he described as "divine directives to angelic heralds," with its setting in the divine council. Parallels for this genre occur in 1 Kings 22:19ff., Isa. 6:1ff. Job 1:6ff., and in extrabiblical literature. However, Cross then returned to the earlier theory of the prophet's call in vv. 6–8 and spoke of a mixed genre with elements from a call narrative and a divine council.

Finally, credit for a new, decisive interpretation of the prologue goes to Seitz's brilliant essay of 1990, which builds on Cross's analysis but moves the discussion in a very different direction. Seitz sharply rejects the call narrative context along with all the accompanying biographical and psychological features that have been widely assumed (cf. Westermann). Rather, he sees the exegetical key to lie in an intertextual relation between chapters 40 and 6 of Isaiah. Both chapters share the language of the heavenly court. In a conscious dependency on chapter 6, chapter 40 does not offer a new independent call narrative, but rather provides a reapplication of Isaiah's call. The commission of Isaiah of Jerusalem has been fulfilled by the Babylonian destruction of Jerusalem in 587. The prophetic message of judgment has been summarized in 40:6b–7 by an intertextual reference to 28:2b–4: "the fading flower of his glorious beauty." However, the point of the prologue is the announcement of a divine decision that now reverses the commission of judgment assigned to Isaiah: "Speak tenderly to Jerusalem and declare to her that her term of service is over" (v. 2). The prologue signals that the old age is passing away and a new day is dawning. Historic Isaiah is now a distant figure of the past, but extending into the future is the word of God which endures forever. Seitz writes: "God speaks again from the divine council as he had done formerly in Israel's day. . . . [T]he word of God goes forth directly, commissioning the heralds of good tidings" (245).

The full force of Seitz's argument comes out strongly when one reviews his interpretation of the different voices involved in the prologue. In vv. 1–2 God speaks to his divine court in plural imperatives. In vv. 3–5 a divine attendant delivers his charge. Then in v. 6a a heavenly voice addresses someone individually with the imperative to "cry." Seitz understands vv. 6b–7 to be an objection: "What shall I cry? All flesh is grass; it withers when the breath of Yahweh blows on it." In this objection Seitz sees an intertextual reference to the words of 28:1–4 that summarize Isaiah's judgment on Israel, which constitutes the "former things" of chapters 1 — 39. However, the objection is overridden in v. 8 and a charge of "new things" is delivered in vv. 9–11.

In contrast to Seitz's interpretation of the different voices in the prologue, specifically vv. 6–8, the traditional interpretation (e.g., Delitzsch, Elliger) found the answer to the question of v. 6a beginning immediately with v. 6b, which was then regarded more as a seeking for clarification of content than as an objection. In spite of the evanescence of all things (vv. 6b–7), God's word remains steadfast forever (v. 8). However, Beuken (*Jesaja,* IIA, 23) correctly observes that this traditional interpretation does not adequately deal with the tension between vv. 7 and 8 in the passage, and thus his division of voices is akin to Seitz's.

I fully agree with Seitz's interpretation that the key to the prologue lies in its intertextual reinterpretation of Isaiah 6 and thus serves as a crucial interpretive bridge between First and Second Isaiah. It signals the change from the "old things" of chapters 1–39 to the "new things" of chapters 40ff. The former deals with judgment associated with Assyria, the latter with redemption from Babylon. However, as will become clear in the exposition, I differ from Seitz in his characterization of the continuing role of Isaiah of Jerusalem and the nature of his relation to the new things.

For Seitz, Isaiah of Jerusalem is a voice of the past who has been assigned to an old and distant era, and his words are only summarized as "the last gasp of the old" in vv. 6b–7. The message of the new is now given by various anonymous voices. However, I will argue that Isaiah of Jerusalem is understood as the proclaimer of both the "old things" of judgment and the "new things" of salvation. The message of the prologue is that, although the prophetic judgment has been fulfilled, Isaiah's word of future salvation is now about to be accomplished in the new things. The continuity between chapters 1—39 and 40ff. does not lie in the historical *persona* of Isaiah—in this Seitz is right—but rather in the word of God, faithfully proclaimed by Isaiah, which extends into the future and fulfills itself in the new things of which Isaiah had also spoken. The strongest evidence for the continuity of chapter 40 with First Isaiah is the ongoing description of the "new" in terms of an intertextual reference to the earlier corpus of his prophecy.

2. Exposition

[40: 1–2] The prologue opens with God's calling on divine attendants (note the plural form of the imperative) to "comfort my people" (first person). The command is then interrupted in the unit with the formula, "says your God." The formula is somewhat unusual since normally it is given in a past tense, and here the present seems to reinforce the sense of urgency. Some form-critics (e.g., Elliger) have argued that the formula marks the end of the divine speech and that another voice takes up the command in v. 2, addressing God in the third person. However, this is hairsplitting, and the coherence of the divine speech in vv. 1–2 should be maintained. Most important is that God confirms his relation with the people of Israel. He is their God and they are his people, a formula that reverberates as a distant echo from the ancient covenant tradition.

An immediate elaboration of the message of comfort follows with three announcements of change in the divine purpose, each introduced with a *kî*: "that her term of service is over," "that her iniquity has been pardoned," and "that she has received from the LORD's hand double for all her sins." The reference to "double for all her sins" is not to suggest that Israel received more punishment than deserved, but rather the author makes use of a legal image already found in Ex. 22:3(4), which requires a guilty one to restore double for a crime.

In an unpublished paper submitted to a Yale graduate seminar, Naoto Kamano argues for much closer attention to intertextual references in the prologue of chapter 40. He makes the point that recognition of an intertextual echo is often the key to the reinterpretation that Second Isaiah effected on the prior Isaianic tradition. The first example of such an interaction occurs immediately in v. 1: "comfort, comfort" (*naḥᵃ mû, naḥᵃ mû*). The verb in its piel form occurs frequently in Second and Third Isaiah (49:13; 51:3, 12, 19; 52:9; 61:2; 66:13), and sounds a note of divine restoration that is central to the second half of the book of Isaiah.

However, the more difficult question turns on the verbal parallel in 12:1. In a liturgical passage that concludes the first section of First Isaiah (chapters 2—12), the voice of faithful Israel testifies to its faith in God's eschatological promise of salvation. "In that day" his anger would turn and he would "comfort" *tᵉ naḥᵃ mēnî*) his people. In its song of praise, an obedient remnant anticipates in faithful worship the experience of divine comfort. What then is the relation of this passage in 12:1 to that of 40:1? The usual historical-critical response is that 12:1 is simply a later redactional retrojection from a late postexilic period expressing the hope of Second Isaiah. Indeed, from a diachronic, redactional analysis, 12:1 may well be a retrojection. Nevertheless, the hermeneutical issue raised by a synchronic reading of these two texts that have been juxtaposed according to a certain order cannot be so lightly dismissed. At least for the reader of the book as a whole, the reference in 40:1 resonates immediately with its earlier parallel in 12:1.

But 40:1 does more than just resonate with 12:1. Its use in the prologue effects a reinterpretation of First Isaiah. Chapter 12 looks forward in anticipation to the day when God delivers Israel, when his anger has abated, and he comforts her. Chapter 40 announces the beginning of God's comfort to his people, who have already experienced judgment. Moreover, chapter 12 is understood as a song of thanksgiving for the deliverance from Assyria, but chapter 40, following 39:7, suggests that the assurance of comfort is for those being freed from Babylon's oppression.

Of greatest hermeneutical significance is that through the technique of intertextual exegesis the radically new word of deliverance announced by Second Isaiah has been already adumbrated in chapter 12. The comfort of 40:1 was already a part of the prophetic word of First Isaiah. Far from being simply a voice of the past, Isaiah's word of promise is precisely "the word of our God [that] stands forever" (40:8).

Another important intertextual link between chapter 40 and First Isaiah can be traced in the reference to Israel's iniquity (*'āwôn*) being forgiven (v. 2). Much of Isaiah's attack on Israel focused on a "people laden with iniquity" (1:4; cf. 5:18). Indeed, the people's self-indulgence and refusal to repent was an iniquity that would not be forgiven, but rather issued in a death sentence (22:14). Again, Isaiah's response of despair in seeing the Lord seated upon a throne (6:1ff.) arose not only on account of his own guilt, but from his dwelling among a sinful people. Only after his sin was expiated did he hear the voice within the divine council and accept his commission. Yet at the same time, the description of the redeemed city Zion, "a peaceful habitation, an immovable tent," is climaxed by an anticipation that the people who dwell there will be forgiven their iniquity (33:24; cf. 27:9).

[3–5] A voice from the heavenly council now picks up the divine message of coming redemption with a cry that continues the urgent imperatives to a plural addressee: "prepare the way," "make level a highway" for the coming of "our God." Then the imagery of the highway is further expanded. Valleys will be raised, mountains levelled, and the rough terrain made flat. This is in preparation for the unveiling of the glory of God that will be revealed to all. The oracle closes with a formulaic assurance that "the mouth of Yahweh has spoken."

Commentators debate among themselves at length about the exact nature of the historical analogues to the highway imagery (cf. Elliger). Was it a processional highway prepared for the triumphal entry of a god or king, such as pictured from Babylonian sources? Was there originally a cultic setting for the imagery? Within Second Isaiah the theme of a highway is part of a larger set of images describing the transformation of the wilderness into a garden (41:18ff.; 42:15ff.) in order to facilitate the return of the exiles. Equally important for the biblical imagery is the appropriation of the language of the exodus from Egypt (11:16; 51:9ff,; 52:11ff.), as the two events are fused into a single all-encompassing paradigm of divine deliverance. It is thus a crucial move in establishing the intertextual connection between chapter 40 and First Isaiah to note that already in chapter 11 the promise of the return of the "dispersed of Judah" (v. 12) is portrayed in terms of a highway from Assyria. Chapter 40 again signals the fulfillment of this promise, but adjusts the geography to include also the wilderness separating the Babylonian exiles from Zion.

However, the strongest intertextual tie with 40:3–5 is found in chapter 35. The chapter addresses the return to Zion expressed in terms of a highway, called the Holy Way (v. 8), of the seeing of the glory of the Lord (v. 2), and the coming of God to save his people (v. 4). Especially noteworthy are the large number of exact verbal parallels: highway, way (*derek*), wilderness, and glory. Of course, these parallels have long been noticed, but the critical response has often been simply to transfer chapter 35 to the corpus of Second Isaiah (cf. Torrey, McKenzie) with little awareness of the hermeneutical effect of the positioning of chapter 35 within the collection of First Isaiah's oracles.

The theme in v. 5 of the revealing of the glory of God reflects also a close connection with the theophany of chapter 6. The glory of God (k^e $b\hat{o}d$ *YHWH*) is that aspect of the divine image which is made visible to human perception. The prophet first spoke of "seeing Yahweh" (6:1), but immediately the language is rendered more precisely to indicate that it was only his glory that was rendered accessible. The prophet overhears the liturgy of the seraphim bearing witness to the whole earth's being filled with God's glory. However, the point of his experiencing God's presence in chapter 6 is that only to the prophet was the revelation disclosed. However, in chapter 40 a sign of the inbreaking of a new age of salvation is that the glory of God will now be revealed to all flesh.

When 40:3–5 is read in light of chapter 35, then the prologue signals not just a general expectation of a coming redemption, but points explicitly to the end of God's judgment upon Judah, symbolized by its blindness and inability to see: "Then the eyes of the blind will be opened" (35:5). Moreover, these who return are not merely refugees, but are the "redeemed" (35:9), those who have been ransomed and transformed in order to walk in the Holy Way. Verse 5 closes with a stereotyped formula that usually functions to close an oracle. Is it possible in the context of the prologue that another note is also echoed? What the mouth of the Lord has spoken in vv. 3–5 is the message already sounded in chapters 1—39 (cf. Kamano, 16).

[6–8] In an earlier section on establishing the context of chapter 40, the problem of sorting out the different voices in vv. 6–8 was reviewed. According to the interpretation of Seitz, the voice in v. 6b raises an objection to the prior command to cry: "What shall I cry?" The issue turns on how there can be a proclamation of a coming salvation when God's devastating judgment preached by Isaiah has surely been fulfilled: "All flesh is grass. . . . The grass withers, flowers fade when the breath of the LORD blows on them" (cf. 28:1–4). The response in v. 8 first repeats a line of the objection affirming the truth of the prophetic judgment—indeed, "the grass withers, flowers fade," but then it defends the call for salvation by appealing to the steadfast word of God which stands forever. Seitz interprets this appeal to the enduring truth of the word of God, spoken by an anonymous angelic voice, to be a new word unrelated to Isaiah's proclamation, which he assigns to the old age, now passed.

Yet from what has already been seen of the use of intertextuality in the prologue as a means of describing the message of the new age according to the prior prophecy of Isaiah, it is reasonable to inquire whether this appeal to the steadfast word of God in v. 8b could also be related to Isaianic prophecy. Seitz has made a strong case that Isaiah's preaching of judgment has been summarized in 40:6b–7 by means of an intertextual reference to 28:1–4. However, if one takes notice that in 28:5–6 there is a promise made that "in that day" (an eschatological formula paralleled in 12:1) "the proud crown of the drunkards of Ephraim and its fading flower" would be transformed by Yahweh of hosts into "a crown of glory, and a diadem of beauty . . . and a spirit of justice to him who sits in judgment." If one then pursues the logic of the intertextual exegesis of 40:8, it seems reasonable to assume that v. 8 is appealing to the promise of 28:5–6 as evidence that an Isaianic word of salvation followed his prophecy of judgment. In sum, the steadfast word of God is a reference to Isaiah's proclamation of the coming new age. A continuity is thus established between First and Second Isaiah, both in terms of the old and of the new things. This conclusion also explains why from a modern redactional perspective large portions of Second Isaiah have been retrojected into First Isaiah. It was simply assumed that the two canonical collections shared the same substance in their prophetic messages.

[9–11] In an earlier section the question was raised of whether vv. 9–11 form a separate oracle because of the change in genre, or whether they constitute an integral part of the prologue. The ensuing exegesis of vv. 1–8 would seem to confirm the latter interpretation. Zion and Jerusalem are now personified as the evangelists of the good tidings. They are appointed to proclaim the news to the cities of Judah.

Some decades ago a position regarding the translation of *mᵉ baśśeret ṣiyyôn* as an accusative object (= "herald to Zion") was strongly defended by R. W. Fischer. He argued that the messenger is not only a prophet, but Second Isaiah himself. In the light of my exegesis of both vv. 1–8 and vv. 9–11, I do not find this interpretation of v. 9 a convincing option.

Once again the key to the interpretation of vv. 9–10 is found in the use of intertextual exegesis linked to First Isaiah. (I am indebted to Kamino for this initial insight.) The connection with 35:3–4 is exceedingly strong and shares a verbal identity of key words and phrases. Compare, for example:

35:4:	"*say* to those who are fearful" (*'imrû*)	**40:9:**	"*say* to the cities" (*'imrî*);
v. 4:	"be *strong*" (*ḥizqû*)	**v. 10:**	"in *power* (*ḥāzāq*);
v. 4:	*fear not* (*'al-tîrā'û*)	**v. 9:**	"*do not fear*" (*'al-tîrā'î*)
v. 4:	"*behold, your God*" (*hinnēh 'ᵉlōhêkem*)	**v. 9:**	"behold your God" (*hinnēh 'ᵉlōhêkem*)
v. 4:	"he *will come*" (*yabô'*)	**v. 10:**	"*the Lord GOD* comes" (*yabô'*).

We have already seen the intertextual link of chapter 35 with 40:3–5 in the use of the highway imagery and the revelation of the glory of God. In 35:3–4 the imperative is given in the masculine plural to strengthen the weakhearted with the proclamation of God's coming with vengeance and recompense to save. In chapter 40 the perspective has shifted. Zion and Jerusalem are not portrayed simply as awaiting the coming of imminent salvation. Indeed the emphasis is not primarily on the return of the exiles, but focuses foremost on the coming of God. Jerusalem and Zion are now described from the perspective of having already received redemption. Their task is rather one of the proclamation of the good news to the remaining cities of Judah. The genre of vv. 9–11 is a military one, of instructions to a herald. The imperatives are thus given in the feminine singular form to Zion as a personified herald of good news or "evangelist" (cf. the LXX's rendering of the Hebrew *biśśar*).

There are several other significant changes to note in chapter 40's intertextual relationship to chapter 35. In 35:4 the command "fear not" is addressed to those who in consternation still await the coming of God in salvation. However, in 40:9 the command not to fear is directed to the heralds of good tidings as if the reality of God's return had already been experienced. The command not to fear relates to their task of proclaiming to others the good news of the divine advent. The heralds are to have faith in the power that they have already received. There is another alteration in the way in which God's coming is portrayed. From the perspective of First Isaiah (chapter 35), God comes to save, but with vengeance and requital (*gᵉmûl*); however, in chapter 40 both the terminology and focus have shifted. God comes with "his reward" (*s^ekārô*) and "retribution" (*p^eullātô*). Of course, in another context Second Isaiah can also speak of "requital to his enemies" (*g^emûl*), but in chapter 40 the stress is fully on the coming of God for salvation and on the inbreaking of the new era of joy. His strength is manifest as he leads his flock like a shepherd, carrying in his arms the weak.

3. The Canonical Function of the Prologue

The primary role of the prologue (40:1–11) is to announce God's new purpose for Israel in bringing forth totally new redemptive events on its behalf, which serve as evidence for the faithfulness of God's word standing forever. Melugin (85) has observed that from a formal perspective the prologue reflects the structure of chapters 40—55 in miniature. Verses 1–8 are a microcosm of chapters 41—48, with their use of the image of the highway and new exodus; whereas vv. 9–11 correspond to chapters 49:14ff., with the themes of the return of Yahweh as ruler in Zion, the voice of the messengers, and the victory of Yahweh's arm. There is also widespread agreement that chapter 55 is an epilogue bringing the prophetic collection to an end by returning to the prologue's theme of the word of God accomplishing unfailingly the divine purpose (55:10–11).

Yet even more crucial for understanding the canonical function of the prologue is to recognize its role in establishing the theological relation between chapters 1—39 and 40ff. This achievement has been carried out by means of intertextual exegesis of chapters 1—39. The radically new word of chapter 40 has been announced through a fresh understanding of the earlier Isaianic corpus. Chapter 39 marked the historical change in the agent of God's destruction from Assyria to Babylon. The prologue of chapter 40 assumes this knowledge of God's former purpose when it sets forth the new intent.

Yet the relationship established is a subtle one, often dialectical (cf. 43:18; 46:9). The prologue confirms the truth of Isaiah's prophecy of judgment: the grass has withered and the flower has faded. Yet at the same time it also confirms the truth of Isaiah's prophecy of salvation: "the word of our God stands forever." No new prophet is called in chapter 40, but rather the word of God through Isaiah continues to work in order to fulfill the promise. According to the superscription of the book (1:1), Isaiah's ministry ended with the reign of Hezekiah. In chapter 39 Isaiah informs the king that the judgment on Israel which he had prophesied by the hand of Assyria had been transferred to Babylon in the period after the king's death. Implied in this final narrative of First Isaiah is also the death of Isaiah, who never reappears after chapter 39. The point of the prologue is therefore to affirm that Isaiah's prophetic word continues to work in fulfilling God's purpose, but apart from the historical *persona* of the prophet. In spite of the multitude of modern commentators on the book of Isaiah, Delitzsch appears to have been the last to have sensed this subtle hermeneutical issue when he described the prophet Isaiah's role in chapters 40ff. to be "like a spirit without visible form" (2:124).

The final aspect of the canonical function of the prologue of chapter 40 to be discussed turns on its role within the New Testament. According to the Synoptic Gospels, John the Baptist came proclaiming the imminent coming of the kingdom of God, which he linked to the prophecy of Isaiah 40: "Prepare the way of the Lord, make his paths straight" (Matt. 3:1–3; Mark 1:2–3; Luke 3:2–6). What are the theological warrants for this usage of the Isaianic prologue within the category of prophecy and fulfillment?

The function of the prologue of chapter 40 was to confirm the truth of the word of God regarding the promise of divine salvation. The temporal sequence relating the promise and the fulfillment was reinterpreted in the light of a fresh understanding of God's purpose. Judgment on Jerusalem was executed by the Babylonians, not the Assyrians, and only after the destruction of Babylon was the new age of salvation to appear. The credibility of the prophecy was not undercut by an adjustment within the historical sequence because the truth of prophecy could only be measured by its faithfulness to the substance of the divine reality of which it spoke. In contrast, the events of human history remained fragile and transitory. Thus, to the objection raised in the prologue against the call to preach God's imminent salvation, the prophetic response was to affirm that "the word of our God stands forever." The truth of God's promise did not depend on its conformity to a specific temporal sequence within human history.

When John the Baptist linked the appearance of Jesus with the prophet's call to "prepare the way of the Lord," he was not making a mechanical connection with an ancient prediction of Isaiah. Rather, the reality of God's salvation was manifest in Jesus Christ in such a way that his advent provided a perfect morphological fit according to its redemptive substance with the Old Testament promise. In a word, the salvific significance of Jesus Christ was understood in the light of the Old Testament prophecy, while, conversely, the Old Testament promise gained its true meaning from the revelation of the Christ in the fullness of God's time. (Cf. the commentary of Grimm and Dittert, *Deuterojesaja*, 61ff. for further reflections on the New Testament.)

43. Isaiah 40:12–31

40:12 Who has measured the waters in the hollow of his hand,
    and marked off the heavens with a span,
  and contained in a basket[a] the dust of the earth,
    and weighed the mountains with a scale
    and the hills in a balance?

13   Who has plumbed the mind of the LORD,
          or with whom has he shared his plan?
14   Whom did he consult to enlighten him,
          and who taught him the path of justice?
      And who taught him knowledge,
          and showed him the path of wisdom?
15   Look, the nations are like a drop from a bucket,
          and are considered as the dust on the scales.
          He raises up the islands as if they were fine dust.
16   All Lebanon does not yield enough wood for fuel,
          nor are its animals enough for sacrifice.
17   Before him all the nations are as nothing;
          they are regarded by him as worthless and
          less than nothing.
18   To whom then will you liken God,
          or with what likeness compare him?
19   An idol? A craftsman shaped it,
          and a smith overlaid it with gold
          and fashioned silver chains[b] for it.
20   A man chooses mulberry wood,[c] which
          will not rot.
      He seeks out a skillful workman
          to set up an image that will not topple.
21   Do you not know? Have you not heard?
          Have you not been told from the beginning?
          Have you not understood from the foundation
          of the earth?
22   He is the one who sits enthroned above the circle of
          the earth,
          and its inhabitants seem as grasshoppers.
      He stretches out the heavens like a curtain,
          and spreads them out like a tent to live in.
23   He brings down princes,
          and reduces the earth's rulers to nothing.
24   Hardly are they planted, hardly are they sown,
          hardly have their stems taken root in the earth,
          when he blows upon them and they dry up,
          and the storm carries them off like chaff.
25   "To whom then will you compare me,
          or who is my equal?" says the Holy One.
26   Lift up your eyes and look to the heavens.
          Who created these?

He brings out the hosts one by one,
　　and calls each of them by name.
Because of his great might and vast power,
　　not one fails to appear.

27　Why do you say, O Jacob,
　　and complain, O Israel:
"My way is hidden from the LORD
　　and my right is ignored by my God?"

28　Do you not know? Have you not heard?
The LORD is the everlasting God,
　　the creator of the ends of the earth.
He does not faint or grow weary.
　　His understanding cannot be fathomed.

29　He gives strength to the weary,
　　and increases the power of the weak.

30　Youths may grow faint and weary,
　　and young men stumble and fall,

31　but they who trust in the LORD
　　will renew their strength.
They will soar on wings like eagles,
they will run and not grow weary,
　　they will walk and not faint.

a. The word translated "basket" is *šāliš* ("a third part," probably of an ephah).

b. The Hebrew is uncertain.

c. Cf. the text below for the problems of translation. Williamson gives a valuable review of proposals. Cf. also the important contribution of Van Leewen.

Selected Bibliography

W. A. M. Beuken, "*MIŠPĀṬ.* The First Servant Song and Its Context," *VT* 22, 1972, 8–11; **M. Dijkstra,** "Lawsuit, Debate and Wisdom Discourse in Second Isaiah," *Studies in the Book of Isaiah, Fs W. A. M. Beuken,* ed. J. van Ruiten and M. Vervenne, Leuven 1997, 251–71; **K. Elliger,** "Der Begriff 'Geschichte' bei Deuterojesaja," 1953, reprinted in *KSAT,* ThB 32, Munich 1966, 199–210; **C. J. Labuschagne,** *The Incomparability of Yahweh in the Old Testament,* Leiden 1966; **R. F. Melugin,** "Deutero-Isaiah and Form Criticism," *VT* 21, 1971, 326–37; **T. N. D. Mettinger,** "The Elimination of a Crux? A Syntactic and Semantic Study of Isaiah xl 18–20," *Studies on Prophecy,* VT Sup 26, Leiden 1974, 77–83; **B. D. Naidoff,** "The Rhetoric of Encouragement in Isaiah 40, 12–31," *ZAW* 93, 1981, 62–76; **K. van Leewen,** "An Old Crux: *hamsūkān tᵉrûmāh* in Isaiah 40, 20," *Studies in the Book of Isaiah, Fs W. A. M. Beuken,* ed. J. Van Ruiten and M. Vervenne, Leuven 1997, 273–87; **H. G. M. Williamson,** "Isaiah 40:20 — A Case of Not Seeing the Wood for the Trees," *Bib* 67, 1986, 1–20.

The prophet mounts an argument that God as sovereign creator and redeemer is not only able but willing to come to the aid of his despairing people who trust him.

1. Form, Structure, and Context

As indicated in the Introduction to Chapters 40–55, for the large part of the twentieth century a major concern of the scholarly study of Second Isaiah has turned on analyzing the form of the oracles. At first, form-critics assumed a strong continuity with preexilic oral prophecy. They proceeded to isolate small units and sought to reconstruct suitable settings for the individual units (Begrich, von Waldow, Elliger). This endeavor was successful in demonstrating strong elements of continuity with earlier prophecy, especially in recovering the force of stereotyped elements within the literature. Yet the weakness of the classic form-critical approach was its atomization of the material. It failed properly to see the biblical text as a literary composition and not just a collection of isolated oracles that had subsequently been joined in a largely indeterminate manner.

As a reaction to the approach of the form-critics, a new approach arose that stressed the rhetorical features of the text as a unified literary composition (e.g., Muilenburg, Clifford, Watts). This synchronic approach was helpful in recovering a sense of a holistic reading of Second Isaiah and for closer attention to literary techniques in rendering its unique type of prophetic poetry. The emphasis shifted from genre to strophe. The weakness of this approach lay in its failure to assess the diachronic forces often still at work in shaping stereotyped forms. Often modern literary categories were used in determining the scope and coherence of a passage. Indeed, the level of subjective reconstruction was greatly increased, for example, in Muilenburg's analysis of strophes, or J. W. D. Watts's arbitrary supplying of divine voices for each unit, which often ran roughshod over the indices within the unit itself.

Fortunately, Westermann and Melugin have attempted to arbitrate between these two extreme positions. However, it has become increasingly clear during the last three decades that much remains unresolved in establishing the proper balance between the forces from original stereotyped forms and the fresh creativity of the prophetic author. A closer analysis of 40:12–31 is a good place to illuminate both the problems and possible solutions respecting form, structure, and context of the oracles of Second Isaiah.

There has been general agreement among form-critics that 40:12–31 is dominated by the genre of disputation. Elliger is close to Begrich in identifying three originally independent units (vv. 12–17; 18–26; 27–31). However, Westermann's analysis seems to have convinced a larger majority that only vv. 27–31 constitute a proper disputation and that the preceding oracles consist of rhetorical questions with the flavor of a disputation. They simply prepare the way for the one true disputation that has a concrete historical setting. Exiled Jacob complains that its rights have been forgotten by God. Westermann, thus, is attempting to distinguish between the literal and metaphorical levels in the role played by the stereotyped genre forms within the given literary composition. His move certainly represents a hermeneutical advance over the earlier form-critics.

Yet the problems of form and context are more complex than Westermann's analysis recognizes, and Beuken in his Dutch commentary (IIa, 35–36) calls for a much more subtle interpretation. He begins by pointing out a number of problems that stem from applying a special category such as disputation. Certainly the disputation in 40:12ff. is very different from that found, say, in Job. There is no reference to the voice of the antagonist except in a brief retort in v. 27, which is still a citation delivered by the one prophetic voice. Again, the debate does not start from shared assumptions regarding creation and then move to issues unique to Israel's historical tradition. The text does not move to a resolution ultimately by means of rational demonstration, but reflects throughout a confessional stance. Finally, Westermann approaches the text according to the classic assumptions of form-critical analysis when he assigns priority of meaning to v. 27 because it allows him a means of recovering a concrete sociological setting. The sixth-century Jewish exiles in Babylon complain that they have been abandoned by their God. Westermann then interprets vv. 12–16 metaphorically as subordinated to v. 27, which he sees as the real focus of the entire unit. The effect is that the text's meaning is determined from his initial form-critical reconstruction, which, at the very least, appears to reverse the order of the final form of the text without an adequate literary basis.

Yet the problems that evoked Westermann's form-critical analysis are simply avoided in the synchronic analysis of Muilenburg, who in the place of a disputation genre posits as a literary type a hymnic monologue of self-predication consisting of seven strophes. Similarly, Clifford attempts a literary reading that gains a certain historical dimension by appealing to parallels common to the ancient Near East and to the Psalter, but also fails to deal with the decisive disputational flavor that pervades the whole of 40:12ff.

The major interpretive problem of the chapter can be further elucidated by focusing one's attention on the structure of the passage. The present structure of the text does not move from complaint to praise as Westermann's reconstruction suggests. The focus of the final form of the text does not revolve around the anthropocentric complaints of Israel, but rather the focus is unremittingly theocentric. Israel's expression of doubt is not the center of the passage—this is to take unbelief far too seriously—but has been assigned to the margins of the debate (cf. below). However, conversely, we cannot properly say that confessional statements so dominate the chapter that Israel's complaints are simply ignored. To suggest that praise, spoken loudly enough, eliminates doubt by drowning it out, also does not do justice to the subtle theological relationship envisioned by the prophet, which has retained a genuinely disputational form for his message. In sum, the passage begins with a rhetorical style which then provides the response to a complaint; however, it is given voice when the accusations have already been rendered irrational and groundless in the light of God's actual creative and redemptive presence. Israel's unbelief has not been disregarded, but absorbed within the reality of the everlasting God.

The structure of 40:12–31 is as follows:

vv. **12–17** No one can gauge God's work
   12   not in creation
   13–14 not in counsel
   15–17 not among the nations
   18–26 No one can compare with God
   18–24 no one compares: proof given
   25–26 no one compares: proof given
   27   Israel's complaint
   28–31 Hymnic climax: God gives strength to the faint

Nowhere is Israel as the addressee assigned explicitly to the exilic period. Yet the transition in historical setting is continued from the prologue, 40:1–11: "The grass withers, flowers fade." The Israel addressed in v. 27 continues to reflect the despair of the exiles. It has not heard the good news. Following the prologue, the prophetic message turns to address the question, Who is God who can bring forth these new things? The movement of the succeeding chapters focuses on God's purpose to transform complaints into praise, first testified to by the prophet in 40:12ff., but then continued in chapter 41 with God's defense of his sovereign purpose with Israel as servant, Cyrus as his tool, and the nations as the recipients of his salvation.

2. Exposition

[40:12–17] The first exegetical question lies in determining the force of the series of interrogatives beginning "who" (*mî*). Older commentators, such as Delitzsch, tended to construe the material as hymnic, seeing parallels in Job 38:4ff. and Isa. 28:24ff. The description that followed vv. 12–14 was one of how God alone created the universe. In terms of a holistic reading of the entire passage, this interpretation has much to commend it. Nevertheless, this interpretation is not fully on target in regard to how the prophetic witness is being made, and it misses even closer parallels found in sapiential disputational passages (Prov. 30:4; Isa. 31:37; Sir. 1:1). To the questions, "Who has measured . . . marked off . . . contained . . . weighed . . . ?" the intended answer is no one. The same disputational sequence follows in vv. 13 and 14, each calling for the same response.

This disputational form is, however, a rhetorical device. The prophet speaks fully from a confessional stance, but he confronts his putative antagonist as if it were obvious that no one else could possibly work as creator of the universe. Although the verbs chosen are all exactly appropriate to a craftsman constructing an object—measuring, enclosing, weighing—the immensity of the task renders absurd any analogy with human skills. The omnipotence of God must be admitted by any rational creature. The movement from the waters, to the heavens, and then to earth (v. 12), follows the traditional biblical and ancient Near Eastern sequence (Gen. 1:1ff.; Ps. 9:11; 135:6).

In vv. 13–14 the focus shifts from God's omnipotence to his infinite wisdom (cf. Rom. 11:34). There is a continual discussion among commentators on rendering the exact nuances of v. 13. The verb *tikkēn* in v. 12 appears to have a concrete meaning such as "determine" or "gauge," but in v. 13 that is a slight shift of meaning to suit the content, best translated to *"plumb* the spirit of Yahweh." Then the issue arises in v. 13b whether Yahweh is the object or subject of the clause. Is the sense, "Who as his counsellor instructed him?" or rather "with whom has he [Yahweh] shared his plan?" The latter sense seems preferable. While there are other references in Isaiah by "a man of God's counsel" (e.g., 46:11) nowhere does a counsellor ever inform God. The point seems to be that no one can fathom the hidden mysteries of God.

Then in v. 14 the theme of God's infinite wisdom is pursued. No one "taught him the path of justice (*mišpāṭ*) . . . [nor] showed him the path of wisdom." (*BHS* follows the LXX and omits v. 14b as a secondary expansion). In an important essay Beuken has argued for the crucial role of the word *mišpāṭ* in Second Isaiah in encapsulating the redemptive purpose of God for Israel, which then culminates in the election of the servant in 42:1 toward bringing *mišpāṭ* to the nations. Certainly this is an important theme in the ensuing chapters that will call for closer analysis. However, it does seem clear that God's omnipotence in creation and his supreme wisdom in history are viewed as fully complementary and that both are directed toward the fulfillment of his sovereign will.

Verses 15–17 then proceed to draw the implications from the disputation in respect to the nations. They can lay no claim to a share in God's power or wisdom. They are judged as nothing and emptiness in comparison to God. At the very historical moment when exiled Israel is feeling the tremendous threat from the great powers of the world, such as Babylon, and remembering the humiliating annihilation of the Jewish state, the prophet boldly pronounces the rulers of the world to be as meaningless before God as "a drop from a bucket"!

[18–26] In v. 18 and again in v. 25 the theme of God's incomparability is pursued: "To whom then will you liken God?" The majority of modern critical scholars (e.g., Westermann, Elliger, Beuken) regard vv. 19–20 as a secondary expansion that interrupts the logical connection between vv. 18 and 21. From a stylistic perspective there is some evidence to support this hypothesis (cf. 46:5ff.). However, one cannot simply remove the verses as intrusive. Regardless of whether these verses represent a secondary expansion, there is an important theological point being made. The utter incomparability of God lies at the base of the Old Testament's uncompromising rejection of every attempt to represent the God of Israel by means of an image (cf. Ex. 20:3ff.). The continual and detailed controversy with idolatry would seem to reflect an eyewitness account of Babylonian practices, which viewed the making of idols partly as a ridiculous folly, but partly still as a threat.

The exact sense of v. 20a remains a classic crux that continues to resist a clear-cut solution. Elliger reviews at great length the various proposals, but ends up finding none fully convincing. In general, either one attempts to find a cognate from Arabic or Ugaritic, both of which are far from clear, or one follows a tradition found in Jerome that the term refers to a kind of wood. More recently an Akkadian cognate has been proposed that seems to support this latter theory and has been accepted by several modern translations (NJPS, "mulberry"). In addition, the difficulty of relating a metal idol with its wooden components is unresolved. What is striking in vv. 19–20, in contrast to 44:9ff. or 46:5ff., is that the description of producing an idol is quite objectively portrayed without the high level of sarcasm and ridicule that is usually heaped upon the process.

Verse 21 appears to have its primary response in vv. 22ff. Now it is made explicit in a hymnic style reminiscent of the Psalter that God—named "El" in v. 18—is the creator who has been announced to Israel "from the beginning," "from the foundation of the earth." Calvin sagaciously paraphrases the sense: "Ye have not any new God, but the same God who revealed himself from the beginning to Abraham, Moses, and the rest of the fathers." God sits "above the circle of the earth," and "he stretches out the heavens like a curtain." A clear echo is sounded from Genesis 1, Psalms 19, 89, and 104, and from Job 12. Then the focus shifts again from creation to the "earth's rulers," whose fragile destiny is in the power of God to blow them away like stubble. The only possible rival to God's incomparability—now named "the Holy One"—lies in the astral powers so widely respected in the ancient Near East. The heavenly bodies move in complete dependency upon God and respond in concert to his sovereign will.

[27–31] These final verses introduce for the first time Jacob/Israel as the implicit addressee of the entire oracle. As we have seen earlier, Westermann thinks that the complaint of exiled Israel in v. 27 forms the center of the entire unit. The preceding sections serve only as preparation for the real point of the disputation. Yet it is important to notice that when Israel's complaint is introduced within the oracle in order to appreciate the logic of the prophetic disputation, Israel's voice comes as a citation from the prophet and is compressed into one line. Moreover, the interrogative used is now "why?" The prophet asks why Israel can complain about God. Why indeed, because the refutation of her complaint has already been overwhelmingly given in the sections that preceded v. 27. "Do you not know? Have you not heard?" The reality of God as creator and redeemer is everywhere present and known. Israel only has to listen, look, and remember. Yahweh is the everlasting God and creator (*bôrē'*). The prophet's disputation never was an attempt rationally and theoretically to convince Israel, but fully from the perspective of Israel's tradition to dramatize the power and wisdom of Israel's God, who was confessed from the beginning as creator.

Nevertheless, Israel's complaint that she has been forgotten has been taken seriously in the prophet's message. God as creator does not grow weary; his understanding is unsearchable. Yet the purpose of this power is to give strength to the faint and weary. The terms are repeated three times. The whole point of the disputation is to confirm that God's incomparability and omnipotence is not a theoretical subject for debate. God is fully willing to come to the aid of his people. In v. 27 Israel is still talking *about* God, not *to* him. The prophet affirms that God's creative power is focused redemptively on Israel's distress; however, the promise is directed to those in Israel who "trust in the LORD," that is, those who ground their hope actively on the presence of God and yearn passionately for his intervention. Because of God's power, they shall not faint or perish, but rather renew their strength, mount up with wings, and even run.

The disputation closes on a parallel note with that of the prologue. Although the flower has faded and the grass withered through God's judgment, God comes with power to save and he will gently gather his dispersed and devastated people in a new and hitherto unknown manner.

44. Isaiah 41:1–42:13

41:1 Listen to me in silence, coastlands.
      Let the nations renew their strength;
      let them approach to state their case;
      let us come forward for trial.

2   Who stirred up one from the east,
      whom victory meets at every step?
      He delivers up nations to him,
      and subdues kings before him.
      He scatters them with his sword like dust,
      and like wind-driven stubble with his bow.

3   He pursues them and passes on unscathed
      by paths his feet have not travelled before.

4   Who has performed and done this,
        calling forth the generations from the beginning?
    I, the LORD, the first,
        and with the last, I am he.
5   The coastlands have seen and fear,
        the ends of the earth tremble;
        they draw near and come.
6   Each one helps the other,
        and one says to another, "Take courage!"
7   The craftsman encourages the smith,
        and he who flattens with the hammer
        supports the one who strikes the anvil,
    saying of the soldering, "It is good."
        He attaches it with nails
        so it cannot topple.
8   But you, Israel, my servant,
        Jacob, whom I have chosen,
        seed of Abraham, my friend;
9   you whom I took from the ends of the earth,
        from the far corners I called you;
    to whom I said: you are my servant,
        I have chosen you, and not cast you off;
10 fear not, for I am with you.
        Do not be frightened, for I am your God.
    I will strengthen you and help you.
        I will support you with my victorious right hand.
11 Now shall all who rage against you
        be put to shame and chagrined.
    They who strive with you
        shall become as nothing and perish.
12 Although you seek those who contend with you,
        you will not find them.
    Those who do battle against you
        will be as nothing at all.
13 For I am the LORD your God,
        who holds your right hand.
    It is I who says to you, fear not,
        I will help you.
14 Fear not, you worm Jacob,
        small maggot[a] Israel.
    I will help you, says the LORD,
        your redeemer, the Holy One of Israel.

15 See, I will make of you a threshing board,
  new, sharp, and with many spikes.
  You will thresh the mountains and crush them;
  and reduce the hills to chaff.
16 You shall winnow them
  and the wind will carry them off;
  the whirlwind will scatter them.
  But you will rejoice in the LORD,
  and glory in the Holy One of Israel.
17 The poor and the needy seek water
  and there is none;
  their tongue is parched with thirst.
  I, the LORD, will answer them;
  I, the God of Israel, will not forsake them.
18 I will open up rivers on the bare hills,
  and fountains in the midst of the valleys.
  I will turn the desert into pools of water,
  and the dry land into springs.
19 I will plant in the wilderness the cedar,
  the acacia, the myrtles, and the olives.
  I will set in the desert the pine,
  the fir, and the cypress together,
20 that men may see and know,
  consider and comprehend,
  that the hand of the LORD has done this,
  the Holy One of Israel has created it.
21 Present your case, says the LORD,
  bring forth your proof, says the King of Jacob.
22 Let them approach and tell us what happens.
  Tell us the former things, what they are,
  that we may take note of them,
  that we may know their outcome;[b]
  or declare to us the things to come.
23 Tell us what is to come in the future,
  that we may know that you are gods.
  Let it be good or bad,
  that we may be awed and terrified.
24 Behold, you are less than nothing,
  and your work is worthless.[c]
  Whoever chooses you is an abomination.
25 I stirred up one from the north,
  and he has come,

from the rising sun, one who calls on my name.
He has trampled[d] rulers like mud,
 like a potter treading clay.
26 Who announced it from the beginning,
  that we might know,
 or beforehand so that we may say
  "He is right"?
No one is told of this, no one foretold it,
 no one heard any words from you.
27 I was the first to tell Zion,
  Behold, here they are![e]
 and I gave to Jerusalem a messenger
  of good tidings.
28 But I looked and there was no one,
  no one to give counsel,
  no one to respond when I asked him.
29 See, they are all a delusion;
  their deeds amount to nothing;
  their images are empty wind.
42:1 See, my servant, whom I uphold,
  my chosen one, in whom I delight.
 I have put my spirit upon him,
  and he will bring forth justice to the nations.
2 He will not shout or cry out,
  or raise his voice in the streets.
3 He will not break even a bruised reed
  or snuff out a flickering wick.
 He will faithfully bring forth justice.
4 He will not fail or be discouraged
  until he has established justice on the earth;
  and the coastlands will await his teaching.
5 Thus said God, the LORD,
  who created the heavens and stretched them out,
  who spread out the earth and all
  that it brings forth,
 who gives breath to the people on it
  and life to those walking on it:
6 I am the LORD, I have called you in righteousness.
  I have taken you by the hand and kept you.
 I have given you as a covenant for the peoples,[f]
  and a light to the nations,
7 to open eyes that are blind,

      to free captives from prison,
          from the dungeon those sitting in darkness.

8   I am the LORD, that is my name.
          I will not give my glory to another
      or my praise to idols.

9   Look, the former things have come to pass,
          and now I foretell new things;
      before they spring forth,
          I announce them to you.

10   Sing to the LORD a new song,
          his praise from the end of the earth,
      you who go down to the sea[g]
          and all that is in it,
          the coastlands and their inhabitants.

11   Let the desert and its towns cry aloud,
          the villages where Kedar dwells.
      Let Sela's inhabitants cry for joy,
          let them shout from the top of the mountains.

12   Let them give glory to the LORD
          and declare his praise in the islands.

13   The LORD goes forth like a mighty man,
          like a warrior he will arouse his fury.
      He cries out, he roars aloud,
          and will triumph over his enemies.

    a. The MT reads "men of," which strains the context. But cf. Oswalt, II, 87 in support of the MT.

    b. *BHS* suggests inverting the order of the last two cola for logical consistency.

    c. The word in the MT is unknown. Most probably it is an orthographical error for *'āpes* (*BHS*).

    d. The MT reads "he has come," which is often emended to *wayyābos* ("trampled").

    e. The first colon is obscure, and probably an elliptical usage.

    f. The exact meaning of *bᵉrît 'ām* is contested.
The MT is often emended to "let roar" (*vir'am*) for the sake of coherence.

Selected Bibliography

J. Begrich, "Das priesterliche Heilsorakel," *ZAW* 52, 1934, 81–92; reprinted in *GSAT*, ThB 21, 1964, 217–31; **W. A. M. Beuken**, " *MIŠPĀṬ*. The First Servant Song in Its Context," *VT* 22, 1972, 1–30; **H. J. Boecker**, *Redeformen des Rechtsleben im Alten Testament*, 2d ed., WMANT 14, Neukirchen-Vluyn 1970; **E. W. Conrad**, "The 'Fear Not' Oracles in Second Isaiah," *VT* 44, 1984, 133–43; **M. Dijkstra**, "De koninklijke Knecht. Voorstelling en investituur van de Knecht des Heren in Jesaja 42," *De Knecht, Studies rondom Deutero-Jesaja, Fs J. L. Koole*, Kampen 1978, 41–58; **J. Goldingay**, "The Arrangement of Isaiah 4–45," *VT* 29, 1979, 289–99; **H.-J. Hermisson**, "Israel und der Gottesknecht bei Deuterojesaja," *ZTK* 79, 1982, 1–24; **G. P. Hugenberger**, "The Servant of the Lord in the 'Servant Songs' of Isaiah: A Second Moses Figure," *The Lord's Anointed: Interpretation of Old Testament Messianic Texts,* ed. O. E. Satterthwaite et al., Grand Rapids 1995, 105–39; **J. Jeremias**, "*Mišpaṭ* im ersten Gottesknechtslied (Jes. XLII 1–4)," *VT* 22, 1972, 30ff.; **H. Klein**, "Der Beweis der Einzigkeit Jahwes bei Deuterojesaja," *VT* 35, 1985, 267–73; **R. G. Kratz**, *Kyros im Deuterojesaja-Buch,* FAT 1, 1991, 128ff.; **R. Marcus**, "The 'Plain Meaning' of Isaiah 42, 1–4," *HTR* 30, 1937, 249–59; **R. F. Melugin**, *The Formation of Isaiah 40—55,* BZAW 141, 1976, 53–69; **R. P. Merendino**, "Literarkritisches, gattungskritisches und exegetisches zu Jes. 41, 8–16," *Bib* 53, 1972, 1–42; **J. Muilenburg**, "Isaiah 40—66," *IB* 5, 447–67; **C. R. Seitz**, "How Is the Prophet Isaiah Present in the Latter Half of the Book? The Logic of Chapters 40—66 within the Book of Isaiah," *JBL* 115, 1996, 219–240; **J. J. Stamm**, "*Berît 'am* bei Deuterojesaja," *Probleme biblische Theologie, Fs. G. von Rad,* Munich 1971, 510–24; **O. H. Steck**, "Aspecte des Gottesknechts in Deuterojesajas Ebed-Jahwe-Liedern," *ZAW* 96, 1984, 372–90; **C. C. Torrey**, "Isaiah 41," *HTR* 44, 1951, 121–36; **D. W. Van Winkle**, "The Relationship of the Nations to Yahweh and to Israel in Isa. XL—LX," *VT* 35, 1985, 446–58; **J. B. Vincent**, *Studien zur literarischen Eigenart und zur geistigen Heimat von Jesaja, Kap. 40—55,* Bern 1977, 124–87; **J. Werlitz**, "Vom Knecht der Lieder zum Knecht des Buches. Ein Versuch über die Ergänzungen zu den Gottesknechtstexten des Deuterojesajabuches," *ZAW* 109, 1997, 30–43; **C. Westermann**, "Das Heilswort bei Deuterojesaja," *EvT* 24, 1964, 355–73; **W. Zimmerli and J. Jeremias**, *The Servant of God,* SBT I/20, London 1957.

Using the form of a fictive trial with the gods, Yahweh denounces them as worthless delusion. Then he lays claim to sovereignty over the events of history by fulfilling his prior prophecy to call a victor from the north. He reiterates his promise of salvation to his discouraged people and presents his servant as a vehicle to establish justice for the nations.

1. Form, Structure, and Content

There is general agreement among the older form-critics that chapter 41 divides into a series of discrete genre units. Thus, 41:1–5(6–7) is described as a trial, vv. 8–13 and 14–16 as two oracles of salvation (*Heilsorakeln*), vv. 17–20 as a communal promise (*Heilsankündigung*) and vv. 21–29 as a trial with the gods. Isaiah 42:1–13 is somewhat more complex and controversial (cf. below). Verses 1–4 comprise a servant song, the genre of vv. 5–9 is contested, and vv. 10–12 are judged to be a concluding hymn (cf. Begrich, Westermann, Elliger).

The far more difficult question, and one that continues throughout most of Second Isaiah, lies in determining the semantic significance of these formal classifications, which arose largely from the assumption that each genre had a specific setting within oral speech. It has become increasingly clear that the issue is far more complex than originally supposed. Often the genres of Second Isaiah have been radically transformed within its literary composition and have acquired a new function, largely shaped by the prophet's own creative intention. Crucial for chapters 41 and 42 is to determine the form and function of a passage within a larger literary composition that greatly influences how one understands the individual parts. For many modern interpreters, the older form-critical approach of, say, Begrich and Elliger no longer carries its former persuasiveness, but effects an acute atomization of the text. Conversely, a rhetorical approach, which has been defended as a better alternative (e.g., Muilenburg, Clifford, Watts), seems strikingly arbitrary and one-dimensional.

An important key to understanding chapter 41 is to recognize its close relation to chapter 40. Israel has complained that its *mišpāṭ* ("right") has been disregarded (40:27). Chapter 41 serves clearly to address this major question in a first person divine discourse. God summons the distant nations together for judgment (*mišpāṭ*). The Hebrew term has a wider and a narrower meaning. It can refer to a larger social order or a specific instance of a legal decision that adjudicates a case. Forensic language commensurate with a trial pervades the entire chapter, but the basic issue at stake turns on who determines the course of events and what is the nature of this history. The trial is set forth in a two-stage structure, vv. 21–23 and 25–29. Yahweh challenges the gods to demonstrate their control of past and future events. When they are unable to respond, he denounces them as nothing. Then on the grounds of his raising up a victor from the east, God asserts that he alone can lay claim to world sovereignty. Yet intertwined with the trial of the gods there is another major theme of chapter 41 that is addressed to the suffering exiles. Israel is comforted (vv. 8ff.), its election is reconfirmed, and a divine hope for salvation is extended. The God of creation is not only willing but fully able to execute his purpose with Israel and the world.

Moreover, it is crucial at this point to recognize that the movement of chapter 41 is not fully understood unless it is joined to chapter 42. Israel had complained that its *mišpāṭ* was disregarded. God responds by presenting his chosen servant on whom his spirit rests to bring forth justice to the nations. However, his role will be far different from that expected by exiled Israel, and will only emerge in the course of time as the new things that God declares are disclosed.

2. Exposition

[41:1–7] The unit opens with Yahweh summoning the nations to appear in court for a trial. The claims of the foreign gods will be tested according to legal rules. The language of the appeal and summons reflects the conventional idiom of Israel's juridical system (cf. Boecker). Yet from the start the attempt to bring a precise sociological setting into sharper focus runs into difficulty. Some earlier scholars (e.g., Begrich) felt that the passage was an imitation of the procedure used in the trials at the town gate (cf. Ruth 4:1ff.). Others argued for a cultic lawsuit derived from a covenant renewal festival. However, these reconstructions seemed strained and of little help in construing the present function of the speech. It seems far more likely that the writer has employed traditional legal language, but used it with great freedom to make his own distinctive points.

The nations are summoned, but they remain silent. The trial scene serves initially to describe the aggressive, adversarial approach of Yahweh. The confrontational style is reflected in the questions of vv. 2 and 4: "Who stirred up?" "Who has done this?" He immediately proceeds to affirm his supreme sovereignty over world events by means of a concrete example. He alone roused a victor from the east and summoned him to his own service. Earlier commentators (e.g., Calvin) and occasionally a modern one (e.g., Kissane), have argued that Abraham is intended. The reference to him in v. 8 and the translation of *ṣedeq* as "righteousness" (v. 2) were thought to provide warrants for this interpretation. However, there is a virtual consensus today that the reference is rather to Cyrus, who is later specifically named (44:28; 45:1). The images of incredible speed and of easy victory reflect that the period of his earliest conquests already lay in the past.

The sheer audacity of the case lay in God's claim to have been the cause of this meteoric rise on the world scene of the king of Persia, and that God's power lay behind this horrendous show of military prowess. By means of a self-prediction formula, which shatters the conventional form of the trial, Yahweh lays claim to being both "the first and the last," the one true force that encompasses the past and the future. He is the one who has been in control of the world's events from the beginning. Twice the term *merō'š* ("beginning") is used (vv. 4, 26). God's power over world events is not limited to the calling of Cyrus, but has exercised sovereignty over history from the beginning of creation. Cyrus is only one instance of God's creative purpose from the start. Although First Isaiah (6:3) had announced that God's rule as king stretched from eternity, even when not perceived by sinful humanity, Second Isaiah speaks of God's power actually controlling every form of human activity occurring within history.

In vv. 5–7 attention shifts quite unexpectedly away from the theme of a trial to a taunt (*Spottlied*) by which to portray the terrified reaction of the nations to this coming conqueror. They frantically resort to fashioning idols as protection, and the biblical writer subtly reveals the irony of trying to polish and support images that are obviously unable to afford any defense against the approaching colossus. Of course, it has long been noted that most often the references to idol making in Second Isaiah appear to have a somewhat brittle literary connection in their present literary context (cf. 40:19; 41:5ff.; 44:9ff.), and a reasonable case can be made for the hand of a subsequent redactor (cf. Kratz, 37ff.). Nevertheless, regardless of the history of the formation of these verses, in the final form of the text the verses provide a coherent addition to the passage and increase the contrast between the enormous history creating dynamic of the God of Israel and the powerless, static folly of the foreign nations whose hope is completely without substance.

[8–16] Two units follow (vv. 8–13; 14–16), described form-critically by Begrich as oracles of salvation (*Heilsorakel*). Indeed, one is struck by the well-defined conventional pattern of these passages. There is a word of direct address in the singular "fear not," a clause indicating the closeness of God's help, a response revealing that Yahweh has heard, and finally the announcement of salvation. Begrich goes on to argue that the form arose from a cultic setting, often reflected in the individual complaint psalm in which a priest responded to the lament with an assurance of salvation. He then considers the form in Second Isaiah to be an imitation of the original cultic oracle.

Begrich's thesis has been very illuminating in pointing out the consistent pattern of stereotyped form and language. Yet one remains troubled by the high degree of speculation attached to his reconstruction, especially when the clearest examples of the form seem to be an imitation far removed from its alleged original setting. Yet regardless of how one evaluates all the details of Begrich's form-critical hypothesis, the more immediate exegetical problem arises in determining the semantic force of the stereotyped form that he discovered. Perhaps one way of testing the significance of Begrich's form-critical analysis is to contrast it with the interpretation of Muilenburg, who disregards the form almost completely and suggests that the initial trial scene of vv. 1–7 continues throughout the chapter (cf. also Clifford). In my judgment, the sharp contrast in style and content of vv. 8–16 is far better explained by observing the conventional forms rather than in falling back on psychological or rhetorical explanations. In sum, form-critical analysis retains its value in providing a close analysis of the building blocks from which the prophet shaped his new message, but the crucial problem remains in observing the full extent of the prophetic freedom in making use of older forms for new content.

[8–13] In vv. 8 and 13, Israel/Jacob is addressed directly as the servant. This designation is not an obvious one, but still one with a long precedent in the tradition (cf. Zimmerli and Jeremias, 9ff.). In chapter 41 the servant's election is confirmed. However, the conventional formula "fear not" receives fresh significance in the light of Israel's present condition of embittered resignation: "My way is hidden . . . and my right is ignored by my God" (40:27). This complaint is the context for the renewed assurance, "I have not cast you off" (v. 9). The promise is not in reference to the trial (vv. 1–7), but is a return to the eternal sovereignty and care of God, the creator and redeemer of Israel, which was a theme developed in chapter 40. The assurance is then expanded in terms of God's strengthening and upholding Israel (v. 10), which plays on a dominant theme of 40:28ff. In vv. 11–12 there is again a return to the theme of victory from v. 2, although Cyrus plays no role here; rather, it is God directly who contends with Israel's enemies.

[14–16] These verses offer another classic example of an oracle of salvation (*Heilsorakel*) and again reflect the conventional form and idiom described by Begrich. The unit is self-contained and has a formal connection with vv. 8–13. Yet when read in the context of chapter 41, it functions to strengthen the assurance of salvation with its repetition of "fear not" to Jacob/Israel. Again, the image of a threshing board has been transferred by the prophet to the strange activity of crushing mountains and making the hills like chaff, which obviously points to the exiles becoming a means of leveling the obstacles separating them from home. Then again, this oracle picks up for the first time in Second Isaiah the designation of God as "the Holy One of Israel," which joins the prophet's message closely to that of First Isaiah (1:4; 5:24; 6:2; 12:6; 30:15). Finally, the oracle ends on the note of Israel's joy, which forms a major theme of the promised return (cf. 35:10).

[17–20] Westermann has strongly criticized Begrich for including the succeeding oracle as another oracle of salvation. From a strictly form-critical perspective it clearly lacks the closely honed pattern of the two preceding oracles and lacks the characteristic formula "fear not." Nevertheless, this debate plays little role in terms of the unit's function in chapter 41, since the promise of salvation is simply extended by these verses. The theme of the exile's return through the parched desert is the background for introducing the language of the return of paradise as the desert breaks forth into blossom to mark the entry of the new age of salvation. Then will Israel finally understand the true dimension of the redemptive action of God, the Holy One of Israel, on its behalf.

[21–29] Chapter 41 began with a trial scene (vv. 1–4) and was followed by three units of promise. In vv. 21–29 the genre of the trial reappears, which now brackets the oracles of promise (vv. 8–20). This structure appears to be quite clearly a redactional ordering to which we shall return when discussing the effect on the larger literary composition. The trial oracle in vv. 21–29 is carefully structured into two parts. Verse 21 sets the stage for the legal challenge of the gods. Verses 22–23 question their legal evidence for claiming the rank of divinity. Can they predict events and also execute them? Verse 24 concludes that their pretention is invalid. Then a new tack is taken in vv. 25–27. Yahweh now presents the legal evidence for his claim to sovereignty. He alone raised up a conqueror from the north; moreover, he announced the conqueror's coming before he appeared. In v. 28 when a chance was offered for a reply, there was none. Verse 29 concludes that the gods are a delusion whose works are nothing.

There are some initial textual problems that call for comment. The problem lies in separating the references to the past, the former things (*hārē'šōnôt*) from those events in the future (*habbā'ôt . . . hā'ōtiyyôt*). In v. 22, rather than construing the first clause as referring to future time (*tiqrênāh*) and thus blurring the sequence that follows between past and future, the verb can better be translated nominally: "the events" (Beuken), or as a timeless verb: "what happens." Then the contrast between the former things and the future things in v. 22b is clear. The polarity is made even sharper if the two final cola in v. 22b are inverted as suggested by *BHS* and accepted by many commentators; however, the emendation is not mandatory to make sense of the passage.

The force of the argument in both parts of the trial appears to be that the claim to true divinity rests on the ability not only to control the course of future events, but also to have predicted the events before they occurred. Consequently, the ability to match the prediction with its fulfillment can then be tested rationally in the trial. For his part, Duhm (280) could only heap scorn on the naïveté of the prophet in claiming that only Yahweh could predict future events and that this claim could be rationally tested.

The initial difficulty of interpreting this passage turns on how one construes the analogy being made between the form of a normal trial in Israel conducted between human parties, and its application in chapter 41 to a trial between gods. In terms of form-critical analysis, it is usually assumed that the logic of the debate remains fully consistent, even if it has been transferred to a metaphorical plane by the prophet. However, in its present form the trial scene has assumed a very different function from that of a rational legal debate. The ploy of a trial to demonstrate rationally the superiority over the gods becomes only a rhetorical device. In the end, the gods are not proven wrong, but rather to be a delusion. They are nothing, lacking all substance.

Even the use of an alleged argument to demonstrate the coherence between prediction and fulfillment does not function in its present form as a rational debate. Yahweh simply announces that he predicted the coming of the conqueror. He declares that he alone had foreseen his coming. There are not two voices contending in the trial, but only one. The fictive form of a trial only serves as a vehicle to arrive at a conclusion that the prophet assumed at the outset, namely, that the gods were not a real adversary but only a delusion and fraud.

It has troubled commentators in the past that in v. 25 the victor from the north is described as "one who calls on my [Yahweh's] name." Since Cyrus never became a worshipper of Yahweh, it has caused some scholars to seek to remove the problem by emending the text. For example, Elliger emends v. 25 to read that Cyrus was "called by his name"; however, the MT is in order and is not to be changed for such apologetic reasons. For the prophet, everything that Cyrus did was in obedience to God's authority, even if concealed (44:28; 45:4). The statement is to be understood theologically as part of the overarching divine guidance of this pagan ruler.

In many modern commentaries the alleged proof-from-prophecy has been regarded as an embarrassment. Westermann does not think the ability simply to predict an isolated event as an act of clairvoyance could serve as a demonstration of divinity. Therefore, he argues that the prophet's argument rested on Yahweh's claim to control all of history, in a word, to place events within a meaningful continuum. Yet one receives the impression that Westermann is accommodating the text to modern sensibilities by fitting it in more readily to a modern understanding of *Heilsgeschichte*. In addition, there is the problem which has disturbed commentators that there is no apparent prophecy in Second Isaiah in which Yahweh had indeed predicted the coming of Cyrus. In sum, these innumerable difficulties would suggest that the interpretation of chapter 41 has not as yet found an access to its meaning.

In the light of this impasse, I would suggest that closer attention needs to be paid to the issue of how the passage functions in the present form of the text, namely, to its canonical shape. The fictive trial between Yahweh and the gods serves to expand God's claim that he alone is the absolute sovereign creator. In a first person monologue, God further refutes Israel's claim that its right has been disregarded. The prophet uses a reshaped traditional form in order to dramatize the point that God has no divine rivalry from other gods. He alone is in control of history. Yet the point being made is not just a general and abstract affirmation of God's sovereignty over history. Rather, the God of Israel has given his word, and the word of God will fulfill itself. The crucial argument of the pattern prophecy—fulfillment in chapter 41 is based on a recognition that the corpus of Second Isaiah presupposes that of First Isaiah. In chapter 13, which is redactionally located within First Isaiah, the prophecy is given in the form of first person divine speech (vv. 17ff.): "Behold, I will stir up the Medes. . . . And Babylon . . . will be like Sodom and Gomorrah. . . . [I]ts days will not be prolonged." What is being argued in chapter 41 is that God foretold the coming of Cyrus, which is now being fulfilled for all to see. The note sounded in the prologue (40:8) and reaffirmed in the epilogue (55:11) is now being confirmed in reference to Cyrus. The theological point is not a general affirmation of divine control of history in general, but the confirmation of God's sovereignty by the truth of his word in sacred scripture.

There is one final topic to be discussed in relation to the trial scene of chapter 41. The issue turns on the use made of this chapter in the history of exegesis as evidence for the dating of Second Isaiah. In the British debate in the last part of the nineteenth century, one of the strongest cases for an exilic dating was made by Davidson and Smith. The argument ran as follows: For a prediction to have been recognized as fulfilled and therefore authoritative, the audience addressed must have experienced the coming of Cyrus. It thus follows that the speaker of the prophecies must also himself have been situated historically at a time after the fulfillment of the prediction, namely, in the sixth century (cf. Williamson, *The Book Called Isaiah,* 2).

The problem with this argument is that it assumes that the passage functions in close analogy to a human audience. Form-critical analysis of the passage has worked on the same assumption and has sought to make as concrete as possible the original sociological setting of the trial used by the prophets. Yet what has become increasingly clear is that the prophet has creatively reshaped the conventional form to bring forth his own theological message in a way that runs roughshod over the original function of a trial between human parties. The oracle has been turned into a monologue in which Yahweh asserts his ability both to predict and to fulfill his word. In sum, the historical weight of this critical argument is greatly reduced once the metaphorical use of the oracle is recognized, since it shares little with ordinary human experience.

In a recent article, Seitz (221) has critically reviewed Calvin's approach to chapter 41. Calvin argued that the prophecy was a prediction given by Isaiah some two hundred years before the coming of Cyrus. Calvin also argued that the prophecy had the force to establish itself to the nations as an utterance prior to its fulfillment in order to confirm God's authority for this prediction. Seitz comments quite logically on the difficulty with this interpretation: "For a prediction to be valid, it must have been uttered meaningfully to contemporaries; yet it cannot at the same time carry weight as having been uttered long ago to special witnesses, whose posterity can claim to know something no one else knows." However, the move to affirm both of the assertions, that is, meaningful to contemporaries and uttered long ago to special witnesses, is exactly what has been attempted by the canonical shaping of Second Isaiah. By joining chapter 41 to the corpus of First Isaiah, the prediction of Babylon's destruction by the Medes was both established as prior to Cyrus's appearance and yet available as a written testimony once delivered to Israel only, but now open for all the contemporaries to see.

[42:1–4] In chapter 42 the interpreter encounters the first of the so-called servant songs. The debate over these passages is too controversial and complex to handle at length in a commentary. I shall, however, present a summary of my position in an excursus at the end of the commentary on chapter 53.

Nevertheless, a few basic decisions have to be made by way of introduction if one is to proceed in an exegesis of chapter 42. A crucial choice turns on whether one follows the hypothesis of Duhm and his many followers that the servant songs of Second Isaiah (42:1–4; 49:1–6; 50:4–9; 52:13–53:12) constitute a secondary collection of oracles that were secondarily inserted into chapters 40—55, either by the prophet or more likely by a later redaction, and as a consequence cannot be meaningfully interpreted in their present position within the book. Rather, they are to be understood independently and only in relationship to themselves. Of course, Duhm's hypothesis has been greatly expanded by redactional critics (Steck, Hermisson, Kratz), but the hermeneutical implications have not changed. Or conversely, one argues that regardless of their compositional history—a topic still open to investigation—these passages are to be understood within their present literary context of chapters 40—55. Obviously, one's initial decision decisively influences the nature of one's interpretation. In my opinion, the literary and theological evidence strongly supports the latter interpretive option.

Chapter 41 served as a divine defense in God's response to Israel's complaint in 40:27, and throughout the chapter a strong case was mounted that no power in heaven and earth could withstand Yahweh. The creator God not only demolished the claims of other foreign gods, but demonstrated his power and willingness to restore his exiled people. In chapter 41 the two major themes were intertwined, namely, the absolute sovereignty of God (vv. 1–7, 21–29) and the theme of God's commitment to Israel, whom he has not cast off (vv. 9, 17) but will redeem as the Holy One of Israel (vv. 8–20). Israel had complained that its right (*mišpāṭ*) had been disregarded. How was God to respond to this? In chapter 42 this question is addressed, but in a totally unexpected fashion. Through the means of his servant (*'ebed*), chosen and anointed with the spirit, God will bring forth justice (*mišpāṭ*) to the nations (v. 1). The servant will not fail until this justice has been established (v. 3). As Beuken has forcefully argued (IIa, 106ff.), chapter 41 remains unintelligible apart from chapter 42, and, conversely, the servant figure of chapter 42 is fully enigmatic apart from the larger context of chapter 41.

Form-critical analysis of vv. 1–4 has produced highly conflicting results (see Melugin, 64ff.). Some have argued that the oracle is one of commissioning a prophet, others of a royal figure. Some assign the context to the heavenly council much like in chapter 6, others see an imitation of an ancient Near Eastern liturgical pattern. The inability to reach any consensus should serve as a caution against pressing reconstructions far beyond the limits of the biblical text. There is throughout the passage a remarkable reticence to provide the very information most sought by modern interpreters.

Rather, a "servant" is presented by means of an attention seeking particle: "see" (*hēn*). The term *servant* in itself does not indicate what specific office or role is being described. It can be used of patriarchs (Gen. 24:14; 26:24), of Levites (Ps. 113:1), of prophets (1 Kings 14:18; Isa. 20:3), of kings (2 Sam. 3:18; Hag. 2:23), or even of Israel (Jer. 30:10; 46:27–28). The form of the oracle does point to some sort of commissioning or installation, which appears from the close stylistic parallels in 1 Sam. 9:15–17 and Zech. 3:8 and 6:12. However, the emphasis of the passage clearly falls on other things that are quite specific in nature: the servant's designation, his task, his approach, and his success. He is designated as God's elect in whom he delights and on whom his spirit resides. He will bring forth justice (*mišpāṭ*) to the nations who await his teaching (*tôrātô*). He will act unobtrusively in his dealing with those who are fragile and suffering. Finally, he will not fail or turn back until he has accomplished his mission.

At this point, the reader is left in considerable confusion, especially if the interpreter is chiefly interested in identifying the servant with a historical persona beyond that of the title. Clearly, to pose this historical question at this point is to enter into an impasse unrelieved by idle speculation. However, what can one discern from the larger literary context? It would seem that the introduction of the servant, who is equipped with the traditional attributes associated with Israel's charismatic deliverers and whose task focuses specifically on *mišpāṭ* (the restoration of God's order in the world), establishes at least a clear relation to Israel's complaint (40:27). Moreover, Israel's lament is a reflection of the historical situation of an exiled people, which has been assumed as the context since chapter 40. God's sovereign power has been established in chapter 41, and demonstrated in history by the calling of a conqueror from the north. Yet, that this victor is the one designated servant in chapter 42 is fully ruled out by the unexpected description of the servant's manner of establishing justice to the nations.

In addition, the mystery of the servant is exacerbated even further by the larger literary context of chapter 41. The term *servant* within Second Isaiah does not occur for the first time in 42:1, but is introduced in 41:8 along with a variety of familiar attributes. Israel/Jacob is designated as servant, the elect one, offspring of Abraham, even friend. Then in v. 9 Israel is again named the servant who has not been cast off and who is promised aid from God's victorious hand (v. 10). For anyone who takes the larger literary context seriously, there can be no avoiding the obvious implication that *in some way* Israel is the servant who is named in 42:1. No one else is named. Clearly there are enormous interpretive problems arising from this identification, but these will have to be explored on the basis of the leads offered by the text. Admittedly, at this point in Second Isaiah the mystery of the servant as Israel remains. However, to suggest that this servant song is an interpolation, fully independent of its present literary context, is to render the passage unintelligible from the outset.

[5–9] As one might expect, the debate over the interpretation of the succeeding verses is equally as controversial. Some have argued that the messenger formula in v. 5 marks a new and fully independent oracle (Begrich). Others have seen in these verses a fragment from an oracle concerning Cyrus (Elliger). Westermann relegates the verses to a subsequent redactional layer that mistakenly tries to interpret the servant song of vv. 1–4 as a reference to Israel. Beuken notes the shift from the singular pronoun in v. 6 to the plural in v. 9 and sharply divides the verses with the servant as the addressee (vv. 6–7) from those with Israel as the addressee (vv. 8–9).

Several things are to be noticed in this passage. Once again the oracle involves a first person singular speech of Yahweh that reflects some sort of commissioning. A self-predicative formula brackets the commissioning in vv. 6 and 8: "I am Yahweh." The recipient is addressed in the second person singular: "I have called you in righteousness. I have taken you by the hand." Then his role is outlined: "a covenant for the peoples, and a light to the nations, to open eyes that are blind, to free captives from prison." There is no sign that vv. 5–9 are simply a secondary interpretive expansion of vv. 1–4. The language is very different and the images are not immediately related. In contrast, there is a direct literary relation between vv. 5–9 and 49:1ff. (cf. below), where there is a close linguistic overlap.

Although vv. 5–9 appear to be originally independent in form and content, there is an obvious relation in their present context. The initial messenger formula identifies Yahweh immediately with the creator God, language that resonates of Genesis 1 and the Psalter: *"El YHWH,"* "heavens and earth," "creator" (*bôrē'*), "stretched out the heavens" (Ps. 104:2; Isa. 40:22), "spread out the earth (*rōga'*)," and "gives breath (*rûaḥ*) to the people." It is especially appropriate following the great emphasis on the power of the creator God in chapter 40 that the commissioning be again closely linked with this God.

However, the actual commissioning is executed by an appeal to the ancient covenantal formula of self-predication: "I am Yahweh." This is the formula used by God when commissioning Moses (Ex. 6:2). Although the terminology which follows, that of righteousness (*ṣedeq*), covenant (*bᵉrît*), and people (*'ām*), stems from Israel's exodus tradition, the use made by the prophet is strikingly different from that of the past. The one commissioned is given as a covenant to the people (*bᵉrît 'ām*). In spite of the difficulty of this unique phrase (cf. Stamm), several aspects emerge with some clarity. First, the use of a metonymy has many parallels in the Old Testament (cf. Gen. 7:1; 12:2) and causes no real difficulty. Second, "people" stands in parallel to "nations," and is not a reference specifically to Israel, but one that carries a universal scope (cf. Stamm, 516ff.). Moreover, the one commissioned does not form a covenant, but rather embodies a covenantal relationship with the nations. In the earlier description of the task of the servant (vv. 1–4), his mission is expressed with great caution by means of the rhetorical device of a litotes, that is, a negative understatement. In contrast, v. 7 describes the task of the one commissioned in exclusively positive terms of action: opening eyes, delivering prisoners, and being a light to the nations.

At this point in the exegesis it is difficult to resist seeing in the commissioning language of vv. 5ff. a further reference to the servant of vv. 1–4. This formulation is not to deny that the link between the two passages may indeed be redactional. Each passage appears to have its own discrete integrity. Yet in the larger literary context of Second Isaiah, the two passages clearly supplement each other. Even v. 9 serves a coherent purpose in contrasting the former things that God the creator had once brought forth (v. 5; cf. 41:22) with the new things that are about to emerge. The shift to a plural pronoun reflects only a rhetorical device, consonant with the plurality of witnesses to the things shortly to come (43:10; 44:8).

Of course, the problem remains how to understand Israel as the servant in spite of the further clarifications offered to its mission in vv. 5–9. Melugin (100) proposes that these latter verses shift the emphasis in vv. 1–4 from the servant's faithfulness to that of persuading the community of its new role. Still, the mystery of Israel as the servant remains yet unresolved up to this point in the book, and the interpreter is compelled to await further illumination in the succeeding chapters. What has emerged with clarity from the introduction of the servant following chapter 41 is that the divine purpose in moving from former things to the new things involves at this juncture both the role of Cyrus and the servant. Just how these two major figures relate in the divine purpose has not yet been disclosed.

[10–13] The larger unit beginning in 41:1 concludes with a final eschatological hymn. Much like the conclusion of chapter 12, the prophetic oracles are suddenly replaced by a liturgical coda. The phrases are closely paralleled to those of the Psalter, particularly the imperative to sing to the Lord a new song (Ps. 33:3; 96:1; 98:1; 144:9; 149:1). However, other themes familiar to Second Isaiah resound: giving glory to God, shouting his praises from the mountains, and God's going forth like a man of war (59:15ff.). The effect of the hymn is to involve the reader also in rendering praise to this great creating and redeeming God who is far from being a distant theological construct, but who is even now worthy of all praise (Rev. 5:9; 14:3)—the Lord, both the first and the last!

A final word is in order regarding how the New Testament heard this text. Hellenistic Judaism took its lead from the LXX and identified the servant with the people of Israel. However, Palestinian Judaism tended to interpret the passage messianically (cf. Strack-Billerbeck I, 87; e.g., Ps. Sol. 17, 32–38). It comes as little surprise that the Targum inserts the title Messiah in apposition to the servant in 42:1.

In the New Testament, Matthew's Gospel (12:17–21) offers an extended citation of 42:1–4 with some slight abbreviations. Matthew's application of Isaiah presents a classic example of the New Testament's christological interpretation of the Old Testament while at the same time responding to the Old Testament witness in the shaping of its own Christology. The *Wirkungsgeschichte* is clearly dialectic in movement. Jesus' healing activity is characterized as fulfilling Isaiah's prophecy. The Messiah fulfills the office of the servant in caring for the weak and fragile. Yet, conversely, it is Isaiah's portrayal that interprets Jesus' healing as bringing justice to victory and giving the Gentiles a hope.

45. Isaiah 42:14–43:21

42:14 For a long time I have kept silent.
    I have kept still and restrained myself.
    But now I will cry out like a woman in labor;
    I will pant and gasp.
15   I will lay waste mountains and hills
    and dry up all their vegetation.

I will turn rivers into islands,
   and dry up all the pools.
16   I will lead the blind by ways
     they did not know,
     and guide them by unfamiliar paths.
I will turn darkness into light before them,
   and rough terrain into level ground.
These are the things I will do
   and not forsake them.
17   But those who trust in idols, saying
     "You are our gods,"
     will be driven back and utterly shamed.
18   Hear, you deaf,
     and look, you blind, and see.
19   Who is so blind as my servant,
     and deaf like the messenger whom I send?
Who is so blind as my commissioned one,[a]
   or blind like the servant of the LORD?
20   You have seen many things, but paid no attention.
     With ears open, he does not hear anything.
21   It pleased the LORD, for his righteousness' sake,
     to make his law great and glorious.
22   Yet this is a people robbed and plundered.
     All of them are trapped in holes,
     imprisoned in dungeons,
carried off as spoil with none to rescue.
     They have been made spoil with no one to say,
     "Send them back."
23   Who among you will listen to this,
     will pay attention and heed from now on?
24   Who was it that delivered Jacob to the spoiler,
     and Israel to the plunderers?
Was it not the LORD, against whom
     we have sinned,
     in whose ways they would not walk,
     and whose law they would not obey?
25   So he unleashed on him his burning anger,
     the violence of battle.
It wrapped him in flame,
     but still he did not comprehend.
It burned him, but still he did not
     take it seriously.

43:1   But now thus says the LORD,
         who created you, O Jacob,
         who formed you, O Israel:
     "Fear not, for I have redeemed you;
         I have called you by name,
         you are mine.

2   When you pass through water,
         I will be with you,
         and through rivers, they will not sweep you away.
     When you walk through fire,
         you will not be burned,
         and the flame will not scorch you.

3   For I am the LORD your God,
         the Holy One of Israel, your Savior.
     I give Egypt for your ransom,
         Ethiopia and Seba in exchange for you.

4   Because you are precious to me,
         and honored, and I love you,
     I will give men in exchange for you,
         people for your life.

5   Fear not, for I am with you;
         I will bring your children from the east,
         and gather you out of the west.

6   I will say to the north, give them up,
         and to the south, do not hold any back.
     Bring my sons from afar,
         and my daughters from the ends of the earth,

7   everyone who is called by my name,
         whom I have created, formed and made
         for my glory."

8   Lead forth the people who have eyes
         yet are blind,
         who have ears, yet are deaf.

9   Let all the nations gather together,
         and the peoples assemble.
     Who among them declared this,
         and foretold the things that have happened?
     Let them produce their witnesses and
         be vindicated,
         and let them hear and respond, "It is true."

10   "You are my witnesses," says the LORD,
         "and my servant[b] whom I have chosen,

that you may know and believe me,
    and understand that I am he.
Before me no god was formed,
    nor will there be any after me.
11   I, even I, am the LORD,
    apart from me there is no savior.
12   I alone revealed and saved and proclaimed
    when no strange god was among you.
    So you are my witnesses," says the LORD.
13   "From the beginning, I am he.
    None can deliver from my hand.
    When I act, who can reverse it?"
14   Thus says the LORD,
    your redeemer, the Holy One of Israel:
"For your sake I will send to Babylon
    and break down all the bars,c
    and the shouting of the Chaldeans
    will be turned to lamentations.d
15   I am the LORD, your Holy One,
    the creator of Israel, your King."
16   Thus says the LORD,
    who made a way through the sea,
    a path through the mighty waters,
17   who drew out chariots and horses,
    a whole army of warriors;
they lay down unable to rise;
    they were extinguished, put out like a wick:
18   "Do not remember what happened long ago,
    or dwell on the events of old.
19   Look, I am doing a new thing.
    Now it springs up, do you not see it?
I will make a way through the wilderness
    and rivers in the desert.
20   The wild beasts will honor me,
    jackals and ostriches,e
for I provide water in the wilderness,
    rivers in the desert,
to give drink to my chosen people,
21   the people whom I formed for myself
that they might proclaim my praise."

a. The Hebrew *me šullām* is unclear. Often it is translated "covenanted one."

b. The MT reads "my servant." It is most probably not to be emended into a plural, as often suggested (*BHS*).

c. The text followed is an emendation. Cf. the exposition for the nature of the textual problem.

d. The MT *bo'oníyôt* ("in ships") has been repointed to *ba'aníyôt* ("to lamentations").

e. The identification of the animals is conjectural.

Selected Bibliography

E. W. Conrad, "The 'Fear Not' Oracles in Second Isaiah," *VT* 34, 1984, 143–51; **H. Leene,** "Denkt niet aan het vroegere. Methodologische overwegingen bij de uitleg van Jesaja 43:18," *Loven en Geloven, Fs N. H. Ridderbos,* Amsterdam 1975, 55–76; **R. F. Melugin,** *The Formation of Isaiah 40—55, BZAW* 141, Berlin 1976, 110–15; **C. R. North,** "The 'Former Things' and the 'New Things' in Deutero-Isaiah," *Studies in Old Testament Prophecy, Fs T. H. Robinson,* ed. H. Rowley, Edinburgh 1950, 111–26; **A. Schoors,** "Les choses antérieures et les choses nouvelles dans les oracles Deutéro-Isaïens," *ETL* 40, 1964, 19–47; **J. M. Vincent,** *Studien zur literarischen Eigenart und zur geistigen Heimat von Jesaja, Kap. 40—55,* Bern 1977, 40–64; **H. E. von Waldow,** " . . . 'denn ich erlöse dich,'" BSt 29, 1960; **P. T. Willey,** *Remember the Former Things: The Recollection of Previous Texts in Second Isaiah,* SBLDS 161, Atlanta 1977.

1. Genre, Structure, and Movement

One of the continuing problems in interpreting Second Isaiah lies in determining the nature of the present literary composition, its units and coherence. As frequently suggested earlier, it is inadequate to limit the present literary units to those genres that were originally shaped by oral proclamation. As shall become evident in this section, there has been a fusion of different genres and much freedom has been used in structuring a new composition.

Moreover, there are no absolute rules by which to establish the scope of units. For example, Clifford argues that this speech begins with 42:10 and thus includes this hymnic oracle as the introduction to what follows. In my opinion, the majority of commentators are right in holding that 42:10–13 ends the larger section just as a hymn concludes the succeeding composition in 44:23. However, subjective factors are clearly also involved in this judgment. Although such a decision does affect one's understanding of the whole—Clifford even entitles his larger unit from a motif in v. 13—the lack of a highly organized discursive style and the presence of much repetition in chapters 40—48 mean that the precise division of the larger units are of more relative than absolute significance.

An analysis of this larger section reveals many signs of traditional oral forms, particularly the promise of salvation and the trial, but it is a mistake of Begrich, Elliger, and to some extent Westermann, in stressing these form-critical patterns to such a degree as to fail to see the larger literary compositions in which the smaller units have been creatively reworked. The crucial exegetical task lies in discovering the peculiar function within the whole to which the smaller units have been assigned. In this regard, Beuken's modern Dutch commentary reflects a major advance over the German form-critics.

Isaiah 42:1–13 presented the servant and his mission, and made the joyous announcement of new things when God went forth on Israel's behalf as a mighty warrior. Verses 14ff. pick up this same theme. God announces his purpose to lead his people on a way through the wilderness, which theme forms the leitmotif of this section. However, Israel the servant is blind and deaf, a plundered and robbed people. The subject then turns to the meaning of the exile. Israel's complaint (40:27) echoes in the background (vv. 22ff.), and God defends his right to punish a disobedient, sinful people. "But now" the judgment lies in the past and 43:1 marks the turn about in a glorious assurance of salvation. Israel is not to fear. God intervenes, pays the high price of deliverance, and brings back his sons and daughters for his own glory. Again the text returns to God's debate with the nations. The new feature introduced is that Israel, who is described as blind, is nevertheless appointed as witness to God's claim to be sole redeemer. The section ends with God's promising to free the captives and make a way through the desert for his chosen people.

In his commentary Beuken continues his larger compositional unit, 42:14–44:23. He rightly points to the strong elements of continuity within these chapters: Israel the servant, the rebirth of the land, the trial with the nations. Also the major theme of the way through the wilderness continues. Nevertheless, it seems to me that the new elements are such as to indicate a clear break in thought at 43:21. Israel, the blind witness, needs not just to return, but specifically to return to Yahweh. The lengthy satire establishes a sharp contrast with the true God who offers freely to pardon Israel's sins as he awaits the return of a redeemed people.

2. Exposition

[**42:14–17**] The theme of the unit is not fully clear. Westermann argued that the form is a proclamation of salvation (*Heilsankündigung*), and reflects the elements of a community lament, but this analysis stretches the formal features of the unit beyond recognition. It is true that the main content is promise, but the form is dominated by elements of divine monologue. Westermann's attempt to fit these features into a more common form-critical pattern does not aid exegetically. Nor is Elliger's fragmenting of the unit into additions and glosses any improvement over Westermann.

The significance of the passage lies in the announcement of a new decision on God's part, which triggers a variety of new topics for the ensuing literary composition. The connection with v. 13 is immediately clear when the theme of Yahweh's stirring himself to battle is expanded. In v. 14 God sounds forth a change of plan. Up to now he had "kept silent," "restrained himself." Israel's complaint in 40:27 resonates in the background: "My way is hidden from Yahweh." Truly God has not intervened up to now on Israel's behalf to end the exile. Now the decision to hide his face is reversed. He will no longer be a silent observer. The simile in v. 14b, to "cry out like a woman in labor," focuses on the intensity of God's response.

The description of his action in vv. 15–16, to "lay waste mountains" and to turn "rough terrain into level ground," encompasses both acts of judgment and of mercy. Such a portrait of God's intervening action is a common feature of the Psalter (e.g., Ps. 107:33ff.), which offers a contrast between judgment on the oppressors and salvation for the oppressed. Very shortly the main focus falls in v. 16 on the theme of the way through the wilderness, which then dominates the remaining passage. The key words are "way," "blind," and "deaf." The description of levelling a path and guiding the returnees by transforming the wilderness was already sounded in 40:3 and 41:17ff., but the specificity of the returning journey continues to increase in the succeeding verses.

The theme of the blind connects both backward and forward in the larger composition. On the one hand, it picks up the mission of the servant to the blind in 42:7, but, on the other hand, it introduces the new note of the blindness of the servant, which will become a major theme in what follows. The firmness of God's decision is underlined also by the traditional "summary-appraisal" formula in v. 16c. Elliger eliminates v. 17 as a gloss because of its content and somewhat heavy style. It is perhaps possible that it reflects a redactional expansion that picks up from the larger context the folly of trusting in man-made images, but the evidence is inconclusive.

[**18–25**] The form of the passage is extremely difficult to analyze. The initial problem lies with the identification of the speakers in the unit. In v. 21 the prophet speaks, and in 43:1 a prophetic messenger formula continues. However, in vv. 18–20 Yahweh is clearly the speaker. In v. 24 a first person plural pronoun appears in the form of a citation. Westermann attempts to resolve the problem by projecting a disputation underlying the form, with a community lament as the source of the words. However, in order to make his hypothesis work he also is forced to point to a process of literary expansion to the original form. Accordingly, vv. 19–20 are deemed a variant—they are missing in the Greek— and v. 21a is designated as a gloss. Elliger's still more complex analysis leads to even greater fragmentation (cf. v. 24) without any resulting illumination.

In contrast, Beuken is helpful in distinguishing between a divine speech to Israel in vv. 18–20 in the form of a disputation, and a prophetic interpretation of the strife in vv. 21–22. The final verses (vv. 23–25) set forth a warning to Israel which then issues in a number of questions seeking to understand the necessity for Israel's exile. The larger issue at stake in the passage turns on how to understand the nation's destruction. The effect of the disputation is to reject Israel's complaint that the exile occurred from God's ignoring Israel's plight.

Verses 18ff. pick up two themes from the earlier chapters. First, Israel is the servant, and second, Israel is blind. Various commentators have argued that v.

19b is a secondary expansion that sought to interpret the servant in 42:1ff. as corporate Israel by the reference to blind Israel as "the servant of the Lord." However, this move is basically misconstrued and dominated by Duhm's theory respecting the servant as an individual in 42:1–4. The deep paradox of the servant who is always named Israel and who is now designated blind cannot be resolved by such literary reconstructions. Rather, the tensions in the text must be retained until a resolution is allowed to emerge from the text itself.

Before the future promise of God's salvation can be pursued in chapter 43, the question of the divine judgment on Israel's past must be settled once and for all. The exile was a result of God's righteous will. Indeed it was "pleasing" (*ḥāpēṣ*) to God for the sake of his righteousness thereby to magnify his law (*tôrāh*). (The NJPS translation reinterprets the vindication in v. 21 to be that of Israel's rather than God's.) Yahweh allowed Jacob to be deported and Israel plundered (v. 24) because of the people's persistent sinfulness. Yet in spite of it all, his *tôrāh* was not obeyed, nor did Israel understand. In sum, the judgment of the exile did not effect repentance or a desire to listen for the time to come (v. 23).

[43:1–7] The passage that follows is a classic promise of salvation (*Heilsorakel*) with the assurance given three times (vv. 1b–2; 3–4; 5–6), two of which are introduced by the formula "fear not." Yet the redactional connection between 42:18–25 and 43:1–7 is so close that the integrity of the two discrete genres has been considerably blurred. Only in the light of the full judgmental dimension of the former does the full force of the extended grace emerge in the latter: "but now thus says the LORD." The exile did not awaken Israel's conscience or prepare the grounds for a return. Rather a new word, solely from God's side, wrought the change, opening the way to the future.

The promise of salvation in vv. 1–7 picks up many former motifs of Second Isaiah, but at the same time each has been given a special nuance within the movement of the larger composition. Jacob/Israel who was plundered and robbed (42:24) is now the addressee for the message of salvation. In chapters 40 and 41 the theme of God as creator of the heavens and earth had been dominant. Now Israel is the focus of God's creative powers. God not only created Israel but redeemed her. Moreover, the theme of God's creation is personalized further. Israel receives a special name. She belongs to God: "you are mine" (cf. 43:7). Next, on the way home through the dangers of fording rivers or passing through flames (42:25 had spoken of fire), Israel is promised God's special protection by the Holy One of Israel: "I am with you." The holiness of God, whose fiery presence once called forth terrified fear (Isa. 6:5ff.), now serves as a shield on the way.

Israel's special relation to God is interpreted further in vv. 3–4 by means of a different metaphor taken from the context of civil law (Ex. 21:30; Num. 35:31–32). God gave a "ransom" for Israel. He exchanged Egypt, Ethiopia, and Seba for Israel and offered "the price of peoples" for her life. The theological thought expressed turns on the high cost required for Israel's deliverance and the value of Israel in God's sight. Duhm's interpretation of the exchange as an abandonment of Africa to Cyrus because of disregard for the worth of other nations badly distorts the metaphor.

Finally, the promise is extended for the return of the scattered diaspora. Israel's sons and daughters will be collected from the ends of the earth toward the goal of Israel's bringing glory to God her creator. The gathering of the diaspora became a major concern of Third Isaiah (56:8; 60:4ff.) and was retrojected back in 11:11ff. to form an important redactional bridge between the first and second halves of the book. The naming of the returning exiles as God's sons and daughters assumes the special relationship of God as father of his family. In the Bible the name is grounded in Israel's particular covenantal relationship, and is not merely an extension of a general human metaphor onto the deity.

[8–13] The form of the oracle is again that of a trial (cf. 41:1–7, 21–29), and the legal language is largely continued. "Lead forth" (*hôṣî*) is a technical term within the context of a juridical process (Gen. 38:24; Judg. 6:30). Nevertheless, the passage has been given a specific function within its larger literary context that not only picks up the theme of Israel's blindness from 42:18–25, but adds several other new elements. The nations are again assembled for a fictive trial, and again the challenge is mounted: "Who can show us the former things?" Yet the focus of the trial is quite different as it proceeds. The nations never speak, nor is the argument grounded on the ability to predict the future. The unmodified pronoun "this" in v. 9 is immediately explained by its parallel, "things that have happened" (*ri'šōnôt*). The issue turns on who can claim the power of divinity on the basis of what has happened in the past. The events of the past are also far broader than only a reference to Cyrus, but include the entire sequence of events connected with Israel's entire history, specifically with the deliverance from captivity as promised in the preceding oracle (v. 12).

Israel, the blind servant, is called forth as witness for Yahweh's claim. Moreover, the function of witness-bearer is not just directed to the goal of silencing the nations, but in order that blind Israel may nevertheless know, believe, and understand the reality of God (v. 10). The three verbs have a strong cognitive sense, which is consistently a characteristic of Old Testament faith. The formula "I am he" (*'anî hû'*), which epitomizes the reality of God, occurs frequently in Second Isaiah (41:4; 43:10, 13; 46:4; 48:12; cf. Deut. 32:39), and resonates from the initial revelation of the divine name in Ex. 3:14. As in Exodus, God is here also described as encompassing the past, present, and future (cf. v. 13). The issue is not one of clairvoyance or simple prediction, but of the God of Israel being at work in the world. Israel alone can rightly testify to God's redemptive presence in its life. The recurring references to "strange gods" (v. 12) and to idols serve as an ideal foil by which to contrast the dynamic action of God toward his creation with the empty sham and pretense in the claims of other gods, who are flatly rejected as without substance.

[14–21] Form-critical analysis of the unit has not been terribly helpful in terms of illuminating the text (cf. Melugin, 110ff.). The recurrence of two messenger formulae (vv. 14 and 16) has caused some to speak of vv. 14–15 as a fragment (Elliger), or to attach the verses to the preceding oracle (Westermann). Yet in terms of the larger literary context the passage fits in quite well. It brings to a suitable conclusion the dominant theme of the "way through the wilderness" (v. 19), and offers two summarizing promises in the form of specific announcements. The first stresses the sheer grace of God's act (vv. 14–15); the second that the latter act completely transcends the former deliverance (vv. 16–21).

The interpreter of this unit is initially faced with a text-critical problem in v. 14. The MT makes reasonably good sense and is, by and large, supported by the LXX: "For your sake I send to Babylon (1QIs^a reads "against Babylon") and will bring down all of them as fugitives, and the Chaldeans in the ships of their shrill cry." The problem is that with minor repointing of the Hebrew a much more coherent reading is obtained, supported in part by the Vulgate and Targum: "I send to (against) Babylon, and will bring down all the bars [read *b^{e}rîhim* for *bārîhîm*], and the Chaldeans' joy will turn into lamentations [read *ba'^{a}nîyyôt* for *bo'^{o}niyyôt*]." Both the NRSV and the NJPS follow these suggested emendations.

In my opinion, the choice is not easy. On the one hand, the MT, while intelligible, does not fit very well into the larger sense of the passage, and references to the Chaldeans as refugees fleeing in ships of joy remain enigmatic. On the other hand, there are numerous other emendations possible once the MT is judged corrupt (cf. Torrey, Elliger). In a word, the choice of a suitable text becomes highly subjective. Fortunately, the basic meaning of the text that the power of Babylon will be broken for Israel's sake is clear enough. Reluctantly, I feel that the balance between the alternatives leads to accepting the repointed text suggested above. (It does not help the interpreter in coming to an honest decision when the translators of the NJPS silently accept emendations but with the comment, "the meaning of the Hebrew is unclear.")

The promises of the passage are divided into two parts, both introduced by a messenger formula. In the first, the emphasis falls on the merciful intervention of God for Israel's sake to shatter Babylon's power and to free the prisoners. A series of traditional epitaphs characterize Yahweh: redeemer (*gô'el*), Holy One of Israel, lord, creator, and king. In the second, there is a conscious allusion to the former deliverance from the captivity of Egypt: "who made a way through the sea, a path through the mighty waters, who drew out chariots and horses." Of course, this event had become for Israel the example par excellence of God's great redemptive power, which was continually celebrated in song and worship from its inception (Ex. 15:1ff.; Josh. 2:10; Pss. 78; 89; 106; Neh. 9:9ff.). What is distinctive in this passage is that Israel is warned not to remember the former things, nor to reflect on this past history. That this prophetic rhetoric is dialogical and not absolute is made clear in the succeeding verses with the exactly opposite admonition: "Recall the past with me" (v. 26; cf. 44:21). The rhetorical point of v. 18 is the contrast between the old and the new things. The coming salvation will completely transcend any expedience of the past. The way in the wilderness will climax in the honoring of God not only by the wild beasts, but above all by his chosen people who declare his praise.

The basic eschatological perception of history by the Old Testament was clearly heard both by postbiblical Judaism and the early Christian community. Grimm (204) appropriately cites the song of thanksgiving from a Qumran text (1QH 13, 11f.), which offers an exegetical extension of Isa. 43:11ff. In spite of a broken text, the author interprets the Isaianic text as pointing to an eschatological new creation that shatters the old order.

In an even more radical appropriation, the apostle Paul portrays the Christian life as one in which old and new are sharply juxtaposed:

> If one is in Christ, there is a new creation; the old has passed away, behold, the new has come. (2 Cor. 5:17)

If this New Testament passage is correctly interpreted according to its Old Testament context, the genuinely dialectical relation between the old and the new is maintained, and the continuing threat to the Christian church from modern gnostic flights of fantasy—"imaginative construal" is the current formulation—are held in check by the biblical faith.

46. Isaiah 43:22–44:23

43:22 Yet you have not called upon me, O Jacob,
　　　　nor have you wearied yourself with me, O Israel!
23　　You have not brought me sheep for burnt offerings,
　　　　nor honored me with your sacrifices.
　　　I have not burdened you with grain offerings,
　　　　nor wearied you with incense.
24　　You have not bought me fragrant
　　　　reeds with money,
　　　　nor bestowed on me the fat of your sacrifices.
　　　But you have burdened me with your sins
　　　　and wearied me with your offenses.
25　　I, even I, am he who wipes out your transgressions
　　　　for my own sake,
　　　and remembers your sins no more.
26　　Recall the past with me.
　　　　Let us debate the matter together;
　　　　make the case for your innocence.

27   Your first father sinned,
     and your spokesmen rebelled against me.
28   Therefore I desecrated the temple officials.
     I delivered Jacob to destruction
     and Israel to scorn.
44:1 But now hear, O Jacob, my servant,
     Israel whom I have chosen.
2   Thus says the LORD who made you,
     and formed you in the womb
     and will help you:
 Fear not, O Jacob, my servant,
     Jeshurun, whom I have chosen.
3   For I will pour water on the thirsty land,
     and rain on the dry ground;
 I will pour forth my spirit on your offspring,
     and my blessing on your descendants.
4   They will sprout like grass in a meadow,
     like willows by flowing streams.
5   One will say, "I am the LORD's,"
     another will use the name "Jacob,"
 still another will write on his hand,
     "The LORD's,"
 and adopt the name Israel.
6   Thus says the LORD, the King of Israel,
     and his redeemer, the LORD of hosts:
 "I am the first and I am the last;
     apart from me there is no god.
7   Who is like me who calls?[a]
     let him declare and set it forth.
 From the bringing forth of an ancient people
 to the events in the future,
     Let them declare them.
8   Fear not, do not be afraid.
     Have I not proclaimed this to you of old?
     I foretold it and you are my witnesses.
 Is there any God besides me?
     There is no other rock; I know of none."
9   All who make idols are nothing,
     and the things they treasure are worthless.
 Those who would testify for them neither see nor know,
     and so they will be put to shame.
10   Who shapes a god or casts a statue
     that can do him no good?

11 He and his sort will be made ashamed;
        craftsmen are merely human.
    Let them assemble and stand together;
        they will be cowed and disgraced.
12 The ironsmith sharpens[b] a tool,
        works it over the coals,
    and fashions it by hammering,
        forging it with the strength of his arm.
    He gets hungry and loses his strength.
        If he drinks no water, he grows faint.
13 The carpenter measures with a line,
        and marks it out with a stylus.
    He fashions it with planes,
        and marks it with a compass.
    He gives it a human form,
        with the beauty of a man,
        to dwell in a shrine.
14 He cuts down cedars, or perhaps
        plane trees and oaks.
    He puts aside some trees of the forest,
        or plants a laurel,[c] and the rain makes them grow.
15 Then it serves a man for fuel.
        He takes some to warm himself;
        he kindles a fire and bakes bread.
    He also makes a god and worships it;
        he fashions an idol and bows down to it!
16 Part of it he burns in a fire.
        Over that part he eats flesh,
        roasting meat, and is satisfied.
    He also warms himself and says,
        "Aha, I am warm. I can feel the heat."
17 From the rest he makes a god, his idol.
        He bows down to it and worships it.
    He prays to it and cries,
        "Save me, for you are my god."
18 They neither know nor understand.
        Their eyes are covered over so they cannot see.
        Their minds are closed so they cannot comprehend.
19 No one reflects,
        nor is there knowledge or judgment to say:
    "Part of it I burned in the fire;
        I also baked bread on its coals.
        I roasted meat and ate it.

Shall I make the residue into an abomination?
Shall I fall down before a block of wood?"
20   He feeds on ashes.
A deluded mind has led him astray.
He cannot save himself, or say to himself:
"The thing in my hand is a sham."
21   Remember these things, O Jacob,
for you are my servant, O Israel.
I formed you, you are my servant.
O Israel, you will not be forgotten by me.
I have swept away your sins like a cloud,
and your transgression like mist.
Return to me, for I have redeemed you.
23   Sing, O heavens, for the LORD has done this.
Shout aloud, O depths of the earth.
Break forth into singing, O mountains,
O forests, with all your trees.
For the LORD has redeemed Jacob,
and he will be glorified in Israel.

a. The MT is difficult and has often been emended (*BHS*). Cf. the discussion below.

b. The sentence is difficult, and the MT is probably corrupt, The lack of a verb in the first colon has caused many to follow the LXX and supply the verb "sharpen."

c. The word *'ōren* is a *hapax legomenon*. It may be a less well-known type of tree, or a textual corruption for *'erez* (*BHS*).

Selected Bibliography

D. Eichhorn, *Gott als Fels, Burg und Zuflucht,* Europäische Hochschulschriften 23/4, Frankfurt 1972; **J. Guillet,** "La polémique contre les idoles et le Serviteur de Yahvé," *Bib* 40, 1959, 428–34; **F. Matheus,** "Jes. 44, 9–20: Das Spottgedicht gegen die Götzen und seine Stellung im Kontext," *VT* 37, 1987, 312–26; **R. P. Merendino,** *Der Erste und der Letzte,* VTSup 31, Leiden 1981, 347–401; **C. R. North,** "The Essence of Idolatry," *Von Ugarit nach Qumran, Fs O. Eissfeldt,* BZAW 77, 1958, 151–60; **H. C. Spykerboer,** *The Structure and Composition of Deutero-Isaiah with Special Reference to the Polemics against Idolatry,* Meppel 1976; **D. W. Thomas,** "Isaiah xliv 9–20: A Translation and Commentary," *Hommages à André Dupont-Sommer,* Paris 1971, 319–30; **E. Würthwein,** "Kultpolemik oder Kultbescheid?" *Tradition und Situation, Fs A. Weiser,* Göttingen 1963, 115–32.

1. Genre, Structure, and Movement

Although there is a clear break after 43:21, the unit that follows continues to develop the previous themes. Israel's return on the way is not just a physical journey, but involves also a return to Yahweh. God again defends himself against Israel's complaint of being disregarded. Rather, the point is made that Israel's sins have caused the destruction. Then the servant Israel receives the spirit of God and the promised blessing. God is the source of Israel's strength and will sweep away Israel's sins. The contrast of Yahweh's redemptive acts is contrasted sharply with the futility of manufacturing idols. The passage then closes with a resounding note of praise for what God has done.

There are once again a variety of familiar genres present: trial, assurance of salvation, and parody, but these forms have been shaped with much freedom to form a coherent whole. Even the lengthy satire on the idol makers (vv. 9–20) adds to the movement, although its positioning is most probably secondary within the present literary composition.

2. Exposition

[**43:22–28**] Westermann correctly notes that this is the only trial speech in which Yahweh opposes Israel. Behind the dispute lies Israel's persistent complaint (40:27). Yet the argument mounted by God in a first person speech sets out to reverse the accusation. God has not burdened Israel with cultic demands. Then a rehearsal of what Israel has not done is presented in a list of traditional Hebrew offerings that have not been brought. The divine argument strikes to the heart of the real problem much like that of the prophet Malachi (1:13). Israel has become weary of God. As a result, God, not Israel, has been burdened, precisely from carrying the weight of Israel's sins.

The accusation against the misuse of the cult offered by Second Isaiah stands in close theological continuity with the message of the preexilic prophet in spite of the different historical contexts. As has long been recognized, the harsh attacks against the cult (Amos 4:4–5; 5:21ff.; Isa. 1:12ff.; Jer. 7:1ff.) are not to be abstracted into a general anticultic principle, but they are sharp criticisms directed to rampant abuse, which has missed the whole point of sacrifice as an offering to God arising from sincere repentance and quest for forgiveness.

Thus, God's dispute with Israel turns immediately to the central issue of Israel's sin. The disputation moves quickly from a polemical tone to one of promise. God, by his very nature ("I am he") is bent on forgiveness. However, Israel's history since the time of Jacob has been one of transgression. As a result, Israel has suffered utter destruction. Now Israel's journey back home involves a return to God, a response to its God who offers to blot out the sins of the past, indeed, for his own sake.

[**44:1–5**] The connection between this promise of salvation is so close to the preceding disputation that many commentators have seen fit to fuse the two into one literary unit, regardless of the signs of once independent genres. The review of Israel's sinful past is broken off with a decisive "but now" (w^e '*attāh*).

The promise that now follows repeats many familiar themes. Jacob is the servant, Israel the chosen. Again, Israel is the special creation of God, and the desert will shortly be watered by flowing streams. However, there are also some new emphases, which pursue the dominant theme of the way back to God. Those returning confess their union with their Lord. They call themselves with the names of faith and thus find their true identity as the conscious people of God.

However, the mystery of the servant continues to persist. Israel is clearly God's servant; no other figure has ever emerged. Yet how this profile of the obedient servant, the recipient of the spirit who identifies himself in faith with Yahweh, relates to the blind and reluctant witness of the preceding chapter remains up to this point unclear. Categories such as "ideal" and "actual" do not really illuminate and are more compatible to Kant and Hegel than to Second Isaiah. At most one can sense that there is an eschatological dimension to the servant that lies close to the heart of the purpose of God, who, as the first and last, incorporates a dimension of history in which the fragments of human experience are nevertheless held together without one divine purpose yet to be revealed.

[6–8] Verse 6 appears to offer the introduction to a new announcement of promise in vv. 6–8, but because of their close extension of vv. 1–5, it makes little sense to separate the units according to discrete form-critical patterns. God as speaker is again described with a series of familiar epitaphs: king of Israel, redeemer, Lord of hosts. He is the first and last, the alpha and omega (cf. 41:4), the completely incomparable.

The language returns to that of disputation with the challenge for all to find a comparison and declare it (cf. 40:18). At this point (v. 7) there is a textual problem that calls for a critical decision. *BHS* follows a clever emendation by Oort and thus brings the text into line with Isaiah's earlier idiom in 41:21–29: "Who has announced from of old things to come?" Yet this emendation runs the risk of flattening the unique features of the MT of v. 7, which remains difficult but not impossible (cf. the attempt of the NJPS). Beuken has correctly seen that the key to understanding the verse lies in construing the words of the first colon together: "Who is like me who calls? Let him declare and set it forth." The more usual option is to take the first two words as a rhetorical question relating in general to God's incomparability in evoking events in history: "Who is like me?" However, the former alternative is preferable in bringing out that the specific election of Israel is at stake in the calling. This idea is then developed further in v. 7b: "From the bringing forth of an ancient people to the events in the future let them declare them." Israel is God's witness because it alone has experienced God's sovereign will at work in history from the beginning. The claim of God to uniqueness finds its strongest evidence in the witness of his chosen people on whom his redemptive care has been evidenced from the beginning. He is the ground of their existence. There is no other. His title as "first and last" is testified to most clearly in his continuous care to Israel's welfare. (For the terminology of rock, cf. Ps. 18:32; Deut. 32:4ff., and the monograph of Eichhorn).

[9–20] Traditionally with the modern critical study of Isaiah, this passage has often been quickly dismissed as a late and largely extraneous addition. The fact that the unit was printed by *BHK* in a prose format increased the negative impression. However, in more recent commentaries there has been a more positive evaluation. *BHS* has printed the text as poetry, a stylistic evaluation with increasing support (Muilenburg, Clifford, Beuken). In addition, the content of the satire is not immediately denigrated as unworthy of Isaiah, but numerous linguistic and conceptual analogies between the passage and the rest of Second Isaiah have been established.

The argument that the present literary positioning of the passage between vv. 6–8 and 22–23 reflects a redactional move is still largely accepted. In the modern scholarly climate that no longer interprets a redactional layer a priori in a negative light, the issue of authorship has greatly receded in exegetical importance. Instead, more attention turns on analyzing the polemic against idols with the broader issues of Second Isaiah's confrontation with the gods throughout the whole corpus. Duhm's opinion, that the excessive concern with the details of idol construction does not match the elevated temperament of the exilic prophet, no longer carries the same weight. Of course, commentators have long observed that the painstakingly descriptive details of fashioning idols both from metal and wood reveal careful firsthand observations, rather than being simply a catena of stereotyped caricatures of idolatry that had long since floated loose from any concrete historical experience.

The oracle has been clearly structured. Verses 9–11 offer a judgment on idol makers, rather than on the deities themselves. The repetition of the craftsmen's accomplishing nothing and only delighting in what is worthless culminates in the threefold pronouncement of their being put to shame. The legal terminology of a trial, which carries over from the larger literary context, is reflected in the terminology of their assembling, of standing forth, and of being terrified. Nowhere in this introduction is Yahweh mentioned, but an underlying contrast between the dynamic God of history and the worthless idols reverberates in the background.

The actual taunt extends from vv. 12–17. First, the ironsmith is described, shaping and forging his work with great intensity and discipline. Then follows the description of the carpenter whose consummate skill in measuring, designing, and fashioning is portrayed. The irony of the resulting form reflecting only a human image is subtly introduced. The topic then shifts to the securing of his material, which is carefully selected. What then follows is the heart of the satire, in which the effect of his hard work and skill is pursued. One part of the material he uses for fuel; the other part he makes into a god and worships it. The very object that his own hand has just constructed immediately becomes the focus of his prayer for aid.

The satire concludes in vv. 18–20 with a biting attack on the sheer folly of idol makers. They are totally lacking in understanding or knowledge. They are incapable of seeing the irrationality of their action, which, in the mind of the prophet, should be obvious to all. However, the attack goes beyond stressing its foolishness. The biblical writer names it an abomination (*tô'ēbāh*) and thus links it with Israel's ancient repudiation of everything judged to be a cultic and moral offense (Lev. 18:30; Deut. 7:26; 12:31; Ezek. 7:20; cf. Isa. 1:13; 42:24).

The final effect of the idol maker's folly is summed up in v. 20: "A deluded mind has led him astray. He cannot save himself." The theme of impotency thus connects with the larger composition and forms a powerful support to the argument of the chapter concerning Yahweh's sovereign ability to command the course of all history, both present and future. It is interesting to observe that, although the term *abomination* is used, the main emphasis does not fall on cultic impurity, nor on conscious evil at work. Rather, a strong Jewish wisdom influence is at work in this oracle, which was later shared by a growing segment of sophisticated Hellenistic rationalists. From such a perspective all sense of what an image might have meant to its religious devotees has been lost and idols are not feared or held in awe in any sense, but only treated as an object of derision. In the end, there is considerable affinity between this satire and the contempt expressed by the prophet in 41:24 regarding all foreign gods. The only difference lies in the prophet's ability still to project a fictive duel with the gods before denying their existence. For the satire of vv. 9–20, the pretense of pagan deities is simply too absurd to consider seriously.

[21–22] These verses pick up the main theme of the larger unit that began in 43:22. Jacob/Israel is again addressed and named as servant. Israel's complaint is denied (40:27), but it is assured of not being forgotten. Then God's forgiveness, first sounded in 40:2 (cf. 43:25), is again confirmed. The oracle concludes with a final call to return to Yahweh, who alone is the source of Israel's salvation.

[23] Much like the hymn in 42:10ff., the section closes with a hymn that calls for all creation to render praise to God, who has redeemed Jacob and who purposes to be glorified by means of Israel. The strong affinity with the language of the Psalms not only bears witness to the continuing role of the worshiping community of faith, but continues the editorial device of ending a literary unity with an appeal to a response in the language of faith to God's promised redemption (cf. Isa. 12:1ff.).

47. Isaiah 44:24–45:25

44:24 Thus says the LORD, your Redeemer,
who formed you from the womb:

I am the LORD who made all things,
    who alone stretched out the heavens,
and unaided[a] spread out the earth;
25   who foils the omens of false prophets,
    and makes fools of diviners;
who turns wise men back,
    and makes nonsense of their knowledge;
26   who confirms the word of his servant,
    and fulfills the predictions of his messengers;
who says of Jerusalem, "She will be inhabited,"
    and of the towns of Judah, "They shall be rebuilt,
    and I will restore their ruined places";
27   who says to the deep, "Be dry,
    I will dry up your floods";
28   who says of Cyrus, "He is my shepherd,
    and he will fulfill all my purpose";
who says of Jerusalem, "You will be rebuilt,"
    and of the temple, "You will be founded again."
45:1   Thus says the LORD to his anointed, to Cyrus,
    whose right hand I have grasped
to subdue nations before him,
    ungirding the loins of kings,
to open doors before him,
    and allowing no gate to be shut.
2   I will go before you
    and will level towering hills.[b]
I will break down bronze gates
    and cut through iron bars.
3   I will give you treasures hidden in the dark
    and riches stored in secret,
so that you may know that I am the LORD,
    the God of Israel, who calls you by name.
4   For the sake of my servant Jacob,
    of Israel my chosen,
I call you by name,
    and bestow on you a title of honor,
    although you do not know me.
5   I am the LORD, and there is none other;
    besides me there is no God.
I will strengthen you,
    although you do not know me,
6   so that they may know, from east to west,

that there is none besides me.
I am the LORD and there is none else.

7   I form light and create darkness,
       I bring prosperity and create disaster.
    I am the LORD who does all these things.

8   Pour down righteousness, O heavens, from above;
       let the clouds rain it down.
    Let the earth open up that salvation sprout.
       Let the righteousness spring up with it.
       I the LORD have created it.

9   Woe to him who quarrels with his Maker—
       a pot among earthen pots!
    Does the clay say to the potter,
       "What are you making?"
       or "Your work has no hands"?[c]

10   Woe to him who says to a father,
       "What are you begetting?"
       or to a woman, "What are you bearing?"

11   Thus says the LORD,
       the Holy One of Israel and its Maker:
    Will they ask me things to come[d] about my children,
       or instruct me about the work of my hands?

12   It was I who made the earth
       and created humankind upon it.
    My own hands stretched out the heavens,
       and I marshalled all their hosts.

13   It was I who roused him for victory,
       and I will level all roads for him.
    He will build my city
       and set my exiles free
    without price or payment,
       says the LORD of Hosts.

14   Thus says the LORD:
       Egypt's wealth and Ethiopia's goods
       and the tall Sabeans
    will come over to you and be yours.
       They will follow you,
       coming over in chains,
    and bow down to you in supplication, saying,
       "Only among you is God,
       and there is no other, no other god."

15   Truly, you are a God who hides himself,
        O God and Savior of Israel.
16   All who defy him will be shamed and disgraced,
        those who make idols lost in confusion.
17   But Israel will be saved by the LORD
        with an everlasting salvation.
      You will not be ashamed or disgraced
        in all the ages to come.
18   For thus says the LORD,
        the creator of the heavens
      (he is God),
        who formed the earth and made it
        (he established it);
      he did not create it a waste,
        but formed it for habitation:
      I am the LORD and there is no other.
19   I did not speak in secret
        out of a land of darkness.
      I did not say to Jacob's descendants,
        "Seek me in a land of chaos."
      I the LORD speak the truth,
        I declare what is right.
20   Gather together and come,
        assemble, you survivors of the nations.
      They lack knowledge who carry about
        their wooden idols,
        who pray to a god who cannot save.
21   Speak up, and make your case.
      Let them even take counsel together.
      Who foretold this long ago,
        who announced it of old?
      Was it not I, the LORD?
        Then there is no god besides me,
      a righteous God and a savior.
        No god exists besides me.
22   Turn to me and be saved,
        all the ends of the earth,
        for I am God, and there is no other.
23   By myself I have sworn,
        from my mouth has proceeded righteousness,
        a word that will not be revoked.

To me shall every knee bow,
    every tongue confess.
24 They will say of me, "In the LORD
    alone are righteousness and power.
    All who have raged against him
        will come to him and be ashamed,
25 but in the LORD all the offspring of Israel
    will be declared righteous and will triumph."

a. The translation follows the Qere. The Kethib reads, "who was with me."

b. The meaning of the Hebrew *hᵃdûrîm* ("swellings") is uncertain, and various conjectures have been proposed. The LXX reads "mountains."

c. The final colon is very difficult. The versions offer a variety of attempts to render the text. The Syriac reads, "I am not the work of your hands," which is coherent but hardly original. Some modern commentators suggest the translation, "Your work shows no skill!"

d. The translation follows the MT, but most commentators emend the text (cf. *BHS*) to achieve greater clarity.

Selected Bibliography

H. M. Barstad, "On the So-Called Babylonian Literary Influence in Second Isaiah," *JSOT* 2, 1987, 90–110; **W. A. M. Beuken,** "The Confession of God's Exclusivity by All Mankind: A Reappraisal of Is. 45, 18–25," *BTFT* 35, 1974, 335–56; **B. S. Childs,** "Retrospective Reading of the Old Testament Prophets," *ZAW* 108, 1996, 362–77; **M. Dijkstra,** "Zur Deutung von Jes 45, 15ff.," *ZAW* 89, 1977, 215–22; **P. E. Dion,** "L'universalisme religieux dans les différentes couches rédactionelles d'Isaïe 40–55," *Bib* 51, 1970, 161–82; **J. P. Fokkelman,** "The Cyrus Oracle (Isaiah 44, 24–45,7) from the Perspectives of Syntax, Versification and Structure," *Studies in the Book of Isaiah, Fs W. A. M. Beuken,* Leuven 1997, 303–23; **M. Haller,** "Die Kyros-Lieder Deuterojesajas," *Eucharisterion, Fs H. Gunkel,* Göttingen 1923, 261–77; **R. Kittel,** "Cyrus und Deuterojesaja," *ZAW* 18, 1898, 149–62; **R. G. Kratz,** *Kyros im Deuterojesaja Buch,* FAT I, Tübingen 1991; **H. Leene,** "Universalism or Nationalism? Isaiah XLV 9–13 and Its Context," *BTFT* 35, 1974, 309–34; **R. F. Melugin,** *The Formation of Isaiah 40–55,* BZAW 141, Berlin 1976; **A. Schoors,** *I Am God Your Saviour,* VTSup 24, 1973, 259–67; **D. W. Thomas,** ed., "The Cyrus Cylinder," *Documents from Old Testament Times,* New York 1961, 92–94; **C. Westermann,** "Sprache und Struktur der Prophetie Deuterojesaja," *Forschung am Alten Testament,* ThB 24, 1964, 92–170.

1. Context within Its Larger Isaianic Framework

The unit 44:24–45:25 begins a new section of the prophetic message within chapters 40—48. It announces Yahweh's sending of Cyrus to break the power of Babylon and redeem Israel, God's chosen, from captivity. This section extends the plan of God in relation to the servant (40:12–42:13) and focuses on the return of Israel to God (40:14–44:23). It forms the climax of chapters 40—48 in describing the call of Cyrus, his mission in overthrowing Babylon, and the fulfillment of God's power as supreme commander over the world and its inhabitants for the sake of Israel.

2. Methodological Problems of Interpretation

Previously, attention has frequently concentrated on determining the proper use of form-critical analysis. The case has been argued that this critical tool is indispensable in analyzing precisely the shape of units and assessing the conventional forces at work on prophetic speech in shaping an oracle. Yet the problem arises in determining the level on which the present text was shaped by conventional speech patterns. The assumption that oral conventions functioned in the exilic period in the same way as in the preexilic has been shown to be misleading. I have argued that the effect of oral speech forms often lies in the distant background of the text and that the final form of the written text has used much freedom in transforming traditional patterns into a new composition. As a result, I have been critical of the attempts of form-critics such as Begrich, Westermann, and even Melugin to establish the form and function of individual units according to largely form-critical criteria. These issues become crucial, for example, when assessing the individual parts of 44:24–45:25 in relation to the whole.

Most recently a redactional-critical analysis has been developed in an attempt to overcome the atomizing tendency of earlier form-critical analysis. Initially, Elliger's commentary (BK) resorted to an older literary-critical approach in which he resolved the tensions in 44:24ff. by reconstructing two independent literary strands (181ff.), but this solution was widely regarded as unsatisfactory. Instead, R. G. Kratz, a student of O. H. Steck, has focused his dissertation on the Cyrus oracles by means of a new redactional analysis. Following the leads of Steck, he rejects the earlier critical assumption that chapters 40—48 were largely a unity and proceeds to reconstruct a complex theory of multiple levels of redactional activity that have shaped the present text over a lengthy process.

I have not been persuaded by Kratz's arguments. He begins by focusing on alleged tensions in the text, which he uses as a key to reconstructing distinct redactional layers. For example, in 45:2 Yahweh announces that he will break down the doors of Babylon, whereas in v. 1 Yahweh opens doors so that the gates cannot be closed (26). He then proceeds to build on such alleged discrepancies as a sign of disunity. In my judgment, this redactional approach suffers major exegetical problems and I regard it as deeply flawed. As a result, it would be unfruitful to engage in a lengthy debate with this school of redactional criticism, recently named the "neo-literary" approach (cf. my more detailed criticism in "Retrospective Reading"). Fortunately, there is a more restrained and often perceptive use of redactional criticism in Hermisson's commentary on Second Isaiah in the BK series.

Above all, the analysis of Second Isaiah has now an excellent model in the multivolume commentary of Beuken. He is acutely aware of the need for employing a variety of entries into the text—literary, form-critical, redactional—but his interpretive focus falls ultimately on doing justice to the final form of the biblical text. Although at times I differ on individual interpretation of passages, our debate does not lie on the hermeneutical level.

Finally, a methodological comment is in order regarding the Cyrus oracle in terms of the contribution of history of religions. Since the late nineteenth century the striking parallels between the Cyrus oracles of Second Isaiah and the so-called Cyrus Cylinder have been observed (cf. *ANET*, 315–16). In a classic article of 1898, R. Kittel studied carefully the relationship between the two. He concluded that there was indeed a connection both in language, style, and content, but he rejected seeing a direct dependency, choosing rather to regard the similarity as lying in a common ancient Near Eastern *Hofstil*. Of course, there remain problems yet unresolved. For example, was the prophet consciously imitating this *Hofstil* as integral to the form and function of his oracle? Or again, at what period in Cyrus's career was the oracle delivered? Regardless of this continuing debate, the importance of studying these parallels lies in providing a check against isolating the Hebrew prophet from his specific historical context as if his text represented timeless religious literature that floated above all historical particularity.

3. Structure, Form, and Context

There is general agreement that the arrangement of the units within this larger section is not accidental. There is a strong continuity of themes focusing on the creative power of Yahweh, his will in calling Cyrus to liberate captive Israel, and the futility of the enemy to resist the divine will. In addition, there are linguistic ties linking the creative power of God (44:24; 45:11–12, 18), the commissioning of Cyrus to rebuild Jerusalem (44:28; 45:13), and the claims of Yahweh's exclusivity (45:6, 14, 21–24). The present unity of the passage clearly reflects a redactional shaping into a coherent literary whole with a consistent movement from the beginning to the end. However, the more difficult problem turns on assessing the form and function of the smaller units that together comprise the whole.

[44:24–45:8] There is much disagreement regarding the exact form represented by 44:24–28. The oracle is introduced with a messenger formula and is followed by both hymnic and disputational elements. Begrich and Melugin construe the form as a self-contained disputation and a separate unit from what follows. The other major form-critical option is represented by Westermann, who, because of the predominance of the participle forms, argues that vv. 24–28 are a hymnic introduction to the royal oracle that follows in 45:1–8. Certainly, according to its final form, the unit of vv. 24–28 serves to introduce the succeeding oracle. However, the argument for unity cannot successfully be made on form-critical grounds. The elements of discontinuity are too strong. The addressee shifts from Israel in vv. 44:24ff. to Cyrus in 45:1ff. In addition, the internal tensions within 45:1–8, which caused Elliger even to reconstruct two distinct literary strands, do not support the single form posited by Wester-mann.

In my opinion, Beuken's analysis of a redactional relationship between 44:24–28 and 45:1–8 is the most persuasive. His analysis is strengthened greatly by a careful analysis of the two different participle forms with distinct functions. The indeterminate participles in vv. 24–26a serve as predicates: "I am the LORD who made all things, who alone stretched out the heavens, and unaided spread out the earth." In contrast, the determinate participles in vv. 26b–28 function in apposition and extend the identity of God as creator in vv. 24b–26a to what he now says concerning Cyrus and the rebuilding of Jeru-salem. The final effect is that vv. 24–28 now prepare the reader for the royal oracle of 45:1–8 and the exertion of God's creative power in the historical com-missioning of Cyrus for Israel's redemption.

[9–13] Usually this oracle has been construed as a disputation between Yah-weh and Israel in which God defends his use of a foreign king in order to bring Jacob's exile to an end. However, more recently, following the lead of Leene and Beuken the case has been convincingly made that the disputation is between Yahweh and the nations. Israel is addressed always in the third per-son, whereas the objection of the nations turns on the calamity that they have experienced from Cyrus's arrival, all for the sake of Israel. Two woe oracles follow, which first scold them for challenging God's authority, and then lead into the actual message of promise (vv. 12ff.) in the rebuilding of the city and freeing of the exiles. The oracle is a redactional continuation of the actual com-missioning in 44:24–45:7.

[14–17]These few verses have continued to perplex commentators both regarding form and function. The simplest questions regarding speakers and addressee do not appear immediately evident. Verse 14 presents the oracle as a messenger formula of Yahweh, but the sharp distinction, often represented in the preexilic prophets (cf. Amos), is no longer present and the formula has become a literary convention. Yahweh does not speak in the first person, but the oracle that follows is a promise stemming from the prophet. The second feminine suffix that designates the addressee has usually been referred to Zion/Jerusalem. However, Beuken's suggestion that it refers to the exiles (*galût*) in v. 13 appears more convincing. It also ties v. 13 closely with the suc-ceeding oracle in vv. 14ff. In the prophetic word of v. 14 a citation is then included from the nations, which acknowledge their own deliverance to be from Yahweh for the sake of Israel. The voice of the exiles is then heard in

v. 15, again as a response to the events surrounding Cyrus. The passage concludes with a reflection on the shame of those manufacturing idols in the light of Yahweh's power to deliver.

The fact that most of the traditional forms of prophetic oral speech are present would indicate that this passage is a literary composition from a redactor who has shaped the Second Isaianic tradition into a unified whole in which vv. 14–17 serve as a type of commentary on the preceding oracles. In Hermisson's detailed exegesis one can see the more recent advance over the earlier form-critical analysis of Westermann, who can find only three fragments of oracles without any apparent coherence. In contrast, Hermisson works from a final literary result, but then tries to gain a depth dimension to the final effect by reconstructing earlier oral forms. Although methodologically Hermisson is not to be faulted in terms of this passage, Beuken's focus on the end form has been far more successful exegetically, in my judgment.

[18–25] Form-critical analysis of this concluding unit can find a variety of familiar forms and formulae: messenger formulae, hymns, polemics, and self-predication oaths. These formal observations offer some aid in trying to hear the exact nuances of the text; nevertheless, the chief exegetical problem lies in trying to understand the precise function of these verses within a larger compositional unity. When read in this light, the structure is quite straightforward. In v. 18a the prophet introduces God as the speaker to the nations in vv. 18b–24a. The introduction is made in the idiom of the hymn ("the creator of the heavens . . . who formed the earth"). Then in v. 18b the speech of God to the nations is begun with the formula, "I am Yahweh." His identity as God is then developed in terms of his absolute sovereign exclusivity and creative purpose: "I am Yahweh and there is no other. I did not speak in secret."

In vv. 20–24a the familiar form of the trial of the nations begins with a summons and challenge to make their case (cf. 41:21ff.). The speech continues in v. 22 with an invitation to turn and be saved. In v. 23, by means of an oath, God offers assurance of his salvation. The passage concludes in vv. 24b–25 with the prophet announcing the triumph of God's offspring, both outside and inside Israel.

4. Exposition

[44:24–28] The introduction of Cyrus by name as the deliverer of the exiles forms a major climax in the prophecy of Second Isaiah. The prophet turns from his early disputations to focus sharply on the redemption of world history. The implications are then pursued through chapter 48, after which Cyrus disappears from the scene to be replaced by the focus on the suffering servant. Regardless of the possibility of the once independent status of vv. 44:28 (cf. above), the text in its final form now functions clearly as the introduction to the larger literary unit and leads directly to the royal oracles of 45:1–8.

The oracle begins with a messenger oracle of God who, with the self-predication formula, "I am Yahweh," again announces to Israel his power over creation, indeed over all in an absolute sense, when spreading the heavens and forming the earth. The latter imagery is, of course, ancient and traditional, but the creative sovereignty of God is everywhere expanded in what follows. The meaning of the phrase in v. 24b is virtually the same whether one reads the pointing of the Kethib, "with more beside me," or the Qere, "who was with me." In the prophetic oracle which then follows in vv. 25–28, the participle form of the hymnic style dominates, first functioning as predicative and then in apposition. The Hebrew syntax seems to emphasize the creative role of God in nature, which is then extended to announce his promise to fulfill his divine purpose in history in rebuilding Jerusalem, freeing the exiles, and calling Cyrus as the means for his intervention in the events of the world. What now occurs frustrates the foolish efforts of false prophets and diviners, a note that continues in chapter 45, but is fully developed in chapters 46 and 47. Cyrus acts to confirm Yahweh's plan (v. 28), but also in confirmation of his previous promise to the earlier prophets. The parallel to "his messengers" in v. 26 makes it clear that neither the prophet himself nor the "suffering servant" is intended. The address to the "deep" resonates with the notes of the drying up of the floods at the Red Sea (Ex. 15:5; Neh. 9:11). Elsewhere, in Isa. 51:9ff., the redemptive events of creation, exodus, and deliverance from Babylonian captivity are fused as moments within the one divine purpose, all sharing the selfsame content of overcominng chaos. In v. 28 the restoration of Jerusalem is now explicitly joined with the rebuilding of the temple, which becomes an increasingly important theme in the chapters that follow.

[45:1–8] Although the royal oracle in 45:1–8 is addressed directly to Cyrus, the literary composition assumes that Israel is also present and affected. In 44:28 Cyrus had been named "shepherd," an ancient designation for the caring ruler. However, in 45:1 he is named "his anointed" (*mašîₐḥ*). The boldness of the title has long evoked surprise. Nowhere else in the Old Testament is a foreign ruler so described. There is a certain loose parallel in the naming of the Assyrian king as "the rod of my anger" to carry out Yahweh's mission (10:5ff.), but the role is virtually the exact opposite, one calling for destruction, the other for salvation. The term "anointed" should, however, not be construed according to its later usage as the promised eschatological messianic deliverer. Rather, the term was used originally in reference to the consecration of Israel's rulers (1 Sam. 12:3; 24:7), and also was used for the anointing of the high priest (Lev. 4:3). The anointed was specially set aside for a divine commission. Still, the use of the sacred terminology in reference to Cyrus—"whose right hand I have

grasped," "my shepherd," and "anointed"—remains striking in its bold reapplication of Israel's sacred tradition.

This favorable role assigned to Cyrus may also explain the choice of style
in the prophetic oracle. As was previously mentioned, the parallels to the so-
called Cyrus Cylinder seem to reflect a conscious use of a common ancient
Near Eastern court style with its highly exalted style of approbation: "Marduk
nominated him ruler over all. He looked with gladness on his good
deeds. . . . The entire population . . . bowed to him and kissed his feet" (Thomas,
92–93). But whereas in the Cyrus Cylinder the king is lauded with extravagant
praise for his great deeds and loyalty to Marduk, in Isaiah he serves the living
God as an act of divine grace within his own historical plan for the entire world.

Cyrus is promised the shattering of Babylon. The motif given is for the sake
of Israel. The warrant for its success is grounded in the power of God's sole
creative sovereignty. Moreover, the goal of his commission is that "they may
know, from east to west, that there is none besides me" (v. 6). That the whole
world may come to the knowledge of God is the climax of the divine intervention, although it is explicitly stated that Cyrus, God's chosen vehicle, does not
know Yahweh (v. 4). The unit concludes in v. 8 with a call addressed to the
heavens and earth to respond in order that righteousness may spring forth
according to God's creative will.

[9–13] The section that follows has often been described as a disputation
evoked by Israel's objection to God's unusual plan to use a foreign king to
deliver Israel, but a close reading does not support this quasi-psychological
interpretation. The oracle is directed rather to the nations—Israel is addressed
in the third person—and Yahweh defends his sovereign right as creator against
their recriminations: "What are you making?" "Your work shows no skill!" The
disputational form of the "handler/handled" (Melugin, 36) occurs elsewhere in
Isaiah (10:15; 29:15ff.) and in the New Testament (Rom. 9:20ff.). However,
this use in vv. 9ff. leaves no doubt about the answer, which flatly rejects the
attacks. The disputation form is transformed with a messenger speech affirming what will indeed take place: "He will build my city and set my exiles free."
The motivation is one of sheer free will and not one determined by price or
reward (cf. 43:4). The repetition of God's creative power in v. 12 picks up and
reinforces this basic theme of the entire composition (44:24ff.).

[14–17] The case has already been made that 45:14–17 does not reflect an
originally independent oral tradition but has taken its shape within the literary
shaping of the large section. Most probably the promised addressee in v. 14
refers to the exiles (v. 13) and the oracle consists of a prophetic promise to Israel
regarding the nations: "Egypt's wealth and Ethiopia's goods and the tall
Sabeans will come over to you." Moreover, they are described as coming in
chains and prostrating themselves. Some commentators (e.g., Westermann)
find the picture unsuitable for Second Isaiah and an unfortunate retrojection

from Third Isaiah. Yet a closer look at what follows may throw a less negative light on the passage. The nations confess that "only among you is God." The statement is not to be construed as a general acknowledgment of Israel's sole claim on God. Rather, in light of the deliverance by Cyrus, not only of the Jewish exiles but of African tribes as well, these nations acknowledge Yahweh's sovereignty revealed above all in Israel's liberation. The description of their arriving in chains should not be construed as if they voluntarily enslaved themselves anew to Israel, but only that the once captive peoples acknowledge the role of Israel in their liberation.

Such an interpretation seems supported by v. 15. It is no longer spoken by the nations but is the prophet's reflection on this strange outcome. The salvation of Israel came in a totally unexpected manner. The prophet marvels that the hidden ways of God made known in the events of history could not be foreseen, but remain entirely the exercise of God's completely free will. Israel's deliverance occurred at the hands of a foreign ruler and his power was then recognized even by the nations. The false claims of the idol makers have been exposed as a fraud. They are shamed and confounded, but Israel has received eternal salvation from the hand of God. Already in 28:23, in a very different context, the theme of God's hidden plan had first appeared (cf. 29:14).

[18–25] The final passage in this section brings to a climax the theme of the unexpected salvation wrought by God through Cyrus. The prophetic introduction expands on the creative power of God in a hymnic style, but now ties the power of God to his purpose in creation. He formed the heavens and the earth, not as a chaos, but rather to be inhabited. The message is actually not different from that of Genesis 1, but it has now been given a polemical, disputational form. God did not speak in secret, or conceal himself in ambiguous oracles. These verses serve as a major clarification of what is meant by God's hiddenness. God has always spoken the truth and declared what is right: "words which are true and reliable, upon which men may rely" (Muilenburg, 532).

This claim is then confirmed by a return to the theme of God's disputation with the nations (41:21ff.). They are summoned to trial. In spite of God's clear revelation in his creation, they have as yet no knowledge, but carry about idols, praying to that which cannot save. Then in the forensic idiom of the trial, they are shown to be defenseless. Only Yahweh foretold of old what he was about to bring to pass. He alone is the Savior God exercising his righteous will. There is no other avenue to truth or salvation.

What now occurs in vv. 22–25 is astonishing and unexpected, going beyond anything so far seen in Second Isaiah. Instead of the disputation with the nations ending in a resounding pronouncement of judgment (cf. 41:21–24), the widest possible invitation to salvation is extended by God: "Turn to me and be saved, all the ends of the earth." The old division between Israel and the nations has been forced to give way before the salvation that God has both promised and achieved. A new world order of righteousness has emerged. The old is passing; the new age is dawning. God will rule and to him "shall every knee bow, every tongue confess" (cf. Rom. 14:11; Phil. 2:10). Earlier the nations had begun to sense this reality at least in part (45:14). Now it is confirmed by God's divine oath (v. 23). However, this invitation to participate is not a blanket offer of universal salvation. There are still those who receive the promise and those who resist. This division no longer breaks along ethnic, national, or geographic lines. Rather, the "offspring of Israel" is now defined in terms of those who find in God their righteousness and strength. They shall triumph and exult, indeed from all the ends of the earth.

48. Isaiah 46:1–47:15

Chapters 46 and 47 reflect different literary forms and each has had its own compositional history, but within the present book of Israel they clearly belong together. The two different testimonies of the destruction of Babylon have been shaped to complement each other and are to be heard together.

A. Isaiah 46:1–13

46:1 Bel bows down, Nebo cowers,
    their idols are borne by beasts of burden.
  The things that you would carry about
    are now loaded as a burden on weary beasts.[a]
2 They cower and bow down together.
    They are not able to rescue the burden,
    but they themselves go off into captivity.
3 Listen to me, O house of Jacob,
    all you who are left of the house of Israel,
  you who have been carried since birth
    and upheld since leaving the womb.
4 Even when you grow old, I am he.
    When you turn gray, it is I who will carry.
  I have made you and will carry you.
    I will sustain and I will rescue you.
5 To whom can you compare me, or
    make me equal?
  To whom will you liken me
    that we may be similar?

6   Those who lavish gold from their purses
         and weigh out silver on scales,
     they hire a metal worker to make it
         into a god.
     Then they bow down and worship it.
7   They must lift it on their shoulders
         and carry it;
         they set it up in its place,
         and there it stands.
     From its spot it cannot move.
     If they cry out to it, it does not answer.
     It cannot save them from their troubles.
8   Remember this and stand firm.[b]
     Take it to heart, you rebels.
9   Remember the former things of old,
         for I am God, and there is no other;
         I am God, and there is none like me.
10   I make known the end from the beginning,
         and from ancient times things still to come.
     I say: My plan will stand,
         I shall accomplish my will.
11   From the east I hear summoned
         a bird of prey,
         a man to fulfill my purpose
         from a distant land.
     I have spoken, and I will bring it to pass.
     I have planned, and I will do it.
12   Listen to me, you stubborn-hearted,
         you who are far from justice,
13   I am bringing my justice near;
         it is not far off,
     and my victory will not be delayed.
     I will grant salvation to Zion,
         my glory to Israel.

a. The somewhat rough syntax of the MT has called forth many minor emendations (cf. *BHK* and *BHS*).

b. The AV took this *hapax legomenon* as a denominative of "man" and rendered it, "shew yourselves men," but this is unlikely. Most modern scholars seek a meaning from another Semitic cognate. Cf. Oswalt, 2:232 for a detailed listing of all the options proposed.

Selected Bibliography

B. S. Childs, *Memory and Tradition in Israel,* SBT II/3, 1962, 45–65; **R. G. Kratz,** *Kyros im Deuteroje-saja-Buch,* FAT 1, 1991, 53–64; **H. Leene,** "Isaiah 46:8—Summons to Be Human?" *JSOT* 30, 1984, 111–21; *De vroegere en nieuwe dingen bij Deuterojesaja,* Amsterdam 1987; **R. F. Melugin,** *The Forma-tion of Isaiah 40–55,* BZAW 141, Berlin 1976, 131–35; **R. P. Merendino,** *Der Erste und der Letzte: Eine Untersuchung von Jes 40–48,* VTSup 31, 1981, 461–82; **H. C. Spykerboer,** *The Structure and Compo-sition of Deutero-Isaiah: With Special Reference to the Polemics against Idolatry,* Meppel 1976; **O. H. Steck,** "Deuterojesaja als theologischer Denker" (1969), reprinted in *Wahrnehmungen Gottes im Alten Testament,* ThB 70, 1982, 204–20; **C. Stuhlmueller,** "'First and Last' and 'Yahweh-Creator' in Deutero-Isaiah," *CBQ* 29, 1967, 495–511.

1. Form, Structure, and Function

Although the older literary critics (Duhm, Marti, Cheyne) viewed the chap-ter as a somewhat brittle composition, removing vv. 6–8 as a later interpola-tion, most recent commentators assume a general coherence in its present literary form. The chapter seems consciously to repeat themes and formulae from chapter 45, as well as pointing forward to what follows (46:9; 47:8–10). Yet most recent commentators feel constrained to inquire about the early forms of the text in order to acquire a depth dimension by tracing its growth.

The early form-critics discovered a variety of different forms: taunt, disputa-tion, and assurance of salvation, but the debate over the larger coherence contin-ued. Melugin (131ff.) was one of the first who focused his major attention in proceeding beyond the form-critical stage in order to see how the material as a whole was shaped. Second initial observations confirm that the chapter has been consciously shaped toward coherence at some stage. There are numerous verbal repetitions and word plays: *sbl* (vv. 4, 7), *'sh* (vv. 4, 6, 10); *n's'* (vv. 4, 7), and so on. There are also important themes, such as deities who cannot save (vv. 2, 4, 7, 13). Melugin argued that older literary conventions had been creatively reworked by Second Isaiah into a literary whole. A more speculative aspect of the form-critical method turns on going beyond merely formal description and positing that the chapter is actually a prophetic response to the complaints of the exiles, which the prophet answered in a disputation. However, to reconstruct such a context without more evidence runs the risk of overly psychologizing the text.

More recently, much energy has been expended in attempting a redactional analysis of the chapter. Clearly the most exhaustive has been Hermisson's (BK XI/8, 1991). He belongs to a school of thought that judges Second Isaiah to be far from a unified composition of one exilic prophet, but rather, in its present form, a composition that represents extensive redactional reworking in the postexilic period. In a very elaborate reconstruction, he attempts to have a com-plex redactional growth, which not only reflects some minor additions to a basic Second Isaiah core, but which reveals many later attempts to "actualize" the prophet's message in the light of the failure of his promises to materialize. I do not intend here to conduct a detailed debate with Hermisson (cf. my essay "Retrospective Reading," 362–77). In spite of some genuine exegetical insights of value, I have reached the conclusion that the redactional approach as here practiced is misconstrued and that further debate does not contribute to the interpretation of Second Isaiah. At the conclusion of this chapter, I will rather argue for a different kind of editorial process that derives from its canonical function within Israel.

Melugin (131ff.) has made a good case for a variety of features that provide the force for literary coherence. He leaves open the question of whether the force derives from authorial or redactional intent. He divides the chapter into three form-critical units (vv. 1–4; 5–11; 12–13), but demonstrates that the creative shaping of the material has brought the force of the originally separate units into a larger compositional unity. Thus the intention of the disputational form is not only to persuade, but also to accuse. I agree with this latter analysis.

Beuken divides the chapter into two sections: vv. 1–7, a polemic against idols, and vv. 8–13, a disputation with Israel. I would argue that the two halves should not be so sharply distinguished, but that vv. 1–2 form only a background for the main portion of the chapter, which is marked by the three imperatives (vv. 3, 8, 12), all addressing the house of Jacob, whose obedient response to the sovereignty of God alone is the subject matter of the divine message.

2. Exposition

[46:1–2] The first two verses are often called a taunt (*Spottlied*), and parallels to the genre include Isa. 14:4ff.; 37:23ff.; Ezek. 27:1ff.; 28:2ff. (Contrast this form with that in 21:9.) Form-critically speaking, the designation is correct, yet the tone and function of these verses are very different from the parallels. There is no excited animosity; no joy over the collapse of a tyrant. The choice of the perfect tense for the verb renders an effect as if this all lay in the past. The once powerful gods of Babylon, Marduk-bel and Nebo, have become a pitiful sight, certainly not to be feared or even despised. Their humiliating journey of being carted away in defeat on the back of dumb beasts of burden, bowed down by their weight, provides the background for the real focus of the chapter, namely, the radical contrast between the gods of Babylon and the only true God of Israel. Perhaps in the distance the imagery still shimmers through with the memory of the once proud, festive processions of the New Year, but the portrayal of this train of the spoils of war only adds to the contrast. They surely cannot save others who themselves are being led into captivity. Verse 2 increases the picture of helplessness by a skillful literary use of chiasm between the verbs of "bow down" and "cower," which highlights the shame.

Scholars of religion debate whether this Isaianic passage distinguishes between the deity and its image, a distinction that indeed seems to be reflected in v. 1, but one that would then contrast with the polemical satire of 44:9ff. However, the question of a sharp distinction between a god and its concrete representation is quite foreign to the biblical writers, who move easily between the poles of identification and separation. Yet because both are judged powerless and without value, they are both indiscriminately rejected by Second Isaiah as an affront to the one god of Israel. Nor is Westermann's case convincing (182–83) that the understanding of idols in vv. 5–8 is strikingly different from the rest of Second Isaiah. The subject of foreign deities and their idols is introduced within different contexts in order to serve a variety of polemical purposes, but often without a concern to maintain a single logical coherence between arguments. Within all of Second Isaiah the gods never appear as a real power or threat, but only to illustrate stupidity, impotence, and an object of sheer scorn.

[3–4] The main addressee of chapter 46 is introduced in v. 3 with an imperative: "Listen to me, O house of Jacob." This imperative style continues to the same addressee in vv. 8 and 12, thus indicating again that the description of the pitiful gods of Babylon only forms the backdrop for a very different concern respecting Israel. The verses are carefully shaped literarily to continue the themes of vv. 1–2. The verses pick up and play with the different senses of words for carrying and bearing. In contrast to the gods who are helpless and need to be themselves carried, the prophet announces in a first person speech by Yahweh that he has carried Israel from its birth. He will continue to carry, bear, and save his chosen people. The ancient tradition of Israel's election as a special possession (Ex. 19:5) is here skillfully shaped to form a striking contrast between a static and a dynamic force, and between an impotent and a powerful protector. The appearance of the self-predication formula, "I am he," connects with a repeated theme from the earlier chapters (e.g., 43:25), but will grow into a climactic crescendo in the succeeding chapter. This total and unique sovereignty is demonstrated in the shattering of Babylon's rival claims (47:8, 10).

[5–7] The comparison between Yahweh and the impotent gods having been introduced in vv. 1–4, it is almost a reflex in Second Isaiah that the theme of the irrationality of idol making is again brought forth. Whether this material is a secondary interpolation from another source or redaction is a question of minor importance. In the final literary form of this chapter the theme is far from being a meaningless repetition, but now serves to further buttress the theme of Yahweh's ability to save (vv. 1, 4, 7, 13). The fact that the form reflects the oral convention of a prophetic disputation is not in itself a warrant for projecting an alleged complaint from the exiles against God's lack of intervention, which this passage supposedly seeks to address. It is, of course, possible that somewhere in the distant background of the text such a situation did arise, but the theme of God's ability to save has been developed in such a way in the chapter as to reapply the conventions of disputation toward a new kerygmatic purpose within the literary composition.

[8–13] Again Israel is addressed in the imperative: "Remember." In an earlier context the memory of the past is forbidden (43:18). Only the new things are to be considered. Now reflection on the past ("the former things of old") is crucial. Israel is to recall what God has accomplished on her behalf from the very beginning of ancient times. The verb *zkr* ("remember") involves far more than merely intellectual contemplation, but includes the active response commensurate with the past experience of what God has already done (Childs, 64). His call of Cyrus, "a bird of prey" from the east, is only the final evidence of God's keeping his word of promise and fulfilling his purpose in the affairs of history. "I have planned, and I will do it" (v. 11).

However, it is also important to observe that Israel, the house of Jacob of v. 3, is now addressed as "you rebels" (v. 8). The shift away from the mockery of the gods of Babylon to an indictment of Israel clearly indicates that chapter 46 was not simply a traditional taunt song, or even less, an "oracle against the nations" (Westermann). Rather, the focus now turns from a description of what God has done and will do to the issue of Israel's response. Disputation moves to accusation. Israel's required reaction will be the theme that now begins to dominate the following chapters (48:49–55).

Verse 12 further indicts Israel as a "stubborn-hearted" people who remain distant from the salvation that God is about to execute. The promised salvation will indeed come and not be delayed. Zion will be saved and Israel will reflect God's glory. Yet the question remains: Who is this Israel who shares in the coming salvation? Surely not the transgressors and stubborn of heart. The reader of Isaiah's book must await the answer in the succeeding chapters.

To conclude with a reflection on the reading of chapter 46 as a whole: Is there more to be said about the specific canonical shaping of this chapter? It has troubled interpreters in the past (e.g., Vitringa) that the fall of the city of Babylon through Cyrus in 539 did not follow historically the predictions of Isaiah. The great city was not levelled, nor were the Babylonian gods dishonored and replaced. Under the traditional assumption that chapter 46 was to be understood according to a theory of direct historical referentiality, scholars pointed out that chapter 46 must be directed, not to the events surrounding Cyrus, but to some later conquest, say, that of Xerxes, c. 480. Yet the evidence fails to support such a ploy.

More recently, redaction critics (e.g., Hermisson) have sought to resolve the problem by isolating later literary levels (*Schichten*) that developed in an attempt to actualize for a later period the original prophecy of Second Isaiah, especially in the light of its failure to materialize according to his prophecy. The very complexity of the argument raises initial suspicion.

In response to both of these suggested resolutions, the first point to make (cf. Beuken, 225) is that such readings fail to do justice to the unique nature of a prophetic proclamation. Biblical prophecy is not simply a description of a coming historical event made in advance, shortly to be visible to all. Rather, Isaianic prophecy interprets the effects of God's entrance into human history. It embraces a different dimension of reality, which only in part coheres with empirical history. The eschatological appeal of God's rule involves a vision of divine intervention that indeed enters human history, but is not exhausted by any one moment. The quality of God's salvific presence is not limited to one specific event in time and space, but embraces the whole of God's announced purpose for creation, which moves toward consummation. The nature of correspondence between word and event can only be measured in terms of this ongoing divine plan toward ultimate restoration of God's creation. Prophecy thus speaks of a quality of future event. It is not a clairvoyant projection of the events within the unredeemed experience of human history.

The second point to make, which up to now has not been adequately developed within the exegetical discipline, turns on the theological role of the editors in shaping the biblical material to render it in the light of the larger literary collection. This statement is not to suggest that they simply sought to dehistoricize the prophetic oracles into timeless proclamation. The historical specificity of chapter 46 remains, and is not diminished by the retention of oral conventions from the distant past. Moreover, there is a continuing attempt to highlight and intensify the kerygmatic content of the message in light of the whole. The fall of Babylon in 539 is registered, but the object of human pride and arrogance represented by Babylon is also addressed, and this description far transcends the events surrounding sixth-century Babylon. The confessional affirmation of God's absolute and unique sovereignty, "I am Yahweh, there is no other," is picked up from earlier chapters and continually extended as the measuring rod by which to describe what actually is unfolding according to the ways of God in the world.

In sum, much of Second Isaiah shows elements that are far later chronologically than those of the sixth century as the sacred tradition was constantly actualized in Israel's interpretation. However, to suggest that a redactional layer can be clearly isolated and reconstructed within a historical trajectory fails to grasp the nature of Israel's use of its scriptures, which cannot be easily correlated with some sociological or historical projections. To assume that the exegetical key for interpretation lies in reconstructing such a development runs against the intent of the final form of the text when it has disregarded or blurred the very evidence sought to be unearthed by redactional criticism.

B. Isaiah 47:1–15

47:1   Get down and squat in the dust,
          virgin daughter of Babylon.
       Sit on the ground without a throne,
          daughter of the Chaldeans.

Never again will you be called
    tender and delicate.
2   Take millstones and grind flour.
      Take off your veil,
strip off your robe, bare your legs,
    wade through the streams.
3   Your nakedness will be uncovered
    and your shame exposed.
I will execute vengeance
    and let no one intercede,[a]
4   (says)[b] our Redeemer, the LORD of hosts his name,
    the Holy One of Israel.
5   Sit in silence, go into darkness,
    daughter of the Chaldeans,
never again will you be called
    queen of kingdoms.
6   I was angry with my people;
    I defiled my heritage.
I delivered them into your hands,
    but you showed them no mercy.
Even on the elderly your yoke
    was exceedingly heavy.
7   You said, "I will continue forever
    still as queen."
But you did not reflect on these things,
    or consider what might happen in the end.
8   Listen now, you lover of luxury,
    dwelling in security
and saying to yourself,
    "I am, and there is no one but me.
I will not become a widow
    or ever be childless."
9   Both these things will come upon you,
    suddenly, on the same day.
Loss of children and widowhood
    will overwhelm you in full measure,
in spite of your many sorceries
    and your countless spells.
10   You felt secure in your wickedness.
    You thought, "No one can see me."
Your wisdom and your knowledge,
    they led you astray,

and you said to yourself,
"I am, and there is no one but me."

11   Disaster will come upon you,
        and you will not be able to charm away.[c]
      Holocaust will overwhelm you,
        which you will not be able to appease,
      a catastrophe suddenly coming on you
        of which you know nothing.

12   Keep on then with your spells
        and your many enchantments,
        at which you have worked since childhood.
      Perhaps you will succeed;
        perhaps you can inspire terror.

13   You have exhausted yourself with all your schemes.
        Let them stand up and help you now,
      Those astrologers and stargazers,
        who predict, month by month,
        what will come upon you.

14   Surely they have become like straw,
        the fire consumes them.
      They cannot even save themselves
        from the power of the flames.
      There is no coal for warming oneself,
        no fire to sit by.

15   This is all they have done for you,
        those with whom you have labored
        and worked from your youth.
      Each has gone astray on his own.
        There is no one to save you.

a. The meaning of the verb according to the pointing of the MT is somewhat unusual. Cf. *HALAT,* 861, for a list of suggested emendations.

b. *BHS* proposes to add the verb *'mr* ("say"), but it could well be implicit.

c. The sense of the verb, which usually means "atone," is uncertain in this context.

Selected Bibliography

A. Fitzgerald, "BTWLT and BT as Titles for Capital Cities," *CBQ* 37, 1975, 167–83; **M. Haran,** "The Literary Structure and Chronological Framework of the Prophecies in Is. XL–XLVIII," *Congress Volume, Bonn,* VTSup 9, 1963, 127–55; **R. Martin-Achard,** "Esaïe 47 et la tradition prophétique sur Babylone," *Prophecy, Fs G. Fohrer,* BZAW 150, Berlin 1980, 83–105; **R. F. Melugin,** *The Formation of Isaiah 40–55,* BZAW 141, Berlin 1976, 135f.; **R. Merendino,** *Der Erste und der Letzte,* VTSup 31,

1981, 482–97; H. D. Preuss, *Verspottung fremder Religionen im Alten Testament*, BWANT 92, Neukirchen-Vluyn 1971, 222–24.

1. Form, Structure, and Function

There is general agreement that chapter 47 in its final form is a unified poetic composition. Martin-Achard has rightly pointed out the poetic skill evidenced in its literary composition (1980, 87ff.). Also Hermisson recognizes a certain unity in the present text in spite of his complex reconstruction of the text's redactional history according to three different layers. In terms of form-critical analysis, there are several conventional patterns evident and some disagreement obtains as to which forms one assigns these elements. The taunt song clearly dominates (vv. 1–9), but some commentators have also designated components as stemming from the lawsuit, warning oracle, accusation, and indictment. Others feel that the chapter simply represents the traditional oracle against the nations, which is so prominent in the prophetic collections (e.g., Isaiah 13ff.). These various form-critical distinctions, in this case, do not seem of primary importance. Melugin (135–36) agrees that this is a freely created poem that has been shaped by prophetic announcements of the future.

From the overall perspective of the oracle it is usually dated in the period before 539. Yet it seems to me questionable when Westermann describes it as a "genuine proclamation" of Second Isaiah, and he is at pains to insist on Second Isaiah's delivering it orally at a specific moment in history. Obviously, Westermann is identifying Second Isaiah's prophetic role with that of the pre-exilic prophets. I would argue instead that the signs of literary composition are primary, including the shaping of chapter 47 together with chapter 46 to form a crucial segment within chapters 40—48. Moreover, the assessment of its "genuine" quality has little to do with the form of its delivery.

Traditionally, the search for the chapter's structure has settled on four unequal parts: vv. 1–4; 5–7; 8–11; 12–15. Yet one can see the immediate attraction of Duhm's brilliant reconstruction of five equal parts with a consistent meter, allowing for a few minor emendations and deletions. He suggested these divisions: vv. 1–4; 5–7; 8–10a; 10b–12; 13–15. Yet, more recently, doubts regarding Duhm's solution have mounted. First, commentators are far less confident that the goal of perfect poetic symmetry was an ancient concern in addition to its being a nineteenth-century obsession. Second, the splitting of v. 10 between two strophes cannot be justified, but rather appears dictated by Duhm's initial structural construal. Beuken has returned to a two-part division between a taunt song (vv. 1–7) and a judgment (vv. 8–15). Although these elements are certainly present, one must ask whether this division pulls apart the chapter's overall coherence. The theme of Babylon's arrogance is repeated three times in vv. 5–11, each time with a formulative introduction of a direct quotation (vv. 7, 8, 10). In sum, the overarching coherence is not greatly affected by how one envisions the chapter's subdivisions.

2. Exposition

[47:1–4] The form of the taunt in vv. 1–4 has returned more of the traditional tone of mockery than in chapter 46. The personification of the city of Babylon is a familiar one in the ancient Near East and elsewhere in Second Isaiah. In fact, chapter 47 has its counterpart in chapter 54, and Jerusalem's exaltation is set in direct contrast to the humiliation of the "virgin daughter of Babylon." The picture is of the exalted queen reduced into the utterly humiliating status of a slave. The delicate and tenderly handled ruler is now forced to perform the most menial tasks of the slave with her finery removed and her clothing stripped down to a minimum. Some commentators assign the sexual humiliation portrayed in v. 3 to be a subsequent textual expansion, yet this scene is so closely tied to the fate of the slave that the picture is fully coherent with the taunt.

There is a textual problem in v. 4. Although the MT text remains intelligible, the connection is unexpectedly brittle: "our Redeemer—the LORD of hosts is his name—is the Holy One of Israel." With the addition of a verb (*'mr*) to introduce the doxology (cf. *BHS*), the transition from the first person verbal forms in v. 3b to the formula in v. 4 is much more smoothly made. However, an implicit connection cannot be ruled out of court.

[5–11] When viewed form-critically, vv. 5–7 appear as a discrete unit and a new beginning is made in v. 8. Yet the continuity with the theme of the arrogance shown by the personified queen unites the verses within the chapter. Moreover, the same pattern of taunt followed by prophetic announcement overrides the various oral patterns. The familiar theme of Yahweh's anger against his own people as the cause for Zion's destruction (54:7ff.) is again introduced as background for the prophetic accusation. Israel's God caused Israel's destination—"I delivered them into your hands"—Babylon bears the divine reproach in showing her captives no mercy.

However, another cause for the prophetic accusation lies in Babylon's *hubris*: "I will continue forever still as queen. . . . [T]here is no one but me." This resonates as a false claim to an authority only held by God alone (45:18, 21; 46:9). The theme of Babylon's pretense of glory—whether through her false gods or through the unassailable security of her city—is an affront that always calls forth the prophet's scorn and resulting judgment. The theme of being led astray by false knowledge is also sounded in v. 10 and culminates in the suddenness of the impending ruin.

[12–15] The final verses elaborate on the nature of Babylon's false knowledge. The tone of vv. 12–13 is highly ironical throughout. The sorcerers and magicians with their spells and enchantments have been consistently the cause of wrong counsel. The prophet then characterizes stargazers and scanners of the heavens who predict the future as hopelessly misdirected and wandering aimlessly about, unable to save even themselves, which is a note that had already been sounded in chapter 46.

C. The Function of Chapters 46 and 47 in Context

If one now reads chapters 46 and 47 together, several observations of importance emerge. Whatever the compositional history of each unit might have been, in the final form of the book of Isaiah, the two chapters form a larger unit and the different images serve to complement each other in sounding the one note of Babylon's imminent destruction. The present position of chapters 46 and 47 is also significant within chapters 40−55. The promise of a new beginning was predicated upon the fall of the great oppressor. Now the promise has been realized with the end of Babylon and the humiliation of its ruler. These two chapters form the background for the immediate announcement that the exiles are now free: "Go forth from Babylon, flee from Chaldea" (48:20). From here on, chapters 49ff. can turn their attention to a different set of questions.

In spite of the fact that chapter 46 deals with the humiliation of the gods and chapter 47 with the shame of the city, various common themes are shared in the two chapters. Both use the form of the taunt to express the change from power to impotence. Great Babylon with all its pretenses of power is no more to be feared; rather, she has become the object of scorn and derision. Again, the redeeming God of Israel is without comparison, a note sounded in two different but mutually supportive ways in the chapters (46:5ff.; 47:6ff.). Then again, both chapters contrast the plan of Yahweh from the beginning toward a promised goal (46:10ff.), now realized in the coming of Cyrus and the false counsel of the Babylonian sages, which brought only confusion (47:12ff.). Finally, the contrast between Yahweh, who is able both to hear and deliver his people (46:3ff; 47:4), and the impotent gods of Babylon who cannot save (46:7, 15), serves to unify the two chapters into a coherent literary composition.

49. Isaiah 48:1–22

48:1 Hear this, O house of Jacob,
   who bears the name Israel
   and have issued from the loins[a] of Judah,
   who swear by the name of the LORD

and invoke the God of Israel—
    but not in truth or righteousness—

2   you who call yourselves citizens of the holy city
        and lean on the God of Israel,
        the LORD of hosts is his name.

3   The former things I announced long ago,
        they issued from my mouth;
        suddenly I acted, and they came to pass.

4   Because I know how stubborn you are—
        the muscles of your neck are like iron,
        your forehead bronze—

5   therefore I told you long beforehand;
        in advance of their happening I announced them to you,
    unless you should claim,
        "My idol caused them,
        my carved and metal images
        control them."

6   You have heard, seen everything,
        Do you not admit this?
    As of now, I will tell you of new things,
        well-guarded secrets unknown to you.

7   They are created only now, not long ago;
        before today you have not heard of them,
        so you cannot say, "I knew of them already."

8   You had never heard, you had never known;
        hitherto your ears were not opened.
    Well I know how treacherous you are,
        that from birth you were called a rebel.

9   For the sake of my name, I control my anger,
        for my own glory, I rein it in
        so as not to destroy you.

10   Look, I have refined you, but not as silver.
        I tested you in the furnace of affliction.

11   For my sake, my own sake, I act,
        for how can I profane my name?
        I will not give my glory to another.

12   Hear me, O Jacob,
        Israel whom I have called.
    I am he; I am the first,
        and I am the last.

13   My own hand founded the earth,
        my right hand spread out the heavens.

        I call to them,
            they all stand up together.

14   Assemble, all of you and hear.
            Who among them foretold these things?
        the one whom God loves
            will execute his will on Babylon,
            and show his might against the Chaldeans.

15   It is I who has spoken and called him.
            I have brought him and made his way succeed.

16   Draw near to me and hear this.
            From the beginning I did not speak in secret.
            From the time since anything existed, I was there.
        And now the Lord GOD has sent me,
            endowed with his spirit!

17   This is what the Lord your Redeemer says,
            the Holy One of Israel;
        "I am the LORD your God,
            who teaches you what profits,
            guiding you on the way you should go.

18   If only you had paid attention to my commands,
            your peace would have been like a river,
            and your righteousness like the waves of the sea.

19   Your offspring would have been as many as the sand;
            your descendants like its grains.
        Their names would not be obliterated,
            nor cut off from my presence."

20   Go forth from Babylon,
            flee from Chaldea.
            Declare this with shouts of joy,
            proclaim it.
        Publish the word to the ends of the earth,
            say, "The LORD has redeemed
            his servant Jacob!"

21   They did not thirst when he led them
            through the deserts.
        He made water flow for them from the rock.
            He split the rock
            and water gushed out.

22   "There is no peace for the wicked,"
            says the LORD.

a. The Hebrew reads "from the waters."

Selected Bibliography

J. Begrich, *Studien zu Deuterojesaja* (1938), reprinted ThB 20, Munich 1963, 169–70; **A. Condamin,** "Les Prédictions nouvelles du Chapitre XLVIII D'Isaïe," *RB* ns 7, 1910, 200–16; **K. Elliger,** *Deuterojesaja in seinem Verhältnis zu Tritojesaja,* BWANT 63, Stuttgart 1933, 185–98, 254–58; **R. G. Kratz,** *Kyros im Deuterojesaja-Buch,* FAT 1, Tübingen 1991, 113–21; **H. Leene,** "Juda en de heilige stad in Jesaja 48:1–2," *Verkennigen in een Stroomgebied, Fs M. A. Beck,* Amsterdam 1974, 80–92; **R. F. Melugin,** *The Formation of Isaiah 40 – 55,* BZAW 141, Berlin 1976, 39–41, 137–42; **R. P. Merendino,** *Der Erste und der Letzte,* VTSup 31, Leiden 1981, 497–539; **C. R. North,** "The 'Former Things' and the 'New Things' in Deutero-Isaiah," *Studies in Old Testament Prophecy, Fs T. H. Robinson,* ed. H. H. Rowley, Edinburgh 1950, 111–26; **H.-C. Schmitt,** "Prophetie und Schultheologie im Deuterojesajabuch. Beobachtungen zur Redaktionsgeschichte von Jesaja 40 — 55," *ZAW* 91, 1979, 43–61; **A. Schoors,** "Les choses antérieures et les choses nouvelles dans les oracles deutéro-isaïens," *ETL* 40, 1964, 19–47; *I Am God Your Saviour,* VTSup 24, Leiden 1973, 278–92; **C. Westermann,** "Jesaja 48 und die 'Bezeugung gegen Israel,'" *Studia Biblica et Semitica, Fs T. C. Vriezen,* Wageningen 1966, 356–66.

1. A Brief Review of the History of Interpretation

Few chapters in the book of Isaiah have called forth such diverse interpretations. Yet those commentators who dismiss all too easily the difficulties (e.g., Smart, Hanson) have obviously not penetrated deeply enough into this complicated text.

The exegetical problems are immediately evident. The sudden shift to a harsh rhetoric appears strange to the message of the preceding chapters, 40 — 47. The homiletical style calling for repentance seems more akin to the Psalms (e.g., 51; 81; 85) and Deuteronomy (chapters 7 and 31) than to Second Isaiah. Finally, many of the theological concepts of the chapter—Yahweh's concern for his name, Israel's unmitigated sinfulness—are those usually associated with postexilic prophets such as Ezekiel.

These early critical observations received a brilliant development in Duhm's famous commentary of 1892. He argued that an original core of prophecies by Second Isaiah had been reworked by a postexilic author who supplied a series of glosses and longer textual expansions (48:1a, b; 2a, b; 4a, b; 5b; 7b; 8b; 9a, b; 10a, b; 11a; 16a, b; 17–19; 22). When these glosses were removed, Duhm felt that he could recover the genuine promises of salvation characteristic of Second Isaiah that had been distorted by a later hand. It should be noted that the syntactical problem of the unexpected shifts in the verbs from singular to plural (e.g., v. 6) has not been resolved by an appeal to later glosses.

The form-critical stage which followed that of the early literary critics is best represented by Begrich and Westermann, who in general followed Duhm's literary analysis of the present text's double intention. However, both sought, in somewhat different ways, to show that one could successfully recover oral forms of speech that could be attributed to Second Isaiah. In addition, Westermann argued that the expansions had arisen from a subsequent cultic application of the text by a postexilic community that was trying to actualize the prophetic tradition in order to apply it to a later situation. Finally, in Melugin's careful analysis (137ff.) one can discern a struggle to overcome the atomizing tendency of the form-critical approach by describing the present literary joining of two oral patterns into a "kerygmatic unity."

The most recent line of interpretation, which is the storm center in a continuing debate, is best characterized as redactional. This approach is a conscious attempt to build upon the earlier critical insights but to focus attention in another direction. Its major concern is not only to distinguish the different levels of redactional layering (*Schichten*), but to pursue the historical and sociological forces at work in shaping the text. At the same time, it seeks to determine the effect of these literary trajectories on the theological interpretation of the biblical material. Although Elliger's work has been a major impulse toward developing the redactional approach (cf. *Deuterojesaja,* 1933), perhaps the clearest and most detailed application of the method to chapter 48 remains the essay of his student, H.-C. Schmitt (43ff.). Schmitt follows with minor alterations the lines of the classic literary critics, but rather than dismissing the additions as a series of glosses, he attempts to work with larger redactional layers, which he interprets, not as cultic actualization, but as a literary activity of specific postexilic editors who attempted to reinterpret the prophetic text in the light of the failure of Second Isaiah's prophecies to materialize in order to serve the religious needs of a later postexilic Jewish community. The arguments are serious and need to be carefully weighed since much that affects the text's interpretation is at stake.

In response to this brief survey of the history of modern interpretation of chapter 48, I would agree that the biblical text shows many signs of having been reworked by later editorial hands over a period of time. (In contrast, the exegesis of conservative commentators, such as J. W. D. Watts and A. Motyer, appears to me far removed from the difficulties of the actual text and cloaks the text with a homiletical coating without deep exegetical probing.) Still, the crucial questions turn both on how one understands the process of the book's editorial shaping, and how one establishes an appropriate context for its interpretation.

Of all the modern commentaries on Isaiah, I find that Beuken has wrestled hardest with these issues. While fully accepting a critical, diachronic approach to biblical exegesis, he has nevertheless signalled some major problems in the usual redactional approach. First, he insists that the function of a passage within the specific context of chapters 40—55 must provide the textual content rather than appeals to general theories of genre. Second, he proposes that the effect of the larger literary context of the collection was a major force in shaping the literary development within the exilic and postexilic periods. Finally, he is attentive to the interplay among words and themes that structure the passage in a way that often transforms its message from those of inherited oral patterns (*Jesaja,* 2:277–78).

From my own perspective, chapter 48 also offers a good opportunity for illustrating a "canonical approach." While making full use of the insights of the various critical methodologies, a canonical approach often moves in a strikingly different direction when it interprets the theological forces at work in shaping the text into a form received as authoritative by a community of faith and practice.

2. Form, Structure, and Function

Form-critics have long argued that the first part of chapter 48 consists of two distinct literary genres: vv. 1–11, a disputational oracle, and vv. 12–15, a trial speech. Yet it is also clear that in its present shape, other forces were at work that have greatly altered the form and function of these parts within the chapter. A comparison of these similar themes in earlier passages of Second Isaiah reveals clearly a change. The proof-from-prophecy mode is no longer the means of confronting the claims of false deities (e.g., 41:21), but is used as an accusation of Israel's unfaithfulness. Similarly, the role of Cyrus performs a different function in chapter 48 from 44:26ff. Indeed the language of confrontation and strife continues throughout chapter 48, but it has been absorbed within a larger parenetic style in addressing the house of Jacob. The original structure of the oral speech has been creatively reinterpreted and now largely supplies a background for the harsh accusation. Melugin, recognizing the transformation, speaks of chapter 48 as a "kerygmatic unity," but Beuken correctly questions whether this description is fully adequate to describe the nature of the chapter's present coherence.

The new feature of the chapter that is immediately evident is the predominance of the imperative "hear" (*šim'û*) in vv. 1, 12, 14, 16, followed by a repeated usage of the same verb in a finite form (vv. 6, 7, 8). In fact, the first two sections have been arranged in a chiastic pattern around the theme of hear and proclaim (vv. 1–2, 3–6b // vv. 6c–11c, 12–16c). The whole chapter now functions in a homiletical style to confront Israel's unbelief in relation to the divine prophecies made on its behalf. Indeed, the parenetical elements are too deeply embedded in the chapter to be merely characterized as secondary accretions.

The difficult exegetical issue is to explain this radical transformation of form. The various attempts that have been reviewed above to determine what sociological causes in the postexilic period effected the change remain speculative (cf. Schmitt). Similarly, the proposal of an etiological retrojection is a theory without hard evidence for support. Nor is the general appeal to a theory of postexilic entrenchment and Jewish exclusivity convincing.

Rather, the change in form and function turns on the specific role of chapter 48 within its corpus of chapters 40–47, a point persuasively made by Beuken (277). Chapter 48 marks the end of a section within Second Isaiah, and the change is to be explained contextually. The prior chapters focused on the promised deliverance of Israel, announced in prophecy and about to be fulfilled in God's new things associated with Cyrus. But now chapter 48 addresses the issue of Israel's unfaithful response to the promises, and challenges Israel to obedience in order to share in the promised salvation.

In addition, there is another important transition made in the chapter. The role of Cyrus as deliverer from Babylon is brought to an end. He is no longer mentioned after 48:14–16. Rather, a new first person voice is introduced in v. 16b: "now the Lord God has sent me, endowed with his Spirit!" Although the problems associated with this verse remain difficult, when taken in the context of the whole Second Isaianic corpus, chapter 48 forms the transition by the role of the servant, who picks up the same first person pronoun in setting forth his call to ministry in 49:1–6. Indeed, it is in the light of Israel's continual misunderstanding of the divine purpose, including the significance of Cyrus, that a new dimension of Israel as suffering servant is introduced. There is, in other words, a literary and historical development within the book that provides the theological force behind the unique function of chapter 48.

Historical critics have made a good case, in my judgment, that this chapter has been editorially reworked. Yet the critical hermeneutical issue turns on how one understands this expansion and growth of the text. I shall argue the case— the term "canonical approach" is a convenient shorthand cipher—that the prophetic text continued to be shaped through the postexilic period, and that the major force was the concern of its editors to reinterpret the prophetic text in the light of a deeper grasp of God's purpose revealed in history and made known especially from an intertextual study of the growing body of authoritative scripture. Accordingly, one can recognize the influence of Deuteronomy's parenesis and Ezekiel's judgments in the final shaping of chapter 48. Yet this process cannot be easily traced or assigned to self-serving editors wishing to reinforce a private agenda.

The ongoing task of the exposition of the text will be to pursue the nature of this coherence, which has shaped the text in a remarkably subtle way that far transcends constructing simply a formal "kerygmatic unit," or a fusion of redactional layers. Needless to say, it is a step backward to insist that a serious theological handling of the canonical text can only occur when the whole Isaianic corpus is ascribed to a single author.

3. Exposition

[48:1–2] The chapter begins with the imperative "Hear," which sets the tone for the chapter and resonates through the succeeding verses. It forms a clear leitmotif connecting not only v. 12 but the rest of the chapter. The addressee "house of Jacob" is also continued in v. 12. The largely participial expansions, "swear by the name of Yahweh" and "invoke the God of Israel," arise from

Israel's traditional confessional language (Deut. 6:13; 10:20; Isa. 44:5; Ps. 20:8) and celebrate the proud solidarity of the chosen people with its God.

Verse 2 actually continues Israel's language of praise. However, the reference to the holy city is not part of a common liturgical tradition that occurs only in later writings (Isa. 52:1; Neh. 11:1; Dan. 9:24). In chapter 48 it plays a specific role and consciously joins in a reference to Judah in v. 1. The theme of Zion, of course, grows in importance to become a major theme of chapters 48 — 55 and 56 — 66. It forms a crucial link in joining the first and second parts of the entire Isaianic corpus into a coherent whole. The climax of chapter 48 lies in the call to flee Babylon with the implied goal of a return to Jerusalem.

The unexpected element within the extended liturgical litany is the final colon in v. 1: "but not in truth or righteousness." For the early literary critics this clause was thought to dramatize the postexilic redactor's effort to turn a word of salvation into an accusation and call for repentance. Yet removing the clause requires major surgery on the whole chapter, and in the end results in the recovery of merely incoherent fragments (cf. Westermann's analysis). Above all, this critical operation fails to recognize the numerous repetition of words that function to form a larger literary coherence (e.g., $s^e d\bar{a}q\bar{a}h$, vv. 1, 18; $r\bar{\imath}$'š$\hat{o}n$, vv. 3, 12, 16; qr', vv. 1, 8, 12, 15; $higg\hat{\imath}d$, vv. 3, 5, 14; krt, vv. 9, 19; 's'h, vv. 3, 11, 14 [cf. Beuken, 278]). In sum, the present structure of the text is such that the call for obedience lies at the heart of the shaped text and cannot be isolated as part of a late redactional layer. However, I would not rule out the possibility that postexilic elements have been employed in the history of the text's development to portray more precisely the nature of Israel's disobedience (e.g., v. 8b). Nevertheless, one should recall that Second Isaiah was also fully capable of oracles of accusation (cf. 43:22ff.).

[3–6a] In v. 3 the familiar theme of the "former things" is picked up, which played such a major role in earlier chapters (e.g., 41:21ff.; 42:9; 43:8ff.; 46:6ff.). In 41:21ff. the contrast between the former things and the things to come was set in the context of a disputation with the foreign gods. Yahweh challenged them to explain what had happened in the past and to predict the events of the future. They were revealed as false deities (41:24) by their inability to control either the past or the future. In contrast, Yahweh called Cyrus and declared his coming long before his arrival. Yahweh's absolute sovereignty is disclosed both in his creation (43:5ff.) and in his action in history, past and present (43:9ff.). The former things are set in starkest contrast with the "new things" (43:19; cf. 46:9), and Israel is challenged to be God's witness to the new age of redemption that God is ushering in (43:12).

It is striking in 48:3ff. that God's debate over his sovereignty by means of an appeal to his bringing in the former things is addressed, not to the foreign gods or nations, but to Israel. Because Israel is obstinate, not only refusing to believe but even ready to attribute to its idols the power of evoking historical events, God announced these events in advance as visible proof of his sovereignty. Verse 6 then draws the implications of this demonstration of his authority, but in a parenetic rather than strictly logical style: "Do you not admit this?" (better pointed as *qal*). The theme of Israel's failure is not an alien postexilic introduction; instead, chapter 48 draws the implications growing out of a refusal by the nation to assume its divinely appointed task as God's true witness to the redemptive events occurring in public view (43:12). Babylon has fallen, Israel freed, but God's people still do not grasp their true deliverance.

[**6b–8**] The accusatory divine address now turns to the subject of the new things. The sudden, unexpected entrance of the new things had been an earlier theme (42:9), and from the start set in starkest contrast to the things of the past. The entry of the new things was closely associated in 43:14ff. with the coming of Cyrus. The Persian deliverer was the catalyst for the new age of redemption that was then described in broad terms of the miraculous "way through the wilderness" (43:19) and as "water on the thirsty land" (44:3). Cyrus was called to open the gates of Babylon (45:2), but the effect of his coming was toward the goal that "salvation sprout" and "righteousness spring up" (45:8).

Verses 6bff. return to the theme of the new things, and develop the aspect of its total newness in a far more radical form than anything before. The new things are "well-guarded secrets unknown to you," "created only now, not long ago." The note of complete unexpectancy is even repeated in v. 8: "You had never heard, you have never known; hitherto your ears were not opened." However, then the theme of newness is given a different twist. God chose to keep the entrance of the new hidden until the very last moment because he knew that Israel would abuse its foreknowledge. Moreover, the harsh accusation of congenital disobedience that supports the charge is grounded in an *Unheilsgeschichte*. In a manner closely akin to Ezekiel (cf. chapters 16 and 20), Israel's rebellion arises from the moment of birth—always a rebel! It is difficult not to see a postexilic component in this extended portrait of Israel, which serves also to anticipate the accusatory message of much of Third Isaiah. Beuken draws an interesting parallel by comparing chapters 47 and 48. From the larger context of the book, Babylon and Israel are not much different when it comes to discerning God's hand at work, since for both, God's righteous intervention in human affairs is unexpected and misunderstood.

[**9–11**] The next verses continue the theme of God's unrelenting anger. However, for commentators like Westermann who have concluded that the message of Second Isaiah is only one of unmediated salvation, these verses are thought completely alien to the prophet. Certainly if one did not follow the extended intention of the chapter and its place within the larger context of the book, it would be hard to contest this conclusion. However, there is a clear transition introduced in chapter 48 that must be respected. It is simply wrong to demand that the same message of forgiveness and restoration (chapter 40) be continued unchanged when the prophetic narrative is announcing a very new divine agenda for his people at this historical moment within the divine economy.

In this oracle delivered as a first person divine address, God speaks of restraining his anger, lest he destroy Israel in sheer wrath. Israel will not be destroyed, but tested in a furnace of affliction (cf. 40:1–2). Moreover, the grounds for his decision appear unfamiliar to Second Isaiah. God will not destroy "for the sake of [his] name," that his name not be profaned, that his glory not be given to another. The expression "for the sake of my name" is found nowhere else in this prophecy, but the parallels with Ezekiel are manifest (cf. chapter 20). However, in my judgment, the nature of this oracle is not explained in terms of interpolation, but rather as a sign of intertextual reading, which has retrojected a subsequent formulation to articulate the full intensity of the divine wrath.

[12–16a] Verse 12 returns to the imperative address to Jacob. Within the larger context of the whole chapter, the self-definition of God that appears in vv. 12b–13 serves as a corrective to Israel's alleged profession of loyalty, but not in truth (vv. 1–2). Using the familiar self-predication formula, Yahweh defines himself in a hymnic style as the "first and last" (41:4; 44:6), the creator of the heavens and the earth.

The call to assemble (v. 14) is again addressed to Israel, but what follows is a succinct formulation of the proof-from-prophecy argument in relation to the call of Cyrus. In the earlier passages when this argument was first used (41:1–4, 25–27; 43:8–13), the context was a trial before the nation. Indeed, the combative style of the original pattern of oral speech is still present in this passage even though its function in its reworked form has shifted into a homily for Israel. The nations still appear on the periphery as unable to make true prophecies: "Who among them foretold these things?" Then follows a brief summary of the larger Cyrus oracles.

In v. 14b one encounters a syntactical problem since the verse appears to interrupt the first person divine speech. Various solutions have been offered, such as following the LXX in removing the third person, or construing the clause as a citation, or even striking the divine name as a gloss. Muilenburg offers an innovative solution by reading the colon as a compound title, "Yahweh-loves-him," namely Cyrus, who will perform his will. Probably the most helpful solution is to read the clause as a compound sentence (cf. GKC §, 143) and to continue the initial verbal clause as the subject of the sentence: "The one Yahweh loves will work his will against the Babylonians" (cf. NJPS). Then the first person divine message continues in v. 15: "I have called him . . . brought him . . . he shall succeed," which again summarizes the familiar Cyrus tradition. Verse 16 draws out the legal implications of the evidence. God has always spoken openly and given a public witness through his prophets.

In sum, the point of the oracle is to remind Israel, and not the nations, of the truth of God's claim that the deliverance from Cyrus was evidence for his sovereign authority, which Israel continues to reject through unbelief. It should be noted that nowhere in the chapter so far has Israel's resistance been linked to Cyrus's being a foreigner and yet God's chosen vehicle, an argument which many modern commentators assume to be the actual issue lying behind the controversy.

[16b–19] Much to the reader's surprise, v. 16b suddenly and without any obvious preparation introduces a new voice with a dramatic shift in direction: "And now the Lord GOD has sent me, endowed with his Spirit!" The interpretation of this verse and its function within the larger context involves a host of difficult problems that have plagued commentators in the past.

First of all, it does not seem helpful either to eliminate the verse as a gloss (Duhm, Muilenburg, et al.), or to emend the text in order to remove the problem of the first person pronoun (Volz). Nor is Westermann's interpretation of the verse illuminating when he designates it part of an unintelligible fragment. Second, a crucial component in any interpretation turns on determining the referent to the first person pronoun of v. 16b. The issue is difficult and controversial. It is generally thought to be the prophetic author, that is, Second Isaiah, who is speaking autobiographically. A warrant for this judgment is then focused in the prologue of chapter 40:6, sometimes translated, "And I said, what shall I cry?" Yet I have already argued that this interpretation of chapter 40 is faulty. The first person, which supports an autobiographical reading, is only found in the Greek, and not the Hebrew of the MT. In a word, the appearance of a first person prophetic voice in 48:6 is, up to this point in the book of Second Isaiah, unique. In my judgment, to assume an autobiographical reference to the author is as erroneous here as it is in chapter 40.

How then is the verse to be interpreted? The key is found not in some reconstructed redactional layer but in the literary context of the entire corpus of Second Isaiah and, above all, in the specific role played within the book of chapter 48. The theme of the part assigned to Cyrus within the purpose of God is central to chapters 40—47. Yet in chapters 49—55 the figure of Cyrus has disappeared from the scene, and the role of the servant now dominates. Chapter 48 functions to rebuke the transition. Babylon has fallen and yet Israel is rebuked, like Babylon in chapters 46 and 47, for failure to understand the sovereignty of God and the nature of his redemption of the world. Chapter 48 turns the traditional oracles of disputation and trial into an accusatory call for Israel's repentance. God confirms his absolute sovereignty over nature and history. His calling of Cyrus will succeed. But now something new is planned. There is a new movement within the divine economy. It is signalled by the introduction of a new messenger.

Chapter 48 gives no immediate description of his mission. Rather, the reader is forced to wait until chapter 49 in order to understand the identity of the one sent (v. 16b). Then suddenly one is made aware that his identity is that of the servant, who now speaks autobiographically with the same first person pronoun of 48:16b to set forth in detail his calling and mission both to the house of Jacob and to the nations of the world. This connection between the speaker in v. 16b and the servant of chapter 49 has, of course, been suggested earlier. Both Delitzsch and Condamin made the connection. However, it was not taken seriously because such different assumptions reigned respecting the servant ever since Duhm's hypothesis won wide assent, which separated the four "suffering servant" passages from their present literary context within the literary corpus of Second Isaiah. Unfortunately, the traditional exegesis of the church fathers, Calvin, and Vitringa fell back on general historical or theological assumptions and so missed the connection made by the specific literary context of chapter 48.

The one sent by God and endowed with the spirit (cf. 42:1) in v. 16b has an immediate task to perform in chapter 48. From the context it is clear that he is the one who delivers the divine oracle in vv. 17–19, and in this role assumes a prophetic function. However, he remains fully anonymous apart from his identity as the servant of chapter 49. In v. 17 God is identified as Israel's Redeemer and Holy One, titles familiar from earlier oracles. Yet the message that follows points in a new direction, which will become fully clear in the chapters that follow and mark the beginning of a new period after Cyrus.

God reaffirms his relation to his people: "I am Yahweh your God." Then two participles define his future goal. First, God will instruct Israel to do that which benefits its welfare, not by coercion, but by the spirit. (Recall the negative example of Egypt in 30:5). Second, God will guide Israel in the way to go. The reference to a way has often a very concrete meaning in Second Isaiah (43:16, 19; 45:13; 49:11; 51:10), which resonates with the call to depart from Babylon for Jerusalem. Yet the term is also bound to an accompanying moral judgment: the way of the righteous (26:7) and the way of understanding (40:14). The divine speech closes in vv. 18–19 with an oracle of admonition reminiscent of Deut. 30:15 and Ps. 81:14 that again sounds the call to harken to the divine commandments. Regardless of how one dates this formulation—many commentators almost by reflex consider it late postexilic—its presence in this prophetic oracle attests that for the canonical editors Israel's life of blessing can only be defined in relation to torah. Conversely, the destruction and loss of the sacred name stem from its disregard.

[20–22] The chapter ends with an exuberant shout of joy: "Go forth from Babylon, flee from Chaldea!" The inner resonance is, of course, to the flight from Egypt to freedom (Ex. 14:5). The prophetic hymn can be called eschatological since, according to its actual historical situation, Israel is still captive in Babylon. Yet for the biblical writer, deliverance is a certainty and the Hebrew verbal form expresses the note of finality: "The LORD has redeemed his servant Jacob!" However, redeemed Israel is not merely to relish its deliverance. It must also bear witness to all the world in proclaiming what God had done on its behalf on the way home through the desert.

Just as many feel that the final chapter of the book of Isaiah ends on a sour note, so also here the concluding sentence casts a shadow on the celebration of deliverance: "'There is no peace for the wicked,' says the LORD." Peace with God expresses the deepest meaning of deliverance. In the prophetic vision of the future there remain those who do not share in the blessing, even though the promise is for all humanity. There are those outside the circle of joy who have excluded themselves. For a full treatment of this deeply disturbing portrayal, the reader must wait for its exposition in chapters 56—66.

50. Isaiah 49:1–13

49:1 Listen to me, O coastlands,
      and hear you distant nations.
  The LORD called me before I was born;
      he named me while I was in my mother's womb.
2 He made my mouth like a sharpened sword,
      in the shadow of his hand he hid me;
  he made me into a polished arrow
      and concealed me in his quiver.
3 And he said to me, "You are my servant,
      you are Israel,[a] in whom I will be glorified."
4 But I said, "I have labored to no purpose;
      I have spent my strength in vain and for nothing.
  But my case is in the LORD's hand,
      and my reward is with my God."
5 But now the LORD says—
      he who formed me in the womb to be his servant
  to bring Jacob back to him
      and gather Israel to himself.[b]
  I have been honored in the sight of the LORD,
      and my God has been my strength—
6 He says,
      It is too small a thing that you should be
  my servant,
      to raise up the tribes of Jacob,
      and to restore the remnant of Israel;
  I will also make you a light to the nations.
      that my salvation will reach to the ends of the earth."
7 Thus says the LORD,
      the Redeemer of Israel and his Holy One,
  to the one despised and abhorred[c] by the nations,
      to the servant of rulers:
  "Kings will see you and arise,

        nobles will prostrate themselves,
    because of the LORD, who is faithful,
        the Holy One of Israel, who has chosen you."
8   Thus says the LORD:
        In an hour of favor I will answer you,
        and in a day of salvation I will help you.
    I have sustained you, and appointed you
        a covenant for the people
    to restore the land,
        to reallot its desolate inheritances,
9   saying to the prisoners, "Go free,"
        and to those in darkness, "Come forth."
    They shall feed along the paths
        and on every barren hill find pasture.
10 They will not hunger or thirst,
        nor will the scorching wind and sun
        beat down on them.
    He who has pity on them will guide.
        He will lead them to springs of water.
11 I will make all my mountains into roads,
        and my highways will be raised up.
12 Watch, they will come from afar,
        some from the north, others from the west,
        some from the land of Sinim."[d]
13 Shout for joy, O heavens,
        rejoice, O earth!
    Break into song, O hills!
    For the LORD comforts his people
        and will have compassion on his afflicted ones.

    a. Cf. below for predicative use.
    b. Read the Qere *lô* ("to him") rather than Kethib *lō'* ("not").
    c. The MT has an active verbal form (cf. below).
    d. The MT reads *sînîm,* which was traditionally interpreted as China. The suggested emendation to *swnym,* "Syrene" or "Aswan," the southern frontier of Egypt, has received support from 1QIs[a], which reads *swnyym.*

Selected Bibliography

W. A. M. Beuken, "De vergeefse moeite van de knecht. Gedachten over de plaats van Jesaja 49:1–6 in de context," *De Knecht. Studies rondom Deutero-Jesaja, Fs J. L. Koole,* Kampen 1978, 23–40; **K. Elliger,** *Deuterojesaja in seinem Verhältnis zu Tritojesaja,* BZAW 63, Stuttgart 1933, 38–56; **H.-J. Hermisson,**

"Der Lohn des Knechts," *Die Botschaft und die Boten, Fs H. W. Wolff,* ed. J. Jeremias, L. Perlitt, Neukirchen-Vluyn 1981, 269–87; "Israel und der Gottesknecht bei Deuterojesaja," *ZTK* 79, 1982, 1–24; **K. Kiesow,** *Exodustexte im Jesajabuch,* OBO 24, Göttingen 1979, 79–92; **R. G. Kratz,** *Kyros im Deutero-jesaja-Buch,* FAT 1, Tübingen 1991, 135ff., 144ff.; **N. Lohfink,** "'Israel' in Jes 49,3," *Wort, Lied und Gottesspruch, Fs J. Ziegler,* FB 3, Würzburg 1972, 217–29; **R. F. Melugin,** *The Formation of Isaiah 40– 55,* BZAW 141, Berlin 1976, 142–47; **R. P. Merendino,** "Jes 49, 1–6: ein Gottesknechtslied?" *ZAW* 92, 1980, 236–48; "Jes 49, 7–13: Jahwes Bekenntnis zu Israels Land," *Henoch* 4, 1982, 295–329; **T. N. D. Mettinger,** *A Farewell to the Servant Songs: A Critical Examination of an Exegetical Maxim,* Scriptora Minora 13, Lund 1983; **J. van Oorschot,** *Von Babel zum Zion,* BZAW 206, Berlin 1993, 235–39; **H. M. Orlinsky,** "'Israel' in Isa. 49:3: A Problem in the Methodology of Textual Criticism," *Erets Israel* 8, 1967, 42–45; **G. von Rad,** "Die Konfessionen Jeremias," *EvT* 3, 1936, 265–70; **H. W. Robinson,** "The Hebrew Conception of Corporate Personality," *Werden und Wesen des Alten Testaments,* BZAW 66, Berlin 1936, 49–62; **A. Schoors,** *I Am God Your Saviour,* VTSup 24, Leiden 1973, 97–103; **J. J. Stamm,** "*Berît 'am* bei Deuterojesaja," *Probleme biblischer Theologie, Fs G. von Rad,* Munich 1971, 510–24; **O. H. Steck,** "Aspecte des Gottesknechts in Deuterojesaja 'Ebed-Jahwe Liedern,'" *ZAW* 96, 1984, 372–90; reprinted in *Gottesknecht und Zion,* FAT 4, Tübingen 1992, 3–21; **P. Wilcox and D. Paton-Williams,** "The Servant Songs in Deutero-Isaiah," *JSOT* 42, 1988, 79–102.

1. Genre, Structure, and Context

There is little agreement on the genre of vv. 1–6. Those scholars who have followed in Duhm's tradition of designating the unit as the second "servant song" (Begrich, Westermann) have usually designated it form-critically as a song of thanksgiving (*Danklied*), a call report, or a combination of commissioning and thanksgiving. This analysis has not been very illuminating and does not greatly enhance its understanding. Those who resist Duhm's isolation of the servant songs from the larger context of Second Isaiah (Muilenburg, Clifford) opt for a collective interpretation of the servant Israel, and see it as an imitation of a call narrative that has been extended metaphorically to the nation. The apparent difficulty in v. 6 of having the servant Israel sent to minister to Israel has usually forced a retranslation of the verse to make Yahweh the subject of the infinitives, which is syntactically possible but strained (cf. Muilenburg). Once again this form-critical analysis has not been especially helpful for interpreting the unit, and hardly describes the major forces at shaping the text.

The form-critical analysis of the genre represented in vv. 7–13 is equally diverse. Most recent commentators have argued that vv. 8–12 reflect an oracle of promise directed to Israel. However, the analysis has then usually argued that the original collective addressee has been altered by the addition in v. 8b of a citation from 42:6 ("I have given you as a covenant for the peoples") in order to change the addressee redactionally to refer to the servant. Verse 7 is sometimes separated from vv. 8ff. as an independent oracle (Melugin, Grimm), or assigned in part a new position at the end of the unit (Westermann). More frequently, however, the emphasis has fallen on its redactional role in relating vv. 1–6 and 8–12 in an effort to achieve an element of coherence.

In the end, the various attempts to reconstruct an original level before the later redactional shaping often contradict one another because of prior assumptions regarding the identity and role of the servant. For example, some argue that vv. 1–6 were originally directed to an individual servant, which was only later construed to be a collective entity by the addition of "Israel" in v. 3. However, others argue that vv. 8–12 were first understood collectively, and only later reshaped to refer to an individual servant by introducing in v. 8 a citation from 42:6. An apparent allusion to chapter 53 in v. 7 performs a similar function. In sum, it would seem evident that the key for the interpretation of 49:1–13 does not lie in deeply intrusive reconstructions.

In contrast, Beuken (*Jesaja* II/B, 11ff.) has moved in a much more promising direction by recognizing that the stark polarity between collective and individual interpretations of the servant set up by Duhm's theory of four independent servant songs has seriously skewed the analysis. Rather, the key to the chapter is found in the inner movement of the prophetic narrative extending from chapter 40 to chapter 55. Isaiah 49:1–6 is quite clearly an intentional literary continuation of 42:1–4(5–9) as shown by the obvious parallels. Yet much has happened in Second Isaiah's prophetic history between chapters 42 and 49. Cyrus has come to liberate Israel according to the divine promise (44:24ff.). The deities of Babylon have been shown powerless before the will of the one creator God (cf. chapters 46—47). Israel, the servant of Yahweh, has been called to its mission of establishing justice in the earth and being a light to the nations (42:1ff.). Yet Israel remains blind and will not see (42:19). It continues to believe that its right has been disregarded by God (40:27).

Then in chapter 48, unfaithful, obstinate Israel is called to account: "You had never heard, you had never known" (v. 8). A new direction is now signalled by God. A new voice is introduced in 48:16: "And now the Lord GOD has sent me," who delivers a message in vv. 17ff. God renews his promise as Redeemer to Israel in spite of the nation's failure (v. 18). The chapter ends with a summons for those who believe to depart from Babylon and to participate in the new exodus (vv. 20–21), leaving behind those who persist in evil (v. 22).

Chapter 49 then picks up the voice of the messenger sent in 48:16, and interprets in great detail the new strategy of God for his servant. The structure of the chapter closely parallels that of the servant song in 42:1–4, with the servant's mission explicated in the succeeding verses of 5–9. In a similar fashion, the "second" servant song (49:1–6) has been extended—most probably redactionally (cf. below)—in vv. 7–12. The whole unit has been brought to a conclusion with a hymn, much like that found earlier in 42:10ff. and 44:23.

2. Exposition

[49:1–6] The unit opens with an imperative "listen" that continues the theme made dominant throughout chapter 48. However, now it is the voice of the servant who appears to the "coastlands" and "distant nations." Up to this point it has been a summons from the mouth of God and addressed to the people of Israel (46:3, 12; 48:12; 51:1; etc.). This broader scope of recipients of the message sets the context of chapter 49, climaxing in v. 6: "my salvation will reach to the ends of the earth."

In vv. 1b–3 there follows a recitation of the servant in the first person (cf. 48:16), which recounts his commissioning, equipment, and divine mission. The parallels in vocabulary and content with 42:1–4 are striking (42:4 // 49:1; 42:1 // 49:6; 42:3 // 49:4), but when 42:5–9 is included, the parallels extend to verbal identity (42:6 // 49:6). The imagery of the call is prophetic and reminiscent of Jeremiah's call (chapter 1): called from the womb, named by name, mouth like a sharp sword. However, upon closer examination the apparently simple structure of vv. 1–6 raises some difficult questions that greatly affect the interpretation of the unit. Initial credit goes to H.-J. Hermisson in having opened up the structural problem in great detail. He correctly rejects the earlier form-critical analysis of Begrich in designating these verses as a song of thanksgiving. Such an analysis, taken from a pattern of the Psalms, emphasizes a three-stage temporal sequence of a period before the trouble, a description of the sorrow, and finally its resolution. Quite clearly this pattern does not fit vv. 1–6.

Rather, after the initial commissioning (vv. 1b–3), there follows a report by the servant of his failure, joined with an expression of continued trust in God (v. 4). Then in verse 5 there is a repetition of the call, mission, and divine trust of vv. 1–3 before the servant is again addressed in v. 6 in terms of his office. There is no sequential movement present in the sense of a thanksgiving song, but the entire context is written from the perspective of the servant's call. In sum, the passage does not focus on a personal experience of a petitioner as in the Psalms, but rather is about the office of a prophet. A similar point was made by von Rad respecting Jeremiah's complaints in his well-known essay of 1936.

However, once this insight of Hermisson has been gratefully acknowledged, I would argue that he has not correctly analyzed the exact nature of the crisis of the servant's office. The problem lies in his working still too closely with Duhm's theory of a corpus of four independent servant songs and thus in relating 49:1–6 directly to 42:1–4. The real exegetical issue lies in the relation of 49:1–6 to the larger literary context of chapters 40–55 in a way described above.

The central point of the call in chapter 49 is given in v. 3 and is entirely unique up to this point. "And [Yahweh] said to me, 'You are my servant, you are Israel, in whom I will be glorified.'" Among earlier commentators (Duhm, Koehler, Westermann) it was held that the word "Israel" was a later interpolation to be stricken. However, in more recent times (cf. especially Lohfink), it has become increasingly clear that there are no strong textual reasons for its omission. What then does v. 3 mean and what is its larger exegetical significance?

First, as to the syntactical problem of the word "Israel" within the sentence, the function of the word can be interpreted in several different ways. It can be rendered as a vocative, "O Israel," or in apposition: you are my servant, who is identified with Israel. However, the word can also function as a predicative: you are my servant; *you* are now Israel. If it is so rendered, the point made is not that the servant is simply being incorporated into a corporate entity by means of some such theory as "corporate personality" (H. W. Robinson). Rather, something new at that moment has happened ("but now"), which was not previously the case. The prophetic voice of vv. 1b–3 ("Yahweh called me") has not only been designated as servant, but he has been designated as Israel. In place of the corporate nation Israel, which up to this point has always borne the title, "my servant" (41:9; 42:1, 19; 44:1; 45:4), a single figure now carries the title and even office.

Several features in the text support this interpretation further. First, the new identity of the servant explains in large measure the stark individualization of the imagery that occurs in chapter 49 (cf. the statistics in the excellent essay of Wilcox and Paton-Williams). It has always been fully obvious within the Old Testament that a single noun, such as *son, daughter,* or *servant,* could function as a metaphor for a corporate entity. Thus, in the light of the prior identification of Israel as the servant (e.g., 41:8), the most natural reading of the "first" servant song in 42:1–4 within the literary context of the book of Second Isaiah is to understand "servant" metaphorically as the nation or chosen people. Neither the imagery within chapter 42 of an unobtrusive behavior in establishing justice in the earth (v. 4), nor of being a "light to the nations" (v. 7) appears to stretch the metaphorical usage of servant Israel beyond measure. However, when one comes to chapter 49, the metaphorical usage of a corporate entity seems to grow more and more strained.

Second, the figure of the servant appears to have undergone a history of activity within a concrete temporal sequence. In an almost autobiographical style the servant recounts a period of a failed endeavor in his office as servant: "I have labored to no purpose; I have spent my strength in vain and for nothing" (v. 4). The exact cause of his despondency is not explicitly mentioned, yet the context provided by chapter 48 points to the nature of the problem. The servant had just delivered the divine summons to depart from Babylon and for Israel to begin the new exodus. However, he confesses that he had not been successful in the deliverance of the people from captivity. Earlier, when captive Israel complained that its right (*mišpāṭ*) had been disregarded (40:27), God had promised that his appointed servant would not fail or grow weary until he had established *mišpāṭ* on the earth (42:4). Now the servant has grown weary; he has labored in vain. Nevertheless, he retracts his complaint and comforts himself that his *mišpāṭ* and reward are still assured by God.

Third, this interpretation of the new identity of the servant also explains the change that occurs respecting the servant's mission between the conditions described in chapters 42 and 49. In both chapters the servant is given as "a covenant for the peoples," and "a light to the nations" (42:6 // 49:6, 8). Yet it is only in chapter 49 that God commissions the servant "to bring Jacob back to him and gather Israel to himself (v. 5), and "to raise up the tribes of Jacob, and to restore the remnant of Israel" (v. 6). In a word, the old crux of having corporate Israel, the servant, sent to restore Israel the nation receives a fresh interpretation in the light of the predicative rendering of the servant Israel in 49:3.

I am not suggesting that collective Israel has been replaced by an individual prophetic figure, say, by Second Isaiah himself. Such historical speculation misses the point of the text. The identity of the first person singular voice in 48:16 and 49:1–6 remains fully concealed. Rather, what is crucial to observe is that one, bearing all the marks of an individual historical figure, has been named servant, not to replace corporate Israel—the servant in Second Isaiah remains inseparable from Israel—but as a faithful embodiment of the nation Israel who has not performed its chosen role (48:1–2). For this reason, I conclude that Hermisson's essay on the relation between Israel and the servant, in spite of some excellent observations, in the end is not on target and dissolves into tortuous exegesis.

In sum, Duhm's sharp contrast between the corporate and individual servant has misconstrued the issue by means of a false polarity. Rather, credit still redowns to Delitzsch for correctly seeing a fluidity within the scope of the office of servant. Yet Delitzsch's interpretation of the nature of this fluctuating concept remained far too static and was an insight not actually grounded in the ongoing prophetic narrative of Second Isaiah, which was testified to in the literary movement of chapters 40—55.

The key to interpreting vv. 5 and 6 appears to lie in understanding the sentence in v. 6: "It is too small a thing (*nāqēl* from *qll*) that you should be my servant." The context for this divine word continues to focus on the office of the servant, specifically in the light of his confessed failure in v. 4. Commentators have usually argued that, lest the task of restoring Israel seem too small a task for the servant, God expands his mission to include the nations. However, nowhere in Second Isaiah is the restoration of Israel set in competition with the salvation of the nations. Rather, again the issue turns on the office of the servant. The servant has been promised in v. 5 that he will be glorified (*kbd*); however, the verb "to appear trifling" (niphal of *qll*) in v. 6 expresses the exact antonym of being glorified. The point thus arises from the contrast of the two verbs: "It is too little a thing for the office of the servant that you should raise up Israel." Or, as J. Skinner interpreted: "To restore Israel is the least part of thy vocation as my servant." Rather, his mission as a light to the nations forms the true climax of his divine calling as servant to the God of all creation.

To summarize: Several points of great importance emerge from the description of this faithful servant, Israel, of chapter 49. God confirms that in spite of his momentary failure, his role of establishing right in the earth (42:4) will be sustained. The servant's *mišpāṭ* has now been fully identified with God's own rule of justice, the full implication of which will appear in the servant's vindication in chapter 53.

[7–12] The interpretation of v. 7 has long been a difficult problem. The introductory messenger formula, "Thus says the LORD," is thought to be awkward and not suitable to the content of the following oracle that refers to Yahweh and the Holy One of Israel in the third person. Yet in spite of not following consistently the pattern of oral speech, v. 7 has a clear literary function within the larger composition. It picks up the speech formula of v. 5, and extends it both in v. 7 and again in v. 8 in order to indicate the continuity between the two units, vv. 1–6 and 8–12. However, v. 7 performs a special function in assuring that the servant is seen as the addressee in both oracles. The structuring of v. 7 to serve as a bridge shows every sign of being part of a larger redactional shaping. Yahweh, the Redeemer of Israel, addresses one who is described as "despised and abhorred by the nations, the servant of rulers." The translation of the Hebrew is not without its problems because of the active stem forms of the verbs used, which often has called forth emendations (*BHS*). The translation of the NJPS seeks to render the two Hebrew texts without emendation, but in the end follows the Targum in rendering a passive sense. Attempts to hold to an active sense, "to one abhorring a nation," remain unintelligible within the context. To this despised one there then follows a promise given to him in the form of direct address: "Kings will see you and arise, nobles will prostrate themselves because of Yahweh . . . who has chosen you."

The most remarkable feature of this verse is its content. The verse appears to be a careful paraphrase of 52:13ff., the so-called "fourth" servant song. It follows the same pattern of the servant's humiliation and abuse, his ultimate recognition by kings and rulers, and his final vindication by God. The introduction of the servant in v. 7 as a redactional retrojection assures that the servant is understood as the addressee of vv. 8–12. Moreover, by retrojecting a holistic reading from chapter 53 at this point, the verse forges further a link with the growing theme of the servant's sufferings, which was first introduced in 49:4, continued in 50:4ff., and finally dominates the second portion of Second Isaiah (52:13ff.).

The oracle that appears in vv. 8–12 has also been editorially shaped further to enhance a coherent description of the servant's role in the new exodus of the chosen people, which had been sounded in 48:20ff. Form-critics such as Westermann, who argues that the oracle is a community lament, are forced to eliminate as glosses the very editorial signs that have been provided to establish the chapter's coherence. The messenger formula in v. 8 links the oracle with vv. 5 and 7 and thus functions to render the whole section (vv. 1–13) as one unified divine speech regarding the servant. The phrase "in an hour of favor" resonates with the "but now" of v. 5 and speaks of the eschatological moment of salvation in God's time. Moreover, the citation of 42:6 in v. 8: "I have . . . appointed you a covenant for the people," provides the crucial link with the "first" servant song. The mission of the servant in chapter 49 is a continuation of that originally given to the servant Israel: to be a light to the nations, to open the eyes of the blind, and to release prisoners from darkness. However, chapter 49 expands the servant's task in terms of the restoration of the land (v. 8) and the gathering of the diaspora (v. 12), which are themes closely allied to that of the new exodus.

Again the point should be emphasized that the extension of the servant's role in chapter 49 is not an attempt to replace an earlier corporate understanding of the servant Israel with that of an individual prophetic figure. Rather, the servant always remains Israel, but Israel is now understood within the dynamic movement of the prophetic history as embodied in a suffering, individual figure who has been divinely commissioned to the selfsame task of the deliverance of the chosen people and the nations at large.

[13] The unit concludes in v. 13 in the form of a hymn of praise. This literary device seems to be characteristic of the entire book and recurs in 42:10–13, 44:23, and 48:20–22. A similar call for a liturgical response is also occasionally found as conclusions to earlier sections (e.g., 12:5–6). The summons to both heaven and earth to exalt is explicitly grounded in the comfort and compassion of God toward his afflicted people. Especially the use of the verb "comfort" resonates with the leitmotif in 40:1, but also points forward to the comforting of Zion in 51:3 and 66:13.

51. Isaiah 49:14–50:11

49:14 But Zion says,
> The LORD has forsaken me,
> my God has forgotten me."

15 Can a woman forget her nursing baby,
> and have no feelings for the child she has borne?
> Though she might forget,
> I could never forget you.

16 Look, I have engraved you
> on the palms of my hands;
> your walls are forever before me.

17 Your sons[a] are hastening back.
> Those who devastated and revisited you are departing.

18 Lift up your eyes around you and see:
> they all gather and come to you.

As I live, says the LORD,
   you will wear them all like jewels,
   ordain yourself with them like a bride.
19 As for your wasted and desolate places
   and your land in ruins—
you will surely be too crowded for your inhabitants,
   and those who devoured you will be distant.
20 The children born in your bereavement
   will yet say in your hearing,
"This place is too small for us;
   give us more space to settle."
21 You will say to yourself,
   "Who ever bore me these?
I was bereaved and sterile,
   exiled and rejected;
   who has brought them up?
I was left all alone,
   but from where have these come?"
22 Thus says the Lord GOD,
"I will raise my hand to nations,
   and lift up my banner to the peoples;
and they will bring your sons in their arms,
   and carry your daughters on their shoulders.
23 Kings will be your foster fathers,
   and their queens will serve as nurses.
They will bow down to you, face to the ground,
   and lick the dust of your feet.
Then you will know that I am the LORD;
   those who trust in me will not be ashamed."
24 Can spoil be taken from a warrior,
   or captives rescued from a victor?[b]
25 Yet thus says the LORD:
"Captives will be taken from a warrior,
   and spoil rescued from a tyrant.
I will contend with those who contend with you
   and I will deliver your children.
26 I will make your oppressors eat their own flesh.
   They will be drunk on their own blood as with wine.
Then all humankind will know
   that I am the LORD, your Savior,
   the mighty one of Jacob, your Redeemer."
50:1 Thus says the LORD:

"Where is your mother's bill of divorce
    with which I sent her away?
Or to which of my creditors
    did I sell you?
Because of your sins, you were sold,
    and your mother was dismissed for your fault.

2   When I came, why was there no one there;
    when I called, why did none respond?
Is my arm too short to redeem you?
    Do I lack the strength to save?
Merely with a rebuke I dry up the sea,
    and turn rivers into a desert.
Their fish rot from lack of water
    and lie dead of thirst.

3   I clothe the sky with darkness
    and make sackcloth their covering."

4   The Lord GOD has given me a tongue of one taught,
    to know how to sustain the weary with a word.
Morning by morning he awakens,
    he wakens my ear to listen like disciples.

5   The Lord GOD has opened my ear,^{c}
    and I have not been rebellious;
    I did not withdraw.

6   I gave my back to those beating me,
    and my cheeks to those who pulled out my beard.
I did not hide my face
    from insults and spitting.

7   And the Lord GOD has helped me;
    therefore I have not been disgraced.
Therefore I have set my face like a flint,
    and I know I will not be put to shame.

8   He who vindicates me is near.
Who dares contend with me?
    Let us confront each other.
Who is my accuser?
    Let him approach me.

9   It is the Lord GOD who helps me.
    Who can condemn me?
They will all wear out like a garment.
    The moths will devour them.

10   Who among you fears the LORD
    and obeys the voice of the servant?

When he walks in darkness without light,
  let him trust and rely on his God.
11 But now, all you who light fires
  and furnish yourselves with flaming torches,
  go, walk in the light of your own fires
  and of the blaze you have lit!
  This is what will come from my hand:
  you will lie down in torment!

a. It is possible that a double reading ("sons"/"builders") is preserved in the consonants. The NRSV follows the second alternative. Cf. the exposition and *BHS*.
  b. The MT reads "victor" (*ṣaddîq*); 1QIsᵃ has "tyrant" (*ʿārîs*). The latter reading occurs
in the parallel in v. 25. It may be either a textual corruption or a stylistic variation.
  c. In his commentary on 50:4–9, Beuken has followed the stichometry of P. van der
Lugt, by which verses 5a and 7a are read as monocola. The approach has the advantage of
requiring few emendations. Still, I am not convinced that this poetic ordering has greatly
aided in the interpretation of the passage and it remains largely an aesthetic judgment.

Selected Bibliography

K. Baltzer, "Zur formsgeschichtlichen Bestimmung der Texte vom Gottes-Knecht im Deuterojesaja-
Buch," *Probleme biblischer Theologie, Fs G. von Rad,* ed. H. W. Wolff, Munich 1970, 27–43; **W. A. M.
Beuken,** "Jes 50, 10–11: Eine kultische Paränese zur dritten Ebedprophetie," *ZAW* 85, 1973, 168–82;
K. Elliger, *Deuterojesaja in seinem Verhältnis zu Tritojesaja,* BWANT 63, Stuttgart 1933, 38–56; **H.-J.
Hermisson,** "Der Lohn des Knechts," *Die Botschaft und die Boten, Fs H. W. Wolff,* ed. J. Jeremias and
L. Perlitt, Neukirchen-Vluyn 1981, 269–87; **H. Leene,** *De stem van de knecht als metafoor: Beschouwin-
gen over de composite van Jesaja 50,* Kampen 1980; **P. van der Lugt,** "De strofische structuur van het
derde knechtslied," *De Knecht. Studies rondom Deutero-Jesaja, Fs J. L. Koole,* Kampen 1978, 102–17;
R. F. Melugin, *The Formation of Isaiah 40–55,* BZAW 141, Berlin 1976, 148–56; **R. P. Merendino,**
"Jes 49:14–26: Jahwes Bekenntnis zu Sion und die neue Heilszeit," *RB* 89, 1982, 321–69; **D. Murray,**
"The Rhetoric of Disputation: Re-examination of a Prophetic Genre," *JSOT* 38, 1987, 95–121;
A. Schoors, *I Am God Your Saviour,* VTSup 24, Leiden 1973, 104–21; **O. H. Steck,** "Zion als Gelände
und Gestalt. Überlegung zur Wahrnehmung als Stadt und Frau im Alten Testament," *ZTK* 86, 1989,
261–81; "Beobachtungen zu Jesaja 49, 14–26," *Gottesknecht und Zion,* FAT 4, 1992, 47–59.

1. Structure of the Larger Section

When entering this section, it becomes clear that the themes sounded first in
chapter 49 have continued in the cycle of chapters 49—55, themes that set it
apart from chapters 40—48. The name Israel has largely been replaced by
Zion/Jerusalem. The servant, now the embodiment of Israel (49:3), moves to
center stage and his response in suffering obedience is set in striking contrast
to the complaints of Israel. The opposition and scorn of his opponents from
within Israel mounts until it reaches a climax in chapter 53.

  Formal literary indices that mark the boundaries of the larger sections within
the cycle are often indistinct. This structural issue is not as important as fre-

quently suggested by commentators since the continuing movement within the chapters is often unaffected. The hymnic oracle of 49:13 seems to form a clear and appropriate conclusion to the prior section. Then in spite of a somewhat unusual aversive particle in 49:14 at the head of a new section, the initial complaint of Zion sounds a theme that provides the critical context for the oracles that follow. The obedient servant alone responds to the promise of salvation offered again by God to his people. The section concludes in 50:10–11 with an oracle that serves as a commentary on the preceding servant song and is clearly set apart from chapter 51.

In sum, the larger section of 49:14–50:11 can best be divided into four smaller units:

49:14–26   Refutation of Zion's complaints
50:1–3   Zion's refusal to receive God's proffered salvation
50:4–9   The servant's suffering and continued trust in God
50:10–11   The challenge to identify with the servant's faith

2. Exposition

[49:14–26] There has been considerable discussion by commentators regarding the exact divisions within this unit. Much of the debate arose out of concern to establish form-critically the form and function of the discrete parts within the composition. Traditionally, three different subsections have been discerned: vv. 14–22; 22–23; 24–26. More recently a case has been made for a two-part division, vv. 14–21 and 22–26, with the final unit assigned to a later redactional level. It is evident that form-critics (e.g., Westermann) can discern elements from a disputation or a trial, but such observations are of little help in setting the context. Almost immediately one is forced to suggest that these elements are actually imitations of oral patterns which are now used for a new literary purpose. Therefore, there seems little point in pursuing the details among Begrich, Westermann, and Schoors. Diminishing returns seems to have set in.

It is more important exegetically to see how the imagery of Zion, city, and bereaved mother are intertwined and developed in response to the initial complaint. Zion says, "The LORD has forsaken me, my God has forgotten me" (v. 14). The tone of the refutation is not that of a classic disputation. Rather, the evidence of God's unfailing faithfulness to his people is first reiterated in the reflective tones of sapiential wisdom. Just as it is impossible for a mother to abandon her newborn infant, it is even more unthinkable for God to forget his people. "I have engraved you on the palms of my hands; your walls are forever before me" (v. 16). Then Zion is instructed simply to look up and observe. She is to see for herself what is actually happening. The promise of restoration is appearing before her very eyes.

Two themes are artfully intertwined in vv. 17 and 18: the return of the children and the rebuilding of the walls. In fact, some have argued that in the Hebrew consonants of *bnyk* (v. 17) a double reading is retained, namely, the MT pointing *bānāyik* ("sons") and the Greek and Qumran rendering *bōnayik* ("builders"). The reference to the children returning continues in vv. 18, 20–22, whereas the restoration of Zion picks up the theme of the walls in v. 16 and extends the imagery into v. 19. Zion, the bereaved mother, is admonished simply to look. The scattered children are assembling. They come to be worn like jewels for a bride. With a note of exuberant celebration, Zion's children announce that they need more room to accommodate their sheer numbers. Then in astonishment the barren mother will exclaim: "Whoever bore me these? I was bereaved and sterile. . . . [W]ho has brought them up? I was left standing all alone, but from where have these come?" Those who once inflicted Israel with devastation (vv. 17 and 19) will simply disappear from the joyous scene.

Because of the introduction of a new messenger formula, vv. 22–23 are often distinguished as a discrete unit. However, the theme of these verses is largely a continuation of what preceded. The new note sounded turns on the role of the nations in bringing back Zion's sons and daughters, of course, now in their function as servants and slaves. Because the imagery of aliens and foreigners now serving Israel is a recurring theme in Third Isaiah (e.g., 61:5ff.), some commentators have argued for a redactional level in these verses different from that of Second Isaiah (Elliger, 124ff.), but such a case is difficult to make on linguistic grounds. Rather, the coercion exerted by the coherence of the whole passage emerges as a force against the fragmentation involved in such theories.

In v. 24 the element of a second complaint associated with a disputation appears. Does Yahweh really have the power to deliver his captive people? The complaint serves to evoke again a divine announcement of his power and will for Israel's deliverance. In a series of bold statements, the oppressor's power is assessed. God will take on in battle the mighty, the warriors, and victors, tyrants, and adversaries. Not only will they be humbled and shamed, but the ultimate goal of Yahweh's victory, first stated in regard to Israel (v. 23), is expanded to include all the nations of the world: "Then all humankind will know that I am the LORD, your Savior, the mighty one of Jacob."

Often at this juncture commentators contrast these harsh words directed to the nations with the earlier and completely positive invitation for all to return and be saved (e.g., 45:22ff.). Yet it is highly misleading to set up a polarity between passages allegedly universalistic and those of ethnic narrowness. Much turns on the specific issue at stake in the oracle. If the prophet is addressing the scope of God's salvific will toward his creation, the free inclusion of the nations is an integral part of the prophet's message. However, if the issue turns on rival claims of power and authority exercised by the mighty and powerful rulers of the world, then the harshest possible rejection of their pretensions is made. Yahweh alone is Lord and Redeemer, who tolerates no rivals either on heaven or earth. The theme in chapter 49 thus lies in closest continuity with the earlier disputations of chapters 40 and 41.

[50:1–3] This passage has some obvious connections with the preceding one. There is a strong disputational tone and the theme of the mother and her children is continued. Once again God defends himself against an accusation. Nevertheless, the logic of the references to the "mother's bill of divorce" and to a creditor to whom the addressees have been sold (v. 1) is not as clear as one might at first have thought. As a result, various interpretations have been offered in an attempt to clarify the intention of the passage.

Form-critics have usually argued that the key to interpretation lies in discerning the genre of the oracle as a disputation speech that seeks to imitate a trial in confronting a false claim and then in affirming Yahweh's sole authority. Although this appeal to an adaptation of a conventional genre is not wrong, the effect of such an interpretation is frequently to obscure the specificity of the passage's function by focusing its attention on general patterns of speech. An important initial check is to keep sharply in view the oracle's role in providing a bridge between Zion's complaint in 49:14–26 and the faithful response of the servant in 50:4–9. The issue of genre is largely subordinated in importance to the basic subject matter at stake in the section as a whole.

The oracle is again introduced by a simple messenger formula (cf. 49:22, 25), which is followed by a first person divine speech: "Where is your mother's bill of divorce?" Some have argued that the point implied in the question is that because there is no such bill, the bereaved mother has not been put away by God. However, this portion is difficult to reconcile with v. 1b where it is plainly stated that the mother has been put away. Others suggest some modification of the question by seeking a further clarification in appealing to the exact wording of the original law as found in Deut. 24:1–4. For example, because there is no bill of divorce available, the rejection of the mother cannot be viewed legally as a permanent status. Then again, others think that the reference to the law focuses not on the fact of the repudiation, but rather on its legal justification.

A major problem of the oracle is that the foundation to which the initial legal appeal is made is not carried through with complete consistency, but points in another narrative direction. The accusation falls, not on some legal issue of the past regarding the mother's rejection, but on the present sins of the children. Their transgressions caused them to be sold into slavery and Zion rejected. The function of the oracle then becomes clear. When God came as promised in chapter 49 to effect Zion's deliverance, there was no response. When he called, no one answered (v. 2). When 50:1–3 is read in the narrative context of chapters 48 and 49, the accusation is highly existential. At issue is not some technical legal debate. Zion refused the call of 48:20 to depart from Babylon and to participate in the divine deliverance offered. She continued to complain that she had been forgotten (49:4), and doubted whether God had the power to deliver (49:24; 50:2).

The response by God to Israel's repudiation of his salvation in 50:2ff. is highly significant in its present literary sequence. God does not seek further to persuade Israel, but the rejection results in a demonstration of the creator's power in judgment. By his rebuke he dries up the sea and makes the rivers a desert. He makes the fish stink and clothes the heavens with blackness. The biblical imagery is of God's judgment on Egypt at the exodus, but now it falls on Israel, who had just refused to share in the "new exodus" by being led through the wilderness without thirst and with an abundance of water and light.

[4–9] However, not all of Israel was disobedient. A first person voice is suddenly sounded, indeed the same voice first heard in 48:16 ("the Lord GOD has sent me"). This one had delivered the promise and challenge of deliverance in 48:17ff. In 49:3 the voice was identified with that of the servant, who was designated to be the embodiment of Israel ("You are my servant, you are Israel"), and given the task of both bringing Jacob back and of being a light to the nations. The task that the nation Israel had been given and failed to accomplish (42:1–9) had been transferred, not away from Israel, but rather to one who would incarnate Israel (cf. 49:1–6).

Now in contrast to Israel's refusal, the faithful servant, the embodiment of the chosen nation, is again heard. The form of the oracle—Duhm's "third servant song"—is that of a monologue, which fits roughly within the broader genre of a trust psalm. Three times in the oracle God is referred to as the *"Adonai YHWH"* (vv. 4, 7, 9). This usage occurs elsewhere in Second Isaiah (40:10; 51:22; 52:4), but especially it is spoken by the servant in 48:16 in reference to his commission. In v. 4 it serves to pick up and to continue the intensity of the servant's testimony to his calling. Although the term *servant* is not used in vv. 4–9, the larger context, before and after, removes any possible doubt that the speaker is the servant.

In the confession that follows, the servant rehearses his divine commission. God has given him a "tongue of one taught," one instructed for being a disciple (*limmûd*). Some commentators have tried to connect the term with its reference in 8:16 in which the prophet Isaiah is instructed "to seal the teachings among my disciples" following his rejection by King Ahaz. The suggestion is then made that the servant is thus identifying himself with the line of Isaiah's followers. However, a more immediate context is found in 48:17, which is the oracle delivered to recalcitrant Israel by the servant: "I am Yahweh your God, who teaches you what profits, guiding you on the way you should go." The servant testifies to having reviewed the tongue of one willing to be taught. In 49:2 the emphasis was on his mouth as a sharp sword. Here it is on knowing how to comfort the weary with a suitable word. Each morning he awakens to be taught further.

What the servant learned was not information, but to accept the experience of suffering and shame. Earlier (49:4) he had confessed his failure to persuade a resisting people. Now the negative response intensifies into physical violence from which the servant did not retreat. Verse 6 recounts the full scope of his oppression: he was beaten, insulted, and he submitted to the vilest outrages of physical humiliation. Isaiah 49:7 had spoken of his being deeply despised and abhorred. In 50:6 the horrible details are portrayed, much like those experienced by the innocent sufferers of the Psalter (Psalms 22; 31; 35).

However, v. 6 serves only as a backdrop for the climax of the servant's confession of trust in God. Once again he bears testimony to *Adonai YHWH* who sustains him. "Therefore I have not been disgraced. Therefore I have set my face like a flint" (v. 7). In 49:4 the servant testified that "my case is in the LORD's hand." In 50:8 he returns to the same theme. God who vindicates him is present. Three resounding and defiant expressions of his confidence follow: "Who dares contend with me?" "Who is my accuser?" "Who can condemn me?" The confession of unswerving trust ends on the assured note that his oppressors will be exhausted and devoured.

In this song, the theme of the suffering of the servant enters a new dimension. The servant Israel had been called in 42:1ff. to bring justice to the nations, even while working unobtrusively, not even breaking a bruised reed or extinguishing a smoldering wick. However, the one who became the "learner," who had assumed the role of the servant to restore the remnant of Israel (49:3, 6), is now led along a new path of suffering and deepest humiliation. When seen in the larger context of the narrative movement within chapters 40–55, there is a clear transfer from Israel, the servant nation, to Israel, the suffering individual who now embodies the nation's true mission.

[10–11] There is widespread agreement that vv. 10–11 constitute a separate oracle from that which precedes. The servant is no longer the speaker, but one spoken about. In a literary development much like the extension of 49:7 in relation to 49:1–6, once again there is a commentary-like addition in vv. 10–11 to the preceding servant song, which seeks to draw out the implications of that which has occurred. Moreover, once again the tone of the extension reflects a certain sense of distance from the events, and appears to share the wider perspective of the larger literary context, including perhaps chapter 53.

The initial difficulty in interpreting the unit turns on the syntactical problem of relating the various clauses to one another. The problem has been pursued in great length by Beuken (168ff.). The first option is to take the relative clause in v. 10b as referring to the servant as well as all the following verbal clauses: "The servant who walks in darkness . . . trusts in the name of Yahweh and relies upon his God." The second option is to take the final two verbal clauses in v. 10b as addressed to someone other than the servant: "Let that one trust and rely on his God." The third option takes all the clauses of 10b after the *'ašer* particle as referring to one other than the servant: "When he walks in darkness without light, let him trust and rely on his God."

In my judgment, Beuken has mounted a strong case in favor of the third option. A challenge is extended to anyone who rightly fears the Lord, and thus identifies with the message of the servant, to trust in God even though it still involves walking on a path of darkness, just like the servant. The call to follow the servant is not directed to some well-defined political group (*contra* Hanson), but is addressed in the singular to those individuals, whoever they are, to make a witness to the truth. Of course, that the community of Israel is divided over the servant is fully clear. Therefore, in v. 11 a word of judgment is directed to those who have tried to create their own light as a way out of the present darkness. There is also a command, "walk in the light of your own fires," but the result is to experience the most bitter punishment from God, who turns the torment that they have created upon themselves.

It has been argued by some critical commentators that vv. 10–11 are much later in age than Second Isaiah, and are to be assigned to the pessimistic message of Third Isaiah. I would agree that there is some reflective distance between vv. 4–9 and 10–11. However, the crucial exegetical issue turns on determining how vv. 10–11 relate to the literary composition of Second Isaiah as a whole. To see in vv. 10–11 a later, pessimistic addition, which largely distorts the message of the servant songs, is badly to miss the point of the oracle. Actually vv. 10–11 pick up the growing theme from chapters 48ff. of a disobedient community that resists the offer of deliverance (48:17ff.) and that torments the servant, who alone bears faithful testimony to God in trust. The call to any within the exiled and despondent community to respond to the servant's word serves to anticipate the voice of a faithful Israel in chapter 53, who finally confesses to understand the divine role of the suffering servant in the plan of God. To be sure, a level of redactional shaping is evident in 49:7 and 50:10–11, but it reflects the hand of an editor who is working with a knowledge of the entire Second Isaianic corpus. From the holistic perspective, he seeks to offer a redactional clarification of this salvific history that extends throughout chapters 40–55.

52. Isaiah 51:1–52:12

51:1 "Listen to me, you who pursue righteousness,
    you who seek the LORD.
Look to the rock from which you were cut,
    and to the quarry from which you were dug.
2 Look to Abraham, your father,
    and to Sarah who gave you birth.
When I called him, he was but one,
    but I blessed him and made him many."
3 Surely the LORD will comfort Zion

and will look with compassion on all her ruins.
He will make her deserts like Eden,
  her wilderness like the garden of the LORD.
Joy and gladness will be found in her,
  thanksgiving and the sound of music.

4 "Listen to me, my people,
  hear me, my nation;
for the law will go forth from one,
  and my justice for a light to the nations.
I will bring it speedily.[a]

5 My salvation nears, my deliverance proceeds,
  my arm will bring justice to the peoples.
The coastlands wait for me,
  and await with hope for my arm.

6 Lift up your eyes to the heavens,
  and look at the earth below.
The heavens will vanish like smoke,
  the earth will wear out like a piece of clothing,
  and its inhabitants will die as well.[b]
But my salvation will last forever,
  and my righteousness will never fail.

7 Listen to me, you who know the right,
  people with my law in their hearts.
Do not fear the abuse of people,
  and do not be threatened at their insults.

8 For the moth will eat them up like a garment,
  and the worm will consume them like wool.
But my righteousness will last forever,
  and my salvation throughout all generations."

9 Awake, awake, clothe yourself with strength,
  O arm of the LORD!
Awake, as in days past,
  as in former times!
Was it not you who cut Rahab to pieces,
  who pierced the dragon?

10 Was it not you who dried up the sea,
  the waters of the great deep,
who made a path in the heart of the sea
  for the redeemed to cross over?

11 The ransomed of the LORD will return,
  and come to Zion with shouts;
everlasting joy will crown their heads,

joy and gladness will overtake them,
 while sorrow and sighing will flee.

12 "I myself am the one comforting you.
  What is the matter that you fear people,
  mortals who are like grass?

13 You have forgotten the LORD your Creator,
  who stretched out the heavens
  and laid the foundations of the earth.
 You live every day in constant dread
  because of the anger of the oppressor,
 who is intent on destruction.
  But where is the fury of the oppressor?

14 Very shortly the cowed one will be freed.
  He will not succumb to the pit,
  nor will he lack food.

15 For I am the LORD your God,
  who churns up the sea so that its waves roar—
  the LORD of hosts is his name.

16 I have put my words in your mouth
  and hidden you in the shadow of my hand,
 setting the heavens in place,
  and laying the foundations of the earth,
  who said to Zion, "You are my people.'"

17 Rouse yourself, rouse yourself,
  stand up, O Jerusalem.
 You who have drunk the cup of wrath
  from the hand of the LORD,
 you who have emptied to the dregs
  the bowl of staggering.

18 Of all the sons she bore,
  there is none to guide her.
 Of all the sons she reared,
  none takes her by the hand.

19 A double calamity has come upon you—
  ruin and devastation—who can console you?
  famine and sword—who can comfort you?[c]

20 Your sons have fainted,
  they lie at the end of every street
  like an antelope caught in a net.
 They are full of the anger of the LORD
  and the rebuke of your God.

21   Therefore, listen to this, you afflicted one,
          who are drunk, but not from wine!
22   Thus says the L ORD, your Lord,
          your God, who intercedes for his people:
      "Look, I have removed from your hand
          the bowl of staggering, the cup of my wrath,
      you shall never drink of it again.
23   I will put it into the hands of your tormentors,[d]
          who said to you,
          'Lie prostrate that we may walk over you.'
      So you made your back like the ground,
          like a street for them to walk on."
52:1 Awake, awake, O Zion,
          clothe yourself in strength.
      Put on your robes of splendor,
          Jerusalem, holy city.
      For the uncircumcised and the unclean
          will never again enter you.
2   Shake off the dust, arise,
          sit enthroned, Jerusalem.
      Loosen the chains from your neck,
          O captive daughter of Zion.
3   For thus says the L ORD:
          "You were sold for nothing,
      and without a payment you will be redeemed."
4   For thus says the Lord G OD:
          "At first my people went down to Egypt to live.
      Later Assyria oppressed them,
          giving nothing in return.
5   Now what do I gain here, says the L ORD,
          for my people have been carried off for nothing.
      Their rulers howl,[e] says the L ORD, and
          all day long constantly my name is blasphemed.
6   Therefore, my people will know my name,
          surely in that day they will learn
      that it is I who promised. Here I am."
7   How lovely on the mountains
          are the footsteps of the herald
          announcing good news,
      who proclaims peace,
          who brings good tidings,

who proclaims salvation,
who says to Zion, "Your God reigns."

8   Listen, your watchmen lift up their voices,
      together they sing for joy;
      for with their own eyes they will see
      the Lord return to Zion.

9   Break out together into singing,
      you ruins of Jerusalem,
      for the LORD has comforted his people,
      he has redeemed Jerusalem.

10   The LORD will bare his holy arm
      in the sight of all the nations,
      and all the ends of the earth will see
      the salvation of our God.

11   Turn away, turn away, go from there!
      Touch no unclean thing.
      Come away from it and keep pure,
      you who carry the vessels of the LORD.

12   But you will not depart in haste
      or leave in flight,
      for the LORD will go before you
      and the God of Israel is your rear guard.

a. The LXX appears to attach the final verb of v. 4 (*'argî*ʿ) to v. 5, which proposal has been accepted by *BHS* and Westermann.

b. The Hebrew *kᵉmô-kēn* ("like this") does not occur elsewhere. The text has often been emended to read "gnats," but without strong evidence.

c. The MT reads "how will I comfort you?" but the major versions along with 1QIsᵃ read a third masculine singular form.

d. The LXX has an extra colon: "and those who afflict you." In spite of the supporting format of *BHS*, the evidence for the longer text is inconclusive.

e. 1QIsᵃ reads "to deride or mark" (*whwllw*), which has been accepted by the NIV and NEB.

Selected Bibliography

J. Fichtner, "Jes. 52, 7–10 in der christlichen Verkündigung," *Verbannung und Heimkehr, Fs W. Rudolph,* ed. A Kuschke, Tübingen 1961, 51–66; **H. Gunkel,** *Schöpfung und Chaos in Urzeit und Endzeit,* Göttingen 1895; **W. Herrmann,** "Das Aufleben des Mythos unter den Judäern während des babylonischen Zeitalters," *BN* 40, 1987, 47–129; **F. Holmgren,** "Chiastic Structure in Isaiah LI 1–11," *VT* 19, 1969, 196–201; **K. Kiesow,** *Exodustexte im Jesajabuch,* OBO 24, 1979, 93–113; **J. K. Kuntz,** "The Contribution of Rhetorical Criticism to Understanding Isaiah 51:1–16," *Art and Meaning: Rhetoric in Biblical Literature,* JSOT-Sup 19, 1982, 140–71; **R. F. Melugin,** *The Formation of Isaiah 40–55,* BZAW 141, Berlin 1976, 159–67;

O. H. Steck, "Zur literarischen Schichtung in Jesaja 51," *Gottesknecht und Zion*, FAT, 1992, 60–72; "Zions Tröstung. Beobachtungen und Fragen zu Jesaja 51, 1–11," ibid., 73–91; **N. A. van Uchelen,** "Abraham als Felsen (Jes. 51, 1)," *ZAW* 80, 1968, 183–91; **J. M. Vincent,** *Studien zur literarischen Eigenart und zur geistigen Heimat von Jesaja, Kap. 40—55,* BET 5, Frankfurt and Bern 1997, 108–23.

1. Structure and Form

There is widespread agreement that 51:1 forms the clear beginning of a section and that 52:12 offers a suitable ending. Moreover, the recognition that 52:13–15 belongs to chapter 53 was made early on by interpreters of Isaiah (cf. E. F. C. Rosenmüller, *Scholia, Jesajae,* 3:323ff.). There remain minor disagreements on the divisions within this parameter that, fortunately, are not of great exegetical significance.

Far more important is how one envisions the unity or lack of it within this section. Duhm's approach is characteristic of the older literary-critical approach in seeing a series of oracles stemming from the hand of Second Isaiah (vv. 1–7) to which have been joined interpolations from a later hand who cited verses from earlier collections (e.g., vv. 9–11). Duhm saw 51:17–52:12 as a unified poem of five strophes that, however, suffered damage in 52:1–3 from various prosaic accretions. Influences from this same approach of identifying and rearranging literary fragments are still visible in Westermann's rather unconvincing analysis of 51:1–11. Among the form-critics, Melugin offers a careful analysis of the different oral forms present in the chapter, but goes beyond Begrich's classic analysis by heroically trying to overcome the atomizing effect that seems indigenous to the method. The effect is greatly to relativize the significance of the form-critical distinctions. Clearly other important editorial forces were at work in the lengthy process of shaping the literature.

Finally, one should mention the redactional approach reflected in Steck's several articles on chapter 51. The author attempts to reconstruct various horizontal levels into a historical trajectory along which the present conflated text developed. In my opinion, the approach is highly subjective and largely unhelpful (cf. my criticism in "Retrospective Reading," 362–77). In contrast, Beuken offers an illuminating interpretation of chapter 51 that probes both the synchronic and diachronic dimensions of the text. Especially helpful is his continuing concern to work within the explicit context of the larger prophetic history that unfolds within chapters 40—55. The effect is to avoid rendering the different voices into a flat monotony, while at the same time escaping an atomization of the text that loses the inner dynamic of the prophetic composition.

2. Exposition

[51:1–8] This unit is usually subdivided into three smaller sections (vv. 1–3; 4–6; 7–8), each of which is introduced with an imperative calling for attention.

The entire unit is rendered as a divine word offering words of promise to Zion, but with different emphases in each separate part. Of central importance is the continuity of context established in the preceding passage. Isaiah 50:10–11 challenged those who fear God to come forward in an identification with the obedient servant, and thereby to set themselves apart from those who had heaped abuse on the servant for their own aggrandizement.

Verse 1 designates the addressee as those "who pursue righteousness, who seek the LORD." To those who so respond, the challenge is given to return to the roots of the faith, to Abraham and Sarah, the source of the nation's true identity. The imagery of Abraham, the rock, and of Sarah, the quarry, are multivalent and evoke a variety of reverberations within the tradition. Both images portray the nature of the salvation that has been promised. Abraham is the rock on which the house was first built. Sarah is the cavity from which Israel emerged into life. The imagery of hard stone also hearkens back to the long period of expectation and fruitless waiting until God finally brought forth life from what seemed to be two sterile bodies—surely a result of divine intervention. Finally, the reference to the one being the source of the many calls to mind the small and pitiful beginnings of those in Israel who also responded in faith to the promise once delivered.

The promise of God's comforting of Zion is repeated, like a red thread that extends from 40:1 both forward and backward in the book of Isaiah (51:3, 19; 61:2; 66:13; 12:1). The imagery of the wilderness like Eden and a desert like the garden (v. 23) reverberates with the earlier divine promises in 41:17ff. The language is also found in chapter 35 and supports the sense of continuity of the selfsame hope of restoration, joy, and blessing found throughout the entire Isaianic corpus.

In v. 4 the addressee is named "my people," "my nation." The referent is thus clearly the faithful within Israel who have responded to the servant. They are to listen when the nature of God's salvation is described as the same goal that was first set forth to the servant Israel in 42:1ff. God's torah will go forth, for which the coastlands wait (51:4, 5 // 42:4), and his justice will be for "a light to the nations" (51:4 // 42:6; 49:6). The effect of this promise is that the sharp line once separating Israel from the nations has been overcome, and the new people of God emerges as encompassing all those responding in faith to God. Often the appeal to look to the heavens serves to remind Israel of the creative sovereignty of God, but here the divine power is exercised in apocalyptic judgment. The heavens and earth—the gracious setting for God's rule—will disappear as part of the old, corrupt order, but God's true salvation will endure forever, as was always in accord with the divine purpose in his creation.

The final imperative to listen in vv. 7ff. further defines the heart of God's people: "Listen to me, you who know the right (*ṣedeq*), people with my law in their hearts." The imagery is again taken from 42:4, 6. God's new people, like

Israel of old (10:24), is not to fear the scorn of others. The ungodly will perish, but God's deliverance will endure forever. Behind this fresh prophetic formulation one can still discern the older conventions of the oracle of salvation (*Heilsorakel*), which were so prominent in the earlier chapters of Second Isaiah (e.g., 41:8ff.).

[9–16] Scholars have often divided these verses into very small form-critical units or, conversely, projected a large literary composition extending into chapter 52. In one sense, both of these approaches have made a contribution. The former correctly saw the traces of conventional forms at work, while the latter rightly observed elements of literary continuity, such as the use of the double imperatives in vv. 9, 17, and 52:1. The real exegetical task lies in striking a suitable balance between these extremes, avoiding both the tendencies to fragment or to harmonize the text.

The oracle beginning in v. 9 is addressed to Yahweh, and much like the conventional community lament (cf. Ps. 44:24ff.) urges God to arouse himself and come to Israel's aid. The assumption reflected in the idiom is that God indeed has the power to effect a change if he so desires. Thus the psalmist, when in dire straits, continually urges God to move into action. The plea generally follows the pattern of the lament in rehearsing the great acts of divine assistance in the past as a further reason for requesting immediate intervention (Ps. 44:2ff.).

There has been much discussion ever since Gunkel (*Schöpfung und Chaos*, 30ff.) first introduced the subject of the mythological nature of the language employed. Was it not Yahweh who in the primeval age "cut Rahab in pieces and pierced the dragon?" The mythical figure appears in Ps. 89:11 and Job 26:12 as a sea monster, and is subsequently historicized as a symbol for Egypt (Isa. 30:7; 51:9; Ps. 87:4). Gunkel's derivation of the figure from Babylonian mythology has been expanded and modified following the discovery of the Ugaritic texts. It became increasingly evident that the conflict with the primordial dragon existed in various forms, usually not connected with an original creation theme.

Verses 9ff. offer a classic example of how the Hebrew Bible appropriated ancient Near Eastern tradition for its own purpose in a demythologized form. In v. 10 the drying up of the sea (*yām*) is set in apposition to "the waters of the great deep" (*tᵉhôm rabbāh*), which reference continues the mythological idiom of creation as an overcoming of the powers of chaos (Gen. 1:2; Ps. 33:7; 104:6). Yet immediately the imagery of the depths is reinterpreted as providing a way for the redeemed to pass through the waters at the time of Israel's deliverance from the Egyptians at the Red Sea (Ex. 14:22). Then quickly the reference moves to the Babylonian exiles who return to Zion with singing and great joy. The point has long since been made that the depiction is not of three separate events spread along a historical trajectory, but rather that the occurrences are three moments in the one purpose of God for Israel's salvation. Because the content of God's redemptive intervention, that is, its substance, is the same, the three events have been fused together as a unified ontological witness to the one purpose of God concerning his people.

Yet it is crucial to recognize from the larger context of vv. 9–11 within chapters 50 and 51 that the people of God have continued to be defined as the new order of those who seek the Lord and identify with the obedient response of the servant. Verses 9ff. thus emerge as the voice of the new people of God, who now bring forth a prayer for God finally to usher in the long awaited eschatological hope of joy and gladness.

In vv. 12–16 God's response to Israel's prayer is given. God reiterates his promise to Israel in the familiar form of the self-predication: "I myself am the one." The theme of comfort returns to the note sounded in 51:3 and first signalled as a major prophetic pronouncement in 40:1. The form of the oracle does not follow closely that of the oracle of salvation, yet the repeated admonition not to fear echoes throughout the passage. Israel who is bowed down will shortly experience deliverance as the anger of the oppressor is broken. The promise is grounded in God's creative power and again is developed with the image of the sea and God's sovereignty over the waves, as in 51:10.

Of particular note are vv. 15 and 16, which have generally been dismissed by the commentators as a misplaced fragment (Westermann), or from a late redactional layer akin to that of 59:21 (Steck). Others observe that the collective referent of v. 13 has been replaced by the servant who is an individual. Much emphasis has also been placed on the apparent citation of Jer. 31:35b in v. 15 and the correspondence between v. 16a // 59:21 and v. 16b // 49:12. However, Beuken is certainly moving in the right interpretive direction when he again insists on understanding these verses specifically within the context of chapter 51.

The new element in the divine response to the prayer in vv. 9ff. lies precisely in the new role assigned to those who have responded to the Lord by following in the footsteps of the servant (vv. 1ff.). They are the people in whose heart is God's law (v. 7). The promise of God to comfort Israel is reiterated, and his admonition not to fear the fury of the oppressor repeated (cf. 50:10). However, as Beuken has observed, v. 15a forms a bracket by means of a chiasm with v. 16b by repeating Israel's ancient covenant formula: I am Yahweh your God (15a), and you are my people (16b). This appeal to the Sinai covenant is not strange or out of place for Second Isaiah when one recalls the major role the law plays in the portrayal of the new order of justice (v. 7). The God of creation who can stir up the sea in obedient response to his will—Yahweh of hosts is his name (Amos 9:5b)—assigns a new role to the faithful remnant: "I have put my words in your mouth and hidden you in the shadow of my hand." The point of this commission is not that obedient Israel has been fused with the servant. Rather, those who have followed in the servant's footsteps have been assigned a new prophetic task in now bringing the good news to Zion, which is an extension of the servant's task (49:6ff.), namely, "to restore the remnant of Israel," and to be "a light to the nations."

[17–23] The picture of Jerusalem as a woman lying stupefied on the ground, who has been forced to drink the cup of God's wrath, is often thought to be simply a continuation of Israel's communal lament. Westermann converts the third person address into a first person one in order to highlight the original nature of the complaint. Yet by careful attention to the larger context the reader can sense that this is not just more of the same. In v. 16 the faithful community of Israel has been given a prophetic role akin to that of the commissioning of the servant. The execution of this role is then seen in vv. 17–23 as the message of impending deliverance, and restoration is brought to prostrate Jerusalem by those first addressed in 51:5ff.

Dame Jerusalem is first encouraged to rouse herself and to stand. The imagery is the exact opposite of that given to the daughter of Babylon (chapter 47), who is ordered to sit on the ground and to strip in order to reveal her shame. Next, Jerusalem in her present condition is described with words of the conventional lament: wrack and ruin, starvation and sword. She has been forced to drink the cup of God's wrath, described in Ps. 75:9 and Jer. 15:7, which is a metaphor greatly expanded in the postexilic writings (Lam. 4:21; Ezek. 23:31ff.). Jerusalem has been snared like an animal caught in a hunter's net. However, this description of Jerusalem and present desolate state serves only as background for the actual divine word of deliverance that begins in vv. 21ff. Using the messenger's convention of direct address, the prophetic oracle announces to Jerusalem the turn of events and the radical reversal of her fortunes. The cup of wrath will be taken from Jerusalem and forced upon her oppressors as God intercedes for his people.

[52:1–6] This unit has often been divided into two parts (vv. 1–2; 3–6). Both the NRSV and the NEB render vv. 3–6 as a prose insertion within a larger poetic sequence. However, NJPS and NIV (also Torrey, Beuken) understand it, more correctly, as a poetic passage. Frequently, vv. 3–6 are thought foreign to the larger context and expunged (cf. Muilenburg). Yet from a form-critical perspective the pattern of vv. 1–6 follows that of 51:17–23 with an admonition to arise joined with a divine oracle of promise. Moreover, the imagery of the city as an abandoned woman continues and is further developed in vv. 1–6.

However, an important new element does enter, which focuses on the divine name. Jerusalem is to become the holy city, a dwelling that reflects the nature of God's holiness. For that reason, the uncircumcised and unclean will not be allowed in the city to profane the name of God (v. 1). In contrast, Israel, which was once oppressed and exploited by foreigners, will find in a purified city the environment in which to come to know its God. Holy city and divine name are indissoluably joined, and this unimpaired unity is constitutive of the new eschatological order about to be realized. Already in First Isaiah a similar theme had been sounded (1:24ff.; 4:2ff.) that, even if a secondary literary retrojection, was a note assigned by the Isaianic editors to a central function within the earlier literary corpus (chapters 1—12).

[7–10] The initial problem turns on establishing the limits of this oracle. The case will be made below that the form and function of vv. 11–12 distinguish these verses from the song of praise in vv. 7–10.

The striking feature of this oracle is its close relation to the prologue of Second Isaiah (40:1–21). Again we hear of the herald of good tidings announcing the return of God to Zion in might, and the leading of his flock before him. In a very real sense, vv. 7–10 form a suitable conclusion to the eschatological drama first announced in chapter 40 and then unfolded in chapters 40—55. God has forgiven his people and announces his imminent salvation to the exiles languishing in Babylonian captivity.

The structure of the oracle makes clear the summarizing function of the unit. The call in v. 7 evokes a response to the coming messengers of good news who announce the inbreaking of the rule of God. Verse 8 then calls attention to the watchmen seeing the return of Yahweh to Zion, who is shortly to be seen by all. Finally, vv. 9–10 invite all Jerusalem to sing a song of praise because God has comforted his people (cf. 40:1) and all the world will see his salvation. The oracle thus climaxes the prophetic history that has spanned all the succeeding chapters from the prologue of chapter 40.

Nevertheless, the role of 51:7–10 is not simply a rehearsal of what preceded, but it has been decisively shaped by the drama that has unfolded, particularly from chapter 49 onward. Earlier in the corpus the invitation to sing the praises of God had been issued (42:10–12; 44:23; 48:20). However, it is only following the response evoked by the servant that the voice of those who seek the Lord is heard in bringing to Jerusalem the message of God's good news. This is the voice of those confessing God as King, and singing in joy with the watchmen at the return of God to Zion. The prologue had announced the prophetic vision of God's rule. The victories of Cyrus in defeating the oppressor Babylon had confirmed the entrance of God's sovereign rule. However, in 52:7–10 the voice of the new divine order is heard in its song of praise. The reign of God has not just been announced, but the prophetic drama testifies to its actual reception by Zion for all the earth to see.

[11–12] Much controversy revolves about these final verses. Often they are thought to be an unnecessary repetition of 48:20ff., which urged the exiles to flee from Babylon. Others have judged them to be a late redactional addition that emphasizes postexilic, cultic concerns more akin to Third Isaiah than to Second Isaiah.

Yet it should be observed at the outset that there is no mention of Babylon, and the focus is very different from that of 48:20. The issue is hardly one of geography. Rather, the coherence of these verses is established with 52:1–6. The addressees are those in the service of God, "who carry the vessels of the LORD." Those who bear the holy name of Yahweh are admonished to go from that place where God's holiness is not respected. Then unlike the ancient departure from Egyptian captivity, they are not to flee in haste, but deliberately in full confidence because God serves as Israel's rear guard (cf. Ex. 14:19). In sum, these final verses draw out the effect of the hymn of praise in vv. 7–10, and demonstrate that the torah of God to Israel is being observed by those who bear his name in accordance with the righteous reign of God in holiness.

53. Isaiah 52:13–53:12

52:13　Behold, my servant[a] will prosper,
　　　　　be exalted, lifted up, and raised to great heights.
14　Just as there were many appalled at him[b]—
　　　　so marred was his appearance, unlike that of man,
　　　　and his form, hardly human—
15　so will he startle[c] many nations.
　　　　Kings will shut their mouths because of him,
　　　for what they were not told, they will see,
　　　　and what they have not heard, they will understand.
53:1　Who has believed what we have heard,
　　　　and to whom has the arm of the LORD been
　　　　revealed?
2　He grew up before him like a tender shoot,
　　　　and like a root out of arid ground;
　　　he had no form or beauty that we should look at him,
　　　　no charm that we could find attractive.
3　He was despised and shunned by everyone,
　　　　a man of suffering, familiar with disease,
　　　like one from whom people hid their faces.
　　　　He was despised, and we held him in no regard.
4　Surely it was our sickness he bore,
　　　　and our sufferings he carried.
　　　Yet we regarded him as plagued,
　　　　smitten by God and afflicted.
5　But he was wounded because of our sins,
　　　　he was bruised for our iniquities.
　　　The punishment that brought us peace
　　　　　was on him,
　　　　and by his wounds we are healed.

6   We have all gone astray like sheep,
          each going his own way;
     and the LORD laid on him
          the guilt of us all.
7   He was oppressed and afflicted,
          yet he did not open his mouth.
     Like a lamb being led to slaughter,
          or like a sheep silent before her shearers,
          he did not open his mouth.
8   Through oppressive judgment he was taken away,
          but from his generation who considered?
     For he was cut off from the land of the living,
          for the sin of my people he received the blow.[d]
9   And they made his grave among the wicked,
          and with the rich in his death,[e]
     although he had done no violence,
          nor had he spoken anything false.
10   Yet it was the will of the LORD to crush him
          and afflict him with sickness.[f]
     When his life serves as compensation for guilt,[g]
          he will see offspring and have long life,
     and the will of the LORD will prosper in his hands.
11   From the agony of his soul he will see,[h]
          and he shall be satisfied.
     By his knowledge shall the righteous one, my servant,
          make many to be accounted righteous,
          and he will bear their sins.
12   Therefore I will give him a position among the many,
          and he will divide the spoil with the great;
     because he poured out his life to death,
          and was numbered among the sinners;
     because he bore the sin of many,
          and made intercession for sinners.

a. The Targum adds "the Messiah," but the other ancient versions follow the MT.
b. The MT reads "you."
c. The MT reads "sprinkle" (cf. exposition below).
d. The LXX reads "to death."
e. The MT reads "deaths." Some emend to "his tomb" (*BHS*).
  f. The MT *ḥ heli* is problematic. It appears to be a hiphil *ḥl'* / *ḥlh* ("to make sick"). 1QIs[a]
reads "that he might pierce him." Others emend to the hiphil of *ḥlm* ("to make well").
  g. Cf. exposition for the translation of *'ašām*.

h. The LXX adds "light" as an object, as does the Qumran texts. This option is to be taken seriously.

Selected Bibliography on Textual Problems of Chapter 53

D. Barthlélemy, *Critique Textuelle de L'ancien Testament,* 2. *Isaïe, Jerémie, Lamentations,* Fribourg 1986, 383–406; **G. R. Driver,** "Isaiah 52,13–53,12: The Servant of the Lord," *In Memoriam Paul Kahle,* ed. M. Black and G. Fohrer, BZAW 103, Berlin 1968; 90–103; **K. Elliger,** "Nochmals Textkritisches zu Jes 53," *Wort, Lied und Gottesspruch, Fs Joseph Ziegler,* ed. J. Schreiner, FB 2, Würzburg 1972, 137–44; **C. R. North,** *The Suffering Servant in Deutero-Isaiah,* Oxford 1948, 116–38; **J. N. Oswalt,** *The Book of Isaiah, Chapters 40–66,* Grand Rapids 1998, 373–410; **D. W. Thomas,** "A Consideration of Isaiah LIII in the Light of Recent Textual and Philological Study," *ETL* 44, 1968, 79–86.

Selected Bibliography of the History of Interpretation, 1948–96

V. de Leeuw, *De Ebed Jahweh-Profetieen,* Assen 1956; **H. Haag,** *Der Gottesknecht bei Deuterojesaja,* Darmstadt 1985; **B. Janowski and P. Stuhlmacher,** eds., *Der leidende Gottesknecht,* FAT 14, Tübingen 1996; **C. R. North,** *The Suffering Servant in Deutero-Isaiah,* London 1948.

Selected Exegetical Bibliography

K. Baltzer, *Die Biographie der Propheten,* Neukirchen-Vluyn 1975, 171–77; **J. C. Bastiaens,** *Interpretaties van Jesaja 53,* Tilburg 1993, 29–93; **J. Begrich,** *Studien zu Deuterojesaja* (1938), TB 20, Munich 1963, 62–66; **H. Cazelles,** "Les poèmes du Serviteur. Leur place, leur structure, leur théologie," *RevScRel* 43, 1955, 5–55; **D. J. A. Clines,** *I, He, We, and They: A Literary Approach to Isaiah 53,* JSOTSup 1, Sheffield 1976; **J. Day,** *Da'at* 'Humiliation' in Isaiah LIII ii in the Light of Isaiah LIII iii and Daniel XII iv, and the Oldest Known Interpretation of the Suffering Servant," *VT* 30, 1980, 97–103; **S. R. Driver and A. Neubauer,** *The Fifty-Third Chapter of Isaiah according to the Jewish Interpreters,* 2 vols., 1876–77, reprinted New York 1969; **I. Engnell,** "The *Ebed* Yahweh Songs and the Suffering Messiah in 'Deutero-Isaiah,'" *BJRL* 31, 1948, 54–93; **H.-J. Hermisson,** "Israel und der Gottesknecht bei Deuterojesaja," *ZTK* 79, 1982, 1–24; "Das vierte Gottesknechtslied im deuterojesajanischen Kontext," *Der leidende Gottesknecht,* FAT 14, Tübingen 1996, 1–25; **H. W. Hertzberg,** "Die 'Abtrünnigen' und die 'Vielen.' Ein Beitrag zu Jesaja 53," *Verbannung und Heimkehr, Fs W. Rudolph,* ed. A. Kuschke, Tübingen 1961, 97–108; **G. P. Hugenberger,** "The Servant of the Lord in the 'Servant Songs' of Isaiah: A Second Moses Figure," *The Lord's Anointed: Interpretation of Old Testament Messianic Texts,* ed. P. E. Satterthwaite et al., Grand Rapids 1995, 105–40; **B. Janowski,** "Er trug unsere Sünden. Jes 53 und die Dramatik der Stellvertretung," *Der leidende Gottesknecht,* FAT 14, Tübingen 1996, 27–48; **R. F. Melugin,** *The Formation of Isaiah 40–55,* BZAW 141, Berlin 1976, 73–74, 167–69; **S. Mowinckel,** *Der Knecht Jahwäs,* Giessen 1921; **H. M. Orlinsky,** *Studies on the Second Part of the Book of Isaiah: The So-Called "Servant of the Lord" and "Suffering Servant" in Second Isaiah,* VTSup 14, 1967, 3–133; **O. H. Steck,** "Aspekte des Gottesknechts in Deuterojesajas 'Ebed-Jahwe-Liedern,'" *Gottesknecht in Zion,* FAT 4, Tübingen 1992, 3–43; **R. N. Whybray,** *Thanksgiving for a Liberated Prophet: An Interpretation of Isaiah Chapter 53,* JSOTSup 4, Sheffield 1978; **W. Zimmerli,** "Zur Vorgeschichte von Jes 53," *Studien zur alttestamentlichen Theologie und Prophetie,* TB 51, Munich 1974, 213–21; "Das 'Gnadenjahr des Herrn,'" ibid., 222–34.

Selected Bibliography on Isaiah 53 and the New Testament

R. Bultmann, *Theology of the New Testament,* I, ET New York 1955, 31; **S. R. Driver and A. Neubauer,** *The Fifty-Third Chapter of Isaiah according to the Jewish Interpreters,* 2 vols., 1876–77, reprinted New York 1969; **E. Fascher,** *Jesaja 53 in christlicher und jüdischer Sicht,* Berlin 1958; **M. Hengel,** *The Cross of the Son of God,* ET London 1981, 189–292; **M. Hooker,** *Jesus and the Servant: The Influence of the Servant Concept of Deutero-Isaiah in the New Testament,* London 1959; **E. Hoskyns and N. Davey,** *The Riddle of the New Testament,* London 1947; **B. Janowski and P. Stuhlmacher,** *Der leidende Gottesknecht. Jesaja 53 und seine Wirkungsgeschichte,* FAT 14, Tübingen 1996, 264–71; **J. Jeremias and W. Zimmerli,** *The Servant of God,* SBT I/20, ET London 1957, 43–104; **E. Käsemann,** "Review of H. W. Wolff," *VF* 1952, 200–203; **P. Stuhlmacher,** "Der messianische Gottesknecht," *JBTh* 8, 1993, 131–54; **H. W. Wolff,** *Jesaja 53 im Urchristentum,* Berlin 1952.

1. Exegetical Approach

It is hardly necessary to remind the reader that this passage is probably the most contested chapter in the Old Testament. The problems of interpretation are many and complex. Even to engage the textual problems is a formidable challenge in itself. The decisions in establishing a critically responsible reading of the Hebrew text can greatly influence the interpretation.

The history of exegesis of chapter 53 reveals clearly the nature and extent of the Christian church's enormous interest in the passage, which was seen to be closely related in some profound sense to the New Testament's proclamation of the gospel (Acts 8:26ff.). The initial responsibility of an Old Testament commentary is initially and above all to attempt to hear Israel's own voice in the plain sense of the text. The very format of a modern commentary restricts its author from exploring in detail this whole range of problems involved and requires an initial selection of issues to be explored. Only in conclusion will I attempt to offer some theological reflections of the chapter within the context of the whole Christian canon.

In the task of seeking to hear the text's plain sense, the interpreter of Isaiah 53 is faced with an initial hermeneutical issue of major importance. Although this methodological question has been addressed in earlier chapters, it bears repeating in respect to the handling of the text at hand. Beuken's discussion of the subject has much to commend it (*Jesaja* II/B, 185–86). To what extent does a proper exegesis derive from bringing a historical or literary perspective from outside the context of the book itself? Is the interpretation dependent on a correct assessment of the literary and theological function of the text within its present canonical context (chapters 40—55)?

The decision to choose the latter option does not in itself deny that several different authors can well be involved, or that redactional layering is often clearly present. In a word, a diachronic dimension is not ruled out, but its relation to the present, shaped text is subtle and indirect. Independently, it does not provide the key to interpretation, but functions within the literary context of the larger corpus. Especially is this true for chapter 53, which provides a continuation of a lengthy prophetic narrative extending from chapters 40—55 and climaxing in the sequence that follows in chapters 49ff. God intervenes to end the exile and to usher in his eschatological reign. This hermeneutical decision not only separates the ensuing interpretation fundamentally from the radically atomistic interpretation of the heirs of Duhm, but equally from the utterly fanciful historical speculation of Watts (*Isaiah 34 — 66,* 222ff.) who, oddly enough, stands on the far right of the theological spectrum.

2. Scope, Structure, and Genre

There is wide agreement going back to the first century A.D. That the unit extends from 52:13 to 53:12, thus correcting the traditional chapter division (cf. de Leeuw, 181–182). Whybray's form-critical argument for contesting the consensus does not carry the weight that he attributes to it (163). The passage both begins and ends with reference to "my servant." The structure of the unit is also remarkably clear in dividing into three sections: 52:13–15, the first divine speech; 53:1–11a, the confession of the "we"; and 53:11b–12, the second divine speech. A major exegetical problem turns on assessing the coherence of the passage (cf. below). Especially difficult, but crucial to its interpretation, is the determining of the antecedents of the references in 52:15 and 53:12, as well as the understanding the voice of the confessing "we" in the middle section. Credit goes to D. J. A. Clines for having clearly pointed out the full complexity of the passage's opacity.

During the last half century much energy has been expended in analyzing the literary genres of the passage (e.g., Begrich, Westermann, Baltzer, Melugin, Whybray). A form akin to the individual psalm of thanksgiving or of lament has been suggested. Others see an analogy to the dirge or psalm of repentance. Whybray (127) makes the significant observation that in spite of psalmic parallels, there is the important difference from the common liturgical pattern in that the thanksgiving is not made by the suffering petitioner himself, but in the third person by another group. Recently a consensus is growing (Melugin, Beuken, etc.) that this passage is unique. Although traditional psalmic conventions lie in the background of the text, the structure is basically a new literary creation, differing in both form and content from the common oral patterns. Of course, this opinion has also contributed to the insistence (cf. above) that the unit be interpreted within its larger, narrative context.

During the 1940s, de Leeuw and North spent much time debating the theories of Engnell and other Scandinavians regarding an allegedly ancient Near Eastern mythological setting for the poem, largely on the basis of Ugaritic parallels. Since that time the theory has virtually collapsed from its own weight and from the highly tendentious translations of the extrabiblical material. Other less radical cultic contexts that have been suggested have also not been sustained. In sum, in spite of the ambiguities surrounding the passage, the present literary context provides the basic arena from which the passage must be analyzed and ultimately interpreted.

3. Exposition

[52:13–15] The oracle of God begins with an elevated presentation: "Behold, my servant . . ." The parallel is immediately evident with the servant song of 42:1 in which the servant is introduced with the mission to bring *mišpāṭ* ("justice") to the nations. However, this intertextual reference to 42:1 has been decisively affected by the subsequent call in 49:1ff., which transferred the office of the servant from the nation Israel to the individual prophetic figure of 49:3: "And he said to me, 'You are (now) my servant, you are Israel, in whom I will be glorified.'" Then in 50:4ff., following the sequence of the prophetic narrative, the reception of his call as God's servant is related as he is tortured and humiliated by his oppressors, who are not from outside, but from within the nation of Israel itself.

It is highly significant that the divine oracle in 52:13 begins, not with the servant's humiliation, but with his exaltation, a theme that returns to climax the second divine speech concerning the servant in 53:11ff. His exaltation in 52:13, "[he] shall prosper, be exalted," also forms the initial perspective from which the voice of the "we" speaks. This group confesses finally to have understood his true role in their salvation. To the sense of prospering there is also included in the Hebrew verb (*śql*) the connotation of insight, wisdom, and true knowledge.

The divine word next describes the astonishment and confusion that the figure of the servant evokes. The broken style of the confession, which begins in the first colon of v. 14 and is completed in v. 15, has caused many commentators to reassign v. 14b to another position within the oracle (cf. *BHS*). Yet there is no textual evidence to support this reordering of the sentence, and the striking effect of the sudden shift to the servant's humiliation—"so marred was his appearance, unlike that of man," is lost by such an alteration. Such stylistic breaks are found elsewhere in the prophetic literature (e.g., Isa. 31:4; 55:10; Zech. 8:14, etc.). Verse 14b therefore anticipates the response of the confession "we," but the note of disfigurement is first sounded in the divine oracle. The full force falls on the astonishment and shock of many of the nations, whose kings shut their mouths in confused silence.

The Hebrew verb in v. 15 (*yazzeh*) has as its primary meaning "to sprinkle," but there are several reasons that have caused most commentators to prefer a broader, secondary sense of the root (cf. W. Gesenius, *Commentar über den Jesaia* 2:174ff.). First, the Greek reads "surprise," which *BHS* conjectures— probably wrongly—to reflect a different Hebrew root from the MT. More likely, the issue is one of semantic range rather than a textual variant. Second, the verb *nzh* (hiphil) never designates the person or thing sprinkled, but the blood being applied. In English the sense is expressed in the archaic distinction between sprinkling a liquid, and besprinkling a person. Third, it is an exegetical misconstrual in seeking to heighten the cultic context of the passage that never actually surfaces to the foreground.

The difficult exegetical problem turns on determining the persons referred to in these verses. The "many" in v. 14 who were astonished join smoothly with the subject of v. 15a: "So will he startle many nations." In the Psalter the reference to the "many" usually refers to the advisories or bystanders who observe the suffering petitioner (Ps. 3:1–2; 4:7; 31:14; etc; cf. Beuken, 202). Melugin (167) argues that the antecedent in v. 15b is a continuation of v. 15a, namely, the nations and kings: "what has not been told them [the nations] they will see and that which they have not heard they will understand." Because v. 15 then joins closely to 53:1, the effect of this interpretation is naturally to assign the voice of the confessing "we" in chapter 53 to that of the nations. In my judgment, this interpretation carries with it major difficulty (cf. below).

Rather, as Beuken has convincingly shown (II/B, 203ff.), a different subject has been introduced in v. 15b. The issue at stake is not the astonishment evoked in the nations, but rather in their seeing and understanding. They key to this interpretation is found in the intertextual reference to 48:6ff. Israel is challenged to see and to hear the new things God is about to reveal. "Before today you have not heard of them" (v. 7). The people's ear has been closed. Now suddenly in 52:15b, a group, different from the nations, is promised by God both to see and understand: "what they were not told, they will see, and what they have not heard, they will understand." The reference is to a group within Israel to which has been revealed the "new things," hitherto hidden. What then follows in 53:1ff. is the confession of that group, who suddenly is made to understand the will of God through their experience with his suffering servant.

[53:1–11a] The connection between the new unit and the preceding divine speech is skillfully made with a chiastic device. The metaphor of seeing (52:15b and 53:1b) brackets that of hearing (v. 15b and 53:1a) and confirms the continuity between the group of Israel in v. 15b and the confessing voice of 53:1ff. In addition, from a form-critical perspective, the confessing "we" of the Old Testament is always Israel and not the nations (Hos. 6:1ff.; Jer. 3:21ff.; Dan. 9:4ff., etc.) Finally, reference to the nations and the "many" only returns in the second divine speech when they also are brought into the purpose of God for all his creation, which has been accomplished in the mission of the suffering servant (53:12).

[1] The confession of Israel begins in v. 1 with a question of which several interpretations are possible. Is its meaning: Who could possibly have believed what we have experienced? This rendering is unlikely because the issue at stake in the confession of Israel is not that of the astonishment reflected by the nations. Rather, from the outset, those within Israel who confess understand that their new knowledge came from divine revelation, that is, derived from the arm of Yahweh. The sense of the question is not simply rhetorical, but serves to identify among them those who now also believe what they have seen and heard from God's disclosure. The note had already been sounded in 50:10–11 that the response to the servant would divide the people of Israel into two groups, those who believe and those who oppose.

[2–3] The actual narrative of the servant's humiliation begins in v. 2. The description is clearly retrospective in nature, and looks back on an experience in the past that continues to evoke painful reflection. The figure who is portrayed appears in every way to have been a historical personage. The language cannot be rendered metaphorically as the nation without straining the plain sense of the text in a tortuous fashion. The figure remains anonymous, and is identified throughout simply with the pronoun "he." However, the description is not merely biographical. Certainly it does contain some biographical elements. He grew up unobtrusively from nowhere, isolated, and without a known lineage. He possessed nothing in his physical appearance that would attract others or even evoke attention. Verse 3b speaks even of his being afflicted with sickness or disease. However, almost immediately one senses that the chief interest of the narrative is not biographical; rather, the concrete features that encompass the ensuing description focus largely on the response of others to him. He was despised and shunned by all and called forth such revulsion that people covered their faces to prevent seeing him. Increasingly the language takes on a flavor that transcends a simple historical description, and begins to resonate with the typical idiom of the innocent suffering one of the Psalter: "I am a worm, less than human, scorned and despised by the people. All who see me curl their lips and wag their heads" (22:6–7). "You have caused my companions to shun me; you have made me a thing of horror to them" (Ps. 88:8).

In addition, there is another feature in the description that moves in a typifying direction. Especially in the trials of Jeremiah, one can see the prophetic office being described in a similar idiom as that of the Psalter, but also in a manner that does not abstract from given historical events in his own personal struggle to survive. "I sat alone, because your hand was upon me" (15:17). "I have become a laughingstock all day; everyone mocks me" (20:7). "Terror is on every side! Denounce him!" (20:10). Much like Jeremiah, the description of prophetic suffering depicts a calling, even an office, into which a servant of God has been summoned. However, the confession that then follows in chapter 53 begins to probe a new dimension of obedient suffering, unknown to Jeremiah or the other prophets.

[4–6] In v. 4 the narrative continues with a series of striking contrasts in which the Hebrew *'ākēn* ("surely") marks the beginning of a theme. "Surely it was our sickness he bore," yet "we regarded him as plagued." "He was wounded because of our sins," yet "we have all gone astray like sheep." Two additional notes are sounded in the sorrowful recital. First, the confessing community bears testimony to what it has seen and now understands (52:15). It was for "our sins" he was tortured; it was for "our iniquities" he was bruised. "The punishment that brought us peace was on him" and "by his wounds we are healed." Second, it was God's will and purpose that the servant was dealt this affliction. Not only did God allow it (the passive voice softens the theological tension), but God is understood as the active agent of his suffering: He was "smitten by God and afflicted" (v. 4); "Yahweh laid on him the guilt of us all" (v. 6). What occurred was not some unfortunate tragedy of human history but actually formed the center of the divine plan for the redemption of his people and indeed of the world.

It is at this juncture in the interpretation of the chapter that the modern debate over the term "vicarious" suffering has set in. Some of the controversy turns on the various ways in which the term has been construed. Beuken (*Jesaja*, II/B, 214ff.) is rightly concerned that the term be used with great caution lest theological categories foreign to the witness of the Old Testament be uncritically applied. Clearly, Christian interpreters should be warned not to read in, say, Anselm's highly developed, scholastic theology of the atonement, but rather closely to follow the exact terminology of chapter 53.

However, once this caveat has been registered, it is equally as important to assess a variety of modern options that dispute the presence of vicariousness in the chapter altogether. For example, H. M. Orlinsky argues in a lengthy essay (51ff.) that the chapter only asserts that this person also suffered "on account of and along with the people at large, the latter because of their own sins, the former because of his unpopular mission." Orlinsky also contends that the concept of vicariousness conflicts fundamentally with the idea of covenant. This legal contract assured both the guiltless and the wicked their proper due, and was grounded completely in a basic concept of quid pro quo. I shall leave it to the reader to decide whether this interpretation does justice to chapter 53 and to the prophetic message in general.

Whybray (29ff.) addresses the question of the servant's allegedly vicarious suffering at great length. His study is philologically oriented and he attempts to show from parallel passages within the Old Testament how the concepts of sin, guilt, and punishment are treated. He picks up the argument of Orlinsky that the use of the preposition *min* in vv. 5 and 8 cannot be understood vicariously since this would have called for the preposition *b^e* (*bet pretii*), meaning "in exchange for." Actually a *bet pretii* does occur in v. 5, as Zimmerli has pointed out (*Zur Vorgeschichte,"* 215). However, Whybray is convinced of the "inherent improbability of such a notion in the Old Testament" (75). Accordingly, he summarizes his interpretation of chapter 53: "What the speakers in ch. 53 are saying is that the servant, who deserved no punishment, has, as a result of *their* sins, which had necessitated his dangerous and fateful prophetical ministry, received the largest share of it." In my judgment, this bland and even superficial understanding of the passage serves as a major indictment of his conclusions.

Finally, for P. Hanson the question around which the chapter turns is how the tragic pattern of sin and punishment can be broken within the context of a higher morality. He recognizes the uniqueness of the message within the chapter in which "the mysterious ways of God in everyday human experience is recognized." "God's will is done where a human being finds the highest expression of human dignity in expressing solidarity with fellow human beings through a love that acknowledges no bounds because its source is God" (160). I leave it to the reader to assess whether this modern "politically correct" formulation does justice to the chapter's understanding of the willing obedience of the suffering servant who bore "our sins" (cf. below).

[7–8] The narrative of the servant's oppression continues, but the emphasis now falls on the willing submission of the innocent sufferer. The clause "he did not open his mouth" occurs twice in v. 7, and serves stylistically as a bracket around the similes "like a lamb being led to slaughter" and "like a sheep silent before her shearers." Verse 8 next introduces an apparently forensic image that the NJPS translation effectively renders as a hendiadys, "by oppressive judgment he was taken away." However, other commentators stress the element of restraint in the noun '*ōṣer* and interpret the phrase to mean "without hindrance or opposition" he was removed. The verb "taken away" (*lūqqāḥ*) is generally understood as a reference to his violent and sudden death, but the less likely idea of his being "released by death" has been occasionally suggested.

[8a] The sense of the next colon in v. 8a is even less clear and has evoked a variety of interpretations, as is evident from the different translations offered. The term *dôr* can express the time of a generation, or a circle of one's contemporaries. On the basis of a Semitic cognate some commentators have suggested the meaning of "state" or "fate." The other problem of the clause turns on its syntactical function. The more usual move is to regard the noun as the object: "Who thinks of his fate (or of his line)?" However, the noun can be rendered as the subject (GKC § 117, 1–m; cf. BDB, 85a, 3): "as for his generation, who considered" (RSV), or "regarding his contemporaries, who gave him a thought?" Westermann wisely concludes that the exact meaning is uncertain, but that "the general sense is perfectly clear—no one was concerned about him."

[8b] Some commentators have argued that the description of the servant as "cut off from the land of the living" is to be taken metaphorically, and does not necessarily indicate his death. The point is made that in the Old Testament both life and death are seen as qualities of existence and that the line separating them is fluid. Consequently, it has been suggested that it is possible that the servant only risked death or was exiled, allegedly a fate worse than death. In my opinion, these are tortuous interpretations and run against the plain sense of the text. The implicit mention of his grave in v. 10 rules out these figurative options.

Unfortunately, the last colon in v. 8 is difficult to interpret because of textual problems. The MT appears to read "for the transgressions of my people the stroke for them" (or "due them"). The Greek reads, "he was stricken to death," and this rendering provides the warrant for a critical emendation suggested by

BHS. Variations of the emendation are followed by many modern commentators. In addition, the form "my people" is often emended "for our transgressions" (cf. Westermann) in order to ease the problem of a first person singular pronoun. A less radical emendation has been suggested by the Qumran text (1QIsᵃ), which reads, "his people" (*'ammô*), and would be translated, "because of the transgressions of his people was there punishment for him." In sum, it is unwise to be dogmatic on any one textual reading, but the general sense of the sentence is clear from the context as a whole.

[9] The main controversy regarding this verse turns on the interpretation of the "rich man." (*'ašîr*). The difficulty lies in the linking of the wicked with the rich in a burial site, which hardly offers a natural parallel within Israel. The usual emendation renders it, "with evil doers" (*BHK*), but *BHS* suggests "demons"; others seek to retain the MT and expand its semantic range to denote "rich through extortion." The final line in v. 9, by means of a concessive clause, emphasizes that he was killed even though he had done nothing either violent or deceitful. This juxtaposition continues the typing of the servant as the righteous and innocent sufferer of the Psalter.

[10] The next verse returns to the theme that it was the will of God to crush or injure him (cf. vv. 4, 6). The verb that follows in the MT (*ḥlh*) conveys the sense of "make sick" or "render weak," and forms with its parallels a continuing lament of the suffering innocent of the Psalter (Pss. 35:13; 41:4; 77:16). Nevertheless, it is a mistake to seek to specify the sickness too precisely, as if leprosy (Duhm) were intended. Much like the idiom of the Psalter, physical and spiritual suffering are combined without carefully defined boundaries and so probe into its multifaceted aspects.

The second colon in v. 10 is again difficult and controversial: "when/if his life serves as compensation for guilt" (*'āšām*). The initial problem is textual and a variety of emendations have been suggested. Both Begrich and *BHS* emend to read, "he healed him who made his life a guilt offering." Undoubtedly this alteration presents a far clearer meaning, but one should be cautious in making such an intrusive move through emendation, which too easily resolves the hard exegetical problem. Actually there is not explicit mention of healing of the servant up to this point, and the difference between "afflict him with sickness" or "healed him" is hardly inconsequential.

However, the really difficult exegetical problem turns on the interpretation of the term *'āšām* ("guilt offering"). The first problem lies in determining the exegetical range of the term. It occurs most frequently in ritual prescriptions of the books of Leviticus and Numbers, in the so-called Priestly source within the Pentateuch (Lev. 5:6–25; 6:10; 7:1–2, 5–7, 37; 14:12ff.; 19:21–22; Num. 6:12; 18:9), but also is found in the book of Ezekiel (40:39; 42:13; 44:29; 46:20). Particularly in Leviticus 5 the nature of the misdeed is described and the procedure for atonement by means of a guilt offering is stipulated.

Traditionally some commentators (e.g., Alexander, Delitzsch) held that the same cultic concept of Numbers could be transferred directly to the Isaianic passage. It seemed to provide a further support for seeing the servant's sacrifice as both vicarious and priestly. However, right from the outset there were difficulties with this interpretation. The analogy between a slain animal and the suffering servant is far from obvious, and the ritual of sprinkling blood on the altar is without parallel. Moreover, there is no contextual preparation in chapter 53 to alert the reader to a cultic interpretation. Indeed, the lack of a cultic context in the chapter is apparent. For such reasons, commentators such as Duhm and Marti have eliminated the term as reflecting an incoherent textual error. But the problem cannot be so easily resolved in this manner.

Certainly the most learned of the modern discussions of the problem is represented in a recent article by B. Janowski. He first makes the important observation that the concept of *'āšām* did not originally stem from the cult (cf. Gen. 26:10; 1 Sam. 6:3–4, 8, 17), but rather from a secular situation in which compensation for a misdeed was demanded. Thus Israel, who is unable to make restitution, must in some way be freed from its debt. The forgiveness comes from the suffering, innocent servant who gave his life according to the plan of God to release the guilt of his people. The servant did not ritually obliterate the sin—there is no parallel to the scapegoat—rather the terminology is that he "bore" or "carried it" (*ns'*, *sbl*). This is the sense of the servant's vicarious role in carrying the sins of the nation ("our sins"). There is nothing automatic or intrinsic in the servant's act that would result in forgiveness. To this extent, Orlinsky is correct in asserting, "Nowhere in the Hebrew Bible did anyone preach a doctrine . . . which allowed the sacrifice of the innocent in the place of and as an acceptable substitution for the guilty" (55).

Yet the point of the Isaianic text is that God himself took the initiative in accepting the servant's life as the means of Israel's forgiveness. In the first divine speech (52:13), the "success" of the servant is promised because of what God had done. This promise was hidden, never before told (v. 15), but Israel finally understood it as a revelation from "the arm of the LORD." The role of the servant resulted in Israel's forgiveness because of God's acceptance of the servant's obedient suffering. Israel not only recognized the freedom that the servant had won for it, but in the experience of encountering the hidden plan of God, was itself transformed into the new Israel, which shared in the coming redemptive age. Already the scene for Israel's restoration was set as God designated the servant as the embodiment of Israel (49:3), through whom God would be glorified and the nation would be gathered again to him. When seen in the light of the unfolding drama of God's plan to redeem Israel in chapters 40–55, the vicarious role of the servant lies at the very heart of the prophetic message and its removal can only result in losing the exegetical key that unlocks the awesome mystery of these chapters.

The confession of the redeemed community concludes with the recognition of the servant's exaltation, first announced in 52:13: "Behold, my servant will prosper, be exalted, lifted up, and raised to great heights." The problem of determining just what is meant in the sharp turn from humiliation, suffering, and death to the servant's exaltation has continued to evoke much disagreement. Traditionally, it was a Christian reflex to see here an indication of the servant's resurrection. The historical critics of the nineteenth century were quick to point out that there is no explicit mention of resurrection in the text. In addition, it was judged highly unlikely that the concept of individual resurrection played any role in Israel until the late Hellenistic period. Nevertheless, the text clearly speaks of a reversal of fortune. The servant will see his offspring (this term will play a major role in chapters 56—66) and have long life.

[11–12] Verse 11 continues the promise: "From the agony of his soul he will see, and he shall be satisfied." The LXX adds an object, "see *light*," but this clarifying addition appears secondary within a difficult text. The next phrase presents further problems for which there is no clear consensus. *BHK* joins "his knowledge" (*da'tô*) to the following verb, "make righteous," which syntactical division follows the Masoretic accentuation system. (The *zāqēp* is a stronger disjunctive than that *rᵉbîaʻ*.) Conversely, *BHS* joins the noun to the preceding verb, which also makes excellent sense. Added to the problem is determining the exact sense of *da'tô*. Following the lead of D. W. Thomas, some have opted for positing a homonym for the root *yd'* and interpreting its meaning as "humiliation." In my opinion, the option of *BHS* is preferable and the ordinary sense of the word as "knowledge" is to be retained. I do not find it an abrupt intrusion, but a summary of the servant's experience that has just been described.

In sum, nothing is gained by offering a figurative or allegorical interpretation to explain the servant's exaltation. The prophetic text is silent on how the transformation will be accomplished. Fortunately, the second divine speech (vv. 11b–12) returns to the subject of the servant's future exaltation, which had been sounded first in 52:13–15 and which offers a divine perspective on the mystery of the servant's "afterlife."

The scope of the second divine oracle is established by the introduction of the first person form of address. The explicit reference to "my servant" provides a coherent closure to the entire passage. Again, in v. 11b the syntax of the sentence is unclear. The present position of the substantive prevents it from being rendered as a simple attributive, "my righteous servant," but rather as "the righteous one, my servant." Although the verb (*ṣdq,* hiphil) can be translated in several different ways, the two senses of declarative and causative seem to flow together from the force of the larger context: He shall "make many to be accounted righteous."

The reference to the "many" thus returns to the theme of the first divine oracle. However, now the effect of the servant on the many is not just of astonishment or confusion. Rather, through him will the many be accounted righteous because he also bears their sins through the mercy of God. Verse 12 summarizes the divine promise to the servant starting with his exaltation, which is then once again grounded in his suffering and death for the many. He will receive the divine blessing—"a position among the many"—with whom he now shares a future.

4. Theological Reflections on Isaiah 53 within a Canonical Context

The format of a commentary does not lend itself to extended analysis either of the relation of an Old Testament text to the New Testament, or to questions involving larger biblical theological issues. The need to restrict one's focus is especially acute when attempting to interpret the entire Isaianic corpus lest the commentary grow to an inordinate size. Nevertheless, it seems necessary occasionally to make an exception when handling certain selected texts that have played an unusually important role in the history of interpretation. Such a treatment must be brief, and its goal simply to stimulate further thought, rather than to be in any sense exhaustive. I would like therefore to address two separate topics relating to the servant of Isaiah 53: first, the relation of Isaiah 53 to the New Testament; second, the role of the "suffering servant" in Christian theology.

a. The Relation of Isaiah 53 to the New Testament

In the modern critical study of this question, two very different interpretations have emerged, which have been locked in an impasse for well over half a century.

On the one hand, the position has been defended by conservative biblical scholars that Jesus himself consciously shaped his ministry according to the servant figure in Isaiah 53, with whose mission he identified. When the early church continued to expand this relationship theologically, it did so on the basis of Jesus' own self-understanding of himself as the suffering servant. This position has sought to demonstrate historically that the concept of the servant's vicarious sacrifice was already present in pre-Christian Judaism. The leading defense of this position is found in the writings of J. Jeremias, H. W. Wolff, P. Stuhlmacher, M. Hengel, among others.

On the other hand, liberal scholars have sharply disputed this traditional interpretation. They have pointed out how seldom are there explicit references to Isaiah 53 found in the Synoptics, and when possible allusions occur they are vague and related to a general Old Testament milieu rather than a specific text. Many argue that the concept of a suffering servant was, at best, late within Hellenistic Christianity and in no way related to the historical Jesus' own self-understanding. A defense of this position is found in the writings of R. Bultmann, E. Käsemann, and M. Hooker, among others.

At the outset, it is important to observe a word of caution that is crucial to the formulation of the question. The concept of an individual figure of a suffering servant, distinct from the larger concept of servant in Second Isaiah, is a thoroughly modern concept, first clearly formulated by Duhm. It is highly misleading and anachronistic to project this reconstructed figure back into the New Testament period.

In addition, there are other basic hermeneutical issues at stake. Both sides in the debate have sought to establish that the concept of a suffering servant can or cannot be attributed to the self-understanding of Jesus. Both sides argue pro and con about the "mind of Jesus" on the issue. Moreover, both sides distinguish between Jesus' own self-understanding and that voiced by the various witnesses of scripture. Both therefore seek to ground their positions on a historical-critical reconstruction of the history of tradition. In the end, one side sees the historical force of Isaiah 53 moving in the direction from the Old Testament toward the New Testament. The other reverses the direction of influence, seeing the New Testament's understanding as primary and only secondarily being retrojected back into the Old Testament.

In my judgment, these antagonistic positions can be seriously faulted from a hermeneutical perspective. First, both have failed adequately to distinguish between the New Testament's kerygmatic witness to Jesus Christ as found in the Gospels and that of a historical-critical reconstruction, regardless of whether executed with conservative or liberal historical assumptions. Theologically speaking, it is a false dichotomy that plays "the mind of Jesus" over against scriptural witness. To confuse allegedly neutral historical reconstruction with kerygmatic witness results in a fundamental confusion of hermeneutical categories.

Second, to attempt to determine historically the direction from which Isaiah 53 exerted a shaping influence is to fail to understand the dynamic within the development of canonical literature. The Old Testament clearly exerted a decisive force in shaping the New Testament, but conversely, the latter appropriated the former by a radical reinterpretation of its meaning in the light of Jesus Christ.

Often it is virtually impossible in a given text to determine the initial force of coercion because of the continuing mutual impact in the search for theological understanding. Even a cursory analysis, say, of John 12:37ff. shows how much the New Testament's understanding of Jesus has been shaped by that of Isaiah, while, conversely, how much of the prophetic text of the Old Testament has been reinterpreted from the perspective of the gospel. In addition, the Old Testament functioned as a coherent whole in shaping the Christology of the New Testament, and its influence cannot be restricted to single verses or to exact linguistic parallels (*contra* Hooker).

This caveat against the use of historical-critical reconstruction as an avenue to the New Testament's kerygmatic witness is not to be misunderstood as a denial of any role for a diachronic dimension in biblical interpretation. The issue rather turns on the confusion of categories that misunderstands the distinction between treating the text as an objective source of information or as a kerygmatic testimony to a divine reality. Within the New Testament's witness there are clear signs of growth and development. The use of Isaiah 53 appears in some early levels of New Testament tradition and therefore is not confined to a late Hellenistic elaboration. Yet there are periods when the servant theology plays very little, if any, role before once again emerging as a major theme within the early church (1 Peter 2:18ff.). The tracing of growth and development within the kerygmatic witness greatly aids in determining its theological function within the whole Christian Bible. Nevertheless, the major hermeneutical point to be made is that the authority of the biblical witness is not determined by its being anchored in "the mind of Jesus." Rather, the true exegetical task is to understand its theological role as the witness of scripture within the entire Christian canon.

b. The Suffering Servant and Christian Theology

During most of the history of the Christian church's interpretation of Isaiah, it was assumed that the suffering servant theme of chapter 53 was a messianic prophecy predicting the future passion of Jesus Christ. This tradition is still represented in the Isaiah commentary of E. J. Young (1972): "we may say with assurance that there is only One of whom these words may be spoken, namely, Jesus the Christ" (3:348).

However, with the rise of the modern historical-critical approach to the Old Testament the position that gained the widest acceptance was that the description of the suffering servant, regardless of a continuing debate over details, was a figure closely tied to the historical experience of Israel in the Babylonian exile. My commentary has also defended the position that both the servant's response to his prophetic call (49:1–6) and the confession of a repentant community respecting the servant (53:1–11a) reflect actual events within the life of historical Israel. In sum, Isa. 53:2ff. cannot be interpreted either as simply a future prophecy or as a timeless metaphor of the suffering nation of Israel.

As a consequence of this historical mooring of the servant in the sixth century as an anonymous figure, many commentators have recently assigned very limited theological importance to chapter 53 (cf. Whybray). Its chief significance is seen to lie in its *Wirkungsgeschichte* (afterlife), when the Christian church chose to use the passage as a vehicle for developing its later christological theology by means of an imaginative construal without warrant from the Old Testament witness itself.

In contrast to this critical position, I have argued in my exegesis that the canonical shape of the book of Isaiah shows a suffering servant figure who was not simply viewed as a figure of the past, but assigned a central and continuing theological role in relation to the life of the redeemed community of Israel. Thus, there was a coercion exerted by the biblical text itself, as authoritative

scripture, that exercised pressure on the early church in its struggle to understand the suffering and death of Jesus Christ.

The theological category used for its interpretation was not primarily that of
prophecy and fulfillment. Rather, an analogy was drawn between the redemptive activity of the Isaianic servant and the passion and death of Jesus Christ. The
relation was understood "ontologically," that is to say, in terms of its substance,
its theological reality. To use classic Christian theological terminology, the distinction is between the "economic" Trinity, God's revelation in the continuum
of Israel's history, and the "immanent" Trinity, the ontological manifestation of
the triune deity in its eternality. Thus, for example, the epistles of Ephesians and
Colossians argue that the creation of the universe cannot be understood apart
from the active participation of Jesus Christ (Col. 1:15ff.). Or again, the book of
Revelation speaks of "the lamb slain before the foundation of the world" (13:8).
In a word, in the suffering and death of the servant of Second Isaiah, the selfsame divine reality of Jesus Christ was made manifest. The meaning of the Old
Testament servant was thus understood theologically in terms of the one divine
reality disclosed in Jesus Christ. The morphological fit between Isaiah 53 and
the passion of Jesus continues to bear testimony to the common subject matter
within the one divine economy. Of course, in a broad sense, Isaiah 53 does continue to function as prophecy since the chapter is bracketed within the eschatological framework of an unfolding divine economy.

To summarize, the servant of Isaiah is linked dogmatically to Jesus Christ primarily in terms of its ontology, that is, its substance, and is not simply a future
promise of the Old Testament awaiting its New Testament fulfillment. It is significant to observe that in Acts 8, when the eunuch asked about the identity of the
Isaianic servant, Philip did not simply identify him with Jesus of Nazareth. Rather,
beginning with the scriptures, "he preached to him the good news of Jesus." The
suffering servant retains its theological significance within the Christian canon
because it is inextricably linked in substance with the gospel of Jesus Christ, who
is and always has been the ground of God's salvation of Israel and the world.

54. Isaiah 54:1–17

54:1 Shout, O barren one,
        and you who never bore a child.
     Break into singing, shout for joy,
        you who were never in labor,
     for the children of the desolate woman
        will be more than those of the married,
        says the LORD.

2   Enlarge the site of your tent;
    let the curtains of your dwelling be extended;[a]
do not hold back.
    Lengthen your ropes and make your stakes firm,
3   for you will spread out to the right and the left.
    Your seed will dispossess nations
    and settle in their desolate cities.
4   Fear not, you will not be ashamed.
    Do not be anxious; you will not be disgraced,
for you will forget the shame of your youth
    and remember no more the stigma of your widowhood.
5   For your Maker is your husband—
    the LORD of hosts is his name—
and the Holy One of Israel is your Redeemer.
    He is called the God of all the earth.
6   For the LORD has called you back
    as a wife forsaken and distressed in spirit,
as one married young only to be rejected,
        says your God.
7   For a brief moment I abandoned you,
    but with deep compassion I will bring you back.
8   In a burst[b] of anger I hid my face from you for an instant,
    but with everlasting love I show you compassion,
    says the LORD your Redeemer.
9   For this is to me like the days[c] of Noah,
    when I swore that the waters of Noah
    would never again cover the earth.
So now I have sworn not to be angry with you
    or to rebuke you.
10 For the mountains may move
    and the hills be shaken,
but my steadfast love for you will never move,
    nor will my covenant of peace be shaken,
    says the LORD, who has mercy on you.
11 O afflicted city, buffeted by storm, and without
    relief,
I will set your stones in antimony,
    and make your foundations of sapphires.[d]
12 I will make your battlements of rubies,
    your gates of sparkling jewels,
    and all your walls of precious gems.

13 All your children will be taught by the LORD,
and great will be the prosperity of your sons.
14 In righteousness you will be established,
and you will be far removed from violence without fear,
and terror will be made distant.
15 If anyone does stir up trouble,[e] it will not be my
doing.
Whoever will harm you will fall because of you.
16 Behold, it is I who created the blacksmith,
who fans the charcoal into fire
and produces a weapon for its work.
It is I who has created the means to create havoc.
17 No weapon forged against you will succeed.
Every voice raised against you in court
you will defeat.
Such is the heritage of the servants of the LORD,
and this is their vindication from me
says the LORD.

a. The MT *yaṭṭû* appears to be a jussive, and thus emended (*BHS*), but Oswalt (411) defends the use of an indefinite 3 plural as a passive.

b. The precise meaning of this *hapax legomenon* (*šeṣep*) is unclear, and many emendations have been proposed (*BHS*).

c. The MT reads "waters of Noah," but by a slightly different separation of the consonants a more coherent reading is obtained, which is supported by the LXX and 1QIs[a].

d. The identification of the various precious stones in vv. 11 and 12 remains uncertain.

e. The interpretation of v. 15a is difficult and controversial. The issue turns on whether the root *gûr*, which occurs twice in the verse, has the same meaning of "attack" in both cases, or is an intentional play on a homonym with the meaning of "sojourn" (cf. Torrey, 425–26).

Selected Bibliography

W. A. M. Beuken, "Isaiah LIV: The Multiple Identity of the Person Addressed," *OTS* 19, 1974, 29–70; **K. Elliger,** *Deuterojesaja in seinem Verhältnis zu Tritojesaja,* BWANT 63, Stuttgart 1933, 162–63; **H. Golebiewski,** *Analyse littéraire et théologique d'Is 54–55. Une alliance éternelle avec la nouvelle Jérusalem,* Rome 1976, 38–48; **D. M. Gunn,** "Deutero-Isaiah and the Flood," *JBL* 94, 1975, 498–508; **R. Martin-Achard,** "Esaïe liv et la nouvelle Jérusalem," *Congress Volume Vienna* 1980, VTSup 32, Leiden 1982, 238–62; **R. F. Melugin,** *The Formation of Isaiah 40–55,* BZAW 141, Berlin 1976, 169–75; **E. Otto,** "*ṣijjôn,*" *TWAT* VI, 1988, 994–1028; **N. W. Porteous,** "Jerusalem-Zion: The Growth of a Symbol," *Verbannung und Heimkehr, Fs W. Rudolph,* Tübingen 1961, 235–52; **H. W. Robinson,** "The Hebrew Conception of Corporate Personality," *Werden und Wesen des Alten Testaments,* BZAW 66, Berlin 1936, 49–62; **J. F. A. Sawyer,** "Daughter of Zion and Servant of the Lord in Isaiah: A Comparison," *JSOT* 44,

1989, 89–107; **O. H. Steck,** "Beobachtungen zu den Zion. Texten in Jesaja 51—54. Ein redaktions-geschichtliche Versuch," *Gottesknecht und Zion,* FAT 4, Tübingen 1992, 113–18; "Zion als Gelände und Gestalt. Überlegungen zur Wahrnehmung Jerusalems als Stadt und Frau im Alten Testament," ibid., 126–45; **C. C. Torrey,** *The Second Isaiah,* Edinburgh 1928, 423–26; **P. T. Willey,** *Remember the Former Things: The Recollection of Previous Texts in Second Isaiah,* SBLDS 161, Atlanta 1997.

1. Form, Structure, and Larger Context

The significance of the present position of chapter 54 within the larger structure of chapters 40—55 has been much discussed. The literary art of depicting Zion as an abandoned wife in the chapter is closely related to the earlier presentation in 49:14–26 and 51:17–52:12. The close continuity between chapter 54 and the latter passage has been interpreted as evidence that the "fourth servant song" (52:13–53:12) is a subsequent interpolation into the corpus of Second Isaiah (Duhm). As a consequence, many earlier commentators have seen no connection between chapters 53 and 54. More recently the pendulum has swung in the opposite direction (cf. Beuken, *Jesaja,* II/B, 242ff.). Initially, attention has focused on the parallel themes: "seed" (53:10 // 54:3); "the many" (52:14–15 53:11–12 // 54:1); "righteousness" (53:11 // 54:14); "peace" (53:5 // 54:10). However, the harder question lies in determining the exact nature of the continuity within the context of the larger prophetic drama of Second Isaiah. Muilenberg's rhetorical explanation, "the need of a poem which does justice to the tragic dimension of the historical situation," is far too general and abstract. Rather, the key may well be in v. 17 and in "the heritage of the servants of the LORD" (cf. below).

As to the form it is widely agreed that the present form of the text reflects a literary unity. The older form-critics assumed that the unity is the effect of editorial activity that linked originally independent oracles such as a hymn, salvation-assurance oracle, and a promise of salvation, into a "kerygmatic" whole (Begrich, Melugin, etc.). Westermann sees in the poetic art of the chapter "a perfect example of the exuberance" that reflects Second Isaiah's creative style of preaching. Surely nineteenth century romanticism is not dead! Beuken makes the wise observation that differences of literary genre are not of themselves indicators of independent pericopes. Rather, they play "a role of differentiating the pericope, not of dividing it" (31–32). He then delineates two major sections in vv. 1–6, the address of the prophet, and vv. 7–17, the praise of God, which he then further subdivides in his exposition.

From a form-critical perspective, one of the unique features of the unit of vv. 1–6 is the unusual function of the messenger formula ("says the LORD your God"). In vv. 1 and 6 the formula serves, not as a sign of direct address, since nowhere in vv. 1–6 does God appear to be speaking in the first person. Rather, this *formula citandi* represents a way of referring to God's activity lying behind the prophet when the deity is actually not present on stage.

Generally in the past it has been argued that chapter 54 contains a series of oracles construed in metaphorical style by which to address Zion in the guise of the forsaken wife. Beuken proposes a very different theory of interpretation when he argues that to begin with the assumption that Zion is being addressed from the start loses the richness of the imagery. He notes that the appeal is first to a nameless woman in a twofold shape of the barren ancestress, Sarah, as mother, followed by a different image of the forsaken wife. This double identity tallies with two phases of Israel's history up to the exile. Only in v. 11 does the imagery shift from the abandoned woman to that of the personified city, Zion. Thus the chapter is linked in a series that moves from the images of mother, wife, and city, and symbolizes three epochs of Israel's existence.

Beuken then contends that this multiple identity is only understood within the concept of "corporate personality," a concept first formulated by H. W. Robinson. This concept constitutes the anthropological mold in which chapter 53 has been cast. Beuken then proceeds to elaborate on the different spheres of reality that are foreign to the modern mentality expressed within the categories of corporate personality, such as the relation of the one and the many, and the fluidity between different ontological spheres (69). In his commentary, written some ten years after the initial article, Beuken has toned down the importance of this concept, but the effect on his exegesis has remained constant.

In my judgment, Beuken has made many acute and sensitive interpretations of the imagery of chapter 54 by his careful delineation between the different aspects of the mother-wife imagery. However, I think that he has been misled by appealing to Robinson's theory of corporate personality, which has not held up well under close scrutiny in the post–World War II period. Particularly, his attempt to correlate the imagery with three different historical periods seems strained. In sum, the theory of multiple identity has taken the diversity of imagery in a wrong direction by projecting a philosophical theory of "pre-logical" understanding of reality (Lévy-Bruhl), which has not been helpful. Consequently, I suspect that he has overinterpreted the meaning of the passage.

Finally, there is another interpretation of the imagery of chapter 54 that calls for an assessment. In a provocative essay, J. F. A. Sawyer argues the case that the feminine imagery of this chapter, along with the rest of Second Isaiah, has not been correctly analyzed, largely because of traditional male insensitivity. In his opinion, the "daughter of Zion" is just as prominent a figure in chapters 40–66 as the servant of the Lord. He then attempts to reconstruct a parallel story from the imagery, which has a plot and characters. In my judgment, this attempt has badly misconstrued the important role of the feminine imagery within the book of Isaiah. To take imagery that has been clearly identified in Second Isaiah as a figurative depiction of Zion and to render it as a portrayal of a figure paralleled to the servant is to engage in a confusion of literary categories. For example, there is a general agreement within the modern scholarly guild that one cannot reconstruct a novel about the life of Gomer from the imagery in the book of Hosea. Likewise in Isaiah, the figurative language of the prophet must be interpreted within a subtle dialectic, namely, to render the figurative language in the light of its explicit referent, and, conversely, the referent in the light of its figurative depiction. Above all, the language cannot be given a life of its own through various forms of objectification, whether rationalistic or romantic. In terms of chapter 54, the unity of the chapter's content, in spite of the great diversity of the figurative language, illustrates clearly the function of the metaphor within this prophetic proclamation.

2. Exposition

[**54:1–3**] The prophet addresses Zion in the imagery of the mother. The three epithets in v. 1 are virtually synonymous: "barren," "never bore a child," "never in labor." This observation is in contrast to the imagery of the wife in vv. 4–6: "widowhood," "wife forsaken," "married young" (cf. Beuken, 35). In vv. 1–3 the prophet begins by calling on the barren mother to break forth in singing. The theme of a turn in Jerusalem's fortunes had previously been sounded in 51:17ff. The reader is not to look for any strict consistency within the variety of imagery. In 51:17 the woman's isolation is pictured in terms of her being forsaken by the sons whom she has borne, not by her being childless. In vv. 1–3 the portrait of the desolate mother is set over against the joyous surprise of suddenly experiencing an abundance of children, greater in number than those conceived by women who were not barren. The imagery shifts to that of enlarging the tents in order to accommodate the huge influx of unexpected offspring.

Beuken has argued at length that the imagery of the woman in vv. 1–3 calls to mind Sarah, the ancestral mother of Israel. However, the theme of the barren mother, while an essential trait of the patriarchal period (Gen. 11:32), occurs elsewhere in the settlement and monarchial periods (Judg. 13:2; 1 Sam. 7:5), and does not in itself constitute a reference to a particular period in Israel's history. The force of the recurring imagery serves to contrast the irony of calling upon a barren woman, who is suffering the worse fate of her sex, to break forth in joyous singing. Again, the theme of possessing the land of the nations and of occupying the desolate cities also functions to highlight the extent of the promised change in Jerusalem's sad condition. In addition, vv. 1–3 build on the note of utter surprise and incomprehension sounded earlier in 49:19ff.: "Who ever bore me these? . . . [F]rom where have they come?"

[**4–6**] The imagery of humiliated Zion continues in these verses, but the metaphor has been extended in a slightly different direction. The focus now falls on the abandoned wife, who bears the shame and reproach of widowhood. The formula "fear not" serves explicitly to offer comfort. When form-critics insist on describing the formula as an imitation of a *Heilsorakel,* little insight is added to its present function, which has retained no cultic flavor whatever. The emphasis of the prophetic words falls on removing the shame, confusion, and stigma of Zion by an act of divine intervention. God is then described with a series of powerful names: Maker, husband, Redeemer, and Holy One of Israel. The terms are all familiar from the earlier chapters, but call to mind the nature both of the savior and salvation that have been developed since chapter 40. The renewed call for a response is then illustrated by two similes: a grieving wife who has been forsaken and a first wife once young who has been cast off for another. The desolation portrayed is clearly shaped by the misery of the exile, but there is no evidence that two different historical periods are being symbolized through this figurative language.

[7–10] The promise to desolate Jerusalem is now given by God himself in a first person address: "I abandoned you. . . . I will bring you back. . . . I hid my face. . . . I show you compassion." Twice in vv. 7–10 the use of a messenger formula indicates that the divine word has been mediated through the prophet, but in a slightly different form from vv. 1–3 with its *formula citandi*. Only in vv. 11ff. is the divine address offered directly (but cf. v. 13), but then it concludes by a prophetic voice using a summary-appraisal formula.

Verse 7 describes the moment of the change in the divine will towards Israel, which was first heralded in chapter 40. The exile is portrayed as but a brief moment of being forsaken, which is contrasted with the great gathering in compassion. God's momentary wrath stands opposed to an everlasting love. The reference to the "days of Noah" is used to buttress the oath not again to be angry with Israel: "my steadfast love (*ḥesed*) for you will never move, nor will my convenant of peace by shaken." Clearly the terminology of the Genesis flood provides the language for the renewed promise of an everlasting convenant, but it is idle to speculate whether only the Priestly tradition of the flood was known to the prophet. The shift in the imagery of the passage from abandoned wife to covenant and the rebuilding of the holy city does not obscure the basic unity of the chapter, in which great freedom of language has been used to project a vision of Zion's future.

[11–17] The concluding section describes in enthusiastic exuberance the rebuilding of a new Jerusalem both from an external and internal perspective. The old city is now portrayed as afflicted and storm-tossed, but the new is depicted in extravagant, joyful language. Her stones will be set as precious stones in antimony. (Many commentators have identified the noun with a black powder used by oriental women to blacken the eyelids in order to enhance the eyes' appearance.) Her foundation made of sapphires is often identified with lapis lazuli. Her battlements will be decorated with rubies, her gates set in precious stones, and the entire encircling wall constructed with costly gems. Some older commentators, such as Vitringa, attempted to construct an elaborate symbolism from the different colors of the stones and to attach a specific virtue to each stone, but such allegorical interpretations have largely disappeared in the modern period. However, it is also clear that in the later chapters of Isaiah the description of the new Jerusalem continues to expand in elegance with the themes of foreigners rebuilding the walls (60:10), the gates left continually open (60:11), and the presence of God providing the city light by day and night (60:1); cf. Rev. 21:10ff.)

Verse 13 picks up the theme of Zion's being taught by God, which was first developed in 48:17: "I am Yahweh your God, who teaches you what profits." Then the theme of Zion's future prosperity is described in the theological terms of righteousness and lack of violence. The meaning of v. 15 remains very controversial, but the sense seems to be that God, who is the creative force behind human capacity to forge weapons of war, now assures his people that none will be used against them. Is this an echo from First Isaiah of a past time when God employed an enemy to wield its weapons against Israel (10:5)? The transformation of the weapons of war to those of peace among the nations also resonates with the notes of 2:4.

The divine oracle concludes with a summary formula, delivered not by God but by the prophet in God's name: "Such is the heritage of the servants of the LORD, and this is their vindication from me." It has long been observed that the expression "servant of the LORD" is unique in Second Isaiah. Elliger succinctly summarizes the issue (162): Second Isaiah never uses the plural form, but names the servant always in the singular. Conversely, Third Isaiah never uses the singular, but always speaks of "servants" (54:17; 63:17; 65:8, 9, 13, 14, 15; 66:14). However, Elliger then draws a false implication by suggesting that 54:17 must therefore by necessity be ascribed to the author of Third Isaiah. As a result, he fails to understand the true significance of the use of v. 17 as a conclusion to chapter 54. Even more disastrous exegetically is the move of Watts (241) who designates v. 17b as the introduction to chapter 55, thus cutting the crucial link of the "servants" with chapter 54.

Actually this verse serves a double function. On the one hand, it forms a crucial link between chapters 53 and 54, which has been largely lost by those commentators who suggest that chapter 53 is a later interpolation into the corpus of Second Isaiah. Earlier, notice had been taken of the continuation of certain terms from chapter 53 into chapter 54 (e.g., seed, the many, righteous, and peace). Now v. 17b provides the explicit motivation for this connection. The suffering servant of chapter 53 had been promised a posterity and the fruit of his labor. On his account many were to be accounted righteous (v. 11). Isaiah 54:17 builds on this promise. The suffering innocent one of chapter 53 is seen as having his life, in some way, extended and incorporated through his suffering by those who are now designated "the servants of the LORD." They are the bearers of the true faith in the next generation. In 50:10 a challenge had been given to all who would respond obediently to the voice of the servant. In chapter 53 they had then responded in a confession that through the suffering of the servant they had been made whole. They now will receive their vindication from God.

On the other hand, 54:17b serves as an organic link to the ensuing chapters of Third Isaiah, and demonstrates that these chapters are integrally related to the preceding chapters, the prophetic vision of chapters 40—55. Indeed, in Third Isaiah the question of how God's promised salvation was received and fulfilled is addressed in terms of the communal heirs of the servant. Although many of the promises offered to Zion in chapter 54 had been given earlier, the special role of chapter 54 emerges when they are joined to the heritage of the servants of the Lord, which could only occur after chapter 53 within the continuing narrative depiction.

55. Isaiah 55:1–13

55:1   Attention, all you who are thirsty,
> come to the waters.
> Even you who have no money,
> > come, buy and eat.
> Come, buy[a] wine and milk
> > without money or cost.

2   Why spend money for what is not bread,
> and your earning for what does not satisfy?
> Listen carefully to me,
> > and you will eat what is good,
> > and enjoy the richest diet.

3   Pay attention and come to me.
> Listen and you will be revived.
> I will make an everlasting covenant with you,
> > my enduring mercies promised to David.

4   Behold, I have made him a witness to the peoples,
> a ruler and leader of peoples.

5   Behold, you will summon nations you do not know,
> and nations that do not know you
> will come running to you,
> because of the LORD your God,
> > the Holy One of Israel, who has glorified you.

6   Seek the LORD while he still can be found,
> call to him while he is close.

7   Let the wicked forsake his way,
         and the sinful man his thoughts.
     Let him return to the LORD,
         and he will show mercy to him,
         and to our God, for he freely forgives.
8   For my thoughts are not your thoughts,
         nor are my ways your ways,
         says the LORD.
9   But as the heavens are higher than the earth,
         so are my ways higher than your ways,
         and my thoughts than your thoughts.
10   As the rain and snow come down from heaven
         and do not return there without watering the earth,
     making it bring forth and grow
         in order to produce seed for sowing
         and bread for eating,
11   so is my word that goes forth from my mouth.
         It will not return to me unfulfilled,
     but accomplishes what I purpose,
         and succeeds in what I sent it to do.
12   Surely you will go out in joy,
         and be led forth in peace.
     The mountains and hills
         will break out in singing,
         and all the trees of the field will clap their hands.
13   Instead of the briar, a cypress will grow,
         instead of the thistle, a myrtle will come up.
     These shall stand as a testimony to the LORD,
         as an everlasting sign that will not be destroyed.

a. It is possible that the MT suffers from dittography in repeating the phrase "come, buy," thus producing an unusually long verse (cf. *BHS*).

Selected Bibliography

J. Begrich, *Studien zu Deuterojesaja,* ThB 20, Munich 1969, 59–60; **W. A. M. Beuken,** "Isa. 55:3–5: The Reinterpretation of David," *BTFT* 35, 1974, 49–64; **W. Brueggemann,** "Isaiah 55 and Deuteronomic Theology," *ZAW* 80, 1968, 191–203; **A. Caquot,** "La prophétie de Nathan et ses échos lyriques, "*VTSup* 9, 1963, 213–24; **R. J. Clifford,** "Isaiah 55: Invitation to a Feast," *The Word of the Lord Shall Go Forth, Fs D. N. Freedman,* ed. C. L. Meyers and M. O'Connor, Winona Lake 1983, 27–35; **J. H. Eaton,** "The King as God's Witness," *ASTI* 7, 1970, 25–40; **O. Eissfeldt,** "The Promises of Grace to David in Isaiah 55:1–5," *Israel's Prophetic Heritage: Essays in Honor of James Muilenburg,* ed. B. W. Anderson and W. Harrelson, London 1962, 196 207; **W. Grimm and K. Dittert,** *Deuterojesaja,* Stuttgart 1990,

476–79; **J. M. Vincent,** *Studien zur literarischen Eigenart und zur geistigen Heimat von Jesaja, Kap. 40–55,* BET 5, 1977, Frankfurt and Bern, 65–107; **H. G. M. Williamson,** "'The Sure Mercies of David': Subjective or Objective Genitive?" *JSS* 23, 1978, 31–49; **W. Zimmerli,** "Jahwes Wort bei Deuterojesaja," *VT* 32, 1982, 104–24.

1. Structure, Genre, and Context

Although a few modern commentators have joined 55:1–5 to the preceding chapter, this division seems inappropriate for several reasons, particularly since 54:17 provides a conclusion to the thematic movement of chapter 54. A new subject begins in chapter 55, even though admittedly it is closely related to chapter 54. Then again, there are commentators who connect 55:11–12 with chapter 56, but this analysis is difficult to accept in the light of the messenger formula of 56:1, which marks a sharp caesura.

Verses 1–5 form a rather clear unit of thought, even though the imagery and style of these verses are quite diverse. The remarkable cluster of imperatives in vv. 1–3 is set apart from the verbal forms of vv. 4 and 5, both of which are introduced by the interjection "behold" (*hēn*). Various form-critical themes have been proposed to explain the unusual shape of the divine invitation in vv. 1–3. Some wisdom motifs have been identified, which offer verbal parallels to those of Proverbs 9 and Sir. 24:19ff. Then again, Westermann's suggestion of the language of a merchant at a market aggressively hawking his wares is also illuminating. Actually, these two proposed settings are not in basic conflict as Clifford contends, because Dame Wisdom is often described in the Old Testament in the idiom of an aggressive hawker. As we have often discovered, the form-critical problem of establishing an original setting is frequently of minor exegetical importance in Second Isaiah because of the great freedom exercised by the prophet in reshaping the material for his own ends. Clifford's alleged parallels from Ugarit of a royal banquet have little to do with the prophet's invitation to enter into the joy of God's new order.

The theme of a covenant with David is introduced in v. 3, and it is developed further within a chiastic pattern in v. 4. The unit is formulated as a divine oracle, even though in v. 5 the sharp division between prophetic and divine speech is beginning to break down (cf. the third person reference to God).

In vv. 6–7 a prophetic oracle is clearly present that serves to introduce the divine promise following in vv. 8–13. Verses 12–13 form a conclusion to the chapter, but also to the larger corpus of chapters 40—55. We have already noted Second Isaiah's pattern of concluding a section with a call to exit from Babylon with joy (48:20–23; 49:13; 52:11–12). In sum, the traditional oral forms in chapter 55 have been largely pushed into the background and made subordinate to the overriding themes that summarize the book of Second Isaiah.

2. Exposition

[55:1–3] A series of imperatives give the passage an immediate heightening of intensity: come, buy, eat, pay attention, listen. Who then is the addressee and to what end is this divine invitation to enter into such abundance? Some take the invitation as yet another general appeal to the people of Israel to share in the promised gifts of God, but this broad interpretation misses the specific nature both of this appeal and of the content of what is being offered. Far more likely is an interpretation that relates chapter 55 to chapter 54, and thereby sees the recipients of the invitation to be the "servants of the LORD" (54:17).

The invitation is for those to whom the heritage of the suffering servant falls, to embrace to the full the new divine world order that had just been described in 54:9ff. In the past, commentators have debated at length whether the blessings, which are portrayed by Second Isaiah as a form analogous to that used by a rowdy street hawker, are of a material or a spiritual nature. But surely to formulate these two dimensions in a dichotomy is a false way to state the question. Much like the book of Deuteronomy, which describes the joy of Israel's inheritance (*naḥªlāh*) as eating and drinking before the Lord in sheer delight (8:7ff.; 12:15), so also for Second Isaiah the material and spiritual gifts for Israel are closely fused and cannot be torn apart.

Very shortly it becomes fully clear that the goal of the invitation is the obtaining of life (v. 3), and this is only possible because of the "covenant of peace" through God's compassions (54:10). Israel is invited to come and listen. What then brings life is the divine word (55:11), which causes the earth to sprout forth in creative abundance. Again the parallel with Deuteronomy is close: "one does not live by bread alone but by every word that comes from the mouth of God" (8:3).

Verse 3 next moves in a remarkably new direction by tying the invitation of life offered to the servants of the Lord in an everlasting covenant according to "my enduring mercies promised to David." In one sense this move had been anticipated in chapter 54 when an analogy was drawn between the steadfast love shown in the former days of Noah and God's present compassion toward Israel through a covenant of peace. Yet it is also clear that much more of the greatest significance is involved in the promise of an everlasting covenant of enduring loyalty promised to David than simply a reference to divine favors in the past.

The term "eternal covenant" (*bᵉrît 'ôlām*) occurs in the Pentateuch within the Priestly tradition (Gen. 9:16; Ex. 31:16; Lev. 24:8; etc.), in Third Isaiah (61:8), and in the later layers of Jeremiah and Ezekiel (Jer. 32:40; 50:5; Ezek. 16:60; 37:20). The expression "enduring mercies to David" (*ḥasdê dāwid*), which is to be understood as an objective genitive (Williamson), occurs only twice in the Hebrew Bible (Isa. 55:3; 2 Chron. 6:42). Yet more important than this statistic is the nature of the tradition that is represented here. In his article of 1962, O. Eissfeldt pointed out the close relationship between Isa. 55:3–4 and Psalm 89. He developed a strong case for seeing here a preexilic origin for a Davidic tradition of an everlasting dynasty, a tradition found elsewhere within the Old Testament in other forms (2 Samuel 7; Jer. 33:20–22; Ps. 18:51; 2 Chron. 6:42).

Particularly significant is the form of the Davidic tradition in Psalm 89. The psalmist speaks of "a covenant with my chosen one," "sworn to David my servant," "to establish your descendants forever." The choice of vocabulary in v. 29(28) is especially close to Isaiah 55: "steadfast love . . . forever . . . standing firm." However, the main purpose of Psalm 89 is not simply to recall an ancient promise, but rather to sound a heartrending cry of complaint to God: "You have renounced the covenant with your servant. . . . Where is your steadfast love of old . . . sworn to David?"

In the light of this background, the use of the Davidic tradition by Second Isaiah receives its special role. The prophet takes up the selfsame promise, but he has reinterpreted it in a strikingly new fashion. Some have spoken of a prophetic "midrash" on Psalm 89, but it would be perhaps more accurate simply to describe the persistent usage of intertextual reference to components within this psalm according to a manner that goes beyond a common oral tradition.

[4–5] The central issue at stake is the manner in which the analogy between the promise to David is now related to the role of those Israelites now being addressed. In v. 3 the everlasting covenant made with David is explicitly transferred to the people. The promise is no longer tied to David and assigned to the past, but is renewed as a present, active reality. The contrast is continued further in vv. 4 and 5, in which both referents are introduced by an interjection—"behold"—first, in respect to David: "I have made him a witness to the peoples, a rule and leader of peoples." The sense of both of these cola is difficult to interpret. J. H. Eaton (32) has explored several possible meanings of the king as witness within the royal psalms, and he ultimately concludes that the king's witness to God's incomparability is the main sense. In addition, the usual title of David as "ruler (*nagîd*) of his people" (1 Sam. 13:14; 25:30) has been expanded to become "ruler and leader of peoples."

The problem, however, in these designations is that, historically speaking, David was neither an example of a witness, nor a prince for peoples. At most, one can find in the royal ideology of the psalms a hint at a wider universal role for the idealized king (Ps. 18:43–44), which is itself an inadequate explanation for the prophet's formulation. Actually, what emerges in v. 4 is a prophetic construct used to depict David's true vocation according to the original, theological purpose of God for his anointed one. Like the servant Israel (Isa. 43:9–10) who was appointed to bear witness, so David's true role as God's chosen is presented as a witness to God's wonders (Ps. 89:6–7). Moreover, David's office as divinely appointed leader has now been extended to encompass not just Israel, but, in a positive sense, also the nations.

If v. 4 speaks prophetically of David's role in the past as God's witness, v. 5 picks up the theme of the continuation of the promise into the present, but placed within the context of an actual transference. The recipients of the address, the servants of 54:17, are now given their calling within the everlasting covenant. They are to call nations, not previously known, who will respond to this invitation, not because of Israel's power or intrinsic worth, but because of the glory of God that they now reflect. It comes as no surprise that the servants of the Lord continue in the selfsame calling extended both to the servant Israel (42:6) and to the suffering individual servant of Yahweh (49:5ff).

In sum, it is important to see how Second Isaiah has transformed the Davidic convenantal tradition. Certainly the prophet does not envision a restoration of a Davidic rule according to the pleas of the psalmist. Nor does Second Isaiah share the same eschatological hope found in Jer. 23:5, "I will raise up for David a righteous branch," or in Ezek. 34:23, "I will set over them one shepherd, my servant David." However, it is also the case that there is a continuity between the original promise to David and the new purpose envisioned for the prophetic community of faith in Isaiah 55, which contradicts the opinion expressed by some that the former was only warlike and the latter only peaceful. Rather, the covenant of David, which has been sustained by the eternal loyalty of God, was seen as continuing in the new people of Israel, but in a form that fulfilled the original purpose of David's rule in the glorifying of God by all the nations of the world. The transformation of the form of the promise was not a general move toward universalism or democratic participation, but in the context of the prophetic drama of chapters 40–55 resulted from the work of the suffering servant whose seed, the servants of Yahweh, received the inheritance (54:17; cf. 65:8, 9, 13, 15).

Finally, there is an additional aspect to the problem of the eternal covenant to David and the shaping of the message of Second Isaiah. When P. Volz (2:138ff.) speaks of a transfer from the political sphere to that of the spiritual, he has mistaken the prophetic polarity, which is a transformation of a different order. At first it might seem odd that in the concluding chapter of the corpus of Second Isaiah the tradition of David's rule should be taken up. Indeed, one of the striking differences between First Isaiah (1–39) and Second Isaiah (40–55) is that the hope of a future messianic figure plays such a central role in the former (chapters 7, 9, 11), whereas it appears to be either unknown or repudiated by the latter. Yet this sudden reference to the Davidic covenant in chapter 55 can hardly be accidental.

One of the contributions of Eissfeldt's essay is in pointing out the great similarity between Psalm 89 and Second Isaiah, not just in terms of the tradition of an eternal covenant to David, but on a far more comprehensive scale. Many of the same words and unusual expressions are found in both: "To whom then will you liken God, or with what likeness compare him?" (Ps. 89:7 // Isa. 40:18); "who cut Rahab to pieces" (Ps. 89:11 // Isa. 51:9); "my chosen one" (Ps. 89:4 // Isa. 42:1), among others (cf. Eissfeldt's complete text, 199–200). It is most important to see in this relation that the promise to David has not been repudiated by Second Isaiah, but extended and transferred to the mission of the servants of the Lord in the new world order depicted by the prophet.

In a word, Second Isaiah has incorporated the messianic promise to David in First Isaiah into a new version of God's future rule. In Isa. 65:25 (Third Isaiah), there is an extensive citation from Isaiah 11 that describes the future messianic age. Thus, in Third Isaiah the imagery of the servants of Yahweh from Second Isaiah (54:17) has been joined with that of the imagery of the messianic age of First Isaiah. It is very likely that this fusion reflects an editorial activity (cf. the exposition of chapters 56—66 below) by which chapters 65 and 66 serve to unite the entire Isaianic corpus of sixty-six chapters. Nevertheless, the role of the Davidic covenant in chapter 55 is a strong indication that already within Second Isaiah a link between the imagery of the servant and the messianic Davidic rule has been formed. The observation has been made earlier that chapter 55 has been strongly shaped by its intertextual relations to Psalm 89. Is it also possible that the numerous references in the psalm to David, not only as the chosen one, but as God's servant (*'abdî*, vv. 4[3], 21[20], 49[39]), also serve as another intertextual link to the dominant servant imagery of Second Isaiah? In spite of the strikingly different imagery of First and Second Isaiah—the difference is between royal and nonroyal language—there is evidence that a coercion was exerted in the shaping of the whole Isaianic corpus by a common vision of the ultimate rule of God in justice and compassionate love.

[6–9] In vv. 6–7 the style of address returns to that of the dominant imperative mode, this time through the mouth of the prophet. Whereas in the earlier oracle the search for the abundant riches of life was expressed in terms of water, milk, and wine ("you will eat what is good, and enjoy the richest diet") in vv. 6–7 it is clear that the object of Israel's search for life is found in God alone. However, God is not a static object merely to be located, but God is one who lets himself be known (cf. Jer. 29:10ff.). The seeker is urged to respond when his presence is known, when God can be found. The contrast is made by means of a chiastic structure between the ways and thoughts of humans (v. 7) and the thoughts and ways of God (v. 8). By God's thoughts are intended his plans and purpose, which differ in kind from those of human beings as greatly as that distance dividing heaven from earth.

[10–11] The image of heaven and earth is continued in v. 10, but turned in a different direction. Just as the rain from heaven falls on the earth and causes it to flourish, so also God's word, which is the source of all life, also goes forth and accomplishes the purpose of God for which it was intended. Of course, the striking element in this imagery is its parallel to the prologue of the book (chapter 40), which sets out in the beginning the drama of God's intervention for Israel's redemption in terms of the writing of the word of God which stands forever (40:8). Thus, it is completely fitting as a conclusion of the corpus of Second Isaiah that the prophet returns to the subject that undergirds his entire message. The history of the redemption and of the return of the exiles from Babylonian captivity, which involved the conquest of the false gods, the humiliation of Babylon, the role of Cyrus, and finally the call of the servant Israel, can finally best be described as the creation of the divine word working itself in accordance to the purpose of the sovereign creator of heaven and earth, the Holy One of Israel.

[12–13] The final two verses offer in highly exalted language a climax to the book, which concludes with a summarizing song of praise. Israel will go forth from Babylon in peace, breaking forth in singing, to see the transformation of the created world sharing in the moment of salvation. Indeed, a testimony to God and an everlasting sign that shall not perish!

(For a study of the use of Isaiah 55 in the New Testament, see W. Grimm and K. Dittert, 476–79.)

56. Introduction to Chapters 56—66 (Third Isaiah)

Selected Bibliography

R. Abramowski, "Zum literarischen Problem von Jesaja 56—66," *ThStK* 96/97, 1925, 90–143; **E. Achtemeier,** *The Community and Message of Isaiah 56—66,* Minneapolis 1982; **B. W. Anderson,** "The Apocalyptic Rendering of the Isaiah Tradition," *The Social World of Formative Christianity and Judaism, Fs H. C. Kee,* ed. J. Neusner et al., Philadelphia 1988, 17–38; **W. A. M. Beuken,** "Trito-Jesaja: profetie en schriftgeleerdheid," *Profeten in profetische Geschriften, Fs. A. S. van der Woude,* ed. F. G. Martinéz, Kampen 1984, 71–85; *Jesaja,* III/A, POT, Nijkirk 1989, 7–18; "The Main Theme of Trito-Isaiah: 'The Servants of YHWH,'" *JSOT* 47, 1990, 67–87; "Isaiah chapters LXV—LXVI: Trito-Isaiah and the Closure of the Book of Isaiah," *Congress Volume Leuven,* ed. J. A. Emerton, VTSup 43, Leiden 1991, 204–21; **J. Blenkinsopp,** "The 'Servants of the Lord' in Third Isaiah," *Proceedings of the Irish Biblical Association* 7, 1983, 1–23; "The Servant and the Servants in Isaiah and the Formation of the Book," *Writing and Reading the Scroll of Isaiah,* I, ed. C. C. Broyles and C. A. Evans, Leiden 1997, 155–75; **H. Bloom,** *The Anxiety of Influence: A Theory of Poetry,* New York 1973; **B. S. Childs,** "Retrospective Reading of the Old Testament Prophets," *ZAW* 108, 1996, 362–77; **R. E. Clements,** "Beyond Tradition-History: Deutero-Isaianic Development of First Isaiah's Themes," *JSOT* 31, 1985, 95–113; **K. Elliger,** *Die Einheit des Tritojesaja,* BWANT 45, Stuttgart 1928; "Der Prophet Tritojesaja," *ZAW* 49, 1931, 112–41; *Deuterojesaja in seinem Verhältnis zu Tritojesaja,* BWANT 63, Stuttgart 1933; **G. I. Emmerson,** *Isaiah 56—66,* JSOTSup Sheffield 1992; **P. D. Hanson,** *The Dawn of Apocalyptic,* Philadelphia 1975; **J. Hollander,** *The Figure of Echo: A Mode of Allusion in Milton and After,* Berkeley 1981; **K. Koenen,** *Ethik und Eschatologie im Tritojesajabuch,* WMANT 62, Neukirchen-Vluyn, 1990; **R. Lack,** *La symbolique du livre d'Isaïe: essai sur l'image litteraire comme element de structuration,* AnBib 59, Rome 1973; **W. Lau,** *Schriftgelehrte Prophetie in Jes 56—66,* BZAW 225, Berlin 1994; **L. J. Liebreich,** "The Compilation of the Book of Isaiah," *JQR* 46, 1955–56, 259–77; 47, 1956–57, 114–38; **F. Maass,** "Tritojesaja?" *Das ferne und das nahe Wort, Fs L. Rost,* BZAW 105, 1967, 153–63; **H. Odeberg,** *Trito-Isaiah,* Uppsala 1931; **K. Pauritsch,** *Die neue Gemeinde: Gott sammelt Augestossene und Arme (Jesaja 56—66),* AnBib 47, Rome 1971; **R. Rendtorff,** "The Composition of the Book of Isaiah," *Canon and Theology,* ET Minneapolis 1993, 146–69; "Isaiah 56:1 as a Key to the Formation of the Book of Isaiah," ibid., 181–89; **B. Schramm,** *The Opponents of Third Isaiah: Reconstructing the Cultic History of the Restoration,* JSOTSup 193, Sheffield 1995; **E. Sehmsdorf,** "Studien zur Redaktionsgeschichte von Jesaja 56—66," *ZAW* 84, 517–76; **C. Seitz, ed.,** *Reading and Preaching the Book of Isaiah,* Philadelphia 1988; **S. Sekine,** *Die Tritojesanische Sammlung (Jes 56—66) redaktionsgeschichtlich untersucht,* Berlin 1989; **O. H. Steck,** *Studien zu Tritojesaja,* BZAW 203, Berlin 1991; "Author und/oder Redaktor in Jesaja 56—66," *Writing and Reading the Scroll of Isaiah,* I, VTSup 71, ed. C. C. Broyles et al., Leiden 1997, 219–59; **J. Vermeylen,** *Du Prophète Isaïe à l'Apocalyptique,* II, Paris 1978, 451–517; ed., *The Book of Isaiah,* Leuven 1989; "L'unité du livre d'Isaïe," ibid., 11–53; **P. Volz,** "Jesaja 56—66. Einleitung," *Jesaia II,* KAT, Leipzig 1932, 197–202; **C. Westermann,** "Structure and Composition of Chapters 56—66," *Isaiah 40—66,* ET Philadelphia 1969, 296–308; **A. Zillessen,** "'Tritojesaja' und Deuterojesaja. Eine literarische Untersuchung zu Jes 56—66," *ZAW* 26, 1906, 231–76; **W. Zimmerli,** "Zur Sprache Tritojesajas," (1950), reprinted in *Gottes Offenbarung. Gesammelte Aufsätze,* ThB 19, Munich 1969, 217–33.

1. Introduction

As is well known, the last eleven chapters of the book of Isaiah were separated from chapters 40—55 by Duhm in 1892 and assigned the name of Third Isaiah. Duhm ascribed these writings to different authors from chapters 40—55, whom he located in Jerusalem during the postexilic age shortly before the period of Nehemiah and long after the return of the Jews from captivity. He regarded the eleven chapters as largely a unified literary corpus.

Because the subsequent history of the debates over the nature of Third Isaiah have been reviewed so frequently in Old Testament introductions, in articles, and monographs (e.g., Pauritsch, Sekine), it seems hardly necessary to rehearse this material, especially within a commentary. Needless to say, many questions first raised by Duhm remained unresolved and occupied the scholarly community for the next half century. Such names as Elliger, Odenberg, and Volz emerged at the forefront of research. In the early post–World War II period new interest in Third Isaiah began to emerge with the substantial commentary of Westermann and the stimulating essay of Zimmerli, among others.

However, within the last several decades there has been a virtual explosion of new interest in the problems of Third Isaiah, coupled of course with its relation to Second Isaiah. In many ways the volume of collected essays edited by Vermeylen provided an initial benchmark in registering many of the new forces at work on the book of Isaiah. It is again not my purpose to sketch the contribution of a host of scholars, but names such as Pauritsch, Sehmsdorf, Sekine, Beuken, Steck, Hanson, Rendtorff, Koenen, and Lau have all offered serious work on the interpretation of these chapters. Rather, my aim is to outline some of the persistent problems involved in these chapters and to offer an overview of my own solutions, which will be then developed in more detail in the succeeding exegesis. I shall begin with more general hermeneutical issues, which greatly influence how one deals with the literary, historical, and theological issues.

2. Hermeneutical Reflections

I shall argue that both a diachronic and a synchronic dimension are necessary for biblical exegesis. In a word, I deem inadequate the usual diachronic approach of traditional historical criticism that offers a literary and historical reconstruction of the text's allegedly original background as the necessary context for critical interpretation. Likewise, I reject a synchronic or structuralist rendering—a position increasingly defended both in liberal and conservative circles—which focuses solely on the text as a self-sufficient literary entity apart from any consideration of the reality behind its written form. Rather, the crucial issue remains in determining how the diachronic and synchronic relate.

The genuine complexity of the hermeneutical problem emerges when one senses that these two different approaches cannot simply be joined. The relationship is far more subtle. An "objective" analysis of "what really happened," viewed, as it were, from the "outside" offers a different kind of perception of reality from that found in the Bible, that is, from "inside." Here reality is understood not only as including the divine, but also as requiring for its perception a particular stance and faith perspective of the viewer. This hermeneutical distention is usually formulated as a contrast between reading the text as "source" or as "witness." Of course, occasionally the Bible itself makes use of source as part of its witness. Thus, the prophet Jeremiah enjoins his readers to confirm the truth of his witness by seeking from the experience of the nations a confirmation of Israel's guilt (18:13).

In addition, there is another aspect to the hermeneutical issue that bears closely on the interpretation of Third Isaiah. The issue turns on exactly what one understands by "witness." Not every component of the biblical text carries the same weight or serves a similar role as tradent of the prophetic message. In the process of canonical shaping some material has been assigned to the background, some to the foreground. The narrative or kerygmatic witness of the final form is often filled with vestiges from earlier stages of composition. These may bear only indirectly on the shape of the narrative whole, which has provided a "storied" referentiality essential to its kerygmatic (canonical) witness.

Moreover, this hermeneutical issue provides the warrant for the insistence on giving exegetical priority to the final form of the text. The decision is not derived from a higher evaluation of the last level of redaction per se, but rather in the entire critical assessment provided by the final form of the text as to what is normative for Israel's faith involving all the different levels. It is constitutive of canonical shaping to offer this theological *Sachkritik* on the tradition in its entirety. The process is not the same as harmonizing because often the retention of elements of tension within the canonical text has been judged to be essential to Israel's authoritative scriptures. The implications of this hermeneutical understanding of the role of exegesis for various modern exegetical techniques (literary, form-critical, redactional, sociological) will be examined throughout the commentary.

3. The Relationship between Second and Third Isaiah

The relationship between chapters 40—55 and 56—66 lies at the heart of the exegetical task and continues to pose major problems. I strongly support the recent move (cf. Beuken, Rendtorff, Steck) to interpret chapters 56—66 as part of a larger literary collection rather than to assume its function as an independent corpus that is only peripherally connected to the larger book of Isaiah. At the same time, chapters 56—66 clearly reveal striking differences in style, historical background, and theological emphasis, which must be acknowledged and exegetically pursued with boldness and skill.

One of the most important insights into the nature of Third Isaiah has been the recognition of the close dependency upon Second Isaiah, and, to a lesser degree, First Isaiah. This relationship is far closer than that of sharing a common oral tradition, but the nature of the dependency, often expressed in verbal citations and allusions, points to Third Isaiah's knowledge of chapters 40—55 in some sort of written form. A continuing oral transmission is not thereby excluded. This description is supported further by the present literary structuring of the chapters. There are far fewer signs of a prior oral stage of the material that would reflect the conventional forms of oral communication found especially in preexilic prophecy and continued to some extent in Second Isaiah.

Nevertheless, the issue of intertextual reference is far from settled and difficult problems remain to be resolved. Zimmerli felt that by comparing citations and allusions to Second Isaiah in Third Isaiah he could determine by the changes the intentional redactional goals of the latter. He concluded that Third Isaiah sought to adjust the highly concrete, eschatological message of Second Isaiah to a new postexilic situation by spiritualizing Second Isaiah's prophecy and rendering it into metaphorical language more suitable to ethical application by the postexilic community. In my opinion, Zimmerli's conclusions are largely dictated by prior assumptions regarding authorship, dating, and relation to Second Isaiah. In other words, I think that Zimmerli has often overinterpreted the text and thus misconstrued the relationship. I would argue that the citations and allusions, far from attempts to correct Second Isaiah's perspective, serve to call attention to Second Isaiah as an authoritative warrant and offer support for his continuing use of the same material. The references in Second Isaiah serve to highlight the continuity with chapters 40—55 rather than to mark a change in direction. Second Isaiah's prophetic message and authority are assumed (cf. Beuken, *Jesaja*, 3:22). The general lack of exact verbal correspondence is only a sign of the role of memory still at work, and the divergence is not automatically to be pressed as an intentional reinterpretation at each point of difference. I would again stress the deictic rather than the midrashic function of Third Isaiah's use of Second Isaiah.

I do not dispute that there are some real differences both in content and emphasis shown by comparing the parallels between Second and Third Isaiah (cf. 40:3; 57:14; 62:10). Some of them have clearly arisen from an altered historical situation. Nevertheless, it remains part of the exegetical task to determine whether these differences are part of fortuitous influences from a changing cultural background, but without an intentional purpose when measured by the passage's kerygmatic goal. Thus, when viewed as a whole, Third Isaiah continues to hold to a coming, eschatological change brought about by divine intervention into the created world and in direct continuity with Second

Isaiah, whose prophetic expectancy has not been rendered into toned-down metaphor (cf. 56:1 // 46:12).

4. The Nature of Third Isaiah: Prophet and Text

The recent focus on the use of citations and allusions by Third Isaiah has also greatly affected how one envisions the work of Third Isaiah. Ever since Duhm's initial analysis it has been customary to conceive of Third Isaiah as a prophetic figure much akin to the prophets of the preexilic period. They delivered their oracles orally, which were then subsequently collected as originally independent oracles and formed into larger literary corpora. Although this model has come under increasing attack as inaccurate for the postexilic period, vestiges of the theory still survive, even in Zimmerli's describing Third Isaiah as an individual, historical personage and disciple of Second Isaiah. More recently, a strong reaction has begun that moves in a very different direction. For example, Steck (*Studien zu Tritojesaja*) argues that Third Isaiah is simply a nomenclature by which to designate chapters 56–66. It is a cipher to denote the exposition of learned scribal prophecy. These chapters are a literary *Fortschreibung* of a received written corpus, largely consisting of a core from Second Isaiah, which was extended in the exilic period through a process of redactional reinterpretation. This scribal activity is directed to a small group of professional tradents who fully control through memory this entire literary legacy and thus are in a position to recognize and respond to the subtle art of intertextual exegesis (cf. Steck, "Ausblick," *Studien zu Tritojesaja,* 275). In my opinion, Lau's criticism of Steck's position (Lau, 16–17) is fully convincing when he argues that there is no evidence for the reconstruction of such an audience. Indeed, Steck's proposal is a highly unlikely model since it is far removed even from the earliest rabbinical practices from which one might have expected a precursor in a *Schriftgelehrte Prophetie*.

The resolution to this issue lies in avoiding the extremes found both in Duhm and Steck. Third Isaiah is neither to be assigned an individual historical personality, nor are these chapters to be rendered into a literary construct attributed to learned scribes. Rather, it is essential to maintain them as genuine prophecy that responds to the divine word, "Thus says Yahweh," an integral part of the larger prophetic book of Isaiah. The fact that Third Isaiah serves a particular function within the book (this position will be subsequently argued in detail) does not change in kind the nature of its content. The prophetic author, who is not just a learned scribe, follows Second Isaiah in keeping his identity anonymous when performing his role as a faithful tradent of the prophetic tradition of Isaiah. He lays claim to the same divine spirit that was given to his predecessor in 42:1, and he identifies fully with his same mission (cf. this commentary on chapter 61). In sum, his special prophetic testimony to God's purpose with Israel functions in these chapters apart from an individual historical identity, which is not given a specific historical context apart from its location within the narrative witness. At times, indeed, one hears in the text's background of a rebuilt temple, of a reconstructed cult, and of warring factions within the community. However, this information is never used to establish an absolute dating nor an exact chronology. Above all, such data does not serve to assign Third Isaiah to a separate historical person within the prophetic witness. Rather, Third Isaiah remains in close narrative continuity with Second Isaiah in prophesying the "new things" (different in kind from the "former things"), which are about to unfold within the eschatological plan of God (65:17).

5. The Purpose of Chapters 56—66

Finally, the question must be addressed regarding the purpose and function of these chapters designated as Third Isaiah. During the last two decades this issue has been closely tied to methodological debate. For many, it is a scholarly truism that the problem of determining the purpose of Third Isaiah cannot be resolved without first reconstructing the historical growth of the literature. Obviously, the obstacles to such an enterprise are immense because of the lack of solid evidence provided by the biblical text itself. Nevertheless, various critical proposals have been made. P. D. Hanson's sociological attempt to interpret the literature as resulting from a postexilic controversy between warring Jewish parties (visionary and hierarchical) has received some acceptance within the English-speaking world, but has also been widely criticized, especially in Europe, for its excessive historical speculation. My own uneasiness with the approach lies, above all, in its bringing to bear on Hanson's analysis an external set of sociological categories that provide the context from which to date and restructure the prophetic corpus in order to conform to an alleged historical process lying behind the text. Exegesis is thus dominated by ideology.

In Europe a much more widely accepted approach has been developed in various forms of redactional criticism. Earlier efforts are represented by Elliger and Pauritsch; more recently by Vermeylen, Sekine, Steck, and Koenen, among a host of others. In my judgment, much of interest has emerged from the effort to trace the work of various editors and in recovering various layers within the process. One can only admire the close scrutiny and detailed philological work that has been pursued in the enterprise. One of the most important results has been the discovery of the extent in which the editorial process has involved a shaping of the entire book of Isaiah (*das Grossjesajabuch*). This intention is especially clear in the intertextual linkage between chapters 1 and 65—66.

Nevertheless, in my opinion, there has again been a very serious downside to the redactional approach (cf. my essay, "Retrospective Readings"). Frequently the method seeks to sort out redactional strands by isolating passages that seem to show conceptual inconsistency. One therefore hears of a layer that is positive toward the nations over against another that is negative. Yet this polarity fails to reckon with the special function of this diversity within its present literary context. In a word, it disregards the entire dimension of a holistic reading that derives from its canonical shape. At times this search for conceptual consistency as a major criterion for recovering editorial activity has led to tortuous exegesis. Thus, for example, Steck assigns chapter 66 to one of the latest redactional layers of the corpus, yet then must explain why the postexilic temple appears as not yet built in v. 1 ("Tritojesaja im Jesajabuch," *Studien*, 396–97). Could it be that references to the temple and its reconstruction function in a special way within the book and cannot be immediately employed as a chronological artifact? In sum, redactional criticism should be used with caution and skill largely as a tool to aid in interpreting the rich texture of the present text, rather than as a means of reconstructing a complex, speculative theory of an alleged historical development.

Of all the methods proposed to address the problem of determining the purpose of these chapters, the recognition of the central role of intertextuality appears to me a most fruitful avenue of pursuit. Yet as the earlier discussion of Zimmerli's analysis of citations showed, the issue involves many problems, and scholars are far from united regarding the significance of the reuse of a passage (cf. Bloom, Hollander). Various distinctions have been introduced in an effort to gain further clarity. One speaks of direct citation, approximate citation, and of indirect allusion. Recently, Lau (15) has taken over Rosenzweig's term *Musivstil* (mosaic style) to characterize the intentional introduction of single words, often reflecting a catchword connection, that are placed within a different literary context from the original occurrence in order to effect a reinterpretation. Obviously, several problems come to mind that must be carefully explained before accepting the concept of *Musivstil* as an intertextual exegetical device of Third Isaiah.

One of the most pressing questions in the study of intertextual reference remains that of determining the role of conscious redactional intentionality. I have already argued that the primary function of intertextual reference in Third Isaiah lay in signalling continuity with a prior tradition, which in Third Isaiah seems often to have been executed casually from memory with only rare cases of exact citation. Its function is deictic—that is, pointing, identifying—rather than midrashic. In addition, there is another element that, particularly in poetic language, has to be seriously considered. At times it is very difficult to determine to what extent a resonance is intentional, or rather derives from the effect on the reader of a complex poetic composition. The status of whether the resonance is an intentional device of its author or arises from a reader's response appears in many instances to be a fluid one. Thus, for example, there is a certain resonance between the complaint of the eunuch, "I am only a dry tree" (56:3) and the earlier invitation, "Attention, all you who are thirsty, come to the waters" (55:1). However, I doubt very much that the reference is an intentional one designed by a redactor, but rather relates to the reader who continues to discern new moments of linkage once the complex literature is read as a unified prophetic composition. Although there are some examples of an intentional *Musivstil,* the majority of examples proposed can be better understood apart from redactional intentionality. I would also argue against Steck's constant reference to complex systems of intertextuality—Lau calls it *Grüblerei* (10)—that seldom is a direct intentional linkage involved and that his model is strained even for tannaitic midrashim of the Hellenistic period.

In spite of these initial caveats, I would affirm that there are some crucial passages within Third Isaiah that do reveal a conscious intentionality by the prophetic author or redactor. Moreover, this reuse of passages from First and Second Isaiah provides an important guide to the purpose and function of chapters 56—66 within the book of Isaiah.

First, in respect to Third Isaiah's intentional use of Second Isaiah, certain themes are repeatedly picked up and reused. The following are prominent:

a. The theophanic revelation of God occurs in the inbreaking of a new age of salvation (40:1ff. // 62:11–12, etc.), and in the manifestation of glory to all (40:5 // 66:18). As in Second Isaiah, there is a contrast between the new things and the former things, which are to be forgotten (43:18–19 // 65:16–17).

b. A sign of the entrance of the new age is the return of the diaspora (43:5ff. // 60:4ff.) and liberty for the captives (43:1ff. // 61:1ff.).

c. The outpouring of the spirit as the agent of divine salvation (42:1 // 61:1) is also an essential component of the promise.

d. The glorification of restored Zion as held in common (49:14ff.; 51:3 // 62:1ff.).

e. The ministry of the "servant" is extended to his "servants" as offspring (42:1ff.; 54:17 // 56:6; 63:17; 65:8, 13–15).

Second, in response to Third Isaiah's intentional use of First Isaiah, the following themes are prominent:

a. The return of the messianic age becomes a component in Third Isaiah's eschatological hope (11:6ff. // 65:25). Although Second Isaiah is generally silent about David and his messianic rule, an important link had been forged in 55:3 to an everlasting covenant with David by way of Psalm 89 (cf. the exegesis of chapter 55). The connection with Isaiah's messianic hope is made explicit in Third Isaiah (65:25; cf. also 25:8 // 65:19).

b. The sinful acts of the rebels and the wicked often described in First Isaiah as cultic sins are paralleled in citations and by allusions in Third Isaiah (1:12ff., 28ff.; 2:6; 17:10ff. // 56:9ff.; 57:1ff.; 65:3ff.).

c. The anger of God issuing in fiery judgment is closely paralleled in Third Isaiah as the rebels and sinners are destroyed (2:19ff.; 9:20ff.; 29:5ff.; 34:1ff. // 59:17ff.; 63:1ff.; 66:24).

d. The restoration of Zion and the worship of the nations on God's holy mountain are widely used by Third Isaiah (1:26–27; 2:1ff. // 56:7; 57:13; 65:25; 66:20). Coupled with this motif is the theme of the nations coming to the light out of darkness (9:1 // 60:1ff.).

6. Implications of Intertextuality for Interpreting Third Isaiah

There are several broad redactional implications from this use of conscious intertextual reference by Third Isaiah that shed light on the larger purpose of these chapters and their role for the book of Isaiah as a whole. Above all, Third Isaiah serves consciously to unite the major themes of both First and Second Isaiah into one literary composition. To speak of an "apocalyptic rendering" of the Isaianic tradition (Anderson) can be misleading if this redaction is separated from the overall process of the canonical shape of the book as a whole. Although it is highly likely that the process of redactional shaping took place gradually in different stages of composition, the effect of the final form was directed toward establishing a unified prophetic corpus. It has long been observed (Liebreich) that chapters 65 and 66 form a bracket with chapter 1 around the whole book of Isaiah. Also, it is clear that major connecting links have been established between chapters 40 and 60—62, which have extended the earlier resonance made between chapters 6 and 40.

Equally important to observe is that the intertextual use by Third Isaiah of both First and Second Isaiah does not simply establish continuity, but also results in a reinterpretation of the previous themes in a variety of different ways:

a. The use of the Second Isaianic theme of the breaking in of the new age in contrast with the old is continued in Third Isaiah. It is not the case that Third Isaiah has abandoned Second Isaiah's hope and has rather turned to explain to the postexilic community the reasons why his predecessor's prophecy was unfulfilled. Regardless of the evidence of vestiges shimmering in the text's background that indicate that the historical milieu of Third Isaiah is indeed postexilic, the theological framework of the narrator of Third Isaiah is not consciously set in contrast to Second Isaiah, but as a continuation of it. (The former things are behind, the new things are still ahead.) Yet what is different is that the expected promise of the new age has been radicalized in terms of its eschatology. In contrast to Second Isaiah, the deliverance from Babylon is not seen as concurrent with the inbreaking of the new age, but as only an illustration, a foretaste, of God's promise, which is increasingly identified with a new creation of heaven and earth (65:17ff.).

b. First Isaiah had proclaimed the entrance of a messianic reign of a Davidic ruler as the goal of God's purpose for a righteous rule. A faithful remnant (7:14; 8:18; 10:20; 28:16) had responded in trust to the promise of "God with us." However, Second Isaiah did not continue this messianic theme. Some commentators have argued, wrongly in my opinion, that Cyrus was an unsuccessful substitute (45:1). Rather, Second Isaiah turned his attention to the role of the servant, through whose suffering and death faithful Israel experienced atonement and confessed to have understood the true nature of divine forgiveness and salvation (chapter 53). An important role of Third Isaiah was in linking the faithful remnant of First Isaiah with the obedient "servants" who followed in the steps of Second Isaiah's "suffering servant." Clearly a direction of interpretation was begun that in time identified the Messiah of First Isaiah with the suffering servant of Second Isaiah (Luke 24:14ff.; Acts 8:32: Rev. 21:1ff.; 22:3).

c. Third Isaiah described the rebellious and sinful opposition to God's rule with the same language by which First Isaiah had depicted rebellious Israel in his day (chapter 1). The implication of this construal offers an important reason why Hanson's historicizing of the enemies in Third Isaiah misunderstands the theological function of the enemy. The effect of Third Isaiah's intertextual reference to First Isaiah is to reinterpret the appearance of the rebellious and sinful in Israel who oppose God's righteous rule. Instead of the enemy being simply a part of the "former things" who would disappear with the entrance of the new, their reappearance in Third Isaiah testifies prophetically that they are not to be understood chronologically, but rather ontologically. God's servants will always be under attack from enemies. Evil will persist and refuse to participate in the divine new order. Thus, the book of Isaiah ends with a description of those who continue to rebel and whose "worm will not die." They will never be victorious, but their corpses remain in defeat much like Sennacherib's vanquished army (37:36).

7. Conclusion

If the argument is at all correct that the literary and theological function of chapters 56—66 was both to unite and to reinterpret the book of Isaiah as a whole, then it does affect how the reader understands the structure of these chapters. Recently, scholars have been inclined to follow Westermann's hypothesis (*Isaiah 40—66,* 296ff.) that the structure is largely concentric in nature, with the nucleus being formed by chapters 60—62 and around which were then set two communal laments, chapters 59 and 63—64. The final stage he then attributes to the prologue of chapter 56 and epilogue of chapter 66. In my opinion, Westermann has substituted his understanding of how the book developed diachronically for a proper analysis of how these chapters now function synchronically according to their final form. Even Beuken, who first described convincingly the role of the servant's theme in Third Isaiah ("The Main Theme") has sought to retain Westermann's concentric scheme in part. I would argue instead that the structure in its final form, irrespective of its history of composition, moves in a linear progression by means of intertextual references toward the goal of joining together the diverse parts of the book into a unified whole. The resulting shape bears a truthful witness to the selfsame divine reality first testified to by the eighth-century prophet Isaiah, but then continually unfolded, modified, and enriched by successive generations of prophetic tradents to serve as Israel's authoritative scripture, a prophetic word that stands forever (40:8) and accomplishes its divine purpose (55:1).

57. Isaiah 56:1–8

_{56:1} Thus said the LORD:
  Keep justice and do righteousness,
 for soon my salvation will come,
  and my deliverance will be revealed.
2 Blessed is the mortal who does this,
  the one who holds fast to it,
 who keeps the Sabbath, not profaning it,
  and restrains his hand from doing any evil.
3 Do not let the foreigner who has joined
  himself to the LORD say,
   "The LORD will surely exclude me
   from his people."
 And do not let any eunuch complain,
  "I am only a dry tree."
4 For thus said the LORD:
  Regarding the eunuchs who keep my Sabbath,
  who choose the things pleasing me
  and hold fast to my covenant,
5 I will give them, in my house
  and within my walls,
  a monument and a name
  better than sons and daughters.
 I will give them^a an everlasting name
  that will not be cut off.
6 As for the foreigners
  who join themselves to the LORD,
  to serve him, to love the name of the LORD
  and to be his servants,
 all who keep the Sabbath
  without profaning it,
  and who hold fast to my covenant,
7 these I will bring to my holy mountain

and let them rejoice in the house of prayer.
Their burnt offerings and sacrifices
    will be accepted on my altar,
for my house will be called
    a house of prayer for all peoples.
8   Thus said the Lord GOD,
    who gathers the outcasts of Israel:
I will gather still others to them
    besides those already gathered.

a. The MT reads *lô* ("him"), but many, following the versions, regard it as a mistake for *lamô* ("them"). Cf. *BHS*.

Selected Bibliography

M. A. Beck, "De vreemdeling krijgt toegang (Jes. 56:1–8)," *De Knecht. Studies rondom Deutero-Jesaja, Fs J. F. Koole,* Kampen 1978, 17–21; J. Begrich, "Die priestliche Tora" (1936), reprinted, *GSAT,* ThB 21, Munich 1964, 232–60; H. Bertholet, *Die Stellung der Israeliten und der Juden zu den Fremden,* Leipzig 1896; W. A. M. Beuken, "The Main Theme of Trito-Isaiah: 'The Servants of YHWH,'" *JSOT* 47, 1990, 67–87; H. Donner, "Jesaja LVI 1–7: Ein Abrogationsfall innerhalb des Kanons—Implikationen und Konsequenzen," VTSup 37, *Congress Volume Salamanca,* ed. J. A. Emerton, Leiden 1985, 81–95; K. Koenen, *Ethik und Eschatologie im Tritojesajabuch,* WMANT 62, Neukirchen-Vluyn 1990, 11–15, 27–32; W. Lau, *Schriftgelehrte Prophetie in Jes 56—66,* BZAW 225, Berlin 1994, 262–79; H. Odeberg, *Trito-Isaiah (Isaiah 56—66),* Uppsala 1931, 33–62; K. Pauritsch, *Die neue Gemeinde: Gott sammelt Ausgestossene und Arme (Jesaja 56—66),* AnBib 47, Rome 1971, 31–51; R. Rendtorff, "Isaiah 56:1 as a Key to the Formation of the Book of Isaiah," *Canon and Theology,* ET Minneapolis 1993, 181–89; E. Sehmsdorf, "Studien zur Redaktionsgeschichte von Jesaja 56—66 (I)," *ZAW* 84, 1972, 542–62; O. H. Steck, "Zur jüngsten Untersuchungen von Jes 56, 1–8; 63, 7–66, 24," *Studien zu Tritojesaja,* BZAW 203, Berlin 1991, 229–65; R. D. Wells Jr., "'Isaiah' as an Exponent of Torah: Isaiah 56.1–8," *New Visions of Isaiah,* ed. R. F. Melugin, M. A. Sweeney, JSOTSup 214, Sheffield 1996, 140—55.

1. Introductory Issues of Structure, Genre, and Setting

a. Position and Function of the Oracle in Third Isaiah

The significance of 56:1–8 at the beginning of Third Isaiah has often been discussed. A host of difficult problems call for resolution. It has often been argued that the oracle serves as a prologue to the larger collection, matched by an epilogue in 66:15–24. Isaiah 56:1 has been designated as a superscription to the whole corpus. Although the proposal has its strengths, the difficulty with the thesis is that it derives in large part from prior historical assumptions that are not immediately apparent from the literature itself. Often the alleged evidence emerges from an earlier diachronic reconstruction that cannot be directly related to the literary shape of the text itself.

For example, in terms of the literary form of v. 1, there is no strong evidence that the formula "thus said Yahweh" serves as a superscription to a new collection. Actually, one could argue in the opposite direction. The formula occurs with great frequency in Second Isaiah, but never as a superscription or to make a sharp disjunction (43:14; 44:6, 24; 45:1, 14; 48:17; 49:5, 8, 28; 50:1; 52:3). It occurs only infrequently in Third Isaiah and then largely in chapters 65 and 66 (56:1, 8; 65:8, 13; 66:1, 12). In sum, it functions above all in a formal sense in 56:1 to establish a continuity with Second Isaiah rather than to signal a new beginning.

In terms of the historical setting and the addressee of 56:1ff., Rendtorff can state categorically that "it is obvious that the whole book in its present form is addressed to post-exilic Israel" (186). Yet I would question whether it is wise from this initial passage immediately to assign to it such an absolute dating, which on one level may well be true. However, such a conclusion does not raise the question of whether from the narrative context a different audience from chapter 55 is being addressed or whether literarily a different historical time has been assumed. In the introduction to Third Isaiah, I have already tried to defend the crucial hermeneutical need for such a distinction.

In terms of the shift in content, careful distinctions are once again required. Surely the observation is correct (cf. Whybray, Rendtorff) that v. 1a uses the term "righteousness" (*ṣᵉdāqāh*) in a different sense from Second Isaiah, but can one then argue on that account that Third Isaiah has lost the expectancy of an imminent divine act of deliverance as found in Second Isaiah (Whybray, 197)? A shift in content could also indicate a conscious redactional intention to modify or to supplement a position of Second Isaiah that is assumed to be true and authoritative. Whybray's interpretation, which has largely become a consensus, is derived from a prior assumption that a new and subsequent historical situation is being addressed. Even if it were true that regular worship has been reinstituted and that the temple may have by then been rebuilt, it still does not follow that this information informs the concern of this passage. Muilenburg (653) is rightly sensitive to this issue when he cautions, "The reference to the temple must not be pressed since we are dealing with poetry in an eschatological context."

In sum, I would argue that the crucial interpretive problem of 56:1–8 lies in carefully distinguishing between the literary (canonical) function of the text and historical reconstructions developed according to a prior diachronic interpretation of its setting, dating, and postexilic addressee. Of course, so to distinguish initially in one's exegesis does not remove the responsibility finally to relate—but not to fuse—these two dimensions of the text in some fashion. In terms of vv. 1–8, I would argue that the complex issue of interpretation is a theological problem closely related to the expectancy of Second Isaiah, but one in which the diachronic evidence has been pushed into the background and has not been assigned a major role of great significance.

b. Structure and Genre

There has been much debate regarding the literary coherence of the text. A host of literary-critical analyses have contested the chapter's essential unity because of the diversity of its components. Some commentators hold that the passage consists of three independent elements that have been loosely joined with considerable remaining tension. Others see only vv. 1 and 8 as original, and view vv. 3–7 as a later interpolation. However, more recently scholars have recognized that the passage has been shaped by other factors, especially from the intertextual reuse of Second Isaiah, and they would treat the present oracle as a unity in spite of its mixture of forms. It is argued that with the increasing textualized form of the tradition the appeal to conventional oral forms has become less convincing as a literary guide. Surely there are oral vestiges present (*Botenspruch,* blessing formulae, etc.), but can one still classify vv. 1–2 as a *Mahnwort* (warning) as Sehmsdorf does (542)?

An even more difficult question turns on the analysis of vv. 3–7. It has frequently been assumed that its genre is a prophetic imitation of a priestly torah (cf. Begrich), in which a legal tradition (cf. Deuteronomy 23) has been replaced by a new prophetic pronouncement seeking to adjust to a new postexilic situation. As I hope to show in the exegesis, there are major problems with this interpretation. Particularly unfortunate is the frequent attempt made to assign the setting to the fifth century after the reforms of Ezra and Nehemiah, and then to contrast Third Isaiah's more "liberal" approach to the alleged rigidity of postexilic Judaism. Similarly, Donner's effort to reconstruct a process of prophetic abrogation of a law appears to me too much controlled by prior assumptions regarding the date and setting of Isaiah 56. The assessment applies to Pauritsch's theory of a Babylonian group seeking cultic assurances before returning to Jerusalem. In sum, in a strictly synchronic sense, apart from heavy historical assumptions, one can still speak of 56:1–8 as a kind of prologue. The major themes that are introduced are then brought to completion in chapters 65 and 66 as a loosely constructed epilogue.

The structure of the oracle in its present form appears as follows:

vv. 1-2 Divine oracle calling for torah observance
vv. 3-7 Response to outsider's complaints
v. 8   A divine guarantee to the outcasts

c. Redactional Layering

In most recent studies of Third Isaiah (e.g., Westermann, Beuken, Steck), it is assumed that 56:1–8 and 66:15–24 belong to the latest level of the redactional process. In contrast, chapters 60—62 are seen to reflect the closest continuity with Second Isaiah and are thus placed at the earliest stage of editorial growth. The equation of discontinuity with late and continuity with early is far from obvious. Regardless of whether this historical reconstruction is true or not— many of the literary observations are illuminating—the decisive point is that the function of 56:1–8 be maintained according to its literary integrity and not sacrificed to a diachronic reconstruction. I would argue that 56:1–8 sets the basic question for Third Isaiah raised in Second Isaiah regarding the servants of Yahweh (cf. especially Beuken, "The Main Theme"). It forms a red thread through the book which only reaches its climax in chapter 66. To raise the question of redactional layering in Third Isaiah is helpful insofar as it aids in understanding the present complex literary text. It is not useful if it only succeeds in replacing the final form of the text with a historical process according to a highly subjective interpretive theory.

2. Exposition

[56:1–2] The formula "thus said the LORD" serves to attribute divine authority to the passage that follows in the same way that the formula functions in Second Isaiah. The inclusion in v. 8 adds a further note of finality and summarizes the ruling that precedes as the explicit will of God. The theological implication of the use of the formula is that following it is a prophetic oracle transmitting a divine word. Whatever one understands under *Schriftprophetie* (cf. especially Lau), it is different in kind from mere scribal reinterpretation. Significantly, later rabbinic midrash, which often sought to reinterpret a biblical text in order to serve in another setting, made a sharp distinction between the authoritative received text and later scribal application.

"Keep justice (*mišpāṭ*) and do righteousness (*ṣᵉdāqāh*), for soon my salvation (*yᵉšûʻātî*) will come, and my deliverance (*ṣidqātî*) will be revealed." The observation has often been made that the term *ṣᵉdāqāh* is used in two very different senses. The second usage (v. 1b), translated "deliverance," accords with the sense largely found in Second Isaiah. God fulfills his covenantal relationship with his people by his gracious acts of deliverance (cf. 45:23; 46:12; 51:5, 6), which appear to be unconditionally rendered.

In contrast, 56:1a speaks in the imperative, demanding that Israel "keep justice" and "do righteousness." Whybray follows a majority opinion by stating that Third Isaiah implies that *ṣᵉdāqāh* is achieved through the perfecting of human behavior. Duhm had even spoken of "works righteousness" (*Werkgerechtigkeit*) and saw this postexilic prophet as a precursor of the legalistic Priestly code.

In my judgment, this line of interpretation is very wide of the mark. From the earliest preexilic tradition *ṣᵉdāqāh* was a term that established the grounds for a harmonious relationship between parties in accordance with mutual obligations of just behavior. Yahweh pledged his lasting faithfulness to Israel's welfare. Conversely, Israel pledged its loyalty to God (Deut. 6:25; 24:13; Ps. 106:31). In First Isaiah (1:21) Jerusalem was described as a faithful city because righteousness lodged in her. Those within Zion who repent will be redeemed by righteousness (1:27). Although it is true that the terminology of "keeping justice" and "doing righteousness" is most common in the later writings (Jeremiah, Ezekiel, Chronicles), the reciprocal relationship demanded between God and his people has always been constitutive of the term and is fundamental to Israel's understanding of law and grace.

When v. 1 links doing righteousness with the promise of Second Isaiah (51:5–6), namely, that salvation and deliverance will come, the former prophecy is not being repudiated but confirmed. Yet the confirmation is made in terms of a reemphasis on Israel's responsibility, which was always constitutive of her faith. Moreover, the manner by which the doing of righteousness and the revelation of salvation is made in v. 1 is consistent with ancient Hebrew tradition, and also with the prophets. The linkage between Israel's response and God's deliverance is not conditional but causal: do righteousness that deliverance will come.

Yet while it is true that Third Isaiah is confirming the promise of Second Isaiah through a form of citation, he is also offering an important interpretation. The salvation promised by Second Isaiah is misunderstood if it is not joined with an obedient response. It is possible of course to argue that v. 1 arose as an apologetic attempt to address the disappointment of his hearers when Second Isaiah's promises were not fulfilled. However, whether the psychological interpretation is historically true or not, there is no evidence to indicate that this is the motivation that informed the present passage. The prophetic promise functions exclusively on the theological level. Second Isaiah's promise is not adjusted to meet a changing historical situation, but redefined theologically to correct any possible misunderstanding stemming from Second Isaiah's formulation. Third Isaiah does not soften or spiritualize the promise (*contra* Zimmerli), but redefines the issue theologically by appealing to a holistic, inclusive understanding of the entire biblical tradition. The intertextual relation between 56:1–2 and 46:12–13 is not a verbatim citation, but the difference is not of substance and reflects only the less than precise role associated with memory in establishing a scriptural warrant.

Verse 1 is also of crucial importance in demonstrating that Third Isaiah has not formulated his message independently of Second Isaiah, as if a new historical period called forth a new message. From the narrative perspective of the Third Isaiah corpus, the prophetic writer is offering a theological reformulation, but he has not altered his point of standing from that of Second Isaiah. He still stands before the coming new age, awaiting its near fulfillment. The former things are passed. The author reveals no disappointment in a failed divine promise. Rather, he links the same eschatological hope to Israel's obedient response. Yet it is also true that Third Isaiah's concern with cult, law, Sabbath, and temple reveals a different focus from that of Second Isaiah, which has called forth the exegetical tension between the literary and the historical perspectives of Third Isaiah discussed above.

[3–7] Certainly the most controversial part of the oracle turns on the interpretation of these verses, which ever since Begrich's influential essay have been accepted as a prophetic imitation of a priestly torah pronouncement (cf. Hag. 2:14ff.; Zech. 7:2ff.). The usual historical-critical approach attempts to reconstruct the legal problem in the postexilic community respecting the exclusions of aliens with special reference to Deut. 23:1–8, Ezra 9:1ff., and Neh. 9:1ff. Since the term for eunuch (*sārîs*) can also describe an official in a foreign court, it has been suggested that the issue of Isa. 56:3–7 involved either Jewish proselytes in Babylon or eunuchs who served in some capacity in a more local, syncretistic setting, and who were seeking admission to the Jewish cult. Often the background is set in the late fifth century and is related to the restrictive practices of Nehemiah and Ezra. A variety of such historical reconstructions have been suggested by Pauritsch, Sehmsdorf, Donner, and Lau, among others.

Recently, a different approach has been developed by Beuken (*Jesaja III*), who attempts to work far more closely to the specific literary and theological context of Third Isaiah. However, before offering his own fresh interpretation, Beuken is at pains to supply some very telling reasons for rejecting the usual historical-critical reconstructions.

First, the problem of the cultic admission to the foreigner (*ben hannēkār*) in Third Isaiah is a very different one from that associated with Canaanite, Hittite, Moabite, and Amorite foreigners who caused such major religious problems in the period of Ezra and Nehemiah because of their role in promoting religious syncretism ("abominations"). Foreigners had always been seen as ethnically different from Israel (Gen. 17:12; Ex. 12:43), but at times were allowed to attach themselves to Israel (Isa. 14:1; Zech. 2:11). In 56:3 the foreigner at issue is specifically described as belonging to this class of proselytes. The fact that the issue at stake involved eunuchs as well as foreigners speaks against the hypothesis that a common legal precedent arising from one historical situation was involved. The alleged reference to the laws in Deut 23:1ff. does not make mention of the eunuch, and actually addresses a very different set of issues, as a close scrutiny of 56:1–8 reveals.

Second, in terms of the literary form of the oracle, the issue at stake in vv. 3ff. is given voice by means of two different complaints, both of which reflect the stereotyped language of the suppliants of the Psalter. The foreigner complains, lest he be separated from the worshipping congregation (Ps. 88:1ff.). The imperfect form of the verb (v. 3b) speaks against the theory that a legal decision had already been made. The eunuch complains that he is unable to provide a posterity and thus his name will be cut off (cf. Jer. 17:19). The problem addressed seems at best only indirectly related to the question of a community cultic order, nor is a solution sought by a form of legal abrogation (Donner).

Third, the context of the divine oracle is explicitly eschatological. The promise of universal acceptance into the worshipping community is set by God's bringing them to his "holy mountain" (v. 7), which is an intertextual play on the promise of the assembly of the nations in Isa. 2:1ff. (ET 2:2ff.). Moreover, the promise is further expanded in v. 8 with Yahweh himself gathering the outcasts. The setting of the oracle is that of the "new things" promised in Second Isaiah for which there is no analogy between the former and the latter (42:9; 43:19; 48:6).

Finally, the close relationship between chapters 55 and 56 provides a reason why chapter 56 cannot be construed as an independent oracle from the fifth century concerning community cultic order. Verse 6 continues the theme first announced in 54:17 of the servants as the offspring of the suffering servant of 53:10. This theme is introduced programmatically by Third Isaiah and establishes from the outset a different relationship between the faithful of Israel and the nations. In chapter 56 and again in 66:18ff. the point is made decisively that the "servants" can include foreigners and outcasts who line themselves with the law of God over against the rebels and sinners within and without Israel who continue to resist his will.

It is highly significant that in v. 4 acceptance of the eunuch is conditioned on three things: keeping the Sabbath, choosing the things that please God, and holding fast to the covenant. These stipulations parallel closely those set forth in v. 2 as forming the grounds for divine blessing. In a real sense, the conditions are simply the norms appropriate to a life lived under torah. While it is true that in the postexilic period the emphasis on Sabbath observance greatly increased in importance as the means of expressing obedience to God under the restraints of postexilic life without political autonomy (Jer. 17:21–22; Ezek. 20:12ff.; 22:8; Neh. 13:17–18), these commands serve as a concrete expression of the selfsame will of God on which the original Mosaic covenant was based and are not a descent into narrow legalism, as has frequently been charged by Christian antinomians.

In v. 5, in response to the eunuch's complaint that without posterity his name will be cut off, God promises "a monument and a name" (*yad wašem*) in his house better than sons and daughters. The exact meaning of the expression is debated. Occasionally the expression is rendered grammatically as a hendiadys. However, the real issue turns on whether it is to be understood literally or figuratively. It does not seem likely that a memorial is meant in the sense of Absalom's stele (2 Sam. 18:18). Delitzsch argues quite persuasively that the term *yad* can also signify a "place" (Num. 2:17) or a "share" (2 Sam. 19:44), which would match nicely the larger context of chapter 56. The intertextual connection with 55:13b ("name" and "sign") is also a further indication of a carefully structured oracle with a close relation to the preceding unit.

Similarly, in v. 6 the description of the relationship of the foreigners to God as those who join themselves to Yahweh is defined further in terms of the purpose of this attachment: in order to minister to him, in order to love the name of Yahweh, and in order to be his servant. In each case an older tradition of faithful behavior is picked up and reapplied. The combination of loving God and honoring his name is especially prominent in Deuteronomy (6:13; 7:9; 10:8; 13:3, etc.). Verse 7 further elaborates on the significance of full participation in the worship of God at his holy mountain: it consists of being joyful in the house of prayer, and to have one's offerings and sacrifices received by God. Verse 7 concludes with a summary that removes any doubt that God's purpose for his house is directed to all peoples without restriction.

[8] The oracle closes with a solemn formula of finality, "Thus said the Lord GOD" (*nᵉ'um 'ᵃdōnāy YHWH*), which forms a literary bracket with v. 1. God takes the initiative in gathering the outcasts of Israel. There then follows an addendum (v. 8b). Concerning precisely what has been added, commentators are somewhat divided. Some find the emphasis to fall on the gathering beyond Israel to other Gentiles. Others stress the continuing process of gathering in the future indicated by "still others." Others interpret the final Hebrew word to suggest that those who have been already gathered are the means by which the gathering of those still left is executed. The close New Testament parallel occurring in John 10:16 also denotes a similar openness to the further ingathering, but with a purposefully undefined referent.

58. Isaiah 56:9–57:13

56:9 Come, all you beasts of the field,[a]
       come and devour, all you beasts of the forest.
10   His watchmen are blind,
           they all are without knowledge;
       they are all dumb dogs
           that cannot bark.
       They lie about and drowse,
           they love to sleep.
11   These dogs have a ferocious appetite,
           they never have enough.
       As for the shepherds,
           they do not understand what it is to watch.
       Everyone has gone his own way,
           each seeking his own gain.

12   "Come, I'll get some wine;
          let us fill ourselves with liquor,
          and tomorrow will be more of the same,
          or even better!"
57:1 The righteous perish,
          and no one pays any attention.
      Faithful men are swept away,
          and no one even gives it a thought
      that the righteous are taken away
          to be spared evil.
2   Those who walk uprightly
          will enter into peace.
      They will find rest in their beds.
3   But as for you, come closer,
      you sons of a sorceress,
          you offspring of adulterers and harlots.
4   Whom are you treating with such derision?
          At whom do you obscenely gesture
          and stick out your tongue?
      Are you not children of rebellion,
          the offspring of treachery?
5   You inflame yourselves among the terebinths,
          under every green tree;
      you sacrifice your children in the valley
          under the cleft of the rocks.
6   Among the smooth things of the valley
          is your portion.[b]
      These, these are your share.
      To them you have poured out libations
          and offered grain offerings.
          In the face of this am I to relent?
7   On a high and lofty mountain
          you have set up your couch.
      There also you have gone up
          to perform sacrifices.
8   Behind the door and doorpost
          you have set up your heathen symbols.[c]
      Forsaking me, you have uncovered your bed,
          you have climbed upon it and made it wide.
      You have made a pact for yourselves with them
          whose bed you loved sharing;
          you have looked on their nakedness.

9   You went to Molech with oil
        and increased your perfumes.
     You have dispatched your envoys far off,
        even down to Sheol.
10   Although wearied by the length of travels
        you would not say, "It is too much."
     You found new energy,
        and so you never weakened.
11   Whom have you dreaded and feared
        that you lied?
     But you did not remember me
        or give me any attention.
     Is it because I have been silent for so long
        that you do not fear me?
12   I will make known your righteousness
        and your deeds,
        but they will not help you.
13   When you cry out for aid,
        let your various idols save you!
     The wind will blow them away,
        a mere breath will dispel them
     But those trusting me will possess the land
        and inherit my holy mountain.

    a. The Masoretic accents have to be altered to gain sense (cf. *BHS* and Delitzsch).
    b. The play on the root *ḥlq* is difficult. Irwin suggests a homonym with the meaning "to die," but the evidence is unclear.
    c. The exact meaning is unclear.

Selected Bibliography

W. A. M. Beuken, "Isa. 56:9–57:13—An Example of the Isaianic Legacy of Trito-Isaiah," *Tradition and Re-interpretation in Jewish and Early Christian Literature, Fs J. C. H. Lebram,* ed. J. W. van Henton, et al., SPB 36, Leiden 1986, 48–64; **M. E. Biddle,** "Lady Zion's Alter Egos: Isaiah 47.1–15 and 57.6–13 as Structural Counterparts," *New Visions of Isaiah,* ed. R. F. Melugin and M. A. Sweeney, JSOTSup 214, Sheffield 1996, 124–39; **P. D. Hanson,** *The Dawn of Apocalyptic,* Philadelphia 1975, 186–202; **G. C. Heider,** *The Cult of Molek: A Reassessment,* JSOTSup 43, Sheffield 1985; **W. H. Irwin,** "The Smooth Stones of the Wadi? Isaiah 57, 6," *CBQ* 29, 1967, 31–40; **K. Koenen,** "Sexuelle Zweideutigkeiten und Euphemismen in Jes 57, 8," *BN* 44, 1988, 46–53; *Ethik und Eschatologie im Tritojesajabuch,* WMANT 62 Neukirchen-Vluyn 1990, 32–60; **W. Lau,** *Schriftgelehrte Prophetie in Jes. 56–66,* BZAW 225, Berlin 1994, 151–68, 229–39; **T. J. Lewis,** "Death Cult Imagery in Isaiah 57," *HAR* II, 1987, 267–88; **H. Odeberg,** *Trito-Isaiah (Isaiah 56–66),* Uppsala 1931, 62–99; **K. Pauritsch,** *Die neue Gemeinde: God sammelt Ausgestossene und Arme (Jesaja 56–59),* AnBib 47, Rome 1971, 51–66; **B. Renaud,** "La mort du juste, entrée dans la paix (Is. 57, 1–2)," *RevScRel* 51, 1977, 3–21; **B. Schramm,** *The Opponents of Third*

Isaiah, JSOTSup 193, Sheffield 1995, 125–33; **O. H. Steck,** *Studien zu Tritojesaja,* BZAW 203, Berlin 1991, 170–77, 197–203.

1. Literary Analysis, Dating, and Theological Function

Regarding the scope of the passage, a few commentators include in the unit also 57:14–21. However, I agree with Beuken (*Jesaja*) that the change in subject matter favors seeing a break after 57:13. In the earlier analyses of literary and form-criticism, this section was divided into a variety of smaller units that were thought to have been secondarily collected together. Westermann's analysis is a good example of this approach. In more recent times there has been a growing consensus to see a larger unity in the passage. Yet there remains disagreement on how precisely the coherence should be described. Broad categories such as prophetic liturgy or kerygmatic intent appear too imprecise.

The focus of most modern studies has been on seeing the passage as shaped by a reuse and reinterpretation of earlier portions of scripture (cf. Beuken, Steck, Koenen, Lau). The major compositional force is no longer considered to be traditional oral patterns, but to have arisen from authorial/redactional structuring. In my opinion, this approach generally moves in the right direction. Yet as discussed earlier in the Introduction to Chapters 56—66 (cf. above), I sense two major dangers to be avoided. First, Third Isaiah remains a prophetic collection, both in form and content, which means there is an encounter with actual historical realities, albeit seen in the light of the divine. This dimension dare not be flattened simply into a type of learned scribal activity dealing exclusively with literary texts. Second, not every occurrence of a parallel can be assigned an intentional reuse. A critical assessment must be made that reckons with the theological substance at stake beyond merely identifying formal parallelism discovered by the perusal of a concordance.

Often, in a concern to exploit every possible intertextual reference, it is easy to miss the major theological function of the chapter as a whole. Westermann has pointed out the striking similarity, both in form and content, between Third Isaiah's oracles in chapters 56 and 57 with those of the preexilic prophets. He concluded that these oracles are to be dated from the preexilic period but subsequently reused to draw a later historical analogy. Most modern commentaries reject Westermann's preexilic dating because the postexilic evidence appears too strong. I agree with this assessment. But more is at stake, and I judge that Westermann's analysis has missed a major theological point in assessing the similarity. The use of central intertextual references by Third Isaiah, derived especially from First Isaiah, offers a major reinterpretation of the relation of First and Second Isaiah.

Chapters 5—10 described the rebellion of the nation Israel against God in terms of the theme of hardening. Yet juxtaposed within these same chapters was an eschatological hope of a messianic salvation that was actualized in the faithful response of a remnant (chapters 1, 6—9, 11, 12). The exact relation between the good and the evil in Israel was never clearly developed within the one plan of God, but remained in an eschatological tension. Isaiah next interpreted the relation of these dimensions of evil in terms of the former and latter things, of the old and new age (41:21ff.; 42:9; 44:6ff.). The old would pass and the new break forth in glory when Israel's Babylonian captivity ended (48:20ff.; 55:12–13). Within chapters 49—55 the full profundity of God's promised salvation was enacted in the role of the suffering servant, who fulfilled Israel's mission to the world through his obedient suffering and death in atonement. However, the relation of the old to the new was largely portrayed in a chronological sequence within an eschatological framework. The past was not even to be remembered (43:18).

Yet Third Isaiah faced a new problem that bore directly on the relation between the old and the new. His was not a psychological problem of overcoming disappointment with the failure of Isaiah's promises to materialize. There is no hint of this in the biblical text. Nor did he try to soften the earlier promises by spiritualizing them. Rather, Third Isaiah confronted a theological problem that turned on the continuing presence of the old along with the very real experience of the new. He offered his theological resolution by understanding the relation of the old and the new as ontological, not just chronological, in essence. The new age was coming as promised—Third Isaiah still shares Second Isaiah's theological point of standing—but the old will remain in all its violence and opposition.

In order to make this point, Third Isaiah described the present evil within the community with intertextual references to the wicked and rebellious of First Isaiah. The selfsame reality denounced by Isaiah of Jerusalem in the days of Ahaz and Hezekiah was still at work opposing God's new world. By a reuse of this earlier language of accusation and judgment (e.g., 1:28ff.), Third Isaiah succeeded in reshaping the entire Isaianic corpus into a theological unity and offered a comprehensive prophetic reflection on the nature of abiding evil, which cast a continuing shadow even on the rule of God (63:1–6; 66:24).

The process of reinterpretation becomes very clear in 56:9–57:12. In 56:7 and 57:7, 13, Third Isaiah introduced the theme of the holy mountain by combining the theme of First Isaiah (2:2) and Second Isaiah (40:9) in order to show the sharpest possible contrast between the promise of God to his servants of true worship in Zion (56:6; cf. 55:1ff.; 57:13) and the adulterous and idolaters of 56:9–57:12. He then described the latter group in the idiom of the preexilic prophets burning with lust "among the terebinths" (cf. Hos. 4:12f.; Isa. 1:29; Jer. 3:60), playing the harlot "under every green tree" (Deut. 12:2; Jer. 3:6, 13; Ezek. 6:13), and sacrificing their children (Ezek. 16:20–21). Some commentators have argued that the preexilic cultic abuses simply continued into the postexilic period. They argue it is even possible, when child sacrifice was banned in the Josianic reform, that the gruesome practice erupted once again later. However, to attempt to historicize the various forms of idolatrous rites can

obscure the function of intertextual play by Third Isaiah. The issue of dating
has been subordinated to an overarching theological concern, namely, the identification of the selfsame evils in the past with those of the present in spite of
the eschatological hope of a new age of God's rule (65:25). The old and the new
persist even in the eschaton.

The structure of the passage is as follows:

56:9–12 Accusation of Israel's faithless leaders
57:1–2 Lament over the state of the righteous
3–5 Accusation of revelers and cultic abusers
6–11 Accusation of the adulterous woman
12–13a The futility of idolatry exposed
13b Salvation promised to the faithful

2. Exposition

[56:9–12] The introductory summons appears very abrupt and offers a sharp
contrast to vv. 1–8. Yet there are very clear connecting themes which demonstrate that the juxtaposition is not without some elements of conscious intention. Particularly striking is the theme of the holy mountain of 56:7, which is
repeated both in 57:7 and again in 57:13 as a concluding frame.

The divine summons to the beasts to come and devour has a close parallel
in Jer. 12:7–13. Yet it is a mistake to find here a direct intertextual reference as
if the author was doing only scribal exegesis. Rather, the prophetic invective in
vv. 9–11 is delivered against leaders much like those delivered by the earlier
prophet. In v. 9 the wild beasts are summoned to devour because of the neglect
of faithless shepherds who care nothing for the flock. In v. 10 the third person
relative "his watchmen" is to be retained with Israel as its antecedent. Beuken
(*Jesaja III*) has argued that Israel is not envisioned as the flock being attacked.
Rather, the shepherd's neglect is at the cost of Israel, who allows her enemies
to devour the agricultural produce of the land. It is certainly true that the shepherds in vv. 9–11 are not pictured as those in Ezek. 34:1ff. actually devouring
the sheep themselves. Rather, in chapter 56 they are stupid and without sense.
Verses 10 and 12 describe them as sleepy and lazy, thinking only of strong
drink. This behavior thus allows the real enemies of Israel to indulge their insa-
tiable appetite. The image of ferocious dogs in v. 14 refers back to v. 9, but does
not fit in well with agricultural destruction, which may indicate that one cannot
clearly separate between the injury of the flock and of the land.

The main point of these verses is to establish the sharpest possible contrast
with vv. 1–8, at which holy mountain burnt offerings and sacrifices to God will
be accepted and the outcasts of Israel lovingly gathered. In vv. 9–12 these leaders are described as false shepherds, without knowledge, each after his own gain.
Beuken (*Jesaja III*) has pointed out a number of other intertextual references by

which the faithless leaders are portrayed. The theme of not knowing and of blindness is common to Second Isaiah (42:18ff.; 43:8ff., etc.). He finds also a contrast with the true shepherd in 40:11 and sees in 56:11 an intentional parallel being drawn with 53:6 where the infrequent idiom of "each going his own way" is used. He even sees a loose connection between the carefree longing for drink in 56:12 and Isa. 22:13. In my opinion, it is a mistake to attribute an authorial intent to every case of loose parallelism. I am thus skeptical of Lau's frequent appeal to a *Musivstil* (15, passim), which focuses on the repetition of individual words as a sign of intentional reinterpretation. Such a move shatters the text into endless fragments, which, in the end, was the danger often threatening rabbinic midrash. I would attribute many elements of textual resonance to the effect on the reader of a literary whole. Its significance lies in forming a semantic texture, but it is not to be automatically transferred into the text's foreground. Therefore, I do not think it correct to introduce the figure of the suffering servant into v. 11 because of a resonance with 53:6. Yet for the reader of the entire book of Isaiah there is a certain reverberation between the destruction of Israel's inheritance and the vineyard in Isaiah 5, an effect that strengthens the sense of a single, larger narrative encompassing the entire Isaianic collection.

[57:1–2] The interpretation of these verses has continued to cause commentaries difficulty. The form is of a lament for the fate of the righteous, and some of the difficulty of interpretation may lie in the state of the text, especially v. 2, which fluctuates between a singular and plural subject. The older form-critics spoke of independent fragments, which hardly offers much help. The fact that there are parallels (cf. Jer. 12:7–13; Micah 7:2) is also no reason to assume with Lau that these verses are only a literary construct of scribal origin.

The editor of this larger unit has set up his portrayal of the prevailing wickedness of the times, first by focusing on the irresponsible rulers (56:9–12) and then on those idolaters who mock the righteous (57:3–13). However, in between these oracles he has placed a brief description of the plight of the righteous, much in the idiom of the innocent sufferer of the Psalter who is being swept away by evil oppressors (Pss. 6:4; 10:1; 75:17; 89:47). The lament does not register directly the voice of the righteous, but his plight is pictured as a consequence of the neglect of the shepherds in 56:10ff. The righteous perish and no one is concerned.

More controversial is the significance of "enter into peace" and "rest in their beds." Certainly there is no well-developed theology here of an afterlife. Yet at the conclusion of chapter 57 the concept of peace is given a decidedly positive turn, which affects how 57:2 is heard. The righteous who walk in integrity enter into peace (*šalôm*), which condition is then explicitly denied the wicked who can neither rest nor share in peace (vv. 20–21). The fact that a distinction is indicated between the future of the righteous and the future of the wicked moves this prophetic witness away from the psalmist's despair in perceiving no difference in the death of the good or the evil person (Pss. 49:11; 89:49; Job 3:19). However, by the end of chapter 66 a radical difference in the fate of the righteous and of the wicked is spelled out in greatest detail.

[3–5] Verse 3 sets the tone of the passage that follows with a sharp adversive, "but as for you" (*we'attem*; cf. 65:11, 13). The wicked children, the sons of the sorcerers, adulterers, and harlots, are now directly addressed in the second person plural. Their identity is at first revealed in terms of their role as abuser: "Who are you treating with such derision?" Some commentators interpret God as the maligned one who is being mocked. Yet this interpretation does not match well with v. 11, which speaks rather of his being disregarded and ignored. From the context it seems more reasonable to see the righteous being those mocked, which rendering would extend the sharp contrast between the faithful of Israel and the wicked, which dominates the chapter.

Very shortly, however, these wicked oppressors of the righteous are further described in "preexilic" language, that is to say, the sins of which they are accused are the same ones used by those condemned by the prophets before the exile: "to burn with lust under every green tree" is the stereotyped idiom of cultic, sexual orgy found in Deuteronomy (12:2), the Deuteronomistic History (1 Kings 14:23; 2 Kings 17:10), Jeremiah (2:20; 3:6, 13), and Ezekiel (6:13). The oak or terebinth appears also in conjunction with idolatry in Isa. 1:29, Hos. 4:13, and Ezek. 6:13. Finally, child sacrifice in the valleys was a gruesome practice of Canaanite origin that was abolished by Josiah (2 Kings 23:10), but could well have flared up in the postexilic period of Third Isaiah.

In the light of the accusations of v. 5, the literary function of these idolatrous practices is not fully understood by a simple historicizing move, regardless of whether or not the evil practices may have been revived. It is far more likely, when the crucial role of intertextual reference for Third Isaiah is considered, that an intentional identification of Israel's transgression is made between past and present. The selfsame idolatrous evils exist in Israel even after the announcement by Second Isaiah of the promise of an imminent new age of righteousness. In sum, it is this troubling and persistent problem that is addressed by chapters 56—66.

[6–13] In v. 6 a fresh accusation against wicked cultic perversion begins, but this time directed against a second person feminine object, namely, the adulterous woman. The description focuses on idolatrous worship with a strong sexual overtone of pouring out offerings to lovers. Many of the details of the cultic rites are no longer fully clear. Obviously, the practices were intensely abhorrent to the tradents of the tradition and thus toned down. For example, the reference to the "smooth things of the valley" (stones?) is unclear. Some have opted for a homonymous form of the verb *ḥbl* (cf. Irwin), and postulate a grave site for the dead. Still, there is neither strong philological nor archaeological evidence to prove this reconstruction. The setting up of a bed, "making it wide," resonates with a variety of sexual images (cf. Koenen). Some interpreters would see a reversal of the Deuteronomistic symbols (Deut. 6:8) for the true worship of Yahweh by the substitution of secret pagan signs. Verse 9 refers to going to a king (*melek*) with oil, but most commentators (cf. RSV), correctly in my opinion, see here a reference to Molech or Milcom (cf. Heider).

Perhaps the key to understanding lies less in the ability to recover the exact form of the cultic, sexual idolatry, even though Ugaritic parallels are readily available (cf. Schramm, 129), but rather in the evidence of intertextual interpretation. Especially significant is that the use of adjectives chosen in the expression of v. 7, "a high (*gabōᵃh*) and lofty (*niśśaʾ*) mountain," is found only in relation to Isa. 2:2 (cf. Micah 4:1). This is to say, although the description of idolatry in high hills is common in the Old Testament, only here is the specific terminology parallel. The point of the reference in 57:7 thus takes on great clarity and significance. The portrayal of Israel's flagrant idolatry against Yahweh is set in direct opposition to the promise of First Isaiah of the true worship of God on Mount Zion to which the nations flow to learn torah. In sharp contrast, now the "high and lofty mountain" of Isa. 57:7 is used in blatant defilement of God's holy name. Moreover, the contrasting reference is not only to First Isaiah, but also to the promise of Second Isaiah. The single passage in chapters 40—55 in which Zion is described as a mountain is found in 40:9. Yet Zion, as the herald of good tidings of God's salvation, is now replaced by the words of mockery and desecration.

The contrast between the roles of the high and exalted mountain is then brought to a close in 57:13. Over against the many idols whose worthless efforts will be blown away are those who take their refuge in God. These faithful shall possess the land—the promise of Second Isaiah is still intact—and they shall inherit the holy mountain as Isaiah the prophet had faithfully announced (2:2).

It becomes increasingly clear from the role of intertextual referencing that the function of this passage is neither to replace the earlier promises nor to adjust them to new sociological exegesis. Rather, a theological understanding is being offered in these prophetic chapters that seeks through reflection on its sacred scriptures to interpret the nature of God's one purpose for his people, which is faithful both to its past and to its future.

59. Isaiah 57:14–21

57:14 And it will be said:
"Build up, build up, prepare the way,
remove the obstacles from the way of my people."
15 For thus says the high and lofty one,
who inhabits eternity, whose name is holy:
I dwell in the high and holy place,

but also with him who is repentant
and humble in spirit,
reviving the spirits of the lowly,
reviving the hearts of the repentant.
16   For I will not always accuse,
nor will I always be angry;
for then the human spirit would grow
faint before me,[a]
and the breath of life I have made.
17   Because of his sinful greed I was angry;
I struck him, and hid my face in wrath,
but he continued in his sinful ways.
18   I have seen his ways, but I will heal him.
I will lead him and show him comfort,
for his mourners[b] creating fruit[c] of the lips.
19   Peace, peace, to the far and near, says the LORD,
and I will heal them.
20   But the wicked are like the troubled sea
which cannot rest,
and its waves toss up mire and mud.
21   There is no peace, says my God,
for the wicked.

a. The meaning of the verb is uncertain (cf. the exposition).
b. In the MT the "mourners" belong to v. 18, but the sense of the sentence is improved by shifting the punctuation.
c. The meaning of the noun is uncertain with a variant reading in the MT.

Selected Bibliography

R. Bergmeier, "Das Streben nach Gewinn—des Volkes '*wn*," *ZAW* 81, 1969, 93–97; **W. A. M. Beuken,** "Trito-Jesaja: profetie en Schriftgeleerdheid," *Profeten en profetische Geschriften, Fs. A. S. van der Woude,* ed. F. G. Martinéz, et al., Kampen 1984, 74–78; **K. Koenen,** *Ethik und Eschatologie im Tritojesajabuch,* WMANT 62, Neukirchen-Vluyn 1990, 46–58; **W. Lau,** *Schriftgelehrte Prophetie in Jes 56—66,* BZAW 225, Berlin, 1994, 119–26; **H. Odeberg,** *Trito-Isaiah (Isaiah 56—66),* Uppsala 1931, 100–18; **K. Pauritsch,** *Die neue Gemeinde: Gott sammelt Ausgestossene und Arme (Jesaia 56—66),* AnBib 47, Rome 1971, 66–73; **P. A. Smith,** *Rhetoric and Redaction in Trito-Isaiah,* VTSup 62, Leiden 1995; **W. Zimmerli,** "Zur Sprache Tritojesajas," (1950), reprinted in *Gottes Offenbarung. Gesammelte Aufsätze,* ThB 19, Munich 1969, 217–33.

1. Genre, Structure, and Function

The scope of the passage is fairly clear. Verse 21 ends a line of thought and 58:1 begins something new. The role of v. 14 as a beginning is more difficult. The chief problem turns on the assessment of the initial verb, "it will be said" (w^e'*āmar*). It seems most unlikely that the verb can be joined with v. 13 and thus to understand the subject as those taking refuge in God. Some commentators suggest simply expunging it as an unnecessary gloss (Duhm, Odeberg) since the divine speech is introduced in vv. 15ff. by means of a messenger formula. Rather, I shall argue below that the verb serves to introduce the imperatives in v. 14 as a previously spoken divine word and thus marks the beginning of the oracle.

There is wide agreement that v. 14, and indeed the rest of the passage, makes an intentional appeal to 40:3, and that the structure is largely determined by the elements of intertextuality. The sharp juxtaposition of the righteous and the wicked, which emerged as the context of chapters 56 and 57, also plays a major role in the shaping of the passage. Of course, how one evaluates the element of continuity between Second Isaiah and Third Isaiah's reinterpretation forms the heart of the exegetical problem of the passage. Moreover, one's understanding greatly affects how one construes the relationship between these two Isaianic sections.

Recent European study has focused much attention on working out the growth of various redactional layers in Third Isaiah. Such an approach is not to be dismissed out of hand, but it frequently serves to distract from the primary task of interpreting the final form of the text. (Beuken is a refreshing exception.) Among the leading redactional critics nothing even close to a consensus respecting Third Isaiah has emerged, and the high level of subjectivity and speculation has not commended itself up to now (cf. Steck, Koenen, Lau, Smith). Likewise, the proposal to reorder the sequence of 57:14ff. (cf. Kessler) has not met with general approval.

The broad structure of the passage appears as follows:

57:14   Summons to prepare the way for God's people
57:15–19 Announcement of salvation
    v. 15   Divine assurance of renewal
    vv. 16–17 Grounds for God's proud anger
    vv. 18–19 Promise of healing and comfort
57:20–21 Judgment for the wicked

2. Exposition

[57:14] The difficulty of the formula, "And it will be said," is apparent at the outset from the wide variations in the versions and in the Qumran texts. The verb does not relate easily either to what precedes or follows. Yet it cannot be simply removed as a meaningless gloss (Duhm, Odeberg). Fortunately, a far more convincing interpretation was hinted at by Volz, and then carefully developed according to its full implications by Beuken ("Trito-Isaiah," 74ff.; *Jesaja III*).

The verb, when used as a genre marker, never appears in Third Isaiah without a subject (e.g., 56:1, 8; 57:19; 59:21). In v. 14 it appears to function as a marker of the citation that follows from 40:3. The addressee is undefined as is also the case in 40:3, but the formula serves to confirm that it is an authoritative word from Yahweh, not an anonymous message. Moreover, the imperatives concern the preparation of the way for God's people ("my people"). It is characteristic of Third Isaiah's use of Second Isaiah that the citation is not verbatim, but has been, nevertheless, carefully crafted. Beuken observes not only the formal imitation of the double imperative from 40:1, but also the choice of the verb "build up" (*sll*), whose nominal form, "highway," (*mᵉsillah*) appears in 40:3.

The crucial exegetical issue turns on the reinterpretation of Isaiah 40 in v. 14. The position was represented in Skinner's commentary of 1898 (177) that Second Isaiah portrayed an actual highway for the return of the exiles through the desert, but for Third Isaiah the way had become only a figure for the spiritual obstacles blocking Israel's redemption. This position was then further developed in Zimmerli's well-known essay, which argued that Third Isaiah had "spiritualized" Second Isaiah's hopes. Zimmerli's view was widely accepted, and was even enthusiastically adopted by Westermann. Only recently has this so-called ethical interpretation been seriously questioned.

A reigning assumption of Zimmerli's article was that Third Isaiah was disappointed with the failure of Second Isaiah's promises to materialize. He thus "spiritualized" the earlier prophecies, falling back on the view that Israel's sins had caused the delay in the promise, and called for Israel to remove these barriers by more ethical behavior. The expected event in Second Isaiah of a "new exodus" had been reshaped into a call for pious living. Yet a decisive argument against this interpretation was made by Koenen (53–54) that, if Zimmerli were correct, v. 14 would have to have been directed to the people. They were to improve their moral behavior in order to make God's promises of salvation possible. Yet clearly the imperatives of v. 14 are not directed to the people, as was also the case in 40:3. Rather, the imperatives, directed most likely to the heavenly host of chapter 40, relate to what God is about to do in preparing a way for his people. The focus is completely theocentric and God is at work in removing all obstacles that block his salvation. The clear change from prepare "the way of Yahweh" (40:3) to prepare "the way of my people" (57:14) indicates the extent of the reinterpretation. The content has been shifted, but not by means of a spiritualization.

[15–21] What then was the purpose of this reinterpretation and what was its new content? At the outset, it should be emphasized that the divine authority of Second Isaiah's promise in chapter 40 has been confirmed. However, the promise has not just been repeated, but extended beyond its initial form. The expansion also involves a theological correction of Israel's misunderstanding of the promise. Israel failed to understand that God's salvation separated between the righteous and the wicked, between God's servants who inherit "the holy mountain" (56:13) and the wicked idolaters who will perish (56:11ff.). Quite clearly when Third Isaiah, paraphrasing chapter 40, speaks of "my people" in v. 14, he is assuming this distinction, which was not spelled out in 40:1.

This distinction is not to be explained as a sociological change within Israel between warring religious groups (*contra* Hanson), but the author of Third Isaiah is at pains to give it a theological interpretation, which he grounds in the message of First Isaiah. The will of God, expressed in the imperatives of v. 14, is centered in the nature of the "high and lofty one" (*rām weníssāh*). The intertextual reference is clearly that of 6:1, which is a description of God as revealed to Isaiah. Only here do the two terms occur in the book. The reference is then made unmistakenly clear by its further paraphrase of his inhabiting eternity and of his name being holy (cf. Isa. 9:5[6]).

God, the Holy One, high and lifted up, commands that every obstruction be removed from his people's way. The focus of the passage in chapter 57 has indeed shifted from God's way through the desert to that of the people's way. The reinterpretation makes also fully evident the nature of Israel's way. Isaiah 56:7 had first spoken of God's "servants" being brought to the holy mountain. Then the theme continues in 57:13 for those who take refuge in God. The path that is blocked is the way to God's holy mountain, to Zion. Verse 15 makes it clear that the eternal God actually dwells (*skn*) in his holy place. The prophetic language struggles with a formulation that has always been at the heart of Israel's faith. God is totally transcendent, yet at the same time God truly "tabernacles" with his people. From ancient times in the great psalms of Zion (Psalms 46; 47; 48) Israel celebrated in worship both God's transcendence and his concrete presence.

Verse 15, however, goes a step beyond the traditional affirmation of both God's transcendence and continual presence with Israel. Now the divine promise is: "I dwell also with him who is repentant and humble in spirit." (A reader response with the theme of Immanuel, God-with-us, is also not to be denied.) The Holy One of Israel has taken the initiative, but a faithful response to his offer is also demanded. The invitation to salvation in God's holy presence calls for both repentance and humility. (Once again, this note surely reverberated in a reader response with Isaiah's experience of forgiveness in chapter 6.) Then in v. 16b a further motive for God's salvific intervention is given. The Hebrew verb *'tp* is difficult to construe. One translation (RSV) follows the LXX in rendering it "from me proceeds the spirit," that is, God is the source of all life. However, there is also the possibility of translating the verb "to make weak" (cf. NRSV). The sense then would be that God mercifully intervenes in reversing his anger against sinful humankind lest the human spirit grow weak and the gracious purpose of God's creation be destroyed.

The continuation of the oracle in vv. 15ff. also makes fully evident that the place where God dwells is not separated from the divine reality itself. To be brought to God's holy mountain Zion is understood by the prophet as sharing in the one divine promise of salvation. Therefore, only God can remove the obstacles that prevent Israel's entrance. What then are the obstacles that block Israel's way? At this point the close connection with the preceding oracle of 56:9–57:13 becomes clear. "Israel's sinful greed" (*biṣ'ô*) (v. 17) has already been described in greatest detail as the contrast between God's holy mountain and Israel's unholy cult, which has here been dramatically reviewed.

The new term in the divine will announced by Third Isaiah in chapter 57 is that God no longer will hide his face in anger, but wills to "heal," "lead," and "comfort" (*nḥm*). Moreover, it is this God who creates (*br'*) the ability of repentant Israel to praise him with the "fruit of the lips." The reference in v. 18 to God's comfort picks up a major theme of 40:1: "Comfort, comfort, my people. . . ."

At this point it is of major importance in understanding the true function of Third Isaiah to see its proper relation to Second Isaiah. In chapter 57, Third Isaiah confirms the promise of God's coming salvation, yet at the same time, Second Isaiah's message has been theologically refined and expanded. The one great turn in Israel's favor has not been revoked or changed. Third Isaiah's point of standing within the divine economy remains the same as that of Second Isaiah. What has changed is the locus of salvation and its recipient. The divine salvation promised Israel requires more than merely deliverance from Babylon. The historical event of the end of the exile serves for Third Isaiah as only an instance of God's mercy. However, true salvation is to enter into the holy presence of God. It is the path to his holy mountain offered only to those who take refuge in him. In a word, the holiness of God demands that only the faithful share in God's salvation. This point remains a major theme of chapters 56—66 and extends through this entire collection to the very end (66:24).

However, it is a major misunderstanding to argue that such a theological position reflects a tragic narrowing of Second Isaiah's universal promise. Third Isaiah begins his message in 56:1–8 by extending God's invitation to all: "my house"—on the holy mountain—"will be called a house of prayer for all peoples." The invitation encompasses foreigners and eunuchs. The old division separating Israel from the nations has been breached. However, God's invitation does not include the wicked, regardless of how "politically incorrect" this may seem to the modern mind. A distinction is drawn and chapter 57 ends by returning to those wicked who obtain no rest, but are likened to the troubled sea turning up "mire and mud." It is also to be noted that according to the biblical ontology of evil, those excluded continue in exerting their own will to remain outside the circle of God's holy presence.

The function of Third Isaiah's theological reinterpretation by intertextual reference to passages in First and Second Isaiah regarding the nature of God, his salvific will, and his judgment of the wicked, serves to present a holistic reading of the entire book. For this reason alone, the various attempts to replace Third Isaiah's own theological rendering with a sociological theory of competing groups in strife run flatly in the face of the canonical shaping of the entire Isaianic corpus.

60. Isaiah 58:1–14

58:1 Cry aloud with all your might, do not hold back.
　　　Raise your voice like a trumpet.
　　　Declare to my people their transgression,
　　　　　and to the house of Jacob their sins.
2　　For day after day they seek me
　　　　　and delight to know my ways,
　　　as if they were a nation that does what is right,
　　　　　that has not abandoned the laws of its God.
　　　They ask from me beneficial judgments,[a]
　　　　　and they delight to draw near to God.
3　　"Why have we fasted, and you did not see it?
　　　　　Why have we mortified our flesh and you have
　　　　　paid no attention?"
　　　Because on the day of your fasting
　　　　　you go about your own concerns
　　　　　and exploit all your workers.
4　　Look, you fast only to quarrel and fight,
　　　　　striking each other with clenched fists.
　　　You cannot fail as you do today
　　　　　and expect your voice to be heard on high.
5　　Is this really the kind of fast I have chosen,
　　　　　a day for a man to chastise his own flesh?
　　　Is it a time to bow one's head like a weed,
　　　　　and lie in sackcloth and ashes?
　　　Do you call this a fast,
　　　　　a day pleasing to the LORD?
6　　Rather, is not this the kind of fast I choose:
　　　　　to loosen the cords of evil,
　　　　　and untie the straps of the yoke,

    letting the oppressed go free
       and breaking every yoke?

7   Is it not to share your food with the hungry,
       and to bring the homeless poor into your house?
    When you see the naked, to clothe him,
       and not to ignore your own kin?

8   Then will your light break forth like the dawn,
       and your healing spring up quickly.
    Your salvation will go before you,
       and the glory of the LORD will be your rear guard.

9   Then you will call, and the LORD will answer
       You will cry, and he will say, "Here I am."
    If you take away oppression from your midst,
       pointing the finger and malicious talk,

10 and if you commit yourself to the welfare of the
       hungry,
       and satisfy the wants of the oppressed,
    then your light will rise in the darkness,
       and your gloom will be like noonday.

11 The LORD will guide you continually,
       and satisfy your needs in parched places,[b]
       and strengthen your bones.
    You will be like a well-watered garden,
       and like a spring whose waters do not fail.

12 From your midst they will rebuild the ancient ruins,
       and restore the ancient foundations.
    You will be called the repairer of fallen walls,
       restorer of streets for dwelling.

13 If you keep from desecrating the Sabbath,
       from doing your own delights on my holy day,
    and call the Sabbath a joy,
       and an honorable, holy day to the LORD,
    if you honor it, not going your own ways,
       or pursuing your own affairs or business,

14 then you will take pleasure in the LORD.
    I will cause you to ride upon the heights
    of the earth,
    and let you enjoy the heritage of your father Jacob,
       for the mouth of the LORD has spoken.

---

a. The precise meaning of this combination is uncertain. Some translate it "righteous judgments" in a positive sense (cf. the exegesis).

b. The noun is a *hapax legomemon*, derived from the root "to shine," probably meaning "a waterless place."

Selected Bibliography

M. L. Barré, "Fasting in Isaiah 58:1–12: A Reexamination," *BTB*, 1985, 94–98; **H. A. Brongers**, "Jes. 58, 13–14," *ZAW* 87, 1975, 212–16; **L. J. Hoppe**, "Isaiah 58:1–12, Fasting and Idolatry," *BTB* 13, 1983, 44–47; **W. Lau**, *Schriftgelehrte Prophetie in Jes 56—66*, BZAW 225, Berlin, 1994, 240–61; **D. Michel**, "Zur Eigenart Tritojesajas," *Theologica Viatorum* 10, 1965–66, 213–30; **K. Pauritsch**, *Die neue Gemeinde*, AnBib 47, Rome 1971, 73–87; **G. J. Polan**, *In the Ways of Justice toward Salvation: A Rhetorical Analysis of Isaiah 56—59*, New York 1986, 186–90, 232–40; **S. Sekine**, *Die Tritojesajanische Sammlung (Jes 56—66) redaktionsgeschichtlich untersucht*, Berlin 1989, 121–31; **O. H. Steck**, *Studien zu Tritojesaja*, BZAW 203, Berlin 1991, 211–13; **W. Zimmerli**, "Zur Sprache Tritojesajas," (1950), reprinted in *Gottes Offenbarung. GA*, ThB 19, Munich 1969, 217–33.

1. Genre, Structure, and Literary Function

Up to now in chapters 56 and 57 the prophetic author has focused on the sharp polarity within Israel between the righteous and the wicked. The "servants of the Lord" (56:6), including the foreigners and outcasts, are assured of God's salvation and an inheritance in his holy mountain, whereas the wicked idolaters will have no future (57:13). Then in chapters 58 and 59 the issue focuses on the obstacles that have delayed the promised salvation. Already in the introduction of chapter 56 the divine promise had been theologically linked with the keeping of justice and the doing of righteousness. Not that Israel's obedience was linked in a direct causal chain (cf. above), but both salvation and justice must coexist. In 57:14ff. God commanded his agents that all obstacles from his side were to be removed. His will was to heal, lead, and comfort his people in spite of the wicked, who will always churn evil (57:20–21). Why then is salvation still being delayed? Chapter 58 addresses this question, first raised as a complaint by the people concerning their practice of fasting, and goes on to define the nature of a faithful response pleasing to God.

In general, 58:1–12 has been regarded by commentators as a loosely unified unit, at least in its present literary form. However, debate persists on whether this is the result of a later redactional shaping of once independent units or an original composition. Whybray uses an older literary critical approach to distinguish between an original kernel (vv. 1–3a; 5–9a) and a later interpolation (vv. 3b–4), which, he argues, has missed the original point of the debate. Westermann discovers fragments of different oral forms of entirely disparate elements. Other commentators are troubled that the initial call to the prophet to make known Israel's sin, parallel to, say, Micah 3:8, did not issue in a *Scheltrede* (invective), but is more akin to a wisdom discourse. In my judgment, such observations are largely irrelevant and assume certain oral patterns that no

longer obtain. If one follows the inner logic of the oracle and observes the freedom used to reshape the traditional forms of address, the discourse is fully consistent. Furthermore, a clear indication of careful redactional shaping is also
revealed by the intertwining of themes by means of the repetition of key words
throughout the entire oracle. Note, for example, "delight" (vv. 2 [bis], 13 [bis]),
"cry" or "call" (vv. 1, 5, 9, 12, 13), and "day" (vv. 2, 3, 4, 5, 13).

The unit begins in vv. 1–4 with an accusation against the people that develops in response to a complaint cited in v. 3. There follows in vv. 5–9a a defining of the true meaning of fasting shaped in the idiom of a disputation. A series
of provocative questions is asked, concluding with a divine reaffirmation of the
coming salvation. Then vv. 9b–12 and 13–14 set forth in two sets of conditional
sentences the stipulations of God, which will ensue in Israel's salvation and
well-being.

The two most important critical issues that will be discussed below turn first
on the exact nature of the distinction between genuine and nongenuine piety.
The second issue relates to the role of vv. 13–14 to the preceding verses and
whether there is a formal or material link to the earlier controversy over fasting. Finally, the function of intertextual references within the oracle raises a
similar problem as was encountered in 57:14.

2. Exposition

[58:1–4] The prophet is summoned by God to expose the sins of Israel ("my
people"). The form of the delivery is often compared to the summons of the
preexilic prophets to proclaim a divine word of judgment (cf. Micah 3:8). The
substance of what follows is certainly that of an accusation, but the form is very
different from that of a preexilic invective. The style is much more reflective
without the use of a messenger formula. God reflects, as it were, on the people's piety and even cites their complaint to him in its direct address before
responding with a devastating attack on their form of fasting. The term "house
of Jacob," which is used in parallel with "my people," occurs only once in Third
Isaiah, but six times in First Isaiah, and twice in Second Isaiah (cf. Odeberg,
125). Beuken argues that whenever reference is made to Jacob within the book
of Isaiah, it serves intentionally to call attention to Israel's patriarchal heritage
along with its sin.

The difficult exegetical problem turns on determining precisely the force of
the divine accusation. Some would argue that the contrast being made is
between a piety based on empty ritual practices and one possessing a genuinely
spiritual context of true devotion. Others suggest that the prophetic author is
radically calling into question all ritual piety as essentially misdirected, and has
replaced it with an altogether new definition of right behavior before God, consisting of care for the poor and homeless. Fortunately, there is another option

beyond these choices.

Verse 2a describes traditional Israelite piety in a way that appears completely positive. "To seek God" is the liturgical idiom of the Psalter (14:2; 63:1; 70:4; etc.) expressing the suppliant's desire to enter into God's presence or to receive his word. The God of Israel is not a static given, but a dynamic reality who must be actively engaged to be found. The formula of seeking God occurs with particular frequency in the exilic period (Isa. 55:6; Jer. 29:12; 2 Chron. 15:2). It is grounded on the promise that when properly sought, God lets himself be known. The idiom is paralleled in v. 2 with the phrase "to know my ways" (Jer. 5:4; 10:2). To know God's will is to evoke the response of "delight," and Psalm 1 serves as a prologue to the entire Psalter in commending the use of the psalms that follow in order to engender the proper form of genuine piety.

In sum, v. 2a is not a description of false piety, but a proper response to God. The controversy, however, arises from what then follows. The people who initially appear to pursue the way of true faith fail because their actions lack the elements concomitant with proper ritual, namely, the doing of righteousness (56:1) and obeying the ordinances of God. They only act "as if" they were such a people. Verse 2c then further spells out the conflict between their piety and their behavior. The expression "to ask" or "to inquire of" God has a very different connotation in the Old Testament from "seeking God." Because the phrase "they ask from me" (*mišpᵉṭê - ṣedeq*) is unique in the Old Testament, its meaning is not fully clear. Often the phrase is translated "right ways" or "righteous decisions" with a thoroughly positive connotation. However, from the context that follows v. 3, the sense is clearly to be construed negatively. They ask of me "judgments," that is, legal decisions directed against others on their behalf. In addition, they delight to draw near to God, an objective genitive in Hebrew. In sum, they rejoice in their own religious agenda.

If there is any doubt about wherein the fault lies, the citation of their complaint strikes to the heart of the problem with great force. Israel complains that its fasting—still a fully proper expression of true piety—had produced no effect on God. In spite of Israel's self-mortification, God has taken no notice and has not fulfilled his part of the bargain. In a word, Israel's understanding of the rule of fasting is fundamentally flawed, as vv. 3–4 forcefully demonstrate: "on the day of your fasting, you go about your own concerns (*ḥepeṣ*)." Throughout chapter 58 the author subtly plays with different nuances of the word, especially in the contrast between vv. 2 and 3. In v. 3b the seeking of pleasure by Israel is equivalent to pursuing its own affairs. Such fasting has even resulted in the oppression of the slaves and day workers, and has erupted in physical violence. This manner of fasting will hardly cause God to listen.

It is clear from vv. 1–4 that fasting itself is not being attacked, but rather its misunderstanding by Israel. The issue is then further pursued theologically in the form of a fictive disputation in which the true meaning of devotion to God is developed in a powerful, fresh prophetic formuation. (Cf. a parallel account regarding fasting in Zechariah 8, which provides some of the historical background from the exilic period assumed by Third Isaiah).

[5–9a] Verse 5 begins the disputation with a negative formulation. The sharpness of the attack is equal to any polemic of the preexilic prophets. No amount of self-mortification can suffice as an action pleasing to God since it all stems from the wrong motivation. It is, in essence, a pursuit of one's own affairs, completely self-serving in orientation. The prophet satirizes with utter disdain the pious bowing of the head like a weed, or the lying in sackcloth and ashes. His derision is heightened by means of a continuing aggressive style: "Do you call this a fast, a day pleasing to the LORD (*yôm raṣôn*)?" The term *raṣôn* ("favor") occurs frequently in Third Isaiah (56:7; 58:5; 60:7, 10; 61:2), and in later poetic literature. It often sounds a positive eschatological note of God's ultimate act of gracious intervention.

The passage next turns to a positive description of what constitutes true piety before God. The ritual of fasting is not rejected out of hand, but redefined by enlarging its parameters. Phrases such as "loosen the cords of evil," "untie the straps of the yoke," "letting the oppressed go free," occur frequently in the earlier prophets (Amos 5:14; Isa. 1:16–17; 33:15, Micah 6:6), but this particular formulation resonates with the commission first given to the servant in 42:6ff. (cf. 49:8ff.). However, this response is more generated by the reader from the book of Isaiah as a whole than from an intentional authorial reference. To share bread with the hungry, to provide shelter for the homeless, and to clothe the naked goes far beyond the servant's commission and addresses common human compassion in a general imperative. It lies at the heart of God's rule to demand mercy and justice for all. Recall the moving story of 2 Chron. 28:8ff. when the victorious army of Israel was constrained by the prophet Oded to clothe, feed, and furnish shelter to the defeated, helpless people of Judah rather than to follow the common ancient Near Eastern practice of subjugating one's foes to slavery. The reference in v. 7 of "not to ignore your own kin" expresses a frequent concern of the Old Testament. It was regarded as especially grievous if the poor within the nation were forced by economic pressures into misery and slavery (Amos 4:1ff., 8:4; Isa. 3:15, 10:2; Ps. 9:19; Prov. 30:14).

Verse 8 describes next the effect of obedience of God's demands for righteous and compassionate behavior as action pleasing to him. It comes in the form of a renewal of the divine promise. The imagery of salvation as light and healing becomes a dominant metaphor in Third Isaiah (60:1; 62:2); however, the closest parallel to v. 12 lies in 52:12: "the God of Israel is your rear guard."

Zimmerli (219ff.) uses the intertextual relation between 52:12 and 58:8 as his initial example to illustrate the basic change between the messages of Second and Third Isaiah. Second Isaiah used the imagery of a new exodus to present the coming of a new eschatological age that would occur simultaneously with the deliverance of Israel from Babylon. Salvation was depicted as a miraculous march through the desert and the transformation of Zion into the city of God. However, Third Isaiah, living after the return of the exiles to Jerusalem, has taken over Second Isaiah's eschatological imagery, but at the same time has greatly transformed it. He has dropped all references to Babylon and to the wilderness journey, and interpreted the coming salvation metaphorically as the new religious condition of an inwardly transformed moral people. Although I do not dispute that Third Isaiah has altered Second Isaiah's message in important ways, I disagree with Zimmerli's interpretation regarding the nature of the change, which, of course, greatly affects how one understands the relationship between these two portions of the book of Isaiah.

First of all, regardless of what Second Isaiah may once have meant in the use of the exodus imagery, by the time of Third Isaiah, that is, in the postexilic era, Second Isaiah was interpreted within a larger literary collection, and its language understood largely metaphorically as pertaining to God's promised salvation, which was always its true content. Part of the truth of Second Isaiah's prophecy had been indeed fulfilled. The captivity of the Jews in Babylon had been ended and the exiles freed. There was no longer the need to repeat the language of the miraculous new exodus. Yet not all the promises had been accomplished. Jerusalem had not been elevated, nor had the new age broken with the glory of God revealed to all. Third Isaiah refers to the earlier promise (52:12), citing the last part of the verse: "the LORD will be your rear guard." As always, Third Isaiah's citation is never exact, but this is immaterial since its function is deitic, not midrashic. This is to say, the citation of the promise by Third Isaiah functions, above all, to confirm the truth of the earlier prophetic word. He is neither softening nor spiritualizing it in a so-called ethical reinterpretation, but refocusing the earlier promise in a new, concrete form which addresses that part of the hope not yet realized. He centers on the imagery of light and healing. The term "your righteousness" is a reference, not to Israel's behavior, but to the salvation of God (objective genitive), promised by Second Isaiah and employed again in its original prophetic sense (41:2; 45:8, 24).

The house of Jacob had complained in 58:3ff. that God had not responded to its fasting. He had taken no notice. Now the prophet assures the people of the presence of God: "Then you will call, and the LORD will answer" (cf. 41:17). The heart of Second Isaiah's promise of salvation, although couched in the language of a new exodus, had always been the coming of God: "Say to the cities of Judah, 'Behold, your God'" (49:9). He will be with his people and feed his flock like a shepherd (40:11). This same hope of the real, concrete presence of God is strongly affirmed by Third Isaiah. God will say, "Here I am" (58:9).

The imagery has shifted, but the same theological substance of the promise has remained.

[9b–12] Although these verses are very closely connected with the subject that preceded, the form of the oracle indicates a slight shift in focus. A conditional statement is first made (vv. 9b–10), which is then joined by a fresh repetition of the promise. Far from being just more of the same (Duhm), the prophet makes a new point with a different application of Second Isaiah's imagery.

The stipulations of removing oppression, hateful gestures, and wicked talk pick up the motif of 58:3ff. They are linked with the positive theme of aiding the hungry and afflicted, which is also reminiscent of 58:6ff. Next, the promise of the coming of God's salvation is repeated much in the language of 58:8, with the dominant image being the inbreaking of light for those in gloom (cf. 9:1ff.). In vv. 11f. the prophet makes a new application of the theme of the miraculous way through the desert, familiar from Second Isaiah. God will "guide" his people, satisfying their desires and increasing their strength. However, there is a change. Now the imagery of the transformation of the wilderness into a garden (43:20; 44:3) has been applied to the people themselves: "You will be like a well-watered garden, and like a spring whose waters do not fail" (v. 11). The goal of God's guidance through the wilderness had always been for the sustenance of the people. This point is now made explicit by Third Isaiah: they will be transformed, renewed, and strengthened.

However, the real focus of the promise by Third Isaiah focuses on that part of Second Isaiah's eschatological promise not yet fulfilled. Jerusalem still lies in desolation. Second Isaiah's word to Jerusalem, "She will be inhabited" (44:26), is still to be fulfilled. This portion of the promise is then renewed: "they will rebuild the ancient ruins and restore the ancient foundations." In sum, there is no hint that Third Isaiah understood his role as salvaging the unfulfilled hopes of his predecessor by turning the imagery into pious metaphors of conventional religious speech. His words of promise are still as massive and concrete as before, but he does offer a different application of the promise of salvation in the light of the present dire circumstances of postexilic Jerusalem, which still awaits longingly the full entrance of God's rule in a new age of redemption.

[13–14] As was previously mentioned, vv. 13–14 are frequently considered to be a later interpolation, or at least regarded as a disconnected new subject from the rest of chapter 58. The argument is that the shift from the topic of fasting to the observance of the Sabbath severs the continuity of subject matter. Usually commentators proceed to discuss the growth of the importance of the Sabbath in the postexilic period as a history of religion's phenomenon, and forgo the attempt to relate the subject to chapter 58 as a whole. Fortunately,

Beuken (*Jesaja III*) has broken fresh ground in mounting a very persuasive case for linking vv. 13–14 to the preceding material of the chapter.

First of all, careful exegesis of the theological issue at stake in the issue of fasting (57:3ff.) made it clear that the prophet was not setting up the conflict as between false ritualistic piety and aid to the oppressed in concrete acts of social action. If this had been the polarity of 55:1–4, then obviously it would have been impossible to find a coherent link between the critique of fasting and the ritual of Sabbath observance. However, such a modern construal of the issue presents a false polarity from a biblical perspective. Rather, Israel's fasting was condemned because of its arrogant, self-serving abuse of the ritual, which it used for its own gain and to seek to manipulate God to its own purposes. The key phrase of the criticism was that in the past Israel pursued its own business. It is as a directly opposite action of obedience to God's affairs that the theological role of the Sabbath emerges.

Verses 13–14 are shaped in a parallel form as the preceding oracle. First, a conditional stipulation is presented as a protasis: "If you keep from desecrating the Sabbath," "if you honor it, not going your own ways or pursuing your own affairs. . . . " Then the promise is given in the apodosis: "I will cause you to ride upon the heights of the earth, and let you enjoy the heritage of your father Jacob." It is highly significant that there is a play on the word "delight," which had occurred earlier in v. 2, and then returns in v. 13. In contrast to pursuing one's own business, the essence of the faithful observance of the Sabbath is that one explicitly refrains from one's normal, daily occupation and honors the day as sacred to God.

The Sabbath is not observed as a means of manipulating God or to realize any ulterior motive. Rather, one celebrates the day by focusing one's attention on the majestic words of God in creation (Ex. 20:11) and in salvation (Deut. 5:15). The observance of the Sabbath by God's faithful is only pleasing as an act of worship that takes delight in God. As such it is fully congruent with the stipulation for the obedient response of feeding the hungry and caring for the poor. It should come as no surprise that this connection has always been seen by rabbinic Judaism in its continued affirmation of the centrality of the Sabbath. (Cf. Beuken, 123, for the relevant references in the Babylonian Talmud and midrashim.)

61. Isaiah 59:1–21

59:1 Surely the LORD's hand is not too short to save,
     nor his ear too dull to hear.
2   But your iniquities have separated you
     from your God.

> Your sins have hidden his face from you
>   so that he refused to hear you.
3 For your hands are stained with blood,
>   and your fingers with iniquity.
> Your lips have spoken lies
>   and your tongue utters treachery.
4 No one sues justly
>   or pleads his case honestly.
> They rely on casuistry and speak falsely,
>   conceiving trouble and bringing forth evil.
5 They hatch the eggs of vipers[a]
>   and weave the spider's web.
> Whoever eats those eggs will die,
>   and if one is crushed a viper is hatched.
6 Their webs are useless for clothing;
>   they cannot cover themselves with what they make.
> Their works are evil deeds,
>   and their hands commit violent acts.
7 Their feet run after evil;
>   they are quick to shed innocent blood.
> Their thoughts are plans of evil.
>   Ruin and injury are on their roads.
8 They do not know the way of peace.
>   There is no justice in their paths.
> They have made their roads crooked.
>   No one who walks in them will know peace.
9 Therefore justice is far from us,
>   and righteousness does not reach us.
> We look for light, but all is darkness,
>   for some brightness, but we walk in gloom.
10 We grope like the blind along a wall,
>   feeling our way like those without sight.
> We stumble at noon as if it were dark.
>   Among the vigorous,[b] we are like the dead.
11 We all growl like bears
>   and moan like doves.
> We look for justice and there is none,
>   for deliverance, but it is distant.
12 For our many sins are before you,
>   and our offenses testify against us.
> We are well aware of our sin,
>   and we acknowledge our iniquity:

13 rebellion, treachery against the LORD,
and turning away from our God,
causing oppression and revolt,
conceiving and uttering lies from the heart.
14 Therefore justice is turned back,
and righteousness stops at a distance
because truth has fallen on the streets,
and honesty cannot enter.
15 Truth is missing,
and whoever turns from evil makes himself a prey.
The LORD looked and was displeased
that there was no justice.
16 He saw that there was no man,
and he was appalled that no one interceded.
Then his own arm brought him victory,
and his own righteousness sustained him.
17 He put on righteousness like a coat of mail,
and the helmet of salvation on his head.
He dressed himself with garments of vengeance,
and wrapped himself in zeal as in a robe.
18 According to their deeds, so^c he will repay:
anger to his adversaries and retribution to his
enemies.
He will render requital to the distant lands.
19 From the west, they shall fear the name of the LORD,
from the east, his glory,
for he will come like a roaring flood
that the wind of the LORD drives.
20 He will come to Zion as Redeemer,
to those in Jacob who turn away from sin,
says the LORD.
21 As for me, this is my covenant with them, says the LORD: my spirit
that is upon you, and my words that I have put in your mouth will not
depart from your mouth, or from the mouth of your children, or from
the mouths of their descendants from this time on and forever.

a. The noun *ṣip'ônî* occurs rarely in the Hebrew, and the exact kind of snake described is unclear.

b. The Hebrew word is a *hapax legomenon* and its meaning ucnertain. The present translation derives the word from the root "to be fat" (cf. *HALAT,* 93).

c. The repetition of the particle (*ke'al*) appears intentional and is not to be emended, as often proposed (*BHS*).

Selected Bibliography

H. A. Brongers, "Der Eifer des Herrn Zebaoth," *VT* 13, 1963, 269–84; **W. Dietrich,** "Rache. Erwägungen zu einem alttestamentlichen Thema," *EvTh* 36, 1976, 450–72; **D. Kendall,** "The Use of *Mišpaṭ* in Isaiah 59," *ZAW* 96, 1984, 391–405; **K. Koenen,** *Ethik und Eschatologie im Tritojesajabuch,* WMANT 62, Neukirchen-Vluyn 1990, 59–76; "Textkritische Anmerkungen zu schwierigen Stellen im Tritojesajabuch," *Bib* 69, 1988, 564–73; **W. Lau,** *Schriftgelehrte Prophetie in Jes 56–66,* BZAW 225, Berlin 1994, 229–39; **K. Pauritsch,** *Die neue Gemeinde,* AnBib 47, Rome 1971, 87–102; **A Rofé,** "Isaiah 59:19 and Trito-Isaiah's Vision of Redemption," *The Book of Isaiah,* ed. J. Vermeylen, Leuven 1989, 407–10; **O. H. Steck,** "Beobachtungen zu Jesaja 56—59," *Studien zu Tritojesaja,* BZAW 203, Berlin 1991, 169–86; "Jahwes Feinde im Jesaja 59," ibid., 187–91; **D. Weissert,** "Der Basilisk und das Windei in LXX-Jes 59, 5," *ZAW* 79, 1967, 315–22; **W. Zimmerli,** "Zur Sprache Tritojesajas," *Gottes Offenbarung, Gesammelte Aufsätze,* ThB 19, Munich 1969, 217–33.

1. Genre, Structure, and Literary Function

This chapter is declared by Volz (230) to be one of the most difficult in Second Isaiah (chapters 40—66) and for good reason. There are shifts in oral form, literary style, and unexpected alterations of speaker and addressee. In addition, the change in the tenses (vv. 15bff.) has continued to evoke puzzlement among commentators.

The passage, which is generally assumed to have a unity in some sense, is usually divided into three parts: vv. 1–8; 9–15a; 15b–20. Verse 21 is thought to be a prose addition. Many agree in describing elements of a prophetic invective in vv. 1–8, yet the form-critical problem is complex. Verses 1–2 appear to be responding to the people's complaint over God's alleged impotence. Verses 5–8 are often judged to be a later literary expansion because of the excessive detail given in a different style. The unit vv. 9–15a is a classic communal complaint, but has incorporated features from public confession. The first person plural form changes in vv. 14–15 to an impersonal descriptive style of summary. Verses 15b–20 are judged to be a theophany using the imagery of the divine warrior. The puzzling feature lies in the use of the perfect tense in vv. 15b–17 and the imperfect in vv. 19–20.

For most commentators probably the most controversial problem has been in interpreting one overarching literary function to the whole. Westermann thinks that the passage is dominated by two elements: the communal complaint and the prophetic word. However, his ensuing form-critical analysis, while often helpful in respect to smaller units, does not succeed in illuminating the passage as a whole. Then again, a frequent attempt to find a coherent unity has been to postulate a liturgical form that uses this hypothesis to interpret the abrupt changes in voices (Muilenburg, Lau). Unfortunately, the term *liturgy*—first introduced by Gunkel—remains imprecise and speculative. Similarly, the appeal to the category of sermon is too loose to be helpful (Sekine).

In recent times, some scholars (Beuken, Lau) have sought to find the key to the text's unity through attention to its intertextual references. Verses 1–3 are thought to be a reuse of 50:1–2. Beuken correctly points out that in chapter 59 two themes of chapter 50 recur with close verbal parallels, namely, that sin separates Israel from God, and the complaint of God's power being too weak to save. In 59:16 the theme of their being no one to intercede occurs also in parallel to 50:2. Although I would agree that these references to Second Isaiah are significant, I am not convinced that the link between chapters 50 and 59 provides the structural key to the latter. I would argue that these allusions provide the formal idiom for raising certain important questions, but that there is not a major, substantive link between the two. Chapter 59 has made an initial use of chapter 50, but then addresses the question of Israel's sinfulness in a very different way from chapter 50, probing deeply into the theological nature of sin and evil.

Finally, mention should be made of the redactional-critical solution of Steck ("Beobachtungen zu Jesaja 56–59," 169ff.) who first argued that chapters 58 and 59 are not two independent units, but originally a unified text that was redactionally parallel to 56:9–57:21. This analysis rests on too many prior assumptions, and I confess not to find it persuasive. Still, I would agree that Steck has made a contribution in calling for continued attention to the shaping of the book of Isaiah as a whole.

Steck ("Beobachtungen," 188) has also emphasized the cross-connection (*Querverbindungen*) between 59:15b–20, 61:2aß, and 63:1–6, which he postulates to be of the same redactional layer. Of course, it has long been recognized (cf. Muilenburg) that chapters 60–62 seem to be bracketed by two similar passages, 59:15ff. and 63:1–6. Following Duhm, a majority has then judged that 59:15b–20 is dependent upon 63:1–6, yet a few disagree in holding that the chronological sequence between the two passages is not clear (Lau, 219).

For my part, I would argue that the best lead lies in determining the present literary function of the larger context of chapters 56–59. Close attention to the sequence of these chapters of Third Isaiah demonstrates that there is a larger movement of thought. Chapter 56 addressed the question of the coming salvation, defined in terms of the integral relation between deliverance and justice. Salvation was open to all who "joined themselves to the LORD" in faithfulness. Next, chapter 57 set forth the sharp conflict between those who would inherit God's holy mountain and the wicked who would have no peace. Then 57:14 proclaimed that there were no obstacles to Israel's salvation from God's side, but that he wills to heal, lead, and comfort those of a contrite spirit. In chapter 58 false piety was contrasted with the true on the basis of the debate over fasting. Righteous behavior was defined in terms of care for the oppressed and suffering. Finally, chapter 59 continues the theme of sin as separating Israel from God, but the argument, both in form and content, moves in a different direction from chapter 57 by raising a different set of issues. This fact in itself emerges as a strong reason for not supporting Steck's redactional hypothesis regarding the relation of chapters 58 and 59.

In a word, chapter 59 addresses the ontological question of the nature of evil within the nation of Israel in vv. 1–8. The issue of Israel's separating itself from God through sin is not developed as a rebuttal of one specific incident of rebellion, but dealt with on the broader plane of its theological significance to the essential righteousness of God. Two major questions emerge. First, what is the response of a faithful remnant within Israel to the prophetic accusation of gross apostasy? Second, what is the divine response when justice is lost and truth utterly destroyed?

In vv. 9–15 one hears the voice of faithful Israel confirming the extent of the reigning wickedness, but testifying to its own sinful complicity and confessing in deep repentance its own sin. Those repenting offer no mitigating excuses, but identify with the entire nation's evil. Then God's reaction comes in a theophany in which God acknowledges that he alone can bring justice. There is no human intercessor. But when God saw, he arose in angry judgment to avenge the wicked and redeem the faithful. Significantly, the theophanic portrayal of God's decision to establish justice is described in the past tense, and only later continued in an eschatological future. The move from past to present serves to address the plight of the faithful remnant of the postexilic period, but the sequence described is not, first of all, a temporal one. Rather, chapter 59 uses the three sharply different sections to probe theologically the nature of God's righteousness, the response of faith as repentance, and the demand for God's sole eschatological intervention.

If there remains any doubt about how to understand the movement of the chapter, v. 21 provides an interpretive epilogue. A classic example of canonical interpretation is offered by means of a summarizing commentary (cf. Eccl. 12:13). The relationship that has been described in chapter 59 is now identified with God's covenant (*berît*). It is initiated by the spirit of God and sustained by his words (commandments) for each generation in the future. What this future entails is then portrayed in chapters 60–62 as life within God's restored Jerusalem.

2. Exposition

[59:1–8] Chapter 59 begins with a prophetic refutation of Israel's charge that perhaps God did not have the power any longer to save, or that he had no interest in his people to hear their prayers. Westermann lays great emphasis on the role of the complaint throughout the chapter, but, in my opinion, this element has been subordinated. The literary connection of vv. 1–2 has long been noticed. Beuken (*Jesaja III*, 126) argues that more than just a conventional use of an idiom is involved in 59:1 (cf. Num. 11:23) because the reference is also joined to the motif of sin as the cause of the separation between God and his people (59:2 // 50:1–2). Yet his attempt, along with that of Zimmerli (226), to find in this intertextual reference the important key for understanding chapter 59 seems to be misplaced. There appears to be no extension of a substantive nature, but when the language of chapter 50 is taken up into chapter 59, then the main argument of the latter moves in an independent direction. Chapter 58 actually provides a closer connection in its development of the theme of sin as a barrier that blocked Israel's voice from being heard (58:4 // 59:2).

Perhaps even more significant for understanding vv. 1–8 is the allusion in v. 3 to hands that are "stained with blood . . . fingers with iniquity." Its closest parallel is found in 1:15. As we have seen earlier in chapter 57, it is a characteristic move of Third Isaiah when describing the sins of contemporary Israel to portray the people in the prophetic idiom of First Isaiah. There are two immediate theological implications from this practice. First, all of Israel is included and no initial distinction between the righteous and the wicked is offered. Second, a substantive identification is made between the Israel of the eighth century condemned by the prophet Isaiah, and the present community who had been delivered from the Babylonian captivity. Whereas in the proclamation of Second Isaiah it would almost appear (but cf. 43:24; 46:12) as if Israel's former sins were a part of the old age not to be remembered in the glorious light of the new things (43:18), Third Isaiah removes this misunderstanding by addressing Israel's wickedness on an ontological plane. Good and evil will continue to coexist even after God has transformed Jerusalem into the city of God (62:1ff.).

The prophetic accusation of Israel's fundamental apostasy is then further pursued through v. 8. A literary argument has often been made that vv. 5–8 derive from a later interpolation. There are certainly parallels elsewhere in the book of Isaiah when an initial invective subsequently has been greatly expanded to include fresh details of the abuses being committed (3:18–23). It is possible that this is also the case in vv. 5–8, but the evidence is hardly conclusive. The structure of the unit reflects very careful shaping, which is usually not the case with a gloss. However, in the end, the issue is of secondary importance since these verses add substantially to the force of the chapter as a whole regardless of their compositional history.

The tone of accusation is pursued on a somewhat general and sweeping scale. No one enters suits justly, but falsehood brings forth increased iniquity. Of course, the attack by the prophets on the perversion of the legal system of justice is widespread throughout the entire preexilic period. However, the accusations lack the specificity of, say, an Amos or Micah, and rather focus on the universal dimension of evil that pervades the entire society. The imagery begins in v. 5 with the unbroken continuity of evil, which hatches its brood like poisonous vipers, and moves to the uselessness of evil's works, which like spider webs provide no benefit to clothe. In vv. 7–8 the idiom shifts to paths of evil and twisted ways that aid in multiplying evil without ever leading to peace.

In sum, the accusations in vv. 1–8 probe to a new theological depth in exploring the essence of Israel's evil, which has effected a separation from God. The issue is no longer isolated cases of sin, but the author bends over backwards to explore the full dimensions of fundamental perversion. Muilenburg was certainly correct in observing, "Few chapters in the Bible are so rich and diverse in their vocabulary of sin" (686).

What follows next is a dual reaction to this intolerable human condition. Verses 9–15a present faithful Israel's reply, and vv. 15b–20 offer the divine response, first to vv. 1–8 and then to vv. 9–15a.

[9–15a] Verse 9 is linked with v. 8 both by its substance and by the catchword "justice" (*mišpāṭ*). In fact, the unit is bracketed in v. 9 and again in v. 14 by the terms "justice" and "righteousness." In a real sense the genre of complaint continues throughout the entire unit, and the description of some of the same sins of vv. 1–8 is repeated. Yet to focus on the complaint runs the danger of overlooking the main function of the passage which is, first and foremost, to serve as a confession.

In vv. 9–13 the complaint is sounded in the first person plural and thereby a completely different perspective is presented as the voice of faithful Israel transforms the complaint into a confession. As in vv. 1–8 the desperate moral condition of Israel is confirmed: "justice is far from us, and righteousness does not reach us." However, now the confessing community embraces the divine condemnation and passionately acknowledges its plight: "We look for light, but all is darkness, for some brightness, but we walk in gloom." The same contrast of light with darkness is continued in v. 10 with the description, "We grope like the blind. . . . We stumble at noon." Verse 11 returns to the theme of v. 9, confessing that there is no justice and that salvation is far removed.

However, the heart of the passage, which changes its form from lament to confession, comes in v. 12. Faithful Israel names the source of its plight as stemming from its own transgressions which mount up before God. As elsewhere in the Old Testament, sin is experienced as a heavy burden, a substance that testifies against its perpetuator. The confessing community acknowledges freely its own guilt, which is always present. But more, it bears witness that this sin is a grievous offense to God and a form of arrogant rejection of him. The return to the theme of speaking lies serves to identify the repentant community with the apostate nation of 59:3. In sum, those confessing do not seek to distance themselves from the general condemnation by God of the nation as apostate, but they plea for the mercy of God whom they have denied. In vv. 14–15 the first person plural switches to a descriptive style which summarizes the unit. There is no justice, no righteousness, no truth. Indeed, those who seek to depart from such evil become the targets for persecution—a note immediately relevant to the entrenched community of Third Isaiah.

[**15b–20**] These verses remain the most difficult to interpret within the chapter, and are, of course, crucial for understanding the whole. Verse 15b reads, "The LORD looked and was displeased that there was no justice." This is clearly the divine response to the complaints in both vv. 1–8 and 9–15; however, the response is also linked in v. 20 to the confessional voice of faithful Israel. God saw that there was no mediator (cf. 63:5), neither in word nor act (53:12), to provide intercession. Therefore, he himself arose to vindicate his people with avenging righteousness (Deut. 32:35).

The most difficult problem turns on the unexpected shift of senses from the consecutive imperfect in vv. 15–17 to the future imperfect in vv. 19–20. The traditional interpretation of Delitzsch sought to explain the shift as an instance of a prophetic perfect, which used the form of completed action to indicate the certainty of a future event. However, the use of the narrative imperfect form is not frequent for the prophetic perfect, and more seems involved than Delitzsch's solution allows. Westermann describes the form as a theophany, but then he seeks to abort it within his larger liturgical hypothesis without solid evidence. The history of religion's approach of Hanson describes the passage as a fragment from a mythical "Divine Warrior" tradition; however, such a concern for historical origins does not aid greatly in understanding the passage according to its literary function in chapter 59. Moreover, if its role were strictly apocalyptic, one would not expect the past tenses of vv. 15a–17.

In my judgment, Lau (218) points toward a fresh interpretation when he stresses the intertextual relationship between 59:16 and 63:5. Yet he also recognizes that the effect of the shift in tenses in chapter 59 serves to thematize the action of Yahweh. To describe the intervention of God in establishing righteousness by his own might in the past tense serves to address the present situation in Israel by affirming that God has not been inactive up to this point. The assigning to the past of God's reaction of judgment serves to describe, not one specific moment in history, but the state of the divine will. God has purposed to establish his righteous order against human evil long ago. The emphasis of v. 18 on the divine rules governing his actions offers a purposeful transition to his future execution of judgment against all forms of evil. The extended use of the symbolism of armor—breastplate of righteousness, helmet of salvation, garments of vengeance—further emphasizes the enduring substance of God's alternative order to that portrayed in the natural apostasy of vv. 1–15a. Then vv. 18–20 function explicitly to bring comfort to the suffering faithful of vv. 9–15a. God will repay his enemies and render his requital to the distant islands. Above all, he will come to Zion as redeemer to those who repent when he reveals himself finally in his full glory.

In sum, the chapter focuses on a theological summary of the full extent of Israel's apostasy as it probes the devastating dimensions of sin and evil. The faithful within the nation, who are fully enmeshed in Israel's self-destructive fate, throw themselves completely on God's mercy without offering any mitigating excuses. They know and acknowledge their share in Israel's guilt. The ensuing theophanic description of the divine response, retrojected into the past, establishes once and for all that God alone can shatter the power of sin and bring justice and salvation to suffering Zion. There is no other force to intercede.

[21] The final verse consists of a lengthy prose addition in language more akin to different levels of the Pentateuch (D and P). Most frequently this concluding verse is dismissed as being without connection to the preceding passage. Westermann even suggests attaching it to 66:20–24. Yet such solutions miss the canonical function of this verse, which offers an interpretation of the theological intent of the entire chapter, similar to that found in Eccl. 12:13–14.

The verse is assigned directly to God's speech both at the beginning and end. The initial formula "as for me" (*wa'ănî*; cf. Gen. 17:4) emphasizes God's full commitment to the promise that follows: "this is my covenant with them." The term *covenant* occurs infrequently in Third Isaiah, but in v. 21 seems obviously linked to its programmatic occurrence in 56:5–6, addressed to God's servants who join themselves to him. The effect is to summarize and to interpret the whole section comprising chapters 56—59.

Chapter 59 had sounded the voice of repentant Israel confessing its sin and awaiting God's mercy. Verse 20 offered the divine promise that God would come as redeemer to those who turned to him. The role of v. 21 is to articulate this relationship as constituting God's purpose in terms of his covenant. It thus interprets the preceding will of God to intervene in righteousness (vv. 15b–16) as covenant. Verse 21 finds an exegetical warrant in the past tense of vv. 15ff. to see God's eternal will for Israel's salvation in his covenant, extending from the past to the present. By anticipating the eschatological consummation in the future, it served to evoke in the community of faith a call to trust God in the midst of great trial and testing. God wills to be "with them" and to bring new life through his spirit (v. 21). He has given them his words to guide, which are transmitted from one generation to the next, indeed, forever.

There is one final aspect to the theological function of v. 21 to discuss. Chapter 56 had initiated the final collection of Third Isaiah by stressing the need for justice (*mišpāṭ*) and righteousness (*ṣᵉdāqāh*) to rule in Israel if God's promised redemption was to be revealed. The same demand for righteousness continued in chapters 57 and 58, and culminated in chapter 59 with God's purpose to establish it himself through direct intervention in judgment. The introduction of the term *covenant* in chapter 59 functions to join the prophetic call for justice with the Pentateuchal tradition of the Mosaic covenant. Not by chance has chapter 58 paralleled the service of God through works of mercy to the oppressed and the proper observance of the Sabbath. In sum, Third Isaiah shapes his material in such a way to reveal a coherent expression of the one will of God for Israel's salvation in torah.

The chapters that follow (60–62) portray the redeemed life experienced in the new and transformed Jerusalem, city of God.

62. Isaiah 60:1–22

60:1 Arise, shine, for your light has come,
　　　and the glory of the LORD has shone upon you.
2　　See, darkness covers the earth,
　　　and thick darkness the peoples,
　　but upon you the LORD will arise,
　　　and his glory will be seen over you.
3　　Nations will come to your light,
　　　and kings to your shining radiance.
4　　Raise your eyes and look about.
　　　They are all gathered and come to you.
　　Your sons will be brought from far,
　　　your daughters carried on the hip.
5　　Then you will look and be radiant.
　　　Your heart will throb and expand
　　because the wealth of the seas will be turned to you.
　　　The riches of the nations will come to you.
6　　The abundance of camels will overwhelm you,
　　　young camels of Midian and Ephah.
　　　All those from Sheba will come,
　　carrying gold and frankincense
　　　and proclaiming the praise of the LORD.
7　　All the flocks of Kedar will be gathered to you.
　　　The rams of Nebaioth will serve your needs.
　　They will be accepted[a] as offerings on my altar,
　　　and I will adorn my beautiful house.
8　　Who are these that fly like clouds,
　　　like doves to their cotes?
9　　Truly the islands[b] are waiting
　　　with the ships of Tarshish in the lead,
　　to bring your sons from far,
　　　their silver and gold with them,
　　for the name of the LORD your God,
　　　and the Holy One of Israel, who has glorified you.

10   Foreigners will rebuild your walls,
          and their kings will serve you.
      Although in my anger I smote you,
          yet in my favor I have compassion on you.
11   Your gates will always stand open,
          day and night they shall never be shut,
      to let the wealth of the nations enter
          with their kings led in procession.[c]
12   For the nation or kingdom that will not
          serve you will perish;
          those nations will be completely destroyed.
13   The glory of Lebanon will come to you,
          the pine, the fir, and the cypress,
      to adorn the site of my sanctuary,
          and to glorify the place of my feet.
14   The sons of your oppressors will come
          bowing before you,
      and those who despised you
          will prostrate themselves at your feet,
      and you will be called "city of the LORD,"
          Zion of the Holy One of Israel.
15   Instead of your being forsaken and hated
          with none passing through,
      I will make you an enduring pride
          and a joy to all generations.
16   You will suck the milk of nations
          and nurse at the breast of kings.
      And you will know that I, the LORD,
          am your Savior,
          your Redeemer, the Mighty One of Jacob.
17   Instead of bronze, I will bring gold,
          instead of iron, silver,
      instead of wood, bronze,
          and iron in the place of stone.
      I will make your overseers peace,
          and your magistrates righteousness.
18   No more will violence by heard in your land,
          neither devastation nor ruin within your borders,
      but you will call your walls Salvation,
          and your gates Thanksgiving.
19   The sun will no longer be your light by day,
          nor will the moon's brightness illuminate you by night,

but the LORD will be your light forever,
and your God will be your glory.

20 The sun will set no more,
nor will your moon ever wane;
the LORD will be your light forever,
and your days of mourning will end.

21 Then all your people will be righteous;
they will possess the land forever.
They are the shoot of the plantings of the LORD,[d]
the work of my hands, for my glory.

22 The least of you will become a thousand,
the smallest a mighty nation.
I, the LORD, will expedite it quickly.

a. The MT may be slightly in disorder (cf. *BHS* and the readings of the LXX and 1QIs[a]).

b. The text is often emended to "ships" (*ṣiyyîm*) and "gather" (*yiqqāwû*), but the suggestion is not compelling.

c. *BHS* emends the passive form of the verb to an active participle to remove the idea of compulsion.

d. The Kethib reads "shoot of his planting," while the Qere reads "my plantings." Cf. the discussion in the exposition and the extended notes of Beuken (187f.) and Oswalt (II, 54–55).

Selected Bibliography

W. A. M. Beuken, "Does Trito-Isaiah Reject the Temple? An Intertextual Inquiry into Isa. 66:1–6," *Intertextuality in Biblical Writings: Essays in Honour of Bas van Iersel*, ed. S. Draisma, Kampen 1989, 53–66; **K. Koenen,** *Ethik und Eschatologie im Tritojesajabuch*, WMANT 62, Neukirchen-Vluyn 1990, 137–57; **W. Lau,** *Schriftgelehrte Prophetie in Jes 56–66*, BZAW 225, Berlin 1994, 23–65; **J. C. de Moor,** "Structure and Redaction: Isaiah 60:1–63:6," *Studies in the Book of Isaiah, Fs W. A. M. Beuken*, Leuven 1997, 325–46; **H. Odeberg,** *Trito-Isaiah*, Uppsala 1931, 216–49; **K. Pauritsch,** *Die neue Gemeinde*, AnBib 47, Rome 1971, 119–27; **G. von Rad,** "The City on the Hill," *The Problem of the Hexateuch and Other Essays*, ET Edinburgh 1966, 232–42; **S. Sekine,** *Die Tritojesanische Sammlung (Jes 56–66) redaktionsgeschichtlich untersucht*, BZAW 175, Berlin 1989, 68–74; **P. A. Smith,** *Rhetoric and Redaction in Trito-Isaiah*, VTSup 62, Leiden 1995, 22–49; 173ff.; **O. H. Steck,** "Der Grundtext in Jesaja 60 und sein Aufbau," *Studien zu Tritojesaja*, BZAW 20, Berlin 1991, 49–79; "Lumen Gentium. Exegetische Bemerkungen zum Grundsinn von Jesaja 60, 1–3," ibid., 80–96; **C. C. Torrey,** *The Second Isaiah*, Edinburgh 1928, 443–52; **J. Vermeylen,** *Du Prophete Isaïe à l'Apocalyptique*, II, Paris 1978, 471–78; **W. Zimmerli,** "Zur Sprache Tritojesajas," (1950), reprinted in *Gottes Offenbarung*, ThB 19, Munich 1969, 217–33.

1. Form, Structure, and Literary Function

From a synchronic perspective, chapter 60 is closely related editorially to the preceding chapter. Chapter 59 had introduced the voice of faithful Israel in confession of its sin and guilt, to which a divine reassurance was then given. God's covenant with those "who turn away from sin" (v. 20) will continue from generation to generation. Chapters 60—62 serve to spell out, in different ways, the effect of this enduring promise. Particularly in chapter 60 the future glory of Zion is described in a moving portrayal of the city of God. She is addressed in the second person feminine as the downtrodden, rejected woman whose fortunes have suddenly been reversed.

Various attempts have been made (e.g., Westermann) to analyze features of the chapter form-critically, but this search for earlier oral forms has not been very illuminating. Rather, within recent times more scholarly attention has again turned to the older literary-critical problems treated once by Duhm and Marti (e.g., Vermeylen, 471ff.). Some attempts have also been made to rearrange the sequence of chapters 60—62, but without great success. There is wide consensus that v. 12 is a later interpolation written in a prose style. Pressing even further, Pauritsch would remove all traces of "nationalism" from the chapter by also deleting vv. 6c, 14a, 17b, and 19c.

The most extensive redactional analysis of the chapter has been made by Steck (cf. "Der Grundtext in Jesaja 60" and "Lumen Gentium"). He argues that vv. 1–9 and 13–16 constitute the original layer of chapter 60, which focuses on the coming of the nations, the subjugation of Babylon, and the salvation of Zion. This original layer was first expanded in vv. 16–17, an addition that reflects a different conceptual framework. The second expansion (vv. 17–22) belongs to his "*Grossjesaja Redaktion*," and it sought to connect certain themes of chapters 56—59 with First Isaiah. Space in a commentary is too limited for a detailed response to Steck. In spite of several excellent observations on the role of intertextuality in chapter 60, I find his larger hypothesis highly speculative and burdened with a huge ballast of earlier critical assumptions.

I continue to be disturbed by Steck's method of discerning layers within the text according to a theory of logical consistency. I do not think that poetic texts can be handled in this manner. Thus, to suggest that there is a conflict between building city walls and the free entry of the nations described in vv. 1–9 ("Grundtext," 66) appears excessively rationalistic and pedestrian (cf. P. A. Smith's criticism [32] of Steck's reconstruction of alleged contradictions regarding foreigners). Although I do not contest that the present text shows signs of growth, I question whether this complex process can be precisely reconstructed, and, even less, that such an alleged development provides the key to understanding the chapter in its final form.

Most recently, P. A. Smith has attempted a more conservative redactional scheme by which he distinguishes two distinct textual levels. The first, which encompasses 60:1–63:6, he assigns to Third Isaiah in the early postexilic period; the second, which encompasses 56:1–8; 56:9–57:21; 58:1–59:20; and 65:1–66:17, he assigns to a later writer working up to 515. In his analysis he offers some interesting statistics of characteristic formulae in order to buttress his position. However, in the end, he also attempts with Steck to establish an absolute historical chronology by which to develop his redactional trajectory. Equally questionable, in my opinion, is that he falls back into typical psychological appeals to Israel's alleged disillusionment following Second Isaiah, and finds therein evidence for dating certain prophetic oracles. I do not regard this approach to be a scholarly advance.

It is, however, encouraging that a virtual consensus has emerged in recognizing the crucial role that intertextuality between Second and Third Isaiah plays in chapter 60 (cf. Volz, Beuken, Steck, Koenen, Lau). Thus, there are the following virtual citations of Second Isaiah in chapter 60: v. 4a // 49:18a; v. 9b // 55:5b; v. 13a // 41:19b; v. 16b // 49:26–27. In addition, there are multiple parallel themes: v 4b // 49:12, 22, 43:6b–7; v. 10b // 54:7–8. Of course, the difficult exegetical problem turns on the manner in which this relationship to Second Isaiah is interpreted.

At the outset, there is some agreement that the striking dependency of Third Isaiah on Second Isaiah provides a different model by which to understand the forces at work in the shaping of chapter 60. Lau finds a clear warrant here for speaking of a *"Schriftgelehrter Prophet"* (65). The structure of the chapter is far less determined by oral patterns (theophany, complaints, etc.) than by the reuse of the themes of Second Isaiah by means of explicit citations and allusions. For example, Third Isaiah can describe transformed Zion with the earlier images of a change from darkness to light, of a pilgrimage of the nations, of the restored wife, and of the return of the diaspora.

More controversial is determining the exact function of the intertextual usage of Third Isaiah. As I have argued earlier, one must be cautious in first assuming a postexilic historical setting different from chapters 40—55, which caused Third Isaiah to adjust Second Isaiah's message to conform to the new historical situation. A far more subtle interpretation is required. From a synchronic perspective, Third Isaiah seems to share fully the same theological context as did Second Isaiah, and his citations function deictically to provide a warrant confirming the continuity. The fact that there are also diachronic signs of an actual shift in historical setting cannot hermeneutically override the literary shaping of the prophetic text. The recovery of a historical depth dimension rather aids in sharpening the diverse contours of the biblical portrayal, but without destroying the coherence of the final form (cf. the exegesis below).

Finally, there has been considerable debate over the quality of the prophetic witness in chapter 60. The legacy of Duhm has generally been to deprecate both the literary style and theology of chapter 60 as greatly inferior to that of Second Isaiah. Particularly Volz has attacked the alleged "nationalism" of the chapter, even after v. 12 has been removed as an offensive gloss. According to Volz, a major sign of theological narrowness is that Jerusalem, not Yahweh, has become the center of the proclamation. In my judgment, great caution should be exercised lest a modern value judgment respecting the virtue of unconditional universalism become the measure of an acceptable theology. As I shall attempt to show, there is not a difference in kind between the eschatological hope of Second and Third Isaiah on this point. The Wellhausen legacy of seeing postexilic Judaism as a trajectory of moral decline must be strongly resisted.

The broad structure of the chapter can be outlined as follows:

vv. 1–9   Zion challenged to greet God's appearance
10–16   The reversal in Zion's fortunes
17–22   The transformation of the city and its people

2. Exposition

[60:1–3] The idiom of Zion's being addressed as a woman in great distress is continued from Second Isaiah (51:17). The imagery of the breaking forth of the divine light into darkness as the sign of the manifesting of God's glory certainly resonates the promise of 40:1–11. In addition, several themes from First Isaiah also shimmer in the background of the theophany. There is the sharp contrast between the light of God's coming salvation and the people dwelling in deep darkness (9:1ff.). Moreover, the motif of the nations coming to the divine city of light forms a background reminiscent of 2:2–5.

[4] This verse picks up the theme of the return of Zion's children with a citation from 49:18a: "Lift up your eyes around you and see: they all gather and come to you." In fact, chapter 49 provides the context for the entire chapter, expanding on the theme of the scattered exiles being brought in the arms of the rulers of the nations (vv. 22–23). Although it is true that Third Isaiah's promise of the return of the diaspora to Jerusalem had a special relevance to postexilic Israel—only a few of the exiles had returned at first in 539—the reuse of the promise of Second Isaiah, especially in chapter 49, serves a particular function in chapter 60 as a whole. In the context of chapters 56—66 the author completely identifies with the point of standing of chapters 40—55. The earlier promise is confirmed and eschatologically expanded. Chapter 60 continues to envision Zion as on the very edge of the divine transformation of Jerusalem.

[5–7] Then the vision is greatly developed in the description of the coming of the nations who bring their wealth to enhance the temple's splendor. Midian and Ephrah are used as symbols of the great traders from the desert, whose territory lay east of the Gulf of Aqaba. The Sabaeans of Sheba in south Arabia recalls the wealth flowing to King Solomon at the queen's visit (1 Kings 10:1–13). At a later period Sheba was especially known for supplying spices and gold. The flocks of Kedar and rams of Nabaioth are associated with the Arabic tribes to the south who provide the animals needed for the proper worship of God in the new Jerusalem. In spite of a slightly different reading of v. 7b in the Isaiah text of Qumran (1QIs[b]), the MT is still to be preferred in stressing the point of acceptable sacrifice in the restored temple of the future. Significantly, the referential language to the temple remains elusive and aids little in establishing an exact chronology of the oracles, as is evident in the continuing disagreement among the commentators regarding its role as a warrant for dating.

[8–9] The next verses continue the theme of the return of the diaspora from afar but shift the imagery. The white sails of ships from Tarshish are compared to cumulus clouds in the sky or to pigeons flying to their dovecots. Verse 9b brings the theme of the return of Israel's scattered exiles to a close by citing 55:5. Verse 9 develops the theme that all this has been done in "the name of Yahweh your God" who has chosen to glorify Zion. To suggest with Volz that the portrayal of the accumulation of material splendor is derived from a crude postexilic nationalism seems to miss the theological point of the chapter. Because Zion is understood as the restored divine city, its splendor is identified with the rendering of honor to God. Although it is true that Third Isaiah has developed the theme of Zion's future magnificence beyond that of Second Isaiah, the portrayal is not different in kind in the two, nor is the purpose greatly altered in Third Isaiah.

[10–16] The reversal of Zion's fortunes is pursued in detail in vv. 10–16. Israel's former oppressors now rebuild Jerusalem's walls, and kings serve its people. The grounds for the change is attributed to the passing of God's anger and the extension of his mercy, a favorite theme of Second Isaiah (40:1–2; 54:6), which has been occasionally retrojected redactionally into First Isaiah (12:1; 30:19). The description of the gates of the city being continually left open is not used here to depict the absence of war, but rather that the flow of the nations bringing their wealth into the city not be impeded (cf. Rev. 21:24ff.). The imagery in the final phrase of v. 11 has evoked some disagreement about its meaning. What is intended "with their kings led ($n^e h\hat{u}g\hat{i}m$) in procession"? Some have argued that the passive form must denote being led unwillingly as captives, but this negative connotation does not fit well into the context of the chapter. Often the verb is emended into an active participle (*HALAT*, Whybray): "their kings leading them." However, the idea of free will is not excluded from the passive voice and the MT can be rendered "with kings in procession" (NJPS, cf. Beuken, *Jesaja III*).

Most frequently, v. 12 is eliminated by commentators as a late gloss. The warrant is found in its alleged prose style and the disconcertingly harsh rhetoric. Some argue that the gloss was an abortive attempt to clarify the sense of v. 11b. Indeed, it is highly possible that the verse is a later addition; however, rather than eliminating it as worthless, a more suitable exegetical approach would be to see how it functions in the chapter. Some of the conceptual difficulty that commentators have had with the verse arises from a misleading polarity between a level of Third Isaiah that speaks in a positive fashion of a universal salvation and another level that excludes the nations in a move of nationalism. I judge this construal to rest on a false analysis of Third Isaiah. Rather, the polarity, which is consistent throughout Third Isaiah, is between those who turn to Yahweh, including foreigners, and those who resist God's will. Verse 12 simply makes fully explicit that judgment is decreed for those peoples, including Israelites, who oppose God's salvation.

The reference in v. 13 to the rich forests of Lebanon providing pine, fur, and cypress is part of the imagery of the paradisiacal new order and not an inventory of lumber for the rebuilding of the temple. Finally, in v. 14, Zion, the city of Yahweh, is named as the antecedent of the second person feminine pronoun, who was first addressed in v. 1. It is also fully consistent with Third Isaiah's close connection with Second Isaiah that the familiar divine epithet, "Holy One of Israel" (cf. 41:14, 16, 20; 43:3; etc.), appears in v. 14 (cf. V. 9).

Considerable discussion has focused on the strange imagery of v. 16. In the preceding verse the familiar portrayal of the forsaken wife recurs, now restored to her position of honor. However, in v. 16a, instead of the formulation of 49:23, "Kings will be your foster fathers, and their queens will serve as nurses," one reads, "You will suck the milk of nations and nurse at the breast of kings." Zimmerli (222) finds the alteration to be "an inelegant destruction of imagery," and sees therein a further warrant for his thesis that Third Isaiah engages in tortuous exegesis in an attempt to adopt Second Isaiah's prophecies to a later historical period. He also notes an even further extension of the same imagery in 66:11, with Israel sucking from the consoling breasts of Jerusalem. Although such imagery may seem offensive to modern sensibilities, the change tells us little about the intentions of Third Isaiah. The explicit goal of the promise is the same in Second and Third Isaiah, namely, that "you will know that I, the Lord, am your Savior" (49:23b; 60:16).

[17–22] The portrayal of the future glory of Zion continues to expand in the final verses of the chapter. The contrast between the old and the new is made in terms of the building materials: instead of bronze, gold; instead of iron, silver; instead of wood, bronze; and instead of stones, iron. Clearly the language has become hyperbolic in projecting the new, eschatological city of God. The crass and base have been exchanged for the pure and precious. The reference to overseers and taskmasters as agents of peace and righteousness draws on the oppression during the Egyptian slavery, which has been overturned. All violence and destruction will be excluded from Zion's future. It is significant that even though the closest parallel might be found in First Isaiah's portrayal of the messianic age (e.g., 11:6ff.), there is no explicit mention whatever of a messiah in this passage (cf. also 65:25).

In the early part of chapter 60, in spite of a close continuity with the promises of Second Isaiah, one can see that Third Isaiah's use involved an expansion both in length and in intensity. In vv. 19ff. a new dimension is reached in the eschatological portrayal of Zion that enters into the realm of the apocalyptic. Zion is not only purified and restored, but takes on the features of the heavenly city. There is no longer need for the light of the sun and moon because the presence of God in its midst provides an everlasting light. The days of mourning are passed (cf. 65:20). The promise of inheriting the land is repeated, but joined with a new claim: all the inhabitants of Zion shall be righteous. This theme was already adumbrated in 60:14. Zion, the city of the Holy One of Israel, will reflect the same quality of righteousness as its God.

The full implications of this characterization of the people as righteous are spelled out in the phrase of v. 21b, "the shoot of the plantings of the LORD." Unfortunately, there is a textual problem that has tended to blur the full force of the verse. The Kethib reads "his planting," the Qere "my plantings." Moreover, there is a significant variant in a Qumran text (1QIs^a) that reads "the planting of Yahweh," which may explain the source of the variations within the MT tradition (cf. Beuken's discussion, 187–88). I follow the reconstruction of the verse to read "the shoot of the plantings of Yahweh." Clearly, the words "shoot" (*nēṣer*) and "planting" (*maṭṭaʿ*; cf. 61:3) set up a resonance with many earlier parts of the book of Isaiah, but then caution is needed to avoid fanciful speculation in the name of intertextuality. In a word, there is no real evidence to connect the term directly with the messianic term in 11:1.

However, the idea of God's special planting is a significant theme in both First and Second Isaiah (5:1ff.; 27:2ff.; cf. 65:22), which is often joined with the motif of offspring and progeny (65:23). In chapter 53 the servant was promised an offspring and a long life. In chapter 54 the servants of the Lord are named as those who will possess the nations and inhabit the land (v. 3). In fact, in chapter 65 the servants of God who inherit the land are identified with the offspring of the servant. Moreover, it is in the context of the future blessing of the servants of God that Zion is transformed as part of the new heavens and earth, and thus provides the closets parallel to the cosmological change depicted in 60:19ff.

The implication of this line of thought is that the description of all the people who inhabit the new Zion as righteous is not a moralistic aspiration, but rather understood as the fulfillment of the promise of a righteous offspring made to the servant in 53:19ff. The portrayal of the city of God in terms of light is further informed by the original mission of the servant to be the light to the nations (42:6; 49:6). The persecuted group of the faithful within Israel (50:10ff.), who obey the voice of God's servant, are further promised to become a "mighty nation" (60:22). This same theme is then pursued in chapter 61. The planting of the Lord will be glorified (v. 3). There will be an everlasting covenant with them (v. 8), and their descendants will be known by the nations (v. 9).

Perhaps the most significant aspect of chapter 60 is the new eschatological interpretation of the future revealed by Third Isaiah. Although my exegesis has

attempted to show the close dependency upon Second Isaiah, it is equally important to recognize the important reinterpretations of the prior promises. However,
in contrast to Zimmerli's claim of a spiritualization, I would argue that Third
Isaiah strongly confirms the promises of Second Isaiah, and shares his anticipation of a coming *kairos*. Yet there is a difference. Third Isaiah no longer identifies the deliverance of the exiles from Babylon as coterminous with the entrance
of God's kingdom. Indeed, Babylon has receded into the background as has the
new exodus. It has become only an instance of the promise. Rather, what now
lies ahead has become radically eschatologized. The new Jerusalem is not a
rebuilt earthly city, but the entrance of the divine kingdom of God, the creation
of a new heaven and earth. Yet the promise is still tied to the faithful of Israel,
to the obedient offspring who await the promised blessings of God (61:9).

63. Isaiah 61:1–11

61:1 The spirit of the Lord GOD is upon me,
        because the LORD has anointed me.
      To bring good tidings to the poor he has sent me,
        to bind up the brokenhearted,
      to proclaim liberty to the captives
        and freeing[a] to those who are bound,
2   to proclaim the year of the LORD's favor
        and the day of vengeance of our God,
      to comfort all who mourn
3   and provide[b] for those who grieve in Zion,
        to give them a turban instead of ashes,
      the oil of gladness instead of mourning,
        and a garment of praise instead of a drooping spirit.
      They will be called oaks of righteousness,
        a planting of the LORD that he may be glorified.
4   They will rebuild the ancient ruins,
        they will raise up the devastations of old.
      They will renew the ruined cities
        that have been devastated for generations.
5   Strangers will stand and pasture your flocks.
        Foreigners will work your fields and vineyards.
6   But you will be called the priests of the LORD;
        men will speak of you as the ministers of our God.
      You will enjoy the wealth of nations
        and boast[c] in their riches.

7 Instead of your shame[d] there will be a double portion,
   instead of disgrace they shall rejoice in their lot.
   Thus, they will possess a double portion in their land
   and everlasting joy will be theirs.
8 For I the LORD love justice.
   I hate robbery with a burnt offering.[e]
   I will faithfully pay them their reward,
   and will make an everlasting covenant with them.
9 Their offspring will be known among the nations,
   and their descendants known among the peoples.
   All who see them will acknowledge them:
   "Surely, they are the offspring that the LORD has
   blessed."
10 I rejoice greatly in the LORD,
   my soul exalts in my God;
   for he has clothed me in garments of salvation
   and wrapped around me a robe of righteousness,
   like a bridegroom adorned himself with a turban
   and as a bride dressed with her finery.
11 For as the earth brings forth its sprouts,
   and a garden causes seed to grow,
   so the Lord GOD will cause righteousness and praise
   to spring up before all nations.

a. The Hebrew word is artificially separated. There is uncertainty whether the redu-
plication arises from dittography or is a rare verbal form (cf. *HALAT*). The imagery is
of freeing from dark prison.

b. The Hebrew verb usually means "to put" or "to set," and does not fit well in the
context. Some excise v. 3a as a duplicate of v. 2b.

c. The form of the verb is a *hapax legomenon,* but often interpreted as a hithpa'el of
ymr ("to exchange"). However, Oswalt (II, 568) defends Jerome's interpretation as a bi-
form of *tit'ammar* ("to boast"), which better suits the context.

d. The shift in the pronominal suffixes from second person to third causes some difficulty (cf. the exegesis below).

e. A slight emendation yields "iniquity" (cf. *BHS*).

Selected Bibliography

W. A. M. Beuken, "Servant and Herald of Good Tidings: Isaiah 61 as an Interpretation of Isaiah 40–
55," *The Book of Isaiah,* ed. J. Vermeylen, Leuven 1989, 411–42; **W. W. Cannon,** "Isaiah 61, 1–3 an
Ebed-Jahweh Poem," *ZAW* 47, 1929, 284–88; **J. J. Collins,** "A Herald of Good Tidings: Isaiah 61:1–3
and Its Actualization in the Dead Sea Scrolls," *The Quest for Context and Meaning, Fs J. A. Sanders,*
ed. C. A. Evans et al., Leiden 1997, 225–40; **R. W. Fisher,** "The Herald of Good News in Second

Isaiah," *Rhetorical Criticism, Fs James Muilenburg*, ed. J. J. Jackson and M. Kessler, Pittsburgh 1974, 117–32; **U. Kellermann,** "Tritojesaja and das Geheimnis des Gottesknechts. Erwägungen zu Jes 59:21; 61:1–3; 66:18–24," *BN* 58, 1991, 46–82; **K. Koenen,** *Ethik und Eschatologie im Tritojesajabuch*, WMANT 62, Neukirchen-Vluyn 1990, 103–22; **W. Lau,** *Schriftgelehrte Prophetie in Jes 56–66*, BZAW 225, Berlin 1994, 66–89; **J. Morgenstern,** "Isaiah 61," *HUCA* 40, 1969, 109–21; **K. Pauritsch,** *Die neue Gemeinde*, AnBib 47, Rome 1971, 106–13; **J. Schmitt,** "L'oracle d'Is. LXI, 1 ss.et sa relecture par Jésus," *RevScRel* 54, 1980, 97–108; **P. A. Smith,** *Rhetoric and Redaction in Trito-Isaiah*, VTSup 62, Leiden 1995, 22–38; **O. H. Steck,** "Der Rachetag in Jesaja 61,2. Ein Kapitel redaktionsgeschichtlicher Kleinarbeit," *Studien zu Tritojesaja*, BZAW 203, Berlin 1991, 106–18; **J. Vermeylen,** *Du Prophète Isaïe à l'Apocalyptique*, II, Paris 1978, 478–83; **W. Zimmerli,** "Das 'Gnadenjahr des Herrn,'" (1970), reprinted in *Studien zur alttestamentlichen Theologie und Prophetie, G.A., II*, ThB 51, Munich 1974, 222–34.

1. Form, Structure, and Function

Although a few voices in the past have suggested that chapter 61 has been misplaced in relation to chapters 60 and 62 (e.g., Volz), there is a wide consensus that its present position is fully in order. The chapter is also generally regarded as a unity with only a rare exception (cf. Westermann's division). The broad structure of the unit is relatively simple to determine from its form and subject matter: vv. 1–7; 8–9; 10–11. The more difficult problem lies in determining the speaker in the first and last sections since it is obvious that vv. 8–9 are spoken by God. The Targum seeks to make the speaker explicit by prefacing vv. 1–7 with the formula "The prophet said," and vv. 1–9 with the addition "Jerusalem has said," but the issue is hardly resolved thereby.

Closely allied with this problem is the fact that chapter 61 again makes frequent use of passages from chapters 40—55, especially with citations and allusions from the so-called servant songs of Second Isaiah. For example, the anointing by the spirit is closely related to the servant's call in 42:1. Further, the task of the one sent in 61:1ff. is described in a similar terminology as that of the servant: "to bind up the brokenhearted," "to proclaim liberty to the captives" (40:7; 49:9). The controversial question lies in interpreting the significance of this usage by Third Isaiah.

Formerly some argued that 61:1–3 belongs with the other servant songs of Second Isaiah (e.g., Cannon). However, shortly this option was dismissed, particular in the light of Zimmerli's influential article ("Zur Sprache Tritojesaja"), which describes the linguistic differences between Second and Third Isaiah's usage. An earlier, traditional interpretation, such as that of Delitzsch, identified the voice with the servant, who was also construed messianically. Probably the most widespread interpretation was to understand it as the call of the prophet Third Isaiah, who in some fashion was thought to identify himself with Second Isaiah. Accordingly, both Zimmerli and Westermann are insistent that Third Isaiah was much aware of his own call. Koenen (216) agrees that 61:1–3 provides an access to the self-understanding of this prophet. Likewise Whybray emphasizes the genuine, personal experience involved. All these latter positions are much influenced by the form-critical focus on the issue of genre. The other extreme, more recently expressed by Lau, would see the passage as a key text for the phenomenon of *Schriftgelehrte Prophetie*. In fact, chapter 61 is judged to be an irrefutable apologetic to legitimate this form of prophetic scribal activity (72).

Nevertheless, in my judgment, the most persuasive analysis of 61:1–3 has been offered by Beuken ("Servant and Herald" and *Jesaja III*). He correctly observes that the passage is quite different from the call in Isaiah 6 or Jeremiah 1. Furthermore, nowhere does the speaker call himself "servant." Thus, the interpreter's task is to determine the subtle connection that is made between his mission and that of the servant of Second Isaiah. It is necessary not too quickly to identify the speaker with the servant or with a personal prophetic call of Third Isaiah. Beuken uses Ackroyd's language in speaking of the "self-presentation" of the speaker as prophet and argues for seeing chapter 61 in relation to the whole corpus of chapters 40—55. In the end, he concludes that in the speaker of chapter 61 the offspring of the "suffering servant" of chapter 53 is embodied, who can be an individual as well as a collective entity. Of course, the evidence for such an understanding turns on how one interprets the intertextual references to Second Isaiah within chapter 61 (cf. below).

2. Exposition

[61:1–7] In sudden shift from chapter 60, there is a change of form and content with the introduction of first person speech. At first the language may seem to be analogous to a prophetic call. The speaker presents himself as having been set apart with the anointing of the spirit. This endowment is then followed by a recounting of the mission of the "prophet" by means of a series of infinitival clauses: "to bring good tidings, . . . to proclaim liberty . . . , to proclaim the year of the LORD's favor, . . . to comfort all who mourn." The importance of the proclamation seems emphasized by the somewhat rare use of the formula *Adonai YHWH* both in v. 1 and v. 11, as if to form a bracket around the entire chapter.

Yet it is also the case that the presentation in vv. 1–3 is neither a direct parallel with the call narrative of Isaiah 6 nor even of Jeremiah 1. The description is not of an event that is being recounted, but rather a first person portrayal of the effect or lasting endowment of the call. Two moments in the past are indeed related: Yahweh's anointing the speaker with the spirit and his being sent; however, the presentation does not focus on an individual's experience. The frequent attempt to attribute a personality to the speaker arises not from the text itself, but is a projection from a prior, critical assumption regarding authorship. Although it is true that the self-presentation appears to be that of a prophet, there is no attempt made to give the bearer of this office a specific historical profile apart from his servant role. His function as prophet is fully absorbed within his role as servant and specifically as defined by chapters 40—55. The ambivalence of the text's profile resists assigning the figure a historical individuality, yet it cannot be simply described as an exegetical construct without any real concrete embodiment (*contra* Lau and Steck).

The subtle complexity of Third Isaiah's portrayal of the "servant prophet" in 61:1–3 has already been adumbrated in Second Isaiah. In the "servant songs" the office of the servant is described, first by God in the third person (42:1ff.). Then when the servant speaks in the first person to describe his mission and resultant suffering (49:1ff.; 50:4ff.), he speaks as one designed as God's servant, Israel (49:3): "You are my servant Israel." It would thus appear that there is no attempt to give this bearer of the office a specific historical contour apart from his servant role. (Chapter 53 has a different function [cf. above], but does not contradict this generalization.) Yet suddenly, without preparation, a first person figure emerges in 48:16: "And now the Lord GOD has sent me, endowed with his spirit!" He speaks in the first person and, if one follows a synchronic reading of chapter 48, delivers a prophetic oracle in 48:17ff. as a prophet. In sum, behind the suffering servant of Second Isaiah lies a historical, prophetic figure, yet these features remain almost entirely relegated to the text's background and are absorbed within the office—collective and individual—of the servant.

Beuken's interpretation is highly sensitive to the subtlety of the self-presentation of the voice in chapter 61. The words of the prophetic speaker describe himself at once in the garb of the figure of the servant of Second Isaiah. The spirit of God has been placed upon him (42:1) and he has been sent with his spirit (48:16). Beuken has also correctly observed the role of another intertextual reference that provides a crucial link in joining the servant figure in Second Isaiah with the presentation of chapter 60. Isaiah 44:2b–3 reads: "Fear not, O Jacob, my servant. . . . I will pour forth my spirit on your offspring, and my blessing on your descendants." Thus the promise is given that the spirit of God will also be upon the offspring of the servant (cf. also 59:21). The voice which then announces in 61:1 that the spirit is upon him is thereby identifying with "the heritage of the servants of Yahweh" (54:17). To inquire then whether the identification is of an individual or corporate form misses the point of the presentation because the term *servant* remains fluid throughout both Second and Third Isaiah.

The case was once made by Delitzsch, and has been recently expanded by Oswalt (II, 561ff.) that the voice of chapter 61 is not just to be identified with the servant, but with the Messiah of First Isaiah. Is there not an intertextual link between the anointing with the spirit in 61:1 and the "resting of the spirit" upon the messiah in 11:2? I do not underestimate the force of this argument, nor dismiss it out of hand. Yet I think that there are important distinctions to be made and that this traditional interpretation has to be greatly refined.

As I have attempted to show, the relation of chapter 61 to the servant remains a very subtle one, but fits in clearly with the major theme of Third Isaiah in linking the suffering servant of Second Isaiah with the servants of chapters 56—66 who are his offspring. Neither the messianic imagery of First Isaiah nor the eschatological function of the Messiah plays a significant role in the main body of Third Isaiah. Only on the periphery of chapters 56—66, most probably in the final stages of editorial shaping, was an attempt made in chapters 65 and 66 to unify the book of Isaiah as a whole. This intention included a citation in 65:25 of the messianic hope of 11:6–9. Yet even here the focus of the paraphrase of the earlier passage lies on the coming eschatological age as messianic without stress falling on the Messiah himself.

In sum, I would concur that the final shape of the Isaianic corpus is such that a resonance between the eschatological Messiah and the suffering servant was soon heard by the Christian church as a legitimate reader response to its scriptures in linking servant and Messiah. However, to read back a "servant/Messiah" figure into chapter 61 is to blur the Old Testament's own witness by a retrojection of a later, fully developed Christian theology, not yet developed in the book of Isaiah.

What then follows in vv. 1b–3 within a series of infinitival clauses is a description of the task assigned to the one identifying with the servant. Indeed, the mission to which he has been sent corresponds in the greatest detail with the tasks of Second Isaiah's servant figure: "to open eyes that are blind, to free captives from prison" (42:7; cf. 49:9). Yet it is also clear from the wording of chapter 61 that the content of the mission derives from the entire corpus of Second Isaiah. Thus, "to comfort all who mourn" (v. 2) picks up the verb "comfort," which was first sounded in the prologue (40:1) and which resonates throughout the entire corpus (49:13; 51:3, 12; 52:9).

Then again, the theme of proclaiming liberty in "the year of Yahweh's favor" (v. 2) is formulated in the language of the Jubilee year (Lev. 25:10ff.; Ezek. 46:47), and articulates succinctly the great change in Israel's fortunes initiated through God's favor. Finally, to "bring good tiding" ($l^ebass\bar{e}r$) is to assume the mantle of the herald (40:9; 52:7) who first sent out the message of God's return to his people in power. Regardless of the continuing controversy over the identification of the herald in 40:9, the fact that a herald, expressed with a masculine participial form ($m^ebass\bar{e}r$), was sent in 41:27 and 52:7 would seem to indicate that the herald of good tidings and the servant were shortly identified (cf. Fisher, Beuken).

The effect of the prophetic proclamation on the servant's offspring is the outpouring of joy and praise, occasionally expressed in the language of the

Psalter: "oil of gladness" (Ps. 45:8; cf. 23:5; 133:2) "planting of the LORD" (92:13). The rebuilding of the ancient ruins picks up a favorite theme of chapters 49—55 (49:16ff.; 51:3; 52:9; 54:1ff.). The connection between the rebuilding of the destroyed land and the righteousness of its new inhabitants is sounded in v. 3b. The "shoot" becomes a mighty tree of righteousness.

It has also been rightly pointed out that the description of Israel's deliverance has shifted away from Second Isaiah's portrayal of captivity and exile to that of release from economic slavery within the land. Of course, this shift reflects the changing historical context of Third Isaiah, who has simply refocused the initial promise of Second Isaiah. Again, the familiar theme of Third Isaiah returns, that aliens and foreigners will serve them (60:10, 16) and the wealth of the nations come to them (60:5). However, the portrayal of the coming deliverance is somewhat blurred in what follows because of the textual difficulty in v. 7. The problem lies with the shift in the pronominal suffixes from the second to the third person. Various attempts have been made in the older commentaries (e.g., Vitringa) to retain a reference both to Israel and to the nations. Others such as the RSV emend the text to read the second person form throughout (cf. NRSV). Perhaps the simplest and most satisfying solution is to assume an enallage of persons in which "your shame" and "their lot" relate to the same subject: "Instead of your shame there will be a double portion (of good), instead of grace they shall rejoice in their lot."

[8–9] The speaker in these verses is clearly God, who confirms the word of the servant figure. The grounds for the mission of the one endowed with the spirit in vv. 1–7 rest on God, who loves justice while hating injustice. The phrase "robbery with a burnt offering" is reminiscent of the corruption condemned in 1:13, provided the Hebrew text is in order (cf. *BHS*). The theme of making an everlasting covenant picks up the same promise of 55:3 (cf. 59:12), and also returns to specify the recipients as the "offspring" who receive the divine blessing (53:10; 54:17). Moreover, Israel's fame among the nations (55:5) is then developed in 60:9 when the nations will acknowledge Israel's special, favored status in the eyes of God.

[10–11] The question of who is the speaker in vv. 10–11 is resolved by the Targum, which introduces the unit with the formula, "Jerusalem has said." Certainly there are warrants for a collective Jerusalem to offer a song of thanksgiving. Yet the reasons for assuming the speaker to be the same as in vv. 1–7 are even stronger. A song of thanksgiving is the response of the servant figure, whose mission has received God's unqualified confirmation. The prophet rejoices that he is the instrument of God's salvation and is clothed in a robe of righteousness. The final verse returns once again to the metaphor of seed and offspring, and connects the new order of righteousness with the growth of a community of faith acknowledged by all the nations.

3. The New Testament's Use of Isaiah 61

Selected Bibliography

R. Albertz, "Die 'Antrittspredigt' Jesu im Lukasevangelium auf ihrem alttestamentlichen Hintergrund," *ZNW* 74, 1983, 192–206; **J. A. Fitzmyer,** *The Gospel according to Luke I–IX,* AB 28, New York 1981, 525–40; **M. Hooker,** *Jesus and the Servant,* London 1959; **B. Janowski and P. Stuhlmacher,** eds., *Der leidende Gottesknecht,* FAT 14, Tübingen 1996; **J. A. Sanders,** "From Isaiah 61 to Luke 4," *Christianity, Judaism, and Greco-Roman Cults,* SJLA 12, ed. J. Neusner, Leiden 1975, 75–106.

It is remarkable that the New Testament's reference to Isaiah 61 in Luke 4:16ff. has played a minor role in the continuing debate over Jesus' self-understanding as the servant of Second Isaiah. Some of the reason may lie in the fact that 61:1–3 was not included among the servant songs of Duhm (cf. Fitzmyer, 529), which is, of course, completely irrelevant to the New Testament's interpretation. Hooker (85) concedes that in Luke 4, Jesus is seen interpreting his mission in connection with the news of redemption originally proclaimed by Second Isaiah. Yet she asserts that Jesus' words apply here only to his preaching and teaching with no mention of his death. In my opinion, Hooker has restricted her interpretation of the function of the Old Testament in far too narrow a fashion.

In Luke 4, Jesus' appearance at the synagogue in Nazareth is portrayed as the beginning of his ministry. The theme in Isaiah 61 of the prophet's being sent with the spirit is joined with his own anointing with the Holy Spirit at his baptism (Acts 10:36). In both passages the anointing by the Spirit provides the authorization for the message of God's coming salvation. Moreover, the anointing in Luke makes clear that a messianic anointing is being claimed.

Jesus identifies himself with the Old Testament promise of the one coming to preach the gospel, to free the captives, and to heal the infirmed—activities all sharing the language of Second Isaiah's servant. Above all, Jesus proclaims the "acceptable year of the Lord," the eschatological event of God's outpouring of his favor foreshadowed in the ancient Jubilee year (Leviticus 25). He announces that the promise has been fulfilled now in his presence. "Today" is fulfilled time. The new age of the salvation has arrived.

To suggest that the application of Isaiah 61 is limited only to Jesus' preaching and healing activity is to miss the larger context of the Old Testament promise, which is claimed by Christ as scripture's foreshadowing of his entire earthly ministry and which is now fulfilled by his presence. The assumption that only when there is a specific New Testament reference to the death of the servant can the servant be understood as playing a christological role misunderstands the function of biblical intertextuality. Rather, a case can be made that Jesus himself ushers in the acceptable year of the Lord, and thus the citation of Isaiah 61 encompasses the entire mission of the servant, including his life, death, and offspring.

64. Isaiah 62:1–12

62:1 For Zion's sake I will not be silent,
    and for Jerusalem's sake I will not rest,
until her vindication emerges in brightness,
    and her salvation as a flaming torch.
2 The nations will see your vindication,
    and all the kings your glory.
You will be called by a new name
    that the LORD himself will bestow.
3 You will be a crown of splendor in
    the hand of the LORD,
and a royal diadem in the hand of
    your God.
4 Never again will you be called "Forsaken,"
    nor your land be named "Desolate."
But you will be called "I Delight in Her" (Hephzibah),
    and your land "Married" (Beulah),
for the LORD will delight in you,
    and your land will be married.
5 As a young man marries a virgin,
    so will your sons[a] marry you,
and as a bridegroom rejoices over
    his bride,
    so will your God rejoice over you.
6 Upon your walls, O Jerusalem,
    I have set watchmen,
who will never be silent
    day or night.
You who serve to remind the LORD,
    take no rest,
7 and give no rest to him,
    until he establishes Jerusalem
    and makes her the praise of the earth.
8 The LORD has sworn by his right hand,

and by his mighty arm:
"I will never again give your grain
    to be food for your enemies,
and never again will foreigners drink
    the new wine
    for which you have toiled;
9   but those who harvest it will eat it,
    and give praise to the LORD,
and those who gather it will drink it
    in the courts of my sanctuary."
10   Pass through, pass through the gates,
    prepare the way for the people.
Build up, build up the highway,
    remove the stones.
Raise a banner over the peoples.
11   See, the LORD has announced
    to the end of the earth:
"Proclaim to the Daughter of Zion:
    'Look, your Savior comes.
See, his reward is with him,
    and his recompense before him.'"
12   They will be called "the Holy People,
    the Redeemed of the LORD";
and you will be called "Sought Out,"
    a city not forsaken.

a. *BHS* suggests emending "your sons" (*bānāyik*) to "your builder" (*bōnêk*), but without adequate warrant.

Selected Bibliography

T. D. Anderson, "Renaming and Wedding Imagery in Isaiah 62," *Bib* 67, 1986, 75–80; **J. Begrich,** "Sōfēr und Mazkir," *ZAW* 58, 1940/41, 12ff.; **K. Koenen,** *Ethik und Eschatologie im Tritojesajabuch,* WMANT 62, Neukirchen-Vluyn 1990, 122–37; **W. Lau,** *Schriftgelehrte Prophetie in Jes 56–66,* BZAW 225, Berlin 1994, 90–117; **P. A. Smith,** *Rhetoric and Redaction in Trito-Isaiah,* VTSup 62, Leiden 1995; **W. Zimmerli,** "Zur Sprache Tritojesajas," *G.A,* ThB 19, Munich 1969, 217–33.

1. Structure, Genre, and Content

Chapter 62 is generally divided into three parts: vv. 1–7; 8–9; 10–12. Regarding its unity, some have followed Duhm in separating vv. 10–12. Westermann sees vv. 8–9 as a later addition, and Watts joins vv. 8–12 to the following chapter. However, in recent years the unity of chapter 62 has been largely accepted.

The much harder question focuses on the speakers of the oracles within the chapter. There is no disagreement that vv. 8–9 consist of a divine oracle with a clear introductory formula setting it apart from vv. 1–7. Much controversy still turns on identifying the "I" voice of vv. 1–7. Older commentators, like Delitzsch, tended to see it as a speech of God. Then to meet the objection that in vv. 2ff. Yahweh is addressed in the third person, it is argued that a mixture of divine and prophetic speech is characteristic of the chapter (Smith, 13).

Most recently a very strong case has been made for understanding both vv. 1–7 and 10–12 as prophetic oracles (Koenen, Lau). First, the divine oracles in chapter 62 are always designated by introductory formulae (cf. vv. 8a and 11a). Second, the continuity in thought, which is deeper between v. 1 and v. 6, also leads to an identification of the same voice in these two verses. Finally, to construe the voice in 61:10ff. as continuing in chapter 62 offers the most natural reading. Of course, the strongest argument of Delitzsch for identifying the speaker in v. 1 with God is that the verb "to keep silent" (*ḥšh*) often appears with Yahweh as the subject (64:11; 65:6; cf. also 42:14; 57:11). Yet this argument has been successfully refuted by Koenen (127ff.), who demonstrates the very different action at work in chapter 62. Elsewhere Yahweh's keeping silent was a sign of judgment, and his decision not to remain inactive was then a signal for the entrance of his promised salvation. In v. 1 a different sense of the movement is evident when the prophet announces that he will not be silent or inactive until God once again intervenes. Moreover, he places his watchmen on the walls of Jerusalem so that God will have no rest until the time of favor is evoked.

Once the initial oracle has been identified as a prophetic speech rather than divine, it has then often been characterized as a fictive speech (Lau, 92). In contrast to this interpretation, I would agree with Koenen's observation (127) that the speaker of chapter 62 continues in the office of the servant figure of 61:1–9. The mission of the servant of Second Isaiah will be crowned with success as Zion is transformed and its inhabitants called the holy people (v. 12).

Verses 10–12 offer a virtual catena of allusions to Second Isaiah (40:3, 10; 49:16; cf. also 57:14). Therefore, how this passage functions is largely determined by one's understanding of the role of Third Isaiah's intertextual references (cf. the earlier debate with Zimmerli in the exposition on 57:14ff.).

Finally, in terms of the overarching structure of the chapter, a variety of form-critical analyses have been made. Elliger and Fohrer speak of a liturgy, but again the category is far too general and remains increasingly suspect. Westermann argues for a complaint genre and seeks to distinguish various components of the complaint as a way of linking chapters 60—62; however, the suggestion is hardly persuasive as providing the key for interpretation. I am also unconvinced when Lau joins the watchmen and the "recorders" (*mazkîrîm*) to his theory of "scribal prophets," reminding God, as it were, of what he had promised in scripture (104ff.).

Certainly the most extensive attempt to work with a model of intertextuality is that of Beuken (*Jesaja* III, 225ff.). He argues that 52:5–12 serves as the paradigm on which the structure of chapter 62 as a whole rests. He picks up the terminology of the "herald of good tidings" and the watchmen (*ṣōfayik*) and relates these with the watchmen (*šōmᵉrîm*) in chapter 62. He then proceeds to designate vv. 1–7 as "the good tidings to Zion," and vv. 10–12 as "the good tidings to the watchers." As always, Beuken's observations are probing and full of careful reflection. Still, in my judgment, the link between 52:7–12 and chapter 62 is far looser than suggested by Beuken. The function of the watchmen in chapter 62 seems very different indeed from chapter 52. Consequently, the intertextual link with 62:1–7 and 10–12 appears strained, and serves to blur the more obvious continuity with Second Isaiah that is reflected in vv. 10–12 (cf. below).

2. Exposition

[62:1–7] Although vv. 1–5 and 6–7 both address Zion, there is a slightly different focus in vv. 6–7 that has caused some commentators to separate the verses into two discrete oracles. This issue does not seem of great importance and involves at most a strategic decision on how best to handle a progression of a largely unified line of thought.

According to the interpretation suggested above, the first person speech functions as a continuation of chapter 62 in the context established in chapter 61. The prophet-servant figure focuses his full attention on the fulfillment of the promises of Zion's vindication. Whereas in chapter 61 the stress fell on the people of Zion—the brokenhearted, the imprisoned, the afflicted—in chapter 62 the imagery of light used in 60:1ff. now falls on the city. Only here and in 64:10(9) are the two words, Zion and Jerusalem, used together in this way. In chapter 61 the mission of the servant of Second Isaiah was clearly the model for Third Isaiah's description. However, in chapter 62 there is initially a shift of emphasis that only at the end of the chapter returns to Second Isaiah with a catena of allusions. Of course, this prophetic announcement of the coming glory of Zion comes as no surprise for readers of chapters 56ff.

Yet it is also clear that the message of the glorification of Zion has been a major theme of Third Isaiah. Isaiah 58:12 had promised that its ancient ruins would be rebuilt and a new foundation laid. Isaiah 59:20 spoke of God's coming to Zion as redeemer and of a new covenantal relationship. In chapter 60 the moment of salvation for Zion was developed in Second Isaiah's language of light and glory. Not only would the exiles return to Zion, but they would be escorted from afar. The security of Zion would be such that there would be no need for the city gates ever to be closed.

The question therefore naturally arises as to what then is new in chapter 62. First, Zion is to receive a new name to symbolize the dramatic change. The phrase "new name" (*šem hadaš*) only occurs here. No more called "Forsaken" or "Desolate," but "I Delight in Her" (*Hephzibah*) and "Married" (*Beulah*). T. D. Anderson has mounted a very persuasive case for understanding the imagery as derived from the context of a wedding, which he links to the remaining ceremony. This setting would explain the reference to the crown and royal diadem in v. 3, and Zion envisioned as the bride at the royal wedding. Yet a variety of problems remain in trying to establish the coherence of the picture. Especially puzzling is the reference in v. 5 of "so will your sons marry you." Anderson argues that the image of sons returning to their mother and the image of Zion as bride are combined in the idea of the sons who represent the returning people also being the bridegroom of Zion (79). Nevertheless, the explanation remains strained even with this appeal to the flexibility of Isaiah's imagery. No fully satisfactory solution has as yet emerged. Similarly, the function of the crown in the hand of God continues to evoke a wide range of interpretations without any consensus.

There is another important addition already sounded in v. 1, which is then greatly developed in v. 6. In v. 1 the prophet emerges in great agitation to announce that he will neither rest nor keep silent until God's promises of Zion's vindication and salvation have become a reality. Then in v. 6 the prophet expands his task by adding helpers to aid him in his avowed mission. Upon the walls of Jerusalem he has appointed watchmen (*šōmᵉrîm*) who will also not be silent day or night. Their task, like the prophet's, is continually to remind God of Israel's plight, and to call for divine intervention. Indeed, they will give God no peace until he has established Jerusalem according to his promises.

Naturally, the issue is much discussed regarding the identity of the watchers. Some have sought to link them to the office of the "recorder" (*mazkîr*), which was a high court office in Egypt and thought to have been appropriated by David (cf. Begrich). However, the analogy is at best distant. Then again, Beuken has sought to relate the watchers to the heralds of 52:7ff. However, not only is a different Hebrew noun used (*ṣōfayik*, 52:8), but, more importantly, the role of the watchers appears to be very different from the role described in chapter 62. In the former, the watchers are the heralds of good tiding of God's return to Zion who burst forth in sheer joy. In the latter, they aid the prophet in continually urging God to intercede in Zion's favor.

At most one can relate the watchers to the servant-prophet of 61:1ff. and 62:1ff., who seeks to fulfill the mission of the servant in Second Isaiah. Although chapter 62 focuses chiefly on the restoration of Zion, the theme of "the Holy People" and "the Redeemed of the LORD" in 62:12 forms a transition to 63:18. There the holy people are identified with the "servants" and thus brought directly into relationship with the suffering servant tradition of Second Isaiah as his offspring and heritage (53:10ff.).

[8–9] The response of God to the prophet's call for divine action on Zion's behalf is given in these verses. The Lord swears by his right hand and mighty arm (Ex. 32:13; Isa. 45:23; Ps. 89:50). The act of God's swearing is often specifically tied to his oath to David (Isa. 55:3; Ps. 89:50; 132:11), but in chapter 62 it focuses on the restoration of Jerusalem. Nevertheless, the intertextual connection with David reverberates in the background of the text. The historical needs of Jerusalem's plight in the postexilic age clearly shapes the prophet's message. Never again will the holy city be ravished by foreigners and left in a condition of starvation and shame.

[10–12] It has often been observed that these three verses constitute a virtual catena of verses from Second Isaiah. Yet the recognition of the passage's close intertextual relation to Second Isaiah does not in itself resolve all the difficulties of interpretation. Beuken has argued with skill that the addressee in v. 10 must be the watchers, who are the last mentioned subject before the divine oracle. Yet I remain uneasy with the interpretation and think that it has sought to join disparate elements within the chapter too closely. The effect is to extend the function of the watchers too widely, thereby obscuring the more obvious intertextual links to Second Isaiah.

I would argue instead that the reference in v. 10 picks up the note first sounded in 40:3, and then reapplied by Third Isaiah in 57:14. In both cases the summons is addressed to the heavenly beings who are ordered first to prepare the way for Yahweh (40:3), and then to clear all the obstacles from the people's way (57:14; cf. the exegesis of chapter 57). In my judgment, there has been no connection made between the role of the watchers in vv. 6–7 and the verses 10–11. The new element in 62:10 is that they are now to go through the gates in preparing the way for the people. The direction of the entry is best understood as from outside into the city. The way prepared leads to the holy sanctuary (62:9). The theme of lifting up a banner to assemble the outcasts occurs in First Isaiah (11:11–12)—most probably a retrojection from Second Isaiah—and again in 49:22. The theme of Yahweh's proclamation to the ends of the earth is one that reverberates often throughout Second Isaiah (42:9; 43:12; 44:8; 45:21; etc.).

The actual message of salvation directed to Zion in v. 11 is a citation from 40:11b: "his reward is with him, and his recompense before him." The effect is firmly to join together the original promise of the prologue with Third Isaiah's reinterpretation. In a word, the reuse has not "spiritualized" the promise (*contra* Zimmerli), but rather extended it in such a way as to apply to the glorification of Zion in place of its former desolation. The final verse returns to a central theme of Third Isaiah, namely, the establishment within the city of a holy people, the "servants" of God who share in the promised heritage (63:17–18).

65. Isaiah 63:1–6

63:1 Who is this coming from Edom,
with crimson stained garments from Bozrah?[a]
Who is this, robed in splendor,
swaying[b] forward in his great might?
"It is I, proclaiming vindication,
powerful to save."

2 Why are your garments so red,
like those who tread in the winepress?

3 "I have trodden the winepress alone;
from the nations there was no one with me.
I trod[c] them in my anger
and trampled them in my fury;
their lifeblood has spattered my clothing,
and I have befouled my garments.

4 For the day of vengeance was in my heart,
and the year of my redemption has arrived.

5 I looked, but there was no one to help.
I was appalled that no one gave support,
so my own arm brought me victory,
and my own rage sustained me.

6 I trampled peoples in my anger,
in my wrath I made them drunk,
and poured out their blood on the ground."

a. The once widely accepted emendation of the MT's "Edom" and "Bozrah," first suggested by Lagarde and still proposed by *BHS*, has increasingly been rejected as lacking textual support.

b. The somewhat uncertain verb *ṣ'eh* ("swaying") has frequently been emended to *ṣo'ēd* ("striding"). It has rightly been rejected by Barthélemy (*CTLAT*, 429).

c. It is unnecessary to repoint the conjunctives in the prefixed verbs (vv. 3, 5, 6) as proposed by *BHS* (cf. the exegesis).

Selected Bibliography

B. C. Cresson, "The Condemnation of Edom in Post-Exilic Judaism," *The Use of the Old Testament in the New and Other Essays,* ed. J. M. Efird, Durham 1972, 125–48; **P. D. Hanson,** *The Dawn of Apocalyptic,* Philadelphia 1975, 203–8; **F. Holmgren,** "Yahweh the Avenger: Isaiah 63:1–6," *Rhetorical Criticism, Fs James Muilenburg,* ed. J. J. Jackson and M. Kessler, Pittsburgh 1974, 133–48; **K. Koenen,** *Ethik und Eschatologie im Tritojesajabuch,* WMANT 62, Neukirchen-Vluyn 1990, 76–87; **W.**

Lau, *Schriftgelehrte Prophetie in Jes 56—66,* BZAW 225, Berlin 1994, 279–85; **C. R. Mathews,** *Defending Zion: Edom's Desolation and Jacob's Restoration (Isaiah 34—35) in Context,* BZAW 236, Berlin 1995; **K. Pauritsch,** *Die neue Gemeinde: Gott sammelt Ausgestossene und Arme (Jesaia 56—66),* AnBib 47, Rome 1971, 138–44; **O. H. Steck,** *Bereitete Heimkehr,* SBS 121, Stuttgart 1985, 50ff.; *Studien zu Tritojesaja,* BZAW 203, Berlin 1991, 209–11; **M. Weippert,** "Edom und Israel," *TRE* 9, 1982, 291–99.

1. Structure, Genre, and Function

There is almost full agreement regarding the structure and unity of this passage. The unit consists of two parts shaped by question and answer. Two questions are asked (vv. 1a, 2), and twice Yahweh gives a response (vv. 1b and 3). Then follows in vv. 4–6 an explanation by God of the reasons for his action. The effect is that the account of the event is repeated twice, first through the interchange of question and answer, and second through an extended interpretation of the history by means of a direct divine oracle. Occasionally some commentators prefer to divide the unit into vv. 1–2 and 3–6, thus connecting vv. 4ff. directly with the response to the question in v. 3. In my opinion, this division blurs somewhat the subtlety of the present structure.

Over the years there has been much discussion regarding the form of the oracle (cf. Koenen, 76–77). Some have spoken of an apocalyptic vision, or of a hymn to the "Divine Warrior," or of a song of triumph. Others have stressed the passage's mythological roots from an ancient Near Eastern tradition. However, increasingly the designation of the oracle as a sentry's cry (cf. Muilenburg) has become widespread. Actually there are no very close parallels of this form within the Old Testament. The frequent reference to 21:11–12 is not fully persuasive.

The real exegetical problem is that the oral form pursued by form-critics now lies deep in the text's background, and the major forces for shaping the oracle derive largely from literary stylization (cf. the exegesis below). The strongest argument for assuming a sentry's cry relates to the editorial linkage of 63:1–6 to the role of the watchmen in chapter 62. But even this element has been subordinated to the content of the oracle, which is the coming of Yahweh (59:8–20; 62:11) and the dramatic confrontation with God himself.

Once again in Third Isaiah the key issue turns on the author's use of intertextual references. The close literary connection between 59:15b–20 and 63:1–6 has long been noted and is crucial. Occasionally, older scholars (e.g., Budde) argued that the two oracles originally belonged together in a single unified oracle and were separated by the late insertion of chapters 60—62. However, this new theory has few modern defenders. A far more likely hypothesis relates 63:1–6 to an editor who positioned the oracle after chapters 60—62 with a conscious intertextual reference to 59:15b–20. The effect of this bracketing of chapters 60—62 has played a major role in the more recent redactional studies, especially for Steck (*Bereitete Heimkehr,* 50ff.), who ascribes 63:1–6 to a scribal extension (*Fortschreibung*) of chapter 34 in the fourth century as part of a *Grossjesaja* redactional layer.

However, the reader should be cautioned from too quickly assuming a single, unilinear trajectory of redactional growth. The problem is that there is a rich variety of other intertextual references that also must be considered. First, within the book of Isaiah only twice are the two terms Bozrah and Edom juxtaposed (34:6; 63:1), which right away sets up a close intertextual resonance between the two chapters. Second, there is another highly significant interaction of the paralleled expressions "day of vengeance" and "year of my redemption," which appear in slightly varying formulations in 34:8, 61:2, and 63:4. Moreover, it is very difficult to determine the exact chronological dependency of this common formulation (cf. Koenen, 81–82). Finally, there are a host of phrases from chapter 62 that resonate in chapter 63, and indicate clearly that the latter oracle is most certainly not just a loose fragment or independent oracle, but one that has been carefully positioned to perform a crucial interpretive role in the succeeding chapters.

In conclusion, there remains the basic exegetical problem of determining the significance of the focus on Edom. It has long been argued that Edom, especially in the postexilic period, was long considered Israel's archenemy, and therefore very early became representative of the judgment by God of the nations (cf. Jer. 49:7–22; Ezek. 25:12–14; 35:1–12; Amos 1:11–12; Obad. 1:21; Mal. 1:2–5; Ps. 137:7). Yet this interpretation has never been fully satisfactory, and in more recent times scholars have pursued the question of the dual relationship between Jacob and Esau as both brother and enemy. The issue to be explored turns on whether Third Isaiah's use of Edom addresses another aspect of his understanding of the continuing sharp polarity within the household of Israel (cf. below).

2. Exposition

The oracle begins with two questions, each of which receives a divine response. The first question, "Who is this coming from Edom?" appears to be couched in the form of a sentry's call: "Who goes there?" This would provide a narrative continuity with chapter 62 and be understood by the reader as being the watchmen's challenge (62:6). Yet this connection is not without some difficulty and should not be overly pressed. The watchmen have a different function in chapter 62 from guarding the city. Moreover, the question moves on a different plane from a routine sentry's challenge. There is an initial double wordplay on Edom with *'ādom* ("red") and on Bozrah with *bṣr* ("to gather grapes"), which adds to the unexpected effect of suspense and mystery. The challenge is also not exclusively addressed to the approaching one, but includes a wider audience. The one who is near is coming from Edom, that is, from the south. The sense of awe is extended further by the ensuing description, which is hardly a conventional component of a sentry's challenge but rather serves to anticipate the answer: "Who is this, robed in splendor, swaying forward in his great might?"

It is not necessary for the one who now answers to identify himself by name. God's identity is obvious to all by the characteristic of his self-predicative speech: "It is I, proclaiming vindication (*ṣᵉdāqāh*)" (cf. 41:4, 17; 60:16; 61:8; 65:18). The close link between salvation and righteousness in Third Isaiah (e.g., 56:1) is again sounded.

If the element of awesome mystery emerged from the first question and answer, the full significance of Yahweh's coming from Edom is terrifyingly clarified by the second exchange (vv. 2–3): "Why are your garments so red, like those who tread in the winepress?" Suddenly in the divine response the level of discourse has shifted. The red is no longer juice, but blood; the crushing is not of grapes, but of peoples! "I have trodden the winepress alone. . . . [T]heir lifeblood has spattered my clothing." Now the effects of the intertextual references serves to disclose the meaning of the event. This is the great slaughter in the land of Edom foretold in 34:6ff.: "Their land will be soaked with blood" (v. 7). Chapter 63 now describes this judgment on Edom as a completed action. Yahweh is portrayed returning from the slaughter having requited his great anger. The reference in v. 3 to his being "alone" picks up the same theme of 59:16. In chapter 59 no one from Israel stood on his side for justice. In chapter 63 there were also none from the nations who sided with God's righteous cause.

It is a grammatical feature of v. 3 that the Masoretes have pointed the series of verbs with a weak *waw,* rather than the *waw* consecutive of past narrative prose. The effect is to seek to interpret the past action as extending also into the future. Thus, although the form of the oracle is not eschatological, the oracle was obviously heard by its tradents as such, especially as the divine intention is then further developed in vv. 4–6. The warrant for this understanding of the tradition stems both from its intertextual relationship to chapter 34 and to its apocalyptic content.

God's interpretation of his action in vv. 4–6 is rendered initially by a repetition of the formula that occurs both in 34:8 and 61:2: "the day of vengeance/the year of my redemption." However, the liberating content of chapter 61 ultimately determines the formulation of 63:4. Again there is a play on words. Verse 3 had spoken of "befouling" the garment (II *g'l*); v. 4 now speaks of Yahweh's "redemption" (I *g'l*). Occasionally commentators argue for the translation of "blood wrath," but, in my judgment, it distorts the context of chapter 63. Rather, it is important to see that the announcement in 61:2ff. of the year of Yahweh's favor is being fully confirmed. What is at stake is that Israel's ultimate vindication must be preceded by God's judgment, which he alone is able to execute.

It has long puzzled commentators how to account for the overwhelming judgmental focus on Edom when it is the rebellious peoples of the world who are the objects of God's action. In chapter 34 there was a similar movement of God's anger against all the nations that even reached cosmological dimensions. Yet again the judgment quickly narrowed to Edom (v. 5). The most frequent and easiest explanation is to suggest that Edom serves as representative for all the nations, an interpretation not fully without warrant. In addition, it is clear that Israel's hatred for Edom in the postexilic period grew in intensity.

Yet commentators such as Beuken (*Isaiah* III, 256ff.) have made a persuasive case that more is involved in Third Isaiah. Jacob and Esau function in Israel's tradition both in terms of brother and of enemy. Chapters 58 and 59 had gone to great lengths to point out the deep division within the people of Israel, and that it was the reigning injustice and the persecution of the faithful that called forth God's judgment. "According to their deeds, so he will repay: anger to his adversaries and retribution to his enemies" (59:18). Yet to those who "fear the name of Yahweh"—chapter 56 had already thrown the net wide enough to include foreigners—they will experience God as Redeemer (59:20). Then the faithful are further specified as "those in Jacob who turn away from sin." In contrast, Edom as Jacob's kin and yet archenemy now symbolizes the sharp and enduring division within the household of Israel. The peoples in revolt are not being ethnically defined. Now foreigners belong to those joined to Yahweh (56:3). Conversely, within those who are God's adversaries, Edom, *the brother of Jacob,* must be named above all others as standing unrepentant outside the circle of the just. For the author of Third Isaiah, the division between the righteous and the unjust is not a lingering cultural prejudice, but is an ontological portrayal of the paradoxical nature of evil with which finally he concludes his book (66:24).

There is one final topic to address in respect to 63:1–6. Up to this point I have resisted the frequent attempts of modern redactional critics to reconstruct the growth of discrete layers and to trace the exact history of the composition of the book. Several reasons have been operative in this decision. First, I think that the evidence for much of such reconstructing is highly subjective. Second, I do not think that a historical reconstruction lying behind the final form of the text provides the key for interpreting the canonical scriptures.

Yet once this has been said, further distinctions are in order. To recognize in the text signs of growth and tension can greatly aid in hearing the final form in all its subtle complexity. In my judgment, the literary evidence is strong that two similar oracles 59:15b–20 and 63:1–6 now bracket chapters 60—62. What for me is the most significant implication lies in the effect that this editorial decision had on the synchronic reading of the final form of the book. Isaiah 59:20 had spoken of the coming of God to Zion as Redeemer. This theme has been picked up and greatly enlarged in chapters 60—62. The message turns on the future glory of Jerusalem and the good tidings to its afflicted, faithful inhabitants. Yet the crucial function of chapter 63, which is set forth in a retrospective sequence, is to emphasize in the strongest manner possible that the divine judgment against the evil and injustice of those in rebellion against God's rule must precede the entrance of God's promised kingship in the transformation of Zion. Although it is helpful to see that in the growth of the book of Third Isaiah the apparently earlier traditions of chapters 60–62 were bracketed with a later editorial framework, far more important than this concentric pattern are the implications for its interpretation. According to the witness of these chapters, the eschatological economy of God unfolds sequentially according to his purpose of judgment that precedes the final redemption of God's elect.

66. Isaiah 63:7–64:11(12)

63:7 I will recount the gracious acts of the LORD,
      the praises of the LORD,
  according to all that the LORD has done for us,
      the abundant goodness to the house of Israel,
  according to his mercy and many kindnesses.

8 He said, "Surely they are my people,
      sons who will not act falsely,"
  and so he became their savior.

9 In all their affliction, he was afflicted,[a]
      and the angel of his presence saved them.
  In his love and pity he redeemed them.
      He raised them up and carried them
      all the days of old.

10 But they rebelled and grieved his holy spirit.
  Therefore he turned to become their enemy,
      and he himself fought against them.

11 Then he remembered the ancient days,
      Moses and his people.[b]
  Where is he who brought them up from the sea
      with the shepherds[c] of his flock?
  Where is he that set his holy spirit
      in their midst,

12 who caused his glorious arm
      to go at the right hand of Moses,
  who divided the waters before them
      to make for himself an eternal name,

13   who led them through the depths
          so that they did not stumble,
      like a horse in open country.
14   Like cattle that descend into the valley,
          the spirit of the LORD gave them rest.
      So you guided your people
          to make for yourself a glorious name.
15   Look down from heaven and see,
          from your holy and glorious habitation.
      Where are your zeal and power?
          Your tenderness and love
          are withheld from us.[d]
16   Yet you are our Father,
          even though Abraham does not know us
          and Israel does not recognize us.
      You, O LORD, are our Father,
          our Redeemer from of old is your name.
17   Why, O LORD, do you make us
          stray from your ways,
          and harden our hearts
          so that we do not revere you?
      Return for the sake of your servants
          the tribes of your heritage.
18   For a brief time they possessed your holy people,[e]
          but our enemies have trampled down your sanctuary.
19   We have become like those whom
          you never ruled,
      like those who are not called by your name.
64:(1) O that you would rend the heavens
          and come down,
          that the mountains would tremble before you—
1(2)   as when flames ignite bushwood
          and fire causes water to boil—
      to make your name known to your foes,
          and cause nations to tremble before you.
2(3)   When you did terrifying deeds
          that we did not expect,
          you came down and mountains shook before you.
3(4)   From ancient times no one has heard,
          no ear has perceived,
      no eye has seen any God besides you,
          who acts for those who wait for him.

4(5)   You meet him[f] who joyfully works righteousness,
      they remember you in your ways.
   Because you were angry, we have sinned.
      For a long time we have been immersed[g] in them;
   how then can we be saved?

5(6)   We have all become like an unclean thing,
      and all our righteous deeds like a defiled garment.
   We are all shrivelled like leaves,
      and our sins, like the wind, sweep us away.

6(7)   Yet no one calls on your name,
      or strives to lay hold of you,
   for you have hidden your face from us,
      and made us melt away because of our sins.

7(8)   Yet, O LORD, you are our Father.
      We are the clay, you are the potter.
      We are all the work of your hand.

8(9)   Do not be violently angry, O LORD;
      do not remember our sins forever.
   O, look upon us, for we are all your people.

9(10) Your sacred cities have become a desert.
      Even Zion has become a wilderness,
      Jerusalem a desolation.

10(11) Our holy and glorious temple,
      where our fathers praised thee,
   has been burned with fire,
      and all that is treasured is ruined.

11(12) After all this, O LORD, will you still restrain
      yourself?
   Will you stand by idly and let us suffer so greatly?

a. The LXX offers a different division of the line and a different pointing. Cf. the discussion by Barthélemy (*CTLAT*, 434–37) and the exegesis below.

b. The Hebrew text is obscure and a great variety of emendations have been suggested by commentaries without a consensus (cf. Barthélemy, *CTLAT*, 438–39).

c. Many follow the LXX in reading a singular for the plural of the MT.

d. The MT reads "me."

e. The meaning of the sentence is obscure, and the text appears damaged. *BHS* suggests an emendation that is very intrusive (cf. also *HALAT*, 421).

f. The verb is often interpreted in a negative sense (cf. NJPS).

g. The MT is obscure. The LXX reads "because of it we strayed." Other emendations have been proposed (cf. *BHS*).

Selected Bibliography

E. Achtemeier, *The Community and Message of Isaiah 56–66,* Minneapolis 1982, 109–21; **M. A. Beek,** "Das Mitleiden Gottes. Eine masoretische Interpretation von Jes. 63, 9," *Symbolae biblicae et mesopotamicae, F.M. Th. De Liagre Böhl dedicatae,* ed. M. Beek at al., Leiden 1973, 23–30; **S. H. Blank,** "'And All Our Virtues.' An Interpretation of Isaiah 64:4b–5a," *JBL* 71, 1952, 149–54; **D. Conrad,** "Zu Jes 64, 3b," *ZAW* 80, 1968, 332–34; **P. D. Hanson,** *The Dawn of Apocalyptic,* Philadelphia 1975, 79–100; **K. Koenen,** "Zum Text von Jes 63, 18," *ZAW* 100, 1988, 406–9; *Ethik und Eschatologie im Tritojesaja,* WMANT 62, Neukirchen-Vluyn 1990, 159–61; **W. Lau,** *Schriftgelehrte Prophetie in Jes 56–66,* BZAW 225, Berlin 1994, 286–315; **K. Pauritsch,** *Die neue Gemeinde,* AnBib 47, Rome 1971, 144–71; **O. H. Steck,** *Studien zu Tritojesaja,* BZAW 203, Berlin 1991, 221–25.

1. Form, Structure, and Context

There is wide scholarly agreement over the form and structure of this unit. The form is that of a communal complaint that shares much with the common oral pattern of the Psalter, but especially with other late psalms such as Psalms 76, 106, and Nehemiah 9. Still, there is no solid evidence by which to date precisely this psalm, particularly if one argues that it was originally independent of Third Isaiah and only later in the book's redactional shaping was introduced to its present position. Actually, modern redactional critics have little to say about this passage other than to observe that it lacks a close connection with any of the earlier reconstructed layers.

However, when the passage is read synchronically, the communal complaint fits quite coherently into the larger movement established by the preceding oracles. The voice of faithful Israel had confessed its own unrighteousness in the light of the appalling conditions of national wickedness (59:1ff.). Then in 59:15ff. and 63:1–6 the promise of salvation is repeated with the coming of God as redeemer, but must first be preceded by God's terrifying judgment on his people (63:1–6). In 63:7ff. the voice of faithful Israel is heard in a prayer that contains all the stereotyped features of the complaint: recital of God's past mercies, confession of sin, call for divine intervention, and plea for aid in need.

Particularly at the conclusion of chapter 63 a major theme of Third Isaiah's message is again picked up as the "servants" and the "tribes of your heritage" are identified as God's holy people (vv. 17–18). Moreover, the context is fully congruent with the rest of Third Isaiah and with a people devastated by the destruction of the temple while yearning for redemption. A variety of other familiar themes occur: God's steadfast love for Israel, the continuing divine guidance, and the calling of God's name, Yet the language of the chapter differs from the preceding chapters because of the dominant role assigned to the exodus tradition and the role of Moses. Also the theme of God as Father is expanded in a way unknown to Second Isaiah.

As to its structure, although the form reflects the unified pattern of the communal complaint, the unit does break easily into subdivisions. Isaiah 63:7–14 recounts Israel's praise of God for past mercies, then the succeeding verse (63:15–64:11[12]) are addressed to God directly and contain prayers for God's attention, presence, and salvation. In many ways the greatest difficulty of this passage concerns numerous text-critical problems, many of which are not easily resolved (cf. the analysis of Barthélemy, *CTLAT*).

2. Exposition

[63:7–14] The verse that introduces a communal complaint psalm is at first rendered in the first person singular (cf. also v. 15). The voice is of the prophet, who then immediately identifies with "us," the house of Israel. As is common in the Psalter, complaints are often introduced with praise and the recitation of the great events of God's show of mercy to Israel. The effect is to highlight the contrast between living in God's favor and under divine judgment. The language of steadfast love, of granting favor, and of abundant mercies is quite basic to all of Israel's liturgical tradition (e.g., Psalm 145).

In v. 8 God is quoted as affirming the classic covenantal formula (e.g., Lev. 26:12; Deut. 29:13) by means of a partial citation. The stipulation of being sons who "will not act falsely" follows, and concludes with God's commitment of being Israel's savior (59:1; 60:16; 63:1). The enumeration of God's love and mercy in sustaining Israel in the days past is again continued in v. 9. However, the precise interpretation of v. 9b is difficult and controversial. The initial problem is signalled by the Kethib/Qere variant interpreting the Hebrew *lō'*. The MT appears to understand the clause according to the Qere: "in all their troubles, he was troubled." However, the LXX prefers the Kethib ("not"), and repoints *ṣar* ("affliction") as *ṣir* ("messenger"). With the verse division also shifted, a very different sentence emerges: "it was no messenger or angel, but his face (presence) that saved them." It is argued by those defending this reading that the formula "angel of the presence" does not appear elsewhere in the Old Testament.

However, in response, it is also clear that there is a rather close parallel in Ex. 33:12ff. of the face or presence of God accompanying Israel as a sign of his continued commitment in spite of the sin of the golden calf. The extension of the term in the formula "angel of his presence" is fully in accord with the other circuitous formulations of divine intermediaries who are the visible agents of the selfsame divine essence (e.g., "angel of Yahweh," etc.). Although the LXX's rendering remains attractive, I would nevertheless argue that the MT's interpretation is probably to be preferred (cf. Barthélemy, *CTLAT*).

Verse 10 anticipates the main theme of the succeeding communal lament by introducing the theme of Israel's rebellion and resultant divine judgment, which it interjects into the initial recounting of God's great deeds of salvation.

The terminology of disobedience to God as grieving the holy spirit (*rûªḥ qodšô*) is a formulation infrequent in the rest of the Old Testament (cf. Ps. 51:11), but one occurring twice in chapter 63 (vv. 10–11). Closely akin is the spirit of Yahweh (v. 14). The spirit here is the holy presence of Yahweh, which is a form of his outward manifestation to Israel theologically retrojected to the period of the nation's inception. Although the holy spirit is here still far removed from its later New Testament understanding, there is nevertheless an adumbration in the Old Testament of the identity of the God of Israel both as the transcendent and immanent presence in creation and redemption.

The bridge back to God's mercy is formed in v. 11 with the appeal to the memory of God's former acts of intervention on Israel's behalf in the traditions of the exodus. Unfortunately, the text of v. 11 presents a variety of textual problems on which there is no consensus toward resolving. Since the following verses recount the tradition from Israel's perspective, some commentators have emended the subject of the remembering to a plural form ("they"), but this interpretation is not fully persuasive in the light of the frequent appeal to God's remembering (e.g., Ex. 2:24, etc.). Others have sought to construe Moses as the subject rather than the object of the remembering, but this syntactical construction is at best strained in Hebrew. The NRSV follows the Syriac in emending the Hebrew "his people" to "his servant," but this reading is hardly the original text. Nor is the attempt satisfactory by the NJPS to see a midrashic wordplay on the name Moses according to Ex. 2:10. Possibly the least intrusive emendation is to follow the American Revised translation in reading "Moses and his people," even when the solution is not fully persuasive. The only comfort is that the general meaning of the whole sentence is fairly clear.

The reference to the exodus tradition continues in v. 11b with the terminology of bringing up from the sea. The plural object of the verse, "the shepherds of his flock," remains somewhat unclear, but from the larger context probably relates to Moses and Aaron. Much like 51:9 the imagery of dividing the waters and being led through the depths (*tᵉhōmôt*) fuses together the acts of the primeval creation and the Egyptian deliverance as being part of one divine, salvific moment in the purpose of God. The theme of God's intent in saving Israel to establish his name is one that emerges strongly in Ezekiel and in postexilic prophecy (Ezek. 20:14, etc.).

[63:15–64:11(12)] A sharp break occurs in the prayer between vv. 14 and 15. From this point onward God is addressed directly and with a tone of greatest intensity (cf. Ps. 80:15). Again the prophet's "me" is encompassed within the community's "we." Although the description of Israel as God's sons is common throughout the tradition, the reference to God as Father grows in frequency only during the later postexilic period. It is possible that the earlier reluctance to name God as Father derived from the original association with the mythological world of Canaanite deities, such as that reflected at Ugarit. However, in the Hellenistic period within both Judaism and Christianity, the terminology, at first rare in the Old Testament, became common.

The appeal to God as Father in 63:16 is set in contrast to the hostility and alleged indifference of Abraham and Israel. Hanson (79ff.) uses this text to identify the presence of rival political groups within Israel, but the historical evidence for an exact sociological analysis is largely missing. Rather, the group seeking God's intervention is only designated as "servants" (v. 17). Those followers of the faithful servant of Second Isaiah (cf. 50:10ff.) first surfaced as "servants" in 56:6, but shortly return in chapters 65 and 66 to become a major subject of Third Isaiah. This portion of the prayer ends in vv. 18 and 19 with an increased intensity in which Israel's desperate need is highlighted. Not only has their sanctuary been destroyed—surely the destruction of the temple in 587 is meant—but Israel registers its feelings of utter abandonment. It has been isolated to such an extent as to question whether in truth it ever was under God's care and sovereignty and bore the name of God.

Although the chapter division of the Hebrew text adds an additional line to the preceding unit, the Vulgate's chapter division, taking its lead from the LXX, has generally been accepted by most modern translations as being more coherent. Even the NJPS prints the last two lines of v. 19 in conjunction with the oracle that follows. The prayer returns to the urgent plea for God's direct intervention from above: "O that you would rend the heavens and come down." That the plea is for a theophany is clear from the imagery of quaking mountains, flaming fire, and steaming liquid. The wording evokes again reference to God's past intervention with the awesome signs of power displayed when he descended at Sinai and the mountains quaked. The confession of God's sole rule as sovereign also reverberates from the Sinai tradition: "You shall have no other gods before me" (Ex. 20:3), but now understood as an affirmation of God's uniqueness ("no eye has seen any God besides you").

The interpretation of v. 5 continues to evoke debate. The central problem is in determining the force of the verb "meet" (*pg'*). It may be understood in a positive sense, "You meet those who gladly do right" (NRSV), or as part of the complaint, "You struck him who would gladly do justice" (NJPS). Even more controversy turns on the rendering of v. 4b(5b). The Hebrew text appears to read, "It is because you have been angry that we have sinned." This proposed reading seems radically to reverse the traditional theological sequence of first the sin, then the divine judgment. For that reason, most translations link the two clauses by removing the causal connection (RSV, NIV, NEB), and thus maintain by implication the traditional link (cf. the lengthy discussion in Barthélemy, *CTLAT* 448ff.). In my opinion, the power of the verse lies in the unexpected sequence, which is an *ad hoc* formulation, and its literary function lies exactly in its outrageous formulation. The sentiment is not to be abstracted into a theological principle, but serves only to identify the frustration of the confessing community. The statement is congruent with the intensity of the rest of the lament that follows. We are like a polluted garment, our virtue like filthy rags, and as for God, he has hidden his face from us (vv. 5–6).

The final plea in vv. 7–11 (8–12) returns to a more sober note in which the intensity of the present pain is tempered by Israel's enduring faith: "Yet, O LORD, you are our Father. We are the clay, you are the potter." Then the final arguments are mounted for God's immediate intervention: "Our holy and glorious temple . . . has been burned with fire. . . . After all this, O LORD, will you still restrain yourself?"

The chapter ends with this haunting question, but the reader of the book does not have long to wait, for the divine response follows immediately in chapter 65, and with a passionate intensity fully matching Israel's complaint.

67. Isaiah 65:1–66:24

65:1 I let myself be sought by those who did not ask,
    to be found by those who did not seek me.
I said, "Here I am, here I am,"
    to a nation that did not invoke my name.
2 I continually held out my hands
    to a rebellious people
who walk in a way that is not good,
    following their own devices;
3 a people who constantly provoke me
    to my face,
sacrificing in gardens and burning incense on tiles,
4 crouching in tombs
    and spending the night in secret places;
who eat the flesh of swine,
    with a brew of unclean things in bowls;
5 who say, "Keep your distance! Don't come near,
    for I am too sacred for you."[a]
They are smoke in my nostrils,
    like fire burning all day long
6 See, this stands written before me:
    "I will not keep still, but I will repay it,
I will repay[b] into their bosom
7   both your sins and the sins of your fathers,"
    says the LORD.
"Because they burned sacrifices on the mountains

and defiled me on the hills,
I will measure full recompense into their bosoms
  for their former deeds."

8   Thus says the LORD:
When juice is formed in a cluster of grapes,
  and someone says, "Don't destroy it, there's still good
  in it,"
so will I do for my servants' sake,
  and not destroy them all.

9   I will bring forth offspring from Jacob,
  and from Judah heirs to my mountains;
my chosen people will inherit it,
  and my servants will dwell there.

10   Sharon will become a pasture for flocks,
  the valley of Achor a resting place for herds,
  for my people who seek me.

11   But as for you who forsake the LORD
  and forget my holy mountain,
who set a table for Luck (Gad)
  and fill bowls of wine for Destiny (Meni),

12   I will consume you with the sword,
  and you will all kneel to be slaughtered,
because you did not answer when I called,
  you did not listen when I spoke.
Rather, you did what was evil in my sight
  and chose what I did not want.

13   Therefore, thus says the Lord GOD:
Behold, my servants will eat,
  but you will go hungry;
behold, my servants will drink,
  but you will go thirsty;
behold, my servants will rejoice,
  but you will be shamed.

14   Behold, my servants will sing in heartfelt joy,
  but you will cry out from sorrow
  and wail from anguish of spirit.

15   You will leave behind your name
  for my chosen ones to use as a curse,
  and the Lord GOD will give you over to death.
  But to his servants he will give another name.

16   Whoever blesses himself in the land
  will do so by the true God,

and who takes an oath in the land
    will swear by the true God.
The former troubles will be forgotten,
    and will be hidden from my eyes.

17 For behold, I create new heavens and a new earth,
    and the former things will not be remembered;
    they will never come to mind.

18 Be glad then and rejoice forever
    in what I am creating,
for I create Jerusalem a delight
    and her people a joy.

19 I will rejoice in Jerusalem
    and take delight in my people.
Never again will the sound of weeping
    and crying be heard in it.

20 No more will there be in it an infant
    that lives only for a few days,
or an old man who does not
    live out his days,
for whoever dies at a hundred
    will be considered a youth,
and whoever fails to reach a hundred
    will be thought to be cursed.

21 They will build houses and inhabit them,
    they will plant vineyards and enjoy their fruits.

22 They will not build for others to inhabit,
    or plant for others to enjoy.
For the days of my people will extend
    as long as those of a tree,
my chosen ones will enjoy
    the fruit of their labor.

23 They will not work for nothing,
    or raise children for misfortune.
They shall be the offspring blessed by the LORD,
    and their children after them.

24 Before they call, I will answer;
    while they are still speaking, I will respond.

25 The wolf and the lamb will feed together,
    and the lion will eat straw like the ox,
    and dust will be the serpent's food.
They will not hurt or destroy in all my holy
    mountain, says the LORD.

66:1 Thus says the LORD:
    Heaven is my throne
       and earth is my footstool.
    Where could you build a house for me?
       What could serve as my resting place?
2 All these things were made by my hand,
       and so they came into being,
       declares the LORD.
    Yet this is the one I cherish:
       the downtrodden and contrite in spirit,
       who reveres my word.
3 But for those who slaughter an ox and kill a man,
       who sacrifice a sheep and break the neck of a dog,
       who make a grain offering and offer pig's blood,
       and who offer incense and worship an idol,
    they have chosen their own ways,
       and delight in their abominations.
4 So I, on my part, will choose their harsh judgment,
       and will bring upon them what they dread.
    For when I called, no one answered;
       when I spoke, no one responded.
    They did evil in my sight,
       and chose what I do not allow.
5 Hear the word of the LORD,
       you who tremble at his word:
    Your kinsmen who hate you,
       and exclude you because of my name,
    they say, "Let the LORD be glorified,
       that we may see your joy!"
    Yet it is they who will be put to shame.
6 Hear that commotion from the city,
       that uproar from within the temple.
    It is the sound of the LORD
       exercising retribution on his enemies.
7 Before she was in labor, she gave birth;
       before she experienced pains, she delivered a son.
8 Who even heard of such a thing?
       Who has seen such things?
    Can a country be born in a day,
       or a nation be brought forth in a moment?
    Yet Zion at the onset of labor
       brought forth their sons.

9   Will I bring on labor and not bring forth a birth?
      says the LORD.
   Will I who cause birth close the womb?
      says your God.

10 Rejoice with Jerusalem, and be glad for her,
      all you who love her.
   Rejoice greatly with her,
      all you who mourn over her,

11 that you may nurse from her breasts
      consolation to the full,
   that you may drink deeply
      and rejoice in her abundance.

12 For thus says the LORD:
      "I will extend prosperity to her like a river,
      and the wealth of nations like a stream in flood.
   You will nurse and be carried on her hip,
      and dandled on her knees.

13 As a mother comforts her child,
      so will I comfort you,
      and you will find comfort in Jerusalem."

14 You will see and your heart will rejoice;
      your limbs will strengthen like the grass;
   the power of the LORD will be known
      to his servants,
      and his rage shown to his foes.

15 Behold, the LORD will come in fire,
      and his chariots like a whirlwind.
   He will vent his anger in fury,
      and his rage with flames of fire.

16 For with fire and sword will the LORD
      execute judgment upon all people,
   and those slain by the LORD will be many.

17 "Those who sanctify and purify themselves to enter the gardens, after the one standing in the midst,[c] eating swine's flesh, filth, and the mouse, these all will come to an end together, just as the LORD has said.

18 "As for me, knowing their works and their thoughts,[d] the time has come to gather all the nations and tongues; they will come and behold my glory. 19 I will set a sign among them, and send from them survivors to the nations, to Tarshish, Pul, and Lud who draw the bow, to Tubal, Javan, and the distant coastlands that have not heard of my fame nor seen my glory. They shall proclaim my glory among the nations.

20 From all the nations they will bring their kin to my holy mountain in

Jerusalem as an offering to the LORD, upon horses, in chariots and
wagons, and on mules and camels, says the LORD, just as the Israelites
bring their cereal offerings in pure vessels to the house of the LORD.

21 Some of them I will also take for priests and Levites, says the LORD.
22 "For as the new heavens and new earth
    that I make will endure by my will,
        says the LORD,
    so will your seed and your name endure.
23 From new moon to new moon,
        and from Sabbath to Sabbath,
    all flesh will come to worship me,
        says the LORD.
24 "And they will go out and gaze on the corpses of those who rebelled
    against me, for their worm will not die, their fire will not be quenched,
    and they will be a horror to all humanity."

a. Some interpreters (*BHS*, NJPS) repoint the verb as a piel and translate the colon,
"I would render you consecrated."

b. It is possible that the repetition of the verb "I will repay" (*šillamtî*) is a dittography. NJPS emends by bringing up "your sins" from v. 7 as the object.

c. The translation of *'aḥad* as *'eḥād* ("one") follows the Qere. Still the meaning is
unclear.

d. The MT is difficult at best: "and I their works and thoughts it is coming." Many translations (e.g., NJPS) move the first three words of v. 18 to the preceding verse. Two
difficulties are present. The pronoun lacks a verb, which is often supplied: "I know"
(NRSV). Others suggest the clause is to be rendered elliptically. In addition, the verb *bā'āh*
requires a feminine subject such as *'et* ("moment") (cf. Barthélemy, *CTLAT*, 462ff.).

Selected Bibliography

R. Aus, "The Relevance of Isaiah 66:7 to Revelation 12 and 2 Thessalonians." *ZNW* 67, 1976, 252–68;
W. A. M. Beuken, "Does Trito-Isaiah Reject the Temple? An Intertextual Inquiry into Isa. 66:1–6," *Inter-
textuality in Biblical Writings: Essays in Honour of Bas van Iersel,* ed. S. Draisma, Kampen 1989, 53–66;
"The Main Theme of Trito-Isaiah: 'The Servants of YHWH,'" *JSOT* 47, 1990, 67–87; "Isaiah Chapters
LXV—LXVI: Trito-Isaiah and the Closure of the Book of Isaiah," *Congress Volume, Leuven 1989,*
VTSup 43, Leiden 1991, 204–21; **E. Conrad,** "Zu Jes. 65:3b," *ZAW* 80, 1968, 332–34; **W. J. Dumbrell,**
"The Purpose of the Book of Isaiah," *TynBul* 36, 1985, 111–28; **J. A. Emerton,** "Notes on Two Verses
in Isaiah (26:16 and 66:17)," *Prophecy: Essays Presented to Georg Fohrer,* BZAW 150, Berlin 1980,
12–25; **G. Fohrer,** "Kritik am Tempel, Kultus und Kultusausübung in nachexilischer Zeit," *Archäologie
und Altes Testament, Fs K. Galling,* ed. A. Kutschke and E. Kutsche, Tübingen 1970, 101–16; **J. Gray,**
"Gad," *IDB,* II, Nashville 1961, 335; "Meni," ibid., III, 350; **P. D. Hanson,** *The Dawn of Apocalyptic,*
Philadelphia 1975, 134–86; **W. Houston,** *Purity and Monotheism: Clean and Unclean Animals in Biblical Law,* JSOTSup 140, Sheffield 1991; **U. Kellermann,** "Tritojesaja und das Geheimnis des
Gottesknechtes: Erwägungen zu Jes 59, 21; 61, 1–3; 66, 18–24," *BN* 58, 1991, 46–81; **K. Koenen,** *Ethik
und Eschatologie im Tritojesajabuch,* WMANT 62, Tübingen 1990, 183–214; **H.-J. Kraus,** "Die ausge-
bliebene Endtheophanie. Eine Studie in Jes. 56—66," *ZAW* 78, 1966, 317–32; **R. Lack,** *La Symbolique*

du livre d'Isaïe, AnBib 59, Rome 1973; **W. Lau,** *Schriftgelehrte Prophetie in Jes 56–66,* BZAW 225, Berlin 1994, 126ff.; **T. J. Lewis,** *Cults of the Dead in Ancient Israel and Ugarit,* HSM 39, Atlanta 1989; **L. S. Liebreich,** "The Compilation of the Book of Isaiah," *JQR* 46, 1956, 259–77; 47, 1957, 114–38; **H. Odeberg,** *Trito-Isaiah (Isaiah 56–66): A Literary and Linguistic Analysis,* Uppsala 1931, 281–85; **K. Pauritsch,** *Die neue Gemeinde: Gott sammelt Ausgestossene und Arme (Jesaja 56–66),* AnBib 47, Rome 1971, 171–218; **R. Rendtorff,** "Zur Komposition des Buches Jesaja," *VT* 34, 1984, 295–320; **A. Rofé,** "Isaiah 66:1–4: Judean Sects in the Persian Period as Viewed by Trito-Isaiah," *Biblical and Related Studies Presented to Samuel Iwry,* ed. A. Kort and S. Morschauer, Winona Lake 1985, 201–17; **A. von Rohr Sauer,** "The Cultic Role of the Pig in Ancient Times," *Memoriam Paul Kahle,* ed. M. Black, BZAW 103, Berlin 1968, 201–7; **J. T. A. G. M. van Ruiten,** "The Intertextual Relationship between Isaiah 65,25 and Isaiah 11,6–9," *The Scriptures and the Scrolls, Fs A. S. van der Woude,* VTSup 49, Leiden 1992, 31–42; **J. M. Sasson,** "Isaiah LXVI 3–4a," *VT* 26, 1976, 199–207; **S. Sekine,** *Die Tritojesa-janische Sammlung (Jes 56–66) redaktionsgeschichtlich untersucht,* Berlin 1989, 43ff., 165ff.; **P. A. Smith,** *Rhetoric and Redaction in Trito-Isaiah,* VTSup 62, Leiden 1995, 128–72; **O. H. Steck,** *Studien zu Tritojesaja,* BZAW 203, Berlin 1991, 217ff., 248ff., 262ff.; "Der neue Himmel und die neue Erde. Beobachtungen zur Rezeption von Gen 1–3 in Jes 65, 16b–25," *Studies in the Book of Isaiah, Fs W. A. M. Beuken,* Leuven 1997, 349–65; **M. A. Sweeney,** "Prophetic Exegesis in Isaiah 65–66," *Writing and Reading the Scroll of Isaiah,* I, ed. C. C. Broyles and C. A. Evans, Leiden 1997, 455–74; **A. J. Tomasino,** "Isaiah 1.1–2.4 and 63–66, and the Composition of the Isaianic Corpus," *JSOT* 57, 1993, 81–98; **R. de Vaux,** "Les sacrifices de porcs en Palestine et dans L'Ancien Orient," *Bible et Orient,* Paris 1967, 499–516; J. Vermeylen, "L'unité die livre d'Isaïe," *The Book of Isaiah,* ed. J. Vermeylen, Leuven 1989, 11–53; **E. C. Webster,** "A Rhetorical Study of Isaiah 66," *JSOT* 34, 1986, 93–108; "The Rhetoric of Isaiah," *JSOT* 47, 1990, 89–102.

1. Genre, Structure, and Literary Context

During the period dominated by the form-critical approach, it was assumed that chapters 65 and 66 consisted of a great variety of smaller units reflecting different genres and settings. Scholars such as Elliger, Sekine, Westermann, and Pauritsch are representative of this approach (cf. Westermann, 398ff.; Pau-ritsch, 171ff.; Sekine, 165ff.). However, increasingly there has begun to emerge a consensus that the older literary and form-critical analyses, although at times making some acute observations, have unduly fragmented the literature. The older formal indices of new genres no longer seem to function as in the preex-ilic period. As a result, most of the more recent analyses of these chapters work with larger units, and increasingly argue for some larger literary unity com-prising chapters 65 and 66 (e.g., Hanson, Steck, Beuken, Smith). Of course, this characterization is not to suggest full agreement, especially when it comes to the analyzing of the details. In sum, the nature of the debate has dramatically shifted in the last several decades.

In spite of the common concern to recover the continuity between develop-ing horizontal layers, the proposed redactional schemata reconstructed for these last two chapters remain still very far apart. Steck's complex analysis indeed envisions chapters 65–66 as a response to the preceding prayer (63:7–64:11), but, more importantly, along with 56:1–8, a final redaction of the entire book of Isaiah and a correction to the preceding prayer. He dates this redactional layer very late, perhaps in the third century (*Studien zur Tritojesaja,* 217ff.; 248ff.).

More recently, P. A. Smith has projected a division of Third Isaiah into the work of two different prophets, T1 and T1[2] (128ff.). Over against 62:1–63:6 he reconstructs four units (56:1–8; 56:9–57:21; 58:1–59:20; 65:1–66:17), which he claims have a distinction in perspective from the initial corpus. Within the context of a commentary his hypothesis cannot be pursued in detail and will be referred to only when it directly impinges on the exegesis. Of immediate relevance is his defense of the unity of 65:1–66:17. Some of the same rhetorical arguments have also been made by E. C. Webster.

Finally, special attention should be given to the careful redactional analysis of Beuken. First in his Dutch commentary and then in a well-known English article ("Isaiah Chapters LXV–LXVI"), he has argued that in chapters 65–66 there is a threefold editorial closure, first of Third Isaiah alone, then together with Second Isaiah, and finally of the book of Isaiah as a whole. Although I do not doubt that this attempt to reconstruct the redactional layers of chapters 65–66 at times has aided in sharpening the focus of the text, its ultimate exegetical value is restricted by the very nature of the questions asked. In my opinion, a more important enterprise is to analyze the *effect* of the editorial layering on the final form of the text, even when the compositional process remains often unclear. In other words, I would like to turn the major focus of my exegesis of chapters 65–66 in another direction.

Still, I am fully aware that how one analyzes the subdivisions of these chapters can often greatly influence the interpretation. Unfortunately, at times it is very difficult to demonstrate the sole legitimacy of one reading and, in the end, several vying interpretations will have to be respected as possible alternative readings.

This issue emerges immediately in attempting to subdivide both chapters. We turn first to chapter 65. There is largely agreement between Beuken and Smith on the subdivision of chapter 65, of course with minor differences. Both resist the earlier attempt to separate v. 1 from the unit of vv. 1–7 (Sekine), or to remove vv. 8–10 as a separate unit from vv. 8–16a (Vermeylen), or to link vv. 16–25 directly to chapters 60–62 (Westermann).

However, complex exegetical problems emerge in chapter 66. Again both Smith and Beuken resist the usual interpretation of seeing two different redactional layers in vv. 5–17, with the core of the chapter being vv. 7–14 and vv. 5–6 and 15–17 functioning as a framework. Instead, Smith argues that 66:1–4 is closely connected with chapter 65 as a fourth strophe. Then he construes 66:5–17 as one coherent oracle pointing to a consistent mode of addresses with various stylistic features.

In contrast, Beuken argues that vv. 5–6 belong integrally with vv. 1–4. He then designates vv. 7–14 as an individual unit and assigns vv. 15–24 to the concluding epilogue. Beuken's arguments for this division also carry considerable weight. He sees the function of chapter 66 to be that of a converse image (*Spiegelbild*) of chapter 65. By not construing vv. 5–6 and 15–17 as a framework to vv. 7–14, he envisions a consistent polarity between the faithful and apostate Jews. He supports his division by appeals to form-critical indices, but the weight of the argument falls on literary evidence, such as the chiastic structure of 66:1–16 and its formal coherence. Both Smith and Beuken continually refer to intertextual resonances to support their particular divisions of chapter 66, especially the connection between 66:4 and 65:1, 12, 24.

My purpose in reviewing these debates is not to support wholeheartedly only one hypothesis. I do agree with the attempts of both Beuken and Smith to resist the atomization of the modern critics. Rather, my chief concern is to raise the hermeneutical question of whether deciding on the exact literary subdivisions of Third Isaiah should carry as much weight as modern critical scholarship tends to attribute to it. I would argue instead that in the ancient hearing and reading of scripture, that is, in its canonical reception, the resonance set up from repeated themes played a more important role in interpretation than the modern concerns with establishing exact literary units. Therefore, the decision of whether 66:1–4 belongs literarily with chapter 65 (Smith) or is only closely related (Beuken) is not of major importance when interpreting chapters 65 and 66. The fact that appeals to the repetition of similar themes and to verbal parallels are recognized by both Beuken, Smith, and Webster, even when used to support different subdivisions, would caution against pressing only one reading to the exclusion of others.

Finally, in respect to the much debated question of the historical dating of these chapters, I remain skeptical of the various redactional theories (e.g., Steck) to employ the alleged layering of the text as a means of exact dating. Also, appeals to the presence or absence of a rebuilt temple (cf. 66:1) do not provide an adequate source for dating material in Third Isaiah. Finally, the attempts to historicize the enemy into rival sectarian groups (Hanson), or to identify the adversary with the Samaritans, or with later Hellenistic controversies rest on unsupported theories that distort rather than sharpen the biblical text.

2. Exposition

[65:1–7] It is not of great importance whether one limits the initial unit to vv. 1–7 followed closely by vv. 8–16, or envisions a single oracle in vv. 1–16. The traditional warrant for separating two oracles lies in the messenger formula in v. 8 (cf. also v. 13), and in the shift of addressee from the apostate Jews of vv. 1–7 to the "servants" of vv. 8–16. However, the elements binding together the two sections are equally strong. The speaker is God in much of vv. 1–16 (but cf. vv. 15b–16), and the sharp contrast between the apostate and the faithful is maintained throughout. It is even heightened in vv. 13–15. In addition, all commentators recognize the refrain in God's calling and the people's failure to respond to 65:1, 12, 24; and 66:4.

The more important question turns on the linkage between chapter 65 and the preceding chapter. Does chapter 65 as a whole function as a crucial divine response to the people's lament in 63:7–64:11? Several modern commentators reject this traditional reading by claiming that chapter 65 does not offer the kind of answer expected. Still, the very unexpected nature of the response does not in itself negate this linkage. Indeed, the role of chapter 65 may well lie precisely in the astonishment of new accusations that support the sharp polarity drawn between the righteous and unrighteous within Israel.

[1] The first verse reflects a decidedly disputational flavor. Over against the complaint of 64:12 that God is silent, the divine response mounts its full defense on the grounds of God's accessibility. The theme of the continuous divine calling points both backward and forward. God lets himself be found by those who seek him, which is, of course, a familiar theme of Second Isaiah (51:1) and Third Isaiah (58:2). Whereas it is usually the petitioner who spreads out his hands toward God (Isaiah 1:15; 4:31), here God is pictured extending his hands toward his rebellious people.

[2–5] In these verses there is compiled a veritable catalogue of sins consisting of seven participles: walking in evil ways, provoking me continually, sacrificing in gardens, burning incense on tiles, sitting in tombs, spending the night in secret places, and eating swine's flesh. Much of the cultic language appears elsewhere in the Old Testament, with its closest intertextual parallels found in Isa. 1:21ff.; 57:5ff.; and 66:3ff. These forbidden practices often reflect illicit cultic rites known from Ugarit, Babylon, and elsewhere (cf. de Vaux, Rohr Sauer, Fohrer). The practice of necromancy, fertility cults, and eating of swine flesh were all vigorously opposed in the Old Testament, but were constantly emerging as a threat to Israel's worship (Lev. 19:31; 20:6; Num. 19:11ff.; Deut. 14:3; Ezek. 8:9ff.; Isa. 66:3ff.). The fact that an exact description of the illicit practices is missing accords well with Israel's practice of rejecting them en masse as an abomination without much attention to details. In v. 5 the practice of separation to protect a state of sanctity can be interpreted several ways, but appears to be some kind of magical rite that afforded an alleged status of cultic holiness. Verse 5b lumps the various practices together and summarily dismisses them. God pronounces them "smoke in my nostrils."

[6–7] The divine judgment on the apostates follows. A sentence has already been inscribed in writing, which is then cited. The clause "because they burned sacrifices on the mounts and defiled me on the hills" (v. 7) not only picks up the language of chapter 57, but resonates the standard accusation of the Deuteronomistic historian (1 Kings 14:22ff.) and of the prophets (Jer. 3:6ff.; Ezek. 20:27ff.). Verse 7 concludes with a reference to payment for "their former deeds" (*p^e'ullātām rī'šōnāh*). From the context of chapter 65 it refers back to the above-mentioned cultic abominations, and *ri'šōnāh* is to be taken as an adjective ("former"). But could there be a resonance of Second Isaiah's use of "former things," which belong to the old age, as opposed to God's "new things" (41:22; 42:9; 48:3; etc.)? It is hardly accidental that the designation "former troubles" occurs in 65:16, and "former things will not be remembered" in 65:17 (cf. 43:18).

[8–16] In contrast to the description of the apostate, rebellious people who continually provoke God through their pagan cults, the writer turns to announce divine blessing on his servants. In fact, the major attention of chapter 65 falls on the "servants," a term that occurs seven times (vv. 8, 9, 13, 14, 15). In an important article, Beuken ("The Main Theme of Trito-Isaiah") has argued that the dominant theme of Third Isaiah focuses on the servants of Yahweh. He attempts to explain how the plural term comes just at the end of Second Isaiah (54:17) to form a bridge with the servant of chapter 53, and fulfills the promise of the "offspring" (53:10). He then attempts with a bit more difficulty to explain why the term is missing in two succeeding sections that follow the prologue (56:9–59:21; 60:1–63:6), only to surface again in 63:17, and then to dominate the thought of chapter 65 (cf. 66:14). Although Beuken has made an impressive case, I am inclined to argue that there are other equally important themes in Third Isaiah that rival in significance the theme of the servants (cf. below).

[8–10] The unit begins with a messenger formula and continues as a divine, first person oracle throughout the rest of the unit except at the very end. The theme of the servants' glorious future is first developed by means of an analogy to the gathering of grapes at the harvest: "When juice is formed in a cluster of grapes." Then what appears to be a vintager's song is cited: "Don't destroy it, there's still good in it." Some commentators have understood the analogy as pointing to the presence of good and bad grapes in the same cluster, but it is more likely that the entire cluster is judged to be good and thus spared. Next, the promise to the faithful of Israel unfolds. The servants, "offspring from Jacob," "heirs to my mountains," and "my chosen people," shall inherit the land, which extends from the Mediterranean in the east to the Jordan in the west. Sharon designates the western coastal plain and Achor the valley in eastern Palestine near Jericho. The repetition of the theme of seeking the Lord in v. 10 serves to join the passage coherently with v. 1.

[11–16] Verse 11 picks up the theme of the apostates, those who forsook rather than sought Yahweh. The two deities referred to as Gad and Meni—often rendered as Fortune and Destiny—were most probably gods of fate. Gad was a Syrian deity whose name is preserved in various place names such as Baalgad (Josh. 11:17). Meni is less familiar, but thought to be venerated by the Arabs in the pre-Islamic period. Pettinato claims to have found reference to Meni at Ebla (cf. literature cited by Koenen, 180). The biblical text appears to refer to some form of sacred meal that further extends the accusations against the pagan practices in 65:3ff. The theme of not responding to God's call of v. 1 is once again continued in v. 12 in order to lay stress on the deliberate rejection of God's invitation.

The sharp contrast between the faithful and the apostate within Israel climaxes in a dramatic juxtaposition of blessing and curse. The divine sentence is heightened by the fourfold repetition of "behold" (*hinnēh*):

> Behold, my servants will eat,
>> but you will go hungry;
> behold, my servants will drink,
>> but you will go thirsty;
> behold, my servants will rejoice,
>> but you will be shamed.
> Behold, my servants will sing in heartfelt joy,
>> but you will cry out from sorrow.

Moreover, the name of the apostates will be used as a curse (cf. Num. 5:21; Ps. 102:9[8]), while God's servants will receive a new name, a promise given earlier by Third Isaiah (56:5; 62:2). They will swear by the "God of amen," that is, the "true God," because the former troubles (cf. v. 7) have been forgotten, not only by them, but by God himself.

[17–25] The final unit in chapter 65 announces a radically new vision of the future: "new heavens and a new earth." Initially the vocabulary used to portray the prophetic portrayal of a new divine order appears to be a direct extension of Second Isaiah. The reference to God as creator (*bôrē'*) of the heavens and earth is a dominant theme (42:5; 45:7, 12, 18; etc.). Moreover, the verb is not only used to designate God's initial creation of the heavens and earth, but its continuous maintenance and preservation (42:5–6). However, even more significantly, the verb is employed by Second Isaiah in connection with the promise of the new things (48:6), which will replace the former things. Thus, v. 17b joins intentionally to this theme of the former things (48:18).

Nevertheless, Third Isaiah has greatly radicalized the theme of God as creator in speaking of a new world order different in kind from the past. For many commentators the break is so stark that the new vision is designated as apocalyptic. This interpretation is set out most fully by Hanson (134ff.). According to his hypothesis, while Second Isaiah had managed to maintain a dynamic tension between the new and the old in one historical continuum, in Third Isaiah the promise of a new creation threatened to dissolve the dialectic between myth and history. The present social order as unmitigated evil had to be completely expunged to purge the human sphere and to usher in a new apocalyptic vision of a supernatural divine order (cf. Rev. 21:1ff.). As part of this pattern the imagery of chapter 65 is understood as an eschatological return to the primordial age (*Endzeit wird Urzeit*). Accordingly, the verses that follow develop the mythical themes of a return to paradise, which later abound in the apocryphal and pseudepigraphical books.

Respecting this mode of interpretation, Beuken has mounted a strong case against imposing the broad categories of the history of religions, which fail to pursue closely enough the specific context of Third Isaiah's vision. Above all, it is the emphasis on the role of the servants of Yahweh which form the center of Third Isaiah's hope that shapes the relationship with Second Isaiah. The continuity between the old and the new is provided by the emergence of the off-spring of the servant, who now inherit God's land.

The description that follows v. 17 and provides the context by which to understand the new heavens and earth is portrayed always in relation to God's faithful people, who experience the entry of God's rule within transformed Jerusalem. The imagery of joy and absence of weeping is set in contrast to the sorrow through which the community of faith has come. The planting of vine-yards and the enjoying of its fruits is simply the converse of Israel's experience of exploration and conquest. Verse 23 summarizes this eschatological hope: "They shall be the offspring blessed by Yahweh." The link with the promise to the suffering servant is fully evident: "[H]e will see offspring. . . . From the agony of his soul he will see" (53:10–11). The promise in chapter 65 is not an apocalyptic flight into an imaginative world of fantasy, but the fulfillment of God's will taking shape throughout the entire book of Isaiah. Verse 24 once again repeats the theme of chapter 65 of God's utter accessibility in his calling and answering those who seek his presence.

There is, however, one more important aspect to the fulfillment of God's promise, which is developed in v. 25. It has long been recognized that v. 25 offers a compendium of the messianic oracle of 11:6–9. Two lines between the passages are virtually identical: "the lion will eat straw like the ox" and "They will not hurt or destroy in all my holy mountain." The first line of v. 25 picks up the vocabulary of 11:6, but refashions it into the larger pattern of juxtapos-ing the predator with the prey. The line "dust will be the serpent's food" is a play on Gen. 3:14, which describes the curse of the serpent at the Fall.

Beuken follows the majority opinion of almost all modern commentators (*Jesaja,* III, 92) when he assumes that the messianic content of Isaiah 11 is com-pletely lacking in 65:25. He conjectures that the author perhaps saw a connection between the harmony in the animal world and the judgment dividing the oppressed of the land and the godless. The lack of a messianic hope in Second and Third Isaiah seems conclusive in ruling out any messianic function in chapter 65.

In my opinion, there is another approach to this issue. It is one thing to sug-gest that messianism played no role in "the theology of Third Isaiah," the con-venient modern cipher for the reconstructed author of these chapters. It is quite another to ask how this intertextual reference to chapter 11 would have been heard by readers of the whole book of Isaiah. I suggest that a very different answer is forthcoming if one does not restrict correct interpretation simply to an original author's intention. Whoever finally shaped the present form of chapter 65—whether Third Isaiah or an even later redactor is unclear—chose to conclude his portrayal of the new eschatological order by citing the well-known messianic passage of chapter 11.

In no other passage was the transformation of the new eschatological age expressed with such radical imagery. Indeed, the inclusion of the terminology of "my holy mountain" (11:9) serves in addition to incorporate into the portrayal of chapter 11 also the transformation of Jerusalem into the heavenly Zion. The function of this appeal to intertextuality thus serves to identify the new creation of chapter 65 with the messianic hope of First Isaiah. Of course, this is not to suggest that chapter 65 has appropriated a full-blown messianism, but rather that the editor of chapter 65 fashioned his vision of the eschatological hope to include, in some fashion, the messianic hope of First Isaiah along with the promises of Second Isaiah, thus linking redactionally the beginning, middle, and end of the book of Isaiah (cf. below). Moreover, when one recalls the theme of God's "everlasting covenant" and "enduring mercies promised to David" in chapter 55, along with its liturgical development in Psalms 89 and 132, the repeated assertion that messianism was limited only to First Isaiah is an underestimation of its resonance within the whole book of Isaiah in its final form.

[66:1–24] In his *Congress Volume* essay, Beuken has developed a rather complex redactional hypothesis that greatly influences how he subdivides chapter 66. He divides the chapter into three major sections: vv. 1–6; 7–14; 15–24. In opposition to the majority opinion, which divides into units vv. 1–4, 5–17, and 18–24, Beuken argues that vv. 15–20a are a theophany of Yahweh that serves as the conclusion of both Second and Third Isaiah. He then views vv. 22–23(24) as forming the closure of the whole book of Isaiah and thus integrating the central themes of vv. 7–14 (servants of Yahweh) and 15–20 (destiny of Israel and the nations).

In the context of trying to trace the redactional history of the text in its final stages, Beuken's attempt certainly has merit. However, it seems to me that the evidence for precisely distinguishing different redactional hands on the basis of the continuity of themes and intertextual references remains a subjective enterprise. Rather, I would argue that the literary effect of chapter 66 along with chapter 65 is to bring the book of Isaiah as a whole to a conclusion by interweaving elements from First, Second, and Third Isaiah together. I shall try to interpret the theological effect of these chapters for the reading of the whole corpus at the conclusion of this chapter. In sum, the shape of the final form of these chapters has priority over the project of tracing the process of their composition, which remains highly illusive in its details.

[1–6] The majority of commentators (cf. Smith) designate the initial unit as comprising vv. 1–4. The force of the initial formula in v. 5 is thought to confirm this division. In addition, some commentators join the unit with chapter 65 to form a fourth stanza. Over against this analysis, Beuken and Webster opt for vv. 1–6 as constituting the scope of the unit. They argue that conventional oral formulae no longer function as absolute form-critical markers, but the content of judgment against the apostates unites vv. 1–6. This unit is then to be separated from vv. 7–14, which focus on the comfort of the servants of Yahweh. Beuken contends that unless v. 6 is separated from v. 7, the enemies appear to be from outside Israel rather than from within the community. However, Smith largely agrees that the enemies are from within, while at the same time rejecting Beuken's literary division. In my opinion, this debate over determining the exact limits of each subdivision is less important than often supposed, and the force of the chapter as a whole with its multiple themes is not ultimately determined by the precise subdivisions.

The unit begins with a disputational tone in which Yahweh calls into question the kind of house (temple) that some would build for him: "What could serve as my resting place?" God has already provided his own context in response: "Heaven is my throne and earth is my footstool" All these things have been created by him and belong to him alone. Whereas v. 2 fits logically behind v. 1a, the rhetorical effect of the clause is enhanced by separating the two claims of absolute creative power. In the debate over building God's dwelling one can hear the resonance from 2 Samuel 7 and from Solomon's prayer in 1 Kings 8:22ff. The issue within the Old Testament, and especially in chapter 66, is not whether God is too exalted even to tolerate an earthly dwelling place, but is the motivation of those desiring to construct a temple. Those arrogant people who feel that God is thereby beholden to them are flatly rejected. God asserts his complete sovereignty over all creation and all its works. Then v. 2b reaffirms the theme of chapter 65 that the transcendent and creative God is fully accessible to the one who is humble, contrite, and respectful of God's word.

Verses 3–4 return to the disputational mode, climaxing in a harsh accusation directed against those who seek to appease the Almighty with their cultic activity. A series of clauses occurs, consisting of four pairs of deeds described with participles. In each pair the first member depicts what appears to be a legitimate cultic act, whereas the second member portrays an illegitimate pagan action. The problem lies in determining how these two parts within the sentence relate. The NRSV and NIV render the connection as a comparative: "He who slaughters an ox is like one who kills a man; he who sacrifices a lamb, like one who breaks a dog's neck." The point then of the accusation becomes clear. In contrast to the humble and contrite (v. 2b), those who would build God a temple are the same arrogant people who defile his worship with their syncretistic, pagan cults. Beuken correctly observes the mirror image with those rebellious persons described in 65:3ff., who provoke God through their idolatrous practices. The addresses are identified through intertextual references. Isaiah 66:4 picks up the refrain from 65:12b: "when I called, no one answered." The attempts to gain great historical specificity by various reconstructions (e.g., Hanson, Rofé) run the danger of going beyond the intention of the biblical text itself.

Although there appears at first to be a formal break in v. 5, the content of the accusation against the persecutors of the righteous is developed and expanded. Like the idiom of the Psalter (e.g., Ps. 5:6; 6:9; 14:4), the words of the "workers of iniquity" are cited as they denounce those "who tremble at [God's] word" (v. 5). Rather, it is they that will be shamed. Verse 6 concludes with the sound of an uproar from the city as God renders judgment on his enemies. Because it is from his own heavenly temple that God exercises his recompense and not the one they have built, some commentators hear an echo of chapter 6, where the themes of temple and judgment are closely joined.

[7–14] Full attention now turns to the promise of God to his faithful, who are explicitly named as his servants (v. 14), thus bringing to a conclusion a main theme of chapter 65 that has unfolded throughout Third Isaiah. Verse 7 begins with a literary form resembling a riddle. How is one to explain the astonishing occurrence that a woman gave birth before she was in labor? Whoever heard of such a thing? Then the solution is immediately revealed. God has accomplished the totally unexpected. He has brought forth the children of Zion when a birth seemed impossible.

Next, the theme of Jerusalem's joy, found frequently in both Second and Third Isaiah, is repeated in order to console both those who once mourned and those now sharing her present gladness. Verses 12–13 continue the image of Zion's prosperity and wealth, which she shares as a suckling child is dandled upon the mother's knees. The theme of comfort to the mother resonates with Second Isaiah, especially 40:1 and 49:13. Verse 14b summarizes the sharp contrast between the fate of the servants and of the enemies, which has continued to dominant Third Isaiah since chapter 56.

[15–17] The majority of modern commentators see the unit including vv. 15–17. It makes little difference whether one envisions a close continuity with the description of the judgment, or lays the emphasis on the new features of the theophanic appearance of God. The coming of God in awesome power resonates both with 40:10 and 62:11, but is further intensified with the threefold stress on fire when all flesh is subjected to the fury of his burning anger. Verse 17 is often characterized as a prosaic addition, but its significance lies in again returning to the theme of those who strive to purify themselves falsely by means of pagan rites. The repetition of swine flesh and the theme of sanity joins directly with 65:3ff. Yet the references to the gardens as the locale for this illicit practice reaches far back to chapter 1 in describing the rebels and sinners who were first promised God's fiery judgment (vv. 28ff.). The end is registered by the stark finality of the clause: "just as the LORD had said (n^e'*um* YHWH)." However, because of a textual problem in the succeeding verse, some (e.g., NJPS) have moved the first part of v. 18 into this paragraph to confirm God's judgment of their deeds and purposes. An additional advantage of such a move is that it separates the judgmental theme of vv. 14–17 from the eschatological promises which then follow in vv. 18–24.

[18–23] There is a disagreement among commentators about whether vv. 18–21 should be considered prose or metrical verse. The NRSV, NJPS, and the NIV regard these verses as prose, whereas Beuken and other recent commentators, as well as the NEB, have sought to recover a form of poetic versification. However, the issue, in my judgment, is not of primary importance and should not be a factor in dismissing these verses as a much later apocalyptic addition.

Actually what one finds in this passage is a succinct summary of eschatological themes that occur throughout the entire book of Isaiah. The gathering of all the nations from the ends of the world, the seeing of God's glory (41:5), the survivors sent to the nations as a witness, the return of the diaspora to God's holy mountain, and the choosing of foreigners for priests of Yahweh (56:6ff.), are all themes that appear in differing forms. What is new in the passage is the joining of them together in one concluding oracle. The radical formulation of 65:17–18 is repeated, but now in such a way as to provide an interpretation of the earlier promises as a part of the one eschatological goal: the creation of new heavens and a new earth. This purpose does not emerge as a cosmological projection, but as the context for God's descendants, his own people, whose name will remain forever and whose life consists in the eternal worship of God from new moon to new moon and from Sabbath to Sabbath.

[24] It has long been the view of many that the true ending of the book of Isaiah should have come with v. 23, which they interpret as a call for universal salvation. Critical scholars are virtually unanimous that v. 24 is a later and unfortunate addition, which is then described as an apocalyptic portrayal of Gehenna. The NJPS follows the rabbinic dictum in repeating v. 23 after v. 24 in order to end the book on a note of promise. Yet as I shall attempt to show in the final section (cf. below), it is a fundamental feature in the final shaping of the book as a whole that the division between the righteous and the wicked is maintained into the eschaton. In spite of God's new heavens and earth, the exaltation of Zion, and the entrance of the nations to the worship of God, there remain those outside the realm of God's salvation. The tension continues between all flesh coming "to worship me" (v. 23) and "the corpses of those who rebelled against me." The closest literary parallel is to the city defended by God and the camp of the defeated Assyrians, "all the dead bodies" (37:36ff.). Even though many commentators would argue that v. 24 is a very late addition, which indeed may be true, the fact that there is a conscious pattern throughout the entire chapter between woe and weal indicates a very broad foundation for the theology reflected in v. 24.

2. The Canonical Function of Chapters 65—66

The overarching thesis that has governed this interpretation of Third Isaiah (chapters 56—66) has been that these chapters function to shape the entire book of Isaiah into a coherent whole by a reuse, reordering, and reinterpretation of Sec-

ond and Third Isaiah (cf. above, Introduction to Chapters 56—66). Moreover, this
intent and this effect are best illustrated by the editorial role of chapters 65—66.

a. The Relation of Chapters 65 and 66 to Chapter 40

One gets an impression of the significance of Second Isaiah for Third Isaiah
by focusing first on the intertextuality between chapters 65—66 and chapter 40.

65:1	God's presence manifested: Here am I.	**40:9**	Behold, your God.
66:15	God comes in fire for judgment.	**40:10**	God comes with might, his reward with him.
65:16	Israel's former troubles are forgotten, hidden from God's eyes.	**40:2**	Israel's warfare is ended and iniquity pardoned.
66:13	God comforts his people.	**40:1**	Comfort, comfort my people.
65:18	Gladness and joy for Jerusalem.	**40:11**	Jerusalem, herald of good tidings.
65:10	Sharon, a pasture for flocks.	**40:11**	He feeds his flock like a shepherd.
66:18–19	God's glory among the nations.	**40:5**	His glory revealed to all flesh.

If one then expands the use of chapter 40 in chapters 65—66 to the rest of
Second Isaiah, one finds a whole range of additional, common themes, often
with exact verbal parallels. God as creator (*br'*) is a frequent subject throughout Second Isaiah (e.g., 42:5) and is adopted in 65:17. Isaiah 65:23 picks up the
theme of the heritage of the servants from 54:17, and 65:17 speaks of "the former things" that "will not be remembered" from 43:18.

b. The Relation of Chapters 65 and 66 to 1:1–2:4

Again it appears highly significant to observe parallels in themes and imagery
because of the unusual level of intertextuality.

65:2	God spreads out his hands to a rebellious people.	**1:2**	Sons I reared, they rebelled against me.
65:3	A people who provoke God.	**1:4**	The whole head sick, utterly estranged.
65:3	They corruptly sacrifice in gardens.	**1:29**	You will blush for the gardens.
65:6	God will repay into their bosom.	**1:5**	Why will you continue to be smitten?
65:8	I will not destroy them all.	**1:9**	If he had not left a remnant, then like Sodom . . .

| 65:15 His servants will be called by a different name. | 1:26 You will be called the city of righteousness. |
| 66:18ff. All nations will come to my holy mountain. | 2:1–4 Let us go up to the mountain of Yahweh. |

If one now expands the use of chapter 1 by chapters 65—66 to include the rest of First Isaiah, one again discovers a host of common themes and vocabulary. The voice of God speaking from the temple in 66:6 has an echo in 6:9ff. The sharp contrast between the faithful servants and the rebellious apostates in 65:8–15 finds its close analogy in 1:27ff. Finally, the use of an abbreviated citation of 11:6–9 in 65:25 shows an indisputable example of intertextual reference between the two parts of the book of Isaiah.

In his important essay on chapters 65 and 66, Beuken ("Isaiah Chapters LXV—LXVI") observes that the agreement between chapters 1 and 65—66 does not reach the level of conscious allusion because of two factors: (1) The correspondence involves neither sentences nor word groups, but single words (e.g., "fire," "sword," "garden," etc.), and (2) specific segments of chapters 65 and 66 do not share words with specific segments of chapter 1, but borrow them from all over chapter 1. Beuken notes the difference of the relationship between Second and Third Isaiah. He concludes that the lexical correspondence between chapters 1 and 65—66 is largely because both texts contain the same prophetic literary genres with their similar themes.

My own evaluation of the correspondence attributes a greater significance to the correspondence of single words than allowed by Beuken (cf. the very different stance of Lau). Nevertheless, even if the degree of redactional intentionality can be debated, the effect of the correspondence on the reader of the whole book should not be underestimated. Still, I will not press my different assessment from that of Beuken because he offers two remarkable exceptions to his prior generalization regarding intertextuality, which provide a sufficient warrant for my drawing of larger hermeneutical implications regarding these last two chapters.

First, Beuken affirms that in 65:17–24 the frame conveys affinity with chapter 1 by the word pair "heavens and earth" (65:17 // 1:2), by the promise "I will answer (65:24) in contrast to "I will not listen" (1:15), and the reference to offspring (65:23 // 1:4). Second, the density of common terms between chapter 1 and 66:22–24 is of a remarkable quality. He cites the following examples: the calling of "heavens and earth" to witness that Israel is a "brood of evildoers" (1:2, 4); the promise that "the new heavens and new earth" will share their everlasting existence with the purified "seed" (66:22); the accusation against "those who rebelled against me" (66:24 // 1:2, 28); the reversal in Israel's true worship (66:23) from the false cult of 1:13. He thus concludes that the lexical agreement of chapter 66 and chapter 1 reaches the level of intentional reference, and that words from both the beginning and end of chapter 1 are quoted so as to include the whole chapter in the references (221).

3. The Hermeneutical Significance of the Editorial Shaping

The editorial shaping of Third Isaiah raises several points of hermeneutical significance. First, Third Isaiah continues the hope of Second Isaiah for the salvation of Zion. The same promises are reiterated of a new age, of the return of God in power, and of the transformation of Zion as the center for God's righteous rule. The "point of standing" of Third Isaiah is shaped by its dependence on Second Isaiah, which is to say, the particular postexilic setting of Third Isaiah's oracles, although clearly present, has been rendered largely peripheral to the kerygmatic content of the hope. Third Isaiah shares with Second Isaiah the same *kairos,* and awaits the coming of Zion's eschatological deliverance, which still lies in the future. For commentators to assign crucial interpretive significance to a reconstructed postexilic setting is to miss the major theological message of Third Isaiah, whether construed historically (Zimmerli), psychologically (Begrich), or sociologically (Hanson).

Second, the nature of Israel's salvation has been extended by Third Isaiah initially in terms of Second Isaiah's hope, especially in relation to chapter 40 (cf. chapter 35). The promises of Second Isaiah of the glorious return from the Babylonian exile have not been repeated, but assumed as true and often rendered metaphorically to serve as background for Israel's final entrance into the transformed and glorified city. The imagery of Zion as the holy mountain and center for the worship of God by the nations has been taken from First Isaiah (2:1ff.) and serves to join the various parts of the book into a unity.

The most significant change in the rendering of Israel's hope for salvation is that the deliverance from Babylon—a major feature of Second Isaiah—has now been understood within the book as a whole as only one instance of God's unfolding eschatological purpose for his people. Third Isaiah has instead rendered the ultimate salvation of Israel into an eschatological picture of the new heavens and new earth (65:17ff.; 66:22ff.). The citation of First Isaiah's messianic hope in 65:25 functions as an integral part of this eschatological reinterpretation. The messianic imagery has not been introduced to form a closely coherent picture, but functions only to identify the eschatological hope of First Isaiah as an integral part of the one overarching goal of the entire prophetic book. For the reader of the Isaianic corpus as a whole, a warrant is provided by which to relate Isaiah's witness in chapters 7, 9, and 11 with the eschatological promise of a new creation. The formulation is different, but the theological substance has been identified. For commentators to suggest that Third Isaiah's apocalyptic vision is totally alien to the earlier prophecies of a transformed

Zion ruled by a messiah is to miss the creative function of authoritative scripture for a community of faith.

Third, the nature of Third Isaiah's understanding of the nature of those redeemed once again has taken its central lead from Second Isaiah's portrayal of the suffering servant (chapter 53). The transition from Second Isaiah to Third Isaiah is made in 54:17, and the issue of the heritage of the servants forms a major theme of Third Isaiah. Immediately in chapter 56 the ethnic distinction between Israel and the nations has been theologically relativized, and God's invitation is offered to all who faithfully enter into his covenant of justice and righteousness (56:6ff.). The presence of the redeemed is not presented just as a hope for the future, but is portrayed in each part of the book as a present, concrete, and active reality of a faithful remnant who lives in hope of God's deliverance, longing for his coming. Already chapters 1—12 have been shaped in such a way that the faithful remnant of the eighth century has been assigned a voice in chapter 12, which resonates not only with those rescued at the Red Sea (12:2 // Ex. 15:2), but also with the suffering servants of every successive generation (59:9ff.; 63:15ff.).

Finally, a highly important feature of Third Isaiah, which especially takes its shape in chapters 65 and 66, is the way in which the description of the new age has been set over against the continuing opposition of the old. The language of First Isaiah, especially of chapter 1 (cf. 34:2), has been appropriated intertextually to provide the imagery by which to describe the apostates of Third Isaiah. However, there is a major change in the role of the enemies of God. Whereas Second Isaiah tended to describe those opposing God in temporal terms (e.g., Assyrians, Babylonians, and Egyptians), which were then to be overcome in the new age by God's might, in Third Isaiah the relation of the old to the new age has been construed, not chronologically, but ontologically. In the profoundest of mysteries and with acute tension, the defeated voice of evil opposing God's rule will be allowed to continue. The enemies of God in Third Isaiah are identified with those of every age—thus the consistent appeal to the enemies of First Isaiah—because they constitute an ontological opposition to God's will. It is, therefore, not by chance that the book of Isaiah closes on this same note of judgment. Still, it is not wrong theologically when the synagogue chose to repeat the promise of 66:23 after v. 24 in order to bear testimony that the worship of the one true God by his faithful has the last word.

The book of Isaiah ends with this terrifying paradox. Yet it is according to a similar pattern that the New Testament also closes. Revelation 21 cites the promise of a new creation of heaven and earth, and of God's wiping away all tears (Rev. 21:1–4 // Isa. 25:8; 65:17–20; 66:22b). Again there are those outside: "the dogs . . . and murderers and idolaters, . . . practitioners of falsehood" (22:15). Then "the sea gave up its dead . . . and all were judged by what they had done" (20:13) by the one who sits on the great white throne (20:11).

The promise of God's salvation is to all, but it is received by the household of faith. For this reason, the early Christian church, some five hundred years later, saw itself also addressed with the same promises once directed to Israel in the book of Isaiah. The same pattern by which the prophetic editors shaped their message continued to operate for the New Testament's community of faith. The concrete sign of the promise was given in the Eucharist, the pledge today of its fulfillment tomorrow. Christ has come in power, but we await the new heavens and earth. Therefore, we still pray with the saints of every generation:

"Maranatha, come quickly Lord Jesus."

Index of Authors

Abramowski, R, 439
Achtemeier, E, xx, 439, 522
Ackroyd, P., 1, 2, 27, 70, 259, 260, 265, 284, 287, 503
Albertz, R., 507
Albright, W. F., 90, 127, 264
Alexander, J. A., xix, 135, 418
Alt, A., 78, 79
Amiran, R., 156, 161
Anderson, B. W., 40, 41, 44, 439, 447
Anderson, G. W., 171
Anderson, T. D., 509, 512
Aquinas, Thomas, 5
Asen, B. A., 213
Augustine, 5
Aus, R., 531

Bach, R., 121, 147
Baldwin, J. G., 27
Baltzer, K., 390, 409, 411
Barnes, W. E., 147, 149
Barré, M. L., 230, 259
Barrois, G., 99
Barstad, H. M., 348
Bartelmus, R, 61, 65
Barth, H., 1, 9, 40, 52, 53, 78, 90, 94, 96, 99, 100, 101, 121, 123, 127, 199, 230, 233, 236, 237, 239
Barthel, J., 40, 43, 51, 54, 61
Barthélemy, D., xi, 50, 61, 151, 182, 188, 197, 236, 252, 280, 409, 521, 523, 525, 531
Bartlett, J. R., 131, 252
Barton, J., 1
Bastiaens, J. C., 409
Beck, M. A., 452

Becker, J., 15, 27, 61, 90, 96, 99, 100, 289
Becker, U., 40
Beek, M. A., 522
Begg,C. T., 259
Begrich, J., 15, 121, 127, 259, 280, 283, 284, 289, 290, 294, 306, 315, 316, 317, 318f., 320, 325, 331, 349, 370, 381, 383, 392, 401, 409, 411, 433, 452, 454, 457, 545
Bengel, J. A., 55
Bentzen, A., 100
Ben Zvi, E., 15, 259
Bergmeier, R., 468
Bertholet, A., 452
Beuken, W. A. M., xii, xx, 1, 4, 107, 108, 204, 213, 223, 228, 244, 245, 247, 248, 252, 253, 254, 257, 289, 291, 305, 307, 310, 315, 320, 324, 325, 331, 332, 333, 343, 348, 350, 351, 361, 365, 371, 372, 381, 382, 390, 396, 401, 405, 411, 412, 413, 415, 426, 427, 428, 433, 439, 440, 442, 449, 452, 454, 455, 457, 461, 462, 464, 468, 469, 476, 481, 485, 486, 493, 495, 497, 501, 503, 504, 505, 509, 511, 512, 518, 531, 532, 533, 534, 536, 538, 539, 540, 542, 544
Biddle, M. E., 461
Birkeland, H., 188
Blank, S. H., 522
Blenkinsopp, J., 27, 439
Bloom, H., 439, 445
Blum, E., 40
Boecker, H. J., 15, 20, 315, 317
Boer, P. A. H. de, 113
Bonnard, P.-E., xx

Bonner, L.,   141
Bosshard-Nepustil, E.,   121, 122, 141,
    143, 147, 149, 156, 158, 159
Bost, H.,   121
Brekelmans, C.,   51
Bright, J.,   157, 259, 264
Brinkman, J. A.,   147, 259, 285
Brongers, H. A.,   484
Brown, W. P.,   40, 83
Brueggemann, W.,   44, 433
Buber, M.,   61
Budde, K.,   xx, 9, 15, 40, 42, 70
Bultmann, R.,   410, 421

Calvin, J.,   xix, 5, 54, 60, 257, 318, 323
Cannon, W. W.,   501, 502
Caquot, A.,   433
Carlson, R. A.,   78
Carr, D. M.,   1, 15, 16, 259, 281
Carroll, R. P.,   70
Cazelles, H.,   409
Cheyne, T. K.,   xix, 141, 164, 236, 244,
    358
Childs, B. S.,   1, 3, 4, 15, 21, 40, 51, 65,
    90, 94, 121, 127, 135, 150, 156, 223,
    224, 228, 233, 244, 249, 259, 260, 263,
    264, 271, 273, 284, 289, 348, 358, 361,
    439
Christensen, D. L.,   90, 113, 114
Chrysostom,   5
Clements, R. E.,   xx, 1, 2, 9, 10, 16, 21, 22,
    29, 31, 35, 43, 52, 53, 61, 75, 83, 91, 94,
    100, 121, 122, 123, 127, 135, 144, 147,
    149, 151, 156, 157, 158, 159, 160, 177,
    188, 215, 216, 231, 233, 237, 259, 264,
    265, 272, 276, 281, 286, 289, 291, 439
Clifford, R. J.,   xx, 306, 307, 317, 319,
    331, 343, 381, 433, 434
Clines, D. J. A.,   409, 411
Coats, G. W.,   11
Cobb, W. H.,   147, 149
Cogan, M.,   259, 281, 285
Coggins, R. J.,   171
Cohen, C.,   259
Collins, J. J.,   501
Condamin, A.,   370

Conrad, D.,   522
Conrad, E. E.,   315, 331, 531
Crenshaw, J. L.,   83
Cresson, B. C.,   514
Cross, F. M.,   294, 295
Crüsemann, F.,   107, 108

Dalman, G.,   90
Davey, N.,   410
Davidson, A. B.,   289, 290, 322
Davies, G. I.,   27, 99, 113, 252
Day, J.,   171, 181, 191, 194, 409
Delcor, M.,   15, 135
Delitzsch, F.,   xix, 18, 36, 63, 78, 84, 85,
    96, 103, 166, 182, 193, 283, 294, 308,
    385, 418, 458, 489, 502, 504, 510
Dhorme, P.,   144
Dicou, B.,   252
Dietrich, W.,   484
Dijkstra, M.,   305, 315, 348
Dillmann, A.,   xix, 294
Dion, P. E.,   254, 348
Dittert, K.,   xx, 303, 433, 438
Döderlein, J. C.,   289
Dohmen, C.,   61
Donner, H.,   83, 90, 96, 113, 135, 141,
    157, 223, 252, 452, 454, 457, 458
Drechsler, M.,   113
Driver, G. R.,   236, 409
Driver, S. R.,   289, 290, 409, 410
Duhm, B.,   xix, 1, 2, 7ff., 9, 10, 28, 31,
    34, 41, 43, 66, 70, 71, 92, 94, 95f., 114,
    165, 166, 171, 183, 216, 232, 239, 262,
    266, 271, 289, 290, 291, 321, 323, 334,
    343, 358, 365, 370, 377, 381, 382, 385,
    394, 401, 411, 418, 421, 426, 440, 443,
    455, 469, 480, 485, 494, 495, 507, 509
Dumbrell, W. J.,   531

Eaton, J. H.,   433, 436
Eichhorn, D.,   340
Eichhorn, J. G.,   289
Eichrodt, W.,   xx, 28, 43, 52, 92, 105,
    145, 149, 157, 158, 230, 233
Eidevall, G.,   230
Eissfeldt, O.,   433, 435, 437

Elliger, K., xi, xx, 252, 289, 290, 299, 305, 306, 310, 316, 321, 325, 331, 332, 333, 336, 349, 370, 371, 381, 390, 392, 409, 426, 439, 440, 444, 510, 532

Emerton, J. A., 40, 50, 51, 78, 157, 182, 531

Emmerson, G. I., 439

Engnell, I., 409, 412

Erlandsson, S., 113, 115, 121, 125, 141, 148, 149, 157, 164, 165, 166

Evans, C. A., 51, 70

Exum, J. C., 199, 204, 207, 214, 230

Fascher, E., 410

Feigin, B., 214

Feldmann, F., xix

Fichtner, J., 401

Finkelstein, L., xix

Fischer, J., xix

Fischer, T., 164

Fisher, R. W., 294, 301, 501, 505

Fitzgerald, A., 364

Fitzmyer, J. A., 507

Fohrer, G., xix, xx, 15, 16, 17, 61, 66, 171, 172, 188, 234, 510, 531, 535

Fokkelman, J. P., 348

Fouts, D. M., 188

Frei, H., 259, 274

Frey, H., xx

Fullerton, K., 70, 90, 92, 121

Galling, K., 148, 223

Gehman, H. S., 113, 121

Gese, H., 62

Gesenius, W., xix, 260, 413

Geyer, J. B., 113, 148

Ginsberg, H. L., 113

Gitay,Y., 15

Gnilka, J., 51.

Goldingay, J., 315

Golebiewski, H., 426

Gonçalves, F. J., 259, 263, 264

Gordon, C. H., 194

Gosse, B., 15, 121, 135, 252

Gray, G. B., xix, 35, 53, 71, 84, 93, 94

Gray, J., 531

Greenberg, M., 121

Grelot, P., 121

Gressmann, H., 99, 100

Grimm, W., xx, 303, 337, 382, 433, 438

Grol, H. W. M. van, 194

Gross, H., 99

Groves, J. W., 259, 261

Guillet, J., 340

Gunkel, H., 194, 244, 245, 283, 401, 403, 484

Gunn, D. M., 426

Haag, H., 409

Habel, N., 51, 294

Haenchen, E., 188.

Haller, M., 348

Hamborg, G. R., 113

Hammershaimb, E., 62

Hanhart, R., 54

Hanson, P. D., xx, 370, 416, 439, 440, 444, 448, 461, 471, 514, 531, 532, 534, 537, 540, 545

Haran, M., 364

Hardmeier, C., 40, 51, 259, 264, 266, 272

Hartenstein, F., 51

Hayes, J. H., 78, 83, 86, 113, 125, 126, 141, 149, 153, 157, 164, 244

Heider, G. C., 223, 461, 467

Hengel, M., 410, 421

Henry, M.–L., 171

Hermisson, H.–J., xx, 99, 236, 294, 315, 323, 349, 352, 358, 361, 365, 381, 383, 384, 390, 409

Herntrich, V., xx, 32, 53, 103, 105

Herrmann, W., 401

Hertzberg, W., xix, 236, 410

L'Heureux, C. E., 40, 83

Hitzig, F., xix

Höffken, P., 62

Høgenhaven, J., 78

Hollander, J., 439, 445

Holmgren, F., 401, 514

Hooker, M., 410, 421, 507

Horn, S., 259

Hoskyns, E., 410

Houston, W.,   531
Hugenberger, G. P.,   316, 410
Hutter, M.,   259

Ibn Ezra,   xix
Irvine, S. A.,   40, 43, 78, 83, 113, 115,
    125, 126, 141, 148, 149, 157, 164, 244

Jackson J. J.,   204
Jacob, E.,   194
Jahnow, H.,   121, 126
Janowski, B.,   409, 410, 418
Jenkins, A. K.,   113
Jensen, J.,   15
Jepsen, A.,   54, 70
Jeremias,C.,   259, 281, 316
Jeremias, J.,   316, 319, 410, 421
Johnson, D. G.,   171, 172, 177, 180, 188,
    194
Jones, D. R.,   1, 15
Junker, H.,   40, 45

Käsemann, E.,   410, 421
Kaiser, O.,   xx, 53, 64, 66, 70, 79, 91, 135,
    149, 166, 172, 177, 188, 194, 259, 281
Kamano, N.,   294, 297, 300, 301
Keller, C. A.,   62, 70, 71
Kellermann, U.,   502, 531
Kendall, D.,   484
Kiesow, K.,   381, 401
Kilian, R.,   xx, 51, 62, 79, 105, 149, 158
Kimḥi, D.,   xix
Kissane, E. J.,   xix, 71, 165, 318
Kittel, R.,   548, 350
Klein, H.,   70, 316
Knabenbauer, J.,   xix
Knierim, R.,   51, 52
Knight, G. A. F.,   xx
Köhler, L.,   204, 384
Koenen, K.,   439, 440, 444, 452, 461,
    462, 466, 469, 470, 484, 493, 495, 502,
    509, 510, 514, 515, 516, 522, 531, 536
Konkel, A. H.,   259, 281
Koole, J. L.,   xx, 316
Kratz, R. G.,   316, 318, 323, 348, 358,
    370, 381

Kraus, H.-J.,   531
Krinetski, L.,   294
Kuntz, J. K.,   401
Kuyper, L. J.,   294

Laato, A.,   70, 259
Laberge, L.,   214
Labuschagne, C. J.,   305
Lack, R.,   439, 531
Lagarde, P. A. de,   137
Lau, W.,   439, 440, 445, 446, 452, 455,
    457, 461, 462, 465, 468, 469, 484, 485,
    489, 493, 495, 503, 504, 509, 510, 515,
    522, 532, 544
Lauterjung, V.,   252
Leene, H.,   331, 348, 358, 370, 390
Leeuw, V. de,   409, 412
Leeuwen, C. van,   259
Lescow, T.,   40, 51
Lewis, T. J.,   461, 532
Liebreich, L. J.,   1, 3, 45, 51, 113, 439,
    447, 532
Lindblom, J.,   164, 166, 171, 172, 204
Liwak, R.,   259
Loewenstamm, S. E.,   107
Lohfink, N.,   70, 75, 381, 384
Lohmann, P.,   148, 171
Long, B. O.,   11, 259, 273, 275, 281, 282,
    283
Loretz, O.,   11, 15, 122, 294
Lugt, P. van der,   390

Maass, F.,   439
Macintosh, A. A.,   148, 150, 151, 153
Marcus, R,   316
Marti, K.,   xix, 358, 494
Martin-Achard, R.,   157, 182, 188, 364,
    365, 426,
Matheus, F.,   340
Matthews, C. R.,   252, 515
McKay, J. W.,   122
McKenzie, J. L.,   xx, 299
McLaughlin, J. L.,   51
Melugin, R. F.,   1, 15, 223, 289, 290,
    294, 305, 306, 316, 324, 326, 331, 348,
    349, 350, 354, 358, 359, 364, 370, 372,

381, 382, 390, 401, 410, 411, 412, 413, 426, 427

Merendino, R. D., 289, 291, 316, 340, 358, 364, 370, 381, 390

Mettinger, T. N. D., 157, 305, 381

Michel, D., 475

Millar, W. R., 171, 172, 173

Millard, A. R., 259

Mittmann, S., 90

Moor, J. C. de, 493

Morgenstern, J., 502

Motyer, J. A., xix, 3, 21, 29, 31, 371

Mowinckel, S., 244, 245, 410

Müller, H. P., 41

Muilenburg, J., xx, 252, 289, 290, 295, 306, 316, 317, 319, 343, 355, 376, 377, 381, 406, 427, 453, 484, 485, 487, 488, 515

Murray, D., 390

Na'aman, N., 259

Naidoff, B. D., 305

Neubauer, A., 409, 410

Nielsen, K., 51

North, C. R., xx, 331, 340, 370, 409, 412

Nyberg, H. S., 260

Odeberg, H., 439, 440, 452, 461, 468, 469, 476, 493, 532

Oetinger, F. C., 55

Oorschot, J. van, 381

Orlinsky, H. M., 381, 410, 415, 429

Oswalt, J. N., xi, xix, 3, 115, 125, 157, 159, 182, 188, 315, 409, 493, 504

Otto, E., 426

Otzen, B., 171

Paton-Williams, P., 381, 384

Pauritsch, K, 439, 440, 444, 452, 454, 457, 461, 468, 484, 493, 494, 501, 515, 522, 532

Petersen, D. L., 41, 113, 131, 204, 207, 294

Plöger, O., 171, 177, 180, 194

Polan, G. J., 475

Pope, M., 214, 252

Porteous, N. W., 426

Power, E., 131

Preuss, H. D., 188, 289, 365

Procksch, O., xx, 31, 43, 52, 86, 92, 127, 149, 165, 172, 233, 257

Provan, I., 260

Rad, G. von, xi, 78, 294, 381, 383, 493

Rehm, M., 62, 99

Renaud, B., 461

Rendtorff, R., 1, 3, 51, 54, 289, 291, 439, 440, 442, 453, 532

Reventlow, H. Graf, 41, 43

Richards, K. H., 41

Rignell, L. G., 15, 70

Ringgren, H., 171

Roberts, J. J. M., 204, 236, 244

Robertson, E., 194

Robinson, H. W., 381, 384, 426, 427, 428

Rössel, M., 62

Rofé, A., 484, 532, 540

Rohr Sauer, A. von, 532, 435

Rosenmüller, E. F. K., xix, 401

Rudolph, W., 131, 164, 165, 171, 172

Rüderswörden, U., 164

Ruiten, J. T. A. G. M. van, 99, 101, 532

Ruprecht, E., 260

Saebø, M., 70, 73, 124

Sanders, J. A., 507

Sasson, J. M., 532

Sauer, G., 230

Sawyer, J. F. A, xix, 1, 5, 141, 181, 426, 428

Schibler, D., 62

Schmidt, J. M., 51

Schmitt, H.-C., 370, 381

Schmitt, J., 502

Schoors, A., xix, 331, 348, 370, 390, 392

Schottroff, W., 41

Schramm, B., 439, 461

Schunck, K.-D., 223

Scott, R. B. Y., xx, 99, 113, 232, 252

Sehmsdorf, E., 439, 440, 452, 454, 457

Seitz, C. R.,   v, xx, 1, 2, 113, 115, 122,
    150, 154, 158, 159, 172, 177f., 186,
    188f., 191, 199, 231, 260, 261, 263, 266,
    271, 272, 276, 281, 294, 295ff., 300,
    316, 323, 439
Sekine, S.,   439, 440, 444, 484, 493, 533
Selms, A. van,   204
Sheppard, G. T.,   xx, 1, 27, 30, 41
Simon, U. E.,   xx
Skinner, J.,   xiv, 164, 166, 289, 290, 470
Smart, J. D.,   xx, 370
Smelik, K. A. D.,   260, 261, 262, 271,
    272, 275, 281
Smend, R.,   171, 284
Smith, G. A.,   xix, 53, 289, 290, 322
Smith, P. A.,   468, 469, 493, 494, 502,
    509, 510, 532, 533, 534, 539
Smothers, T. D.,   131
Sommer, B. D.,   1
Spykerboer, H. C.,   340, 358
Stade, B.,   260, 262, 272
Stamm, J. J.,   62, 316, 381
Stansell, G.,   236, 237
Steck, 0. H.,   41, 43, 51, 53, 62, 70, 143,
    149, 252, 260, 266, 289, 290, 316, 323,
    349, 358, 381, 401, 410, 426, 439, 440,
    443, 445, 446, 452, 454, 461, 462, 469,
    484, 485, 486, 493, 494, 495, 502, 504,
    515, 522, 534
Steinmetz, D. C.,   51
Stoebe, H.-J.,   294
Stuhlmacher, P.,   410, 421
Stuhmueller, C.,   358, 409, 410, 421
Sweeney, M. A.,   1, 2, 8, 9, 10, 11, 15,
    16, 21, 27, 29, 62, 70, 71, 78, 80, 83, 86,
    90, 96, 113, 122, 123, 131, 135, 136,
    141, 142, 149, 151f., 157, 158, 162, 164,
    166, 171, 172, 174, 177, 179f., 184, 188,
    194, 195, 197, 214, 215, 223, 230, 237,
    244, 253, 254, 266, 281, 289, 291, 532

Tadmor, H.,   259, 281, 285
Tanghe, V.,   253
Tate, M. E.,   1
Thomas, D. W.,   340, 348, 354, 409, 420

Tomasino, A. J.,   532
Torrey, C. C.,   xx, 253, 289, 290, 294,
    299, 316, 336, 405, 426, 493
Tucker, G. M.,   11

Uchelen, N. A.,   401

Van Leewen, K.,   305
Van Winkle, D. W.,   316
Van Zyl, A. H.,   131
Vaux, R. de,   532
Vermeylen, J.,   1, 15, 21, 91, 101, 107,
    109, 148, 165, 171, 172, 177, 194, 199,
    200, 215, 233, 234, 244, 253, 260, 289,
    291, 440, 444, 493, 494, 502, 532, 533
Vincent, J. M.,   294, 316, 331, 401, 435
Vischer, W.,   62
Vitringa, C.,   xix, 165, 361, 430, 506
Vollmer, J.,   78
Volz, P.,   xx, 15, 377, 437, 440, 495,
    497, 502

Wakeman, M. K.,   194
Waldow, H. E. von,   306
Wanke, G.,   135
Watson, G. E.,   164
Watts, J. W. D.,   xix, 1, 21, 31, 157, 161,
    306, 317, 371, 411, 509
Webster, E. C.,   532, 533, 534, 540
Wegner, P. D.,   62, 78
Weippert, M.,   515
Weissert, D.,   484
Wellhausen, J.,   496
Wells, R. D. Jr.,   452
Welten, P.,   177, 183
Werlitz, J.,   41, 62, 214, 316
Werner, W.,   41, 51, 53, 223
Westermann, C.,   xi, xx, 1, 289, 290,
    306, 307, 310, 316, 320, 321, 331, 332,
    333, 341, 348, 349, 350, 351, 354, 360,
    365, 370, 371, 375, 381, 384, 391, 392,
    400, 404, 411, 417, 426, 434, 440, 448,
    454, 461, 470, 475, 484, 486, 494, 502,
    509, 510, 532, 533
Whedbee, J. W.,   204

Whitley, C.,   70, 164
Whybray, R. N.,   xx, 410, 411, 412, 416,
    423, 453, 475, 497, 503
Widengren, G.,   99, 100
Wilcox, P.,   381, 384
Wildberger, H.,   xi, xx, 1, 28, 35, 41, 47,
    52, 53, 72, 78, 103, 105, 135, 141, 143,
    149, 152, 158, 160, 165, 177, 183, 188,
    194, 225, 239, 252, 257, 264, 266, 271
Willey, P.T.,   331, 426
Williams, G. R.,   41
Williamson, H. G. M.,   1, 3, 9, 15, 16, 28,
    29, 51, 91, 107, 108f., 113, l99, 200,
    244, 246, 253, 260, 261, 266, 276, 281,
    289, 291, 305, 322, 433, 435
Willis, J. T.,   16, 41, 157

Wodecki, B.,   183
Wolff, H. W.,   62, 78, 164, 165, 410, 421
Woude, A. S. van der,   78
Würthwein, E.,   340

Yee, G. A.,   41, 122
Young, E. J.,   xix, 3, 276, 422

Zapff, B. M.,   122
Zarins, J.,   148
Zillessen, A.,   440
Zenger, E.,   99
Zimmerli, W.,   51, 52, 79, 260, 316, 319,
    410, 416, 433, 440, 442, 443, 456, 468,
    470, 479, 484, 493, 502, 509, 510, 513,
    545